CONTENTS

ON ROME AND THE GODS

THE LIFE AND WORKS OF EMPEROR JULIAN

EDWARD ALEXANDER

BASED ON THE TRANSLATION BY
W. C. F. WRIGHT

INVICTUS PUBLISHING

Published in 2022 by Invictus Publishing.

ISBN: 978-1-0684163-2-3

"dis te minorem quod geris, imperas:
hinc omne principium, huc refer exitum:
di multa neglecti dederunt
Hesperiæ mala luctuosæ"

"you rule because you hold yourself inferior to the gods;
make this the beginning and the end of all things,
for neglect of the gods has brought many ills
to the sorrowing lands of Rome"

– Horace, *Odes*, III, VI

THE ROMAN EMPIRE IN THE 4TH CENTURY

SARMATIA
MARE CASPIUM
PONTUS EUXINUS
THRACIA
TRAJAN'S GATE
Constantinople
Nicomedia
BITHYNIA
ARMENIA
CORDUENE
Cæsarea
CAPPADOCIA
Pergamon
CILICIAN GATES
Delphi
Athens
Ephesus
Carrhæ
Nisibis
Tigris
Tarsus
Antioch
Euphrates
Ctesiphon
Orontes
SYRIA
INTERNUM
Alexandria
ÆGYPTUS
ARABIA
Nile

NOTES ON THE TEXT

Throughout the book, the term "Pagan" has been used to refer to the native polytheistic religions of Europe and the Near East. The word itself – derived from the Latin *paganus*, meaning "rustic" or "rural" – may be considered pejorative due to the connotation that the referent is unlearned, or backwards. The term is also something of an anachronism, having never been used by polytheists to refer to their own beliefs. According to the general historical consensus, because the old religious practices persisted most stubbornly in rural areas, Christians, who themselves predominated in the urban centres, began to attach the word for country-dweller to their religious opponents. Whether the use of *paganus* was intended to be mocking or not is open to debate. Nevertheless, owing to its common and otherwise neutral use in contemporary discourse, the term "Pagan" has been employed throughout the following text.

Additionally, names of both places and individuals have, where applicable, retained their historical form. The modern French city of Lyon, for example, is referred to by its Romano-Gallic name *Lugdunum*.

Finally, the translation of Julian's works by W. C. F. Wright has been extensively edited in an effort to improve both the legibility of the text and, where appropriate, to bring the translation more in line with the original Greek and Latin. All dates are A.D. unless explicitly stated otherwise.

– Edward Alexander

THE LIFE OF JULIAN

THE LIFE OF JULIAN

In December, 355, a young and apprehensive Julian, newly appointed to his first official position, arrived at the Gallic settlement of Vienna where a large crowd had gathered to observe the procession. As he and his companions made their way through the town, a voice was heard to call out: "this is the man who will restore the temples of the gods".[1] Few could have imagined that the unfledged figure before them, slight of frame and ostensibly Christian, was soon to become the last Pagan Emperor to ever rule Rome.

Flavius Claudius Julianus, better known to history by the appellation "Julian the Apostate", was the nephew of Constantine the Great, the man to whom the rise of Christianity within the Roman Empire is most prominently attributed. Although Christianity would not be formally recognised as the state religion until the Edict of Thessalonica in 380, Constantine's fabled conversion on the eve of the Battle of Milvian Bridge in 312 may reasonably be considered the turning point. Whatever the motivations might have been behind the Emperor's adoption of Christianity – Julian himself deeming it the action of a guilty conscience[2] – the consequences were significant. After centuries of marginalisation and sporadic persecution, brought about in large part by the refusal of Christians to perform the rites of the state cult and a fundamental incompatibility with Roman polytheism, Constantine opened the door to its eventual integration. The Edict of Milan, issued just four months later in 313, was in effect a reaffirmation and expansion of Galerius' earlier Edict of Toleration in 311. Christianity was granted legal status and with it imperial protection. While the edict spoke expressly of religious liberty in general, the reality was somewhat different. Constantine, no doubt with the encouragement of high-ranking Christian officials, was eager to see his conversion replicated among the wider population, yet most of the citizens continued to adhere to their traditional

1. Ammianus Marcellinus, 15.8.22 2. Julian, *The Cæsars*

beliefs. A policy of tolerance soon gave way to one of coercion. He determined that widespread adoption of Christianity "would be easily accomplished if he could get them to despise their temples and the images contained therein".[1] What followed was a program of wanton vandalism: temples were broken open and their statues removed; the Pagan "idols" were variously defaced, demolished, and melted down for coinage. By desecrating the very images to which the Pagans made offerings, their beliefs were revealed, so the assumption went, to be mere superstition. As Julian would later comment: "when we look at the images of the gods, let us indeed not think they are mere stones or wood, but neither let us think they are the gods themselves; for we do not say that the statues of the Emperors are mere wood and stone and bronze, but still less do we say they are the Emperors themselves. Therefore, let no man disbelieve in the gods because he sees and hears that certain persons have profaned their images and temples".[2]

Whether such conduct was intended to sow doubt in the minds of Pagans or merely compel them by force, the effects of the policy were significant. According to the fifth century historian, Sozomen, "the people were induced to remain passive for fear that, if they resisted these edicts, they, their children, and their wives, would be exposed to terrible ills".[3] Emboldened by Constantine's actions, "many other cities spontaneously, without any command from the Emperor, destroyed the adjacent temples and statues, and erected churches".[4] While some Christians, lone voices in the crowd, spoke out against the destruction, the die had already been cast.

Throughout the Empire, especially among its rural population, Paganism continued to be practised, albeit less openly and freely than before. Yet the broader decline in polytheism should not be attributed exclusively to the emergence of Christianity and the policies of Constantine. The growth of irreligiousness, particularly in the cities, was a long-term trend which paralleled the broader decline of classical civilisation. Indeed, Julian himself lamented how "the indigenous oracles of Greece have fallen silent and yielded to the course of time".[5] By the fourth century, Rome, like Greece before it, had all but exhausted its energy as a creative and conquering civilisation. Decadence had long set in, and with it came the gradual decay of "the human and spiritual substance"[6] that once animated Roman society. Julian was evidently only too

1. Sozomen, *E.H.*, II, V 2. *Julian, Letter to a Priest* 3. Sozomen, *E.H.*, II, V
4. ibid. 5. Julian, *Against the Galilæans* 6. Julius Evola, *The Emperor Julian*

aware of this: "I saw that there is among us great indifference about the gods and that all reverence for the heavenly powers has been driven out by impure and vulgar luxury".[1] This proved to be fertile ground for a new religion to gain adherents and eventually assume prominence, most notably, again, in the urban centres. The replacement of deeply embedded tradition would not occur overnight, however. Constantinople, for instance, which was established under Constantine's rule as the new capital of the Empire, still bore the semblance of a polytheistic culture, with statues of numerous gods adorning the city. Moreover, while various laws restricting Pagan practices were passed during the early-to-mid 300s, their enforcement appears to have varied greatly depending on local conditions. Thus, while the momentum and, crucially, the power of the imperial office lay with Christianity, the old gods had not been vanquished entirely.

Such, then, was the state of religious affairs into which Julian was born. In 331,[2] Constantine's half-brother, Julius Constantius, and his wife, Basilina, welcomed the arrival of their first and only child in Constantinople. Julian's mother, the daughter of a noble and long-distinguished Biythnian family, died shortly after giving birth to him, "snatched away while she was still a young girl by the motherless maiden".[3] The early years of his childhood, for which he held fond memories, were otherwise spent without event in the capital city. That was, until the death of Constantine in May, 337. Over the subsequent five months, every male who could have potentially challenged the late Emperor's sons for control of the Empire was disposed of. At least eight family members, including Julian's father and the eldest of his two half-brothers, were murdered. Only Julian and his other half-brother, Gallus, were spared. They seem to have avoided the fate of their kin on account of their age – the former being roughly six, the latter twelve – and, in the case of Gallus, a sickly constitution. The pair were simply deemed to be of no threat. The intervention of a bishop by the name of Eusebius may have also played a role, the chamberlain being one of Julian's few male relatives left alive. Fortunately for the two young nobles, then, the ruthless political manoeuvring of imperial succession appears to have had its limits on this occasion.

On 9th September, Constantine's three surviving sons were officially recognised as *Augusti* by the army. The Empire, now divided into a triumvirate, was governed as follows: Constantine II

1. Julian, *Letter 20* 2. Possibly 312 3. Julian, *Misopogon*

held the west, Constans ruled the central provinces of Illyricum, Africa, and Italy, while Constantius presided over the eastern third from Constantinople. The last of these would play a prominent role throughout Julian's life, and indeed may have already done so. Whether the purge of rival claimants was orchestrated by Constantius or not, it seems undeniable that he played a significant part. The act was certainly in keeping with his purported character. Variously described as "destitute of personal merit"[1] and "severe and implacable",[2] he is remembered as a man bereft of many admirable qualities; one who judged quickly and severely, used any means to achieve his political ends, and was easily manipulated by his many courtiers. As Gibbon decried: "the triumph of his arms served only to establish the reign of the eunuchs over the Roman world".[3]

Julian, for his part, seldom spoke ill of his cousin, typically laying the blame at the feet of the officials who surrounded him. These creatures of the court, according to Julian, "made him even harsher than he was by nature".[4] With respect to the murder of their male relatives, however, he was quite unequivocal in holding Constantine chiefly responsible: "our fathers were brothers, sons of the same father. Yet close kinsmen as we were, how this most humane Emperor treated us. Six of our cousins, my father who was his own uncle, another uncle of both of ours, and my eldest brother, he put to death without a trial; and as for me and my other brother, he intended to put us to death, but ultimately inflicted exile upon us."[5]

Julian was swiftly extricated from the capital by his mother's family and relocated to Nicomedia in their home province of Bithynia, while Gallus was withdrawn to Ephesus in Ionia. Newly orphaned, the care and attention he received from relatives who doubtless sought to shield him from political machinations was a welcome reprieve. It was here that Julian began his education in earnest. A "Scythian"[6] named Mardonius, who had previously tutored Julian's mother, was tasked with instructing the boy in a range of subjects, most notably the classics of Greek philosophy, poetry, and tragedy. It is not difficult to see how much of an impression Mardonius left on the young Julian, who would later recount: "by Zeus and the Muses, while I was still a mere boy,

1. Gibbon, *Decline and Fall*, XIX 2. Ammianus, 14.9.2
3. Gibbon, *Decline and Fall*, XIX 4. Julian, *Letter* 13
5. Julian, *Letter to the Senate and People of Athens* 6. Julian, *Misopogon*

my tutor would often say to me: 'never let the crowd of your playmates who flock to the theatres lead you into the mistake of craving for such spectacles as these. Have you a passion for horse races? There is one in Homer, very cleverly described. Take the book and study it; consider the wooded island of Calypso, the caves of Circe, and the garden of Alcinous; be assured that you will never see anything more delightful than these'".[1]

Julian's time in Bityhnia was short-lived, however. After two years away from the capital, he made his return alongside Eusebius, who had been appointed to the bishopric of Constantinople. Such proximity to the imperial court – and the ever-suspicious gaze of Constantius – once again placed Julian and Gallus in a precarious position. This was made all the more uncertain when Eusebius passed away. As their presence in the city posed too much of a risk to Constantius, the brothers were promptly removed in 342 to Macellum, a remote estate near Cæsarea in central Anatolia. The stately surroundings, at one time the residence of the kings of Cappadocia, could not mask the reality that they were effectively imprisoned, isolated from the company of peers, family, and wider society. Mardonius, for instance, had accompanied Julian to Constantinople, but no further.

Despite the loss of liberty, Julian and Gallus were nonetheless afforded the care, for better or worse, of tutors and attendants. In short: "the treatment which they experienced during a six-year confinement was partly such as they could hope from a careful guardian, and partly such as they might dread from a suspicious tyrant".[2] Julian was understandably more inclined towards the latter characterisation, describing their experience as one of "glittering servitude".[3] The pair were closely monitored as though they "were in some Persian garrison"[4]; no visitors were permitted, nor were they allowed to interact with other boys of their own age. For such formative years, it is easy to see why Julian sought refuge in books, a love that would remain with him throughout his life. As he later explained: "the gods, by means of philosophy, allowed me to remain untouched by it and unharmed".[5]

As the nephew of Rome's first Christian Emperor, Julian was naturally raised in the faith: he was baptised, he attended church, and he was regularly tasked with reading during services. Yet even from an early age, one is given the impression that his heart and

1. Julian, *Misopogon* 2. Gibbon, *Decline and Fall*, XIX
3. Julian, *Letter to the Senate and People of Athens* 4. ibid. 5. ibid.

mind may have been drawn elsewhere. One particularly amusing and perhaps revealing anecdote from his time in Macellum involved the two brothers practising the art of debate. Julian, it is said, would always take the position of the Pagan in religious discussions for the reason that he wished to practice "the weaker argument".[1]

In 348, the brothers were finally granted their freedom. After a few years within the Emperor's political circle, Gallus, now comfortably into his twenties, was invested with the title of Cæsar and given Constantina, the sister of Constantius, in marriage. Previously a cognomen for emperors, the term "Cæsar" at this point in history designated a sub-regulus who would primarily govern military affairs in a portion of the Empire at the behest of the Augustus. In this instance, Gallus was to administer the eastern provinces from Antioch while Constantius marched west to deal with the usurper Magnentius. Unfortunately for the young Cæsar, he "possessed neither the genius nor application, nor docility to compensate for the want of knowledge and experience".[2] The appointment would prove to be a poisoned chalice, and fatally so. For Constantius, the only member of the triumvirate left standing, his defeat of Magnentius at the Battle of Mursa in 351 enabled him to consolidate his power as the sole ruler of the Empire.

Julian, meanwhile, was granted the opportunity to pursue his studies without undue constraint for the first time. The inheritance of his late grandmother's estate, situated close to the Propontis, provided him with a stable income and a familiar home. In the years that followed, Julian was able to travel somewhat freely, studying under various tutors, both Christian and Pagan. It was during this time that he met Libanius, a Sophist, teacher of rhetoric, and an outspoken Pagan. The Antiochian and Julian struck up a firm friendship; indeed, Libanius would remain a staunch defender of Julian throughout his long life, as evinced in his many surviving letters. Thereafter, Julian's academic journey through Asia Minor took him to Pergamon and Ephesus, driven as he was by an insatiable curiosity and a desire for knowledge. If we accept the testimony of the man himself, the so-called apostasy that would come to define him may be dated to this period. In a letter written some twelve years later, after he had become Emperor, he claimed to have walked the road of Christianity "till his twentieth year".[3]

1. Gregory of Nazianzus, Oration IV 2. Gibbon, XIX 3. Julian, *Letter 47*

Yet to speak of Julian as having apostasised may not be entirely accurate. Throughout his childhood, he was exposed to both religious traditions: images of Apollo and Athena were just as familiar to him as that of Christ; the exploits of Odysseus just as captivating, if indeed not more so, than those of Moses. One could argue that he had followed two parallel paths for the first nineteen years of his life, and while he had nominally been a Christian, "the inclination of Julian was to prefer the gods of Homer and of the Scipios".[1]

Julian thus arrived in Pergamon receptive and eager to learn from the school's foremost philosopher, Ædesius, a scholar renowned for having studied under the influential Neo-Platonist, Iamblichus. Ædesius declined his requests, however – ostensibly on the grounds of old age – and so the responsibility fell to four of his pupils, each of whom would greatly influence Julian's thinking. The primary source of intellectual inquiry in the Hellenic world at that time was Neo-Platonism, a complex system of philosophy and theology originating with the third-century thinker Plotinus. Based on an elaboration and exegesis of the works of Plato, the Neo-Platonists sought to create a coherent system of metaphysics and Pagan theology with a particular emphasis on the absolute divinity of the One, or the Good, and its relation to the human soul. Julian was, as one might expect, immediately drawn in.

After a short spell in Pergamon studying under two of Ædesius' pupils, Eusebius and Chrysanthius, Julian moved on to Ephesus to meet with the third, Maximus. The setting could not have failed to make an impression on the young man. A steadfastly Pagan city, Ephesus was home to one of the seven wonders of the ancient world, the famed Temple of Artemis. As the poet Antipater of Sidon wrote of the temple: "I have gazed on the walls of lofty Babylon along which chariots may race, and the statue of Zeus by the Alpheus; the hanging gardens, and the Colossus of Helios; the immense labour of the high pyramids, and the vast tomb of Mausolus; yet when I saw the sacred house of Artemis that towered to the clouds, those other marvels lost their brilliance, for apart from Olympus itself, the sun has never looked upon anything so grand".[2]

It was here, then, that Julian came under the wing of Maximus, a charismatic philosopher and theurgist whose voice was "such as

1. Gibbon, *Decline and Fall*, XXIII 2. Antipater, *Greek Anthology*, IX

one might have heard from Homer's Athena or Apollo".[1] With his long grey beard and piercing gaze, it is easy to imagine Julian, still very much at an impressionable age, hanging on to his every word. Indeed, of his time with Maximus he would later write: "I arrived at the threshold of philosophy to be initiated therein by the teaching of one whom I consider superior to all the men of my own time. He used to teach me to practise virtue before all else, and to regard the gods as my guides to all that is good".[2]

During this period, Julian was initiated into a number of Pagan mysteries and will have certainly begun performing the sacred rites, albeit in private. While polytheism was not strictly speaking illegal, certain practices, including sacrifice, were. Thus, in spite of his newfound beliefs, he made sure to remain a Christian in the eyes of the public – or more pertinently the eyes of the imperial officials who shadowed him – attending church and even reading at services. Julian doubtless did not wish to attract the attention of his notoriously ruthless cousin, which, for a time, he managed.

Gallus, on the other hand, was not to be so fortunate. In 354, Antioch was in the midst of a food shortage – a recurring problem for the city, as Julian would later discover – with scarcity and rising prices exacerbated by local landowners withholding their grain. After the provincial governor, Theophilus, was murdered during a riot, the young Cæsar intervened, unilaterally issuing an order for food prices to be lowered. In doing so, he had acted outside the remit of his position. Moreover, when the order was ignored, he called for the entire Antiochian council to be executed. This merely served to further alienate the local senatorial class. Constantius, ever distrustful and quick to judge, was not inclined to tolerate what will have assuredly been perceived as the actions of an independently-minded Cæsar. The prætorian prefect, Domitianus, was duly dispatched to Antioch to urge Gallus to return to the Emperor. Following a dispute with the beleaguered Cæsar, however, both Domitianus and the quæstor, Montius, were arrested and subsequently killed. Nevertheless, the pressure eventually told and Gallus made his way westward. In October, 354, near the town of Pola, in southern Istria, Gallus, "with his hands bound like some convicted thief",[3] was beheaded. He had been stripped of the purple and executed without a trial by the order of Constantius. It was a cautionary tale which Julian would never forget.

1. Eunapius, *Lives of the Philosophers, Maximus* 2. Julian, *To the Cynic Heraclius*
3. Ammianus, 14.11.23

The Emperor's suspicions of disloyalty did not abate with the death of Gallus. All of his associates were investigated, including Julian, who was conveyed to Mediolanum to face his cousin. The charge of having conspired against the Emperor was just as absurd as it was serious. Julian argued his innocence, convincingly by all accounts, only to be held for a further seven months, unable to leave or speak with Constantius. His liberation eventually came at the intercession of an unlikely figure, the Emperor's new wife, Eusebia. In Julian's own words: "had not one of the gods desired that I should escape, and made the beautiful and virtuous Eusebia kindly disposed towards me, I could not have escaped from his hands by myself".[1] The Empress first secured an audience for him with Constantius, then spoke in his favour amid the antagonism of the court eunuchs (and, one presumes, her husband's abiding paranoia). Thereafter, when it became apparent that a return to his home in Bithynia was no longer agreeable to the Emperor, she intervened again, according to Julian, in order that he might take up residence in Athens instead, something for which he would be forever grateful.

For Julian, no setting could have been more perfect for the resumption of his academic pursuits. Athens was the home of Plato and Aristotle; it was, regardless of its diminished status by the fourth century, the eternal abode of philosophy. For one as enamoured with Hellenic culture as Julian, it was the fulfilment of a deep-rooted yearning: "we who dwell in Thrace and Ionia are the sons of Hellas, and all of us who are not devoid of feeling long to greet our ancestors and to embrace the very soil of that land. This had long been, as was natural, my dearest wish, and I desired it more than to possess treasures of gold and silver".[2]

While studying at the university, he quickly established a close friendship with Priscus, the fourth of Ædesius' students. Tall and handsome, Priscus "kept his own convictions hidden as though he were guarding a treasure",[3] something to which Julian would have doubtless related. Sadly, however, his time in Athens was to be cut short. In October, 355, having spent less than four months "amidst the groves of the academy, far from the treachery of courts",[4] the order came for him to return at once to Mediolanum, with no explanation given. Julian was crestfallen.

1. Julian, *Letter to the People and Senate of Athens*

2. Julian, *Panegyric in Honour of Eusebia*

3. Eunapius, *Lives of the Philosophers, Priscus*

4. Gibbon, *Decline and Fall*, XIX

Upon his return, he was immediately placed under house arrest just outside the city, his contact with the outside world limited to the occasional letter of encouragement from Eusebia. One year on from the execution of his brother, Julian must surely have feared the worst. He consoled himself with the belief that, as per his beseechment, Athena had appointed guardians to look over him, "for everywhere she was my guide, and on all sides she set a watch near me".[5] By the time he entered Mediolanum, his fate had already been determined. His life was not to be forfeit; rather, he was to be made Cæsar. Following the warm embrace of the Empress, Julian was set upon by a gaggle of court servants who promptly shaved his beard and exchanged his cloak for the military attire of a Roman soldier. The levity this provoked within the imperial court was not entirely appreciated by the future Emperor. As he would later remark: "at the time, then, I inspired their ridicule, but a little while later their suspicion, and thereafter their jealousy was inflamed to the utmost".[1] Julian, still a young man of about twenty-four years, was entirely ill-at-ease; he had no military training, no experience of court politics outside his sporadic confinements, and now, like Gallus before him, was being thrust into a position where one misstep could cost him his life.

Throughout Constantius' rule, as with much of its history, the province of Gaul had been a persistent source of strife, with the troubles west of the Alps showing no sign of abating. During the civil conflict with Magnentius, the Emperor had enlisted the support of various Germanic tribes from beyond the Rhine to ensure his victory. Hordes of Franks and Alemanni were invited to cross the Rhine with the promise of impunity and the hopes of spoil. The usurper was duly defeated, but the temporary service of the Barbarians had become a permanent headache. Having granted them the freedom to raid in Gallic territory, Constantius "soon discovered and lamented the difficulty of dismissing these formidable allies after they had tasted the richness of Roman soil".[2] With disorder in the west and the threat of Persian encroachment in the east, the Emperor concluded that a military surrogate in Gaul was imperative, and that his young, politically unambitious cousin would be the one to fulfil this role.

On 6th November, Julian took his place atop a high platform surrounded by eagles and standards, with the Emperor beside him

1. Julian, *Letter to the Senate and People and Athens*

2. Gibbon, *Decline and Fall*, XIX

and all of the troops stationed near Mediolanum assembled before him. Constantius took Julian by his right hand and proceeded to address the crowd. First, he explained the purpose behind his decision; then, when their approval had been voiced, he placed the purple robe upon his cousin's shoulders, before resuming his speech. As soon as the Emperor had finished, the troops "clashed their shields against their knees with a fearsome din"[1] in a gesture of applause and approbation. For Julian, however, the mood appears to have been one of apprehension. As Constantius and he were being conveyed back to the imperial residence, Julian is said to have whispered to himself a verse from the Iliad: "wrapped in death's purple by all-powerful fate".[2]

A few days later, the new Cæsar was united in marriage with Helena, the sister of Constantius. Little is known about Helena; indeed, Julian scarcely mentioned his wife, who was to die five years later during childbirth.

On 1st December, Julian departed for Gaul in the company of a modest escort, only four of whom were drawn from his own attendants. Of these "only one knew of my attitude towards the gods, and, as far as he was able, secretly joined me in their worship".[3] It was not to be an auspicious beginning to his appointment. As they arrived in Taurinorum, news reached him that Colonia Agrippina, the famous capital city of Lower Germania, had been overwhelmed and destroyed by a large force of Franks. Additionally, it was revealed that the imperial court had known about the disaster prior to his leaving, but had supposedly chosen to withhold the information from him lest it disrupt his preparations. It was the first indication that the authority of the new Cæsar extended little beyond his title. As Julian perceived the situation: "I was sent not as commander of the garrisons but rather as a subordinate of the generals stationed there. For letters had been sent to them and express orders given that they were to watch me as vigilantly as they did the enemy, for fear that I should attempt to cause a revolt".[4]

From the moment Julian arrived in Vienna, he was "kept under the strictest control and deprived of the means of making any present to his troops",[5] a customary practice for rewarding one's soldiers. As disappointing as this may have been for him, Constantius' approach was an eminently reasonable one. Julian

1. Ammianus, 15.8.15 2. ibid. 15.8.17

3. Julian, *Letter to the People and Senate of Athens* 4. ibid. 5. Ammianus, 22.3.7

had no experience of or training in military and public affairs; to invest such a person with unrestricted authority over a third of the Empire, in a region famous for rebellions no less, would have been folly. For the time being, his cousin's role would effectively be ceremonial; he was to carry the banner of the Augustus and little more.

Julian's response would come to define not just his time in Gaul, but the rest of his life. Rather than retreat into the comfort and security of his new stately residence, far from the din of battle, to delegate matters of war and statecraft to others, and to continue with his studies in relative seclusion, only venturing forth to perform the few duties expected of him, the young Cæsar, more acquainted with books than arms, resolved to become worthy of his title. His scholastic education had left him "in profound ignorance of the practical arts of war and government",[1] and in order to correct this, he committed himself wholly to the venture from the moment he arrived. His first winter in Gaul would be one of transformation: he was to become a soldier and a leader.[2]

Having been abruptly "dragged from the schools and into the clamour of arms",[3] Julian arrived in Vienna a young man "of slight build".[4] It was therefore essential that he prepare himself physically. To this end, he undertook the training regime of a Roman military recruit – a demanding set of exercises which were to be performed every day, without fail, typically in both the morning and the afternoon. Julian will have sparred and trained at the sword-post extensively using a *rudis*, the wooden version of the standard-issue gladius. According to Vegetius' *De Re Militari*, he will have likely also thrown javelins and lead-weighted darts repeatedly without pause, felled trees, jumped ditches, swam in ice-cold water, and marched at full-step in armour while carrying a burden of up to 20 kg.[5]

His commitment to becoming a soldier was not limited to military training, however. As in the case of the famous Cynic, Diogenes, of whom he would later write admiringly, Julian "exposed his body to hardships in order that he might make it stronger than it was naturally".[6] Each night, he slept not upon a soft bed with silk sheets and a duvet, but a rug and coarse blanket; while throughout the winter, he forwent the benefit of a fire in his bed-chamber. As regards food, he seems to have been of a mind

1. Gibbon, *Decline and Fall*, XIX 2. Libanius, *Oration* 18 3. ibid.
4. Ammianus, 22.3.7 5. Vegetius, I.XIX 6. Julian, *To the Uneducated Cynics*

with Democritus in that "fortune provides a man's table with luxuries; virtue with only a frugal meal". For despite Constantius having made generous provision for his cousin's table, Julian rejected delicacies such as pheasant and sow's udders, subsisting instead on the basic diet of the common soldiers. This will have amounted to a simple ration of bread with some meat and, in the manner of his Gallic troops, a helping of beer.

Before the close of winter, word reached Vienna that the ancient city of Augustodunum, a wealthy and populous settlement whose walls were extensive but crumbling with age, had been besieged by Alemanni. Only the vigilance of a small group of veterans had saved the city from being overwhelmed. The unfledged Cæsar's first opportunity to participate in a military campaign was upon him. In keeping with his studious nature, Julian had taken to reading any available literature that might assist him in this endeavour, with Julius Cæsar's *Bellum Gallicum*[1] becoming a firm favourite, such that he considered it "a necessary provision for campaigns".[2] It would later be remarked that Julian "marched with his books, for he always had in his hands either books or arms".[3]

On 24th June, he arrived in Augustodunum, eager to put his preparations into practice. The plan was to march to Remorum where they would rendezvous with the rest of the army under general Marcellus, who, having taken over from Ursicinus, ultimately held sway over military affairs in Gaul. A war council was held to determine which route ought to be taken, with Julian electing to take the shortest of the three options, the path that he knew would lead them through dense forest. The risk of ambush was considerable. Whether naive or bold, the young commander had no intention of shrinking from battle with the Barbarians. With a small contingent of cavalry and artillerymen, Julian set off north at once, quickly reaching Autessiodurum without incident. After a brief rest, they began the long, and far more challenging, march to Tricassium. As they advanced, the column increasingly came under attack from German war-bands using the forest as cover. By strengthening his flanks and repeatedly reconnoitring their surroundings, Julian minimised the threat of ambush; then, when the terrain was favourable, he launched an assault which devastated the enemy and put the survivors to flight. Their

1. *Commentaries on the Gallic War* 2. Julian, *Panegyric in Honour of Eusebia*
3. Libanius, *Oration 18*

subsequent arrival at Tricassium was so unexpected that the city, ever fearful of Barbarian raids, hesitated before opening the gates to them. After another brief halt, they made their way to Remorum without further engagements.

For Julian, the success of this venture – his first taste of battle – will have assuredly given him confidence. For his troops, the significance of their Cæsar marching into camp with various trophies of war should not be understated. In the Roman conception, victory was more than a solely human event: "the victory of a chief often assumed the features of an independent divinity, or *numen*. Through triumph in battle, the victor had become a force existing in an almost transcendent order; a force not of the victory achieved in a given moment of history, but, as the Roman expression stated exactly, of a 'perpetual' or 'perennial' victory".[1]

The following few months were dedicated to reclaiming territory west of the Rhine. While many settlements had been besieged, the Germans appear to have generally avoided taking up residence inside the towns themselves, viewing them "as if they were graves surrounded with nets".[2] The first to be retaken was Brotomagum. As the Roman army neared the town, an Alemanni horde met them in open battle. Julian drew up his forces in a crescent formation, outflanking the German host on both wings and inflicting heavy losses. Some of the survivors managed to flee, while others were taken captive. Thereafter, the Romans encountered little to no resistance.

With the campaign season nearing its end, Julian elected to make the considerable journey northwards to reclaim Colonia Agrippina. The city had been left unoccupied and in a state of utter ruin, with accounts suggesting that they were able to reoccupy it uncontested. Once retaken, Julian remained for several weeks to refortify the settlement and conclude negotiations with the Frankish chiefs. Then, as winter approached, the army disbanded and Julian departed with a small detachment to settle down at Senones, in central Gaul. His first campaign as Cæsar had by any measure been a resounding success.

The year was to have a sting in its tail, however. A number of neighbouring settlements required troops to ensure they had adequate protection, which left Julian undermanned. Learning of the weakened garrison at Senones from either deserters or spies,

---

1. Julius Evola, *Metaphysics of War* 2. Ammianus, 16.2.12

a large German war-band launched an offensive, laying siege to the town and trapping Julian inside. He was significantly outnumbered and had no recourse but to barricade the gates, reinforce the weakest sections of the wall, and wait for support. Marcellus, who was garrisoned nearby with a fair-sized detachment, could have marched to relieve Julian, yet he did not act. After thirty days, the Germans were forced to withdraw in frustration, deeming the affair an exercise in futility. It is not clear why Marcellus neglected to aid his Cæsar; all we know is that he "fell under the suspicions of Constantius and was deprived by him of his command and superseded".[1] Whether motivated by a personal grievance against Julian – fear, perhaps, that his own authority might be undermined by the young Cæsar's growing reputation – or guilty of poor judgement, Marcellus was dismissed from service and exiled to his native Serdica. In his place, a popular and experienced soldier by the name of Severus was appointed *Magister Equitum*.

Julian passed an exacting winter at Senones, the New Year beginning much as the previous had ended, with Barbarian raids persisting across the province. His time was thus divided between much-needed administrative reform and urgent military affairs. As he described the situation: "a great number of Germans had settled themselves with impunity near the towns they had sacked in Gaul. The number of the towns whose walls had been dismantled was about forty-five, without counting citadels and smaller forts. At that time, the barbarians controlled on our side of the Rhine all the land that extends from its sources to the Ocean. Moreover, those who were settled nearest to us were as much as three hundred stades from the banks of the Rhine, and a district three times as wide as that had been left a desert by their raids, such that the Gauls could not even pasture their cattle there. Then, too, there were certain cities deserted by their inhabitants, near which the barbarians were not yet encamped".[2] The assignment before him was a considerable one. Yet Julian had clearly demonstrated enough over the previous year to earn the trust of his Emperor, who made him commander-in-chief of the Gallic army.

In the summer of 357, Julian and Severus set out on campaign, as did a general by the name of Barbatio at the head of a second army in Italy. The plan was to confront the Alemanni in a pincer

1. Julian, *Letter to the Senate and People of Athens* 2. ibid.

movement: Julian's 13,000-strong force was to march southeast from Remorum, while Barbatio's force of 25,000 men was to march northeast from Rauracorum on the Upper Rhine. In theory, the Alemanni horde would be trapped between the two converging armies. Events, however, were to transpire rather differently. The incompetence, or intransigence, of Barbatio – an arrogant man who appears to have been widely detested[1] – would undermine Julian's efforts at every turn. First, he failed to progress from Rauracorum, allowing a German war-band to slip between the two Roman contingents and carry out raids as far as Lugdunum. Then, after Julian successfully intercepted two of the plunder-laden raiding parties, his cavalry was prevented from guarding a route near Barbatio's camp by the tribune Cella, presumably on Barbatio's orders, which enabled the third to escape with their loot in tow.

This inauspicious beginning to their joint campaign was compounded by the lack of cooperation between the two commanders, principally, it would seem, on the part of Barbatio. With the approach of the Roman troops, the Germans who had settled west of the Rhine began to withdraw. Some felled large trees to barricade the roads, while most retreated to the numerous islands dotted along the Rhine. If the Cæsar and his men were to pursue the Barbarians any further, they would need boats. Julian therefore asked Barbatio for seven of the vessels which he had procured, yet the recalcitrant general, not content with merely refusing, burned them all instead. Fortunately for the Cæsar, a few German scouts who had just been captured revealed that, due to it being high summer, certain sections of the Rhine were fordable. Julian promptly sent a body of lightly armed auxiliaries to clear the islands. The operation was a success, and the remaining Germans, realising that the islands were no longer safe, fled east.

Julian and his army then settled at Tres Tabernæ, repairing the fortifications and ensuring the garrison was amply stocked with provisions. Barbatio, meanwhile, was leading his troops across the Rhine alone. The Alemanni launched a surprise attack, overwhelming his army and driving them back to Rauracorum. Most of his baggage train was captured in the rout. This ignominious defeat would be Barbatio's final contribution as he broke up his army and returned to Mediolanum soon after. Within a few years, Barbatio would be executed for his involvement in a plot against Constantius. This suggests that, while his conduct in the Rhine

1. Ammianus, 18.3.6

campaign could be attributed to ineptitude, political ambition should not be discounted. Perhaps he did not wish to be outshone by the Constantinian Cæsar, by a potential rival for the throne.

With Barbatio's departure, and the absence of reinforcements, Julian was less than ideally placed to continue the campaign. To compound matters, word soon reached him that all seven Alemanni kings had united their forces and were marching as one host towards the nearby city of Argentoratum. The Germanic confederation was, relative to the expectation of Barbarians, well armed and armoured. They were experienced warriors; some had even served in the Roman army. Furthermore, their hopes of success were bolstered when a *Scutarii* deserter informed them that Julian had only 13,000 men at his disposal – the Alemanni numbered closer to 35,000.[1] Their confidence was such that they "sent envoys to the Cæsar to demand in an imperious tone that he vacate the territory which they had won by their own valour at the point of the sword".[2]

With summer drawing to a close, Julian resolved to confront the Barbarian horde, and shortly after dawn on the following day, his army departed from Tres Tabernæ. The twenty-one-mile march was conducted at a slow pace under the ever-present threat of ambush. As soon as the Alemanni camp came into view, Julian brought the army to a halt and called his men together. The atmosphere would have undoubtedly been tense. Before them, a vast Barbarian host was assembling in anticipation of battle, impressing upon the Romans, in sight and sound, the reality of their numerical disadvantage. In order to raise the morale of his weary troops and galvanise their appetite for war, Julian employed a textbook piece of rhetorical theatre. During his address to the army, in which he proposed they build a camp to rest and recuperate overnight before facing the Germans, the prætorian prefect, Florentius, spoke up as planned in favour of attacking immediately. Hesitation, he argued, might allow the Barbarians to disperse, and the Roman troops would not "endure to see victory snatched from their grasp".[3] The result was inevitable: the soldiers implored their Cæsar to lead them into battle at once, and when Julian readily acquiesced, they marched forward to meet the enemy with renewed vigour.

---

1. While the number provided for Julian's forces appear to be reliable, the Alemanni host may have numbered nearer 25,000

2. Ammianus, 16.12.3 3. ibid. 16.12.14

When the Roman commanders, who held their position, saw the Alemanni army forming into dense columns, the order was given to draw up in battle formation. Julian commanded the centre, where he had deployed his infantry and some heavy cavalry; the left wing, which was similarly composed, was delegated to the command of Severus; while the greater part of Julian's cavalry was deployed on the right wing, rather than across both flanks. Soon the trumpets were sounded and the Roman army advanced towards the enemy host.

The Alemanni immediately responded by reorganising their line to counter the Roman formation. The Barbarian leader, King Chnodomar, a hulking brute whose "bravery as a warrior was equalled by his pre-eminence as a commander",[1] led the cavalry on their left wing, opposite the Roman cavalry; the mass of the infantry was deployed in the centre; while the second-in-command, Agenarich, lay in ambush amid woodland to their right.

As the Roman army advanced, Severus, either suspecting a trap or discovering Agenarich and his men, halted, forming a barrier between the woodland and the battlefield. With the threat contained, Julian spurred the rest of his men forward with words of inspiritment: "companions in arms, the long-hoped-for day is here when we must wipe away former disgraces and restore the majesty of Rome to its proper glory".[2] The Alemanni infantry, meanwhile, demanded in unison that their leaders dismount from their horses and fight alongside them. Chnodomar, with his distinct flame-coloured plume and gleaming armour, jumped down from his mount at once, followed by the rest of the war-chiefs.

After a brief exchange of missiles, the two opposing armies charged one another. No sooner had both sets of cavalry clashed than the infantry joined the fray, struggling hand to hand and shield to shield. Thick clouds of dust were swept into the air, obscuring the battlefield, and as the fighting swayed to and fro, the "heavens resounded with the roars of the victors and the screams of the wounded".[3] The Roman cavalry wing, buckling under the combined Alemanni assault, fell into disorder and turned to flight, only to be rallied by the intervention of Julian, who rode to meet his men and arrest the collapse. The sight of the Cæsar's standard, a purple dragon, streaming from the tip of his lance impelled the cavalrymen to return and renew the fight.

---

1. ibid. 16.12.24 2. ibid. 16.12.30 3. ibid. 16.12.37

With the right flank of the Roman front line briefly exposed, the Alemanni concentrated their attacks on the infantry, hoping to inflict another rout. The Roman troops held their ground, however, with shields packed together in the traditional *testudo* formation. The two forces were equally matched: the Barbarians had the advantage of strength and numbers, the Romans of training and discipline.[1] With one final charge, the Alemanni, led by their war-chiefs, broke through the Roman front line and forced their way to the centre, where they were met by the veteran *Primani* legion. Drawn up in close formation, the Roman troops held firm, plunging their swords into exposed flesh at every opportunity while guarding against enemy blows. One after another, the Alemanni perished, while the Romans grew in confidence, until finally the Barbarians lost hope and began to flee.

In their flight, many were cut down; those who attempted to escape across the river were assailed with volley after volley of Roman missiles, as per Julian's order to not pursue the enemy into the water. Chnodomar himself was taken prisoner and made to submit to Julian in the presence of the Roman army. The victory was monumental. It had dealt a crushing blow to the Alemanni and definitively proven Julian's ability as a military leader. If he had not been worthy of the title of Cæsar before this battle, he unquestionably was after it.

Following the victory at Argentoratum, Julian would have been forgiven for simply returning to winter quarters. Instead, "the young favourite of Mars"[2] immediately turned his attention to the Franks. After a brief stop at Tres Tabernæ, he informed his men that they would be marching into Germania. The initial – and wholly understandable – protestations of his troops quickly gave way to willingness. Julian's "habit of imposing more hardship on himself than on his men"[3] had earned him a loyal following among the Gallic soldiers. The army at once marched north to Mogontiacum, then crossed over the Rhine using a pontoon bridge. The sudden appearance of a Roman force east of the river left the Germans at sixes and sevens. At first they attempted to sue for peace, then they issued an ultimatum for the Romans to leave or face "war to the death".[4] Julian merely ignored them. As the army advanced deeper into enemy territory, small units were sent ahead to scout the area and conduct raids on any settlements they found. Most of the Germans fled east in response, while the few

1. ibid. 16.12.47 2. ibid. 17.1.1 3. ibid. 17.1.2 4. ibid. 17.1.3

who remained were easily defeated. With hill and field alike now covered in snow, Julian decided to establish a base at Lopodunum. Repairs were conducted on the fort, a garrison was stationed there, and its stores were filled with provisions. What the Germans may have initially assumed to be a punitive raiding expedition now took on the appearance of a more permanent campaign. The Barbarians once again sent envoys to sue for peace. This time Julian agreed to a ten-month truce, which included sworn oaths from three of the German kings to uphold the peace and to supply the Lopodunum fort with corn as needed. These concessions, which Julian had ultimately sought from the beginning, would ensure that there was to be no repeat of the previous winter's disturbances.

The year had entered its final month when the Cæsar and his army at last made for winter quarters. En route, however, they encountered a German war-band which had sought to take advantage of his absence. At the sight of Severus' force, the marauders immediately holed themselves up in two strongholds on the banks of the river Meuse; after a protracted fifty-four-day siege, they eventually succumbed to hunger and surrendered, whereupon Julian had the entire party sent to Mediolanum as a gift to the Emperor. This was to be the final action of a gruelling seven-month campaign. In January, 358, Julian at last arrived in Lutetia, where he would pass the remainder of winter at ease, reflecting on a year in which his exploits had exceeded even the loftiest of expectations.

The success of Julian's first two years in Gaul had emboldened him; no longer was he content to concern himself with military affairs alone. As with Gallus before him, Julian sought to act outside the remit of his office and address certain economic concerns within his province. The first of these pertained to an overdue reform of the taxation system. Owing to widespread tax avoidance, especially among the wealthy, as well as long-term mismanagement of the standard poll-tax, the provincial government was faced with a budget deficit. To resolve this shortfall, the prefect Florentius, under whose purview the administration of finance fell, had proposed a special levy, one which would have inevitably fallen on the shoulders of those predominantly poor citizens who actually paid the existing tax.

Julian vociferously opposed the idea, and when the proposal was later submitted to him, he neither read nor signed it, but merely threw it on the ground. Florentius did not take kindly to the Cæsar's interference. After he appealed to the Emperor to resolve the issue, Constantius sent his cousin a letter of admonishment. Julian replied that it was a "matter for congratulation if the provincials, after being plundered on all sides, could produce the standard taxes; as for a supplement, even torture could not wring that from a man in extreme want".[1] To the chagrin of Florentius, the Emperor seems to have agreed. The supplementary levy was shelved and in its place Julian implemented a few minor but tremendously effective pieces of reform. Through a combination of more efficient collection and a reduction in superfluous state expenditure, not only were there no additional levies introduced, but the rate of tax during Julian's tenure in Gaul was actually reduced by more than two-thirds.[2]

One negative consequence of the affair was a deterioration in relations between Julian and Florentius. Writing shortly after their disagreement, Julian described the latter's proposal as "odious to the gods" because "the hapless people were being betrayed to thieves".[3] The two were to clash once again as the weather improved and the time for campaigning approached.

Because of the time it took for his grain supplies to be replenished from Aquitania, Julian had been unable to enter the field until high summer, a problem compounded by the incursions of Frankish pirates into the *Mare Britannicum*[4] which made shipments of grain from Britannia, the primary alternative, less dependable. The question, then, was how best to bring an end to the Barbarian naval raids. Florentius' solution was a simple one: bribe them. Julian, rather predictably, was less than keen on this suggestion. In his own words: "Florentius had promised to pay the Barbarians a fee of two thousand pounds in weight of silver in return for safe passage. When Constantius learned of this – for Florentius had informed him about the proposed payment – he wrote me to carry out the agreement, unless I thought it absolutely disgraceful. Yet how could it fail to be disgraceful when it seemed so even to Constantius, who was only too much in the habit of trying to conciliate the Barbarians? No payment was made to them".[5]

1. ibid. 17.1.5 2. Monson and Scheidel, *Fiscal Regimes*, pg. 275 3. Julian, *Letter 4*
4. The English Channel 5. Julian, *Letter to the Senate and People of Athens*

Instead, Julian marched against them. With a boldness that bordered on recklessness, the Cæsar gathered together twenty days' worth of rations and promptly set out on campaign. What followed was a rapid and uncompromising offensive: "since the gods protected me and were present to aid, I received the submission of part of the Salian tribe, drove out the Chamavi, and took many cattle, women, and children. I struck such fear into them all and made them tremble at my approach that I immediately received hostages from them and secured a safe passage for my food supplies".[1]

Yet Julian's gamble did not entirely go to plan. After achieving his initial aims, he proceeded to repair three forts along the Meuse and use part of the army's meagre rations to provision them, anticipating that he would be able to obtain grain from the Chamavi before their food supplies were exhausted. This proved to be a serious miscalculation, however, as the crops were not yet ripe. With nothing to eat, his men soon let their discontent be known; and while empty stomachs were the most pressing concern, the subject of pay was a close second. As one soldier protested, they had not "touched or even seen"[2] gold or silver in quite some time. Constantius had not authorised their payment from the public funds, while Julian lacked the means to recompense his men on account of the Emperor's prohibition. Thankfully, words were enough to settle the matter and the campaign continued. Julian then crossed the Rhine for the second time. In a repeat of the previous year's excursion, the advance of the Roman army quickly forced two more Barbarian kings into submission. Both swore oaths of non-aggression, released Roman prisoners, and promised to provide resources as and when required. With the Meuse fortified and his enemies cowed, the Cæsar returned to winter quarters at Lutetia.

In 359, Julian was to carry the Roman eagle beyond the Rhine for a third and final time, marching into Germania almost unopposed and agreeing peace treaties with several more war-chiefs on the same terms as the others. The Barbarians were so severely unsettled by his recent campaigns that the very kings who had long been in the habit of enriching themselves by plundering Gaul, now "bowed their necks to the Roman yoke, and obeyed the imperial commands without a murmur".[3] Given the condition in which he had inherited the province, Julian had cause to be proud

1. ibid. 2. Ammianus, 17.9.4 3. ibid. 17.10.9

of his achievements. As he summarised his time in Gaul: "twenty thousand persons who were held as captives on the further side of the Rhine I demanded and received back; in two battles and one siege I took captive ten thousand prisoners, and those not of unserviceable age but men in the prime of life; I sent to Constantius four levies of excellent infantry, three more of infantry of only slightly less quality, and two very distinguished squadrons of cavalry. I have now with the help of the gods recovered all the towns, and by that time I had already recovered almost forty".[1]

Despite Julian's success – or rather, precisely because of it – his relationship with Constantius began to show signs of an inevitable fracture. News of the Cæsar's accomplishments were met with personal ridicule and far less frivolous invective by the Emperor's court, perhaps in an effort to assuage Constantius' growing unease. While a competent Cæsar may have been an asset, a popular one was a potential rival. When letters crowned with laurel were sent out to the provinces, the victories over the Germans were ascribed to Constantius, while Julian's name was omitted entirely. In truth, there was nothing unusual in having victories attributed to the Emperor, but Julian, not unreasonably, begrudged the lack of recognition. His exclusion was obviously no mere oversight.

The court at Mediolanum was not the only source of political intrigue with which Julian had to contend. Another quarrel with Florentius had left the prefect bitter with resentment. In a naked display of vindictiveness, he wrote to Constantius to inform him that the quæstor Salutius, Julian's trusted adviser and, perhaps more importantly, close friend, was exerting undue influence over the Cæsar. Constantius was only too happy to oblige and duly recalled Salutius in the winter of 359. For Julian, this was a painful blow. In their four years together, the pair had developed a firm friendship, with the older Salutius fulfilling the role of confidant and, one might suggest, mentor. As a fellow Pagan whose Neo-Platonic treatise *On the Gods and the World* remains an influential text to this day, he was one of the few men with whom Julian could share his true religious beliefs. Writing shortly after Salutius' departure, Julian was under no illusions as to why the decision had been taken: "there came into my mind the words 'then was Odysseus left alone'. For now I am indeed like him, since the god has removed you, as with Hector, beyond the range of the shafts

1. Julian, *Letter to the Senate and People of Athens*

which have so often been aimed at you by slanderers, or rather at me, since they desired to wound me through you; to deprive me of the companionship of a faithful friend and devoted brother-in-arms".[1] By the year's end, Julian cut an increasingly isolated figure, and with relations between the Augustus and his Cæsar already strained, events at the beginning of 360 were to bring them to an impasse.

A series of defeats on the eastern march, including the loss of six legions in one siege, had left the Emperor in need of reinforcements. To exacerbate matters, Constantius was made aware that word of Julian's exploits had begun to spread across the Empire. The solution was obvious. In February, 360, Constantius ordered Julian's four most seasoned regiments, along with 300 men specially chosen from each of the remaining divisions, to withdraw from Gaul and march east at once under the command of Lupicinus and Sintula. This would have amounted to roughly half of the Cæsar's force and "all of the most efficient troops without exception".[2] Julian suddenly found himself in a terrible predicament. His first concern was the absence of Lupicinus, who he had recently dispatched to Britannia to deal with unrest in the province. The overseas expedition meant that the Gallic army was already partially depleted. Then there was the question of those local troops who had joined his ranks on the express condition that they would never have to serve beyond the Alps. Julian had given them his word, and though he attempted to explain the consequences such a broken promise would have on the future recruitment of volunteers, his protest fell on deaf ears. Whether these troops were necessary for the coming Persian war, or simply a ploy to leave Julian undermanned and vulnerable, the outcome would be the same; if he "complied with the orders which he had received, he subscribed his own destruction, and that of a people who deserved his affection, while a positive refusal was an act of rebellion and a declaration of war".[3] Julian thus had no choice but to comply with the order. As instructed, Sintula selected the best of the light-armed troops and departed immediately.

The gravity of the situation was such that Julian sought the counsel of Florentius. The prefect, who of all people was perhaps least disposed to help him, rebuffed multiple requests from his Cæsar to return to Lutetia, at first offering an excuse as to why

1. Julian, Consolation on *the Departure of Salutius*

2. Julian, *Letter to the Senate and People of Athens*

3. Gibbon, *Decline and Fall*, XXII

he had to remain in Vienna, then ignoring Julian's summons altogether. With Lupicinus still absent, and Florentius evasive, time pressed on Julian to act. In the end, he decided to recall his men from winter quarters and begin preparations for their departure. The news was not well received by the troops, who felt betrayed by Constantius. In an anonymous piece of literature which was circulated among the camps, the author decried that "we are to be driven off to the ends of the earth like condemned criminals while our families, whom we have set free from their previous captivity after desperate battles, again become the slaves of the Alemanni".[1]

When these concerns were brought before him, Julian acknowledged the grievances of his troops and attempted to alleviate the unrest by permitting their families to travel with them by means of the limited public transport service. The legions then reluctantly gathered outside the gates of Lutetia where Julian went to meet them and offer words of encouragement. On the eve of their departure, his considered oration could not disguise the discontent felt by both parties. Everyone retired to their quarters, resigned seemingly to their respective fates. Come nightfall, however, the soldiers marched together into the city, surrounded the palace, and began to hail Julian as Emperor. With loud chants of "*Julianus Augustus*", the mass of troops urged him to come out and greet them, yet their pleas went unanswered. Inside, Julian wrestled with how he ought to respond: "I prayed to Zeus. When the shouting grew still louder and all was in a tumult in the palace, I entreated the god to give me a sign; thereupon he showed me a sign and bade me yield and not oppose myself to the will of the army".[2]

As day broke, Julian at last appeared before them. He understood only too well that accepting the title of Augustus was an irrevocable act of rebellion, one which brought with it the promise of either execution at the hands of Constantius, or civil war. For the troops, such considerations were perhaps secondary. Julian was promptly placed upon an infantry shield, raised aloft, and unanimously proclaimed Emperor. In a brief moment of levity, they encouraged him to produce a diadem, as befit the crowning of an emperor. With nothing to hand, one of the soldiers asked if his wife might have something he could use. Julian protested that to wear a piece of female jewellery would be

1. Ammianus, 20.4.10   2. Julian, *Letter to the Senate and People of Athens*

"an inauspicious beginning"[1] to his reign. Thankfully, a legionary by the name of Maurus stepped forward and, removing his standard-bearer's collar, placed it atop Julian's head to the raucous applause of the crowd. The Rubicon had been crossed, and it was only a matter of time before word of Julian's impromptu elevation reached Constantius.

Julian knew that he was in no position to challenge his cousin militarily. His only hope of forestalling the inevitable conflict was to convince Constantius that he had no aspirations of becoming sole ruler of the Empire. To this end, he wrote the first of a series of letters to Constantius in which he openly detailed what had occurred outside the palace, offered alternative reinforcements, and promised to accept any replacement for Florentius, who had fled east, albeit while insisting that the Gallic troops should be allowed to remain in Gaul. This and all subsequent letters were signed "Cæsar" as a concession to the Emperor's senior position, and to preserve a semblance of the status quo ante. The task of delivering this letter to Constantius, who was in Cæsarea at the time preparing for his imminent campaign, was assigned to two of Julian's most trusted men, Eutherius and Pentadius. Despite having already been informed of recent events in Lutetia, Constantius flew into such a rage when the letter was read out that the envoys hastily departed in fear of their lives.

Once again, Gaul had produced a rival and forced itself into the preoccupations of the Emperor. Nevertheless, as Julian had likely anticipated, Constantius concluded that the threat posed by a belligerent Persia in the east was a far more pressing concern than his errant cousin in the west. For the time being, words would have to suffice. He ordered his quæstor, Leonas, to make for Gaul at once with a letter in which he admonished Julian for his actions and cautioned him to abandon any ideas above his station. Nebridius, Julian's quæstor, was promoted to prætorian prefect, and several other senior officials were to be either replaced or reassigned.

The day after he arrived in Lutetia, Leonas was given a very public demonstration of Julian's popularity. In front of a large crowd of soldiers and townsfolk who had gathered at the parade-ground, Julian had Leonas present him with the letter from Constantius, which he proceeded to read aloud. When he reached the passage in which Constantius condemned all that had taken

1. Ammianus, 20.4.18

place and declared that Julian should be content with the power of a Cæsar, a deafening chorus of "*Julianus Augustus*" arose on all sides. With that, Leonas was given a letter for Constantius and dismissed. Of the Emperor's nominees, only Nebridius was admitted; the rest of the positions had already been filled by Julian, as per the terms of his first letter.

It was a brazen display of independence in which Julian attempted to assert his authority without courting immediate reprisal. He knew perfectly well that conciliation was no longer an option, and while correspondence between the two sides continued, all that he could realistically hope for was time in which to prepare. Though Julian would later plead that war could have been averted "if only he had allowed us to dwell peaceably in Gaul and ratify what had already been done",[1] this was far more autonomy than Constantius would ever have been willing to permit.

With the Emperor focused on his eastern frontier, Julian spent the campaigning season of 360 solidifying his position in Gaul. Lupicinus was arrested upon his return from Britannia; a Frankish tribe called the Chattuarii were brought to heel; and a number of fortifications along the Rhine were strengthened. An otherwise successful year was marred by the death of his wife, Helena, whose remains he would return to Rome so that she could be buried on the same plot of land as her sister in a Christian ceremony, presumably in accordance with her wishes. Due to at least two miscarriages, the marriage failed to produce a child, and Julian was never to remarry.

In the spring of 361, news reached Julian that a group of Alemanni led by the war-chief Vadomar had ventured across the Rhine and begun raiding in the region of Rætia. A force of Celts and Petulantes under Libino was promptly sent out to restore order, only for the commander to fall in battle and the rest of the troops, outnumbered by the Barbarians, to be put to flight. However angered Julian may have been by the defeat, it paled in significance to what was to follow. One of Vadomar's men was intercepted en route to Constantius by Julian's sentries. On his person they found a letter addressed to the Emperor in which Vadomar had, among other things, written: "your Cæsar is insubordinate".[2] It was all the proof that Julian needed. As with Magnentius, Constantius appeared to be using the Barbarians to

1. Julian, *Letter to the Senate and People of Athens* 2. Ammianus, 21.3.6

undermine his adversary, even if it meant subjecting Roman citizens to pillage and depredation.

Julian's first objective was to capture Vadomar. By good fortune – or a rather obvious piece of subterfuge – Vadomar crossed the Rhine and was duly arrested during a banquet in which one of Julian's men was present. As for his fellow marauders, Julian led a group of light-armed auxiliaries over the Rhine during the dead of night and surrounded the Alemanni camp. Some were slain, while the rest pleaded for and received clemency.

Any lingering doubts Julian may have held were once and for all dispelled as it became abundantly clear that the time for diplomacy was over. Word soon arrived that Constantius had turned his attentions to the west and was preparing to march on Gaul. After sending generous bribes to satraps and kings beyond the Tigris to preserve the peace, the Emperor had set about enlisting reinforcements and requisitioning provisions on a considerable scale and with great urgency. In addition, he dispatched an officer, Gaudentius, to ensure that the coast of Africa was well guarded and that no supplies could reach Julian, while some six million bushels of wheat were sent to depots near the Cottian Alps and the borders of Gaul in anticipation of his advance. The inevitable confrontation was finally upon them.

The only question facing Julian now was whether to remain in Gaul, ready his defences, and await the Emperor's legions, or strike first. Since Constantius enjoyed a significant advantage in terms of troop numbers and resources, the former strategy offered little prospect of success. Julian concluded that "if Constantius had found me waiting in Gaul, clinging to bare life, and, while I attempted to avoid danger, had attacked me on all sides, to the rear and on the flanks by means of the Barbarians, and in front by his own legions, I should, I believe, have had to face complete ruin".[1] If Julian was to take the initiative, however, he needed to act quickly. He determined that his best chance of victory would be to seize Illyricum – and perhaps Constantinople – with a rapid march east before his cousin had time to mobilise his forces and respond.

On 3rd June, Julian marked the festival of Bellona, the Roman goddess of war, by performing a propitiatory rite to the goddess in private, for which he evidently won her favour: "when I had offered sacrifices for my departure, on the day I had thought to

1. Julian, *Letter to the Senate and People of Athens*

announce to the troops that they were to march, the omens were favourable".[1] Confident that he had the blessing of the gods, Julian proceeded to address his assembled troops, who responded to his bid for the throne with a tremendous roar and clashing of shields. The soldiers all held their swords to their throats and swore an oath of allegiance to Julian, vowing to follow him to the death. Each of the officers then followed their example, save for Nebridius, who declared that he could not bind himself to an oath against Constantius. His refusal so enraged the troops that they set upon him with murderous intent, only for Julian to intervene and cover the prefect with his cloak, thereby conferring imperial protection. Nebridius then gratefully withdrew to his home in Tuscany, while Julian set his army in motion and marched for Pannonia.

After arriving in Rauracorum, Julian drew up a plan to conceal his inferior numbers from enemy scouts. The army was to be divided into three for the remainder of the march: Jovinus would lead one party across northern Italy, another would advance through Rætia under the command of Nevitta, and a much smaller force would travel with Julian through the Black Forest. All three detachments were to head for the Danube and then rendezvous near Sirmium. By dispersing his troops in this manner across different regions, they would give the impression of far greater numbers. It was a strategy employed by, among others, Alexander the Great, and would invite the first of many comparisons between Julian and the Macedonian general.

In less than a fortnight, having rushed like a "blazing dart straight to his goal",[2] Julian reached the settlement of Bononia, just nineteen miles north of Sirmium. For as swift as his journey had been, however, it did not entirely escape notice. The commander of Illyricum, Lucillianus, had been informed of Julian's approach and intended to oppose him. With Jovinus and Nevitta still en route, any attempt to take Sirmium by force would have likely failed, yet Julian could ill afford to wait. His solution was a night-raid. A small company of light-armed troops were sent forthwith to seize Lucillianus and bring the obstinate commander before him. When Lucillianus awoke to find himself surrounded by a ring of soldiers he did not recognise, there was little choice but to accept the summons. The veteran soldier nevertheless regained his composure when presented to Julian: "it is rash and incautious

1. ibid. 2. Ammianus, 21.9.6

of your majesty", he said, "to venture with so few men into another's territory". To which Julian wryly responded: "keep these wise words for Constantius. I have allowed you to touch the imperial robe[1] not because I need your advice but to allay your fears".[2]

With Lucillianus out of the way, Julian made at once for Sirmium with hopes of an immediate surrender. His arrival was met by a large crowd of soldiers and civilians who greeted him as "Augustus", then escorted him, with flowers and auspicious prayers, to the palace. It was a tremendous boon for Julian's campaign to have seized Sirmium so soon and without losses. The settlement, located on the ever-volatile Danubian frontier, was an important military and manufacturing centre. By the end of the third century, it had become one of four designated capitals of the Empire. The town was home to substantial arms workshops and a large mint where gold bars were struck with the figure of Fortuna, patron goddess of the town. In celebration of its capture, Julian devoted the following day to chariot races.

Once Nevitta had arrived, it was time to resume their march. Julian led his reinforced army out along the *Via Militaris*, seizing first the town of Naissus then Trajan's Gate.[3] The former provided control of the two primary routes from central Europe to the Ægæan; the latter, situated between the soaring ranges of Hæmus and Rhodope, was a mountain pass of vital importance which separated Illyricum from Thrace – the only obstacle left between Julian and Constantinople. A garrison under Nevitta was posted at Trajan's Gate to guard it, while Julian returned to Naissus to await his remaining forces. With nominal control of most of the Empire, and the capital almost in his grasp, the campaign had thus far been an unqualified success. Yet nothing, of course, is so fickle as fortune. No sooner had he arrived back at Naissus than an unexpected and rather alarming piece of news reached him.

After taking Sirmium, Julian had dispatched the two legions and a cohort of archers that were stationed at the town to Gaul, wary that their questionable loyalty might undermine efforts in Illyricum. The troops had then marched as far as Aquileia, a prosperous and well-fortified city at the head of the Adriatic,

1. "The *adoratio purpuræ* required bending the knee and touching or kissing an emperor's purple *paludamentum*; it was portrayed as a privilege enjoyed only by those of the highest rank, who were admitted to the emperor's presence hierarchically" – Chin; Vidas, *Explorations in Intellectual History*

2. Ammianus, 21.9.8 3. Also referred to as the Succi Pass

before abandoning their orders and barricading themselves inside. Whether inspired by loyalty to Constantius or displeasure at being sent west, this act of defiance, orchestrated by the cavalry commander Nigrinus, was a bitter setback for Julian. The main route from Illyricum to Italy, and by extension Gaul, was now blocked by Nigrinus and his men, who had also begun to rally the local population to their cause. When Julian learned of developments in Aquileia, his only recourse was to send orders for Jovinus, who had just entered Noricum, to return at once and lay siege to the city – a city which had repeatedly shown itself to be impregnable.

Meanwhile, Julian penned letters to Rome, Athens, Corinth, and Sparta in order to present his side of the imperial dispute, and "to maintain, by argument as well as by arms, the superior merits of his cause".[1] Unfortunately, his words were not entirely well received. Not in the Roman Senate, at least. Constantius retained a fair degree of support within the Eternal City, such that blame for the grain shortage they were experiencing, created by the blockade in Africa, was laid at the feet of Julian. The rival Augustus did not endear himself any further with the appointment of Nevitta, a "rather boorish and uncultivated"[2] Gaul, as consul – a decision not terribly well received by the Senators.

Moreover, there was to be no reprieve for Julian as his predicament only deepened. A report came through that troops from across Thrace had been gathered together under the command of Marcianus and were preparing to advance on the Gate of Trajan. In response, Julian assembled the Illyricum army and began to formulate a plan. Yet the situation was far worse than he realised. In the east, the Persian King, Shapur II, had suddenly abandoned his campaign, leaving Constantius free to mobilise his forces and march westwards. With Jovinus still occupied in Aquileia, dissent growing in Italy, and the Emperor's gaze now firmly fixed on the enemy at home, Julian's fate appeared to be sealed.

And yet the one "upon whom fate closed"[3] was not Julian. In late Autumn, with the prospect of a bloody civil war on the horizon, two high-ranking officers arrived from Thrace with an announcement: Constantius was dead. The forty-four-year-old Emperor had fallen ill during his return journey, and, anxious to reach the capital, had marched on in spite of his worsening

1. Gibbon, *Decline and Fall*, XXII 2. Ammianus, 21.10.8 3. *The Iliad*, IV, 493

condition. On 3rd November, in Cilicia, near the foot of Mount Tarsus, the severity of his fever halted their advance, and within a matter of hours he was dead.

There is little reason to suspect that Constantius had been in poor health – indeed, his active role in military affairs would suggest quite the opposite. From Julian's perspective, then, this must have seemed like divine intervention. Having committed himself, by choice or necessity, to a course of action from which there could be no return, his initial hopes of victory had rapidly begun to slip away. With the passing of the Emperor, however, everything had turned. The armies of Constantius had promptly sworn their allegiance to him, and none, bar the grumblings of a few court officials, had risen in opposition. Julian, without spilling the blood of his fellow Romans, had become the Empire's sole Augustus.

For the immediate future of Rome, his victory was far more significant than most realised at the time. With one burden lifted, another swiftly followed. Julian at once disposed of the veil of Christianity which he had been forced to maintain for over a decade, and began to worship the gods publicly. In a letter to his friend and tutor, Maximus, he wrote with evident excitement: "I worship the gods openly, and the whole mass of the troops who are returning with me worship the gods; I sacrifice oxen in public; I have offered to the gods many hecatombs as thank-offerings. The gods command me to restore their worship in its utmost purity, and I obey them, truly, and with a firm will".[1] With a newfound sense of liberation and heightened purpose, he advanced towards the capital "like a second Triptolemus",[2] eager to begin his reign in earnest.

On 11th December, 361, Julian entered Constantinople as Emperor. His arrival was greeted by the formal pleasantries of the senate and the vociferous acclamation of the populace, who had gathered in considerable numbers to welcome him home. It was undeniably a remarkable spectacle. When Constantius had released Julian from confinement and shipped him off to Athens, he was but a bookish youth of slight build, with no aspirations for the throne. Now, having won his fame in Gaul, "acquiring accessions of might and strength wherever he appeared, and seizing everything with an ease that rivalled the flight of rumour",[3] he found himself in possession of the Empire, being escorted

1. Julian, *Letter* 8 2. Ammianus, 22.2.3 3. ibid. 22.2.5

through the city of his birth as the undisputed ruler of Rome. For Julian, and indeed many onlookers, there could be little doubt that he "enjoyed the favour of the immortal gods".[1]

Attendant to his elevation to the imperial throne was the question of how he intended to wield this newfound authority. From his earliest writings, it is clear that Julian, as with most things, followed the teachings of Plato. His model for rulership was thus heavily indebted to Plato's concept of the "philosopher king".[2] Throughout his works, Julian placed the utmost value on knowledge, absolute truth, temperance, the triumph of reason over passion, and the sanctity of the law, each of which pertained to a divine and not merely man-made order. The sovereign, in his view, should be "humane towards his subjects, ruling them and guiding them to what is best, never yielding to his own passions or becoming the slave of theirs"[3]; he "ought by every means in his power to observe the laws"[4] for "it is evident that the gods gave them to us"[5]; and he must set an example for his people "by showing that he himself is what he would have them be".[6] In the pursuit of these ideals, Julian held imitation of the essential nature of the gods to be the ultimate end to which not only the leader, but every man should aspire. Indeed, there is a telling moment in his work *The Cæsars*, in which the gods are tasked with judging the respective virtues of each Roman Emperor. When Marcus Aurelius, whom Julian greatly admired and doubtless sought to emulate, is asked what he considers to be noblest in life, he simply responds: "to imitate the gods".[7]

Julian's philosopher king was not merely an intellectual who sought to govern through the wisdom of learned men, but a warrior and a spiritual crusader, as well. In short, he believed that "the man who presumes to reign should aspire to the perfection of the divine nature; he should purify his soul from its mortal and terrestrial part; he should extinguish his appetites, enlighten his understanding, regulate his passions, and subdue the wild beast which, according to the lively metaphor of Aristotle, seldom fails to ascend the throne of a despot".[8] That he occasionally fell short of such high expectations is perhaps understandable. That being said, Julian was only too aware of his own limitations. In a

1. *The Iliad*, XXIV, 714 2. Plato, *The Republic* 3. Julian, *To the Cynic Heraclius*
4. Julian, *Letter to Themistius* 5. Julian, *Letter 20*
6. Julian, *The Deeds of Emperor Constantius* 7. Julian, *The Cæsars*
8. Gibbon, *Decline and Fall*, XXII

letter to the philosopher Themistius, likely written just after he had been appointed Cæsar, he commented how "it seems that the task of ruling is beyond man, and that a king requires a more divine character".[1]

One of Julian's first acts as Emperor was a thorough and long overdue reform of the imperial court. As the story goes, soon after arriving in Constantinople, he had called for the service of a barber. When a man in ostentatious attire presented himself, Julian drily remarked: "I sent for a barber, not a treasury official".[2] He then inquired as to the terms of the man's employment, and was duly informed that he received twenty men's allowance of bread and a proportionate amount of fodder for his cattle every day, as well as a substantial annual salary and many profitable bonuses. Julian's astonishment soon turned to horror as the extent of the profligacy at Constantius' court became apparent.

The opulence of the imperial palace had grown to such a degree over the prior century that the extravagance of its ornaments was matched only by the lavish spreads and exotic delicacies which comprised the court's subsistence. A thousand cooks, as many butlers and barbers, and even more waiters constituted an army of servants more costly than the legions, while the eunuchs who swarmed the court were more numerous than "flies in springtime".[3] The luxury of life in the capital served only to breed vice among its occupants; officials "who had grown fat on the plunder of temples" and had a "habit of appropriating the property of others", simply "bribed, robbed, and squandered without restraint of any kind". For far too many, the classic Roman virtue of self-discipline had given way to self-indulgence, and thus "triumphs in battle were replaced by triumphs at table".[4]

To Julian, who placed great importance upon moderation and frugality, the excesses of the imperial bureaucracy were anathema. In his exhortation to the Cynics of his day, he recalled with approval the following words from Diogenes: "it is not among men who live on bread that you will find tyrants, but among those who eat costly dinners".[5] Julian was also fully prepared to practice that which he professed. By a single edict, "he reduced the palace of Constantinople to an immense desert".[6] Almost all of the staff were dismissed, while the lavish indulgences to which its residents had become accustomed were reined in significantly.

1. Julian, *Letter to Themistius* 2. Ammianus, 22.4.9 3. Libanius, Oration 18
4. Ammianus, 22.4.4 5. Julian, *To the Uneducated Cynics* 6. Gibbon, XXII

Julian was eager not only to reform the culture of the capital, but, as he had done in Gaul, to relieve Rome's citizens from the burden of taxation. Yet he was not without his detractors. In the execution of this sweeping clear-out, Julian was accused of "proceeding with too much haste and inconsiderate severity".[1] It was not to be the only divisive act of his early reign.

Shortly after becoming Emperor, Julian had established a commission to investigate the crimes of his predecessor's regime. As he wrote to a friend in Egypt at the time: "what little hope I had of hearing that you had escaped the three-headed hydra! Zeus be my witness that I do not mean my cousin Constantius – indeed, he was what he was – but the wild beasts who surrounded him and cast their baleful eyes on all men. I do not wish that these others should be punished unjustly; but since many accusers are rising up against them, I have appointed a court to judge them".[2] In the interest of impartiality, the trial was held in Chalcedon, on the other side of the Bosphorus, while Julian himself played no part in proceedings. He appointed six judges to oversee the inquiry, all of whom held positions of import within the Empire, but possessed varying reputations. His close friend and mentor Salutius, who had just been made prætorian prefect of the East, was named president of the commission; the other appointees included the consul elect Mamertinus, and four commanders, Nevitta, Jovinus, Arbitio, and Agilo – the latter two having served under Constantius.

In the trial which followed, several ministers were sentenced to exile, while a similar number were condemned to death. It was transparently a political purge carried out with the barest of consideration for due process. Yet few will have spared any sympathy for the accused. Constantius' minions were notoriously corrupt and had inspired the antipathy of many, especially among the legions. Their guilt was, for the most part, "indisputable".[3] The one notable exception was a finance minister by the name of Ursulus, whose execution drew widespread disapproval. One year prior, while observing the ruins of Amida, he had offered a mocking critique of the eastern forces and their avarice,[4] which the very same troops present at the tribunal had evidently not forgotten. The inequity of his treatment was such that, according to Ammianus, "Justice herself must have wept".[5]

1. ibid. 2. Julian, *Letter* 13 3. Ammianus, 22.3.2 4. ibid, 22.11.5
5. ibid, 22.3.7

Julian's response was to distance himself from the incident, declaring that the decision had been taken without his knowledge. Nevertheless, in an effort to make amends for the injustice, and perhaps to assuage some guilt, he ensured that the property of Ursulus, which, as per law, had been confiscated by the state upon his conviction, was returned to his family. Ultimately, while some criticism was levelled at the new Emperor for his handling of these affairs, both the Chalcedon Trials and especially the court reform were broadly well received, the latter only enhancing his popularity among the general citizenry.

With the new year came the inauguration of Mamertinus and Nevitta as consuls. Julian decided to attend the ceremony on foot, making his way to the senate house with other persons of distinction rather than summoning everyone to the palace as Emperors before him had done. Some decried the move as a public display of affected humility, yet Julian's actions were, if somewhat at odds with recent custom, perfectly sincere.

He was to regularly be in attendance at the senate house where he played an active role in the resolution of various disputes. For Julian, "who contemplated with reverence the ruins of the Republic",[1] the traditional institutions of Rome were, irrespective of their fallen state, still worthy of the highest regard. Often, he would stay up long into the night composing orations to be delivered in the senate, making him the first sovereign to present speeches in the *curia* since Julius Cæsar.[2]

In a similar vein, when Mamertinus hosted a day of games at the Hippodrome, Julian performed the customary manumission of a slave. The moment he was made aware that in so doing he had infringed upon the jurisdiction of another magistrate, albeit unwittingly, he promptly fined himself ten pounds in gold. The Augustus then embraced his faux-pas and declared to the audience that "he was subject, like the rest of his fellow citizens, to the laws, and even to the forms, of the Republic".[3]

Such conduct, indicative of his early reign, endeared him to many, but attracted the disapproval of a quibbling few who felt that his behaviour "degraded the majesty of the purple".[4] One suspects that Julian might well have countered that he was, after all, *Princeps Civitatis*,[5] and that even the first among citizens is a

1. Gibbon, *Decline and Fall*, XXII 2. Socrates Scholasticus, III
3. Gibbon, *Decline and Fall*, XXII 4. ibid.
5. One of the official titles of a Roman Emperor, meaning "first citizen"

citizen nonetheless. What some perceived as a pretension to humility could more charitably be understood as an earnest dedication to the historical ideals of the Republic.

Of course, Julian's attentions extended far beyond the capital. In his efforts to reshape the Empire, a wide-ranging series of reforms were introduced on issues such as transport, defence, corruption, taxation, and public service. One of the common threads running through many of his policies was a marked shift towards decentralisation. Over the centuries, the civil service had increased continuously in size, doubling from around fifteen thousand to thirty thousand during the reign of Diocletian alone.[1] A concurrent flow of people and resources into the imperial capital, in tandem with a centralisation of authority, had gradually hollowed out the provinces and left the state burdened with mounting expenses, not to mention a plague of ever-more-numerous bureaucrats. Julian therefore sought to reverse this trend by devolving power to the regional councils and trimming the bloated, and one might even say byzantine, imperial bureaucracy. The hope was that these measures would both reinvigorate the provincial towns and relieve pressure on the central government, as well as ensuring that the aforementioned reforms could be more effectively implemented by local officials. The attendant reduction in state spending and fiscal waste was notably in keeping with Julian's successful policies in Gaul.

Alongside the ordinary considerations of public affairs, Julian embarked upon a campaign of religious reform which aimed to simultaneously undo the advance of Christianity and revitalise the traditional Greco-Roman cults. From the perspective of those living in the fourth century, it was by no means an inevitability that Christianity would come to dominate the Empire, nor that the native polytheistic cults would be almost entirely supplanted, living on through half-remembered folk traditions and the scattered ruins of once sacred landmarks. The Galilæans, as Julian was fond of calling them, had gained considerable political influence and institutional privilege over the previous fifty years, primarily due to the reforms introduced by Constantine, yet most of the population, especially outside the large cities, remained Pagan. Julian's plan was thus two-fold: first, amend the laws and customs which advantaged Christians and disadvantaged Pagans, reversing their respective positions where appropriate; second,

1. Jones, *The Later Roman Empire*

implement an extensive reformation of the polytheistic cults into a single, coherent, institutionalised Pagan religion.

For all the personal and intellectual reservations Julian had concerning the Galilæan faith, the overriding issue was not, and never had been, about the Christian worship of their god; rather, it was their attitude towards the gods of Rome. The zeal of many early Christians "who despised the worship and overturned the altars"[1] of Pagan deities ensured that there was never likely to be reconciliation. Julian understood that co-existence would be impossible with a creed that not only refused to honour other gods, but had a tendency to view all deities bar its own as either false, or fundamentally evil. It was something of a foreign concept to polytheists and one which threatened the existence of their beliefs, all the more so if Christians became a majority and continued to hold institutional power. For Julian, "a devout and sincere attachment to the gods of Athens and Rome constituted his ruling passion",[2] and he therefore came to view Christianity as a corrupting influence which led his fellow citizens to fall into "impiety" and "godlessness".[3]

Upon his assumption of the imperial seat, Julian had declared that all temples were to be reopened, "sacrifices brought to their altars, and the worship of the old gods restored".[4] Those that had been torn down were to be rebuilt; those that had been vandalised restored. The perpetrators of their destruction were made to either return the plundered columns and statues, or, if unable to do so, pay an equivalent fine as recompense. With the restrictive laws of Constantine and his sons lifted, "there could be seen in every quarter altar fires kindled, blood and burning fat, the smoke of incense, ceremonial processions, and diviners released from fear".[5] The Emperor himself began to publicly participate in these rites, though his eagerness for sacrifice was to sharply divide opinion among even fellow Pagans. Ammianus commented that the offerings "with whose blood he drenched the altars of the gods were all too numerous".[6] For an Augustus who valued moderation so highly, and "who practised the rigid maxims of economy",[7] there was a conspicuous exception when it came to matters of worship.

1. Gibbon, *Decline and Fall*, XXIII 2. ibid. 3. Julian, *Against the Galilæans*
4. Ammianus, 22.5.2 5. Libanius, *Oration* 18 6. Ammianus, 22.12.6
7. Gibbon, *Decline and Fall*, XXIII

During this period, Julian had a Mithræum built within the imperial palace, and he also restored the Altar of Victory to the *Curia Julia* in Rome. The latter, removed during the reign of Constantius, was established by Octavian in 29 B.C. and featured a golden statue of the winged goddess Victoria. Its significance in the history of the Empire was such that "at this Altar of Victory, senators burned incense, offered prayers annually for the welfare of the Empire, took their oaths, and pledged on the accession of each new emperor. Thus the statue became one of the most vital links between the Roman state and Roman religion, as well as a tangible reminder of Rome's great past and her hopes for the future".[1]

At the beginning of 362, Julian formalised his proclamation with an edict of universal religious tolerance. It was a move that closely paralleled the initial reforms of Constantine the Great, whose policy of nominal religious freedom had assisted the rise of Christianity within the Empire. At the same time, he remitted the sentence of exile for all Christians who had been banished by Constantius due to doctrinal disagreements and restored to them their property. Julian then summoned to the palace a number of Christian bishops, presumably from different sects, and "warned them in polite terms to lay aside their differences and allow every man to practise his beliefs boldly without hindrance".[2] While the purpose of this edict was unquestionably to defend the rights of polytheists to worship openly and freely, Ammianus perceived an additional consequence, one that may have even been intended by the Emperor. The enforcement of tolerance would, so the argument went, serve to intensify the existing divisions within the Christian community and ensure that Julian would not have to face a unified opposition. In Ammianus' own words: "no wild beasts are such dangerous enemies to man as Christians are to one another".[3] Whether or not the ordinance had been promulgated with such an outcome in mind, that is precisely the effect it had, as the various Christian factions began to bicker amongst themselves.

Julian, meanwhile, set about rescinding the various legal privileges afforded exclusively to Christians, such as the right to draw up wills and appropriate the inheritance of citizens for the Church, act as judges in private courts, and veto appointments. A stipend granted to bishops was also withdrawn. These and a

---

1. Sheridan, *The Altar of Victory*, pg. 187 2. Ammianus, 22.5.3 3. ibid. 22.5.4

number of other incremental changes implemented during his first several months as Emperor brought the two religions to a state of relative parity, the favour of the Augustus notwithstanding. Throughout, Julian adhered to the letter of his religious freedom act, and consistently maintained that there was to be no repeat of the historical persecutions of the Christians. Those who worshipped the gods were not, he exhorted, to "outrage or plunder the houses of those who have strayed rather from ignorance than of set purpose. It is by reason that we ought to persuade and instruct men, not by blows, or insults, or bodily violence. Wherefore, again and often, I admonish those who are zealous for the true religion not to injure the communities of the Galilæans or attack or insult them".[1]

Inevitably, of course, the Emperor's words could not prevent isolated instances of violence from occurring. Amidst the fervour of their liberation, Pagans in several eastern cities sought revenge against those whose ill-deeds, performed under the protection of the previous regime, had not been forgotten. Bloody reprisals were carried out against a number of Christians who had demolished shrines, vandalised temples, defaced statues, and tyrannised polytheists. In each case, Julian reprimanded those responsible for having acted outside the law and reiterated his stance as regards the treatment of Christians. Moreover, these incidents pertained to local grievances rather than any imperial policy. Indeed, even the Christian historian Sozomen was willing to concede that Julian "charged the people not to commit any act of injustice against the Christians, not to insult them, and not to compel them to offer sacrifice unwillingly",[2] while Gregory of Nazianzus, another Christian historian, conspired to criticise Julian's prohibition against sectarian violence on the basis that "he begrudged the honour of martyrdom"[3] to Christians. The question, then, is why.

There are two interpretations of Julian's commitment to religious tolerance and his public defence of Christians. The first ascribes to him a genuine belief in the value of religious liberty and a temper that was averse to despotism. Julian perhaps viewed the behaviour of certain Christians towards their religious opponents as antithetical to the Hellenic tradition and, whether naive or simply idealistic, he hoped to remain above such conduct. These considerations may have "restrained the philosophic

1. Julian, *Letter 41* 2. Sozomen, *E.H.*, V 3. Gregory of Nazianzus, *Oration IV*

monarch from violating the laws of justice and toleration which he himself had so recently established".[1] The second explanation attributes to the Emperor a more pragmatic and arguably cynical motive. Since Christians still held considerable influence within the Empire, and were by no means numerically negligible, Julian did not wish to provoke a bitter civil conflict. If his restoration was to succeed, he needed time. In a letter to a provincial official, he wrote: "I affirm by the gods that I do not wish the Galilæans to be either put to death or unjustly beaten, or to suffer any other injury. Nevertheless, I do assert absolutely that the pious must be preferred to them".[2] Regardless of the rationale behind his policy, then, the end goal was the same. There was to be no heavy-handed persecution of the Christians, but rather a slow and deliberate marginalisation, one that would restore Greco-Roman polytheism as the primary state religion of Rome without bloodshed or overt coercion.

Among his various reforms, one particularly infamous edict stands out for having received almost universal condemnation from historical commentators. In the middle of 362, Julian introduced a law which purportedly forbade Christians from teaching the classics of literature. All of the works of Pagan authors, from Homer to Virgil, Demosthenes to Isocrates, Herodotus to Thucydides, and so forth, were, according to accounts written after the Emperor's death, now denied to teachers who professed Christianity. That no explicit prohibition against or legal coercion towards Christian teachers survives in any of the written records, however, casts doubt upon the prevailing historical narrative.

The primary source for this edict is a letter[3] in which the scholastically-minded Emperor outlined his position on the subject of education. Julian held that those who opposed Hellenism and dishonoured the gods ought not to expound upon the works of men for whom the gods were sacred and a source of inspiration. "If they think that those writers were in error with respect to the most honoured gods, then let them betake themselves to the churches of the Galilæans to expound Matthew and Luke",[4] he wrote. Christian teachers were thus given a simple proposal: do not teach what they do not consider admirable, i.e., the works of Pagans, or "first persuade their pupils that neither Homer nor Hesiod, nor any of these writers whom they interpret

1. Gibbon, XXIII 2. Julian, *Letter 37* 3. Julian, *Letter 36* 4. ibid.

and have declared to be guilty of impiety, folly, and error with respect to the gods, is such as they declare".[1]

The choice presented by Julian has been construed almost exclusively as an ultimatum which was enforceable under the new law. Christian teachers of rhetoric, grammar, and philosophy, it followed, would be made to either renounce their religious views or, if they did not resign of their own volition, face dismissal. Yet there is no firm evidence to support such an interpretation. Indeed, the letter upon which that argument hinges does not appear to be a "legal pronouncement, but rather an exercise in mischievous helpfulness".[2] Julian's 'ultimatum' is in fact an offer, one "calculated to stir up a debate rather than to foreclose one".[3] The Emperor will have likely determined that a debate on this question "promised to damage Christian intellectuals much more than would any penalties, since a significant number of Christians could be counted on to agree with the position which he was expressing".[4] Such an initiative would also conform more closely to Julian's wider approach, as evinced by his insistence upon discussion over violence, and disprivileging over hard repression when dealing with Christians.

What the scope and practical impact of this proclamation would have been is unclear. One might reasonably suspect that "Julian was looking to exploit the imperial Midas touch; the tendency of an emperor's words to take on a life of their own"[5] in the hands of Rome's ministers. It would have assuredly been by no means disagreeable to the Emperor if Pagan teachers were consequently placed at an advantage, and their Christian counterparts at a disadvantage. Julian recognised that education was one of the most important avenues for shaping the minds of future generations, and it was evidently of great importance to him personally. His proclamation made it explicit that Christian pupils were still allowed to attend any school, and that the guidelines, whether enforced by law or simply suggested, only pertained to educators. Without the core Roman curriculum, Christian teachers would have indeed been unable to provide an appealing education to most prospective students, and, as a result, they would have soon found themselves alienated from most influential academic positions and the broader intellectual discourse.

1. ibid. 2. Neil McLynn, *Julian and the Christian Professors* 3. ibid.
4. ibid. 5. ibid.

Throughout the centuries, numerous Christian historians have, perhaps understandably, fallen over themselves to decry the edict in ever-more opprobrious language. Even Ammianus, who otherwise spoke very highly of Julian, considered it a "harsh act which should be buried in everlasting silence" having "somewhat dimmed the glorious course of his renown".[1] That the proclamation demonstrated clear partisanship and, if it was a legal prohibition as some assert, a disregard for universal intellectual freedom is not a matter for debate; the only question is whether notions of equal treatment and unqualified liberty ought to have factored into Julian's thinking. From his perspective, the idea of young Romans learning about Homer or Hesiod through a Christian interpretation was wholly objectionable. Indeed, to allow Christians to utilise and repurpose the accumulated learning of a millennium of Pagan civilisation amounted, in Julian's eyes, to crafting a powerful weapon and handing it over to one's enemy: "in the words of the proverb, we are stricken by our own arrows. For it is from our own writings that they take the weapons with which to engage in war against us".[2] The conflict was not merely a theological debate, of course, but a struggle for the soul of Rome itself. When one considers, therefore, how history was to unfold, it is rather difficult to find fault with Julian's judgement.

The Emperor's plans for the revival of Paganism, or Hellenism, as he referred to it, were not limited to the displacement of Christianity. A simultaneous reformation of the religion was undertaken with a special emphasis upon the role of the Pagan priests, who were central to realising Julian's aspirations. In a letter to the high-priest of Galatia, he lamented how "when no Jew ever has to beg, and the impious Galilæans support not only their own poor but ours as well, all men see that our people lack aid from us", after which, he enjoined the priest to "teach those of the Hellenic faith to contribute to public service of this sort; accustom those who love the Hellenic religion to these good works by teaching them that this was our practice of old".[3] As *Pontifex Maximus*, Julian imparted his vision to the priests who in turn were to act as exemplars of the faith and offer instruction to the worshippers. The Emperor determined that charity, communal solidarity, pursuit of virtue, and a rediscovery of neglected traditions would be vital in reversing the decline of Paganism in the Roman world, and it is these ideas that the priests were to promote and embody.

---

1. Ammianus, 22.10.6   2. Julian, *Fragments*, X   3. Julian, *Letter 22*

Julian's expectations in this regard left little room for compromise. He demanded of his priests that they lead a life of absolute moral integrity and unwavering dedication in service of the gods and the pious. As pillars of the community and spiritual leaders, the priests were "to hold fast to deeds of piety, approaching the gods with reverence, and neither saying nor listening to anything base". Furthermore, they were "to keep themselves pure not only from impure or shameful acts, but also from uttering words and hearing speech of that character".[1] The importance Julian placed upon virtuous conduct was such that priests were also admonished to not attend "the licentious theatrical shows of the present day",[2] nor to "drink in a tavern, or control any craft or trade that is base and not respectable".[3] As regards their religious duties, he expected the priests to pray at least twice a day, without fail, once at dawn and once more in the evening. In addition, Julian deemed it "not fit that a consecrated priest should pass a day or a night without sacrifice".[4] Finally, both the priests and the broader Pagan community were urged to "above all exercise philanthropy",[5] for "the gods are called by us 'gods of kindred' and Zeus the 'God of Kindred' yet we treat our kinsmen as though they were strangers".[6] For all Hellenes in kind, he affirmed that "it is our duty to adore not only the images of the gods, but also their temples, sacred precincts, and altars" and to "honour the priests as officials and servants of the gods".[7]

Julian's reforms have been seen by some as a conscious attempt to emulate Christianity; to create a Hellenic church that could compete with its monotheistic adversary in terms of the values it espoused, the structure of its organisation, and the role it played within Roman society. There is undeniably some truth to this, whether the Augustus would be willing to admit it or not. It was an eminently pragmatic, and perhaps even necessary, approach. Where such a characterisation falls down, however, is with the suggestion that Julian's own views were also significantly influenced by Christianity; that he had been, as he would describe it, "infected"[8] by the Galilæan faith. The primary issue here is one of chronology, or rather, intellectual lineage. As a syncretic religion, Christianity represented a fusion of Jewish theology and Greek philosophy, the latter being inseparable from the wider

1. Julian, *Letter to a Priest* 2. ibid. 3. Julian, *Letter 22*
4. Julian, *Letter to a Priest* 5. ibid. 6. ibid. 7. ibid.
8. Julian, *Against the Cynic Heraclius*

Hellenic faith. Whether one looks to Plato and Aristotle – two men whom Julian regarded as essentially divine – or even the Stoics and the early Cynics, the influence their ideas had upon the intellectual foundation of Christianity is impossible to overstate. Moreover, Julian's guiding philosophy, Neo-Platonism, was contemporaneous with the consolidation of Christian thought and "exerted great influence" not only upon the Christians of the time, but all since whose ideas have been "enriched with fundamental Neo-Platonic insights".[1] Indeed, one of the most important Church Fathers, Saint Augustine, was an avowed Platonist who used the philosophy as a lens through which to interpret biblical scripture and elaborate Christian theology.

It is perhaps more accurate, then, to suggest that Julian was a product of the period into which he was born, and that his ideas reflected the currents of thought that dominated the intellectual landscape of fourth-century Rome. For as fond as he was of quoting Homer, Julian's Hellenism belonged to another age. He recognised, certainly, that the future would have to take root in the past, and that Homer's poems contained the models and principles around which Hellenes might form their lives: "nature as foundation, excellence as goal, beauty as horizon".[2] Yet his was no longer the world of Odysseus and Penelope. The vitality which had originally animated Greek and Roman Paganism had been lost, or at the very least depreciated by prosperity and the march of civilisation. This vitality could be rediscovered, of course, but such exhortations from Julian as "let everyone make the basis of his conduct moral virtues",[3] as well as a strong emphasis upon the abstract over the imminent, bespeak the subtle but significant shift away from the Homeric vision and towards the Neo-Platonic.

For the first several months of his reign, Julian had been able to focus solely upon public affairs and the aforementioned reforms. Away from domestic matters, however, a renewal of hostilities with Persia beckoned. The envoys of Shapur II had been dismissed from the capital, whereupon Julian had begun preparations for his first campaign as Augustus. In the summer of 362, he departed from Constantinople and marched for Antioch, the third largest city in the Empire and, more importantly, the base of Roman military operations in the East. Situated near the mouth of the Orontes river, Antioch was a tremendously wealthy and populous city that

1. O'Meara, *Neoplatonism and Christian Thought* 2. Venner, *The Shock of History*
3. Julian, *Letter to a Priest*

had prospered over the centuries in large part due to its strategic location, serving as a hub for trade between Mediterranean Europe and Asia. The "splendid jewel of the Orient"[1] was replete with grand theatres, temples, aqueducts, and baths. Additionally, it had been one of the first centres of Christianity, with the missionary St. Paul having resided in the city.

Julian's arrival at Antioch in July coincided with Adonia, an annual festival celebrated in honour of Adonis, the mortal lover of Aphrodite whose death symbolised the cycle of decay and revival in nature. As the legend goes, Adonis was fatally wounded by a wild boar and subsequently bled to death in the arms of the goddess. While Aphrodite mourned, her tears fell upon the body of Adonis, causing Anemone flowers to spring forth. During Adonia, those participating in the festival, most of whom were women, would plant "Gardens of Adonis", in which fast-germinating plants would quickly sprout before withering and dying. They would also conduct a ceremonial funeral procession to commemorate his death. Julian's entrance to the city, then, was accompanied by the sounds of lamentation and mournful singing – an ill omen, to be sure.

More auspiciously, a large crowd of Antiochians had gathered to welcome the Emperor, and his progress through the city was attended by exuberant cheers. Among those who came to greet him was his old friend and correspondent, Libanius, who recalled their meeting with irrepressible enthusiasm in one of his letters. When Julian was made aware of Libanius, "he was remarkably excited as he sat on his horse. He grasped my hand and would not let go, and he showered me with jests most amusing".[2]

The Augustus was to remain in Antioch until the following spring while preparations for the Persia campaign continued. Within a matter of months, however, Julian found himself bitterly at odds with the city and much of its population. As he would later concede, albeit with an undertone of sardonic reproach for his temporary neighbours, "it was due to my own folly that I did not understand what the temper of this city has been from the beginning".[3] Julian was immediately affronted by the hedonistic and frivolous character of the Antiochians, who in turn had little time for the Emperor's stringent temperance. For many in Antioch, "fashion was the only law; pleasure the only pursuit. The arts of luxury were honoured, the serious and masculine virtues were the

1. Ammianus, 22.9.14 2. Libanius, *Letter 736* 3. Julian, *Misopogon*

subject of ridicule, and the contempt for female modesty and reverent age announced the universal corruption of the capital of the East".[1] That the city was also far more Christian than Julian had initially anticipated only served to deepen the division.

In the years prior to his arrival in Antioch, the local food supply had suffered under the strain of successive crop failures and the additional demands of Constantius' army. The shortage of corn was the primary issue. As reserves rapidly depleted, and prices accordingly rose, the city found itself on the cusp of yet another food crisis. Julian was made aware of this shortly after taking up residence in Antioch when his fellow theatre attendees began chanting "everything plentiful; everything dear!"[2] The following day, the Emperor met with the city's wealthy and powerful, wherein he attempted "to persuade them that it is better to despise unjust profits and to benefit the citizens".[3] All in attendance duly promised to take care of the matter. After three months had passed and, unsurprisingly, nothing had changed, Julian decided to intervene directly. As with Gallus before him, his attempts to resolve the economic crisis were, albeit for different reasons, something of a disaster.

The issue of corn scarcity was straightforward enough. To relieve the shortage, Julian ordered vast measures of corn to be imported from granaries in Syria, Egypt, and his own property. A simultaneous attempt to address the rather more complicated problem of inflated market prices was where his intervention faltered. With admirable intentions, Julian fixed the price of corn to a more affordable sum. The problem was that the introduction of price controls was not accompanied by express limits on how much could be purchased by a single party. In his eagerness to resolve the crisis, the Emperor had, perhaps naively, overlooked the willingness of local merchants to seek personal gain at the expense of their fellow citizens.

The imperial grain was immediately bought up by such opportunistic merchants who, exploiting the artificially low price to make a quick profit, sold the corn outside the city for a far higher price. To compound matters, many of the wealthy land-owners withheld their own produce from Antioch's market, unwilling to sell at the reduced price. The result was that, not only did Julian's measures fail to alleviate the crisis, but he himself ended up bearing the brunt of the populace's dissatisfaction.

---

1. Gibbon, *Decline and Fall*, XXIV 2. Julian, *Misopogon* 3. ibid.

Libanius, of course, came to the defence of the Emperor and admonished his fellow Antiochians for placing the blame on Julian: "we should have shown our disapproval not of him who brought the prices down, but of the merchants who would not brook constraint".[1] Julian certainly felt that he had been betrayed by the city's moneyed elite, and that the policies were otherwise sound. That he should have foreseen the rather predictable behaviour of the merchants was academic by this point. Relations between the Augustus and the Antiochians had been soured by the event, and were soon to become irreconcilable.

From the moment it was decided that Julian would travel to Antioch, he had barely been able to contain his anticipation; not for the city itself, but rather for the nearby village of Daphne, where a celebrated shrine to the god Apollo was housed. Though nominally a suburb of Antioch, the sanctuary was situated about four miles south-west of the city in an area of exquisite natural beauty, with abundant woodland and perennial fountains. It was widely regarded as one of the "most elegant places of devotion in the Hellenic world"[2] and had for centuries remained an important site of pilgrimage for Pagans.

As with Antioch, Daphne owed its existence to Seleucus I, officer of Alexander the Great and founder of the Seleucid Empire. The Macedonian general, who identified his own ancestral lineage with Apollo, had long been captivated by the tragic tale of unrequited love between the Olympian god and the water nymph, Daphne.[3] According to the myth which was recorded by Ovid, and whose power to inspire and enrapture has remained undimmed to this day, Cupid, son of Venus, sought to punish Apollo for the verbal slight which had been aimed against him. To this end, the god of desire drew two arrows from his quiver: one, tipped with gold, which kindled love, and another, tipped with lead, which repelled such affection. The affronted Cupid then loosed both arrows. The bright, golden point transfixed Apollo, while the dull, leaden point pierced the body of Daphne, daughter of the river god, Peneus.

At once, the god of light became infatuated with Daphne, who in turn was compelled to flee: "now the one loved, and the other fled from love's name". As she disappeared deep into the woods, "a careless ribbon holding back her hair", Apollo pursued, pleading

1. Libanius, *Oration 16* 2. Gibbon, *Decline and Fall*, XXIII

3. In Greek, the name Daphne, Δάφνη, means "laurel"

with the elusive nymph to cease her flight lest she harm herself upon the thorns and rough ground. Yet try as he might to assure the daughter of Peneus that he was not her enemy, nor some "boorish guardian of herds and flocks", she would not, could not heed his calls. "This is the way a trembling dove flies from the eagle", he exclaimed. "Everything flies from its foes, but it is love that is driving me to follow you!" Though still his words availed him nothing.

The loveliness of Daphne, "her limbs bared by the gentle breeze; her bright hair flowing behind her" spurred Apollo to hasten his pursuit. "Borne on wings of love", the young god, permitting her no rest, ran faster and faster until he had all but caught up to her. The fair nymph's strength waned. Suddenly she grew pale, overcome by the effort of her flight, and as she caught sight of her father's waves, she cried out for his help, pleading for some god to "destroy this beauty that pleases so". Her prayer was scarcely done "when a heavy numbness seized her limbs; thin bark closed around her gentle bosom, her hair turned to leaves, her arms into branches, her feet so swift a moment ago stuck fast in slow-growing roots, and her face became lost in the canopy. Only her shining beauty remained". Apollo's love for Daphne did not dwindle, however. When he placed his hand against the trunk, "he felt her heart still quivering under the new bark", and thus he called out to her: "laurel, with you shall my hair forever be wreathed, with you my lyre, with you my quiver".[1] The laurel then lowered its newly fashioned limbs in a graceful bow, accepting at last, as it seemed to Apollo, the affections of the bright god.

Thus, when Seleucus discovered an elegant laurel tree beside the river Orontes, just a few miles from Antioch, he was reminded at once of the tragic legend. In the midst of a deep grove of trees and ever-flowing springs, Seleucus built a magnificent temple to Apollo, the centrepiece of which was a colossal, forty-foot statue of the Olympian god. The sublime figure, expertly sculpted from wood and marble, was adorned with a golden robe that hung upon his body so that "some parts of it subsided and others rose".[2] With a lyre in one hand and a tipping cup in the other, his serene visage crowned with golden laurel, the leader of the Muses was depicted "pouring out a libation upon the earth as if

---

1. Ovid, *Metamorphoses*, I, 434-567 2. Libanius, *Oration* 60

in supplication to the venerable mother to give to his arms the cold and beautiful Daphne".[1]

The artistry of the statue, crafted by the Athenian Bryaxis, was unsurpassed, and its beauty quickly gained renown across the classical world. Over the centuries, its fame endured, attracting the munificence of numerous statesmen such as Pompey, and various Emperors such as Trajan, who helped to maintain and expand the temple. The Emperor Hadrian, conversely, having learned from the Castalian fountain of Daphne – "a stream of prophecy which rivalled the truth and reputation of the Delphic oracle"[2] – that he was to assume the throne, had subsequently ordered the fountain to be blocked with a giant boulder so that no one else might receive such a message during his reign. Julian, led by his devout curiosity, intended to reopen the prophetic springs.

It is hardly surprising that Julian was so keen to visit the temple. When the day of Apollo's annual festival arrived, he hastened to Daphne, eager to behold the famous shrine and honour the god of poetry and knowledge. Allowing his thoughts to be carried away in the fervour of anticipation, Julian wrote of the spectacle that he had hoped to discover: "I imagined in my own mind the sort of procession it would be, like a man seeing visions in a dream – beasts for sacrifice, libations, choruses in honour of the god, incense, and the youths of your city there surrounding the shrine, their souls adorned with all piety and themselves attired in white and splendid raiment".[3] Sadly, the reality fell somewhat short of his expectations. The city had neglected to make any preparations for the festival, leaving the local priest to rather sheepishly present a solitary goose from his own livestock as an offering. Worse still, the temple had fallen victim to disrepair, theft, and vandalism. Needless to say, Julian was far from happy. The Augustus responded by venting his frustrations in a rather scathing speech to the senate at Antioch. He rebuked the city for having treated the god of her forefathers with such scorn; for the willingness of its wealthy to spend lavish sums on private dinners, while sparing nothing for the worship of the gods. As acrimonious as relations between the Emperor and the Antiochians were by this point, the nadir was still to come.

To Julian's dismay, the Pythian oracle at Daphne had been reduced to silence. When he went as a suppliant to inquire as to

1. Gibbon, *Decline and Fall*, XXIII 2. ibid. 3. Julian, *Misopogon*

the reason, the oracle responded that no prophecy could be uttered until the corpses buried around the shrine were removed to another spot, and the grove purified. The problem in question dated back to the Cæsarship of Gallus, during which the remains of a local martyr, St. Babylas, had been relocated from Antioch to Daphne. After more than a century at rest within the Syrian metropolis, his body had been transported to the grove and interred beside the Apollonian shrine. A large church was then erected over the bishop's tomb, with part of the sanctuary being usurped for the use of clergymen. In the years that followed, a number of wealthy Christians from Antioch secured the honour of having their remains buried alongside the venerated saint, and thus the cemetery expanded. Not only had the temple been neglected, then, but the sacred ground had, from the perspective of the Pagans, been deliberately profaned.

Julian acted at once to reconsecrate the shrine, conscious in spite of everything of avoiding undue provocation. The bodies were respectfully relocated, the Christian buildings were removed from the sanctuary, and "the ministers of the church were permitted to convey the remains of St. Babylas to their former habitation within the martyrium of Antioch".[1] Moderate though Julian's measures were, many of the city's residents understandably took exception to what they perceived to be an act of desecration. The bishop's sarcophagus was accompanied back to the city by a zealous crowd of Christians, predominately women, who chanted verses from the Psalms of David and loudly proclaimed "shame be to all those who worship graven images"[2] at every pause, their words an unambiguous display of antipathy directed at the Pagan Emperor and his fellow Hellenes.

What followed may be seen in hindsight as the inevitable culmination of many months of hostility between Julian and the Christians of Antioch. On the night of 22nd October, 362, just days after the transfer of St. Babylas' remains, the temple at Daphne was in flames. Before anyone could intervene, the statue of Apollo had been wholly consumed by the fire, and the temple itself reduced to an "awful monument of ruin".[3] The shrine's destruction induced in Julian a fury quite at odds with his usual temper, one that demanded retribution. An investigation into the incident was begun at once, with the Emperor's suspicions centred firmly upon his religious adversaries.

---

1. Gibbon, XXIII 2. Theodoret, *E.H.*, III, VI 3. Gibbon, XXIII

The attendants at the temple were the first to be questioned. Each insisted, even after being flogged, that the fire had been caused by lightning. This version of events was then corroborated by a few local peasants who claimed to have seen "fire fall from heaven onto the temple"[1] – albeit, according to other witnesses, "the weather was very calm and there was no appearance of a storm"[2] on that particular night. Although the inquisition was to continue for some time, no conclusive evidence was ever discovered, and nobody was held to blame. In response, Julian ordered the Great Church at Antioch to be nailed shut and its wealth confiscated. It was the actions of an emperor who had clearly lost all patience with the city.

Inevitably, each side drew its own conclusion as to the cause of the fire. The Christians immediately ascribed the temple's devastation to divine vengeance, asserting with absolute conviction that the "powerful intercession of St. Babylas had pointed the lightning of heaven against the devoted roof"[3]; while Julian, who was understandably more inclined to attribute the incident to criminality than saintly miracles, "imputed the fire of Daphne to the revenge of the Galilæans"[4], declaring that the shrine had been "destroyed by the audacious acts of godless men".[5] Ultimately, the truth would never be known, and the two groups simply became ever-more entrenched in their mutual opposition.

Another consequence of the affair was that it seems to have hardened Julian's resolve with respect to Christianity. While violent persecution was still out of the question – the Emperor, it is true, did not wish to make martyrs of his enemies – a number of laws passed in the months after the Daphne incident suggest a tightening of the screw. One such edict introduced a prohibition on burials during the daytime, which forced Christians to conform to Pagan practices.

Further evidence of Julian's political manoeuvring at this time may be seen in his attitude towards the Empire's Jewish population, a significant portion of which was based in Antioch. During his time in the city, the Augustus had observed first-hand the mutual enmity between Christians and Jews, and through the latter, he saw an opportunity to undermine the Galilæan faith at its source. If the old adage is true, and the enemy of one's enemy

---

1. La Bleterie, *Life of the Emperor Julian*, pg. 231 2. ibid.
3. Gibbon, *Decline and Fall*, XXIII 4. ibid. 5. Julian, *Misopogon*

is indeed a friend, then the Jews earned "the friendship of Julian by their implacable hatred of the Christian name".[1] In a notably cordial open letter to the Jewish community, the authenticity of which is in question,[2] the Emperor urged them to offer prayers for his reign, and promised, most remarkably, to rebuild the temple at Jerusalem after he had returned from the war in Persia. Such a pledge would appear wholly confounding were it not for the prophecy spoken by Christ with respect to the temple: "not one stone shall be left upon another, that shall not be thrown down".[3] If the temple at Jerusalem were to be rebuilt, and no divine retribution or apocalyptic event followed, it would deal a significant blow to the Christian cause. Julian, of course, will have been acutely aware of this.

The Emperor's supposed overtures to the Jews of Rome should thus be understood solely in the context of his religious reforms and the ongoing struggle with Christianity. While he was willing to admit that even the Hebrews "have shown themselves superior to the Galilæans",[4] it was arguably something of a backhanded compliment coming from Julian. In other writings, he was rather more blunt in his appraisal. Of the Jewish prophets, he remarked "how inferior these teachers of tales are to our own poets";[5] while on another occasion, when comparing the Jewish and Hellenic traditions, he observed that God has "bestowed on the Hebrews nothing considerable or of great value".[6]

At the beginning of 363, Julian was in a bullish mood. The Empire was gradually being reformed in accordance with his designs, and for all the discontent at Antioch, his reign had thus far been quite successful and broadly popular. With his stay in the Syrian capital coming to an end, however, there was still time for the Augustus and his fractious neighbours to exchange one last round of rhetorical blows. On 3rd January, during the extended New Year celebrations, Julian visited Antioch's gilded temple of Jupiter Capitolinus to perform the *vota publica*. As tradition dictated, the Emperor granted a donative to his legions, albeit any Christian who refused to participate in the customary sacrifice to the *Genius Augusti* was excluded. This was followed by a

1. Gibbon, *Decline and Fall*, XXIII

2. Van Nuffelen argues that Julian's letter to the Jewish community is a fabrication; cf. *Deux Fausses Lettres de Julien l'Apostat*

3. *Mark*, 13.2 4. Julian, *Letter 47* 5. Julian, *Letter to a Priest*

6. Julian, *Against the Galilæans*

procession to the circus where games were to be held at Julian's expense. As part of the festivities, "it was traditional for the crowd to ridicule the chief magistrates with impunity, using comic impersonations as well as words"[1] – a practice that even extended to the Emperor himself.

Julian was consequently subjected to a mixture of light-hearted mockery and, by all accounts, rather more serious invective. Certain members of the crowd vociferously "derided the laws, the religion, the personal conduct, and even the beard, of the Emperor".[2] Given Julian's displeasure at the spectacle of anarchic revelry that day, it is safe to assume that personal attacks were an unwelcome addition. On this occasion, the Augustus decided to respond in kind. He duly composed a work of satire entitled *Misopogon* ("The Beard Hater"), a parodical self-confession in which Julian's faults, alleged or otherwise, were used as a framing device to ridicule the dissolute, intractable, and effeminate character of the Antiochians. The work was then posted in the city for all to read.

It is hard to know what the reactions will have been. Contrary to the view espoused by some, *Misopogon* was by no means an oddity. Indeed, so-called "edicts of chastisement" were rather commonplace at this time, and the residents were hardly strangers to satire. The work was an inventive means for the Augustus to "entertain, edify, and chastise the citizenry"[3] and thereby demonstrate the "civilised good humour which contemporaries liked to associate with a moderate, because secure, style of rule".[4] As a farewell letter to Antioch, however, it certainly left little ambiguity as to Julian's true feelings. The work repeatedly devolves into an outright rebuke of the city, with the Emperor clearly keen to off-load several months of frustration. One may be inclined to read more than a hint of irony in its final words: "in return for your good will towards me and the honour wherewith you have publicly honoured me, may the gods duly pay the recompense!"[5]

In early March, with the long-awaited campaign in the east finally upon him, Julian departed from Antioch. His motivations for undertaking the invasion of Persia have been much discussed, yet for as little as Julian actually wrote on the subject, it is hard to look beyond the twin imperatives of duty and expectation, with

1. Gleason, *Festive Satire* 2. Gibbon, *Decline and Fall*, XXIV
3. Neil McLynn, *Julian and the Christian Professors*
4. Brown, *Power and Persuasion in Late Antiquity*, pg. 59 5. Julian, *Misopogon*

the additional incentive of personal glory. In truth, his campaign simply represented the continuation of a long-standing border conflict between the region's two most powerful empires, the latest manifestation of which he had inherited from Constantius. The war had persisted for twenty-four years under his predecessor without either side managing to land a conclusive blow. Julian was thus acutely aware that another rearguard action localised to the frontier would merely invite a prolonged campaign of attrition, with little prospect of a decisive victory. While some may have voiced opposition to the war, citing Shapur's apparent willingness to make peace, Julian, as with Rome historically, was more inclined to impose terms from a position of superiority.

Another subject of debate has been the ultimate goal of the Persian campaign. One critic alleged that Julian sought to exceed the exploits of Alexander the Great,[1] while others went as far as to accuse the Augustus of having invaded with no strategic aims at all beyond a desire to wage war. If a letter from Libanius is any indication, however, Julian did indeed have a very clear and feasible end in mind: "we hope that our Emperor will remove the current ruler, handing the kingdom over to the one who was exiled".[2] Libanius was referring to the Persian Prince, Hormisdas, who had fled to Rome in 323 after being imprisoned by his brother-in-law, Shapur, and who was now serving as one of Julian's commanders. It is entirely possible, then, that Julian's plan was to overthrow Shapur and install Hormisdas on the Persian throne, rendering the rival Empire a junior partner. It is equally plausible, of course, that he simply intended to sack the imperial capital, Ctesiphon, in order to end the war and earn Rome a favourable settlement.

Roughly twelve days after his departure, Julian arrived by a series of forced marches at the city of Carrhæ, which was to serve as a temporary base for the Augustus and his army. The final preparations were made and within a few days the offensive began in earnest. Julian's plan of attack entailed a double approach along the two major rivers, the Euphrates and the Tigris, with his divided army eventually converging on the Persian capital. One force of around 18,000 men[3] under Procopius was to march eastwards across the Tigris, join up with a detachment from the Armenian King, Arsaces, then head south to Ctesiphon. At the same time,

1. Socrates Scholasticus, XXI 2. Libanius, *Letter 1402*

3. Zosimus, 3.2.12 (the figures given here could be a slight overestimation)

Julian was to lead some 47,000 men,[1] among whom were his loyal Gallic troops, down the Euphrates.

The Emperor's strategy appears at first glance to have been envisioned as a standard pincer movement. It is unclear, however, whether the force under Procopius was expected to rendezvous at Ctesiphon for a joint assault on the city, or if its primary purpose was to act as a diversion from the main body under Julian, pushing Shapur to focus his own forces on the northern approach. There is certainly a credible argument in support of the latter. The second force had been instructed to "lay waste"[2] to important positions across the upper Fertile Crescent, a region which had served as the principal theatre of war in recent times. It is reasonable to assume, therefore, that Shapur would have expected the Romans to concentrate their attack in this area. "With the main force of the Persian army drawn away to the north, Julian will have hoped that a swift assault down the Euphrates would enable him to reach Ctesiphon and take it before its defences could be set in order."[3] As with his capture of Sirmium in 361, speed, diversion, and the element of surprise were central to the Emperor's strategy.

The initial stages of the offensive gave Julian every reason to be optimistic. He successfully captured, and in some instances destroyed, a number of strongholds, and received the surrender of various settlements, all while facing limited resistance and suffering minimal losses. Nevertheless, the campaign had not been without its minor setbacks and ill portents. At one point, the Euphrates had suddenly burst its banks and flooded the open country when its stone sluices collapsed – in all probability an intentional act of sabotage by the Persians to slow Julian's army down, one that they would repeat over the coming weeks. Another incident which occurred during this period was mistakenly perceived to be favourable. The Emperor was presented with the body of an enormous lion which had been "dispatched by a rain of weapons"[4] after attacking some of the Roman troops. Julian apparently deemed this to be a certain omen of success, yet as Ammianus knowingly remarked: "there is no trusting the fickle winds of fortune, for the event was far otherwise. The death of a king was foreshadowed, but of which king it was not clear".[5]

Towards the end of April, the fortified city of Pirisabora was taken after a three-day siege, continuing the initial success of

1. ibid. 2. Ammianus, 23.3.5 3. Potter, *The Roman Empire at Bay*, pg. 540
4. Ammianus, 23.5.8 5. ibid.

Julian's campaign. This latest victory was to be tarnished, however, when on the following day three squadrons of the Roman advanced guard were ambushed. Although there were few casualties, one tribune was killed and, perhaps more importantly, a standard was captured.[1] Julian responded by immediately riding out at the head of a select band of troops and routing the assailants. When the Emperor returned, the two surviving tribunes were cashiered for cowardice and neglect of duty, then decimation was ordered for all those who had fled. As Ammianus wrote, one in "ten men were discharged and put to death in conformity with ancient Roman law".[2]

The practice of decimation was highly symbolic of early Roman military discipline, and while it had indeed been used historically to punish instances of cowardice and desertion, it had also long since fallen out of use. Even Tacitus, writing in the early second century, described the penalty as rare and archaic.[3] As Julian was an avid student of history – Appius Claudius is said to have been the first to employ decimation in 471 B.C. after a defeat to the Volsci in which the army not only fled but deserted its standards[4] – the Augustus may have been keen to revive the uncompromising martial spirit of Rome's past. It would not be unreasonable to suggest, as with others for whom decimation held a certain appeal, that Julian was inclined towards *nimio amore antiqui moris*.[5] That is to say, an inordinate love of ancient customs.

What effect this may have had upon the morale of his men, few if any of whom will have experienced such severe discipline, is unclear. It was certainly at about this time, though quite possibly the day before the aforementioned incident, that the first sign of discontent among the troops emerged. When Julian publicly thanked his men for their efforts and promised one hundred pieces of silver to each, the crowd reacted rather negatively to what they perceived to be an inadequate sum. With a shrewd piece of rhetoric, Julian was able to both allay their discontent and redirect their energy into the war effort. If wealth was the object of their desires, he began, then Persia abounded in riches; the Romans

---

1. Standards, especially those bearing an eagle known as *aquilæ*, represented imperial rule and held almost religious significance. The loss of a standard was extremely grave, with the Roman military going to great lengths to both protect a standard and to recover it should it be lost in battle.

2. Ammianus, 24.3.2 3. Tacitus, *Annales*, III 4. Livius, *Ab Urbe Condita*, 2.59

5. Watson, *The Roman Soldier*, pg. 120

need only act with unity and valour, and the spoils of that fruitful country would be their reward.[1]

The army resumed its march and by 10th May had arrived at the city of Maiozamalcha. The double-walled fortress was well garrisoned and, being situated upon an elevated plateau, enjoyed the natural protection of high cliffs. Julian determined that, since Maiozamalcha was a mere eleven miles from the capital, it presented too great a risk to be left alone. Rather than rely on a direct siege to overcome the city's borderline impregnable defences, the frontal assault which followed was purposed as a mere distraction. As the siege rumbled on, a tunnel was rapidly and surreptitiously constructed beneath the fortress. On the third day, shortly after sunrise, a small band of stalwart legionaries made their way through the tunnel and into the city. The soldiers quietly cleared a nearby watchtower then opened the gates, allowing the rest of the Roman army to flood in. Maiozamalcha was promptly stormed, its population put to the sword, and everything of value pillaged. The spoils were then divided among the troops in accordance with the respective merit and service of each, while the legionaries who had infiltrated the city were awarded mural crowns and publicly honoured.

A few days later, Julian established a camp just a few miles from Ctesiphon, Coche, and the ruins of Seleucia, "where an ever-flowing spring forms a vast pool that empties into the Tigris".[2] The objective of his campaign was finally in sight. When the Emperor led a scouting party to reconnoitre the area, they came across the rather unsettling image of corpses hung upon gibbets – the remains of the entire family of the man who had surrendered Pirisabora.[3] This was coupled with the news that an enemy force had "cut to pieces"[4] the Roman baggage train during a sudden ambush. For all the confidence the campaign's success may have instilled in the army, they were now deep into Persian territory, in a position that must have impressed a sense of urgency upon the men and Julian. With Shapur's army inbound, the Emperor will have been eager to overcome the defences of the Persian capital without delay.

The fortified cities of Coche and Ctesiphon sat opposite one another, divided by the Tigris; the former on the west bank of the river, and the latter on the east bank. Any approach along the

1. Gibbon, XXIV; Ammianus, 24.3.4 2. Ammianus, 24.5.3 3. ibid.
4. ibid. 24.5.5

narrow river would have exposed the Roman ships to heavy projectile fire from both cities. Julian's solution, then, rested upon a brilliant piece of subterfuge and a surprise night raid. First, however, they would need to reach the twin cities. He ordered the Naarmalcha, a canal linking the Euphrates and Tigris which the Persians had intentionally blocked, to be cleared of all debris, allowing his fleet to sail into the Tigris. Bridges were then swiftly constructed over the canal and the army advanced alongside the fleet to their next camp, just south of Coche. Julian was at last within striking distance of the capital.

On the opposite bank, a significant Persian force had amassed in response to the Roman approach. It was an impressive, perhaps even intimidating sight, if the first-hand account of Ammianus is any indication. Squadrons of heavy cavalry in their shining armour "dazzled the eye", their horses protected with housings of stout leather; several maniples of compact infantry stood in support with long, curved shields; while behind them a number of war elephants came lumbering forward, "walking hills" whose enormous frames "threatened destruction to all who approached, and past experience of which had taught our men to dread them".[1] A direct confrontation against such a force, one with a clear advantage with respect to its defensible position, would have been imprudent to say the least.

Julian, therefore, did what absolutely nobody would have expected – including, one suspects, his own men. The Emperor had a racecourse levelled and proceeded to host a day of games in which cavalrymen, as well as regular troops in a variety of other athletic contests, competed for prizes.[2] The spectacle provided much-needed entertainment for his men, and, presumably, no slight bafflement among the onlooking Persians. His ploy worked precisely as intended. The enemy perceived the display as a sign that the Romans were to be encamped for some time, and duly let their guard down. While the games were being held, provisions and war engines were unloaded from a number of the ships and preparations begun for a nighttime assault. It was typical of Julian who, as Ammianus remarked, "often pushed his boldness to the verge of temerity"[3].

After nightfall, five vessels were sent under the command of the *magister equitum*, Victor, to cross the river and establish a bridgehead. The ships at once disappeared into the dark. As they

1. Ammianus, 24.6.8 2. Libanius, *Oration* 18 3. Ammianus, 24.6.4

reached the eastern bank, Persian sentries raised the alarm and the advanced squadron suddenly came under attack from firebombs and other incendiaries. Julian reacted immediately and with "considerable presence of mind",[1] calling out to his troops that Victor's men had given the agreed signal to show that they had made a successful landing, and ordering his fleet to hasten across with all speed. The battle on the bank of the Tigris began during the dead of night and persisted into the next day, with the Persians unable to dislodge the Roman bridgehead. In the initial exchanges, the Roman troops were able to scale the steep bank and hold the position they had gained in spite of the incessant hail of missiles from above. Once reinforcements had arrived, most crossing by daylight, the second phase of the battle ensued, with Julian both directing the assault and helping to reinforce the points which were hardest pressed. The Persian front line slowly began to give way, and as the battle threatened to turn into a rout, they quickly retreated inside the walls of Ctesiphon.

At this point, the Roman troops failed to capitalise on their evident advantage and pursue the fleeing Persians into the city. According to Ammianus, Victor had ordered his men to hold back after he had been pierced through the shoulder with an arrow.[2] Quite what Julian's opinion of this decision was, or indeed his involvement, no mention is made. Victor apparently feared that if his troops flooded into the city in a disordered fashion, they would find themselves trapped within the walls and overwhelmed by the enemy's superior numbers. Again, where Julian and the rest of the infantry had been at this crucial juncture is unclear. In the end, while the battle had resulted in a resounding victory – estimates, if they are to be believed, placed the Persian dead at around 2,500 and the Roman at just 70[3] – it may be seen in hindsight as a missed opportunity, one that would ultimately prove costly to both the campaign and Julian himself.

Towards the end of May, the Emperor and his commanders gathered to determine how they ought to proceed. The council concluded that a siege of Ctesiphon would be a foolish and in all probability futile undertaking. If the sweltering Persian heat and flooded terrain weren't obstacles enough, the capital's defences had been significantly improved since it was sacked by Galerius in 299, rendering the city essentially impregnable. Furthermore, they were led to believe that Shapur was close by and that his

---

1. ibid. 2. Ammianus, 24.6.13 3. ibid. 24.6.15

arrival with a "formidable host"[1] was imminent. The decision to not besiege the city was entirely sensible given the circumstances, yet by forgoing even an attempt, the initiative in the war had been lost.

To compound matters, it soon became clear that neither Procopius' men nor the Armenian forces would be making an appearance. The latter had failed to join up with the Roman detachment, while the former was accused, rightfully or not, of inaction.[2] Regardless of the reason for their absence, Julian now found himself without reinforcements and low on supplies, in temperatures potentially as high as 44°C, with the Persian royal army expected at any moment. When a second council was convened in early June, the options available to the Roman command were severely limited. It was no longer a question of whether they should abandon the capital, but rather of how they were to return home. Because the Persians had flooded the route by which the army had arrived, a retreat back along the Euphrates was presumably infeasible. The Tigris, meanwhile, was in full spate, and the effort required to tow the fleet upriver was equally impracticable. Julian, therefore, had little choice but to march north towards Roman Mesopotamia and a possible rendezvous with Procopius' force – a journey that was to be made, rather more controversially, without their fleet.

At about this time, Julian ordered all of the ships to be burned, except for twelve of the smaller vessels which could be transported by land and used for bridge-building. The reaction of his troops appears to have been one of dismay, with Ammianus commenting that "Bellona herself must have lit the fatal flame".[3] The Emperor's decision has received considerable criticism from certain historians, with many keen to once more suggest that Julian was attempting to emulate Alexander the Great, who also famously consigned his fleet to the flames after arriving in Persia. Even Gibbon allowed himself to be carried away by the far more romantic notion that, as allegedly with Alexander, Julian deprived his soldiers of the hopes of a retreat so that the only alternative left to them would be death or conquest.[4] In reality, the decision was considerably more pragmatic, albeit Julian had not ruled out a decisive confrontation with Shapur. As Libanius explained, towing boats up the swollen Tigris would have required a vast

1. ibid. 24.7.1 2. Libanius, *Oration* 18 3. Ammianus, 24.7.4
4. Gibbon, *Decline and Fall*, XXIV

number of hands – roughly 20,000[1] – and thus great effort for little purpose. Moreover, those troops could be better utilised elsewhere, for "when there were no vessels, every man was under arms".[2]

The army departed from Ctesiphon in mid-June and headed in the direction of Corduene, a Roman province some 400 miles north of the Persian capital. From the moment they set out, the Persians began burning crops along their anticipated route and persistently harassing the Roman column. On the morning of 16th June, the troops spotted "what seemed to be smoke or a great cloud of dust"[3] on the horizon. Some speculated that it might be a herd of wild asses; others that it might be the belated arrival of the Armenian forces. In the face of this uncertainty, the army promptly came to a halt and set up camp by a nearby stream. With a circle of shields in close order around them, they held their position until the following morning.

At first light on the 17th June, the Romans were met with the unmistakable sight of Shapur's army bearing down on their camp, the two forces separated by little more than a shallow stream. In the skirmishes which followed, a senior Roman commander was fatally wounded, whereupon his brother immediately slew the man who had dealt the blow. These sporadic encounters, most likely Persian raids on the Roman position, continued until the heat became unbearable and the two sides withdrew. While the army soon resumed its march, the effects of the heat, the paucity of provisions, and the constant threat of ambush had clearly begun to take their toll on Julian's men. During a brief clash with the Persian army a few days later, one of the cavalry regiments failed to support the infantry at a key moment in the battle, for which they were accused of cowardice. Julian "broke their spears, and condemned all who were charged with flight to march among the baggage-train with the prisoners".[4] Five tribunes, all from cavalry detachments, were also cashiered for similar misconduct. Hungry, exhausted, and increasingly demoralised, the army continued on to Maranga, where the two forces clashed once again, this time in a more conventional pitched battle. The Romans successfully repulsed Shapur's army, inflicting heavier losses on the Persians, whereafter both sides agreed to a three-day truce in order to tend to their wounded.

---

1. Ammianus, 24.7.4 2. Libanius, *Oration* 18 3. Ammianus, 24.8.5
4. ibid., 25.1.8

On 25th June, in the silent hours of the night, Julian awoke from a brief and troubled sleep. Beset by restless anxiety, he roused himself from his bed and, such was his habit, began writing. The Emperor was lost in study when, as he relayed to his close friends later that morning, he saw amidst the gloom of his tent the form of the *Genii Populi Romani*,[1] the guardian spirit of the Roman people, which had first appeared to Julian in Gaul when he rose to the position of Augustus. This time, however, the sorrowful figure merely departed through the curtains of his tent without saying a word, its head, and the cornucopia[2] in its hand, veiled. For a brief moment, Julian was lost in the vision that had been, a creeping sense of unease arresting his stupor. As he stepped out into the midnight air, eager to perform the sacred rites in supplication to the gods, he saw a blazing light, not unlike a falling star, which suddenly clove its way through the sky and vanished. Julian was aghast, fearing, however much he wished to banish the thought, that it had been the star of Mars, and that the god of war, too, had abandoned him.[3]

When "Dawn spread out her golden robe"[4] on 26th June, the Emperor and his men set out for the final time, accompanied by the ever-watchful Persian scouts. Shapur's army had no intention of risking a pitched infantry battle, and had opted from the very beginning to shadow the Roman column, launching ambushes whenever the opportunity arose. Experience had thus left Julian's troops on edge, conscious that the Persian eyes hidden amongst the surrounding hills were fixed to their every step, and that a raid could occur at any moment.[5] As Ammianus recounted,[6] the Roman army was marching in as close and ordered a formation as the terrain would permit, its flanks especially well-guarded, when the Emperor, who had gone ahead to reconnoitre, was informed that the rearguard had suddenly come under attack. Alarmed by the news, Julian, without stopping to equip his breastplate, simply grabbed hold of a shield and made at once for the scene of the ambush. Yet just as the Emperor hurried to support the rearguard, he was halted by a signal that the van, which he had only moments earlier left, now found itself in the same plight.

1. *Genius* referred to the individual instance of a general divine nature, and was somewhat comparable to the Greek "daimon"

2. The mythical "horn of plenty" which symbolised material and spiritual abundance

3. Ammianus, 25.2.3 4. *The Iliad*, VIII 5. Ammianus, 25.3.1 6. ibid. 25.3.2

He hastened back to help defend the position, only for a troop of Persian heavy cavalry to attack the Roman centre, overrun the left-wing, which began to give way in the face of enemy elephants, and press the legionaries back with pikes and showers of missiles. As Julian flew from one point of intense fighting to another, the light-armed troops took the offensive, striking the backs of the Persians and the legs of their monstrous beasts as the enemy turned tail.

The Emperor threw himself boldly into the fight, shouting and raising his arms in a bid to spur his men forward and by a merciless pursuit crush their disordered foe. His guards, who had been scattered during the melee, were calling out for him to withdraw from the mass of fleeing Persians when suddenly a cavalry spear, directed no one knows from where,[1] grazed Julian's arm, pierced his ribs, and lodged itself in the lower part of his abdomen. As he tried to pull the spear out with his right hand, he felt the double-edged point of the weapon slice his fingers to the bone. The Emperor then fell from his horse, at which all present hastened to the spot, lifted him onto a shield, and carried him to the Roman camp to receive immediate medical treatment.

As soon as the pain had diminished somewhat, Julian called for his horse and arms, desperate to return to the fray and to restore the confidence of his troops. Yet his strength was not equal to his spirit; his body, weakened by a considerable loss of blood, failed him, and so he remained without moving. In his absence, the Romans successfully pressed home their advantage and routed the remaining Persian forces. The battle had been won, but at a significant cost. The Emperor's wound was fatal, and even if few were aware at first that the injury was to cost him his life, the sight of a bloodied and perhaps unconscious Julian being carried into his tent and failing to reemerge will have led many in the camp to fear the worst.

The historical accounts of Julian's death, few though they may be, are broadly consistent save for a few key details, namely the time of his passing and who exactly was responsible for inflicting the mortal wound. Zosimus[2] and Ammianus[3] both claimed that he passed away that very evening, while Philostorgius[4] believed that Julian was to live for another three days before finally succumbing to his injuries. The question of who dealt the fatal blow was rather more contentious. One rumour suggested that the Emperor "had

1. ibid. 25.3.6 2. Zosimus, 3.29.1 3. Ammianus, 25.3.23 4. Philostorgius, 7.15

fallen by a Roman weapon",[1] with Libanius quick to accuse the Christians within Julian's army.[2] It is certainly noteworthy that Ammianus chose to describe the spear as "*incertum unde*",[3] that is, coming from somewhere unknown. No evidence of a Christian plot, or a rogue actor within the Roman ranks, ever emerged, however, and even Libanius would later accept that the man responsible was almost certainly a Saracen cavalryman.

The response to Julian's death demonstrated just how important – and divisive – a figure he had become. Far from being just another emperor, he was a symbol of the religious struggle for Rome's future; a focal point for Pagan hopes and Christian contempt. That his death should become so heavily mythologised is therefore hardly surprising. In one version of events, as Julian lay bleeding upon the battlefield, "he took up in his hands the blood which flowed from his wounds, and cast it up towards the sun, exclaiming, 'take your fill'";[4] while in another, far more famous and oft-repeated, but entirely apocryphal account, Julian cried out "you have won, O Galilean".[5] Some maintained that he had been betrayed by a Christian legionary; others that he had been slain by a daimon[6]; while a popular legend which emerged shortly after his passing portrayed St. Mercurius, a Greek soldier who was martyred in the early third century, as having been the one to deprive the Pagan Emperor of his life.

Julian's final hours were spent in the company of close friends, including Maximus, Priscus, and Salutius, engaged until the very last in a deep discussion on the nature of the soul. It was a fitting scene, and drew inevitable comparisons to the philosophers of old whom Julian had long held in such high regard.[7] Lying in his tent, the Emperor addressed those around him, offering a sober reflection on both his life and his impending death. The only version to survive was recorded by Ammianus, and while it was not uncommon for Roman historians to invent speeches, the words attributed to Julian certainly ring true:

> "My friends, the seasonable moment to depart this life has now arrived, and, like an honest debtor, I exult in preparing to restore what nature reclaims; not, as some might expect, in affliction and sorrow, since I share the common conviction of

1. Ammianus, 25.6.6 2. Libanius, *Oration* 18 3. Ammianus, 25.3.6
4. Philostorgius, 7.15 5. Theodoret, 3.20 6. From a lost work by Callistus
7. Libanius, *Oration* 18

philosophers that the soul is capable of a happiness far greater than the body. For when one considers that the superior part is separated from the inferior, it ought to be a subject of joy rather than of mourning. Indeed, it bears reflection that there have been instances in which the gods themselves have bestowed death as the best of all rewards upon certain men of exceptional merit.

"I well know, moreover, that the duty assigned to me is such that I must never yield to arduous difficulties, nor forget or abase myself; for I have learnt from experience that all hardships, while they triumph over the weak, flee before those who endure them manfully.

"I do not regret my actions, nor am I troubled by the recollection of any grave misdeed, either when I was kept in the shade, and, as it were, in a corner, or after I arrived at the Empire, which, as an honour conferred on me by the gods, I have preserved, as I believe, unstained. In civil affairs I have ruled with moderation, and when waging war, whether offensive or defensive, I have always acted after careful deliberation. Of course, the wisdom of man's counsel is not always attended by success, since the outcome of any endeavour ultimately rests in the hands of the powers above.

"Believing that the aim of a just sovereign is the safety and advantage of his subjects, I have always, as you know, been inclined to peace, and to eradicating all licentiousness – that great corruptress of character and deed – from every part of my own conduct. I depart gladly, knowing that in whatever instances the Republic, like an imperious parent, has commanded that I expose myself to danger, I have stood firm, inured to tread underfoot the storms of fortune.

"Nor am I ashamed to confess that I have long known, from prophecy, that I should fall by the sword. I give thanks, therefore, to the everlasting god that I should die not by some secret treachery, nor by a prolonged or severe disease, or like some condemned criminal, but rather, I have been deemed worthy of an honourable departure from this world in the midst of a flourishing and glorious career. For, to any impartial judge, that man is base and cowardly who seeks to die when he ought not, or who avoids death when his hour has come.

> "These few words must suffice as my strength is failing me. I purposefully forbear to speak of naming a new emperor, lest I should unintentionally pass over a deserving candidate; or, on the other hand, if I should name one whom I think proper, I should expose him to danger in the event of someone else being preferred. As a dutiful son of Rome, I only hope that a worthy ruler will be found to succeed me".[1]

Shortly after delivering this speech, Julian's condition began to rapidly worsen, and in the closing days of June, 363, during the silent hours of the night, he finally passed away.

As news of the Emperor's death spread, the priority for the Roman army became that of extricating themselves from Persia with minimal losses. A senior officer by the name of Jovian was duly elected to the position of Augustus, his nomination, one of compromise and expediency, coming after a brief period of political manoeuvring by various factions within the military. After a failed attempt to cross the Tigris, Jovian arranged for peace talks with Shapur. A "shameful"[2] treaty was subsequently concluded and ratified by solemn oaths in which the new Emperor agreed to surrender five Mesopotamian territories – Arzanene, Moxoene, Zabdicene, Rehimena, and Corduene – as well as the strongholds of Nisibis, Castra Maurorum, and Singara. He also agreed to renounce any influence over the province of Armenia. All of these concessions were made in return for a thirty-year truce. However unenviable Jovian's position might have been, the treaty can only be viewed as an "ignominious"[3] capitulation, one that Ammianus interpreted to be the actions of a man primarily concerned with consolidating his accession.[4] Jovian's reign was to last just eight months, however, with the Emperor passing away before he reached Constantinople. During his brief rule, the Christian Augustus revoked most of Julian's religious edicts under the banner of universal tolerance, and effectively re-established the status quo ante. Jovian's attempt at compromise, whether intentional or not, merely placed Christianity back on course towards institutional dominance.

Julian's body, having been preserved in honey and spices, just as with Alexander the Great's,[5] was carried by his troops back into Roman territory. In October, 363, his men reached the southern

1. Ammianus, 25.3.15 2. ibid. 25.7.13 3. Gibbon, *Decline and Fall*, XXIV
4. Ammianus, 25.7.10 5. John Lake-Williams, *An Historical Account*, pg. 386

Anatolian province of Cilicia, and there, just outside the town of Tarsus, Julian was finally laid to rest. There is a suggestion that the late Emperor had wished to relocate the eastern seat of government from Antioch to Tarsus,[1] and that his burial had been in accordance with his own express wishes.[2] Regardless, not all were in agreement as to where Julian ought to have been buried. Ammianus felt that his remains "ought to have been laid where they might be lapped by the Tiber as it passes through the Eternal City and winds round the monuments of the deified Emperors";[3] while Libanius lamented that he had not been interred in "the garden of the Academy beside the tomb of Plato".[4]

It was, nevertheless, a worthy resting place. Once a "city of great magnificence",[5] Tarsus was said to have been founded by Perseus, the son of Jupiter and Danaë, and had previously been home to one of the foremost universities in the classical world; the settlement lay within sight of the "beautiful and clear"[6] river Cydnus, along the road to Mount Taurus and the famous Cilician Gates. The passage of Septimius Severus through the latter was marked by an inscription upon the rock face in which the former Emperor described Tarsus as "first, greatest, and most beautiful". It seems only fitting that, by contrast, Julian's sepulchre was rather modest and without ostentation, very much in keeping with the character of the man. Upon his tomb were inscribed the following words:

Ἰουλιανὸς μετὰ Τίγριν ἀγάρροον ἐνθάδε κεῖται,
ἀμφότερον, βασιλεύς τ' ἀγαθὸς κρατερός τ' αἰχμητής.

"Here lies Julian, who fell by the strong-flowing Tigris.
He was a good king and a valiant warrior"[7]

One suspects that the second line of the epitaph – a verse from the Iliad[8] much favoured by Alexander the Great[9] – would have met with approval from the Emperor himself.

In death, as in life, Julian remained a divisive figure. To many Christians, he was not merely an apostate but an "Antichrist",[10] a man driven by the influence of demons to commit "much

---

1. Collins, *Early Medieval Europe: 300-1000*, pg. 40 2. Ammianus, 25.9.12
3. ibid. 25.10.5 4. Libanius, Oration 18 5. Ammianus, 15.8.3 6. ibid. 25.10.5
7. *Greek Anthology*, 7.747 8. *The Iliad*, III, 179 9. Plutarch, *Moralia*, 331C
10. Gregory of Nazianzus, *Oration* 5

unrighteousness against Heaven"[1] and to "bitterly persecute the Christians";[2] while to many Pagans, he was the *Restitutor Deorum*[3] "who revived sacred laws, put virtue, not vice, in pride of place, raised up the temples, erected altars, gathered together the priesthood that was languishing in obscurity, resurrected all that was left of the statues of the gods",[4] and gave them hope in the struggle against Christianity.

These contrasting views of Julian were no more apparent than in the immediate response to his passing. When word reached Antioch, a portion of the city's Christian residents "danced with joy"[5] and "even in the theatres the victory of the cross was proclaimed".[6] Conversely, the troops at Remi, still fiercely loyal to Julian, refused to accept the news of their Emperor's death, rising up in mutiny and killing a senior army official, Lucillianus, and a tribune, Seniauchus.[7] As a consequence of the invectives against Julian which dominated the historical discourse for centuries after his death, and still colour our perceptions to some degree, it is easy to overlook just how popular he was, especially within the military. In such a polarised society, then, it was inevitable that his passing would provoke reactions as strong as they were divergent: "one party lamented the approaching ruin of their altars; the other celebrated the marvellous deliverance of their church".[8] With the victory of Christianity, Julian was to become a figure of antipathy for historians and of villainy in popular depictions for over a millennium. It was not until the Renaissance that he would find a sympathetic and even admiring audience willing to rehabilitate him.

In the fifteenth century, a Platonist revival among Byzantine philosophers led both Julian's works and the man himself to receive a positive reappraisal. Gemistos Plethon, one of late Byzantium's leading thinkers and an avowed Hellenist, belonged to a circle which openly admired Julian and drew influence from his writings. The propagation of Ammianus' history, *Res Gestæ*, followed shortly thereafter, and inspired a further reassessment of Rome's last Pagan Emperor from thinkers across Renaissance Europe. Michel de Montaigne, for instance, one of the most significant philosophers of the French Renaissance, compared Julian favourably to Alexander the Great and Scipio in his

1. Gregory of Nazianzus, *Oration 4* 2. ibid. *Oration 5* 3. "Restorer of the Gods"
4. Libanius, *Oration 17* 5. ibid. *Letter 1,220* 6. Theodoret, *E.H.*, III, XXII
7. Ammianus, 25.10.7 8. Gibbon, *Decline and Fall*, XXIV

influential essay *On Liberty of Conscience*, wherein he described Julian as "a truly great and exceptional man whose soul was steeped in philosophy, by which he professed to govern all his actions; and, in truth, there is no field of virtue of which he has not left behind him model examples".[1] A few centuries later, Edward Gibbon was to echo these sentiments in his famous work *The History of the Decline and Fall of the Roman Empire*, in which he concisely summarised the Emperor's qualities thus: "he sustained adversity with firmness, and prosperity with moderation".[2]

There is certainly much in Julian's character and deeds to admire. For all the lofty ambitions to which he aspired, and the stations to which he rose, willingly or otherwise, the man himself never appears unapproachable, either to us, or his contemporaries. Julian's irrepressible enthusiasm for philosophy, for example, led him to behave towards his teachers in an overly effusive and familiar manner which some viewed as unbecoming of his position, first as Cæsar, then as Augustus – a criticism that would be levelled on a number of occasions as his tendency to forget himself, or to present as one of the citizens, drew disapproval.[3] Yet it was precisely his unaffected comportment that endeared him to so many, particularly in the military where he committed himself from the very beginning to share in the trials and tribulations of his men.

One of these soldiers, Ammianus, was especially laudatory in his praise of Julian: "wise men tell us that there are four cardinal virtues: self-control, prudence, justice, and courage; and in addition to these, such corresponding qualities as military skill, dignity, prosperity, and generosity. All of these Julian cultivated both singly and as a whole with the utmost care".[4] While his commitment to certain philosophical ideals may have been taken to extremes at times, such as a conception of temperance that approached the most stringent form of asceticism, one can only admire his dedication to the pursuit of excellence, to cultivating and embodying that which he perceived to be the highest qualities of man.

Of course, Julian aspired to far more than he was able to fully realise in his short life. His religious reformation – without doubt the most important endeavour he undertook – died with him.

1. Michel de Montaigne, *On Liberty of Conscience*

2. Gibbon, *Decline and Fall*, XXIV 3. Ammianus, 25.4.18 4. ibid., 25.4.1

He stood athwart what seems to us the inexorable tide of history as it ushered in the twilight of the Greco-Roman gods, only to be "swept into death"[1] while his restoration was still in its infancy. In truth, one can not reasonably criticise Julian for failing to single-handedly restore and ensure the enduring preservation of the Hellenic faith in just twenty months as Emperor. Yet neither can one deny that his legacy is ultimately defined by the demise of Paganism in the Roman world, by that which he sought so earnestly to prevent. The fate of Julian and the gods were, it might be said, bound together.

It is in this absolute dedication to the inheritance of a thousand years of Hellenic and Roman civilisation that one may understand his importance as a historical figure. Julian was the first Emperor to be born in Constantinople, and the last to worship the gods of Rome; he "dared to be faithful to the spirit of Tradition, to reaffirm the solar and sacred ideal of the Empire"[2] from which so many in the halls of power had turned away; wherefore the long and storied tradition which began on the banks of the Tiber with Romulus and Remus came to an end beside the Tigris with Flavius Claudius Julianus, who throughout his life remained loyal to that divine vision, carrying to his death the sacred flame which burns eternally at the heart of Rome.

1. *The Iliad*, V, 576 2. Evola, *The Emperor Julian*

THE DEEDS OF EMPEROR CONSTANTIUS

PREFACE

The first of Julian's works is a panegyric[1] in honour of the Emperor Constantius. As the full title of the oration[2] suggests, particular emphasis is placed upon the Emperor's deeds, genuine or otherwise, with Julian additionally expounding upon the nature of good kingship. The panegyric, written most probably during either his confinement in Mediolanum or shortly after his arrival in Gaul, centres at first on a series of comparisons between Constantius and the Homeric heroes, invariably settled in favour of the former. Thereafter, he enters into a long Platonic digression on virtue and the ideal ruler. It is noteworthy that the qualities expected of an Emperor are seldom attributed directly to Constantius.

Throughout, Julian adheres faithfully to the customs of sophistic practice, observing the rules and conventions of panegyrics in a manner which offers some insight into the true purpose of the work. The oration, it would seem, was never actually delivered. Moreover, the fulsome praise directed at Constantius – especially when juxtaposed with the Homeric figures beloved by Julian – is entirely insincere. That is to say, it in no way reflects the actual character of the Emperor or Julian's opinion of him. Rather, the panegyric is an intellectual exercise for Julian; an opportunity to practice his rhetorical skills. The exemplary leader portrayed in this work is, therefore, to be understood not as a representation of Constantius, but of Julian's own conception of the ideal ruler.

---

1. An oration or laudatory speech delivered publicly in praise of a person or various other subjects, typically at a festival or games

2. *The Deeds of the Emperor Constantius, or, On Kingship*

THE DEEDS OF EMPEROR CONSTANTIUS

Achilles, as the poet tells us, when his wrath was kindled and he quarrelled with the king,[1] let fall from his hands his spear and shield; then he strung his harp and lyre, and sang and chanted the deeds of the demi-gods, making this the pastime of his idle hours, and in this at least he chose wisely. For to fall out with the king and affront him was excessively stubborn and ill-tempered. Though perhaps the son of Thetis is not free from this criticism either, that he spent in song and music the hours that called for deeds, for at such a time he might have retained his arms instead of laying them aside, and thus later, at his leisure, could he have sung the praises of the king and chanted his victories. In truth, however, the author of that tale also tells us that Agamemnon did not treat his general either temperately or with tact, but first used threats then proceeded to insolent acts, when he robbed Achilles of his prize of valour.[2] Then Homer brings them, penitent by this time, face to face in the assembly, and has the son of Thetis ask:

Ἀτρεΐδη ἦ ἄρ τι τόδ' ἀμφοτέροισιν ἄρειον
ἔπλετο σοὶ καὶ ἐμοί, ὅ τε νῶΐ περ ἀχνυμένω κῆρ
θυμοβόρῳ ἔριδι μενεήναμεν εἵνεκα κούρης;

"Agamemnon, was it better for us,
in any way, to rage at each other,
to waste ourselves in strife over a girl?"[3]

Later on, he has Achilles curse the cause of their quarrel and recount the disasters due to his own wrath, where we see the king blaming Zeus, Fate, and the Erinyes. Here, I think, he is pointing to a moral, using those heroes whom he sets before us like types in a tragedy. The moral is that kings ought never to behave insolently, nor use their power without reserve, nor be carried away by their

1. Agamemnon 2. Briseis 3. *The Iliad*, XIX, 56

anger like a spirited horse that runs away for lack of bit and driver; and, moreover, he is warning generals not to resent the insolence of kings, but to endure their censure with self-control and equanimity, so that their whole life may not be filled with remorse.[1]

When I reflect on this, my beloved Emperor, and behold you displaying in all that you do the result of your study of Homer, seeing you so eager to benefit every citizen in the community in every way, and devising for me individually such honours and privileges one after another, then I think that you desire to be nobler than the king of the Greeks. To such a degree, indeed, that, whereas he insulted his bravest men, you, I believe, grant forgiveness to many even of the undeserving, since you approve the maxim of Pittacus which set mercy before vengeance. Therefore, I should be ashamed not to appear more reasonable than the son of Peleus, or to fail to praise, as far as it lies within me, what pertains to you. I do not mean gold, nor, by Zeus, a robe of purple, nor raiment embroidered all over, the handiwork of Sidonian women[2], nor beautiful Nisæan horses,[3] nor the gleam and glitter of gold-mounted chariots, nor the precious stones of India, so beautiful and lovely to look upon. And yet if one should choose to devote his attention to these and think fit to describe every one of them, he would have to draw on almost the whole stream of Homer's poetry and still he would be short of words. Indeed, the panegyrics that have been composed for each of the demi-gods would be inadequate for your sole praise. First, then, let me begin, if you will, with your sceptre and your sovereignty itself. For what does the poet say when he wishes to praise the antiquity of the house of the Pelopids and to exhibit the greatness of their sovereignty?

ἀνὰ δὲ κρείων Ἀγαμέμνων ἔστη σκῆπτρον ἔχων
τὸ μὲν Ἥφαιστος κάμε τεύχων·

"Before them now arose Lord Agamemnon,
in his hand the sceptre that Hephæstus once fashioned"[4]

First it was given to Zeus; then Zeus gave it to his own and Maia's son; Hermes the prince, in turn, gave it to Pelops, and Pelops "gave it to Atreus, shepherd of the host, and Atreus at his death left it

1. Plato, *The Republic*, 557 2. *The Iliad*, VI, 289

3. Herodotus, 7.40; horses from the plain of Nisæa drew the chariot of Xerxes when he invaded Greece

4. *The Iliad*, II, 101

to Thyestes, rich in flocks; he in turn gave it into the hands of Agamemnon, so that he should rule over many islands and all Argos". Here then you have the genealogy of the house of Pelops, which endured for barely three generations. Yet the story of our family began with Claudius; then its supremacy ceased for a short time, until your two grandfathers acceded to the throne. Your mother's father[1] governed Rome, and Italy, Libya, Sardinia, and Sicily besides, an empire certainly not inferior to Argos and Mycenæ. Your father's father[2] ruled the most warlike of all the tribes of Galatia,[3] the Western Iberians,[4] and the islands that lie in the Ocean,[5] which are larger than those that are to be seen in our seas, just as the sea that rolls beyond the pillars of Heracles is larger than the inner sea.[6] These countries your grandfathers entirely cleared of our foes, at one moment joining forces for a campaign, when occasion demanded, at another making separate expeditions on their own account, thus they annihilated the insolent and lawless Barbarians on their frontiers. These, then, are the distinctions that they won. Your father inherited his proper share of the Empire with all piety and due observance, waiting until his father reached his appointed end. Then he freed from intolerable slavery the remainder, which had sunk from empire to tyranny, and so governed the whole, appointing you and your brothers, his three sons, as his colleagues.

Now, can I fairly compare your house with the Pelopids in the extent of their power, the length of their dynasty, or the number of those who sat on the throne? Or is that really foolish, and must I instead go on to describe your wealth, and admire your cloak and the brooch that fastens it, the sort of thing on which even Homer loved to linger? Or must I describe at length the mares of Tros that numbered three thousand and "pastured in the marsh-meadow",[7] and the theft that followed?[8] Or shall I pay my respects to your Thracian horses, whiter than snow and faster than the storm winds, and your Thracian chariots? For in your case, also, we can extol all these. As for the palace of Alcinous and those halls that dazzled even the son of prudent Odysseus, moving him to such foolish expressions of wonder,[9] shall I think it worth while to compare them with yours, for fear that men should one day think that you

1. Maximianus 2. Constantius Chlorus 3. Gaul
4. Julian may be mistaken. According to Bury, Spain was governed by Maximianus
5. The Atlantic 6. The Mediterranean 7. *The Iliad*, XX, 221
8. *The Iliad*, V, 222 9. *The Odyssey*, IV, 69

were worse off than he in these respects, or shall I rather reject such trifling things? Indeed, I must be on my guard lest someone accuse and convict me of using frivolous speech and ignoring what is really admirable. So I had better leave it to the Homerids to spend their energies on such themes, and proceed boldly to what is more closely allied to virtue, to things to which you yourself pay more attention, that is, physical strength and experience in the use of arms.

Now, which one of those heroes to whom Homer devotes his enchanting strains shall I admit to be superior to you? There is the archer Pandaros in Homer, but he is treacherous and yields to bribes;[1] moreover, his arm was weak and he was an inferior hoplite. Then there are Teucer and Meriones besides. The latter employs his bow against a pigeon,[2] while Teucer, though he distinguished himself in battle, always needed a sort of bulwark or wall. Accordingly, he keeps a shield in front of him,[3] which is not his own but his brother's, and aims at the enemy at his ease, cutting an absurd figure as a soldier, seeing that he needed a protector taller than himself and that it was not in his weapons that he placed his hopes of safety. Though I have seen you many a time, my beloved Emperor, bringing down bears, panthers, and lions with the weapons hurled by your hand, using your bow for both hunting and for pastime, while on the field of battle you have your own shield, cuirass, and helmet. Furthermore, I should not be afraid to match you with Achilles when he was exulting in the armour that Hephæstus made, testing himself and that armour to see "whether it fitted him and whether his glorious limbs ran free therein",[4] for your successes proclaim to all men your proficiency.

As for your horsemanship and your agility in running, would it be fair to compare with you any of those heroes of old who won a name and great reputation? Is it not a fact that horsemanship had not yet been invented? For at that time they used only chariots and not riding-horses. As for their fastest runner, it is an open question how he compares with you. In drawing up troops and forming a phalanx skilfully, however, Menestheus[5] seems to have excelled, and on account of his greater age the Pylian[6] is his equal in proficiency. Yet the enemy often threw their line into disorder, and not even at the wall[7] could they hold their ground when they encountered the foe. You, on the other hand, engaged in countless battles, not only with hostile Barbarians in great numbers, but with

1. *The Iliad*, IV, 97 2. *The Iliad*, XXIII, 870 3. *The Iliad*, VIII, 266
4. *The Iliad*, XIX, 385 5. *The Iliad*, II, 552 6. Nestor; ibid. 7. *The Iliad*, VII, 436

just as many of your own subjects, who had revolted and were fighting on the side of one who was ambitious of grasping the imperial power; yet your phalanx remained unbroken and never wavered or yielded an inch. That this is not an idle boast, and that I do not make a pretension in words that goes beyond the actual facts, I will demonstrate to my hearers. For I think it would be absurd to relate to you your own achievements. I should be like an inane and tasteless person who, on seeing the works of Phidias, should attempt to discuss with Phidias himself the Maiden Goddess on the Acropolis, or the statue of Zeus at Pisa. Whereas, if I publish to the rest of the world your most distinguished achievements, I shall perhaps avoid that blunder and not lay myself open to criticism. I shall therefore hesitate no more but proceed with my discourse.

I hope no one will object if, when I attempt to deal with exploits of such importance, my speech should become proportionately long, even as I desire to limit and restrain it lest my feeble words over-whelm and mar the greatness of your deeds; like the gold which, when it was laid over the wings of the Eros at Thespiæ, took something, so they say, from the delicacy of its workmanship. For your triumphs verily call for the trumpet of Homer himself, far more than did the achievements of the Macedonian.[1] This will be evident as I go on to use the same method of argumentation which I adopted when I began. It then became evident that there is a strong affinity between the Emperor's exploits and those of the heroes, and I claimed that while one hero excelled the others in one accomplishment only, the Emperor excels them all in all those accomplishments. That he is more kingly than the king himself[2] I proved, if you remember, in what I said in my introduction, and over and again it will be evident. So let us now, if you will, consider his battles and campaigns. What Greeks and Barbarians did Homer praise above their fellows? I will read you those of his verses that are most to the point: "tell me, Muse, of all the warriors and horses under the sons of Atreus, who was foremost? Of warriors most formidable was Ajax, son of Telamon, so long as Achilles raged apart. For he towered above them all".[3] And again he says of the son of Telamon: "Ajax, who in beauty and the deeds he wrought, was of a mould above all the other Danaans, save only the blameless son of Peleus".[4] These two, he says, were the bravest of the Greeks who came to the war, and of the Trojan army, Hector and Sarpedon.

1. Alexander 2. Agamemnon 3. *The Iliad*, II, 761 4. *The Odyssey*, XX, 66

Do you wish, then, that I should pick out their most brilliant feats and consider to what they amounted? For indeed, the fighting of Achilles at the river resembles in some respects certain of the Emperor's achievements, as does the battle of the Achæans about the wall. Or Ajax again, when, in his struggle to defend the ships, he ventures up on to their decks, might be permitted some just resemblance to him. Now, however, I wish to describe to you the battle by the river which the Emperor fought not long ago. You know the causes of the outbreak of the war, and that he carried it through, not from desire of gain, but with justice on his side. There is no reason why I should not briefly remind you of the facts.

A rash and traitorous man[1] tried to grasp at power to which he had no right, and assassinated the Emperor's brother and partner in empire. Then he began to be uplifted, blinded even by his hopes, as though he was about to imitate Poseidon and prove that Homer's story was not mere fiction but absolutely true, when he says about the god: "three strides did he make, and with the fourth came to his goal, even to Ægæ";[2] how he took thence all his armour, harnessed his horses, and drove through the waves, whereupon "with gladness the sea parted before him, and the horses fared very swiftly, and the bronze axle was not whetted beneath", for nothing stood in his way, but all things stood aside and made a path for him in their joy. Even so, the usurper thought that he had left behind him nothing hostile or opposed to him, and that there was nothing at all to hinder him from taking up a position at the mouth of the Tigris. There followed him a large force of heavy infantry and as many cavalry, to be sure, and good fighters they were – Celts, Iberians, and Germans from the banks of the Rhine and from the coasts of the western sea. Whether I ought to call that sea the Ocean or the Atlantic, or whether it is proper to use some other name for it, I am not sure. I only know that its coasts are peopled by tribes of Barbarians who are not easy to subdue and are far more energetic than any other race; this I know not merely from hearsay, on which it is never safe to rely, but I have learned it from personal experience.

From these tribes, then, he mustered an army as large as that which marched with him from home, or rather, many followed him because they were his own people, allied to him by the ties of race. Yet our subjects – for so we must call them – by which I mean all his Roman troops, followed from compulsion and not from choice,

1. Magnentius 2. *The Iliad*, XIII, 20

like mercenary allies, for their position and role were like that of the proverbial Carian,[1] since they were naturally ill-disposed to a Barbarian and a stranger who had conceived the idea of ruling and embarked on the enterprise at the time of a drunken debauch, being the sort of leader that one might expect from such a preface and prelude as that. He led them in person, not indeed like Typho, who, as the poet tells us[2] in his wondrous tale, was brought forth by the earth in her anger against Zeus. Nor was he like the strongest of the Giants, rather, he was like Vice incarnate which the wise Prodicus created in his fable,[3] making her compete with Virtue and attempt to win over the son of Zeus,[4] contending that he would do well to prize her above all else. Thus as he led them to battle, he outdid the behaviour of Capaneus,[5] like the Barbarian that he was, in his insensate folly, though he did not, like Capaneus, trust to the energy of his soul or his physical strength, but to the number of his Barbarian followers. He boasted that he would lay everything at their feet to plunder, that every general, captain, and common soldier of his should despoil an enemy of corresponding rank of his baggage and belongings, and that he would enslave the owners as well. He was confirmed in this attitude by the Emperor's clever strategy, and led his army out from the narrow passes to the plains in high spirits, little knowing the truth, since he decided that the Emperor's march was merely flight and not a manoeuvre. Consequently, he was taken unawares, like a bird or fish in the net. For when he reached the open country and the plains of Pæonia, where it seemed advantageous to fight, the Emperor promptly drew up his cavalry separately on both wings.

Of these troops, some carry lances and are protected by cuirasses and helmets of wrought iron mail. They wear greaves that fit the legs closely, and knee-caps, and on their thighs the same sort of iron covering. They ride their horses exactly like statues, and need no shield. In the rear of these was posted a large body of the rest of the cavalry, who did carry shields, while others fought on horseback with bows and arrows. Of the infantry, hoplites occupied the centre and supported the cavalry on either wing. In the rear were the slingers and archers, and all troops that launch their missiles from the hand, having neither shield nor cuirass. This, then, was the disposition of our phalanx. The left wing slightly

1. The Carians were proverbially worthless 2. Hesiod, *Theogony*

3. Xenophon, *Memorabilia*, 2.1.2 4. Heracles

5. Æschylus, *Seven Against Thebes*, 440; Euripides, *Phoenissæ*, 1182

outflanked the enemy, whose whole force was thereby thrown into confusion, and their line broke. When our cavalry made a charge and maintained it stubbornly, he who had so shamefully usurped the imperial power disgraced himself by flight, leaving there his cavalry commander and numerous chiliarchs[1] and taxiarchs[2], who continued to fight bravely. In command of all these was the real author[3] of that monstrous and unholy drama, who had been the first to suggest to him that he should pretend to the imperial power and rob us of our royal prerogative.

For a time, indeed, he enjoyed success, having met with no resistance or failure at his first attempt, but on that day he provoked the punishment that justice had in store for his misdeeds, and was made to pay a penalty that is hardly credible. For all the others who abetted the usurper in that war met death openly or their flight was evident to all, as was the repentance of others. Many came as suppliants, and all obtained forgiveness, since the Emperor surpassed the son of Thetis in generosity. For Achilles, after Patroclus fell, refused any longer to even sell those whom he took captive, but slew them as they clasped his knees and begged for mercy. The Emperor, by comparison, proclaimed an amnesty for those who should renounce the conspiracy, and so not only freed them from the fear of death or exile, or some other punishment, but, as though their association with the usurper had been due to some misadventure or unhappy error, he deigned to reinstate them and completely erase the past. I shall have occasion to refer to this again.

What I must now state is that the man who had trained and tutored the usurper was neither among the fallen nor the fugitives. It was indeed natural that he should not even hope for pardon, since his schemes had been so wicked, his actions so infamous, and he himself had been responsible for the slaughter of so many innocent men and women, of whom many were private citizens, and almost all of whom were connected with the imperial family. He had done this, moreover, without hesitation or the sentiments of one who sheds the blood of his own people, and because of that stain of guilt, he fears and is ever watchful for the avenger, those who will exact a bloody reckoning. Yet, with a kind of purification that was new and unheard of, he would wash his hands of the blood

1. Χιλίαρχος; Greek military rank meaning "commander of a thousand men"
2. Ταξίαρχος; Greek military rank broadly equivalent to brigadier
3. Marcellinus

of his first victims, then go on to murder man after man, and then, after those whom they held dear, he slew the women as well. Thus he naturally abandoned the idea of appealing for mercy. Though likely as it is that he should think such, it may well be otherwise. For the fact is that we do not know what he did or suffered before he vanished out of sight, out of our ken. Whether some avenging deity snatched him away, as Homer says of the daughters of Pandareos,[1] and even now is carrying him to the very verge of the world to punish him for his evil designs, or whether the river[2] has received him and bids him feed the fishes, has not yet been revealed. For until the battle actually began, and while the troops were forming the phalanx, he was full of confidence, moving to and fro in the centre of their line. Yet when the battle was over as was fitting, he vanished completely, taken from our sight by I know not what god or divine power, only it is quite certain that the fate in store for him was far from enviable. At any rate, he was not destined to appear again, and, after insulting us with impunity, live prosperous and secure as he thought he should; rather, he was doomed to be completely blotted out and to suffer a punishment that for him was indeed fatal, but to many was beneficial and gave them a chance of recovery.

Now, though, it would be well worth while to devote more of my speech to the man who was the author of that whole enterprise, even as it breaks the thread of my narrative, which had reached the thick of the action. So I must leave that subject for the present, and going back to the point where I digressed, describe how the battle ended. For though their generals showed such cowardice, the courage of the soldiers was by no means abated. When their line was broken, which was due not to their cowardice but to the ignorance and inexperience of their leader, they formed into companies and kept up the fight. What happened then was beyond all expectation, for the enemy refused altogether to yield to those who were defeating them, while our men did their utmost to achieve a decisive victory, and so there arose the wildest confusion, loud shouts mingled with the din of weapons, as swords were shattered against helmets and shields against spears. It was a hand to hand fight in which they discarded their shields and attacked with swords only, while, indifferent to their own fate, and devoting the utmost ardour to inflicting severe loss on the foe, they were ready to meet even death if only they could make our victory seem

1. *The Odyssey*, XX, 66 2. The Drava

doubtful and dearly bought. It was not only the infantry who behaved thus to their pursuers, but even the cavalry, whose spears were broken and were now entirely useless. Their shafts are long and polished, and when they had broken them they dismounted and transformed themselves into hoplites. So for some time they held their own against the greatest odds. Since, however, our cavalry kept shooting their arrows from a distance as they rode after them, while the heavy cavalry made frequent charges, as was easy on that unobstructed and level plain, and night overtook them, the enemy were glad at last to take to flight, while our men kept up a vigorous pursuit as far as the camp, taking it by assault together with the baggage, slaves, and animals. Directly the rout of the enemy had begun, as I have described, and while we kept up a keen pursuit, they were driven towards the left, where the river was on the right of the victors. There the greatest slaughter took place, and so the river was choked with the bodies of men and horses, indiscriminately. For the Drava was not like the Scamander, nor so kind to the fugitives; it did not put ashore and cast forth from its waters the dead in their armour, nor cover up and hide securely in its eddies those who escaped alive.

For that is what the Trojan river did,[1] perhaps out of kindness, perhaps due to it being so small that it offered an easy crossing to one who tried to swim or walk. In fact, when a single poplar was thrown into it, it formed a bridge, and the whole river roared with foam and blood, and beat upon the shoulders of Achilles, if indeed we may believe this, though it never did anything more violent. When a slight fire scorched it, it gave up fighting at once and swore not to play the part of ally. However this, too, was probably a jest on Homer's part, when he invented that strange and unnatural sort of duel. For in the rest of the poem also he evidently favours Achilles, setting the army there as mere spectators, while he brings Achilles on to the field as the only invincible and resistless warrior. He has him slay all whom he encounters and put every one of the foes to flight, simply by his voice, his bearing, and the glance of his eyes, both when the battle begins and on the banks of the Scamander, till the fugitives were glad to gather within the wall of the city. Many verses he devotes to relating this, whereupon he invents the battles of the gods, and by embellishing his poem with such tales he compromises his critics and prevents us from giving a fair and honest vote. Yet if there be anyone who refuses to be beguiled by

1. *The Iliad*, XXI, 325

the beauty of the words and the creations that are imported into the poem...[1] then, though he is as strict as a member of the Areopagus, I shall not dread his decision. For we are convinced by the poem that the son of Peleus is a brave warrior. After slaying twenty men:

Ζωοὺς δ' ἐκ ποταμοῖο δυώδεκα λέξατο κούρους,
Τοὺς ἐξῆγε θύραζε τεθηπότας ἠύτε νεβρούς,
Ποινὴν Πατρόκλοιο Μενοιτιάδαο θανόντος·

"he picked twelve young men alive out of the river
and led them forth like startled fawns
to atone for the death of Patroclus, son of Menoetius"[2]

Yet his victory, though it had some influence on the fortunes of the Achæans, was not enough to inspire any great fear in the enemy, nor did it make them wholly despair of their cause. On this point shall we set Homer aside and demand some other witness? Or is it not enough to recall the verses in which he describes how Priam came to the ships bearing his son's ransom? For after he had made the truce for which he had come, the son of Thetis asked: "for how many days do you desire to make a funeral for noble Hector?" He told him not only that, but concerning the war he said:

Τῇ δὲ δυωδεκάτῃ πολεμίξομεν, εἴπερ ἀνάγκη·

"And on the twelfth day we will fight again, if fight we must"[3]

You see that Achilles does not hesitate to announce that war will be resumed after the armistice. By contrast, the unmanly and cowardly usurper sheltered his flight behind lofty mountains and built forts on them; nor did he trust even to the strength of the position, but begged for forgiveness. Moreover, he would have obtained it had he deserved it, and not proved himself on many occasions both treacherous and insolent by heaping one crime upon another.

Now, with regard to the battle, if there be anyone who declines to heed either the opinion expressed in my narrative or those admirably written verses, but prefers to consider the actual facts, let him judge from those. Accordingly, then, we will compare next the fighting of Ajax in defence of the ships and of the Achæans at the wall with the Emperor's achievements at that famous city. That is, the city to which the Mygdonius, fairest of rivers, gives its

1. For eight words the text is irreparably corrupted

2. *The Iliad*, XXI, 27 3. *The Iliad*, XIV, 657

name, though it has also been named after King Antiochus. Then, too, it has another, a Barbarian name,[1] which is familiar to many of you from your interaction with the Barbarians of those parts. This city was besieged by an overwhelming number of Parthians with their Indian allies, at the very time when the Emperor was prepared to march against the usurper. And like the sea crab which they say engaged Heracles in battle when he sallied forth to attack the Lernæan monster,[2] the King of the Parthians, crossing the Tigris from the mainland, encircled the city with dykes. Then he let the Mygdonius flow into these, thereby transforming all the space about the city into a lake, and completely hemming it in as though it were an island, so that only the ramparts stood out and showed a little above the water. Then he besieged it by bringing up ships with siege-engines on board. This was not the work of one day, but I believe of almost four months. Yet the defenders within the wall continually repulsed the Barbarians by burning the siege-engines with their fire-bearing missiles. From the wall they hauled up many of the ships, while others were shattered by the force of the engines when discharged and the weight of the missiles. For some of the stones that were hurled on to them weighed as much as seven Attic talents.[3] When this had been going on for many days in succession, part of the dyke gave way and the water flowed in at full tide, carrying with it a portion of the wall as much as a hundred cubits long.[4]

Thereupon he arrayed the besieging army in the Persian fashion. For they keep up and imitate such customs, I suppose, because they do not wish to be considered Parthians, and so pretend to be Persians. That is surely the reason why they prefer the Persian manner of dress. Thus when they march to battle they look like them, and take pride in wearing the same armour, and raiment adorned with gold and purple. By this means they try to evade the truth and to make it appear that they have not revolted from Macedon, but are merely continuing the empire that was theirs of old. Their king, therefore, imitating Xerxes, sat on a sort of hill that had been artificially made, and his army advanced accompanied by their beasts.[5] These came from India and carried iron towers full of archers. First came the cavalry who wore cuirasses, and the archers,

---

1. Nisibis

2. i.e., Sapor becomes the ally of Magnentius as the crab was the ally of the Hydra in the conflict with Heracles

3. 400 lbs 4. 150 ft 5. War-elephants

then the rest of the cavalry in great numbers. For infantry they find useless for their sort of fighting and it is not highly regarded by them. Nor, in fact, is it necessary to them, since the whole of the country that they inhabit is flat and bare. For a military force is naturally valued or slighted in proportion to its actual usefulness in war. Accordingly, since infantry is, from the nature of the country, of little use to them, it is granted no great consideration in their laws. This happened in the case of Crete and Caria as well, and countless nations have military equipment like theirs. For instance, the plains of Thessaly have proved suitable for cavalry engagements and training. Our state, on the other hand, since it has had to encounter adversaries of all sorts, and has won its pre-eminence by good judgment combined with good fortune, has naturally adapted itself to every kind of armour, and to varying equipment.

Perhaps those who watch over the rules for writing panegyric, as though they were laws, may say that all this is irrelevant to my speech. Whether what I have been saying partly concerns you I shall consider at the proper time. Regardless, I can easily clear myself from the accusation of such persons. For I declare that I make no claim to be an expert in their art, and one who has not agreed to abide by certain rules has the right to neglect them. It may also be that I shall prove to have other convincing excuses besides. Though it is not worthwhile to interrupt my speech and digress from my theme any longer when there is no need. Let me, then, retrace my steps to the point at which I digressed.

Now, when the Parthians advanced to attack the wall in their splendid war-gear, men and horses, supported by the Indian elephants, it was with the utmost confidence that they would at once take it by assault. At the signal to charge they all pressed forward, since every man of them was eager to be the first to scale the wall[1] and win the glory of that exploit. They did not imagine that there was anything to fear, nor did they believe that the besieged would resist their assault. Such was the exaggerated confidence of the Parthians. The besieged, however, kept their phalanx unbroken at the gap in the wall, and, on the portion of the wall that was still intact, they posted all the non-combatants in the city, and distributed among them an equal number of soldiers. When the enemy rode up and not a single missile was hurled at them from the wall, their confidence that they would completely reduce the city was strengthened, and they whipped and spurred on

1. *The Iliad*, XII, 438

their horses so that their flanks were covered with blood, until they had left the dykes behind them. These dykes they had made earlier to dam the mouth of the Mygdonius; the mud thereabouts was very deep †and, in fact, was far from being dry in spite of the wood,†[1] for the soil was so rich and of the sort that conceals springs under its surface. Moreover, in that place there was a wide moat that had been made long ago to protect the town and had become filled up with a bog of considerable depth. Now, when the enemy had already reached this moat and were trying to cross it, a large force of the besieged made a sally, while many others hurled stones from the walls. Then many of the besiegers were slain, and all with one accord turned their horses in flight, though only from their gestures could it be seen that flight was what they desired and intended. For, as they were in the act of wheeling them about, their horses fell and bore down the riders with them. Weighed down as they were by their armour, they floundered still deeper in the bog, and the carnage that ensued has never yet been paralleled in any siege of the same kind.

Since this fate had overtaken the cavalry, they turned to the elephants, thinking that they would be more likely to overawe us by that foreign tactic of war. For surely they had not been stricken so blind as to not see that an elephant is heavier than a horse, since it carries the load, not of two horses or several, but what would, I suppose, require many wagons, that is, archers, javelin men, and the iron tower besides. All this was a serious hindrance, considering that the ground was artificially made and had been converted into a bog. This the event made plain. Hence it is probable that they were not advancing to give battle, but rather were arrayed to overawe the besieged. They came on in battle line at equal distances from one another – indeed, the phalanx of the Parthians resembled a wall – with the elephants carrying the towers, and hoplites filling up the spaces in-between. Yet drawn up as these were, they were of no great use to the Barbarian. It was, nevertheless, a spectacle which gave the defenders on the wall great pleasure and entertainment. When they had gazed their fill at what resembled a splendid and costly pageant in procession, they hurled stones from their engines, and, shooting their arrows, challenged the Barbarians to fight for the wall. Now, the Parthians are naturally quick-tempered, thus they could not endure to incur ridicule nor to lead back this imposing force without striking a blow. So, by the king's express

1. The original text is heavily corrupted; the translation provided is thus surmised

command, they charged at the wall and received a continuous fire of stones and arrows, while some of the elephants were wounded and perished by sinking into the mud. Thereupon, in fear for the others also, they led them back to the camp.

Having failed in this second attempt as well, the Parthian king divided his archers into companies, ordering them to relieve one another and to keep shooting at the breach in the wall, so that the besieged could not rebuild it and thus ensure the safety of the town. For he hoped by this means to either take it by surprise, or by mere numbers to overwhelm the garrison. Yet the preparations that had been made by the Emperor show that the Barbarian's plan was futile. For to the rear of the hoplites a second wall was being built, and while he thought they were using the old line of the wall for the foundations, and that the work was not yet in hand, they had laboured continuously for a whole day and night till the wall had risen to a height of four cubits. At daybreak it became visible, a new and conspicuous piece of work. Furthermore, the besieged did not for a moment yield their ground, but kept relieving one another and shooting their javelins at those who were attacking the fallen wall, and all this terribly dismayed the Barbarian. Nevertheless, he did not at once lead off his army but employed the same efforts over again. Yet when he had done as before, and as before suffered repulse, he did withdraw his army, having lost many whole tribes through famine, and squandered many lives over the dykes and in the siege. He had also put to death many satraps one after another, on various charges, blaming one of them because the dykes had not been made strong enough, but gave way and were flooded by the waters of the river; another because when fighting under the walls he had not distinguished himself; and others he executed for one offence or another. This is, in fact, the regular custom among the Barbarians in Asia, to shift the blame of their ill-success on to their subjects. So it was that the king acted on that occasion, and afterwards took himself off. From that time, then, he has kept the peace with us and has never asked for any compact or treaty; instead, he stays at home and is thankful if only the Emperor does not march against him and exact vengeance for his audacity and folly.

Am I now justified in comparing this battle with those that were fought in defence of the Greek ships and the wall? Observe the following points of similarity, and note also the difference. Of the Greeks, the two Ajaxes, the Lapithæ, and Menestheus fell back from the wall and looked on helplessly while the gates were battered down by Hector, and Sarpedon scaled the battlements. Our garrison, however, did not give way even when the wall fell in of itself, but fought and won, and repulsed the Parthians, aided though these were by their Indian allies. Again, Hector went up on to the ships and fought from their decks on foot, and as though from behind a rampart, whereas our garrison first had to fight a naval battle from the walls; and finally, while Hector and Sarpedon had to retreat from the battlements and the ships, the garrison routed not only the forces that brought ships to the attack but the land force as well. Now, it is appropriate that by some happy chance my speech should have alluded to Hector and Sarpedon, and to what I may call the very crown of their achievements, that is, the destruction of the wall which Homer tells us the Achæans built only the day before, doing so on the advice of that princely orator of Pylos[1] "to be an impregnable bulwark for the ships and the army".[2]

For that, I think, was almost the proudest of Hector's achievements, and he did not need the craft of Glaucus to help him, or any wiser plan, for Homer says plainly that the moment Achilles appeared "he shrank back into the crowd of men".[3] Again, when Agamemnon attacked the Trojans and pursued them to the wall, Zeus stole away Hector[4] so that he might escape at his leisure. The poet, I dare say, is mocking him and deriding his cowardice when he says that, as he was sitting under the oak-tree, being already near the gate, Iris came to him with this message from Zeus: "so long as you see Agamemnon, leader of the host, raging in the front, devastating the ranks, so long must you keep from the fight".[5] For is it likely that Zeus would give such base and cowardly advice, especially to one who was not even fighting, but merely standing there very much at ease? Thus while the son of Tydeus, on whose head Athena kindled a mighty flame, was slaying many and forcing to flight all who stayed to encounter him, Hector stood far away from the battle. Though he had to endure many taunts, he despaired of making a stand against the Achæans, making instead a specious excuse for going to the city to advise his mother to propitiate Athena in company with the Trojan women. And yet, if in person he had besought the goddess before the temple, with the elders, he would have had good reason to do so, for it is only proper,

1. Nestor 2. *The Iliad*, XIV, 56 3. *The Iliad*, XX, 379 4. *The Iliad*, XI, 163
5. *The Iliad*, XI, 202

in my opinion, that a general or king should always serve the god with the appointed ritual, like a priest or prophet, and not neglect this duty nor think it more fitting for another, and delegate it as though he thought such a service beneath his own dignity.

For here I think I may without offence adapt slightly Plato's language where he says that the man, and especially the king, best equipped for this life is he who depends on God for all that relates to happiness, and does not hang in suspense on other men, whose actions, whether good or bad, are liable to force him and his affairs off the straight path.[1] Though no one should allow me to paraphrase or change that passage, or alter that word, and though I should be told that I must leave it undisturbed like something holy and consecrated by time, even in that case I shall maintain that this is what that wise man meant. For when he says "depends on himself", assuredly he does not refer to a man's body or his property, or long descent, or distinguished ancestors. For these are indeed his belongings, but they are not the man himself; his real self is his mind, his intelligence, and, in short, the god that is within us. As to which, Plato elsewhere calls it "the supreme form of the soul that is within us" and says that "God has given it to each one of us as a guiding genius, even that which we say dwells in the summit of our body and raises us from earth towards our celestial affinity".[2] It is on this that he plainly says every man ought to depend, and not on other men, who have so often succeeded when they wish to harm and hinder us in other respects. Indeed, it has happened before now that even without such a desire men have deprived us of certain of our possessions. Yet this alone cannot be hindered or harmed, for "the eternal law does not permit the inferior to injure that which is superior to itself".[3] This saying is also from Plato. Though it may be that I am wearying you with these doctrines of his with which I sprinkle my own utterances in small quantities, as with salt or gold dust. For salt makes our food more agreeable, and gold enhances an appearance to the eye, while Plato's doctrines produce both effects. For as we listen to them they give more pleasure than salt to the sense, and they have a wonderful power to nourish and cleanse the soul. With this, I must not hesitate or be cautious of criticism should someone reproach me for being insatiable and grasping at everything, like persons at a banquet who, in their greed to taste every dish, cannot keep their hands from what is set before

1. Plato, *Menexenus*, 247 2. Plato, *Timæus*, 90 3. Plato, *Apology*, 30

them.[1] For something of this sort seems to happen in my case when, in the same breath, I utter panegyric and philosophic theories, and, before I have done justice to my original theme, break off in the middle to expound the sayings of philosophers. I have had occasion before now to reply to those who make such criticisms as these, and perhaps I shall have to do so again.

I will now, however, resume the thread of my discourse and return to my starting-point, like those who, when a race is about to start, run prematurely off the line. Well, as I was saying a moment ago, Plato declares that a man's real self is his mind and soul, whereas his body and his estate are but his possessions. This is the distinction made in that marvellous work, the Laws. Therefore, if one were to go back to the beginning and say "that man is best equipped for life who makes everything that relates to happiness depend on his mind and intelligence, and not on those outside himself who, by doing or faring well or ill force him off the straight path" he is not changing or perverting the sense of the words, but expounds and interprets them correctly. Moreover, if for Plato's word "genius" he substitutes the word "God", he has a perfect right to do so. For if Plato gives the control of our whole life to the presiding "genius" within us, which is by nature unaffected by sensation and akin to God, but must endure and suffer much because of its association with the body, he therefore gives the impression to the crowd that it is also subject to sensation and death; and if he says that this is true of every man who wishes to be happy, what must we suppose is his opinion about pure intelligence unmixed with earthly substance, which is indeed synonymous with God? To this I say every man, whether he be a private citizen or a king, ought to entrust the reins of his life, and by a king I mean one who is truly worthy of the name, not a low-born impostor or one falsely entitled, but one who is aware of God and discerns his nature because of his affinity with him, and being truly wise bows to that divine sovereignty. For it is senseless and arrogant indeed for those who cultivate virtue not to trust wholly in God, once and for all. For we must believe that this above all else is what God approves. Again, no man must neglect the traditional form of worship or lightly regard this method of paying honour to the higher power, but rather consider that to be virtuous is to be scrupulously devout. For Piety is the child of Justice, and that

1. Plato, *Republic*, 354

justice is a characteristic of the more divine type of soul is obvious to all who discuss such matters.

For this reason, then, while I applaud Hector for refusing to make a libation because of the bloodstains on his hands, he had, as I said, no right to go back to the city or forsake the battle, seeing that the task he was about to perform was not that of a general or of a king, but of a messenger and underling, and that he was ready to take on himself the office of an Idæus or Talthybius. As I said at first, however, this seems to have been simply a specious excuse for flight. Indeed, when he obeyed the bidding of the seer and fought a duel with the son of Telamon,[1] he was quite ready to make terms and give presents, and rejoiced at having escaped death. In general, then, he is brave when in pursuit of the retreating foe, but in no case has he the credit of a victory or of turning the tide of battle, save for when "he was the first to leap within the wall of the Achæans"[2] together with Sarpedon. Shall I therefore shrink from competition, as though I could not cite on behalf of the Emperor any such exploit, and must therefore avoid seeming to compare the trivial with the important, and things of little account with what deserves more serious consideration, or shall I venture to enter the lists even against an achievement so famous?

Firstly, that wall was to protect the beach, being a palisade such as we are wont to construct, and was completed in less than a morning. While the wall that was on the Alps was an ancient fort, and the usurper used it after his flight, converting it into a defence as strong as though it had been newly built and leaving there an ample garrison of seasoned troops. Though he did not himself march all the way there, but remained in the neighbouring city.[3] This is a trading centre of the Italians on the coast, very prosperous and teeming with wealth, since the Mysians and Pæonians, and all the Italian inhabitants of the interior procure their merchandise thence. These last, I think, used to be called Heneti in the past, but now that the Romans are in possession of these cities they preserve the original name, but make the trifling addition of one letter at the beginning of the word. Its sign is a single character;[4] they call it "oo" and often use it instead of "b" to serve, I suppose, as a sort of breathing mark, and to represent some peculiarity of their pronunciation. The nation as a whole is called by this name, but at the time of the founding of the city, an eagle from Zeus flew past on the right and so bestowed on the place the omen derived from the

1. Ajax 2. *The Iliad*, XII, 438 3. Aquileia 4. "v"

bird.[1] It is situated at the foot of the Alps, which are very high mountains with precipices along them, and they hardly allow room for those who are trying to force their way over the passes to use even a single wagon and a pair of mules. They begin at the sea which we call Ionian, and form a barrier between what is now Italy and the Illyrians and Galatians, extending as far as the Etruscan sea. For when the Romans conquered the whole of this country, which includes the tribe of the Heneti, some of the Ligurians, and a considerable number of Galatians besides, they did not hinder them from retaining their ancient names, but compelled them to acknowledge the dominion of the Italian Republic. Thus, in our day, all the territory that lies within the Alps and is bounded by the Ionian and the Etruscan seas has the honour of being called Italy. On the other side of the Alps, on the west, dwell the Galatians, with the Rhætians to the north where the Rhine and the Danube have their sources nearby in the neighbouring country of the Barbarians. While on the east, as I said, the Alps fortify the district where the usurper stationed his garrison. In this way, then, Italy is contained on all sides, partly by mountains that are very hard to cross, partly by a shallow sea into which countless streams empty and form a morass like the marshlands of Egypt. Nevertheless, the Emperor by his skill gained control of the whole of that boundary of the sea, and forced his way inland.

I shall now relate how the city was actually taken, lest you should think I am wasting time by describing once more the difficulties of the ground, and how it was impossible to plant a camp or even a palisade near the city, or to bring up siege-engines, or devices for storming it, because the country all about was terribly short of water, and there were not even small pools. If you wish to grasp the main point of my narrative in a few words, remember the Macedonian's expedition against those Indians who lived on the famous rock,[2] up to which not even the lightest birds could wing their flight, and how he took it by storm, and you will be content to hear no more from me. I will, however, add just this, that Alexander in storming the rock lost many of his Macedonians, whereas our ruler and general lost not a single chiliarch or captain, indeed, not even a legionary from the muster-roll, but achieved an unsullied

1. Aquileia means "city of the eagle"

2. A hill fort in Sogdiana where the Bactrian chief, Oxyartes, made his last stand against Alexander in 327 B.C.

and "tearless"[1] victory. Now, Hector and Sarpedon doubtless hurled down many men from the wall, but when they encountered Patroclus in all his glory, Sarpedon was slain near the ships, while Hector, to his shame, fled without even recovering the body of his friend. Thus, without intelligence and emboldened by mere physical strength, they ventured to attack the wall. Whereas the Emperor, when strength and daring are required, employs force of arms and good counsel together, and so wins the day; yet where good judgment alone is necessary, it is by this that he steers his course, and thereby achieves triumphs such as not even iron could ever avail to erase.[2]

Since my speech has, of its own accord, reached this point in its course and has long been eager to praise the Emperor's wisdom and wise counsel, I shall allow it to do so. In fact, I spoke briefly on this subject some time ago, and all the cases where there seemed to me to be any affinity between the heroes of Homer and the Emperor, I described because of that resemblance, comparing great things with small. Indeed, if one considers the size of their armaments, the superiority of his forces also becomes evident. For in those days all Greece was set in motion,[3] including part of Thrace and Pæonia, and all the subject allies of Priam, "all that Lesbos, the seat of Makar, contains within, and Phrygia on the north, and the boundless Hellespont".[4] Yet to try to count up the nations who lately marched with the Emperor and fought on his side in the war, would be idle talk, superfluous verbiage, and absurd simplicity. It is quite natural that, proportionally speaking, as the armies are larger, their achievements are more important. So it follows of necessity that, in this respect as well, the Emperor's army surpassed Homer's heroes. In mere numbers, at any rate, at what point, I ask, could one justly compare them? For the Greeks fought all along for a single city, while the Trojans when they prevailed were not able to drive away the Greeks, nor were the Greeks strong enough, when they won a victory, to destroy and overthrow the power and royal sway of the house of Priam, yet the time they spent over it was ten years long. Though the Emperor's wars and undertakings have been numerous. He has been described as waging war against the Germans across the Rhine; then there was his bridge of boats over the Tigris; and his exposure of the power and arrogance of the Parthians was no trivial thing, on that occasion when they did not

1. Plutarch, *De Fortuna Romanorum*, IV
2. An allusion to Euripides, *Phoenissæ*, 516
3. Isocrates, *Evagoras*, 65; *Panegyricus*, 83
4. *The Iliad*, XXIV, 544

venture to defend their country as he was laying waste to it, but had to look on while the whole of it was devastated between the Tigris and the Lycus. Then, when the war against the usurper was concluded, there followed the expeditions to Sicily and Carthage, and that stratagem of occupying beforehand the mouth of the Po, which deprived the usurper of all his forces in Italy, and finally that third and last fall[1] at the Cottian Alps, which secured for the Emperor the pleasure of a victory that was definitive, and carried with it no fears for the future, while it compelled the defeated man to inflict on himself a just penalty wholly worthy of his misdeeds.

I have given this brief account of the Emperor's achievements, not adding anything in flattery or trying to exaggerate things that are perhaps of no special importance, nor dragging in what is far-fetched or unduly forced points of resemblance with those achievements, like those who interpret the myths of the poets and analyse them into plausible versions which allow them to introduce fictions of their own, though they start out from very slight analogies, and having recourse to a very shadowy basis, try to convince us that this is the very thing that the poets intended to say. In this case, however, if anyone should remove from Homer's poems merely the names of the heroes, and insert and fit in the Emperor's, the epic of the Iliad would be seen to have been composed quite as much in his honour as in theirs.

So that you may not think, if you hear only about his achievements and successes in war, that the Emperor is less well endowed for pursuits that are loftier and rightly considered of more importance, that is, public speaking, deliberations, and all those affairs in which judgment combined with intelligence and prudence take the helm, consider the case of Odysseus and Nestor, who are so highly praised in the poem; and if you find that the Emperor is inferior to them in any respect, put that down to his panegyrists. Though, in fairness, we should simply concede that he is easily their match. Nestor, for instance, when they began to disagree and quarrel about the captive damsel, tried to address them, and he did persuade both the king and the son of Thetis, but only to the extent that Achilles broke up the assembly in disorder, while Agamemnon did not even wait to complete his expiation to the god. While he was still performing the rite and the sacred ship was in view, he sent heralds to the tent of Achilles, just as though, it seems to me, he were afraid that he would forget his anger, and, once free from that

1. A common expression; in wrestling, the third fall secured the victory

passion, would repent and avoid his error. Again, the far-travelled orator from Ithaca, when he tried to persuade Achilles to make peace, offering him many gifts and promising him countless others, so provoked the young warrior that, though he had not before planned to sail home, he now began to make preparations.

Then there are those wonderful proofs of their intelligence, their exhortations to battle, and Nestor's building of the wall, a cowardly notion and worthy indeed of an old man. Nor, in truth, did the Achæans benefit much from that device. For it was after they had finished the wall that they were worsted by the Trojans, and naturally enough. For before that, they thought that they were themselves protecting the ships, like a noble bulwark. When, however, they realised that a wall lay in front of them, built with a deep moat and set at intervals with sharp stakes, they grew careless and slackened their valour because they trusted to the fortification. Yet it is not anyone who blames them and shows that they were in the wrong who is therefore a fit and proper person to praise the Emperor. Rather, he who, in a worthy manner, recounts the Emperor's deeds, which were done not idly or accidentally, or from a reflexive impulse, but were skilfully planned beforehand and carried through, he alone adequately praises the Emperor's keen intelligence.

To report to you those speeches which he made at every public gathering to the armies, the common people, and the councils, demands too long a narrative, though it is perhaps not too much to ask you to hear about one of these. Pray think, then, once more of the son of Laërtes when the Greeks were hastening to set sail and he checked the rush, diverting their zeal back to the war;[1] then of the Emperor's assembly in Illyria, when that old man,[2] persuaded by mere youths to think childish thoughts, forgot his treaties and obligations and proved to be the enemy of his preserver and benefactor. He came to terms with one against whom the Emperor was waging a war that allowed no truce nor herald of a truce,[3] and who was not only gathering an army together, but came to meet the Emperor on the border of the country because he was anxious to hinder him from advancing further. When those two armies met, and it was necessary to hold an assembly in the presence of the hoplites, a high platform was set up at which it was surrounded by a crowd of hoplites, javelin-men, archers, and cavalry equipped with their horses and the standards of the divisions. Then the Emperor,

1. *The Iliad*, II, 188 2. Vetranio 3. Demosthenes, *De Corona*, 262

accompanied by him who for the moment was his colleague, mounted the platform, carrying no sword, shield, or helmet, but wearing his usual attire. Not even one of his bodyguard followed him, thus there he stood alone on the platform, trusting to that speech which was so impressively appropriate. For of speeches, too, he is a good craftsman, though he does not plane down and polish his phrases, nor elaborate his periods like the ingenious rhetoricians, but is at once dignified and simple, using the right words on every occasion so that they sink into the souls not only of those who claim to be cultured and intelligent, but many unlearned persons also understand and give hearing to his words. Thus he won over many tens of thousands of hoplites, twenty thousand cavalry, the most warlike people, and at the same time a country that is extremely fertile, not seizing it by force, or carrying off captives, but by winning over men who obeyed him of their own free will and were eager to carry out his orders. This victory I judge to be far more splendid than that for which Sparta is famous.[1] For that was "tearless" for the victors only, but the Emperor's did not cause even the defeated to shed tears, since he who was masquerading as an emperor came down from the platform when he had pleaded his cause, and handed over to the Emperor the imperial purple as though it were an ancestral debt. All else the Emperor gave him in abundance, more than they say Cyrus gave to his grandfather, and arranged that he should live and be kept in the manner that Homer recommends for men who are past their prime: "for it is fitting that such a man, when he has bathed and fed, should sleep soft, for that is the manner of the aged".[2]

Now, for my part, I should have been glad to repeat to you the words that the Emperor used, and no fear would overtake me when handling words so noble. Yet modesty restrains me and does not permit me to change or interpret his words to you. For it would be wrong of me to tamper with them, and I should feel great shame to have my ignorance exposed, if someone who had read the Emperor's composition or heard it at the time should remember it by heart, and demand from me not only the ideas within it, but all the excellence with which they are adorned, though they are composed in the language of our ancestors.[3] This, at any rate, Homer had not to fear when, many generations later, he reported

1. The victory of Archidamus over the Arcadians; Xenophon, *Hellenica*, 7.1.32

2. *The Odyssey*, XXIV, 253

3. Latin, in which Julian was able to read and write, unlike many sophists of his day

his speeches, since his speakers left no record of what they said in their assemblies, and I think he was clearly confident in his ability to 2elate and report what they said in a better style. Though to make an inferior copy is absurd and unworthy of a generous and noble soul. As to the marvellous portion of his achievements and those of which the great multitude were spectator and hence preserve their memory and commend them, since it looks to the result, being there to judge whether they turn out well or ill, and eulogising them in language that is certainly not elegant – to all this I say you have often heard from the ingenious sophists, and from the race of poets inspired by the Muses themselves, such that, as far as these are concerned, I must have wearied you by speaking about them at too great a length. For you are already surfeited with them, your ears are filled with them, and there will always be a supply of composers of such discourses to sing of battles and proclaim victories with a loud, clear voice, after the manner of the heralds at the Olympic games. For you yourselves, since you delight to listen to them, have produced an abundance of these men. And no wonder. For their conceptions of what is good and bad are akin to your own, and they do but report to you your own opinions and depict them in fine phrases, like a dress of many colours, casting them into the mould of agreeable rhythms and forms, and bringing them forth for you as though they had invented something new. Moreover, you welcome them eagerly, and think that this is the correct way to eulogise, claiming that these deeds have received their due. This is perhaps true, but it may well be otherwise, since you do not really know what the correct way should be.

For I have observed that Socrates the Athenian – you know the man by hearsay and that his reputation for wisdom was proclaimed aloud by the Pythian oracle – I say I have observed that he did not praise that sort of thing, nor would he admit[1] that they are happy and fortunate those who are masters of a great territory and many nations, with many Greeks among them, too, and still more numerous and powerful Barbarians. Such men as are able to cut a canal through Athos and join continents[2] by a bridge of boats whenever they please; who subdue nations and reduce islands by sweeping the inhabitants into a net;[3] and who make offerings of a thousand talents' worth of frankincense.[4] Therefore, he never praised Xerxes or any other king of Persia, Lydia, or Macedonia,

1. Plato, *Gorgias*, 470 2. Plato, *Laws*, 699 3. Ibid., 698; Herodotus, 6.31
4. Herodotus, 1.183

and not even a Greek general, save only a very few, whomsoever he knew to delight in virtue, to cherish courage with temperance, and to love wisdom with justice. Whereas those whom he saw to be cunning, or merely clever, ingenious, or able, or generals and nothing more, though each one could lay claim to only one small fraction of virtue, to impose on the masses, these too he would not praise without reserve. Furthermore, his judgment is followed by a host of wise men who reverence virtue, but as for all those wonders and marvels that I have described, some say of them that they are worth little, others that they are worth nothing.

Now, if you are also of their opinion, I feel no inconsiderable alarm for what I said earlier, nor for myself, lest possibly you should declare that my words are mere childishness, and that I am an absurd and ignorant sophist who makes pretensions to an art in which I confess that I have no skill. This, indeed, I must confess to you when I recite eulogies that are really deserved, and such as you think worthwhile to listen to, even though they should seem to most of you somewhat uncouth and far inferior to what has been already uttered. If, however, as I said before, you accept the authors of those other eulogies, then my fear is altogether allayed. For then I shall not seem wholly out of place, but though, as I admit, inferior to many others, yet judged by my own standard, not wholly unprofitable nor attempting what is out of place. Indeed, it is probably not easy for you to disbelieve wise and inspired men who have much to say, each in his own manner, though the sum and substance of all their speeches is the praise of virtue. For virtue, they say, is implanted in the soul and makes one happy, kingly, and verily, by Zeus, civilised, capable in generalship, generous, and truly wealthy, not because it possesses the Colophonian[1] treasures of gold, "nor all that is held fast in the Archer's vault of stone"[2] from "the old days, in times of peace"[3] when the fortunes of Greece had not yet fallen; nor, indeed, costly clothing, precious stones from India, and many tens of thousands of acres of land, but that which is superior to all these things together and is more pleasing to the gods; that which can keep us safe even in shipwreck, in the market-place, in the crowd, in the house, in the desert, in the midst of robbers, and from the violence of tyrants.

For there is nothing at all superior to it, nothing that can constrain and control it, or take it from him who has once

1. The gold work of Colophon became a proverbial expression for excellence

2. *The Iliad*, IX, 204 3. *The Iliad*, XXII, 156

possessed it. Indeed, it seems to me that this possession bears the same relation to the soul as does light to the sun. For often men have stolen the votive offerings of the Sun, destroyed his temples, and gone on their way; some have been punished, while others left alone as not worthy of the punishment that leads to amendment. Yet his light no one ever takes from the sun, not even the moon when in their conjunction she oversteps his disc, or when she takes his rays to herself, and often, as the saying goes, turns midday into night.[1] Nor is he deprived of his light when he illumines the moon in her station opposite to himself and shares with her his own nature, nor when he fills with light and day this great and wonderful universe. Just so no good man who imparts his goodness to another was ever thought to have less virtue by as much as he had bestowed. So divine and excellent is that possession, and most true is the saying of the Athenian stranger, whoever that inspired man may have been, that "all the gold beneath the earth and above ground is too little to give in exchange for virtue".[2]

Let us, therefore, now boldly call its possessor wealthy, truly, and I should say well-born also, and the only king among them all,[3] if anyone should agree to this. For as noble birth is better than a lowly pedigree, so virtue is better than a character not in all respects admirable. Let no one say that this statement is contentious and too strong, judging by the ordinary use of words. For the multitude are wont to say that the sons of those who have long been rich are well-born. And yet is it not extraordinary that a cook or cobbler, by Zeus, or some potter who has gotten money together by his craft, or by some other means, is not considered well-born nor is he given that title by the many, whereas, if this man's son should inherit his estate and hand it on to his sons, they begin to give themselves airs and compete on the score of noble birth with the Pelopids and the Heraclids? Indeed, even a man who is born of noble ancestors, but himself sinks down to the opposite scale of life, could not justly claim kinship with those ancestors, seeing that no one could be enrolled among the Pelopids who had not on his shoulder the birth-mark[4] of that family. While in Boeotia it was said that there was the impression of a spear on the "Sown-men"[5] from the clod of earth that bore and reared them, and that hence the race long preserved that distinguishing mark. Can we suppose, then, that on men's

1. An eclipse; Archilochus, fr. 74 2. Plato, *Laws*, 728 3. Horace, *Epistles*, 1.1.106
4. One shoulder was as white as ivory
5. The Sparti, sprung from the dragon's teeth sown by Cadmus

souls no mark of that sort is engraved, which shall tell us accurately who their fathers were and vindicate their birth as legitimate? They say that the Celts have a river[1] which is an incorruptible judge of offspring, and that neither can the mothers persuade that river by their laments to hide and conceal their fault for them, nor the fathers who are afraid for their wives and sons in this trial, for it is an arbiter that never swerves or gives a false verdict.

Alas, we are corrupted by riches, by physical strength in its prime, by powerful ancestors, and influence from without that overshadows and does not permit us to see clearly or discern the soul; for we are unlike all other living things in this, that by the soul and by nothing else, we should with reason make our decision about noble birth. It seems to me that the ancients, employing a wondrous sagacity of nature, since their wisdom was not like ours a thing acquired, but they were philosophers by nature, not manufactured,[2] perceived the truth of this, and so they called Heracles the son of Zeus, and Leda's two sons likewise; Minos the law-giver, and Rhadamanthus of Knossos they deemed worthy of the same distinction. Many others, too, they proclaimed to be the children of other gods, because they so surpassed their mortal parents. For they looked at the soul alone and their actual deeds, not at wealth piled high and hoary with age, nor at the power that had come down to them from some grandfather or great-grandfather. Though some, of course, were the sons of fathers not wholly inglorious. Yet because of the superabundance in them of that virtue which men honoured and cherished, they were held to be the sons of the gods themselves.

This is clear from the following fact. In the case of certain others, as they did not know who were by nature their sires, they ascribed that title to a divinity so as to recompense the virtue of those men. Though we ought not to say that they were deceived, and that in ignorance they told lies about the gods. For even if in the case of other gods or deities, it was natural that they should be so deceived, having clothed them in human forms and human shapes when those deities possess a nature not to be perceived or attained by the senses, but barely recognisable by means of pure intelligence, by reason of their kinship with it. Nevertheless, in the case of the visible gods it is not probable that they were deceived, for instance, when they titled Æetes "son of Helios" and another[3] "son of the Dawn" and so on with others. As I said, however, we must in these

---

1. The Rhine 2. Plato, *Laws*, 642 3. Memnon

cases believe them and make our enquiry about noble birth accordingly. Thus when a man has virtuous parents and he himself resembles them, we may with confidence call him nobly born. Yet when, though his parents lack virtue, he himself can claim to possess it, we must suppose that the father who begat him is Zeus, and we must not pay less respect to him than to those who are the sons of virtuous fathers and emulate their parents. When a bad man comes of good parents, however, we ought to enrol him among the bastards, while as for those who come of a bad stock and resemble their parents, never must we call them well-born, not even if their wealth amounts to ten thousand talents, or if they reckon among their ancestors twenty rulers, or, by Zeus, twenty tyrants; nor if they can prove that the victories they won at Olympia, or Pytho, or in the encounters of war – which are in every way more brilliant than victories in the games – were more than the first Cæsar's, or can point to excavations in Assyria, or to the walls of Babylon and the Egyptian pyramids besides, or to anything else that is proof of wealth, great possessions, luxury, and a soul that is inflamed by ambition and, being at a loss as to how to use money, lavishes on things of that sort all those abundant supplies of wealth. For you are well aware that it is not wealth, either ancestral or newly acquired and pouring in from some source or other, that makes a king, nor his purple cloak, nor his crown and sceptre, nor his diadem and ancestral throne, indeed, nor myriad hoplites and ten thousand cavalry; not even if all men should gather together and acknowledge him for their king, because virtue they cannot bestow on him, but only power; ill-omened indeed for him that receives it, and still more for those that bestow it. For once he has received such power, a man of that sort is altogether raised aloft in the clouds, and in no respect differs from the legend of Phaethon and his fate. Furthermore, there is no need of other examples to make us believe this saying, for the whole of life is full of such disasters and tales about them.

If it seems surprising to you that the title of king, so honourable, so favoured by the gods, cannot justly be claimed by men who, though they rule over a vast territory and nations without number, nevertheless settle questions that arise by an autocratic decision, without intelligence or wisdom, or the virtues that go with wisdom, believe me they are not even free men. I do not mean if they merely possess what they have with none to hinder them and have their fill of power, are able to conquer all who make war against them, and, when they lead an invading army, appear invincible and resistless. If any of you doubt this statement, I have no lack of notable witnesses, Greek and Barbarian, who fought and won many mighty battles, and became the masters of whole nations, compelling them to pay tribute, and yet were themselves slaves in a still more shameful manner of pleasure, money, intemperance, wantonness, and injustice. No man of sense would call them even strong, though greatness should shine upon and illumine all that they achieved. For he alone is strong whose virtue aids him to be brave and magnanimous. While he who is the slave of pleasure, who cannot control his temper and appetites of all sorts, but is compelled to succumb to trivial things, is neither brave himself nor strong as befits a truly masculine strength. Though we may perhaps allow him to exult like a bull, lion, or leopard[1] in his brute force, assuming he does not lose even this and, like an idler, merely superintends the labours of others, being himself a "feeble warrior",[2] cowardly and dissolute. If that be his character, he is lacking not only in true riches, but also in that wealth which men so highly honour, reverence, and desire, on which hang the souls of men of all sorts, such that they undergo countless toils and labours for the sake of daily gain, enduring to sail the sea and to trade, rob, and grasp at tyrannies. For they live ever acquiring but ever in want, though I do not say this of necessary food, drink, and clothes; for the limit of this sort of property has been clearly set by nature, and none can be deprived of it, neither birds, nor fish, nor wild beasts, much less prudent men. Yet those who are tortured by the desire and fatal passion for money must suffer a lifelong hunger,[3] departing from life more miserably than those who lack daily food. For the latter, once they have filled their bellies, enjoy perfect peace and respite from their torment, but for the former, no day is sweet that does not bring them gain; nor does night with her gift of sleep that relaxes the limbs and frees men from care[4] bring them any remission of their raging madness, for it only distracts and agitates their souls as they reckon and count up their money. Not even the wealth of Tantalus and Midas, should they possess it, would free those men from their desire and their hard toil therewith, nor, indeed, would "the greatest and most grievous tyranny of heaven",[5] should they become possessed of this also. For have you not heard that Darius, the ruler of Persia, a man not wholly base, but insatiably and

1. *The Iliad*, XVII, 20   2. Homeric phrase; *The Iliad*, XVII, 588
3. Plato, *Laws*, 832   4. *The Odyssey*, XX, 56   5. Euripides, Phoenissæ, 506

shamefully covetous of money, dug up in his greed even the tombs of the dead[1] and exacted the most costly tribute? Hence he acquired the title[2] that is famous among all mankind. For the notables of Persia called him by the name that the Athenians gave to Sarambos.[3]

It seems, however, that my argument, as though it had reached some steep descent, is glutting itself with unsparing abuse, and is chastising the manners of these men beyond what is fitting, such that I must not allow it to travel further. Instead, I ought to demand from it an account, as far as is possible, of the man who is good, kingly, and noble. In the first place, then, he is devout and does not neglect the worship of the gods; secondly, he is pious and ministers to his parents, both in life and after their death, and he is friendly to his brothers; he reverences the gods who protect the family, while to suppliants and strangers he is mild and gentle; he is anxious to gratify good citizens, governing the masses with justice and for their benefit. Wealth he loves, but not that which is heavy with gold and silver, but that which is full of the true good-will of his friends,[4] and service without flattery. Though by nature he is brave and gallant, he takes no pleasure in war, and detests civil discord, yet when men do attack him, whether from some chance, or by reason of their own wickedness, he resists them bravely and defends himself with energy, carrying through his enterprises to the end, not desisting until he has destroyed the power of the foe and made it subject to himself. Then, after he has conquered by force of arms, he makes his sword cease from slaughter, because he thinks that for one who is no longer defending himself to go on killing and laying waste is to incur pollution. Furthermore, being by nature fond of work, and great of soul, he shares in the labours of all; he claims the lion's share of those labours, then divides with the others the rewards for the risks which he has run, and, being glad, rejoices, not because he has more gold and silver treasure than other men, and palaces adorned with costly furniture, but because he is able to do good to many, and to bestow on all men whatever they may chance to lack. This is what he who is truly a king claims for himself.

Since, moreover, he loves both the city and the soldiers,[5] he cares for the citizens as a shepherd for his flock, planning how their

1. Herodotus, 1.187 2. Huckster (κάπηλος); Herodotus, 3.89
3. Or Sarabos, a Platæan wineseller at Athens; Plato, *Gorgias*, 518
4. A saying of Alexander; cf. Stobæus, *Sermones*, 214; Isocrates, *To Nicocles*, 21
5. Isocrates, *To Nicocles*, 15

young may flourish and thrive, eating their full of abundant and undisturbed pasture; just so, his soldiers he oversees and keeps together, training them in courage, strength, and mercy, like well-bred dogs, noble guardians of the flock,[1] regarding them as both the partners of his exploits and the protectors of the masses, not as spoilers and pillagers of the flock, like wolves and mongrel dogs which, forgetting their own nature and nurture, turn out to be marauders instead of preservers and defenders. On the other hand, he will not suffer them to be sluggish, slothful, and unwarlike, lest the guardians should themselves need others to watch them, nor be disobedient to their officers, because he knows that obedience above all else, and sometimes alone, is the saving discipline in war. He will train them to be hardy and unafraid of any labour, and never indolent, for he knows that there is little use in a guardian who shirks his task and cannot hold out or endure fatigue. To this he wins them over and compels them not only by exhorting, or by his readiness to praise the deserving, or by rewarding and punishing severely and inexorably, but rather by showing that he himself is what he would have them be, since he refrains from all pleasure, and as for money, he desires it not at all, or very little, nor does he rob his subjects of it; and since he abhors indolence, he allows little time for sleep. For in truth, no one who is asleep is good for anything,[2] nor if, when awake, he resembles those who are asleep. I think, therefore, he will succeed in keeping them admirably obedient to himself and to their officers, for he himself will be seen to obey the wisest laws and to live in accordance with right precepts, and, in short, to be under the guidance of that part of the soul which is naturally kingly and worthy to assume leadership, and not of the emotional or undisciplined part. For how could one better persuade men to endure and undergo fatigue, not only in a campaign and under arms, but also in all those exercises that have been invented in times of peace to give men practice for conflicts abroad, than by being clearly seen to be oneself as strong as adamant? For, in truth, the most agreeable sight for a soldier, when he is fighting hard, is a prudent commander who takes an active part in the work at hand, himself zealous while exhorting his men, who is cheerful and calm in what seems to be a dangerous situation, but on occasion stern and severe whenever they are over confident. For in the matter of caution or boldness the subordinate naturally imitates his leader. He must plan as well, no less than for what I have

---

2. Plato, *Republic*, 416 3. Plato, *Laws*, 808

mentioned, that they may have abundant provisions and run short of none of the necessities of life. For often the most loyal guardians and protectors of the flock are driven by want to become fierce towards the shepherds, and when they see them from afar, they bark at them and do not even spare the sheep.[1]

Such, then, is the good king at the head of his legions, while to his city he is a saviour and protector, not only when he is warding off dangers from without, repelling Barbarian neighbours, or invading them, but also by putting down civil discord, vicious morals, luxury, and profligacy, he will procure relief from the greatest evils. Moreover, by excluding insolence, lawlessness, injustice, and greed for boundless wealth, he will not permit the feuds that arise from these causes and the dissensions that end in disaster to show even the first sign of growth, and if they do arise, he will abolish them as quickly as possible and expel them from his city. For no one who transgresses and violates the law will escape his notice, no more than would an enemy in the act of scaling his defences. But though he is a good guardian of the laws, he will be still better at framing them, if ever occasion and chance call on him to do so. No device can persuade one of his character to add to the statutes a false, spurious, and bastard law, any more than he would introduce among his own sons a servile and vulgar strain. For he cares for justice and the right, and neither parents, nor kinsfolk, nor friends can persuade him to do them a favour and betray the cause of justice. For he looks upon his fatherland as the common hearth and mother of all, older and more revered than his parents, and more precious than brothers, friends, or comrades; and to defraud or do violence to her laws, he regards as a greater impiety than sacrilegious robbery of the treasures of the gods. For law is the child of justice, the sacred and truly divine adjunct of the most mighty god, and never will the man who is wise make light of it or treat it with disdain. Rather, since all that he does will have justice in view, he will be eager to honour the good, and the vicious he will, like a good physician, make every effort to cure.

There are two kinds of error, however, for in one type of transgressor may dimly be discerned a hope of improvement, nor do they wholly reject a cure, while the vices of others are incurable. For the latter, the laws have contrived the penalty of death as a release from evil, and this not only for the benefit of the criminal, but quite as much in the interest of others. Accordingly, there must be two

1. Plato, *Republic*, 416

kinds of trial. For when men are not incurable, the king will hold it to be his duty to investigate and to cure. Whereas with others he will firmly refuse to interfere, and will never willingly have anything to do with a trial when death is the penalty that has been ordained by the laws for the guilty. Yet in making laws for such offences, he will do away with violence, harshness, and cruelty of punishment, and will elect by lot a court of staid and sober men to judge them, men who throughout their lives have admitted the most rigid scrutiny of their own virtue, who will, after deliberating for only a small part of the day, or maybe without even debating, not rashly, or led by some wholly irrational impulse, cast the black voting-tablet in the case of a fellow citizen. In his own hand, however, no sword should lie ready to slay a citizen, even if he has committed the blackest crimes, nor should a sting lurk in his soul, considering that, as we see, nature has made even the queen-bee free from a sting. Though it is not to bees that we must look for our analogy, but in my opinion to the king of the gods himself, whose prophet and vice-regent the genuine ruler ought to be. For wherever good exists wholly untainted by its opposite, and for the benefit of mankind in common and the whole universe, of this good God was and is the only creator. Yet evil he neither created nor ordered to be,[1] but he banished it from heaven, and as it moves upon earth, having chosen for its abode our souls, that colony which was sent down from heaven, he has enjoined on his sons and descendants to judge and cleanse men from it. Of these some are the friends and protectors of humanity, while others are inexorable judges who inflict on men harsh and terrible punishment for their misdeeds, both while they are alive and after they are set free from their bodies; and others again are, as it were, executioners and avengers who carry out the sentence, a different race of inferior and unintelligent daimons.

The king who is good and a favourite of the gods must imitate this example, and share his own excellence with many of his subjects, whom, because of his regard for them, he admits into this partnership. He must entrust them with offices suited to the character and principles of each: military command for him who is brave, daring, and noble, but discreet as well, so that when he has need he may use his spirit and energy; for him who is just, kind, humane, and easily prone to pity, that office in the service of the state that relates to contracts, devising means of protection for the weaker, more simple citizens, and for the poor against the powerful,

1. Plato, Theætetus, 176

fraudulent, and wicked, those who are so emboldened by their riches that they try to violate and despise justice; but to the man who combines both these temperaments, he must assign still greater honour and power in the state, and if he should entrust to him the trials of offences for which are enacted just pains and penalties with a view to recompensing the injured, that would be a fair and wise measure. For a man of this sort, together with his colleagues, will give an impartial decision, then hand over to the public official the carrying out of the verdict, nor will he through excess of anger or tender-heartedness fall short of what is essentially just.

The ruler in our state, therefore, will be somewhat like this, possessing only what is good in both those qualities and in every quality that I mentioned earlier, avoiding a fatal excess.[1] And though he will in person oversee, direct, and govern the whole, he will see to it that those of his officials who are in charge of the most important works and management, those who share his councils for the general good, are virtuous men and as much as possible like himself. He will choose them, not carelessly or at random, nor will he consent to be a less rigorous judge than a lapidary, or one who tests gold plate or purple dye. For such men are not satisfied with one method of testing alone, since they know, I suppose, that the wickedness and schemes of those who are trying to cheat them are various and manifold, thus they try to meet all of them as far as possible, opposing them with the tests derived from their art. So, too, our ruler apprehends that evil changes its face and is apt to deceive, and that the cruellest thing it does is that it often takes men in by assuming the appearance of virtue, and deceives those who are not keen-sighted enough, or who in the course of time grow weary of the investigation's length; therefore, he will rightly be on his guard against any such deception. Yet once he has chosen them, and has about him the worthiest men, he will entrust to them the choice of the minor officials.

Such is his policy with regard to the laws and magistrates. As for the common people, those who live in the towns he will not allow to be idle or impudent, but neither will he permit them to be without the necessities of life. The farming class who live in the country, ploughing and sowing to furnish food for their protectors and guardians, will receive in return payment in money and the clothes that they need. As for Assyrian palaces and costly and extravagant

1. Plato, *Laws*, 937

public services, however, they will have nothing to do with them, and will end their lives in the utmost peace as regards enemies at home and abroad, and will adore the cause of their good fortune as though he were a kindly deity, praising God for him when they pray, not hypocritically or with the lips only, but invoking blessings on him from the bottom of their hearts. Yet the gods do not wait for their prayers, and unasked they give him celestial rewards, though they do not leave him without human blessings either; and if fate should compel him to fall into any misfortune, that is, one of those incurable calamities that people are always talking about, then the gods make him their follower and associate, and exalt his fame among all mankind. All this I have often heard from the wise, and in their account of it I have the firmest faith. Thus I have repeated it to you, perhaps making a longer speech than the occasion called for, but too short in my opinion for the theme. While he to whom it has been given to hear such arguments and reflect on them, knows well that I speak the truth. Yet there is another reason for the length of my speech, less forcible, but I think more akin to the present argument. Perhaps, then, you ought not to miss hearing this also.

In the first place, let me remind you briefly of what I said before, when I broke off my discourse for the sake of this digression. What I said was that, when serious-minded people listen to sincere panegyrics, they ought not to look to those things of which fortune often grants a share even to the wicked, but to the character of the man and his virtues, which belong only to those who are good and by nature estimable. Taking up my tale at that point, I pursued the arguments that followed, guiding myself as it were by the rule and measure to which one ought to adjust the eulogies of good men and good kings. When, therefore, one of them harmonises exactly and without variation with this model, he is himself happy and truly fortunate, as are those who have a share in such a government as his. While he who comes near to being like him is better and more fortunate than those who fall further short of him. Whereas those who fail altogether to resemble him, or who follow an opposite course, are ill-fated, senseless, and wretched, and cause the greatest disasters to themselves and others.

Now, if you are in any way of my opinion, it is time to proceed to those achievements that we have so admired. And lest any should think that my argument is running alone, like a horse in a race that has lost its competitor and for that reason wins and carries off the prizes, I will try to show in what way my encomium differs from that of clever rhetoricians. For they greatly admire the fact that a man is born of ancestors who had power or were kings, since they hold that the sons of the prosperous and fortunate are themselves blessed. Yet the question that next arises they neither think of nor investigate, that is, how they employed their advantages throughout their lives. Even though, after all, this is the chief cause of that happiness, and of almost all external good. Unless, of course, someone objects to this statement that it is only by wise use of it that property becomes a good, and that it is harmful when the opposite use is made. Therefore, it is evidently not a great thing, as they think, to be descended from a king who was wealthy and "rich in gold", but it is truly great, while surpassing the virtue of one's ancestors, to behave towards one's parents in a manner beyond reproach in all respects.

Do you wish to learn whether this is true of the Emperor? I will offer you trustworthy evidence, and I know well that you will not convict me of false witness. For I shall but remind you of what you know already; and perhaps you understand even now what I mean. If it is not yet evident, however, it will become so when you call to mind that the Emperor's father loved him more than the others, though he was by no means over-indulgent to his children, it being character that he favoured rather than the ties of blood. Nonetheless, he was, I suppose, won over by the Emperor's dutiful service to him, and as he had nothing to reproach him with, he made his affection for him evident. The proof of his feeling is, first, that he chose for Constantius that portion of the Empire which he had formerly thought best suited to himself, and, secondly, that when he was at the point of death he passed over his eldest and youngest sons,[1] though they were at leisure, and summoned Constantius, who was not at leisure, and entrusted him with the whole government. Then, when he had become master of the whole, he behaved to his brothers at once so justly and with such moderation, that, while they who had neither been summoned nor had come of their own accord quarrelled and fought with one another, they showed no resentment against Constantius, nor ever reproached him. Furthermore, when their feud reached its fatal issue,[2] though he might have laid claim to a greater share of the Empire, he renounced it of his own free will, because he thought that many nations or few called for the exercise of the same virtues,

1. Constantine II and Constans
2. Constantine II was slain while marching against Constans

and also, perhaps, that the more a man has to look after and care for, the greater are the anxieties beset him. For he does not view the imperial power as a means of procuring luxury, nor, as certain men who have wealth and misapply it for drink and other pleasures set their hearts on lavish and ever-increasing revenues, does he think this ought to be an emperor's policy, nor that he ought ever to embark on a war save only for the benefit of his subjects. Thus he allowed his brother to have the lion's share, and thought that if he himself possessed the smaller share with honour, he had the advantage in what was most worth having. That it was not rather from fear of his brother's resources that he preferred peace, you may consider clearly proven by the war that broke out later. For he had recourse to arms later on against his brother's forces, but it was to avenge him.[1] Here again there are perhaps some who have admired him merely for having won the victory. Yet I admire far more the fact that it was with justice that he undertook the war, that he carried it through with great courage and skill, and, when fortune gave him a favourable issue, used his victory with moderation and in imperial fashion, showing himself entirely worthy of assuming power.

Now, do you wish, as though I were in a court of law, that I should summon before you by name witnesses of this also? It is plain even to a child that no war ever yet arose that had so just a cause, not even of the Greeks against Troy or of the Macedonians against the Persians, though these wars are certainly thought to have been justified, since the latter was to exact vengeance in more recent times for very ancient offences, and not on sons or grandsons, but on him[2] who had robbed and deprived of their sovereignty the descendants of those very offenders. While Agamemnon set forth "to avenge the struggles and groans of Helen",[3] for it was because he desired to avenge one woman that he went to war with the Trojans. Yet the wrongs done to Constantius were still fresh, and he[4] who was in power was not, like Darius or Priam, a man of royal birth who laid claim to an empire that belonged to him by reason of his birth or his family, but a shameless and savage Barbarian who not long before had been among the captives of war. However, all that he did and how he governed is neither agreeable for me to tell nor would it be well-timed. That the Emperor was justified in making war on him you have heard, and of

1. Constans was slain by the soldiers of Magnentius 2. Darius III
3. *The Iliad*, II, 356 4. Magnentius

his skill and courage what I said earlier is proof enough, but deeds are, I think, more convincing than words. What happened after the victory, then, and how he no longer made use of the sword, not even against those who were under suspicion of serious crimes, or who had been familiar friends of the usurper, indeed, not even against anyone who, to curry favour with the latter, had stooped to win a tale-bearer's fee by slandering the Emperor. Consider, in the name of Zeus the god of friendship, that not even these paid the penalty for their audacity, except when they were found guilty of other crimes. And yet what a terrible thing is slander! How truly does it devour the heart and wound the soul as iron cannot wound the body! This it was that goaded Odysseus to defend himself by word and deed. It was for this reason that he quarrelled with his host[1] when he was himself a wanderer and a guest, even though he knew that "foolish and of little worth is that man who provokes a violent quarrel with his host".[2]

So it was with Alexander, Philip's son, and Achilles, son of Thetis, and others who were not worthless or ignoble men. Yet only Socrates, I think, and a few others who emulated him, men who were truly fortunate and happy, managed to shed the last garment that man discards – the love of fame.[3] For resentment of calumny is due to the passion for fame, and for this reason it is implanted most deeply in the noblest souls. For they resent it as their deadliest foe, and those who hurl at them slanderous language they hate more than men who attack them with the sword or plot their destruction; they regard them as differing from themselves, not merely in their acquired habits, but in their essential nature, seeing that they love praise and honour, while the defamer not only robs them of these, but also manufactures false accusations against them. They say that even Heracles and certain other heroes were swayed by these emotions. For my part, however, I do not believe this account. As for the Emperor, I have seen him repelling calumny with great self-restraint, which in my judgment is no slighter achievement than "to take Troy"[4] or to rout a powerful phalanx. Further, if anyone does not believe me, and thinks it no great achievement nor worth all this praise, let him observe himself when a misfortune of this sort happens to him, then let him decide. I am convinced that he

1. Alcinous 2. *The Odyssey*, VIII, 209

3. Fame with respect to one's reputation, renown and reputational glory being of the utmost importance in Indo-European societies; cf. *Iliad*, 7.91; *Havamal*, 76-77

4. A proverb; cf. Euripides, *Andromache*, 368

will not think me to be speaking with exceeding folly.

Now, since this was and remains the Emperor's behaviour after the war, he is naturally loved and "longed for by his friends",[1] since he has admitted many of them to honour and power, as well as freedom of speech; he has bestowed on them vast sums of money, and permits them to use their wealth as they please, though even to his enemies he is the same. The following may serve as a clear proof of this. Those members of the Senate who were of any account and surpassed the rest in reputation, wealth, and wisdom, fled to the shelter of his right hand as though to a harbour, and, leaving behind their hearths, their homes, and their children, preferred Pæonia to Rome, and to be with him rather than with their dearest. Again, a division of the finest of the cavalry together with their standards, bringing their general[2] with them, chose to share danger with him rather than success with the usurper. All this took place before the battle on the banks of the Drava, which the earlier part of my speech described to you. For thereafter they began to feel perfect confidence, even as prior to that it had looked as though the usurper's cause was gaining the upper hand: he had gained some slight advantage in the affair of the Emperor's scouts, which indeed made the usurper beside himself with joy and greatly agitated those who were incapable of grasping or estimating generalship. Nevertheless, the Emperor was unperturbed and heroic, like a good pilot when a tempest has suddenly burst from the clouds, and the next moment the god shakes the depths and the shores. A terrible and dreadful panic seizes on those who are inexperienced, but the pilot begins to rejoice, gladdened, because he can now hope for a perfect and windless calm. For it is said that Poseidon, when he makes the earth quake, calms the waves. Just so, fortune deceives the foolish and deludes them about more important things by allowing them some small advantage, but in the wise she inspires unshaken confidence about more serious affairs, even when she disconcerts them in the case of those that are less serious. This was what happened to the Lacedæmonians at Thermopylæ, yet they did not despair nor fear the onset of the Mede because they had lost three hundred Spartans and their king at the entrance into Greece. This often happened to the Romans, but they achieved more important successes later on. Wherefore, since the Emperor knew this and counted upon it, he in no way wavered in his purpose.

1. Aristophanes, *Frogs*, 84   2. Silvanus

Seeing, however, that my argument has, of its own accord, once more reached this point and is describing the affection that the Emperor inspires in the common people, the magistrates, and the garrisons who aid him to protect the Empire and repulse its enemies, are you willing that I should relate to you a notable proof of this, which happened, one might say, just yesterday? A certain man[1] who had been given the command of the garrisons in Galatia – you probably know his name and character – left his son behind him as a hostage for his friendship and loyalty to the Emperor, though not at the Emperor's request. Then he proved to be more treacherous than "lions who have no faithful covenants with man",[2] as the poet says, and plundered the cities of their wealth and distributed it among the invading Barbarians, paying it down as a sort of ransom, though he was quite able to take measures to win security by the sword rather than by money. Instead, he tried to win them over to friendliness by means of money. Finally, he took from the women's apartments a purple dress, showing himself truly a tyrant and pompous indeed. The soldiers, then, resenting his treachery, would not tolerate the sight of him thus dressed up in women's garb, and so they set upon the miserable wretch and tore him limb from limb,[3] nor would they endure either that the crescent moon should rule over them.[4]

It was the affection of his garrison that gave the Emperor this gift, a wonderful recompense for his just and blameless rule. Though you are eager to hear how he behaved after this. This too, however, you cannot fail to know, that he chose neither to be harsh towards that man's son, nor suspicious and formidable to his friends, but in the highest possible degree he was merciful and kindly to them all, though many desired to bring false accusations and had raised their stings to strike the innocent. So while many were perhaps genuinely involved in the crimes of which they were suspected, he was merciful to all alike, provided they had not been convicted or proven to be partners in the usurper's monstrous and abominable schemes. Shall we not declare that the forbearance shown by him towards the son of one who had broken the laws, trampled on loyalty, and sworn covenants was truly royal and godlike; or shall we rather approve Agamemnon, who vented his rage and cruelty not only on those Trojans who had accompanied Paris and had outraged the hearth of Menelaus, but on those who

---

1. Silvanus 2. *The Iliad*, XXII, 262 3. Euripides, Bacchæ, 822

4. His Oriental dress suggested Persian rule, symbolised by the crescent

were yet unborn, and even whose mothers were perhaps not yet born when Paris plotted the abduction?

Anyone, therefore, who thinks that cruelty, harshness, and inhumanity ill become a king, and that mercy, goodness, and benevolence befit one who takes no pleasure in acts of vengeance, but grieves at the misfortunes of his subjects, however they may arise, whether from their own wickedness and ignorance or aimed at them from without by fate, will, it is evident, award to the Emperor the palm of victory. For bear in mind that he was kinder and more just to the boy than his own father, and to the usurper's friends he was more loyal than he who acknowledged the tie of friendship. For the usurper forsook them all, but the Emperor saved them all. Thus if the usurper, knowing all this about the Emperor's character, since he had for a long time been able to observe it, was entirely confident that his son was safely at anchor and his friends secure also, then he did indeed understand him properly. Yet he was many times over criminal, base, and accursed for desiring to be at enmity with such a man, for hating one whom he knew to be so excellent and so exceedingly noble, and for plotting against him and trying to rob him of what it was shameful to take from him. If, on the other hand, his son's safety was something that he had never hoped for, while the safety of his friends and kinsfolk he had thought difficult or impossible, and he nevertheless chose to be disloyal, this is yet further proof that he was wicked, senseless, and fiercer than a wild beast. Whereas the Emperor was gentle, mild, and magnanimous, since he took pity on the youth of the helpless child, and was merciful to those who were not proven guilty, whilst disdaining and despising the crimes of the usurper. For he who grants what not one of his enemies expects, because the guilt that is on their conscience is so great, beyond a doubt carries off the prize for virtue. For while he tempers justice with what is nobler and more merciful, in self-restraint he surpasses those who are merely moderate in their vengeance; in courage he excels because he thinks no enemy worthy of notice; and his wisdom he displays by suppressing enmities and by not handing them down to his sons and descendants on the pretext of strict justice, or of wishing, quite reasonably, to blot out the seed of the wicked like the seed of a pine-tree.[1] For this is the way of those trees, and in consequence an ancient tale[2] gave rise to this simile.

1. A proverb: the pine when cut down does not send up shoots again

2. Herodotus, 6.37

Yet the good Emperor, closely imitating God, knows that even from rocks swarms of bees fly forth, and that sweet fruits grow even from the bitterest wood – pleasant figs, for example, and from thorns the pomegranate, and other instances besides where things are produced entirely unlike the parents that begat them and brought them forth. He believes, therefore, that we ought not to destroy them before they have reached maturity, but rather wait for time to pass, to trust that they will cast off the folly and madness of their fathers and become good and temperate. Equally, however, if they should turn out to emulate their fathers' practices, they will in good time suffer punishment, though at least they will not have been uselessly sacrificed because of the deeds and misfortunes of others.

Now, would you say that I have made my sincere panegyric sufficiently thorough and complete? Or are you anxious to hear also about the Emperor's powers of endurance and his august bearing? That not only is he unconquerable by the enemy, but has never yet succumbed to any disgraceful appetite, never coveted a fine house, a costly palace, or a necklace of emeralds, then robbed their owners of them either by violence or persuasion? That he has never coveted any free-born woman or handmaid, or pursued any dishonourable passion? That he does not desire an immoderate surfeit of even the fine things that the seasons produce, or care for ice in summer, or change his residence with the time of year, but is ever at hand to aid those portions of the Empire that are in trouble, enduring both frost and extreme heat? If you should bid me bring before you plain proofs of this, I shall merely say what is familiar to all, and I shall not lack evidence, but the account would be long, a monstrous speech, nor indeed have I leisure to cultivate the Muses to such an extent, for it is now time for me to return to my work.[1]

1. His campaign in Gaul

PANEGYRIC IN HONOUR OF EUSEBIA

PREFACE

The second panegyric, written either just before or shortly after his arrival in Gaul, is dedicated to the Empress Eusebia, the first wife of Constantius. Here, Julian's effusive praise and gratitude are, contrary to the two orations in honour of his cousin, wholly genuine. Eusebia was a unique figure within the Emperor's circle in that she appeared to hold sincere affection for Julian, or at the very least sympathy for his predicament. Her intervention may have saved his life, and, according to Julian, she was also pivotal in the decision to allow him to relocate to Athens before the Cæsarship was eventually thrust upon him.

His appreciation for the various favours he received from Eusebia, and a fondness for the woman herself, is evident throughout his writings, most overtly in this oration. Indeed, "his sincerity affected his style, which is simpler and more direct than that of the other two panegyrics".[1] Julian compares her favourably to both the goddess Athena, and to Penelope, the wife of Odysseus. While such comparisons are commonplace for the rhetorical forms in which he was well versed, it would not be unreasonable to suggest that, for Julian, Eusebia was the feminine ideal, and not merely as an oratorical muse.

---

1. W. C. F. Wright

PANEGYRIC IN HONOUR OF EUSEBIA

What, pray tell, ought we to think of those who owe things of price and beyond price – I do not mean gold or silver, but simply any benefit one may happen to receive from one's neighbour. Suppose that they neither try nor intend to repay that kindness, and instead, being indolent, do not trouble themselves to do what they can to try to discharge this debt? Is it not evident that we must think them mean and base? Far more, I think, than any other crime do we hate ingratitude, thus we blame those persons who have received benefits but are ungrateful to their benefactors. The ungrateful man, moreover, is not only he who repays a kindness with evil deeds or words, but also he who is silent and conceals a kindness, who tries to consign it to oblivion and abolish gratitude. Now, of such brutal and inhuman baseness as the repayment with evil, the instances are few and easily reckoned; yet there are many who try to conceal the appearance of having received benefits, though with what purpose I know not. They assert that it is because they are trying to avoid a reputation for a sort of servility and for vulgar flattery; and though I know well enough that what they say is wholly insincere, I nevertheless let that pass. For even if we assume that they, as they purport to believe, do escape an undeserved reputation for flattery, they would still appear at the same time to be guilty of many weaknesses and defects of character that are in the highest degree base and servile. For either they are too dense to perceive what no one should fail to perceive, or they are not dense but forgetful of what they ought to remember for all time. Or again, they do remember, and yet shirk their duty for some reason or other, being cowards and grudging by nature, such that their hand is against every man without exception, seeing that not even to their benefactors do they consent to be gentle and amiable. Then, if there be any opening to slander and bite, they look angry and fierce like wild beasts. Genuine praise they somehow or other avoid giving, as though it were a costly extravagance, while they censure the applause given to noble actions, when the only thing that they need enquire into is whether the eulogists respect truth and rate her higher than the reputation of showing their gratitude by eulogy. For this, at any rate they, cannot assert: that praise is a useless thing, either to those who receive it or to others besides, who, though they have been assigned the same rank in life as the objects of their praise, have fallen short of their merit in what they have accomplished. To the former it is not only agreeable to hear, but makes them zealous to aim at a still higher level of conduct, while for the latter it stimulates both by persuasion and compulsion to imitate that noble conduct, because they see that none of those who have anticipated them have been deprived of that which alone is honourable to give and receive publicly. For to give money openly, and to look anxiously around so that as many as possible may know of the gift, is characteristic of a vulgar person. Indeed, no one would even stretch out his hands to receive it in the sight of all men, unless he had first cast off all propriety of manner and sense of shame. Arcesilaus himself, when offering a gift, used to try to hide his identity even from the recipient.[1] Though in his case the manner of the deed always made known the doer.

For a eulogy, however, one is ambitious to obtain as many hearers as possible, and even a small audience is, I think, not to be scorned. Socrates, for instance, spoke in praise of many, as did Plato also, and Aristotle. Xenophon, too, eulogised King Agesilaus and Cyrus the Persian, not only the elder Cyrus, but him whom he accompanied on his campaign against the Great King, nor did he hide away his eulogies, but put them into his history. Now, I should think it strange indeed if we should be eager to applaud men of high character, and not think fit to give our tribute of praise to a noble woman, believing as we do that excellence belongs to certain women just as it does men. Or should we who think that such a person ought to be modest, wise, and competent to assign to every man his due, and that courage, high-mindedness, generosity, and in short all such qualities as these should be hers – shall we, I say, then rob her of the encomium due to her good deeds, from any fear of the charge of appearing to flatter? For Homer was not ashamed to praise Penelope, or the consort of Alcinous,[2] or other women of exceptional goodness, or even those whose claim to virtue was slight. Nor did Penelope fail to obtain her share of praise for this

1. Plutarch, *Moralia*, 63 2. Arete

very thing. Yet besides these reasons for praise, shall we consent to accept kind treatment from a woman no less than from a man, to obtain some boon whether small or great, then hesitate to pay the thanks due therefor? Perhaps people will say that the very act of making a request to a woman is low and unworthy of an honourable and high-spirited man, and that even the wise Odysseus was spiritless and cowardly because he was a suppliant to the king's daughter[1] as she played with her maiden companions by the banks of the river. Perhaps they will not spare even Athena, the daughter of Zeus, of whom Homer says[2] that she put on the likeness of a fair and noble maiden and guided him along the road that led to the palace, acting as his adviser and instructing him on what he must do and say when he had entered within; and that, like some orator perfect in the art of rhetoric, she sang an encomium of the queen, and for a prelude told the tale of her lineage from of old. Homer's verses about this are as follows:

Δέσποιναν μὲν πρῶτα κιχήσεαι ἐν μεγάροισιν,
Ἀρήτη δ' ὄνομ' ἐστὶν ἐπώνυμον, ἐκ δὲ τοκήων
Τῶν αὐτῶν, οἵπερ τέκον Ἀλκίνοον βασιλῆα·

"Our lady you shall find just inside the halls.
Arete is her name, and of the same line is she
as those who begat King Alcinous"[3]

Then he goes back and begins with Poseidon, telling of the origin of that family and all that they did and suffered, and how when her father perished, still young and newly-wed, her uncle married her, and honoured her "as no other woman in the world is honoured". He tells of all the honour she receives "from her dear children and from Alcinous himself" and from the council of elders also, I think, and from the people who look upon her as a goddess as she goes through the city. On all his praises he sets this crown, one that man and woman alike may well envy, when he says "for indeed she, too, has no lack of excellent understanding". Further, that she knows well how to judge between men, and, for those citizens to whom she is kindly disposed, how to reconcile with justice the grievances that arise among them. If, when you entreat her, you find her well disposed, the goddess says to Odysseus, "then there is hope that you will see your loved ones and reach your high-roofed house". He was, of course, persuaded by her counsel.

1. Nausicaa 2. *The Odyssey*, VII, 20 3. ibid., 54

Shall I then need yet greater instances and clearer proofs, so that I may escape the suspicion of seeming to flatter? Shall I not forthwith imitate that wise and inspired poet and go on to praise the noble Eusebia, eager as I am to compose an encomium worthy of her, though I shall be thankful if, even in a moderate degree, I succeed in describing accomplishments so many and so admirable? I shall likewise be thankful if I succeed in describing also those noble qualities of hers – her temperance, justice, mildness and goodness; her affection for her husband; her generosity with money; the honour that she pays to her own people and her kinsfolk. It is proper for me, I think, to follow in the track, as it were, of what I have already said, and, as I pursue my panegyric, so arrange it as to give the same order as Athena, making mention, as is natural, of her native land, her ancestors, how she married and whom, and all the rest in the same fashion as Homer.

Now, while I have much that is highly honourable to say about her native land,[1] I think it well to omit part because of its antiquity. It seems, indeed, to be not far removed from myth. For instance, the type of story that is told about the Muses, how they actually came from Pieria[2], and that it was not from Helicon that they came to Olympus when summoned to their father's side. This, then, and all else of the same sort, since it is better suited to a fable than to my narrative, must be omitted. Though perhaps it is not out of the way nor alien from my present theme to tell some of the facts that are not familiar to all. They say[3] that Macedonia was colonised by the descendants of Heracles, the sons of Temenus, who had been awarded Argos as their portion, then quarrelled, and so to make an end of their strife and jealousy led forth a colony. They seized Macedonia, and leaving a prosperous family behind them, they succeeded to the throne, king after king, as though the honour were an inheritance. To praise all these would be neither truthful, nor in my opinion easy. So while many of them were brave men who left behind some of the most glorious monuments of the Hellenic character, Philip and his son surpassed in valour all who of old ruled over Macedonia and Thrace; indeed, I might even say all who governed the Lydians as well, and the Medes, Persians, and Assyrians, except only the son of Cambyses,[4] who transferred the sovereignty from the Medes to the Persians. For Philip was the first to try to increase the power of the Macedonians, and when he had

1. Eusebia belonged to a noble family from Thessalonica, in Macedonia
2. Near Mount Olympus 3. Herodotus, 8.137 4. Cyrus the Great

subdued the greater part of Europe, he made the sea his frontier limit to the east and south, to the north I think the Danube, and to the west the people of Oricus.[1] Then, after him, his son, who was brought up at the feet of the wise Stagyrite,[2] so far excelled all the rest in greatness of soul, and even surpassed his own father in generalship, courage, and the other virtues, such that he thought life for him was not worth living unless he could subdue all men and all nations. Thus he traversed the whole of Asia, conquering as he went, he who was the first of men to adore the rising sun; but as he was setting out for Europe in order to gain control of the remainder and so become master of the whole earth and sea, he paid the debt of nature in Babylon. Then Macedonians became the rulers of all the cities and nations that they had acquired under his leadership. Now, is it still necessary to show by stronger proofs that Macedonia was famous and great of old? Additionally, the most important place in Macedonia is that city which they restored, I believe, after the fall of the Thessalians, and which is named after their victory over them.[3] Concerning all this, however, I need not speak at greater length.

Of her noble birth, why should I take any further trouble to seek for clearer or more manifest proof than this? By which I mean that she is the daughter of a man who was considered worthy to hold the office that gives its name to the year,[4] an office that in the past was powerful and actually called royal, but lost that title because of those who abused their power. For now that in these days its power has waned, since the government has changed to a monarchy, the bare honour, though robbed of all the rest, is held to counterbalance all power, and for private citizens is set up as a sort of prize and a reward of virtue, or loyalty, or of some favour done to the ruler of the Empire, or for some brilliant exploit. For the Emperors, meanwhile, it is added to the advantages they already possess as the crowning glory and adornment. For all the other titles and functions that still retain some feeble and shadowy resemblance to the ancient constitution, they either altogether despised and rejected, because of their absolute power, or they attached them to themselves and enjoy the titles for life. Yet this office alone, I think, they did not despise from the first, and it still gratifies them when they obtain it for the year. Indeed, there is no private citizen or emperor, nor has there ever been, who did not

1. A town on the coast of Illyria 2. Aristotle, who tutored Alexander
3. Thessalonica 4. The Consulship

think it an enviable distinction to be entitled consul. Moreover, if there be anyone who thinks that, because he of whom I spoke was the first of his line to win that title and to lay the foundations of distinction for his family, he is therefore inferior to the others, that person fails to understand that he is deceived exceedingly. For it is, in my opinion, altogether nobler and more honourable to lay the foundations of such great distinction for one's descendants than to receive it from one's ancestors. For undeniably it is a nobler thing to be the founder of a mighty city than a mere citizen, and to receive any good thing is altogether less dignified than to give. Indeed, it is evident that sons receive from their fathers, and citizens from their cities, a start, as it were, on the path of glory. While he who by his own effort pays back to his ancestors and his native land that honour on a higher scale, and makes his country more brilliant and more distinguished, and his ancestors more illustrious, clearly yields the prize to no man on the score of native nobility. Nor is there any man who can claim to be superior to him of whom I speak. For the good must be born of good parents. Yet when the son of illustrious parents himself becomes more illustrious, and fortune blows the same way as his merit, he causes no one to feel doubt should he lay claim, as is reasonable, to be of native nobility.

Eusebia, the subject of my speech, was the daughter of a consul, and is the consort of an Emperor who is brave, temperate, wise, just, virtuous, mild, and high-souled. When he acquired the throne that had belonged to his ancestors, having won it back from him who had usurped it by violence, he desired to wed that he might beget sons to inherit his honour and power, and so deemed this lady worthy of his alliance, after he had already become master of almost the whole world. Why, I ask, need one search for stronger evidence than this? Evidence, I mean, not only of her native nobility, but of all those combined gifts which she who is united to so great an Emperor ought to bring with her from her home as a dowry – wit and wisdom, a body in the flower of youth, and beauty so conspicuous as to throw into the shade all other maidens beside, even as, I believe, the radiant stars about the full-moon are outshone and hide their shape.[1] For no single one of these endowments is thought to suffice for an alliance with an Emperor, but all together, as though some god were fashioning for a virtuous Emperor a fair and modest bride, were united in her single person, and, attracting not his eyes alone, brought from afar that bridegroom blessed of

1. Sappho, fr. 3; *Ἄστερες μὲν ἀμφὶ κάλαν σελάνναν ἄψ' ἀποκρύπτοισι φάεννον εἶδος*

heaven. For beauty alone, if it lacks the support of birth and the other advantages I have mentioned, is not enough to induce even a licentious man, a mere citizen, to kindle the marriage torch. Though both combined have brought about many a match, when they occur without sweetness and charm of character they are seen to be far from desirable.

I have good reason to say that the Emperor in his prudence understood this clearly, and that it was only after long deliberation that he chose this marriage, partly making enquiries about all that was needful to learn about her by hearsay, but judging also from her mother the daughter's noble disposition. Of that mother, why should I take time to say more, as though I had not to recite a special encomium on her who is the theme of my speech? Perhaps, however, I may say briefly and you may hear without weariness, that her family is entirely Greek, indeed, Greek of the purest stock, that her native city was the metropolis of Macedonia, and that she was more self-controlled than Evadne,[1] the wife of Capaneus, and the famous Laodameia[2] of Thessaly. For these two, when they had lost their husbands, who were young, handsome, and still newly-wed, whether by the constraint of some envious powers, or because the threads of the fates were so woven, threw away their lives for love. Yet the mother of the Empress, when fate had come upon her wedded lord, devoted herself to her children and won a great reputation for prudence, so great indeed, that whereas Penelope, while her husband was still on his travels and wanderings, was beset by those young suitors who came to woo her from Ithaca, Samos, and Dulichium, no man, however fair, tall, powerful, or wealthy, ever ventured to approach Eusebia's mother with any such proposals. Thus the Emperor deemed her daughter worthy to live by his side, and after setting up the trophies of his victories, he celebrated the marriage with great splendour, providing feasts for nations, cities, and peoples.

Should anyone desire to hear of such things as how the bride was bid to come from Macedonia with her mother, and the manner of the cavalcade, of the chariots, horses, and carriages of all sorts, decorated with gold, silver, and copper of the finest workmanship, let me say that it is extremely childish of him to wish to hear such things. It is like the case of some player on the cithara[3] who is an accomplished artist – let us say, if you will, Terpander, or he of

1. Euripides, *Suppliants*, 494 2. The wife of Protesilaus

3. An ancient Greek and Roman stringed musical instrument similar to the lyre

Methymna,[1] of whom the story goes that he enjoyed a divine escort and found that the dolphin cared more for music than did his fellow-voyagers, and was thus conveyed safely to the Laconian promontory.[2] For though he did indeed charm those miserable sailors by his skilful performance, they nevertheless despised his art and paid no heed to his music. Now, as I was going to say, if someone were to choose the best of those two musicians, they were to clothe him in the raiment suited to his art, then bring him into a theatre full of men, women, and children of all sorts, varying in temperament, age, and habits besides, do you not suppose that the children and those of the men and women who had childish tastes would gaze at his dress and his lyre, and be marvellously smitten with his appearance? And would not the more ignorant of the men, and the whole crowd of women, except a very few, judge his playing simply by the criterion of pleasure or the reverse; whereas a musical man who understood the rules of the art would not endure that the melodies should be wrongly mixed for the sake of giving pleasure, but would resent it if the player did not preserve the modes of the music and did not use the harmonies properly, in conformity with the laws of genuine and inspired music? If, however, he saw that he was faithful to the principles of his art and produced in the audience a pleasure that was not spurious but pure and uncontaminated, he would go home praising the musician, filled with admiration because his performance in the theatre was artistic and did the Muses no wrong.

Though such a man may think that anyone who praises the purple raiment and the lyre is foolish and out of his mind, if he proceeds to give full details about such outward things, adorning them with an agreeable style and smoothing away all that is worthless and vulgar in the tale, then the critic will think him more ridiculous than those who try to carve cherry-stones, as I believe is related of Myrmecides[3] who thus sought to rival the art of Phidias. Therefore, neither will I, if I can help it, lay myself open to this charge by reciting the long list of costly robes and gifts of all kinds, necklaces and garlands that were sent by the Emperor, nor how the folk in each place came to meet her with welcome and rejoicing, nor all the glorious and auspicious incidents that occurred on that journey, as were reported. When she entered the palace and was honoured with her imperial title, what was the first thing she did, then the second, the third, and the many actions that followed?

1. Arion 2. Tænarum 3. Sculptor famed for his minute carving of ivory

For however much I might wish to tell of them and to compose lengthy volumes about them, I think that, for the majority, those of her deeds will be sufficient that more conspicuously witnessed to her wisdom, clemency, modesty, benevolence, goodness, generosity, and her other virtues, than does now the present account of her, which tries to enlighten and instruct those who have long known it all from personal experience. For it would not be at all proper, merely because the task has proved to be difficult, or rather, impossible, to keep silence about the whole, but one should rather try, as far as one can, to speak of those deeds, and to bring forward as a proof of her wisdom and of all her other virtues the fact that she made her husband regard her as it is fitting that he should regard a beautiful and noble wife.

Therefore, while I think that many of the other qualities of Penelope are worthy of praise, this I admire beyond all: she so entirely persuaded her husband to love and cherish her, that he despised, we are told, unions with goddesses, and equally rejected an alliance with the Phæacians. Even as they were all in love with him – Calypso, Circe, Nausicaa. They possessed exceptionally beautiful palaces, gardens, and parks withal, planted with wide-spreading and shady trees, meadows bright with flowers in which soft grass grew deep, "and four fountains in a row which flowed with shining water".[1] A vigorous, wild vine bloomed about her dwelling,[2] laden with bunches of exquisite grapes. While at the Phæacian court there were things much the same, except that they were more costly, seeing, I suppose, as they were made by art, and hence had less charm, seeming less lovely than those that were of natural growth. In the face of such luxury and wealth, and moreover the peace and quiet that surrounded those islands, who do you think would not have succumbed, especially one who had endured such great toils and dangers, and who expected that he would have to suffer still more terrible hardships, partly by sea and partly in his own house, since he had to fight all alone against a hundred young men in their prime, a thing which had never happened to him even in the land of Troy? If someone in jest were to question Odysseus to this effect: "why, O most wise orator and general, or whatever one ought to call you, did you endure so many toils when you might have been prosperous, happy, and perhaps even immortal, if one may at all believe the promises of Calypso? Yet you chose the worse instead of the better, and imposed on yourself all those

1. *The Odyssey*, V, 70 2. The cave of Calypso

hardships, refusing to remain even in Scheria, though you might surely have rested there from your wandering and been delivered from your perils; but behold, you resolved to carry on the war in your own house, to perform feats of valour and to accomplish a second journey, no less toilsome, as seemed likely, nor easier than the first!" What answer do you think he would give to this? Would he not answer that he longed always to be with Penelope, and that those contests and campaigns he purposed to take back to her as an impressive tale to tell? For this reason, then, he makes his mother exhort him to remember everything, all the sights he saw and all the things he heard, whereupon she says:

ἵνα καὶ μετόπισθε τεῇ εἴπῃσθα γυναικί·

"So that in the days to come
you may tell them to your wife"[1]

And indeed he forgot nothing, for no sooner had he come home and vanquished, as was just, the men who caroused in the palace, than he related all to her without pause, all that he had achieved and endured, and all else that, obeying the oracles, he purposed still to accomplish.[2] From her he kept nothing secret, but chose that she should be the partner of his counsels and should help him to plan and contrive what he must do. Do you think, then, that this a trifling tribute to Penelope, or that there has yet to be found another woman whose virtue surpasses hers, and who, as the consort of a brave, magnanimous, and prudent Emperor, has won as great affection from her husband, since she has mingled the tenderness that is inspired by love with that which good and noble souls derive from their own virtue, whence it flows like a sacred fount? For there are two jars,[3] so to speak, of these two kinds of human affection, and Eusebia drew in equal measure from both, thus she has come to be the partner of her husband's counsels, and though the Emperor is by nature merciful, good, and wise, she encourages him to follow yet more becomingly his natural bent, and ever turns justice to mercy. Indeed, no one could ever cite a case in which this Empress, whether with justice, as might happen, or unjustly, has ever been the cause of punishment or chastisement either great or small.

Now, we are told that at Athens, in the days when they employed their ancestral customs and lived in obedience to their own laws, as the inhabitants of a great and humane city, whenever

1. *The Odyssey*, XI, 223 2. *The Odyssey*, XXIII, 284 3. *The Iliad*, XXIV, 527

the votes of the jurymen were cast evenly for defendant and plaintiff, the vote of Athena[1] was awarded to him who would have incurred the penalty, and therefore both were acquitted of guilt – he who had brought the accusation of the reputation of calumny, and the defendant, naturally, of the guilt of the crime. This humane and gracious custom is kept up in the suits which the Emperor judges, but Eusebia's mercy goes further. For whenever the defendant comes near to obtaining an equal number of votes, she persuades the Emperor, adding her request and entreaty on his behalf, to acquit the man entirely of the charge. Then of free will with willing heart he grants the boon, and does not give it as Homer says of Zeus when, constrained by his wife, he agreed as to what should be conceded to her "of free will but with soul unwilling".[2] Perhaps it is not strange that he should concede this pardon reluctantly and under protest in the case of the violent and depraved. Yet not even when men richly deserve to suffer and be punished ought they to be utterly ruined. Since the Empress recognises this, she has never bidden him inflict any injury of any kind, or any punishment or chastisement even on a single household of the citizens, much less on a whole kingdom or city. I might add, moreover, with the utmost confidence that I am speaking the absolute truth, that in the case of no man or woman is it possible to charge her with any misfortune that has happened, but all the benefits that she confers and has conferred, and on whom, I would gladly recount in as many cases as possible, and report them one by one; how, for instance, this man, thanks to her, enjoys his ancestral estate, and that man has been saved from punishment, though he was guilty in the eyes of the law, or how a third escaped a malicious prosecution, though he came within an ace of the danger, or how countless persons have received honour and office at her hands. On this subject, there is not one who will assert that I speak falsely, even if I should not give a list of those persons by name. This I hesitate to do, in truth, lest I should seem to some to be reproaching them with their sufferings, and to be composing not so much an encomium of her good deeds as a catalogue of the misfortunes of others. And yet, to not cite any of these acts of hers, and to bring no proof of them before the public seems to perhaps imply they are lacking, thereby inviting discredit on my encomium. Accordingly, to avoid such a charge, I shall relate as much as it is not invidious for me to speak or for her to hear.

1. The traditional founding of the ancient court of the Areopagus, which tried cases of homicide, is described in Æschylus, *Eumenides*

2. *The Iliad*, IV, 43

When, in the beginning, she had secured her husband's goodwill by her actions, like a "front shining from afar" to use the words of the great poet Pindar,[1] she forthwith showered honours on all her family and kinsfolk, appointing to more important functions those who had already been tested and were of mature age. Making them seem fortunate and enviable, she won for them the Emperor's friendship and laid the foundation of their present prosperity. Thus if anyone thinks, what is in fact true, that on their own account they are worthy of honour, he will applaud her all the more. For it is evident that it was their merit, far more than the ties of kinship, that she rewarded; and one could hardly pay her a higher compliment than that. Such, then, was her treatment of these. While to all who, since they were still obscure on account of their youth, needed recognition of any sort, she awarded lesser honours. In fact, she left nothing undone to help one and all. For not only on her kinsfolk has she conferred such benefits, but whenever she learned that ties of friendship used to exist with her ancestors, she has not allowed it to be unprofitable to those who owned such ties; rather, she honours them, I understand, no less than her own kinsfolk, and to all whom she regards as her father's friends she dispensed wonderful rewards for their friendship.

Since, however, I see that my account is in need of proofs, just as in a law-court, I will offer myself to bear witness on its behalf to these actions and to applaud them. Lest you should mistrust my evidence, and cause a disturbance before you have heard what I have to say, I swear that I will tell you no falsehood or fiction; although you would have believed, even without an oath, that I am saying all this without intent to flatter. For I already possess, by the grace of God and the Emperor, and because the Empress too was zealous in my behalf, all those blessings which a flatterer would leave nothing unsaid to gain, so that, if I were speaking before obtaining these, perhaps I should have to dread that unjust suspicion. Yet as it is, since this is the state of my fortunes, I will recall her conduct to me, and at the same time give you a proof of my own right-mindedness and reliable evidence of her good deeds. I have heard that Darius, while he was still in the bodyguard of the Persian monarch,[2] met a Samian stranger[3] in Egypt who was an exile from his own country. He accepted from him the gift of a scarlet

1. *Olympian Ode*, 6.4.; Pindar says that he will begin his Ode with splendid words, as though he were building the splendid forecourt of a house

2. Cambyses 3. Syloson, Herodotus, 3.139

cloak to which Darius had taken a great fancy, and later on, in the days when, I understand, he had become the master of all Asia, he gave him in return the tyranny of Samos. Now suppose I acknowledge that, though I received many kindnesses at Eusebia's hands, at a time when I was still permitted to live in peaceful obscurity, and many also, by her intercession, from our noble and magnanimous Emperor, I must fall short of making an equal return; for as I know, she possesses everything already, as the gift of him who was so generous to myself; yet since I desire that the memory of her good deeds should be immortal, and since I am relating them to you, perhaps I shall not be thought less mindful of my debt than the Persian. After all, in forming a judgement it is to the intention that one must look, and not to an instance in which fortune granted a man the power to repay his obligation many times over.

Why, then, do I say that I have been so kindly treated, and in return for what I acknowledge that I am her debtor for all time, that is what you are eager to hear. Nor shall I conceal the facts. The Emperor was kind to me almost from my infancy, and he surpassed all generosity, for he snatched me from dangers so great that not even "a man in the strength of his youth"[1] could easily have escaped them, unless he obtained some means of safety sent by heaven and not attainable by human means. Again, after my house had been seized by one of those in power, as though there were none to defend it, he recovered it for me, as was just, and made it wealthy once more. I could tell you of still other kindnesses on his part towards myself that deserve all gratitude, in return for which I ever showed myself loyal and faithful to him; nevertheless, of late I perceived that, I know not why, he was somewhat harsh towards me. The Empress no sooner heard a bare mention, not of any actual wrong-doing but of mere idle suspicion, than she deigned to investigate it, and before doing so would not admit or listen to any falsehood or unjust slander, persisting instead in her request until she brought me into the Emperor's presence and procured me speech with him. She rejoiced when I was acquitted of every unjust charge, and when I wished to return home, she first persuaded the Emperor to give his permission, then she furnished me with a safe escort. When thereafter some divine being, the one who I suspect devised my former troubles, or perhaps some adverse chance, cut short this journey, she sent me to visit Greece, having asked this favour on my behalf from the Emperor when I had already left

1. *The Iliad*, XII, 382

the country. This was because she had learned that I delighted in literature, and she knew that place to be the home of culture. Then, I prayed, as is proper, first for the Emperor, and next for Eusebia, that God would grant them many blessings, for when I longed and desired to behold my true fatherland, they made it possible. For we who dwell in Thrace and Ionia are the sons of Hellas, and all of us who are not devoid of feeling long to greet our ancestors and to embrace the very soil of that land. This had long been, as was natural, my dearest wish, and I desired it more than to possess treasures of gold and silver. For I consider that discourse with distinguished men, when weighed in the balance with any amount whatsoever of gold, drags down the beam, and does not permit a prudent judge to even hesitate over a slight turn of the scale.

As regards learning and philosophy, the condition of Greece in our day reminds one somewhat of the tales and traditions of the Egyptians. For the Egyptians say that the Nile in their country is not only the saviour and benefactor of the land, but also wards off destruction by fire, when the sun, throughout long periods, in conjunction or combination with fiery constellations, fills the atmosphere with heat and scorches everything. For it has not power enough, so they say, to evaporate or exhaust the fountains of the Nile. So, too, neither from the Greeks has philosophy altogether departed, nor has she forsaken Athens, Sparta, or Corinth. Furthermore, as regards these fountains, Argos can by no means be called "thirsty",[1] for there are many in the city itself and many also south of the city, near Mases,[2] famous of old. Yet Sicyon, not Corinth, possesses Peirene itself. While Athens has many such streams, pure and springing from the soil, and many flow into the city from abroad, no less precious than those that are native. For her people love and cherish them and desire to be rich in that which alone makes wealth enviable.

As for me, what has come over me? And what speech do I intend to achieve if not a panegyric of my beloved Hellas, of which one cannot make mention without admiring everything? Though perhaps someone, remembering what I said earlier, will say that this is not what I intended to discuss when I began, and that, just as Corybants[3] when excited by the flute dance and leap without method, so I, spurred on by the mention of my beloved city, am

1. *The Iliad*, IV, 171 2. The port of Argolis

3. The armed and crested dancers who worshipped the Phrygian goddess Cybele with drumming and dancing

chanting the praises of that country and her people. To him I must make excuse somewhat as follows: good sir, you who are the guide to an art that is genuinely noble, that is a wise notion of yours, for you do not permit or grant one to let go even for a moment the theme of a panegyric, seeing that you yourself maintain your theme with skill. Yet in my case, since there has come over me this impulse of affection which you say is to blame for the lack of order in my arguments, you really urge me, I think, to not be overly afraid of it or to take precautions against criticism. For I am not embarking on irrelevant themes if I wish to show how great were the blessings that Eusebia procured for me as she honoured the name of philosophy. Yet the name of philosopher which has been, I know not why, applied to myself, is verily in my case nothing but a name and lacks reality, for though I love the reality and am terribly enamoured of the thing itself, for some reason I have fallen short of it. Nevertheless, Eusebia honoured even the name. For no other reason can I discover, nor learn from anyone else, why she became so zealous an ally of mine, an averter of evil and my preserver, taking such trouble and pains in order that I might retain unaltered and unaffected our noble Emperor's goodwill; and I have never been convicted of thinking that there is any greater blessing in this world than that good-will, since all the gold above the earth or beneath the earth is not worth so much, nor all the mass of silver that is now beneath the sun's rays or may be added thereto,[1] not if the loftiest mountains, let us suppose, stones, trees, and all, were to change to that substance, nor the greatest sovereignty there is, nor anything else in the whole world. I do indeed owe it to her that these blessings are mine, so many and greater than anyone could have hoped for, since in truth I did not ask for much, nor did I nourish myself with any such hopes.

Genuine kindness one cannot obtain in exchange for money, nor could anyone purchase it by such means, for it exists only when men of noble character work in harmony with a type of divine and higher providence. This the Emperor bestowed on me even as a child, and when it had almost vanished, it was restored to me again because the Empress defended me and warded off those false and monstrous suspicions. When, using the evidence of my life as plain proof, she had completely cleared me of them, and I obeyed once more the Emperor's summons from Greece, did she ever forsake me, as though, now that all enmity and suspicion had been

1. *The Iliad*, IX, 380

removed, I no longer needed much assistance? Would my conduct be pious if I kept silence and concealed actions so manifest and so honourable? For when a good opinion of me was established in the Emperor's mind, she rejoiced exceedingly, and echoed him harmoniously, bidding me take courage and neither refuse out of awe to accept the greatness[1] of what was offered to me, nor, by employing a boorish and arrogant frankness, unworthily slight the urgent request of him who had shown me such favour. Thus I obeyed, though it was by no means agreeable to me to support this burden, and besides, I knew well that to refuse was altogether impracticable. For when those who have the power to exact by force what they wish condescend to entreat, naturally they put one out of countenance and there is nothing left but to obey. Now, when I consented, I had to change my mode of dress, my attendants, my habitual pursuits, and my very house and way of life for what seemed full of pomp and ceremony to one whose past had naturally been so modest and humble. My mind was thrown into confusion by the strangeness, though it was certainly not overawed by the magnitude of the favours that were now mine. For in my ignorance I hardly regarded them as great blessings, but rather as powers of the greatest benefit, certainly to those who use them aright, yet when mistakes are made in their use, as being harmful to many houses and cities, and the cause of countless disasters.

Accordingly, I felt like a man who is altogether unskilled in driving a chariot, and is not at all inclined to acquire the art, only to be compelled to manage a car that belongs to a noble and talented charioteer, one who keeps many pairs and many four-in-hands too, let us suppose; one who has mounted behind them all, and because of his natural talent and uncommon strength has a strong grip on the reins of all of them, even though he is mounted on one chariot; yet he does not always remain on it, but often moves to this side or that, changing from car to car whenever he perceives that his horses are distressed or are getting out of hand; and among these chariots he has a team of four that become restive from ignorance and high spirit, that are oppressed by continuous hard work, but nonetheless are mindful of that high spirit, and grow ever more unruly, irritated by their distress, so that they grow more restive and disobedient, pulling against the driver and refusing to go in a certain direction, and, unless they see the charioteer himself or at least some man wearing the dress of a charioteer, end by becoming violent, so

1. The title of Cæsar

unreasoning are they by nature. When, conversely, the charioteer encourages some unskillful man, and sets him over them, allowing him to wear the same dress as his own, and invests him with the outward appearance of a splendid and skilful charioteer, then if he be altogether foolish and witless, he rejoices and is glad, buoyed up and exalted by those robes, as though by wings; if, however, he has even a small share of common sense and prudent understanding, he is very much alarmed "lest he both injure himself and shatter his chariot withal"[1] and so cause loss to the charioteer and bring upon himself shameful and inglorious disaster.

On all this, then, I reflected, taking counsel with myself in the night season, and in the daytime pondering it alone, being continually lost in thought and rather gloomy. Then the noble and truly godlike Emperor lessened my torment in every way, and showed me honour and favour both in deed and word. At last he bade me address myself to the Empress, inspiring me with courage and giving me a very generous indication that I might trust her completely. When first I came into her presence it seemed to me as though I beheld a statue of Modesty set up in some temple. Reverence filled my soul, and my eyes were fixed upon the ground[2] for some considerable time, till she bade me take courage. Then she said: "certain favours you have already received from us and yet others you shall receive, God willing, if only you prove to be loyal and honest towards us". This was almost as much as I heard. For she herself did not say more, though she knew how to utter speeches not a whit inferior to those of the most gifted orators. While I, when I had departed from this interview, felt the deepest admiration and awe, convinced beyond doubt that it was Modesty herself I had heard speaking. So gentle and comforting was her utterance, and it is ever firmly settled in my ears.

Do you wish, then, that I should report to you what she did after this, all the blessings she conferred on me, and that I should give precise details one by one? Or shall I take up my tale concisely as she did herself, and sum up the whole? Shall I tell how many of my friends she benefited, and how with the Emperor's help she arranged my marriage? Though perhaps you wish to hear also the list of her presents to me: "seven tripods untouched by fire and ten talents of gold"[3] and twenty cauldrons. I have no time, however, to gossip about such subjects. Nevertheless, one of those gifts of hers it would perhaps not be ungraceful to mention to you, since it

1. *The Iliad*, XXIII, 341 2. *The Iliad*, III, 217 3. *The Iliad*, IX, 122

was one with which I was myself especially delighted. For she gave me the finest books on philosophy and history, and many of the orators and poets, since I had brought hardly any with me from home, deluding myself with the hope and longing to return home again. She gave them, moreover, in such numbers, all at once, that even my desire for them was satisfied, though I am altogether insatiable of converse with literature. So far as books went, she made Galatia and the country of the Celts resemble a Greek temple of the Muses. To these gifts I applied myself incessantly whenever I had leisure, so that I can never be unmindful of the gracious giver. Yes, even when I take the field, one thing above all else goes with me as a necessary provision for the campaign, one narrative of a campaign composed long ago by an eye-witness. For many of those records of the experience of men of old, written as they are with the greatest skill, furnish to those who, by reason of their youth, have missed seeing such a spectacle, a clear and brilliant picture of those ancient exploits. By this means, many a young man has acquired a more mature understanding and judgement than belongs to very many older men; and that advantage which people think old age alone can give to mankind, meaning experience – for experience it is that enables an old man "to talk more wisely than the young"[1] – even this the study of history can give to the young, if only they are diligent. Moreover, in my opinion, there is in such books a means of education for the character, supposing that one understands how, like a craftsman, setting before himself as patterns the noblest men, words, and deeds, to mould his own character to match them, and make his words resemble theirs. If he should not wholly fall short of them, but should achieve even some slight resemblance, believe me, that would be for him the greatest fortune. It is with this idea constantly before me that not only do I give myself a literary education by means of books, but even on my campaigns I never fail to carry them like necessary provisions. The number that I take with me is limited only by circumstance.

Perhaps I ought not to be writing a panegyric on books now, nor to describe all the benefits that we might derive from them, but since I recognise how much that gift was worth, I ought to pay back to the gracious giver thanks not altogether different in kind from what she gave. For it is only just that one who has accepted intelligent discourses of all sorts laid up as treasure in books, should sound a strain of eulogy if only in slight and unskillful phrases, composed in

1. Euripides, Phoenissæ, 532

an unlearned and rustic fashion. For you would not say that a farmer showed proper feeling who, when starting to plant his vineyard, begs for cuttings from his neighbours, and presently, when he cultivates his vines, asks for a mattock, then for a hoe, and then, finally, for a stake to which the vine must be tied and which it must lean against, so that it may itself be supported, and the bunches of grapes as they hang may nowhere touch the soil. Furthermore, after obtaining all he asked for, he drinks his fill of the pleasant gift of Dionysus, but does not share either the grapes or the must with those whom he found so willing to help him in his husbandry. Just so, one would not say that a shepherd or cowherd, or even a goatherd was honest, good, and right-minded, who in winter, when his flocks need shelter and fodder, met with the utmost consideration from his friends, who helped him to procure many things, providing him with food in abundance, and lodging, yet when spring and summer appeared, forgot in lordly fashion all those kindnesses, and shared neither his milk, nor cheese, nor anything else with those who had saved his beasts for him when they would otherwise have perished.

Now take the case of one who cultivates literature of any sort, who is himself young and therefore needs numerous guides alongside the abundant and pure nourishment that is to be obtained from ancient writings; then suppose that he should be deprived of all these at once – is it, think you, slight assistance that he is asking? Moreover, is it slight payment that he who comes to his aid deserves? Though perhaps he ought not even to attempt to make him any return for his zeal and kind actions? Perhaps he ought to imitate the famous Thales, that consummate philosopher, and his answer which we have all heard and which is so much admired? For when someone asked what fee he ought to pay him for knowledge he had acquired, Thales replied "if you let it be known that it was I who taught you, you will amply repay me". Just so, one who has not himself been the teacher, but has helped another in any way to gain knowledge, would indeed be wronged if he did not obtain gratitude and that acknowledgement of the gift which even the philosopher seems to have demanded. That is certainly proper. This gift of hers, however, was both welcome and magnificent. As for gold and silver, I neither asked for them nor, were they in question, should I be willing to wear out your patience thus.

All the same, I wish to tell you a story very well worth your hearing, unless of course you are already wearied by the length of this garrulous speech. Indeed, it may be that you have listened without enjoyment to what has been said so far, seeing that the speaker is a layman and entirely ignorant of rhetoric, knowing neither how to invent nor how to use the writer's craft, but merely speaking the truth as it occurs to him. My story, then, is about something almost of the present time. Now many will say, I suppose, persuaded by the accomplished sophists, that I have collected what is trivial and worthless, and related it to you as though it were of serious import. In all probability, they will say this not because they are jealous of my speeches, or because they wish to rob me of the reputation that they may bring; for they well know that I do not desire to be their rival in the art by setting my own speeches against theirs, nor in any other way do I wish to quarrel with them. Yet since, for some reason or other, they are ambitious of speaking on lofty themes at any cost, they will not tolerate those who have not their ambition, and thus they reproach them with weakening the power of rhetoric. For they say that only those deeds are worthy of admiration, serious treatment, and repeated praise which, because of their magnitude, have been thought by some to be incredible. Those stories, for instance, about that famous woman of Assyria[1] who turned aside, as though it were an insignificant brook, the river[2] that flows through Babylon, then built a gorgeous palace underground, before turning the stream back again beyond the dykes that she had made. For of her many a tale is told, how she fought a naval battle with three thousand ships; how on land she led into the field of battle three million hoplites; or how in Babylon she built a wall very nearly five hundred stades in length, along with the moat that surrounds the city and other very costly edifices which, they tell us, were her work. Not to mention Nitocris, who came later than she, and Rhodogyne, and Tomyris,[3] indeed, a crowd of women beyond number who played men's parts in a most unseemly fashion occur to my mind. Some of them were conspicuous for their beauty and so became notorious, though it brought them no happiness. Nonetheless, as they were the causes of dissension and long wars among countless nations and as many men as could reasonably be collected from a country of that size, they are celebrated by the orators as having given rise to mighty deeds.

Thus, a speaker who has nothing of this sort to relate seems ridiculous because he makes no great effort to astonish his hearers or to introduce the marvellous into his speeches. Now, shall we put

1. Semiramis, Herodotus, 1.184 2. The Euphrates 3. Herodotus, 1.185;205

this question to these orators, whether any one of them would wish to have a wife or daughter of that sort, rather than like Penelope? Yet in her case, Homer had no more to tell than of her discretion, her love for her husband, and the good care she took of her father-in-law and her son. Evidently she did not concern herself with the fields or the flocks, and as for leading an army or speaking in public, of course she never even dreamed of such a thing. But even when it was necessary for her to speak to the young suitors "holding up before her face her shining veil",[1] it was in mild accents that she expressed herself. Furthermore, it was not because he was short of such great deeds, or of women famous for them, that he sang the praises of Penelope rather than the others. For example, he could have made it his ambition to tell the story of the Amazon's[2] campaign and have filled all his poetry with tales of that sort, which certainly have a wonderful power to delight and charm. For as to the taking of the wall and the siege, that battle near the ships which in some respects seems to have resembled a sea-fight, and then the fight of the hero and the river,[3] he did not bring them into his poem with the desire to relate something new and strange of his own invention. And even though this fight was, as they say, most marvellous, he neglected and passed over the marvellous as we see. What reason, then, can anyone give for his praising Penelope so enthusiastically and making not the slightest allusion to those famous women? Because by reason of her virtue and discretion, many blessings have been gained for mankind, both for individuals and the common wealth; whereas from the ambition of those others, there has arisen no benefit whatsoever, but rather incurable calamities. Therefore, as he was, I think, a wise and inspired poet, he decided that to praise Penelope was better and more just. And since I adopt so great a guide, is it fitting that I should be afraid lest some person think me trivial or inferior?

It is indeed a noble witness that I shall now bring forward, that splendid orator Pericles, the renowned, the Olympian. It is said[4] that once a crowd of flatterers surrounded him and were distributing his praises among them, one telling how he had reduced Samos, another how he had recovered Euboea, some how he had sailed round the Peloponnesus, while others spoke of his enactments, or of his rivalry with Cimon, who was reputed to be a most excellent citizen and a distinguished general.

1. *The Odyssey*, I, 334 2. Penthesilea 3. *The Iliad*, XXI, 234
4. Plutarch, *Pericles*, 38

Pericles, however, gave no sign of either annoyance or exultation, and there was but one thing in all his political career for which he claimed to deserve praise, that, though he had governed the Athenian people for so long, he had been responsible for no man's death, and no citizen when he put on black clothes had ever said that Pericles was the cause of his misfortune. Now, by Zeus the god of friendship, do you think I need any further witness to testify that the greatest proof of virtue and one more worthy of praise than all the rest put together is to have not caused the death of any citizen, or to have taken his money from him, or involved him in unjust exile? For he who like a good physician tries to ward off such calamities as these, and by no means thinks that it is enough for him to not cause anyone to contract a disease, but unless he cures and cares for everyone as far as he can, considers that his work is unworthy of his skill, do you think that in justice such a person ought to receive less praise than Pericles? And shall we not hold in the highest honour her character and that authority which enables her to do what she will, since what she wills is the good of all? For this I make the sum and substance of my whole encomium, though I do not lack other narratives such as are commonly held to be marvellous and splendid.

If anyone should suspect that my silence about the rest is vain affectation and empty and insolent pretension, this at least he will not suspect, that the visit which she lately made to Rome,[1] when the Emperor was on his campaign and had crossed the Rhine by bridges of boats near the frontiers of Galatia, is a false and vain invention. I could indeed very properly have given an account of this visit, and described how the people and the senate welcomed her with rejoicings and went to meet her with enthusiasm, receiving her as is their custom to receive an Empress. I could, moreover, have told the amount of the expenditure, how generous and splendid it was, the costliness of the preparations, and reckoned up the sums she distributed to the presidents of the tribes and the centurions of the people. Yet nothing of that sort has ever seemed to me worthwhile, nor do I wish to praise wealth before virtue. Though I am aware that the generous spending of money does imply a type of virtue. Nevertheless, I rate more highly goodness, temperance, wisdom, and all those other qualities of hers that I have described, bringing before you as witnesses not only many others, but myself as well and all that she did for me.

1. In 357

If only others might try to emulate my proper feeling, there are and there will be many more to sing her praises.

PANEGYRIC IN HONOUR OF CONSTANTIUS

PREFACE

The third of Julian's panegyrics is another in honour of his cousin, the Emperor Constantius, and was most likely written and delivered in 355, shortly before he departed for Gaul. As with the first, Julian's praise is entirely insincere and divorced from the true character of Constantius; it is thus a compulsory rhetorical exercise in tribute to a man for whom Julian held little affection and much resentment, composed at a time when he was doubtless relieved that the Emperor had not executed him out of rampant paranoia.

Unlike the previous two orations, Julian only quotes Homer once throughout the entire panegyric. It is indicative of a work in which he seems to be far more concerned with convention and producing something that his primarily Christian audience, especially the Emperor himself, would find agreeable. Being unable, or disinclined, to explore extensively such topics as the Homeric poems or Platonic philosophy, the oration consequently lacks the enthusiasm of the first or the sincerity of the second. Nevertheless, some regarded it as his masterpiece, with Libanius even using it as a model for such oratory. Julian's training in rhetoric is certainly evident in the work:

> He follows with hardly a deviation the rules for the treatment and arrangement of a speech in praise of an emperor as we find them in Menander's third century handbook of epideictic oratory. First comes the prooemium to conciliate the audience and to give the threads of the argument; then follows the praise of the Emperor's native land, ancestors, early training, deeds in war and in peace, and the customary contrasts with the Persian monarchs, the Homeric heroes, and Alcibiades. In the two last divisions, the virtues of Plato's ideal ruler are proved to have been displayed by Constantius, his victories are exaggerated and his defeats explained away. Then comes a description of the happy state of the empire and the army under such a ruler, whereupon the panegyric ends without the final prayer for the continuance of his reign, as recommended by Menander.[1]

---

1. W. C. F. Wright

PANEGYRIC IN HONOUR OF CONSTANTIUS

I have long desired, most mighty Emperor, to sing the praises of your valour and achievements, to recount your campaigns, and to tell how you suppressed the tyrannies; how your persuasive eloquence drew away one usurper's[1] bodyguard; how you overcame another[2] by force of arms. Yet the vast scale of your exploits deterred me, for what I had to dread was not that my words would fall somewhat short of your deeds, but that I should prove wholly unequal to my theme. That men versed in political debate, or poets, should find it easy to compose a panegyric on your career is not at all surprising. Their practice in speaking, their habit of declaiming in public thus supplies them abundantly with a well-warranted confidence. Those, however, who have neglected this field and chosen another branch of literary study, that which devotes itself to a form of composition little adapted to win popular favour, and that has not the boldness to exhibit itself in its nakedness in every theatre, no matter what, would naturally hesitate to make speeches of the epideictic sort. As for the poets, their Muse, and the general belief that it is she who inspires their verse, obviously gives them unlimited license to invent. To rhetoricians, the art of rhetoric allows just as much freedom; fiction is denied them, but flattery is by no means forbidden, nor is it counted a disgrace to the orator that the object of his panegyric should not deserve it. Poets who compose and publish some legend that no one had thought of before increase their reputation, because an audience is entertained by the mere fact of novelty. Orators, again, assert that the advantage of their art is that it can treat a slight theme in the grand manner, and again, by the use of mere words, strip the greatness from deeds, and, in short, marshal the power of words against that of facts.

If, however, I had seen that on this occasion I should need their art, I should have maintained the silence that befits those who have

1. Vetranio 2. Magnentius

had no practice in such forms of composition, and left your praises to be told by those whom I just now mentioned. Since, on the contrary, the speech I am to make calls for a plain narrative of the facts and needs no adventitious ornament, I thought that even I was not unfit, seeing that my predecessors had already shown that it was beyond them to produce a record worthy of your achievements. For almost all who devote themselves to literature attempt to sing your praises in verse or prose; some of them venture to cover your whole career in a brief narrative, while others devote themselves to a part only, and think that if they succeed in doing justice to that part they have proved themselves equal to the task. Yet one can only admire the zeal of all who have made you the theme of a panegyric. Some did not shrink from the tremendous effort to secure every one of your accomplishments from the withering touch of time; others, because they foresaw that they could not encompass the whole, expressed themselves only in part, choosing to consecrate to you their individual work so far as they were able. Better this, they thought, than "the reward of silence that runs no risk".[1]

Now, if I were one of those whose favourite pursuit is epideictic oratory, I should have to begin my speech by asking from you no less goodwill than I now feel towards yourself, and should beg you graciously to incline your ear to my words rather than play the part of a severe and inexorable critic. Since, however, bred as I have been and educated in other studies, pursuits, and conventions, I am criticised for venturing rashly into fields that belong to others, I feel that I ought to explain myself briefly on this front and begin my speech more after my own fashion.

There is an ancient maxim taught by him who first introduced philosophy to mankind, which is as follows: all who aspire to virtue and the beautiful must study in their words, deeds, conversation, in short, all the affairs of life, great and small, to aim in every way at beauty. Now what sensible man would deny that virtue is of all things the most beautiful? Wherefore those are permitted to lay firm hold on her who do not seek to blazon abroad her name in vain, appropriating that which in no way belongs to them. In giving this counsel, the maxim does not prescribe any single type of discourse, nor does it proclaim to its readers, like a god from the machine in tragedy,[2] "you must aspire to virtue and eschew evil". Many are the paths that it allows a man to follow to this goal, if he desire to imitate the nature of the beautiful. For example, he may

1. Isocrates, *Panegyricus*, 42

2. Simonides, fr. 66; Horace, *Odes*, 3.2.25.

give good advice, or use hortatory discourse; he may rebuke error without malice, or applaud what is well done, or condemn, on occasion, what is ill done. It permits men also to use other types of oratory, if they please, so as to attain the best end of speech; though it enjoins on them to take thought in every word and deed, of how they shall give account of all they utter, and to speak no word that cannot be referred to the standard of virtue and philosophy. That and more to the same effect is the tenour of that precept.

What, then, am I to do? What embarrasses me is the fact that, if I praise you, I shall be thought simply to curry favour, and in fact, the department of panegyric has come to incur a grave suspicion due to its misuse, such that it is now held to be base flattery rather than trustworthy testimony to heroic deeds. Is it not obvious that I must put my faith in the merit of him whom I undertake to praise, and with full confidence devote my energies to this panegyric? What then shall be the prelude of my speech and the most suitable arrangement? Assuredly I must begin with the virtues of your ancestors through which it was possible for you to come to be what you are. Next, I think it will be proper to describe your upbringing and education, since these contributed very much to the noble qualities that you possess; and when I have dealt with all these, I must recount your achievements, the signs and tokens, as it were, of the nobility of your soul; and finally, as the crown and consummation of my discourse, I shall set forth those personal qualities from which was evolved all that was noble in your projects and their execution. It is in this respect that I think my speech will surpass those of all the others. For some limit themselves to your exploits, with the idea that a description of these suffices for a perfect panegyric, but for my part I think one ought to devote the greater part of one's speech to the virtues that were the stepping-stones by which you reached the height of your accomplishments. Military exploits in most cases, indeed, in almost all, are achieved with the help of fortune, bodyguards, heavy infantry, and cavalry regiments. Virtuous actions, however, belong to the doer alone, and the praise that they inspire, if it be sincere, belongs only to the possessor of such virtue. Now, having made this distinction clear, I will begin my speech.

The rules of panegyric require that I should mention your native land no less than your ancestors. Alas, I am at a loss as to which country I ought to consider singularly yours. For countless nations have long asserted their claim to be your country. The city that rules over them all[1] was your mother and nurse, and in an auspicious hour delivered to you the imperial sceptre; she, therefore, asserts her sole title to the honour, and not merely by resorting to the plea that has prevailed under all the Emperors. Which is to say that, even if men are born elsewhere, they all adopt her constitution and use the laws and customs that she has promulgated, and by that fact become Roman citizens. Yet her claim is different, namely that she gave your mother birth, rearing her royally and as befitted the offspring who were to be born to her. Then again, the city on the Bosphorus which is named after the family of the Constantii, though she does not assert that she is your native place, nevertheless acknowledges that she became your adopted land by your father's act, and will thus think she is cheated of her rights if any orator should try to deprive her of at least this claim to kinship. Thirdly, the Illyrians, on whose soil you were born, will not tolerate it if anyone assigns you a different fatherland and thereby robs them of the fairest gift of fortune. Further still, I hear even some of the Eastern provinces protest that it is unjust of me to rob them of the lustre they derive from you. For they say that they sent forth your grandmother to be the consort of your grandfather on the mother's side. Almost all the rest have hit on some pretension of more or less weight, and are determined, on one ground or another, to adopt you for their own. Therefore, let that country[2] have the prize which you yourself prefer and have so often praised as the mother and teacher of the virtues; as for the rest, let each one according to her deserts obtain her due. I should be glad to praise them all, worthy as they are of glory and honour, though I am afraid that my compliments, however germane they may seem to my subject, might, on account of their length, be thought inappropriate to the present occasion. For this reason, then, I think it better to omit a eulogy of the others. As for Rome, however, your Imperial Majesty summed up her praises in two words when you called her the teacher of virtue, and, by bestowing on her the fairest of all encomiums, you have forestalled all that others might say. What praise of mine would come up to that? What indeed is left for anyone to say? So I feel that I, who naturally hold that city in reverence, shall pay her a higher honour if I leave her praise in your hands.

Perhaps at this point I ought to say a few words about your noble ancestors. Only that here, too, I am at a loss where to begin. For all your ancestors, grandfathers, parents, brothers, cousins, and

1. Rome 2. ibid.

kinsfolk were Emperors, who had either acquired their power by lawful means or were adopted by the reigning house. Why should I recall ancient history or hark back to Claudius and produce proofs of his merit, which are manifest and known to all? To what end should I recount his campaigns against the Barbarians across the Danube or how righteously and justly he won the Empire? How plainly he lived while on the throne! How simple was his dress, as may be seen to this day in his statues! What I might say about your grandparents[1] is comparatively recent, but equally remarkable. Both of them acquired the imperial sceptre as the reward of conspicuous merit, and having assumed the command, they were on such good terms with each other and displayed such filial piety to him[2] who had granted them a share in the Empire, that he used to say that of all the safeguards designed by him for the realm, many as they were, this was his master-stroke. They, meanwhile, valued their mutual understanding more than an undivided empire, supposing that it could have been bestowed on either of them separately. This was the temper of their souls, and nobly they played their part in action, while next to the Supreme Being they reverenced him who had placed authority in their hands. With their subjects they dealt righteously and humanely. They expelled the Barbarians who had for years settled in our territory (and occupied it with impunity as though it were their own) and built forts to hinder encroachment, which procured for those subjects such peaceful relations with the Barbarians as, at that period, seemed to be beyond their dreams. This, however, is a subject that deserves more than a passing mention. Yet it would be wrong to omit the strongest proof of their unanimity, especially as it is related to my subject. Since they desired the most perfect harmony for their children, they arranged the marriage of your father and mother.[3]

On this point, also, I think I must say a few words to show that virtue was bequeathed to you as well as a throne. Though why waste time in telling how your father, on his father's death, became Emperor both by the choice of the deceased monarch and by the vote of all the armies? His military genius was made evident by his achievements and needs no words of mine. He traversed the whole civilised world suppressing tyrants, but never those who ruled by right. His subjects he inspired with such affection that his veterans still remember how generous he was with largesse and other rewards, and to this day worship him as though he were a god. As

1. Constantius Chlorus and Maximianus 2. Diocletian 3. Constantine and Fausta

for the mass of the people, in town and country alike, they prayed that your father might be victorious over the tyrants, not so much because they would be delivered from that hardship as because they would then be governed by him. When he had made his power supreme, however, he found that the tyrant's[1] greed had worked like a drought, with the result that money was very scarce, while there were great hoards of treasure in the recesses of the palace. Therefore, he unlocked its doors and on the instant flooded the whole country with wealth, then, in less than ten years, he founded and gave his name to a city that as far surpasses all others as it is itself inferior to Rome – and to come second to Rome seems to me a much greater honour than to be counted first and foremost of all cities beside. Here it may be proper to mention Athens "the illustrious",[2] seeing that during his whole life he honoured her in word and deed. He who was Emperor and Lord of all did not disdain the title of General of the Athenians, and when they gave him a statue with an inscription to that effect, he felt more pride than if he had been awarded the highest of honours. To repay Athens for this compliment, he bestowed on her annually a gift of many tens of thousands of bushels of wheat, so that while she enjoyed plenty, he won applause and reverence from the best of men.

Your father's achievements were many and brilliant. Some I have just mentioned; others I must omit for the sake of brevity. Yet the most notable of all, as I make bold to say and think all will agree,[2] was that he begat, reared, and educated you. This secured to the rest of the world the advantages of good government, and not for a limited time but for a period beyond his own lifetime, as far as this is possible. Indeed, your father seems still to be on the throne. This is more than Cyrus himself could achieve. When he died, his son proved far inferior, so that while men called Cyrus "father" his successor was called "master".[3] Though you are even less stern than your father, and surpass him in many respects, as I well know, and will demonstrate in my speech as occasion shall arise. Yet, in my opinion, he should have the credit of this as well, since it was he who gave you that admirable training, about which I shall presently speak, but not until I have described your mother and brothers.

Your mother's ancestry was so distinguished, her personal beauty and nobility of character were such that it would be hard to find her match among women. I have heard the Persian saying about Parysatis, that no other woman had been the sister, mother,

1. Maxentius 2. Pindar, fr. 46 3. Herodotus, 3.89

wife, and daughter of kings. Parysatis, however, was the sister of her husband, since their law does not forbid a Persian to marry his sibling. Your mother, then, while in accordance with our laws kept pure and unsullied those ties of kinship, was actually the daughter of one Emperor,[1] the wife of another, the sister of a third, and the mother of not one Emperor but several. Of these, one aided your father in his war against the tyrants; another conquered the Getæ and secured for us a lasting peace with them; the third[2] kept our frontiers safe from the enemy's incursions, and often led his forces against them in person, so long at least as he was permitted by those who were so soon punished for their crimes against him. Though by the number and brilliance of their achievements they have indeed earned our homage, and though all the blessings of fortune were theirs in abundance, in the whole tale of their felicity one could pay them no greater compliment than merely to name their sires and grandsires. I must not make my account of them too long, however, lest I should spend time that I ought to devote to your own panegyric. So in what follows I will, as indeed I ought, endeavour, or rather, since affectation is out of place, let me say I will demonstrate – that you are far more august than your ancestors.

Heavenly voices, prophecies, visions in dreams, and all such portents[3] are common gossip when men like yourself have achieved brilliant and conspicuous success. Cyrus, for instance, and the founder[4] of our capital, and Alexander, Philip's son, and the like. These I purposely ignore. Indeed, I feel that poetic license accounts for them all. Moreover, it is foolish even to state that at the hour of your birth all the circumstances were brilliant and suited to a prince. Now, then, the time has come for me to speak of your education as a boy. You were, of course, bound to have the princely nurture that should train your body to be strong, muscular, healthy, and handsome, and at the same time duly equip your soul with courage, justice, temperance, and wisdom. Yet this cannot result from that loose indulgence which naturally pampers body and soul, weakening men's wills for facing danger and their bodies for work. Therefore, your body required training by suitable gymnastics, while you adorned your mind by literary studies. Though I must speak at greater length about both branches of your education, since it laid the foundation of your later career. In your physical training you did not pursue those exercises that prepare one merely for public display. What professional athletes love to call peak

1. Maximianus 2. Constans 3. Isocrates, *Evagoras*, 21 4. Romulus

condition you thought unsuitable for an emperor who must enter contests that are not make-believe. Such a person must endure very little sleep and meagre food, and that of no precise quantity or quality, nor served at regular hours, but such as can be had when the stress of work allows. Thus you believed you ought to train yourself in athletics with a view to this, and that your exercises must be military and of many kinds – dancing, running in heavy armour, and riding. All these you have continued from early youth to practise at the right time, and in every exercise you have attained to greater perfection than any other hoplite. Usually, a hoplite who is a good infantryman cannot ride, or, if he is an expert horseman, he shirks marching on foot to battle. Yet of you alone can it be said that you are able to put on the cavalry uniform and be a match for the best of them, and when changed into a hoplite, show yourself stronger, swifter, and lighter on your feet than all the rest. Then you practised shooting at a mark so that even your hours of leisure might not be hours of ease, or be found without the exercise of arms. So by work that was voluntary, you trained your body to stand the exertions that you would be compelled to undertake.

Your mind, meanwhile, was trained by practice in public speaking and other studies suitable to your years. Though it was not to be wholly without the discipline of experience, nor was it for you to listen merely to lectures on the virtues as if they were ballads or saga stories, thereby waiting all that time without actual acquaintance with brave works and undertakings. Plato, that noble philosopher, advised[1] that boys should be furnished as it were with wings for flight by being mounted on horseback, and should then be taken into battle so that they may be spectators of the warfare in which they must soon be combatants. This, I make bold to say, was in your father's mind when he made you governor and lord of the Celtic tribes while you were still a youth, or rather, a mere boy in point of years, though in intelligence and endurance you could already hold your own with men in their prime. Your father wisely provided that your experience of war should be free from risks, having arranged that the Barbarians should maintain peace with his subjects. Nevertheless, he instigated them to internal feuds and civil war, and so taught you strategy at the expense of their lives and fortunes. This was a safer policy than the wise Plato's. For, by his scheme, if the invading army were composed of infantry, the boys could indeed be spectators of their fathers' prowess, or, if need

1. Plato, *Republic*, 467

arose, could even take part. Supposing the enemy won in a cavalry engagement, however, one would, on the instant, have to devise some means to save the boys, which would be difficult indeed. Yet to inure the boys to face the enemy, while the hazard belongs to others, is to take counsel that both suffices for their need and also secures their safety.

It was in this way, then, that you were first trained in manliness. As regards wisdom, however, that nature with which you were endowed was your self-sufficing guide. Though also, I think, the wisest citizens were at your disposal and gave you lessons in statecraft. Moreover, your intercourse with the Barbarian leaders in that region gave you an acquaintance at first-hand with the manners, laws, and customs of foreigners. Indeed, when Homer set out to prove the consummate wisdom of Odysseus, he called him "much-travelled" and said that he had come to know the minds of many peoples, visiting their cities so that he might choose what was best in every one and be able to mix with all sorts and conditions of men. Yes, even Odysseus, who never ruled an empire, needed experience of the many and diverse minds of men. How much more necessary that one who was being brought up to guide an empire like this should not equip himself for the task in some modest dwelling apart; neither should he, like young Cyrus in his games, play at being emperor, nor give audiences to his playmates, as they say[1] Cyrus did. Rather, he ought to interact with nations and peoples, give orders to his troops indicating clearly what is to be done, and generally he should be found wanting in none of those things which, when he comes to manhood, he must perform without fear.

Accordingly, once you had gained thorough knowledge of the Celts, you crossed to the other continent and were given sole command against the Parthians and Medes. There were already signs that a war was smouldering and would soon burst into flame. You therefore quickly learned how to deal with it, and, as though you took as model the hardness of your weapons, steeled yourself to bear the heat of the summer season. I have heard say that Alcibiades alone, among all the Greeks, was naturally so versatile that when he cast in his lot with the Spartans, he copied the self-restraint of the Lacedæmonians, then in turn Theban and Thracian manners, and finally he adopted Persian luxury. Yet Alcibiades, when he changed his country, changed his character[2] too, and became so

1. Herodotus, I.114 2. cf. Æschines, *Against Ctesiphon*, 78; Horace, *Epistles*, I.II.27

ill-conditioned and tainted with perversity that he was likely to utterly lose all that he was born to. You, however, thought it your duty to maintain your severity of life wherever you might be, and by hard work inuring your constitution to change, you easily bore the march inland from Galatia to Parthia – more easily in fact than a rich man who lives at one moment here, another there, according to the season, would bear it if he were forced to encounter unseasonable weather. As God, I believe, favoured you and willed that you should govern the whole world, so from the first he trained you in virtue, and was your guide when you journeyed to all points, showing you the bounds and limits of the whole Empire, the character of each region, the vastness of your territory, the power of every race, the number of the cities, the characteristics of the masses, and above all, the vast number of things that one who is bred to so great a rulership cannot afford to neglect. Though I almost forgot to mention the most important thing of all. From a boy you were taught to govern this great Empire, but a better thing you learned: to be governed, submitting, yourself to the authority that is the highest in the world and the most just, that is to say nature and law. By this I mean that as both son and subject you obeyed your father. Indeed, had he been only your father or only your Emperor, obedience was still his due.

Now, what rearing and education for a leader could one find in history better than this? Consider the Greeks: not thus did the Spartans train the Heracleidæ, though they are thought to have enjoyed the best form of government, that of their kings. As for the Barbarians, not even the Carthaginians, though they were particularly well-governed by their kings, chose the best method of training their future rulers. The moral discipline and the studies prescribed by their laws were pursued by all alike, as though the citizens were brothers, all destined both to govern and be governed, and in the matter of education they made no distinction between their princes and the rest of the citizens. Yet surely it is foolish to demand superlative excellence from one's rulers when one takes no pains to make them better than other men. Among the Barbarians, indeed, no man is debarred from winning the throne, so one can excuse them for giving the same moral training to all. Yet that Lycurgus, who tried to make the dynasty of the Heracleidæ proof against all shocks,[1] should not have arranged for them a special education better than that of other Spartan youths is an omission

1. cf. Xenophon, *Constitution of the Lacedæmonians*, 15.7

for which he may well be criticised. He may have thought that all the Lacedæmonians ought to enter the race for virtue, and foster it, but for all that it was wrong to provide the same nurture and education for private citizens as for those who were to govern. The inevitable familiarity little by little steals into men's souls and breeds contempt for their leaders. Though, for that matter, they are not in any sense one's betters unless it was their own merit that earned them the right to rule. This, in my opinion, is the reason why the Spartan kings often found their subjects hard to govern. As proof of what I say, one might quote the rivalry of Lysander and Agesilaus, and many other instances, if one were to review the history of the Spartan kings.

The Spartan polity, however, by securing a satisfactory development of the moral qualities in their kings, even if it gave them a training in no way different from that of the crowd, at least endowed them with the attributes of well-bred men. Though as for the Carthaginians, there was nothing to admire even in the discipline that they all shared. The parents turned their sons out and bade them win the necessities of life by their own efforts, with the injunction to do nothing that is considered disgraceful. The effect of this was not to uproot the wayward inclinations of the young, but to require them to take pains not to be caught in wrong-doing. For it is not self-indulgence only that ruins character, but the lack of mere necessities may produce the same result. This is true, at any rate, in the case of those whose reason has not yet assumed the power to decide, being swayed by physical needs and persuaded by desire. It is especially true when one fails to control the passion for acquiring money, if from boyhood one is accustomed to it and to the trading and bartering of the market-places. This business, unfit for a freeborn child to mention, or so much as hear spoken of, whether the child finds it out for himself or learns it from those of greater experience, leaves many scars on the soul; and even a respectable citizen ought to be free from all this, not a king or general alone.

Though it is not for me to criticise the Carthaginians in this place. I will only point out how different was your education, how you profited by it and have come to excel in appearance, strength, justice, and temperance. By your active life you achieved perfect health; your temperance was the result of obedience to the laws; you enjoy a body of exceptional strength by reason of your self-control, and a soul of exceptional rectitude because of your physical powers of endurance. You left nothing undone to improve your natural talents, but ever acquired new talents by new studies. You needed nothing yourself, but gave assistance to others, and lavished such generous gifts that the recipients seemed as rich as the monarch of the Lydians.[1] Though you indulged yourself less in the good things that were yours than the most austere of the Spartans, you gave others the means of luxury in abundance, while those who preferred temperance could imitate your example. As a ruler you were mild and humane; as your father's subject you were ever as modest as any one of his people. All this was true of you in boyhood and youth, and much more about which there is now no time to speak at length.

When you had reached the age of manhood, after fate had decreed the ending of your father's life[2] and heaven had granted that his last hours should be uniquely blessed, you adorned his tomb not only by lavishing on it splendid decorations[3] and so paying the debt of gratitude for your birth and education, but still more by the fact that you alone of his sons hastened to him when he was still alive and stricken by illness, and granted him the highest possible honours after his death. Yet all this I need only mention in passing. For now it is your exploits that cry aloud for notice and remind me of your energy, courage, good judgement, and justice. In these qualities you are unsurpassed, unrivalled. In your dealings with your brothers, your subjects, your father's friends, and your armies you displayed justice and moderation; except that, in some cases, forced as you were by the critical state of affairs, you could not, in spite of your own wishes, prevent others from going astray. Towards the enemy your demeanour was brave, generous, and worthy of the previous reputation of your house. While you maintained the friendly relations that already existed, kept the capital free from civil discord, and continued to cherish your brothers who were your partners in empire, you granted to your friends, among other benefits, the privilege of addressing you as an equal, full freedom of speech without stint, and perfect frankness. Not only did you share with them all whatever you possessed, but you gave to each what he seemed most to need. Anyone who seeks testimony to all this might reasonably call your friends to witness, but if he does not know your friends, the facts themselves are sufficient to demonstrate the policy of your whole life.

Yet I must postpone the description of your personal qualities and go on to speak of your achievements. The Persians in the past

1. Gyges 2. At Nicomedia, 337 3. Isocrates, *Evagoras*, 1

conquered the whole of Asia, subjugated a great part of Europe, and had embraced in their hopes, I may almost say, the whole inhabited world, when the Macedonians deprived them of their supremacy, and they provided Alexander's generalship with a task, or rather with a toy. But they could not endure the yoke of slavery, and no sooner was Alexander dead, than they revolted from his successors and once more opposed their power to the Macedonians with such success that, when we took over what was left of the Macedonian Empire, we counted them to the end as foes with whom we must reckon. I need not remind you now of ancient history, of Antony and Crassus,[1] who were generals with the fullest powers, or tell how after long-continued dangers we succeeded in wiping out the disgrace they incurred, and how many a prudent general retrieved their blunders. Nor need I recall the second chapter of our misfortunes and the exploits of Carus[2] that followed, when following those failures he was appointed general. Among those who sat on the throne before your father's time, imposing on the Persians conditions of peace admired and welcomed by all, did not the Cæsar[3] incur a disgraceful defeat when he attacked them on his own account? It was not until the ruler of the whole world[4] turned his attention to them, directing there all the forces of the Empire, occupying all the passes with his troops and levies of hoplites, both veterans and new recruits, and employing every sort of military equipment, that fear drove them to accept terms of peace. That peace they somehow contrived to disturb and break during your father's lifetime, but they escaped punishment at his hands because he died in the midst of preparations for a campaign. It was left for you later on to punish them for their audacity.

I shall often have to speak of your campaigns against them, but this one thing I ask my hearers to observe. You became master of a third of the Empire,[5] that part in fact which seemed by no means strong enough to carry on a war, since it had neither arms nor troops in the field, nor any of those military resources which ought to flow abundantly in preparation for so important a war. Then, too, your brothers, for whatever reason, did nothing to make the war easier for you. Yet there is no detractor so shameless and

1. Defeated at Carrhæ in 53 B.C.; the Roman standards were recovered by Octavian

2. Emperor, 282-3

3. Galerius Maximianus, son-in-law of Diocletian, was defeated in Mesopotamia in 296 by Narses

4. Diocletian 5. The Eastern provinces, including Constantinople

so envious as not to admit that the harmony existing between the three of you was mainly due to you. The war in itself presented peculiar difficulties, in my opinion, and the troops were disaffected owing to the change of government; they raised the cry that they missed their old leader and they wished to control your actions. Indeed, a thousand strange and perplexing circumstances arose on every hand to render your hopes regarding the war more difficult to realise. The Armenians, our ancient allies, revolted, and no small part of them went over to the Persians, overrunning and raiding the country on their borders. In this crisis there seemed to be but one hope of safety, that you should take charge of affairs and plan the campaign; alas, it was impossible at that moment, for you were in Pæonia making treaties with your brothers. Thus you went in person, and so managed that no opening was given for criticism. Indeed, I almost forgot to mention the very first of your deeds, the noblest of all, or at any rate equal to the noblest. For there is no greater proof of your prudence and magnanimity than the fact that, in planning for interests of such importance, you thought it no disadvantage if you should, of your own free will, concede the lion's share to your brothers. Imagine, for instance, a man dividing among his brothers their father's estate of a hundred talents, or, if you prefer, twice as much. Then suppose him to have been content with fifty *minæ* less than the others, and to raise no objection, because he secured their goodwill in exchange for that trifling sum. You would think he deserved all praise and respect as one who had a soul above money, as far-sighted, in short, as a man of honour. Yet here is one whose policy with regard to the Empire of the world seems to have been so high-minded, so prudent, that, without increasing the burdens of administration, he willingly gave up some of the imperial revenues in order to secure harmony and peace among all Roman citizens. What praise such a man deserves! Certainly one cannot, in this connection, quote the saying "well done, but a bad bargain". Nothing, in my opinion, can be called a good bargain if it be not honourable as well. In general, if anyone wish to apply the test of expediency alone, he ought not to make money his criterion or reckon up his revenues from estates, like those old misers whom writers of comedy bring on to the stage, but he should take into account the vastness of the Empire and the point of honour involved. If the Emperor had disputed about the boundaries and taken a hostile attitude, he might have obtained more than he did, but he would have governed only his allotted share. Only he scorned and despised such trifles, and the result was that he actually governed the whole world in partnership with his brothers, but had the care of his own portion only; thus, while he kept his dignity unimpaired, he had less than his share of the toil and trouble that go with such a position.

On that subject, however, I shall have a chance later to speak in more detail. This is perhaps the right moment to describe how you controlled the situation, encompassed as you were, after your father's death, by so many perils and difficulties of all sorts – confusion, an unavoidable war, numerous hostile raids, allies in revolt, lack of discipline in the garrisons, and all the other harassing conditions of the hour. You concluded in perfect accord the negotiations with your brothers, and when the time had arrived that demanded your aid for the dangerous crisis of affairs, you made forced marches, and immediately after leaving Pæonia appeared in Syria. Though to relate how you did this would tax my powers of description, and indeed for those who know the facts their own experience is enough. Yet who in the world could describe adequately how, at the prospect of your arrival, everything was changed and improved all at once, so that we were set free from the fears that hung over us and could entertain brighter hopes than ever for the future? Even before you were actually on the spot, the mutiny among the garrisons ceased and order was restored. The Armenians who had gone over to the enemy at once changed sides again, for you ejected from the country and sent to Rome those who were responsible for the governor's exile,[1] and you secured for the exiles a safe return to their own country. You were so merciful to those who now came to Rome as exiles, and so kind in your dealings with those who returned from exile with the governor, that the former did, indeed, bewail their misfortune in having revolted, while still being better pleased with their present condition than with their previous usurpation. Whereas the latter, who were formerly in exile, declared that the experience had been a lesson in prudence, but that now they were receiving a worthy reward for their loyalty. On the returned exiles you lavished such magnificent presents and rewards that they could not even resent the good fortune of their bitterest enemies, nor begrudge their being duly honoured. All these difficulties you quickly settled, and then by means of embassies you turned the marauding Arabs against our

1. Julian is alluding to the interregnum (337-341) of the Armenian kings Tiranus and his son, Arsaces.

enemies. Then you began preparations for the war, about which I may as well say a few words.

The previous period of peace had relaxed the labours of the troops, and lightened the burdens of those who had to perform public services. The war, however, called for money, provisions, and supplies on a vast scale, and even more it demanded endurance, energy, and military experience on the part of the troops. In the almost entire absence of all these, you personally provided and organised everything, drilled those who had reached the age for military service, put together a force of cavalry to match the enemy's, and issued orders for the infantry to persevere in their training. Nor did you confine yourself to speeches and giving orders, but you yourself trained and drilled with the troops, showed them their duty by actual example, and straightaway made them experts in the art of war. Then you discovered ways and means, not by increasing the tribute or the extraordinary contributions, as the Athenians did in their day, when they raised these to double or even more. You were content, I understand, with the original revenues, except in cases where, for a short time, and to meet an emergency, it was necessary that the people should find their services to the state more expensive. The troops under your leadership were abundantly supplied, yet not so as to cause the satiety that leads to insolence; nor, on the other hand, were they driven to insubordination from lack of necessities.

I shall say nothing about your great array of arms, horses, river-boats, engines of war, and the like. Thus when all was ready and the time had come to make appropriate use of all that I have mentioned, the Tigris was bridged by rafts at many points and forts were built to guard the river. Meanwhile, the enemy never once ventured to defend their country from plunder, and every useful thing that they possessed was brought in to us. This was partly because they were afraid to offer battle, partly because those who were rash enough to do so were punished on the spot. This is a mere summary of your invasions of the enemy's country. Who, indeed, in a short speech could do justice to every event, or reckon up the enemy's disasters and our successes? But this at least I have space to tell. You often crossed the Tigris with your army and spent a long time in the enemy's country, but you always returned crowned with the laurels of victory. Then you visited the cities you had freed, and bestowed on them peace and plenty; all possible blessings and all at once. Thus at your hands they received what they had so long desired:

the defeat of the Barbarians and the erection of trophies of victory over the treachery and cowardice of the Parthians. Treachery they had displayed when they violated the treaties and broke the peace; cowardice when they lacked the courage to fight for their country and all that they held dear.

Lest anyone should suppose that, while I delight in recalling exploits like these, I avoid mentioning occasions when luck gave the enemy the advantage – or rather, it was the nature of the ground combined with opportunity that turned the scale – and that I do so because they brought us no honour or glory but only disgrace, I will try to give a brief account of those incidents also, not adapting my narrative with an eye to my own interests, but preferring the truth in every case. For when a man deliberately disregards the truth, he cannot escape the reproach of flattery, and, moreover, he inflicts on the object of his panegyric the appearance of not deserving the praise that he receives on other accounts. This is a mistake of which I shall beware. Indeed, my speech will make it clear that in no case has fiction been preferred to the truth. Now, I am well aware that all would say that the battle we fought before Singara[1] was a most important victory for the Barbarians. Yet I should answer and with just reason that this battle inflicted equal loss on both armies, but proved also that your valour could accomplish more than their luck; for the legions under you were violent and reckless men, and were not accustomed, like the enemy, to the climate and the stifling heat. I shall relate exactly what took place.

It was still the height of summer, and the legions mustered long before noon. Since the enemy were awestruck by the discipline, equipment, and calm bearing of our troops, while to us they seemed amazing in numbers, neither side began the battle. While they shrank from coming to close quarters with forces so well equipped, we waited for them to begin, so that in all respects we might seem to be acting rather in self-defence, and not to be responsible for beginning hostilities after the peace. At last, however, the leader[2] of the Barbarian army, raised high on their shields, perceived the magnitude of our forces drawn up in line. What a change came over him! What exclamations he uttered! He cried out that he had been betrayed, that it was the fault of those who had persuaded him to go to war, and so decided that the only thing to be done was to flee with all speed. To that end, one course alone would secure his safety, namely to cross, before we could reach it, the river which is

1. In Mesopotamia, 344 2. Shapur

the ancient boundary line between that country and ours. With this purpose he first gave the signal for a retreat in good order, then gradually increasing his pace he finally took to headlong flight, with only a small following of cavalry, leaving his whole army to the leadership of his son and the friend in whom he had most confidence. When our men saw this they were enraged that the Barbarians should escape all punishment for their audacious conduct; they clamoured to be led in pursuit, chafed at your order to halt, and ran after the enemy in full armour with their utmost energy and speed. For of your generalship they had had no experience so far, and they could not believe that you were a better judge than they of what was expedient. Moreover, under your father they had fought many battles and had always been victorious, a fact that tended to make them think themselves invincible. Yet they were most of all elated by the terror that the Parthians now showed, thinking of how they had fought, not only against the enemy, but against the very nature of the ground, and if any greater obstacle met them from some fresh quarter, they felt that they would overcome it as well. Accordingly, they ran at full speed for about one hundred stades, and only halted when they came up to the Parthians, who had fled for shelter into a fort that they had lately built to serve as a camp. It was, by this time, evening, and they engaged battle forthwith. Our men at once took the fort and slew its defenders. Once inside the fortifications, they displayed great bravery for a long time, though they were by this point fainting with thirst. When they found cisterns of water inside, they spoiled a glorious victory and gave the enemy a chance to retrieve their defeat. This, then, was the issue of that battle, which caused us the loss of only three or four of our men, whilst the Parthians lost the heir to the throne[1] who had previously been taken prisoner, together with all his escort. While all this was going on, of the leader of the Barbarians not even the ghost was to be seen, nor did he stay his flight till he had put the river behind him. You, on the other hand, did not take off your armour for a whole day and night, one moment sharing the struggles of those who were getting the upper hand, the next giving prompt and efficient aid to those who were hard-pressed. By your bravery and fortitude you so changed the face of the battle that at break of day the enemy were glad to beat a safe retreat to their own territory, and even the wounded, escorted by you, could retire from the battle. Thus did you relieve them all

1. Shapur's son, Narseh

from the risks of flight. Now what fort was taken by the enemy? What city did they besiege? What military supplies did they capture that should give them something to boast about after the war?

Perhaps someone will say that to never come off worse than the enemy must indeed be considered good fortune and felicity, but to make a stand against fortune calls for greater vigour and is a proof of greater valour. Is a man a skilful pilot because he can steer his ship in fair weather when the sea is absolutely calm? Would you call a charioteer an expert driver who on smooth and level ground has in harness horses that are gentle, quiet and swift, and under such conditions gives a display of his art? How much more skilful is the pilot who marks and perceives beforehand the coming storm and tries to avoid its path, then, if for any reason he must face it, brings away his ship safe and sound, cargo and all? Just so, the skilful charioteer is he who can contend against the unevenness of the ground, and guide his horses and control them at the same time, should they grow restive. In short, it is not fair to judge of skill of any sort when it is aided by fortune, but one must examine it independently. Cleon was not a better general than Nicias because he was fortunate in the affair of Pylos, and the same may be said of all whose success is due to luck rather than to good judgement. Yet if I did not claim that your fortune was both better and more deserved than that of your opponents, or rather of all men, I should with reason be thought to do it an injustice, since it prevented the enemy from even perceiving their advantage. For, in my opinion, an impartial judge of my narrative ought to ascribe our reverse to the extreme and insupportable conditions; the fact that you inflicted loss on the enemy equal to ours, he would regard as achieved by your valour; that, though they were aware of their losses, they took no account of their success, he would regard as brought about by your good fortune.

That I may not, by saying more on this subject, spend time that belongs to more important affairs, I will try to describe next the multitude of difficulties that beset us, the magnitude of our perils, and how you faced them all, and not only routed the numerous following of the usurpers, but the Barbarian forces as well.

About six years had passed since the war I have just described, the winter being nearly over, when a messenger arrived with the news[1] that Galatia had gone over to the usurper, that a plot had been made to assassinate your brother and had been carried out,

1. cf. Demosthenes, *De Corona*, 169

that Italy and Sicily had been occupied, and lastly that the Illyrian garrisons were in revolt and had proclaimed their general[1] emperor, though for a time he had been inclined to resist what seemed to be the irresistible onset of the usurpers.[2] Indeed, he himself kept imploring you to send money and men to his aid, as though he were terribly afraid on his own account of being overpowered by them. For a while he kept protesting that he would do his duty, that for his part he had no pretensions to the throne, but would faithfully guard and protect it for you. Such were his assertions, but it was not long before his treachery came to light and he received his punishment, tempered though it was with mercy. On learning these facts, you thought you ought not to waste your time in idleness to no purpose. The cities of Syria you stocked with engines of war, garrisons, food supplies, and equipment of other kinds, considering that, by these measures, you would, though absent, sufficiently protect the inhabitants, while you were planning to set out in person against the usurpers.

Yet ever since the last campaign the Persians had been watching for just such an opportunity, and had planned to conquer Syria by a single invasion. So they mustered all forces, every age, sex, and condition, and marched against us, men and mere boys, old men and crowds of women and slaves, who followed not merely to assist in the war, but in vast numbers beyond what was needed. For it was their intention to reduce the cities, and once masters of the country, to bring in colonists in spite of us. But the magnitude of your preparations made it manifest that their expectations were but vanity. They began the siege and completely surrounded the city[3] with dykes, then the river Mygdonius flowed in and flooded the ground about the walls, as they say the Nile floods Egypt. The siege-engines were brought up against the ramparts on boats, and their plan was that one force should sail to attack the walls while the other kept shooting on the city's defenders from the mounds. The garrison, however, made a stout defence of the city from the walls. The whole place was filled with corpses, wreckage, armour, and missiles, of which some were just sinking, while others, after sinking from the violence of the first shock, floated on the waters. A vast number of Barbarian shields and also ship's benches, as a result of the collisions of the siege-engines on the ships, drifted on the surface. The mass of floating weapons almost covered the whole surface between the wall and the mounds. The lake was

1. Vetranio 3. Demosthenes, *De Corona*, 61 4. Nisibis

turned to gore, and all about the walls echoed the groans of the Barbarians, slaying not, but being slain[1] in manifold ways and by all manner of wounds.

Who could find suitable words to describe all that was done there? They hurled fire down on to the shields, and many of the hoplites fell half-burned, while others who fled from the flames could not escape the danger from the missiles. Though some, while still swimming, were wounded in the back and sank to the bottom, while others who jumped from the siege-engines were hit before they touched the water, and so found not safety indeed but an easier death. As for those who knew not how to swim, and perished more obscurely than those just mentioned, who would attempt to name or number them? Time would fail me did I desire to recount all this in detail. It is enough that you should hear the sum of the matter. On that day the sun beheld a battle the like of which no man had ever known before. These events exposed the historic boasting of the Medes as only empty conceit. Till then, men had hardly believed that Xerxes could have had so huge an armament, seeing that for all its size its fate was so shameful and ignominious; but these events made the fact clearer to us than things long familiar and obvious. Xerxes tried to sail and march by fighting against the laws of nature, and, as he thought, overcame the nature of the sea and of the dry land; yet he proved to be no match for the wisdom and endurance of a Greek whose soldiers had not been bred in the school of luxury, nor learned to be slaves, but knew how to obey and to use their energies like free-born men. That man,[2] however, though he had no such vast armament as Xerxes, was even more insensate, and outdid the Aloadæ in his infatuation, almost as if he had conceived the idea of overwhelming the city with the mountain[3] that was nearby. Then he turned the currents of rivers against its walls and undermined them, but even when the city had lost its walls he could not succeed in taking it, so even that triumph he could not boast of, as Xerxes did when he set fire to Athens. So, after spending four months, he retreated with an army that had lost many thousands. Thus he who had always seemed to be invincible was glad to keep the peace, and to use as a bulwark for his own safety the fact that you had no time to spare and that our own affairs were in confusion.

Such were the trophies and victories that you left behind you in Asia as you led your troops to Europe in perfect condition, determined to fill the whole world with the monuments of your

1. cf. *The Iliad*, IV, 451 2. Shapur 3. *The Odyssey*, VIII, 49

victories. Even if I had nothing more wonderful to relate about you, what I have said is enough to demonstrate that in good sense and energy you surpass all those in the past whose fortune was the same as yours. Indeed, to have repulsed the whole strength of Persia and remain unscathed, not to have lost so much as a soldier from the ranks, much less a town or fort, and finally to have brought the siege to so brilliant and unprecedented a conclusion – what achievement from the past, I ask, could one compare with this? The Carthaginians were famous for their daring in the face of danger, but they ended in disaster. The siege of Platæa shed lustre on its citizens, but all that their valour could do for those unhappy men was to make their misfortunes more widely known. What need to quote Messene or Pylos, since there the defeated did not make a brave defence nor was a vigorous assault necessary to subdue them? As for the Syracusans, they had their famous man of science[1] to aid them against the armaments of Rome and our illustrious general,[2] but what did he avail them in the end? Did they not fall more ignominiously than the rest, and were only spared to be a glorious monument of their conqueror's clemency? Though if I wished to reckon up all the states that could not withstand armaments inferior to their own, how many volumes do you think would suffice? Rome, however, I ought perhaps to mention, because long ago she had just such a fortune, by which I mean when the Galatians and Celts[3] conspired together, and without warning poured down upon the city like a winter torrent.[4] The citizens occupied the famous hill[5] on which stands the statue of Jupiter. There they entrenched themselves with wicker barricades and such like defences, as though with a wall, while the enemy offered no hindrance nor ventured to approach to attack at close quarters, and so they won the day.

It is with this siege that the recent one may well be compared, at least in the issue of its fortunes, for the actual occurrences could not be paralleled in all history. For who ever heard of surrounding a city with water, and from without throwing hills about it like nets, then hurling at it, like a siege-engine, a river that flowed in a steady stream and broke against its walls, or of fighting like that which took place in the water and about the wall where it had collapsed? For my purpose, this is, as I said, evidence enough. Yet what remains to tell is far more awe-inspiring. Perhaps, since I have undertaken to record, as far as possible, all that you accomplished, it is not

1. Archimedes 2. Marcellus, 212 B.C. 3. i.e., Gauls
4. 390 B.C. led by Brennus 5. The Capitoline

fair to break off my narrative at the point where you were at the very height of your activity. For even while you were occupied by the interests I have just described, you arranged your affairs in Europe, dispatching embassies, allocating funds, and sending out the legions that were garrisoning Pæonia against the Scythians, all of which was with the intention of preventing that feeble old man[1] from being overpowered by the usurper.[2] Though how could one, with the best will in the world, present all this in a short speech?

No sooner had you set out for the seat of war, than this very man, who had all along protested that he would loyally continue to guard your interests, and though you had reinforced him with money, troops, and everything of the sort, was driven to folly and madness by I know not what malevolent spirit. He came to terms with the most execrable of mankind, the common enemy of all who care for peace and cherish harmony above all things, and more particularly your enemy for personal reasons. Yet you were undismayed by the magnitude of his preparations, nor would you admit that a conspiracy of traitors could overreach your own wise purpose. One[3] of the pair you justly accused of treason, the other[4] of infamous crimes besides, and deeds of lawless violence, thus you summoned the former to trial and judgement before the legions, the latter you decided to leave to the arbitrament of war. Then he met you face to face, that honourable and prudent old man, who used to change his opinions more easily than any child, and, though he had begged for them, forgot all your favours as soon as the need had passed. He arrived with his phalanxes of hoplites and squadrons of cavalry, intending to compel, if he could not persuade you, to take no action and return the way you came. When you saw this man, then, who had protested that he would continue to be your ally and general, playing an enemy's part and claiming an equal share of your Empire, you were not at all dismayed, though his troops outnumbered yours. For you had not brought your whole force with you, since you decided that to fight it out with such odds against you might be courageous but was in every way hazardous, even if you won the battle, because of that other savage usurper[5] who was lying in wait for a favourable opportunity[6] when you should be in difficulties. You therefore made a wise decision in preferring to achieve success single-handed, mounting the platform with him who for the moment was your colleague in empire. He was escorted

1. Vetranio 2. Magnentius 3. Vetranio 4. Magnentius
5. ibid. 6. Demosthenes, *De Chersoneso*, 42

by a whole host of hoplites with glittering weapons,[1] presenting drawn swords and spears, a sight to make a coward shake with fear, though it inspired and roused one as brave and gallant as yourself.

Now, when first you began to speak, silence fell on the whole army and every man strained his ears to hear. Many shed tears and raised their hands to heaven, though even this they did in silence, so as to be unobserved. Some again showed their affection in their faces, but all showed it by their intense eagerness to hear your words. When your speech reached its climax, they were carried away by enthusiasm and burst into applause, then eager to miss no word they became quiet again. Finally, won by your arguments, they hailed you as their only Emperor, demanded that you alone should rule the whole Empire, and bade you lead them against your adversary, promising to follow you and imploring you to take back the imperial insignia. However, you thought it beneath you to stretch out your hand for them or to take them by force. Then against his will and with reluctance, but yielding at last to what is called Thessalian persuasion,[2] he took off the purple robe and offered it to you. What a heroic figure yours was then, when, in a single day, you became master of all those races, those legions, all that wealth, when you stripped of his power and took prisoner one who, if not yet in intention, had shown that he was your enemy.

Did you not behave more nobly and more generously to him than Cyrus did to his own grandfather? For you deprived your enemy's followers of nothing, but protected their privileges and, I understand, gave many of them gifts besides. Who saw you despondent before your triumph or unduly elated after it? Orator, general, virtuous Emperor, distinguished soldier, though men give you all these titles, how can any praise of ours be adequate? Long had the orator's platform been wholly disconnected from the general's functions.[3] Further, it was reserved for you to combine them once more in your person, in this surely following the example of Odysseus, Nestor, and the Roman generals who sacked Carthage; for these men were always even more formidable to wrong-doers whom they attacked from the platform than to the enemy in the field of battle. Indeed, I pay all the homage due to the forcible eloquence of Demosthenes and his imitators, but when I consider the conditions of your harangue, I can never admit that there is any comparison between your theatre and theirs. For they never had to

1. Euripides, *Andromache*, 1146 2. A proverb for necessity disguised as a choice
3. Æschines, *Ctesiphon*, 74.18

address an audience of hoplites, nor had they such great interests at stake, but only money, or honour, or reputation, or friends whom they had undertaken to assist. Yet when the citizens clamoured in dissent, they often, I believe, left the platform pale and trembling, like generals who prove to be cowards when they have to face the enemy in battle-line. Indeed, from all history it would be impossible to cite an achievement as great as yours when you acquired control of all those races by judicial pleading alone; and, moreover, you had to make out your case against a man by no means to be despised, as many people think, but one who had won distinction in many campaigns, who was full of years, who had the reputation of experience gained in a long career, and had for a considerable period been in command of the legions there present. What overwhelming eloquence that must have been! How truly did "persuasion sit on your lips"[1] with the power to "leave a sting" in the souls of that motley crowd of men, and to win you a victory that in importance rivals any that were ever achieved by force of arms; only that yours was stainless and unalloyed, and was more like the act of a priest going to the temple of his god than of an emperor going to war. It is certainly true that the Persians have a similar example to quote, but it falls far short of what you did, by which I mean that on their father's death, the sons of Darius quarrelled about the succession to the throne and appealed to justice rather than arms to arbitrate their case. Between you and your brothers, however, there never arose any dispute, either in word or deed, not even one, for it was in fact more agreeable to you to share the responsibility with them than to be the sole ruler of the world. Yet your quarrel was with one who, though his actions had not so far been impious or criminal, was shown to have a treasonable purpose, and you brought proofs to make that treason manifest.

After your harangue, there followed a brilliant campaign and a war truly sacred, though it was not on behalf of sacred territory, like the Phocian war. That, we are told, was waged[2] in the days of our ancestors to avenge the laws, the constitution, and the slaughter of countless citizens, some of whom the usurper[3] had put to death, while others he was just about to kill or was trying to arrest. It was really as though he was afraid that otherwise he might be considered, for all his vices, a Roman citizen instead of a genuine Barbarian. As for his crimes against your house, though they were

1. From the description of the oratory of Pericles, Eupolis, fr. 94

2. Demosthenes, *De Corona*, 230 3. Magnentius

quite as flagrant as his outrages against the state, you thought it became you to devote less attention to them. So true it is, that, then as now, you rated the common wealth higher than your private interests.

I need not mention all the usurper's offences against the community and against individuals. He assassinated his own master – for he had actually been the slave of the murdered emperor's ancestors, a miserable remnant saved from the spoils of Germany. Then he aimed at ruling over us, he who had not even the right to call himself free, had you not granted him the privilege. Those in command of the legions he imprisoned and put to death, while to the common soldiers he behaved with such abject servility and deference that he ruined their discipline. Then he enacted those fine laws of his, including a property tax of fifty percent, and threatened the disobedient with death, while any slave who pleased might inform against his master. Then he compelled those who did not want it to purchase the imperial property. Though time would fail me were I to tell of all his crimes and of the vast proportions that his tyranny had assumed. As for the armament which he had collected to use against the Barbarians but actually employed against us, who could give you an adequate report of its strength? There were Celts and Galatians who had seemed invincible even to our ancestors, having so often poured down on the Italians and Illyrians like a winter torrent that sweeps all before it,[1] and, following up their repeated victories on the field of battle, had even invaded Asia, eventually became our subjects because they had no choice. They had been enrolled in the ranks of our armies and furnished levies that won a brilliant reputation, being enlisted by your ancestors, and, later, by your father. Then, since they enjoyed the blessings of long-continued peace, and their country increased in wealth and population, they furnished your brothers with considerable levies, and finally, by compulsion, not choice, they all in a body took part in the usurper's campaign. The most enthusiastic of his followers were, in virtue of their ties of kinship, the Franks and Saxons, the most warlike of the tribes who live beyond the Rhine and on the shores of the western sea. Since every city and fortified site on the banks of the Rhine was shorn of its garrison, that whole region was left with no defence against the Barbarians, and all that splendidly organised army was dispatched against us. Every town in Galatia[2] was like a camp preparing for war.

---

1. Demosthenes, *De Corona*, 153   2. Pannonia, 353

Nothing was to be seen but weapons of battle and forces of cavalry, infantry, archers, and javelin men. When these allies of the usurper began to pour into Italy from all quarters, and there joined the troops who had been enrolled long before, there was no one so bold as not to feel terror and dismay at the tempest that threatened. It seemed to all as though a thunderbolt had fallen from the Alps, a bolt that no action could avert, no words describe. It struck terror into the Illyrians, the Pæonians, the Thracians, the Scythians; the dwellers in Asia believed it was directed entirely against themselves, and even the Persians began to get ready to oppose it in their country's defence. Yet the usurper thought his task was easy, that he would have little difficulty in baffling your wisdom and energy, and so had already fixed his covetous gaze on the wealth of India and the magnificence of Persia. To such an excess of folly and rashness had he come, and after a success wholly insignificant, meaning the affair of the scouts whom, while they were unprotected by the main army, he ambushed and cut in pieces. So true it is that when fools meet with undeserved success,[1] they often find it is but the prelude to greater misfortunes. Thus, elated by this stroke of luck, he left the fortified posts that protected the Italian frontier, and marched towards the Norici and the Pæonians, taking no precautions because he thought that speed would serve him better than force of arms or courage.

The moment that you learned this, you led your army out of the narrow and dangerous passes, whereupon he followed in pursuit, as he thought, unaware that he was being out-generalled, until you both reached open country. When the plains before Myrsa were in sight, the cavalry of both armies were drawn up on the wings, while the infantry formed the centre. Then your Majesty kept the river on your right, and, outflanking the enemy with your left, you at once turned and broke his phalanx, which indeed had from the first the wrong formation, being drawn up by one who knew nothing of war or strategy. Then he who so far had thought he was the pursuer did not even join battle, taking instead to headlong flight, dismayed by the clash of weapons; he could not even listen without trembling when the legions shouted their battle-song. His ranks had been thrown into disorder, but the soldiers formed into companies and renewed the battle. For they disdained to be seen in flight, and to give an example in their own persons of what had hitherto been inconceivable to all men, that is, a Celtic or Galatian

1. Demosthenes, *Olynthiac*, 1.23

soldier turning his back to the enemy. The Barbarians too, who, if defeated, could not hope to make good their retreat, were resolved either to conquer, or not to perish till they had severely punished their opponents. Just see the extraordinary daring of the usurper's troops in the face of dangers and their great eagerness to come to close quarters!

Our men, on the other hand, had so far carried all before them and were anxious to retain the good opinion of their comrades and of the Emperor. They were, moreover, emboldened by their successes in the past and by the almost incredible brilliance of their exploits in this very engagement, thus, ambitious as they were to end the day as gloriously as they had begun it, cheerfully encountered toil and danger. So they charged again as though the battle had only just begun, and gave a wonderful display of daring and heroism. For some hurled themselves full on the enemy's swords, or seized the enemy's shields; others, when their horses were wounded and the riders thrown, at once transformed themselves into hoplites. The usurper's army meanwhile did the same and pressed our infantry hard. Neither side gained the advantage until the heavy cavalry, by their archery, aided by the remaining force of cavalry who spurred on their horses to the charge, had begun to inflict great loss on the enemy, and by main force to drive the whole army before them. Some directed their flight to the plain, and of these a few were saved just in time by the approach of night. The rest were flung into the river, crowded together like a herd of oxen or brutish beasts. Thus did the usurper's army reap the fruits of his cowardice, while their valour availed him nothing.

The trophy that you set up for that victory was far more brilliant than your father's. He led an army that had always proved itself invincible, and with it conquered a miserable old man.[1] While the tyranny that you suppressed was flourishing and had reached its height, partly through the crimes that had been committed, but still more because so many of the youth were on that side, and you took the field against it with legions that had been trained by yourself. What emperor can one cite from the past who first planned and then reproduced so admirable a type of cavalry, and such equipment? First you trained yourself to wear them, and then you taught others how to use such weapons so that none could

1. Licinius, former *Augusti* of the eastern provinces; his rivalry with Constantine ended with defeat and execution at the hands of Julian's uncle

withstand them. This is a subject on which many have ventured to speak, but have failed to do it justice, so much so that those who heard their description, and later had the good fortune to see for themselves, decided that their eyes must accept what their ears had refused to credit. Your cavalry was almost unlimited in numbers and they all sat their horses like statues, while their limbs were fitted with armour that followed closely the outline of the human form. It covers the arms from wrist to elbow and thence to the shoulder, while a coat of mail protects the shoulders, back, and chest. The head and face are covered by a metal mask which makes its wearer look like a glittering statue, for not even the thighs and legs, or the very ends of the feet lack this armour. It is attached to the cuirass by fine chain-armour like a web, so that no part of the body is visible or uncovered, for this woven covering protects the hands as well, and is so flexible that the wearers can bend even their fingers. All this I desire to represent in words as vividly as I can, but it is beyond my powers, and I can only ask those who wish to know more about this armour to see it with their own eyes, and not merely to listen to my description.

Now that I have told the story of this first campaign, which was fought at the end of the autumn, shall I here break off my narrative? Or is it altogether unfair to withhold the end and issue of your achievements from those who are eager to hear? Winter overtook us and gave the usurper a chance to escape punishment. Then followed a splendid proclamation worthy of your imperial generosity. An amnesty was granted to those who had taken sides with the usurper, except when they had shared the guilt of those infamous murders. Therefore, those who had never hoped even to see again anything that they held dear, recovered their houses, money, and native land. Then you welcomed the fleet which arrived from Italy, bringing thence many citizens who, no doubt, had fled from the usurper's savage cruelty. When the occasion demanded that you should take the field, you again menaced the usurper. He, however, took cover in the fastnesses of Italy and hid his army away there in the mountains, in the manner of wild beasts, and never even dared to carry on the war beneath the open heavens. Yet he betook himself to the neighbouring town[1] which is devoted to pleasure and high living, and spent his time in public shows and sensual pleasures, believing that the impassable mountains alone would suffice for his safety. Moreover, intemperate as he was by

1. Aquileia

nature, he thought it clear gain to be able to indulge his appetites at so dangerous a crisis. Evidently, he placed too much confidence in the safety of his position, for the town is cut off from that part of Italy by a natural rampart of mountains, except the half that is bound by a shoaling sea and which resembles the marshes of Egypt, making that part of the country inaccessible even to an invading fleet. It seems, however, as though nature herself will not devise any safeguard for the undisciplined and cowardly against the temperate and brave, for when prudence and courage advance hand in hand she makes everything give way before them. Long ago, she revealed to us those arts through which we have attained an abundance of what was once thought to be unattainable, and in the field of individual effort we see that what seemed impossible for many working together to achieve can be accomplished by a prudent man. And since by your own actions you demonstrated this fact, it is only fair, my Emperor, that you should accept my words to that effect.

For you conducted the campaign under the open skies, though there was a city of some importance near at hand, and, moreover, you encouraged your men to work hard and to take risks, not merely by giving orders, but by your own personal example. You discovered a path hitherto unknown to all, and sent forward a strong detachment of hoplites chosen from your whole army; then, when you had ascertained that they had come up with the enemy, you led forward your army in person, surrounded them, and defeated his whole force. This happened before dawn, and before noon the news was brought to the usurper. He was attending a horse-race at a festival, and was expecting nothing of what took place. How his attitude changed, what was his decision about the crisis, how he abandoned the town and in fact all Italy, and fled, thus beginning to expiate his murders and all his earlier crimes, it is not for this speech to relate. Yet though the respite he gained was so brief, he proceeded to act no less wickedly than in the past. So true is it that by the suffering of the body alone it is impossible for the wicked to cleanse their souls of evil. For when he reached Galatia, this ruler who was so righteous and law-abiding, so far surpassed his own former cruelty that he now bethought himself of all the ruthless and brutal modes of punishment which he had hitherto overlooked, deriving the most exquisite pleasure from the spectacle of the wretched citizens' suffering. He would bind them alive to chariots and, letting the teams gallop, order the drivers to drag them along while he stood by and gazed at their misery. In fact, he spent his whole time in amusements of this sort, until, like an Olympic victor, you threw him in the third encounter[1] and forced him to pay a fitting penalty for his infamous career, namely to thrust into his own breast that very sword which he had stained with the slaughter of so many citizens.[2] Never, in my opinion, was there a punishment more suitable or more just than this, nor one that gave greater satisfaction to all mankind, which, being liberated from such cruelty and harshness, at once began to exult in the good government that we enjoy to this day. Long may we continue to enjoy it, all-merciful providence!

I would fain recite every single one of your achievements, but you will with reason pardon me, most mighty Emperor, if I fall short of that ambition and omit to mention the naval armament against Carthage, which was equipped in Egypt and set sail from Italy to attack her; your conquest of the Pyrenees, against which you sent an army by sea; your successes against the Barbarians, which of late have been so frequent; and all such past triumphs as have not become a matter of common knowledge. For example, I often hear that even Antioch now calls herself by your name. Her existence she does indeed owe to her founder,[3] but her present wealth and gain in every sort of abundance she owes to you, as you provided her with harbours that offer good anchorage for visitors. For until then, it was considered a dangerous risk to even sail past Antioch; so full were all the waters of that coast, up to the very shores, of rocks and sunken reefs. I need not stop to mention the porticoes, fountains, and other things of the kind that you caused to be bestowed on Antioch by her governors. As to your benefactions to the city of your ancestors,[4] you built round it a wall that was then only begun, and all buildings that seemed to be unsound you restored and made safe for all time. But how could one reckon up all these things? Time will fail me if I try to tell everything separately.

The time has now come when it is proper to consider whether your career, so far as I have described it, is at every point in accord with virtue and the promptings of a noble disposition. For to this, as I said at the beginning of my speech, I think it right to pay special attention. Let me therefore mention once more what I said some time ago, that to your father you were dutiful and affectionate, and that you constantly maintained friendly relations with your brothers, for your father you were ever willing to obey, and as the

1. In wrestling, the third fall secured the victory 2. 355
3. Seleucus, son of Antiochus 4. Constantinople

colleague of your brothers in the Empire you always displayed moderation. If anyone thinks this a trifling proof of merit, let him consider the case of Alexander, the son of Philip, and Cyrus, the son of Cambyses, then let him applaud your conduct. For Alexander, while still a mere boy, showed clearly that he would no longer brook his father's control, while Cyrus dethroned his grandfather. Yet no one is so foolish as to suppose that, since you displayed such modesty and self-control towards your father and brothers, you were not fully equal to Alexander and Cyrus in greatness of soul and ambition for glory. For when fortune offered you the opportunity to claim as your right the Empire of the world, you were the first to make the essay, though there were many who advised otherwise and tried to persuade you to the contrary course. Accordingly, when you had carried through the war that you had in hand, and that with the utmost ease and so as to ensure safety for the future, you resolved to liberate that part of the Empire which had been occupied by the enemy. Furthermore, the reason that you assigned for going to war was most just, such as had never before arisen, namely your detestation of those infamous men. Civil war one could not call it, for its leader was a Barbarian who had proclaimed himself emperor and elected himself general. I dislike to speak too often of his terrible deeds and the crimes that he committed against your house. Yet could anything be more heroic than your line of action? For should you fail in your undertaking, the risk involved was obvious. Nonetheless, you faced it, and you were not bidding for gain, nor for undying renown, for whose sake brave men so often dare even to die, selling their lives for glory as though it were gold; nor was it from desire of a wider or more brilliant empire, for not even in your youth were you ambitious of that, rather, it was because you were taken with the worthiness of such an achievement, and thought it your duty to endure anything rather than see a Barbarian ruling over Roman citizens, making himself master of the laws and constitution and offering public prayers for the common wealth, guilty as he was of so many impious crimes and murders. Who could fail to be dazzled by the splendour of your armament and the vast scale of your expenditure? Yet I am told that Xerxes, when he mustered all Asia against the Greeks, spent no less than ten years in preparing for that war. Then he set out with twelve hundred triremes, from the very spot, as I understand, where you gathered your fleet together, having built it in less than ten months and comprising more ships than Xerxes.

Though neither his fortune nor his achievements can properly be compared with yours.

I fear that it is beyond my powers to describe the magnificence of your outlay for other purposes, nor will I risk being tedious by staying to count up the sums you bestowed on cities that had long been destitute. For whereas, in the time of your predecessors, they lacked the necessities of life, they have all become rich through you, and the general prosperity of each city increases the welfare of every private household in it. Moreover, it is proper that I should mention your gifts to private persons, and give you the title of a generous and open-handed Emperor. For since there were many who long ago had lost their property, because, in some cases justly, in others unjustly, their ancestral estates had suffered loss, you had no sooner come into power than, like a just judge, you set right in the latter cases the errors committed by men in the past, and restored them to the control of their property, while in the former cases you were a kindly arbiter, granting that they should recover what they had lost, thinking that to have suffered so long was punishment enough. Then you lavished large sums from your personal purse, and increased the reputation for wealth of many who even in the past had prided themselves on their large incomes. Though why should I remind you of all this and seem to waste time over trifles? Especially as it must be obvious to all that no king except Alexander, the son of Philip, was ever known to bestow such splendid presents on his friends. Indeed, some kings have thought that the wealth of their friends gave more grounds for suspicion and alarm than did the resources of their enemies, while others were jealous of the aristocrats among their subjects. The latter therefore persecuted the well-born in every possible way, or even exterminated their houses, being thus responsible for the public disasters of their cities and, in private life, for the most infamous crimes. There were some who went so far as to envy mere physical advantages, such as health or good looks, or good condition. As for a virtuous character among their subjects, they could not bear even to hear of it, but counted it a crime like murder, theft, or treason to appear to lay claim to virtue. Though perhaps someone will say, and with truth, that these were the actions and practices not of genuine kings but of base and contemptible tyrants. Indeed, but that other malady which has been known to attack not only those who were irrational, but some even who were just and mild, by which I mean the tendency to quarrel with friends who were too prosperous, to wish to humble them and deprive them of their rightful possessions – who, I ask, has ever dared so much as to mention such conduct in your case? Yet such, they say, was the treatment that Cyrus the Persian, the king's son-in-law, received from his kinsman[1] who could not tolerate the honour in which Cyrus was held by the common people. Agesilaus, also, is well known to have resented the honours paid to Lysander by the Ionians.

All these, then, you have surpassed in merit, for you have made their wealth more secure for the rich than a father would for his own children, and you take thought that your subjects shall be well-born, as though you were the founder and lawgiver of every single city. Those to whom fortune has been generous you still further enrich, and in many cases men owe all their wealth to your generosity, so that in amount your gifts clearly surpass those of other princes, while, in security of ownership of what has once been given, you cast into the shade any favours bestowed by democracies.[2] This, I think, is quite natural. For when men are conscious that they lack certain advantages, they envy those who do possess them, but when a man is more brilliantly endowed by fortune than any of his fellows, and by his own initiative has won even higher dignities than fate had assigned him, he lacks nothing, and there is none whom he need envy. Since you realise that in your case this is especially true, you rejoice at the good fortune of others and take pleasure in the successes of your subjects. You have already bestowed on them certain honours, beside other honours you are on the point of bestowing, and you are making plans for the benefit of yet other persons. Nor are you content to award to your friends the government of a single city or nation, or even of many such, with the honours attaching thereto. Yet unless you chose a colleague[3] to share that Empire on whose behalf you had spared no pains to exterminate the brood of usurpers, you thought that no act of yours could be worthy of your former achievements. That you reached this decision not so much because it was necessary as because you take pleasure in giving all that you have to give, is, I suppose, well known to all. For you chose no colleague to aid you in your contests with the usurpers, but you thought it right that one who had not shared in the toil should share in the honour and glory, and that only when all danger seemed to be over. It is well known that from that honour you subtract not even a trifling part, though you do not demand that he should share the danger even in some

1. Cyaxeres 2. Demosthenes, *Against Leptines*, 15 3. Gallus, 351, then Julian, 355

small degree, except indeed when it was necessary for a short time that he should accompany you on your campaign. Does my account of this call for any further witnesses or proofs? Surely it is obvious that he who tells the tale would not be the one to introduce a fictitious account. Though on this part of my subject I must not spend any more time.

A few words about your temperance, your wisdom, and the affection that you inspired in your subjects, will not, I think, be out of place. For who is there among all who does not know that from boyhood you cultivated the virtue of temperance as no one had ever done before you? That in your youth you possessed that virtue your father is a trustworthy witness, for he entrusted to you alone the management of affairs of state and all that related to your brothers, although you were not even the eldest of his sons. That you still display it, now that you are a man, we are all well aware, since you ever behave towards the people and the magistrates like a citizen who obeys the laws, not like a king who is above the laws. For who ever saw you made arrogant by prosperity? Who ever saw you uplifted by those successes, so numerous and so splendid, and so quickly achieved? They say that Philip's son, Alexander, when he had broken the power of Persia, not only adopted a more ostentatious mode of life and an insolence of manner disagreeable to all, but went so far as to despise the father that begat him, and indeed the whole of humanity. For he claimed to be regarded as the son of Ammon instead of the son of Philip, and when some of those who had taken part in his campaigns could not learn to flatter him or to be servile, he punished them more harshly than the prisoners of war. Whilst the honour that you paid to your father, need I speak of in this place? Not only did you revere him in private life, but constantly, where men were gathered together in public, you sang his praises as though he were a beneficent hero-god. As for your friends, you grant them that honour not merely in name, but by your actions you make their title sure. Can any one of them, I ask, lay to your charge the loss of any right, any penalty or injury suffered, or any overbearing act either serious or trifling? Indeed there is not one who could bring any such accusation. For your friends who were far advanced in years remained in office till the appointed end of their lives, and only laid down with life itself their control of public business, then they handed on their possessions to their children, or friends, or another member of their family. Others again, when their strength failed for work or military service, received an honourable discharge, and are now spending their last days in prosperity; yet others have departed this life, and the people call them blessed. In short, there is no man who having once been held worthy of the honour of your friendship ever suffered any punishment, great or small, even if later he proved to be vicious. For him, all that he need do was depart and give no further trouble.

While this has been your character from first to last in all these relations, you always kept your soul pure of every indulgence to which the least reproach is attached. In fact, I should say that you alone, of all the Emperors that ever were, of all mankind almost, with very few exceptions, are the fairest example of modesty, not to men only but to women, also, in their association with men. For all that is forbidden to women by the laws that safeguard the legitimacy of offspring, your reason ever denies to your passions. Though I could say still more on this subject, I shall refrain.

Your wisdom is by no means easy to praise as it deserves, but I must say a few words about it. Your actions, however, are more convincing, I think, than my words. For it is not likely that this great and mighty Empire would have attained such dimensions or achieved such splendid results, had it not been directed and governed by an intelligence to match. Indeed, when it is entrusted to luck alone, unaided by wisdom, we may be thankful if it last for any length of time. It is easy by depending on luck to flourish for a brief space, but without the aid of wisdom it is very hard, or rather, I might say impossible, to preserve the blessings that have been bestowed. In short, if we need cite a convincing proof of this, we do not lack many notable instances. For by wise counsel we mean the ability to discover most successfully the measures that will be good and expedient when put into practice. It is therefore proper to consider in every case whether this wise counsel may not be counted as one of the things you have achieved. Certainly, when there was need of harmony you gladly gave way, and when it was your duty to aid the community as a whole, you declared for war with the utmost readiness. When, moreover, you had defeated the forces of Persia without losing a single hoplite, you made two separate campaigns against the usurpers, and after overcoming one of them[1] by your public harangue, you added to your army his forces, which were fresh and had suffered no losses. Then, finally, by intelligence rather than by brute force, you completely subdued the other usurper who had inflicted so many sufferings on the

1. Vetranio

community. I now desire to speak more clearly on this subject and to demonstrate to all what it was that you chiefly relied on, securing you from failure in every one of those great enterprises to which you devoted yourself. It is your conviction that the affection of his subjects is the surest defence of an emperor. Now, it is the height of absurdity to try to win that affection by giving orders, and levying it as though it were a tax or tribute. The only alternative is the policy that you have yourself pursued, that is, of doing good to all men and imitating the divine nature on earth. To show mercy even in anger, to take away their harshness from acts of vengeance, to display kindness and tolerance to your fallen enemies, this was your practice, this you always commended and enjoined on others to imitate, and thus, even while the usurper still controlled Italy, you transferred Rome to Pæonia by means of the Senate and inspired the cities with zeal for undertaking public services.

As for the affection of your armies, what description could do it justice? Even before the battle at Myrsa, a division of cavalry came over to your side,[2] and when you had conquered Italy, bodies of infantry and distinguished legions did the same. What happened in Galatia, however, shortly after the usurper's miserable end, demonstrated the universal loyalty of the garrisons to you. For when, emboldened by his isolated position, another[3] dared to assume an effeminate purple, they suddenly set on him as though he were a wolf and tore him limb from limb. Your behaviour after that deed, your merciful and humane treatment of all his friends who were not convicted of having shared his crimes, in spite of all the maligners who came forward with accusations and warned you to show only suspicion against friends of his, this I count as the culmination of all virtue. I maintain, moreover, that your conduct was not only humane and just, but prudent in a still higher degree. He who thinks otherwise falls short of a true understanding of both the circumstances and your policy. For that those who had not been proved guilty should be protected was of course just, thus you thought you ought by no means to make friendship a reason for suspicion and so cause it to be shunned, seeing that it was due to the loyal affection of your own subjects that you had attained to such power and accomplished so much. Yet the son of that rash usurper, who was a mere child, you did not allow to share his father's punishment. To such a degree is every act of yours inclined towards clemency and stamped with the hallmark of perfect virtue...[3]

1. Under Silvanus 2. Silvanus 3. The peroration is lost

TO THE UNEDUCATED
CYNICS

PREFACE

The first of Julian's two extant orations on this subject, written in early 362, is an unreserved censure aimed at the Cynic[1] community of his day, prompted by one such individual who had dared to defame the memory of Diogenes[2]. Over the prior centuries, the followers of the Cynic school had gradually degenerated until by Julian's time almost all of them resembled the most flagrantly disingenuous members of a mendicant order. Indeed, the similarity between Cynics and Christians had long been observed.[3] From Julian's perspective, while both contemporary Cynics and Christians were guilty of impiety, the former were additionally at fault for bringing philosophy into disrepute. Many had adopted the outward trappings of the Cynic school – the long hair, staff, and ragged cloak – as well as the disregard for certain social mores, yet neglected to emulate the piety, "genuine discipline, and self-sufficiency which had ennobled the lives of Diogenes, Crates, and Antisthenes".[4] As Julian himself observes, "in our own day, the imitators of Diogenes have chosen only what is easiest and least burdensome, and have failed to see his nobler side". Thus, instead of committing to a life of material hardship as their predecessors had done, they became little more than parasites on Roman society. Julian consequently sought to instruct the Cynics of his day on the conduct befitting the history of that school, contrasting their behaviour and values with those of its founders, as well as an extensive digression on the idea that all philosophy shares a fundamental commonality.

---

1. Cynicism was a school of Greek philosophy dating back to the 4th century B.C. Its members professed a form of asceticism in which individuals were encouraged to reject material possessions, indulgence, and comfort in pursuit of virtue and truth.

2. Diogenes was an early proponent of Cynicism whose example largely came to define the school in later years. He was a pupil of Antisthenes, and died in 323 B.C.

3. Aristides, Oration 46 4. W.C.F. Wright

TO THE UNEDUCATED CYNICS

Behold, the rivers are flowing backwards,[1] as the proverb says. Here is a Cynic who claims that Diogenes was conceited, yet refuses to take cold baths for fear they may injure him, even though his body is in good health, and he is fighting-fit and in the prime of life. This, no less, as the bright god is now nearing the summer solstice. Furthermore, he even ridicules the eating of octopus, claiming that Diogenes paid a sufficient penalty for his folly and vanity in that he perished of this diet,[2] as though by a draught of hemlock. So far, indeed, is he advanced in wisdom that he knows for certain that death is an evil. Yet this even the wise Socrates thought he did not know, and, moreover, after him Diogenes as well. At any rate, when Antisthenes[3] was suffering from a long and incurable illness, Diogenes handed him a dagger with these words: "in case you need the aid of a friend". So convinced was he that there is nothing terrible or grievous in death.

Yet we who have inherited his staff[4] know from our greater wisdom that death is a calamity. We say that sickness is even more terrible than death, and cold harder to bear than sickness. For the man who is sick is often tenderly nursed, so that his ill-health is straightaway converted into a luxury, especially if he be rich. Indeed, I myself, by Zeus, have observed that certain persons live more softly in sickness than in health, though even in health they were conspicuous for luxury. So it once occurred to me to say to certain of my friends that it were better for those men to be servants than masters, and to be poor and more naked than the lily of the field[5] than to be rich as they are now. For they would have ceased

1. A proverb signifying that all is upended and in disorder; cf. Euripides, *Medea*, 410
2. For the tradition that Diogenes died from raw octopus, cf. Lucian, *Sale of Creeds*, 10
3. A pupil of Socrates and founder of the Cynic sect
4. i.e., the Cynics of Julian's day
5. A proverb, though Julian may be alluding to *Matthew*, 6.28

being at once sick and decadent. The fact is that some people think it a fine thing to make a display of their ailments and to play the part of luxuriating invalids. But, says someone, is not a man who has to endure cold and to support heat really more miserable than the sick? Well, in any case, he has no comforts to mitigate his sufferings.

Come now, let me set down for the benefit of the public what I have learnt from my teachers about the Cynics, so that all who are embarking upon this mode of life may consider it. Further, if they are convinced by what I say, those who are now aiming to be Cynics will, I am sure, be none the worse for it; and if they are unconvinced but cherish aims that are high and noble, and set themselves above my argument, not in words only but in deeds, then my discourse will at any rate place no hindrance in their way. If, however, there are others already enslaved by greed or self-indulgence, or to sum it up briefly in a single phrase, by the pleasures of the body, who therefore neglect my words or even laugh them down, well, just as dogs sometimes defile the front porticoes of schools and law-courts, "tis all one to Hippocleides".[1] For indeed we take no notice of puppies who behave in this fashion. Come then, let me pursue my argument under headings from the beginning in due order, so that by giving every question its proper treatment I may myself more conveniently achieve what I have in mind, and may make it easier for you to follow as well. Thus, as Cynicism is in fact a branch of philosophy, and by no means the most insignificant or least honourable, but rivalling the noblest, I must first say a few words about philosophy itself.

The gift of the gods which was sent down to mankind with the glowing flame of fire,[2] from the sun through the agency of Prometheus, along with the blessings that we owe to Hermes,[3] is none other than the bestowal of reason and mind. For Prometheus, the forethought that guides all things mortal by infusing into nature an animating breath that serves as an operative cause, gave to all things a share in incorporeal reason. Each thing took what share it could, and forms without life gained a state of existence: plants received life; animals a soul; and man a reasoning soul. Now, some think that a single substance is the basis of all these, while others that they differ essentially according to their species. Though

1. Herodotus 6.129; Hippocleides, when told by Cleisthenes that by his unbecoming method of dancing he had "danced away his marriage", made this answer which became a proverb

2. An echo of Plato, *Philebus*, 16 C

3. e.g., eloquence, commerce, and discourse

we must not discuss this question as yet, or rather, not at all in the present discourse, for we need only say that whether one regards philosophy, as some people do, as the art of arts, and the science of sciences, or as an effort to become like God, as far as one may, or whether, as the Pythian oracle said, it means to "know thyself" will make no difference to my argument. For all these definitions are evidently very closely related to one another.

Let us begin, however, with "know thyself" since this precept is divinely inspired.[1] It follows that he who knows himself will know not only about his soul, but his body also. It will not be enough to know that man is a soul employing a body, nor to investigate the essential nature of the soul and trace out its properties. Though even this alone will not be enough for him, and in addition he will investigate whatever exists within us that is nobler and more divine than the soul, that something which we all believe in without being taught and regard as divine, and all in common suppose to be established in the heavens. Then again, as he investigates the first principles of the body, he will observe whether it is composite or simple; then proceeding systematically, he will observe its harmony, the influences that affect it, its capacity, and, in short, all that it needs to ensure its permanence. In the next place, he will also observe the first principles of certain arts by which the body is aided to that permanence. For example, medicine, husbandry, and the like. Of such crafts as are useless and superfluous, he will not be wholly ignorant, since these too have been devised to humour the emotional part of our souls. For though he will avoid persistent study of the latter, believing such fixed study to be shameful, and will avoid what seems to involve undue work in those subjects, nevertheless, he will not, generally speaking, remain in ignorance of their apparent nature and what parts of the soul they suit.

Reflect, therefore, on whether self-knowledge does not control every science and every art, and, furthermore, whether it does not include the knowledge of universals. For to know things divine through the divine part in us, as well as mortal things, too, through the part of us that is mortal, this the oracle declared to be the duty of the living being that is midway between these, namely man. For individually he is mortal, but regarded as a whole he is immortal, and, moreover, singly and individually, is constituted of a mortal and an immortal part. Further, to make oneself, as far as possible, like God is nothing other than to acquire such knowledge of the

1. cf. Juvenal, *Satires*, II.27

essential nature of things as is attainable by mankind. This is evident from the following. It is not on the score of abundance of possessions that we count the divine nature happy, nor on the score of any other of those things that are commonly believed to be advantages, but it is because, as Homer says:

θεοὶ δέ τε πάντα ἴσασι·

"the gods know all things"[1]

Indeed, he says also of Zeus: "but Zeus was older and wiser".[2] For it is in knowledge that the gods surpass ourselves. Additionally, it may well be that among them also what ranks as noblest is self-knowledge. In proportion, then, as they are nobler than we in their essential nature, that self-knowledge of theirs is a knowledge of higher things. I say, therefore, let no one divide philosophy into many kinds or cut it up into many parts, or rather, let no one make it out to be plural instead of one. For even as truth is one, so too philosophy is one.

Yet it is not surprising that we travel to it at one instance by one road, then the next by another. For if any stranger, or, by Zeus, any one of her oldest inhabitants wished to go up to Athens, he could either sail or go by road, and if he travelled by land he could, I suppose, take either the broad thoroughfares or the paths and roads that are shortcuts. What's more, he could either sail along the coasts, or, like the old man of Pylos,[3] "cleave the open sea". Let no one try to refute me by pointing out that some philosophers in travelling by those very roads have been known to lose their way, and arriving in some other place have been captivated, as though by Circe or the Lotus-Eaters, that is to say, by pleasure, or opinion, or some other bait, and so have failed to go straight forward and attain their goal. Rather, he must consider those who in every one of the philosophic sects did attain the highest rank, whereupon he will find that all their doctrines agree.

Thus the god at Delphi proclaims "Know Thyself"; Heraclitus says "I searched myself";[4] Pythagoras, also, and his school and his followers down to Theophrastus, bid us become like God as far as possible – and, yes, Aristotle too. For what we are sometimes, God is always. It would therefore be absurd that God should not know himself. For he will know nothing at all about other things if he be

---

1. *Odyssey*, IV, 379 2. *The Iliad*, XIII, 355 3. Nestor; *Odyssey*, III, 174
4. Heraclitus, fr. 80

ignorant of himself. Since he is himself everything, seeing that in himself and near himself he keeps the causes of all things that in any way have existence, whether they be immortal causes of things immortal, or causes of perishable things, though themselves neither mortal nor perishable, for imperishable and ever-abiding are the causes of perpetual generation for the perishable world. This line of argument, however, is too lofty for the occasion.

Now, truth is one and philosophy is one, and those of whom I just spoke are its lovers, one and all. Alongside, of course, those whom I ought in fairness to mention now by name, by which I mean the disciples of the man of Citium.[1] For when they saw that the cities of Greece were averse to the excessive plainness and simplicity of the Cynic's freedom of manners, they hedged about him with screens, as it were. That is to say, with maxims on the management of the household, business, interaction with one's wife, and the rearing of children, to the end, I believe, that they might make him the intimate guardian of the public welfare.[2] That they, too, held the maxim "Know Thyself" to be the first principle of their philosophy you may believe, if you will, not only from the works that they composed on this very subject, but even more from what they made the end and aim of their philosophic teaching. For this end of theirs was life in harmony with nature, and this it is impossible for any man to attain who does not know who and of what nature he is. Indeed, a man who does not know himself will certainly not know what it is becoming for him to do; just as he who does not know the nature of iron will not know whether it is suitable to cut with or not, or how iron must be treated so that it may be put to its proper use. For the moment, however, I have said enough to show that philosophy is one, and that, to speak generally, all philosophers have a single aim, though they may arrive at that end by different paths. Let us, then, consider the Cynic philosophy.

If the Cynics had composed treatises with any serious purpose, and not merely with a frivolous aim, it would have been proper for my opponent to be guided by these and to try in each case to refute the opinions that I hold on the subject. Then, if they proved to be in harmony with those original doctrines, he could not attack me for bearing false witness; whereas, if they proved not to be in

1. Zeno of Citium in Cyprus, founder of the Stoic school

2. Julian appears to be suggesting that Zeno and the Stoics could not accept without modification the lifestyle advocated by the Cynic Crates

harmony, then he could have barred my opinions from a hearing, just as the Athenians barred spurious documents from the Metroum. As I said, however, nothing of that sort exists. Even the popular tragedies of Diogenes are now said to be the work of a certain Philiscus of Ægina; though even if they were by Diogenes, there would be nothing unusual in a wise man's jesting, since many philosophers have been known to do so. For Democritus also, we are told, used to laugh when he saw men taking things seriously.

Well then, I say we must not pay any attention to their frivolous writings, like men who have no desire at all to learn anything of serious interest. Such men, when they arrive at a prosperous city abounding in offerings and secret rites of many kinds, containing within it countless holy priests who dwell in the sacred enclosures, priests who, for this very purpose, that is, in order to purify everything that is within their gates, have expelled all that is sordid, superfluous, and vicious from the city – public baths and brothels, retail shops, and everything of the sort without exception – these men, I say, having come as far as the quarter where all such things are, do not enter the city itself. Surely a man who, when he lights upon the things that have been expelled, thinks that this is the true city, is despicable indeed if he departs on the instant, but still more despicable if he stays in that lower region, when he might by taking a mere step across the threshold behold Socrates himself. For I will borrow the famous phrases of Alcibiades in his praise of Socrates,[1] and assert that the Cynic philosophy is very much akin to those images of Silenus that sit inside the shops of sculptors: the craftsmen make them with pipes or flutes in their hands, but when you open them you see that inside they contain statues of the gods. Accordingly, that we may not make that sort of mistake and think that his jesting was earnest belief (for though there is a certain use even in those jests, Cynicism itself is something very different, as I shall presently try to prove), let us consider it in due course from its actual practice and pursue it like hounds that track down wild beasts in the chase.

The founder of this philosophy, the man to whom we are to attribute it, is in the first instance not easy to discover, even though some believe that the title belongs to Antisthenes or Diogenes. At least the saying of Oenomaus[2] seems to not be without good grounds: "the Cynic philosophy is neither Antisthenism nor Diogenism". Moreover, the better sort of Cynics assert that in

1. Plato, *Symposium*, 215 2. A second century Cynic philosopher from Gadara

addition to the other blessings bestowed on us by mighty Heracles, it was he who bequeathed to mankind the noblest example of this mode of life.[1] For my part, however, while I desire to speak with due reverence of the gods and of those who have attained to their functions, I still believe that even before Heracles, not only among the Greeks but among the Barbarians also, there were men who practised this philosophy. For it seems to be in some ways a universal philosophy, and the most natural, demanding no special study whatsoever. It is enough to simply choose the honourable by desiring virtue and avoiding vice, and so there is no need to turn over countless books. For as the saying goes: "much learning does not teach men to have understanding".[2] Nor is it necessary to subject oneself to any part of such a discipline as those who enter other philosophic sects must undergo. In truth, it is enough to merely heed the Pythian god when he enjoins these two precepts: "Know Thyself" and "falsify the common currency". Hence it becomes evident to us that the founder of this philosophy is he, I believe, who is the cause of all the blessings that the Greeks enjoy; the universal leader, law-giver, and Lord of Hellas, by which I mean the god of Delphi.[3]

Since it was not permitted that he should be in ignorance of anything, the peculiar fitness of Diogenes did not escape his notice. He therefore made him incline to that philosophy, not by urging his commands in words alone, as he does for other men, but in very deed he instructed him symbolically as to what he willed, in two words, when he said "falsify the common currency". For "Know Thyself" he addressed not only to Diogenes, but to other men also, and still does, for it stands there engraved in front of his shrine.[4] Thus we have at last discovered the founder of this philosophy, even as the divine Iamblichus also declares; and we have discovered its leading men, as well, namely Antisthenes, Diogenes, and Crates,[5] the aim and end of whose lives was, I think, to know themselves, to despise vain opinions, and to lay hold of truth with their whole understanding – since truth, for gods and men alike, is the beginning of every good thing.[6] So it was, I think, for her sake that Plato, Pythagoras, Socrates, the Peripatetic philosophers, and Zeno spared no pains, because they wished to know themselves,

1. In *Sale of Creeds*, 8, Lucian has Diogenes say that he modelled himself on Heracles
2. Heraclitus, fr. 16 3. Apollo 4. At Delphi
5. Fourth century Theban Cynic; a pupil of Diogenes 6. Plato, *Laws*, 730

and to not follow vain opinions but to search out truth among all things that are.

Since it has become evident that Plato was not pursuing one aim and Diogenes another, but their end was one and the same, suppose one should inquire of the wise Plato: what value do you set on the precept "Know Thyself"? I am quite sure he would answer that it is worth everything, and indeed he says so in the Alcibiades.[1] Come then, tell us next, divine Plato, scion of the gods, how ought one to be disposed towards the opinions of the many? He will give the same answer, and, moreover, he will expressly enjoin us to read his dialogue the Crito,[2] where Socrates is shown warning us to not take heed of such things. At any rate, what he says is: "but why, my dear good Crito, are we so concerned about the opinion of the multitude?" Are we now to ignore all this evidence, and without further question fence off from one another and force apart men whom the passion for truth, the scorn of opinion, and unanimity in zeal for virtue have joined together? And if Plato chose to achieve his aim through words, whereas for Diogenes deeds sufficed, does the latter on that account deserve to be criticised by you? Consider, then, whether that same method of his be not in every respect superior, since we see that Plato for himself forswore written compositions. "For" he says[3] "there are no writings by Plato, nor will there ever be, and what now pass current as his are the work of Socrates, the ever fair and ever young". Why, then, should we not from the practice of Diogenes study the character of the Cynic philosophy?

The body consists of certain parts, such as eyes, feet, and hands, but there are other parts besides – hair, nails, waste matter, and a whole class of accessories of that sort – without which the human body cannot function. Is it not absurd, then, for a man to take into account such parts, by which I mean hair, nails, or such unpleasant accessories, rather than those parts that are most precious and important, such as, for instance, the organs of perception, and among these more especially the instruments whereby we apprehend, namely the eyes and ears? For these aid the soul to think intelligently, whether it be buried deep in the body, enabling it to purify itself more readily and to use its pure and steadfast faculty of thought, or whether, as some think, it is through them that the soul

1. Plato, *Alcibiades Major*, 129 2. Plato, *Crito*, 44

3. Epistle 2, 314; Julian slightly alters the original; Plato meant that in his dialogues he had suppressed his own personality for that of Socrates

enters as though by channels.[1] For, as we are told, by collecting individual perceptions and linking them through memory, she brings forth the sciences. For my own part, I think that if there were not something of this sort, either incomplete in itself, or perfect but hindered by other things many and various, which brings about our apprehension of externals, it would not even be possible for us to apprehend the objects of sense-perception. Though this line of argument has little to do with the present question.

Accordingly, we must go back to the divisions of the Cynic philosophy. For the Cynics seem to have also thought that there were two branches of philosophy, as did Aristotle and Plato, namely speculative and practical. Evidently this was because they had observed and understood that man is by nature suited to both action and the pursuit of knowledge. So although they avoided the study of natural philosophy, that does not affect the argument. For Socrates and many others also, as we know, devoted themselves to speculation, albeit solely for practical ends. For they believed that even self-knowledge meant learning precisely what must be assigned to the soul, and what to the body. Thus to the soul they naturally assigned supremacy, and to the body subjection. This seems to be the reason why they practised virtue, self-control, modesty, and freedom, and why they shunned all forms of envy, cowardice, and superstition. Yet this, you will say, is not the view that we hold about them, for we are to think that they were not sincere; that they risked what is most precious[2] in despising the body thus, as Socrates did when he declared, rightly, that philosophy is a preparation for death.[3] Furthermore, since this was the aim that the Cynics pursued daily, we need not emulate them any more than the others; rather, we are to think them miserable beings and altogether foolish.

Yet why was it that they endured those hardships? Surely not from ostentation, as you declared. For how could they win applause from other men by eating raw meat? Certainly you yourself do not applaud them for this. At any rate, when you imitate one of those Cynics by carrying a staff and wearing your hair long, as is shown in their pictures, do you think that you thereby gain a reputation with the crowd, even though you yourself do not consider those habits worthy of admiration? One or two, indeed, used to applaud him in his own day, but more than ten times ten thousand had their

1. cf. Lucretius, *De Rerum Natura*, 3.359; Empiricus, *Adversus Mathematicos*, 7.350
2. Plato, Protagoras, 314 3. Plato, *Phædo*, 81

stomachs turned by nausea and loathing, and went fasting until their attendants revived them with perfume, myrrh, and cakes. So greatly did that renowned hero shock them by an act which seems absurd to men "of such kind as mortals now are".[1] Though, by the gods, it was not ignoble, if one should explain it according to the intention of Diogenes. For just as Socrates said of himself that he embraced the life of cross-examining because he believed that he could perform his service to the god only by examining, in all its bearings, the meaning of the oracle that had been uttered concerning him, so I think Diogenes also, because he was convinced that philosophy was ordained by the Pythian oracle, believed that he ought to test everything by facts and not be influenced by the opinions of others, which may be true or may be false. Accordingly, Diogenes did not think that every statement of Pythagoras, or any man like Pythagoras, was necessarily true. For he held that God and not man is the founder of philosophy. So, pray tell, you will ask, what has this to do with the eating of octopus? I will tell you.

To eat meat some regard as natural to man, while others think that to follow this practice is not at all appropriate for man, and this question has been much debated. If you are willing to make the effort, you can see with your own eyes swarms of books on the subject. These Diogenes thought it his duty to refute. His own view was as follows: if one can eat meat without taking too much trouble to prepare it, as can all other animals to whom nature has assigned this diet, and can do so without harm or discomfort, or rather, with actual benefit to the body, then he thought eating meat to be entirely in accordance with nature. If, on the other hand, harm came of it, then he apparently thought the practice to not be appropriate for man, and that he must abstain from it by all means. Here, then, you have a theory on this question, though perhaps it is somewhat forced. There is another more akin to Cynicism, only I must first describe more clearly the end and aim of that philosophy.

Freedom from emotion they regard as the end and aim; and this is equivalent to becoming a god. Now perhaps Diogenes observed that in the case of all other foods he himself felt no unpleasant sensations, and that only raw meat gave him indigestion and nausea, taking this as proof that he was enslaved to vain opinion rather than reason. For flesh is nonetheless flesh, even if you cook it

1. *The Iliad*, V, 304

any number of times or season it with any number of sauces. This, I say, was why he thought he ought to rid and free himself altogether of this cowardice – for you may be sure that this sort of thing is cowardice. In the name of the Law-Giving goddess,[1] then, tell me why if we used cooked meats we do not eat them in their natural state also? You can give me no other answer than that this has become a custom and a habit with us. For surely we cannot say that before meat is cooked it is disgusting and that by being cooked it becomes purer than it was by nature. What, then, was it right for him to do, he who had been appointed by that god, like a general in command, to do away with the common currency and to judge all questions by the criterion of reason and truth? Ought he to have shut his eyes and been so far fettered by this general opinion as to believe that flesh by being cooked becomes pure and fit for food, but that when it has not been acted upon by fire it is somehow abominable and loathsome. Is this the sort of memory you have? Is this your zeal for truth? For though you so severely criticised Diogenes "the vain-glorious" as you call him – though I call him the most zealous servant of the Pythian god – for eating octopus, you yourself have devoured endless pickled food, "fish, birds and whatever else might come to hand".[2]

For you are an Egyptian, though not of the priestly caste, but rather of the omnivorous type whose habit it is to eat everything "even as the green herb".[3] You recognise, I suppose, the words of the Galilæans. I almost omitted to say that all men who live near the sea, and even some who live at a distance from it, swallow down sea-urchins, oysters, and in general everything of the kind without even heating them. These you will think enviable, whereas you regard Diogenes as contemptible and disgusting. Do you not perceive that those shell-fish are flesh just as much as what he ate? Except, perhaps, that they differ in so far as the octopus is soft and shellfish are harder. Regardless, the octopus is bloodless, like hard-shelled fish, but the latter, too, are animate things like the octopus. At least they feel pleasure and pain, which is the peculiar characteristic of animate things. Thus here we must not be put out by Plato's theory[4] that plants are also animated by soul. Nevertheless, it is now, I think, evident to those who are in any way able to follow an argument, that what the excellent Diogenes did was not unusual, irregular, or contrary to our habits. That is, if we do not in such

1. Demeter, who regulated the customs of civilised life, especially agriculture

2. *The Odyssey*, XII, 331 3. *Genesis*, 9.3 4. Plato, *Timæus*, 77

cases apply the criterion of hardness and softness, but judge rather by the pleasure or distaste of the palate. Therefore, it is not after all the eating of raw food that disgusts you, since you do the like, not only in the case of bloodless animals but also of those that have blood. Perhaps, however, there is another difference between you and Diogenes: that he thought he ought to eat such food just as it was and in the natural state, whereas you think you must first prepare it with salt and many other things to make it agreeable, thereby contending with nature. I have now said enough on this subject.

The end and aim of the Cynic philosophy, then, as indeed of every philosophy, is happiness, but specifically happiness that consists in living according to nature and not according to the opinions of the multitude. For plants, too, are considered to do well, and verily all animals, when without hindrance each attains the end designed for it by nature. Even among the gods this is the definition of happiness; that their state should be according to their nature, and that they should be independent. So too, then, in the case of human beings we must not inquire deeply into happiness as if it were hidden away outside ourselves. Neither the eagle nor the plane tree, nor anything else that has life, whether plant or animal, vainly troubles itself about wings, or leaves of gold, or if its shoots may be of silver, or its stings and spurs of iron, or rather of steel. Yet where nature in the beginning has adorned them with such things, even if they are simply strong and serviceable for speed or defence, they consider that they themselves are fortunate and well provided.

Then is it not absurd when a man tries to find happiness somewhere outside himself, believing that wealth, birth, the influence of friends, and generally speaking everything of that sort is of the utmost importance. If, however, nature had bestowed on us only what she has bestowed on other animals, by which I mean the possession of bodies and souls like theirs, such that we need concern ourselves with nothing beyond, then it would suffice for us, as for all other animals, to content ourselves with physical advantages, and to pursue happiness within this field. Yet in us has been implanted a soul that in no way resembles other animals; and whether it be different in essence, or the same in essence but superior in its activity only, just as, I suppose, pure gold is superior to gold alloyed with sand – for some people hold this theory to be true of the soul – we surely know that we are more intelligent than other animals. For according to the myth in the Protagoras,[1] nature dealt with them most generously and bountifully, like a mother, but to compensate for all this, mind was bestowed on us by Zeus. Therefore, in our minds, in the best and noblest part of us, we must say that happiness resides.

Consider, then, whether Diogenes did not above all other men profess this belief, since he freely exposed his body to hardships in order that he might make it stronger than it was naturally. He allowed himself to act only as the light of reason shows us that we ought to act; and the perturbations that attack the soul and are derived from the body, to which this cloak of ours often constrains us for its sake to pay too much attention, he did not take into account at all. Thus by means of this discipline, the man made his body more vigorous, I believe, than that of any who have contended for the prize crown in the games. His soul, moreover, was so disposed that he was happy, and a king no less, if not even more than the Great King, as the Greeks used to call him in those days, by which they meant the King of Persia. Does he then seem to you of no importance, this man who was "cityless, homeless, a man without a state, owning not an *obol*, or a *drachma*, or a single slave".[2] Indeed, not even a loaf of bread – and Epicurus says that if one has bread enough and to spare, he is by no means inferior to the gods on the score of happiness. Not that Diogenes tried to rival the gods, albeit he lived more happily than one who might be counted the happiest of men, and in fact he used to assert that he lived more happily than such a man. If you do not believe me, try his mode of life in deed and not in word, and you will perceive the truth.

Come, let us first test it by reasoning. You think, do you not, that for mankind freedom is the beginning of all good things,[3] by which is meant, of course, that which people are always calling good? How can you deny it? For property, money, birth, physical strength, beauty, and, in short, everything of the sort are, when divorced from freedom, surely blessings that belong, not to him who merely seems to enjoy them, but to him who is that man's master? Whom then are we to regard as a slave? Shall it be him whom we buy for so many silver *drachmæ*, for two *minæ*, or for ten staters[4] of gold? Probably you will say that such a man is truly a slave. And why? Is it because we have paid down money for him to

1. Plato, *Protagoras*, 321

2. *Adespota*, fr. 6; Laërtius, 6.38, says that this was a favourite quotation of Diogenes

3. Plato, *Laws*, 730 4. A stater was worth about one sovereign

the seller? In that case, however, the prisoners of war whom we ransom would be slaves. Yet the law on the one hand grants these men their freedom when they have come home safe, while we on the other hand ransom them not that they may become slaves, but that they may be free. Do you see, then, that in order to make a ransomed man a slave, it is not enough to pay down a sum of money, for that man is truly a slave over whom another man has power to compel him to do whatever he orders, and if he should refuse, to punish him and in the words of the poet "inflict grievous pains upon him"?[1]

Consider next whether we have as many masters as there are persons whom we are obliged to conciliate in order that, should they seek to punish us, we do not suffer pain or grief? Or do you think that the only sort of punishment is when a man lifts up his stick against a slave and strikes him? Yet not even the harshest masters do this in the case of all their slaves, but a word or a threat is often enough. Then never think, my friend, that you are free while your belly rules you, or the part below the belly, since you will then have masters who can either furnish you the means of pleasure or deprive you of them. Furthermore, even if you should prove yourself superior to these, so long as you are a slave to the opinions of the many, you have not yet approached freedom or tasted its nectar, "I swear by him who set in my breast the mystery of the Four!"[2] I do not mean by this, however, that we ought to be shameless before all men and to do what we ought not. Rather, in all that we refrain from and all that we do, let us not do or refrain from it merely because it seems to the multitude somehow honourable or base, but because it is forbidden by reason and the god within us, that is, the mind.[3] As for the multitude, there is no reason why they should not follow common opinions, for better that than to be altogether shameless. Indeed, mankind is predisposed to the truth by nature. Though a man who has attained to a life in accordance with intelligence, who is able to discover and estimate right reasons, ought on no account whatsoever to follow the views held by the many about proper and improper conduct.

Since, therefore, one part of the soul is more divine, that part which we call mind, intelligence, and silent reason, whose herald is

1. *The Iliad*, V, 766

2. An oath used by the Pythagoreans, who regarded the tetrad (the sum of the first four numbers) as symbolic of all proportion and perfection; cf. Pythagoras, *Aureum Carmen*, 47

3. Iamblichus, *Protrepticus*, 8.138; Euripides, fr. 1007

this speech of ours, comprised of words and phrases and uttered through the voice; and since there is yoked therewith another part of the soul which is mutable and multiform, something composite of anger and appetite, a many-headed monster, we ought not to look steadily and unswervingly at the opinions of the multitude until we have tamed this wild beast and persuaded it to obey the god within us, or rather, the divine part. For it is this that many disciples of Diogenes have ignored, and hence have become rapacious and depraved, no better than any of the brutish beasts. To prove, moreover, that this is not my own theory,[1] I will first relate to you something that Diogenes did, which many will ridicule but to me seems most worthy of respect. Once, in a crowd of people among which stood Diogenes, a certain young man made an unseemly noise. Diogenes struck him with his staff and said: "so, vile wretch, though you have done nothing that would give you the right to take such liberties in public, you are beginning here and before us to show your scorn of opinion?" So convinced was he that a man ought to subdue pleasure and passion before he proceeds to the final encounter of all, and prepares to wrestle with those opinions which to the multitude are the cause of innumerable vices.

Do you not know how people lure away the young from philosophy by continually uttering one slander after another against all the philosophers in turn? The genuine disciples of Pythagoras, Plato, and Aristotle are called sorcerers, quibblers, conceited, and quacks. If here and there among the Cynics one is genuinely virtuous, he is regarded with pity. For example, I remember once what my tutor said to me when he saw my fellow pupil, Iphicles, with his hair unkempt and his clothes in tatters on his chest, wearing a wretched cloak in severe winter weather: "what evil genius could have plunged him into this sad state which makes not only him pitiable, but even more so his parents who reared him with care and gave him the best education they could! And now he goes about in this condition, neglecting everything, no better than a beggar!" At the time I answered him with some pleasantry or other. Yet I can assure you that the multitude hold these views about genuine Cynics also.

Now, that may not be so dreadful, but do you see how they persuade them to love wealth, to hate poverty, to serve the belly, to endure any toil for the body's sake, to fatten that fetter of the soul,

1. Euripides, fr. 488

to keep up an expensive table, to never sleep alone at night,[1] provided only that they do all this in the dark and are not found out? Is not this worse than Tartarus? Is it not better to sink beneath Charybdis and Cocytus, or ten thousand fathoms deep inside the earth[2] than to fall into a life like this, enslaved to lust and appetite, and not even to these simply and openly, like the beasts, but to take pains so that when we act thus we may be hidden under cover of darkness? Ah, how much better is it to refrain altogether from all this! If, then, this be difficult, the rules of Diogenes and Crates on these matters are not to be despised: "fasting quenches desire, and if you cannot fast, hang yourself".[3] Do you not know that those great men lived as they did in order to introduce among men the way of plain living? "For" says Diogenes "it is not among men who live on bread that you will find tyrants, but among those who eat costly dinners". While Crates himself wrote a hymn to Plain Living:

Χαῖρε, θεὰ δέσποινα, σοφῶν ἀνδρῶν ἀγάπημα,
Εὐτελίη, κλεινῆς ἔγγονε Σωφροσύνης·

"Hail, goddess and Queen, darling of wise men,
Plain Living, child of glorious Temperance"[4]

Then let not the Cynic be like Oenomaus, shameless or impudent, or a scorner of everything human and divine, but reverent towards sacred things, like Diogenes. For he obeyed the Pythian oracle and did not repent of his obedience. If, however, anyone supposes that because he did not visit the temples, or worship at statues or altars, this is a sign of impiety, he does not think rightly. For Diogenes possessed nothing that is usually offered – incense, or libations, or money with which to buy them. Nevertheless, if he held the right opinions about the gods, that in itself was enough. For he worshipped them with his whole soul, thus offering them, as I believe, the most precious of his possessions: the dedication of his soul through his thoughts. Let not the Cynic be shameless, but, led by reason, let him first make subservient to himself the susceptible part of his soul so that he may entirely do away with it, whereby he will not even be aware of his mastery over pleasure. For it is nobler to attain to this, by which I mean the complete ignorance of such

1. cf. Plato, *Epistles*, 326 2. An echo of Xenophon, *Anabasis*, 7.1.29
3. Laërtius 6.86; *Palatine Anthology*, 9.497; Julian paraphrases the verses of Crates, cf. Crates, fr. 14
4. *Palatine Anthology*, 10.104

impulses. This comes to us only through training. So that none may think I say this at random, I will add for your benefit a few lines from the lighter verse of Crates:[1]

"Glorious children of Memory and Olympian Zeus,
Muses of Pieria, grant me this prayer!
Give me food for my belly from day to day,
so my life may be frugal and free from slavery.
Make me useful rather than agreeable to my friends.
Treasure and the fame thereof I desire not to amass;
nor do I crave the beetle's wealth or the substance of the ant.
I desire only justice to attain, and to collect such riches
that are easily carried, easily acquired, of great avail for virtue.
If I may but win these, I shall propitiate Hermes
and the holy Muses, not with costly and luxurious offerings,
but with actions virtuous and pious."

If it be of any use to write about such things for you, I could recite still more maxims by this same Crates. Though if you should read Plutarch of Chæronea, who wrote his Life[2], there would be no need for you to learn his character superficially from me.

Let me return, then, to what I said before. He who is entering on the career of a Cynic ought first to censure severely and cross-examine himself, and without any self-flattery ask himself the following questions in precise terms: whether he enjoys expensive food; whether he cannot do without a soft bed; whether he is the slave of rewards and the opinion of men; whether it is his ambition to attract public notice and, even though it be an empty honour,[3] he still thinks it worthwhile. For he must not let himself drift with the current of the mob or touch vulgar pleasure even with the tip of his finger, as the saying goes, until he has succeeded in trampling on it. Then, and not before, may he permit himself to dip into that sort of thing if it come his way. For example, I am told that bulls which are weaker than the rest separate themselves from the herd and graze alone, storing up strength in every part of their bodies by degrees, until they rejoin the herd in such condition that they might challenge its leaders and contend with them, confident that they are more fit to take the lead. Therefore, let him who wishes to

1. i.e., parodies such as the verses quoted here based on Solon's prayer, fr. 12
2. Plutarch's biography of Crates is unfortunately lost
3. An echo of Euripides, *Phoenissæ*, 551

be a Cynic philosopher not merely adopt their long cloak, or wallet, or staff, or their way of wearing the hair, as though he were a man walking unkempt and illiterate in a village that lacked barber shops and schools, but let him consider that reason rather than a staff, and a certain mode of life rather than a wallet are the hallmarks of Cynic philosophy. Furthermore, he must not employ freedom of speech until he has first proven how much he is worth, as I believe was the case with Crates and Diogenes. For they were so far from bearing with a bad grace any threat of fortune, whether one calls such threats caprice or wanton insult, that once when he had been captured by pirates, Diogenes joked with them; as for Crates, he gave his property to the state, and, being physically deformed, he made fun of his own lame leg and hunched shoulders. When his friends hosted entertainment, he used to go, whether invited or not,[1] and would reconcile his nearest friends if he learned that they had quarrelled. So as to not seem to persecute those whom he wished to reform, he would reprove them not harshly, but with a charming manner, as though he wished to be of use to both them and bystanders.

Yet this was not the chief end and aim of those Cynics. As I said, their main concern was how they might themselves attain to happiness, and, as I believe, they occupied themselves with other men only in so far as they comprehended that man is by nature a social and political animal; they thereby aided their fellow citizens, not only by practising but by preaching as well. Then let him who wishes to be a Cynic, earnest and sincere, first take himself in hand, like Diogenes and Crates, and expel from his own soul and from every part of it all passions and desires, entrusting all his affairs to reason and intelligence so as to steer his course by them. For this, in my opinion, was the sum and substance of the philosophy of Diogenes.

If Diogenes did at times visit a courtesan – though even this may have only happened once or not even once – let him who would be a Cynic first satisfy us that he is, like Diogenes, a man of solid worth, and then, if he should see fit to do that sort of thing openly and in sight of all men, we shall not reproach him with it or accuse him. First, however, we must see him display the ability to learn and the quick wit of Diogenes, and in all other relations he must show the same independence, self-sufficiency, justice, moderation, piety, gratitude, and the same extreme carefulness not to act at random,

1. Thucydides, 1.118

irrationally, or without a purpose. For these, too, are characteristic of the philosophy of Diogenes. Then may he trample on vain-gloriousness, may he ridicule those who, though they conceal in darkness the necessary functions of our nature, will engage in practices in the centre of marketplaces and our cities that are most brutal and by no means akin to our nature, such as theft of money, false accusations, unjust indictments, and the pursuit of other vulgar deeds of this sort. On the other hand, when Diogenes made unseemly noises, or obeyed the call of nature, or did anything else of that sort in the marketplace, as they say he did, he did so because he was trying to trample on the conceit of the men I have just mentioned, and to teach them that their practices were far more sordid and insupportable than his own. For what he did was in accordance with the nature of all of us, yet theirs accorded with no man's real nature, one may say, but were all due to moral depravity.

In our own day, however, the imitators of Diogenes have chosen only what is easiest and least burdensome, and have failed to see his nobler side. As for you, in your desire to be more dignified than those early Cynics, you have strayed so far from Diogenes' plan of life that you thought him an object of pity. Yet if you did not believe all that I have said about this man, he whom all the Greeks in the generation of Plato and Aristotle admired next to Socrates and Pythagoras, a man whose pupil was the teacher of the most modest and most wise Zeno – and it is not likely that they were all deceived about a man as contemptible as you make him out to be in your travesty – well, in that case, my good sir, perhaps you might have studied his character more carefully and thereby progressed further in your knowledge of the man. Was there, I ask, a single Greek who was not amazed by the endurance of Diogenes, and by his perseverance, which had in it a truly royal greatness of soul? The man used to sleep in his jar[1] on a bed of leaves more soundly than the Great King on his soft couch under a gilded roof; he used to eat his crust[2] with a better appetite than you now eat your Sicilian courses;[3] he used to bathe his body in cold water and dry himself in the open air instead of with the linen towels with which

1. Diogenes's "jar" (πίθος) was a large container used for storing wine, grain, or olive oil. "Pithos" may also be translated as barrel, tub, vat, or kennel

2. cf. Dio Chrysostom, *Oration* 6

3. A proverb; Sicily was famous for good cooking; cf. Plato, *Republic*, 404; Horace, *Odes*, 1.1.18

you rub yourself down, my most philosophic friend! It becomes you well to ridicule him because, I suppose, like Themistocles you conquered Xerxes, or Darius, like Alexander of Macedon. If, however, you had the least habit of reading books as I do, though I am a statesman and engrossed in public affairs, you would know how much Alexander is said to have admired Diogenes' greatness of soul. Though you care little, I suppose, for any of these things. How should you care? Far from it.[1] You admire and emulate the life of wretched women.

Nonetheless, if my discourse has improved you at all, you will have gained more than I. Yet even if you should abide by your former opinions and I should accomplish nothing at this time by writing on such a great subject so hastily, and, as the saying goes, without taking breath[2] – for I gave to it only the leisure of two days, as the Muses, or rather you yourself will bear me witness – I at any rate shall never regret having spoken of that great man with due reverence.

1. Demosthenes, *De Corona*, 47 2. ibid., 308

TO THE CYNIC HERACLIUS

PREFACE

The second of Julian's orations concerning the Cynics, also written in 362, is addressed to one such philosopher by the name of Heraclius, who provoked the ire of the Emperor after delivering an allegorical fable in which the gods were irreverently treated. Julian, having been present for the aforementioned recitation, promptly composed a response in order to explicate the appropriate formulation and use of myths. As with the previous oration, he extensively praises the earliest Cynics throughout and admonishes those of his day. With respect to the treatment of myths, Julian shares the view of his close friend, Salutius, who in his Neo-Platonic treatise *On the Gods and the World* summarised the issue thus: "the first benefit arising from myths is that they excite us to inquiry, and do not suffer our cogitative power to remain in indolent rest...to teach the whole truth about the gods to all men produces contempt in the foolish, for they are incapable of understanding, and negligent in pursuit of the good; whereas to conceal the truth in myths prevents the contempt of the foolish and compels the good to practise philosophy". While both Salutius and Julian viewed myths as allegories to be understood through philosophical inquiry, they "are never rationalistic, and never offer the least excuse for scepticism".[1]

Accordingly, Julian offers instruction to his audience, and Heraclitus in particular, through a parable of his own creation based on the *Choice of Heracles* by Prodicus. In this version, the part of Heracles is filled by a surrogate for Julian whom the gods present with the opportunity to replace Constantius and restore both order to the Empire and the worship of the gods. The parable offers an interesting insight into Julian's views of his cousin and of himself as a reformer invested with power and responsibility by the gods.

In summation, a philosophical investigation beyond the ostensible meaning of a myth may, according to the view espoused by Julian in this oration, allow one to "arrive at comprehension of the true nature of the gods" and the sacred knowledge which he held to be the greatest of all pursuits. From Julian's perspective, the gods portrayed in these stories are not poetic inventions or the

---

1. W. C. F. Wright

abstractions of philosophising theologians, but rather symbols and projections of a transcendent order.[1] Hence the importance he places on myths being handled with propriety and a reverence for the divine – something which Heraclius evidently failed to do.

1. Julius Evola, *The Emperor Julian*

TO THE CYNIC HERACLIUS

"Truly with the lapse of time many things come to pass!"[1] This verse I have heard in a comedy and was tempted the other day to proclaim it aloud when, by invitation, we attended the lecture of a Cynic whose barking was neither distinct nor noble. He was crooning myths as nurses do, and even these he did not compose in any profitable fashion. For a moment my impulse was to rise and break up the meeting. Yet, though I had to listen as one does when Heracles and Dionysus are being caricatured in the theatre by comic poets, I bore it to the end; not for the speaker's sake, but for the sake of the audience, or rather, if I may presume to say so, it was still more for my own sake, so that I might not seem to be moved by superstition rather than by a pious and rational sentiment; to be scared into flight by his miserable words like a timid dove. So I stayed and repeated to myself that famous line:

Τέτλαθι δή, κραδίη, καὶ κύντερον ἄλλο ποτ' ἔτλης.

"Be patient, my heart, for you have endured things
worse than this before".[2]

Endure for the brief fraction of a day even a babbling Cynic! It is not the first time that you have had to hear the gods blasphemed.[3] Our state is not so well governed, our private life is not so virtuous, in short, we are not so favoured by fortune that we can keep our ears pure or, at any rate, our eyes undefiled at least by the many and various impieties of this iron race. And now, as though we had not enough of such vileness, this Cynic fills our ears with his profanities, and has uttered the name of the highest of the gods in such a manner as he ought never to have spoken nor I heard!

Since he has done this, however, come, let me in your presence try to teach him this lesson: first that it is more becoming for a

1. Eupolis, fr. 4 2. *The Odyssey*, XX, 18

3. *Βλασφημία* meant any slander or malicious speech against gods or men

Cynic to write discourses than myths; secondly, what sort of adaptations of the myths he ought to make, if indeed philosophy really needs mythology at all; and finally, I shall have a few words to say about reverence for the gods. For it is with this aim that I appear before you, I, who have no talent for writing and who have hitherto avoided addressing the general public, as I have avoided all else that is tedious and sophistical. Though perhaps it is not unsuitable for me to say, and for you to hear, a few words about myth in general as a sort of genealogy of that kind of writing.

Of course, one could no more discover where myth was originally invented, and who was the first to compose fiction in a plausible manner for the benefit or entertainment of his hearers, than if one were to try to find out who was the first man that sneezed or the first horse that neighed. Nevertheless, as cavalry arose in Thrace and Thessaly; archers and the lighter sort of weapons in India, Crete, and Caria – since the customs of the people were, I suppose, adapted to the nature of the country – just so we may assume about other things as well: that where anything is highly prized by a nation, it was first discovered by that nation rather than by any other. On this assumption, then, it seems likely that myth was originally the invention of men given to pastoral pursuits, and from that day to this, the making of myths is still notably cultivated by them, just as they first invented instruments of music, the flute and the lyre, for their pleasure and entertainment. For just as it is the nature of birds to fly, of fish to swim, or of stags to run, and hence they need not be taught to do so, even if one were to bind or imprison these animals, they try nonetheless to use those special parts of themselves for the purpose to which they know they are naturally adapted. Just so, I think that man, whose soul is none other than reason and knowledge imprisoned, so to speak, in the body – the philosophers call it a potentiality – just so, I say that man inclines to learning, research, and study, as of all tasks most congenial to it. Thus when a kindly god at once looses a man's fetters and brings that potentiality into activity, knowledge is in the very instant his. Whereas in those who are still shackled, false opinion instead of true is implanted, just as, I think, Ixion is said to have embraced a sort of cloud instead of the goddess.[2] Hence they produce wind-eggs[3] and monstrous births, mere phantoms and shadows, so to speak, of true science. So it is

1. Ἱππεῖς ἐν Θετταλίᾳ καὶ Θρᾴκῃ was a well-known proverb

2. i.e., Hera; cf. Pindar, *Pythian*, 2.20

3. cf. Plato, *Theætetus*, 151

that instead of genuine science they profess false doctrines, and are very zealous in learning and teaching such doctrines, as though forsooth they were something useful and admirable.

If I am obliged to say something in defence of those who originally invented myths, I would suggest that they wrote them for immature souls, and I would liken them to nurses who present toys to the hands of children when they are irritated by teething in order to ease their suffering. Thus those mythologists wrote for the simple soul whose wings are just beginning to sprout, and who, though still incapable of being taught the truth, is yearning for further knowledge, pouring in a stream of myths like men who water a thirsty field so as to soothe their hardship and pangs.[1] Then, when the myth was gaining ground and coming into favour in Greece, poets developed from it the fable with a moral, which differs from the myth in that the latter is addressed to children, while the the former to men, and is designed not merely to entertain them but to convey moral exhortation besides. For the man who employs fable aims at moral exhortation and instruction, though he conceals his aim and takes care not to speak openly for fear of alienating his audience. Hesiod, for instance, seems to have written with this in view. After him, Archilochus likewise employed myths often,[2] adorning and as it were seasoning his poetry with them, probably because he saw that his subject matter needed something of this sort to make it attractive. Well he knew that poetry without myth is merely versification[3] and lacks, one may say, its essential characteristic, and so ceases to be poetry at all. He therefore culled these sweets from the Muse of Poetry and offered them to his readers in order that he might not be ranked merely as a writer of satire, but might be counted a poet.

The Homer of myths, however, or the Thucydides, or Plato, or whatever we might call him, was Æsop of Samos. A slave by the accident of birth rather than by temperament, he proved his sagacity by this very use of fable. For since the law did not permit him freedom of speech, he had no resource but to shadow forth his wise counsels and trick them out with charms and graces, serving them up thus to his hearers. Just so, I think, physicians who are free-born men prescribe what is necessary, but when a man happens to be a slave by birth and a physician by profession, he is forced to take pains to flatter and cure his master at the same time.

---

1. The whole passage echoes Plato, *Phædrus*, 251
2. cf. Archilochus, fr. 86, 89
3. Plato, *Phædo*, 61

Now, if our Cynic is also subject to this sort of slavery, let him recite myths, let him write them, and let everyone else under the sun leave to him the role of mythologist. Yet since he asserts that he alone is free, I do not know what need he has of myths. Does he need to temper the harshness and severity of his advice with sweetness and charm, so that he may at once benefit mankind and avoid being harmed by one whom he has benefited? No, that is too much like a slave. Moreover, would any man be better taught by not hearing facts as they really are, or called by their real names, like the comic poet who calls a spade a spade?[1] What need to speak of Phæthon instead of So-and-so? What need to sacrilegiously profane the title of Lord Helios? Who among men that walk here below[2] is worthy to be called Pan or Zeus, as though we should ascribe to those gods our human understanding? If indeed this were possible, however, it would have been preferable to give the men their own names. Would it not have been better to speak of them thus and to bestow on them human names, or rather not bestow, for those that our parents gave us were enough? Well then, if it is neither easier to learn by means of fiction, nor appropriate for the Cynic to invent that sort of thing at all, why did we not spare that wasteful expense?[3] Additionally, why did we waste our time in inventing and composing trivial myths before making stories of them and learning them by heart?

Perhaps you will say that though reason asserts that the Cynic, who alone among men can claim to be free, ought not to invent and compose lying fictions instead of the unvarnished truth then recite these in public assemblies, the custom nevertheless began with Diogenes and Crates, and has been maintained from that time by all Cynics. My answer is that nowhere will you find a single example of such a custom. For the moment I do not insist on the fact that it in no way becomes a Cynic who must "give a new stamp to the common currency" to pay any attention to custom, but only to pure reason, and he ought to discover within himself what is right for him to do and not learn it from without. Do not be misled by the fact that Antisthenes, the disciple of Socrates, and Xenophon too, sometimes expressed themselves by means of myths, for I shall have something to say to you on this point in a moment.

First, in the Muses' name, answer me this question about the

1. Originally "who calls a boat a boat", a proverb found most famously in the works of Erasmus and Lucian, from which the English expression used above derives

2. *The Iliad*, V, 242; Hesiod, *Theogony*, 272

3. An echo of Plutarch, *Antonius*, 28

Cynic philosophy: are we to think it a sort of madness, a method of life not suitable for a man, but rather a brutal attitude of mind which heeds nothing of the beautiful, the honourable, or the good? For Oenomaus would make many people hold this view of it. If you had taken any trouble to study the subject, you would have learned this from that Cynic's *Direct Inspiration of Oracles* and his work *Against the Oracles*; in short, from everything that he wrote. This, then, is his aim: to do away with all reverence for the gods, to bring dishonour on all human wisdom, to trample on all law that can be identified with honour and justice, and more than this, to trample on those laws which have been, as it were, engraved on our souls by the gods, and have impelled us all to believe without teaching that the divine exists, to direct our eyes to it and to yearn towards it, for our souls are disposed towards it as eyes towards the light.

Furthermore, suppose that one should discard also that second law which is sanctified both by nature and by God. The very law that bids us keep our hands altogether and utterly from the property of others and permits us neither by word or deed, or in the private and innermost activities of our souls, to confound such distinctions, since the law is our guide to the most perfect justice – is this conduct not worthy of the pit?[1] Ought not those who applauded such views to have been driven forth, not by blows with rods, like scapegoats,[2] for that penalty is too light for such crimes, but put to death by stoning? For tell me, in heaven's name, how are such men less criminal than bandits who infest lonely places and haunt the coasts in order to despoil navigators? Because, as people say, they despise death; as though bandits were not inspired by the same frenzied courage! So says, at any rate, he[3] who with you counts as a poet and mythologist; though, as a Pythian god proclaimed to certain bandits who sought his oracle, he was a hero and divinity. Speaking of such pirates of the sea, he says:

Οἷά τε ληιστῆρες, ὑπεὶρ ἅλα τοί τ᾽ ἀλόωνται
Ψυχὰς παρθέμενοι.

"Like pirates, sea-wolves raiding at will,
who risk their lives to plunder other men."[4]

---

1. The pit or chasm at Athens into which criminals and the bodies of executed criminals were thrown; cf. Xenophon, *Hellenica*, 1. 7.20

2. For the ceremony of driving out the scapegoat, see Harrison, *Prolegomena*, 97

3. Homer 4. *The Odyssey*, III, 73

What better witness can you require for the desperate courage of bandits? Except, in truth, that one might say that bandits are more courageous than Cynics of this sort, while the Cynics are more reckless than they. For pirates, well aware as they are how worthless the life they lead is, take cover in desert places as much from shame as from the fear of death; whereas the Cynics go up and down in our midst subverting the institutions of society, not to the end of introducing a better and purer state of things, but a worse and more corrupt state. As for the tragedies ascribed to Diogenes, which are admitted to be the composition of some Cynic – the only point in dispute being whether they are by the master himself, Diogenes, or by his disciple Philiscus – what reader of these would not abhor them, and find in them an excess of infamy not to be surpassed even by courtesans? That said, let him go on to read the tragedies of Oenomaus – for he too wrote tragedies to match his discourses – and he will find that they are more inconceivably infamous, that they transgress the very limits of evil; in fact, I have no words to describe them adequately, and in vain should I cite in comparison the horrors of Magnesia,[1] the wickedness of Termerus,[2] or the whole of tragedy put together, along with satiric drama, comedy, and mimicry. With such art has their author displayed in those works every conceivable vileness and folly in their most extreme form.

Now, if from such works any man chooses to demonstrate to us the character of the Cynic philosophy, to blaspheme the gods and bark at all men, as I said when I began, let him go, let him depart to the uttermost parts of the earth wheresoever he pleases. If, however, he does as the god enjoined on Diogenes, and first "give a new stamp to the common currency", then devotes himself to the advice uttered earlier by the god, the precept "Know Thyself", which Diogenes and Crates evidently followed in their actual practice, then I say that this is wholly worthy of one who desires to be a leader and a philosopher. For surely we know what the god meant? He enjoined on Diogenes to despise the opinion of the crowd and to give a new stamp, not to truth, but to the common currency. To which of these categories, therefore, shall we assign self-knowledge? Can we call it common currency? Shall we not rather say that it is the very summary of truth, and by the injunction "Know Thyself" we are told the way in which we must "give a new

1. A proverb; cf. Archilochus, fr. 27

2. A robber whom Theseus killed; Plutarch, *Theseus*, 11

stamp to the common currency"? For just as one who pays no regard whatsoever to conventional opinions, but instead goes straight for the truth will not decide his own conduct by those opinions but by actual facts, so I think he who knows himself will know accurately, not the opinion of others about him, but what he is in reality.

It follows then, does it not, that the Pythian god speaks the truth. Diogenes, indeed, was clearly convinced of this since he obeyed the god and so became, instead of an exile, I will not say greater than the King of Persia, but, according to the tradition handed down, actually an object of envy to the man[1] who had broken the power of Persia and, ambitious to surpass Achilles, was rivalling the exploits of Heracles. Let us then judge the attitude of Diogenes towards gods and men, not from the discourses of Oenomaus or the tragedies of Philiscus – who by ascribing their authorship to Diogenes grossly slandered that sacred personage – but let us, I say, judge him by his deeds. Why in the name of Zeus did he go to Olympia? To see the athletes compete? Could he not have seen those very athletes without trouble both at the Isthmian games and the Panathenaic festival? Then was it because he wished to meet there the most distinguished Greeks? Yet did they not go to the Isthmus too? So you cannot discover any other motive than that of doing honour to the god. He was not, you might say, awestruck by a thunderstorm. By the gods, I too have witnessed such signs from Zeus over and over again without being awestruck! Though for all that I do feel awe of the gods; I love, I revere, I venerate them, and in short have precisely the same feelings towards them as one would have towards kind masters[2] or teachers, fathers or guardians, or anything of that sort. That is the very reason why I could hardly sit still the other day and listen to your speech. I have, however, spoken thus as I was somehow or other impelled to speak, though perhaps it would have been better to say nothing at all.

To return to Diogenes: he was poor and lacked means, yet he travelled to Olympia, while he bade Alexander come to him, if we are to believe Dio.[3] So convinced was he that it was his duty to visit the temples of the gods, but that it was the duty of the most royal monarch of that day to come to him for a discussion. Further, was that not royal advice which he wrote to Archidamus? Truly, not only in words but in deeds also did Diogenes show his reverence for the gods. For he preferred to live in Athens, but when the divine command had sent him away to Corinth, even after he had been set

1. Alexander 2. Plato, *Phædo*, 63 3. Dio Chrysostom, *Oration* 4, 12

free by the man who had bought him, he did not think he ought to leave that city. For he believed that the gods took care of him, and that he had been sent to Corinth, not at random or by some accident, but by the gods themselves for some purpose. He saw that Corinth was more luxurious than Athens, and stood in need of a more severe and courageous reformer. To give you another instance: are there not extant many charming poems by Crates, also, which are proofs of his piety and veneration for the gods? I will repeat them to you, if you have not had time to learn this from the poems themselves:

"Glorious children of Memory and Olympian Zeus,
Muses of Pieria, grant me this prayer!
Give me food for my belly from day to day,
so my life may be frugal and free from slavery.
Make me useful rather than agreeable to my friends.
Treasure and the fame thereof I desire not to amass;
nor do I crave the beetle's wealth or the substance of the ant.
I desire only justice to attain, and to collect such riches
that are easily carried, easily acquired, of great avail for virtue.
If I may but win these, I shall propitiate Hermes
and the holy Muses, not with costly and luxurious offerings,
but with actions virtuous and pious."

You see that, far from blaspheming the gods as you do, he adored and prayed to them. For what number of hecatombs are worth as much as Piety, whom the inspired Euripides celebrated fittingly in the verse:

Ὁσία πότνα θεῶν, ὁσία·;

"Piety, queen of the gods, Piety"?[1]

Or are you not aware that all offerings, whether great or small, that are brought to the gods with piety have equal value, whereas, without piety, I will not say hecatombs, but, by the gods, even the Olympian sacrifice[2] of a thousand oxen is merely empty expenditure and nothing else? This, I believe, Crates recognised, and so with that piety which was his only possession, he himself used to honour the gods with praises, teaching others, moreover, not to honour expensive offerings more than piety in the sacred

1. *Bacchæ*, 370 2. i.e., in honour of Olympian Zeus

ceremonies. Such was the attitude of both those Cynics towards the gods, though they did not crowd audiences together to hear them, nor did they entertain their friends with similes and myths, like the wise men of today. For as Euripides well says:[1]

Ἁπλοῦς ὁ μῦθος τῆς ἀληθείας ἔφυ·

"Simple and unadorned is the language of truth."

Only the liar and the dishonest man, he says, have any use for a mysterious and allusive style. Now, what was the manner of their exchanges with men? Deeds with them came before words, and if they honoured poverty, they themselves seem to have first scorned inherited wealth; if they cultivated modesty, they themselves first practised plain living in every respect; if they tried to expel from the lives of other men the element of theatrical display and arrogance, they themselves first set the example by living in the open marketplaces and the temple precincts, opposing luxury by their own practice before they did so in words; nor did they shout aloud, but proved by their actions that a man may rule as the equal of Zeus if he needs nothing, or very little, and is not thus hampered by his body. Lastly, they reproved wrongdoing during the lifetime of those who had offended, but did not speak ill of the dead, for when men are dead even their enemies, at least the more moderate, make peace with the departed. The genuine Cynic, however, has no enemy, even if men may strike his body, or drag his name through the mire, or slander and speak ill of him, because enmity is felt only towards an opponent, but that which is above personal rivalry is usually loved and respected. Nevertheless, if anyone is hostile to a Cynic, as indeed many are even to the gods, he is not that Cynic's enemy, since he cannot injure him; rather, he inflicts on himself the most terrible punishment of all, namely ignorance of one who is nobler than himself, and so he is deserted and bereft of the other's protection.

If my present task were to write about the Cynic philosophy, I could add many details about the Cynics no less important than what I have said already. Without wishing to interrupt my main theme, however, I will consider in due course the question of what kind of myths ought to be invented. Though perhaps another inquiry should precede this attempt, that is, to what branch of philosophy the composition of myths is appropriate. For we see

1. *Phoenissæ*, 472

that many philosophers and theologians, too, have employed it; Orpheus for instance, the most ancient of all the inspired philosophers, and many besides who came after him. Indeed, as we know, Xenophon, Antisthenes, and Plato often introduced myths, so it is obvious that even if the use of myth be not appropriate for the Cynic, it may still be so for some other type of philosopher.

I must first say a few words then about the subdivisions or instruments of philosophy. It does not make much difference by which of two ways one reckons logic, whether with practical or natural philosophy, since it is equally necessary to both these branches. Nonetheless, I will consider these as three separate branches and assign to each one three subdivisions. Natural philosophy consists of theology, mathematics, and thirdly the study of this world of generation and decay; things that, though imperishable, are nevertheless matter, and so deals with their essential nature and their substance in each case. Practical philosophy again consists of ethics in so far as it deals with the individual man; economics when it deals with the household as a unit; politics when it deals with the state. Logic, finally, is demonstrative in so far as it deals with the truth of principles; polemic when it deals with general opinions; eristic when it deals with opinions that seem only probabilities. These, then, are the divisions of philosophy, if I am not mistaken. Though, in truth, it would not be surprising that a mere soldier should be none too exact in these matters or not have them at his finger-tips, seeing that I speak less from book-knowledge than from observation and experience. For that matter you can yourselves bear me witness, should you wish to count up how few days have elapsed between the lecture that we recently heard and today, and, in addition, the great number of affairs which have of late demanded my attention. As I said, if I have omitted anything – though I do not think I have – then he who can make my classification more complete will be "no enemy but my friend".[1]

Of these branches of philosophy, logic has no concern with the composition of myths, nor has mathematics, the sub-division of natural philosophy; but they may be employed, if at all, by that department of practical philosophy which deals with the individual man, or by that department of theology which concerns itself with initiation and the Mysteries. For nature loves to hide her secrets,[2] and she does not suffer the hidden truth about the essential nature

1. Plato, *Timæus*, 54   2. Heraclitus, fr. 123

of the gods to be cast in naked words to the ears of the profane. Now, there are certain characteristics of ours that derive benefit from that veiled and unknown nature, which nourishes not our souls alone but our bodies also, bringing us into the presence of the gods. This, I think, often comes about by means of myths, when through riddles and the dramatic setting of myths that knowledge is insinuated into the ears of the multitude who cannot receive divine truths in their purest form. It is now evident what branch and what sort of philosophy may properly on occasion employ myths. To support my argument further, I call to witness the authority of those philosophers who were the first to use myths. Plato, for instance, in his theological descriptions of life in Hades, often uses myths, and the son[1] of Calliope before him. When Antisthenes, Xenophon, and Plato himself discuss certain ethical theories, they use myths as one of the ingredients, and not casually but of set purpose. Thus, if you too wished to use myths, you ought to have imitated these philosophers. Instead of Heracles you should have introduced the name of Perseus or Theseus, let us say, and have written in the style of Antisthenes; and in place of the dramatic setting used by Prodicus[2] in treating of those two gods[3], you should have introduced into your theatre another setting of the same sort.

Since I have also mentioned the myths that are suited to initiation, let us ourselves independently try to see what sort of myths they must be that suit one or the other of those two branches of philosophy.[4] We need no longer call in the aid of witnesses from the remote past for all points, but we will follow in the fresh footprints of one[5] whom next to the gods I revere and admire – equally, even, with Aristotle and Plato. He does not treat of all kinds of myths, but only those connected with initiation into the Mysteries, such as Orpheus, the founder of the most sacred of all the Mysteries, handed down to us. For it is the incongruous element in myths that guides us to the truth. By which I mean that the more paradoxical and prodigious the riddle is, the more it seems to warn us not to believe simply the bare words but rather to study diligently the hidden truth; to not relax our efforts until under the guidance of the gods those hidden things become plain, and so initiate, or rather, perfect our intelligence – or whatever we possess that is more sublime than the intelligence, that small particle of

1. Orpheus 2. In his allegory the *Choice of Heracles*; Xenophon, *Memorabilia*, 2.1.2
3. Pan and Zeus 4. Ethics and theology 5. Iamblichus

the One and the Good which contains the whole indivisibly, the complement of the soul, wherein the One and the Good comprehends the whole of soul itself through the prevailing, separate, and distinct presence of the One.

I was impelled, I know not how, to rave with his own sacred enthusiasm when I spoke like this of the attributes of great Dionysus; and now I set an ox on my tongue,[1] for I may not reveal what is too sacred for speech. Regardless, may the gods grant to me and to many of you who have not as yet been initiated into these Mysteries to enjoy the gifts thereof!

To confine myself, then, to what is lawful for us, both for me to say and for you to hear. Every discourse that is uttered consists of language and the thought to be expressed. A myth, therefore, is a form of discourse and so it will consist of these two. Let us consider them separately. In every discourse the thought is of two kinds, either simple or expressed through figures of speech, and there are many examples of both kinds. One is simple and admits of no variety, but that which is embellished with figures has in itself many possibilities of variation, with everything that you are yourself familiar if you have ever studied rhetoric (and most of these figures of thought are suited to myth). Though I need not discuss all or indeed many of them now, but only two: that in which the thought is dignified and that in which it is paradoxical. The same rules apply also to diction. For this is given a certain shape and form by those who do not express themselves carelessly or sweep in the refuse of language from the highways like a winter torrent.

Let us consider these two types. When we invent myths about sacred things our language must be wholly dignified and the diction must be as far as possible sober, beautiful, and entirely appropriate to the gods; there must be nothing in it which is vulgar, slanderous, or impious, lest we should lead the common people into this type of sacrilegious rashness; or rather, lest we should ourselves anticipate the common people in displaying impiety towards the gods. There must, therefore, be no incongruous element in the diction thus employed, but all must be dignified, beautiful, splendid, divine, pure, and, as far as possible, in conformity with the essential nature of the gods. As regards the thought, the incongruous may be admitted so that under the guidance of the gods men may be inspired to search out and study the hidden meaning, though they must not ask for any hint of the truth from others; rather, they must

1. A proverb for compelled silence; cf. Theognis, 815; Æschylus, *Agamemnon*, 36

acquire their knowledge from what is said in the myth itself.

For example, I have heard many people say that Dionysus was a mortal man because he was born of Semele; that he became a god through his knowledge of theurgy and the Mysteries; that, like our lord Heracles, on account of his royal virtue, was brought to Olympus by his father Zeus. "No, my good sir" said I "do you not perceive that the myth is obviously an allegory?" For in what sense do we regard the "birth" of Heracles, as it were, and of Dionysus as well, since in their case birth has superior, surpassing, and distinctive elements, even though it still falls within the limits of human nature, and up to a certain point resembles our own?

Heracles, for instance, is said to have been a child, even as we are; his divine body grew gradually; we are informed that he was instructed by teachers;[1] they say that he carried on wars and defeated all opponents before him, but for all that his body had to endure weariness. In fact, all of this did in his case occur, but on a scale greater than humans. For instance, while still in swaddling clothes, he strangled the serpents then exposed himself to the very elements of nature, the extremes of heat and cold, and things most difficult to contend with, such as lack of food and loneliness. Then there is his journey over the sea itself in a golden cup,[2] though, by the gods, I do not think it was really a cup, but my belief is that he himself walked on the sea as though it were dry land.[3]

For what was impossible to Heracles? Which was there of the so-called elements that did not obey his divine and most pure form, subdued as they were to the creative and perfecting force of his pure and immaculate power? For him did mighty Zeus, with the aid of Athena, goddess of Forethought, beget to be the saviour of the world, and appoint as his guardian this goddess whom he had brought forth whole from the whole of himself. Later, he called Heracles to his side through the flame of a thunderbolt, thus bidding his son to come to him by the divine signal of the ethereal rays of light. Now when we meditate on this, may Heracles be gracious to you and to me!

As for the commonly received legend about the birth of Dionysus, which was in fact no birth but a divine manifestation, in what respect was it like the birth of men? While he was still in his mother's womb, she, as the story goes, was beguiled by jealous Hera to entreat her lover to visit her as he was wont to visit his spouse.

---

1. Dio Chrysostom, *Oration* 1, 61 2. Apollodorus, *Bibliotheca*, 2; Athenæus, 11.470

3. This may be a passing shot at the Christians and need not be taken too seriously

Then her frail body, unable to endure the thunders of Zeus, began to be consumed by the lightning. When everything there was being devoured by flames, however, Zeus bade Hermes snatch Dionysus forth, whereupon he cut open his own thigh and sewed the babe therein.[1] In due course, when the time was ripe for the child's birth, Zeus in the pangs of travail came to the nymphs, who by their song over the thigh did "undo the stitching"[2] and brought to light for us the dithyramb.[3] At which point the god was driven mad by Hera, but the Mother of the Gods healed him of his sickness and immediately he became a god. His followers were not, like Heracles, Lichas, for instance, or Iolaus, or Telamon, or Hylas, or Abderos, but Satyrs, Bacchanals, Pans, and a whole host of lesser divinities.

Do you perceive how much of man there is in this generation through the fire of a thunderbolt, that his delivery is even more human, and that his deeds, even more than these two that we have mentioned, resemble those of human beings? Why, then, do we not set aside all this nonsense and recognise herein first the fact that Semele was wise in sacred things? For she was the daughter of Phoenician Cadmus, and the god himself bears witness to the wisdom of the Phoenicians when he says: "the Phoenicians, too, have learned many of the roads travelled by the blessed gods".

I think, then, that she was the first among the Greeks to perceive that there was to be before long a visible manifestation of this god. So it was that she foretold it, and, sooner than was fitting, gave the signal for certain of the mystic rites connected with his worship; for she had not the patience to wait for the appointed time and was thus consumed by the fire that fell upon her. When it was the will of Zeus to bestow on all mankind in common a new order of things, however, and to make them pass from the nomadic to a more civilised mode of life, Dionysus came from India and revealed himself as a god made visible, visiting the cities of men and leading with him a great host of divine beings. Everywhere he bestowed upon all men in common the plant of "the gentle vine" as the symbol of his manifestation. As their lives were made more gentle by it, the Greeks, I believe, gave it that name,[4] referring to Semele thereafter as "the mother of Dionysus" because of the prediction she had made, but also because the god honoured her as having been the first prophetess of his advent while it was yet to be.

---

1. cf. Euripides, *Bacchæ*, 279 2. cf. Pindar, fr. 85
3. An ancient Greek choral song, typically performed in honour of Dionysus
4. *ἡμερίς* = the vine; *ἥμερος* = gentle

Since this is the historical truth of these events when accurately considered and examined, those who sought to discover what sort of god Dionysus is worked into a myth the truth, as I have relayed, and expressed through allegory both the essential nature of the god and his conception in his father, Zeus, among the intelligible gods, along with his birth, independent of generation in this our world...[1] in the whole universe, and in their proper order, all those other facts which are well worth studying, but too difficult for me at any rate to describe – partly, perhaps, because I am still ignorant of the precise truth about them,[2] though perhaps, also, because I am unwilling to exhibit as in a theatre this god who is at once hidden and manifest, and to do so, moreover, for ears that have not sought after truth and minds disposed to anything rather than the study of philosophy.

That said, let Dionysus himself decide about these things, though I do indeed implore him to inspire my mind and yours with his own sacred enthusiasm for true knowledge of the gods, so that we may not by remaining too long uninspired by him have to suffer the fate of Pentheus, perhaps even while we are alive, but most certainly after death has freed us from the body. For he in whom the abundance of life has not been perfected by the essential nature of Dionysus, uniform and wholly indivisible as it is in the divisible world; pre-existing, whole, and unmixed in all things; he, I say, who has not been perfected by means of the divine Bacchic enthusiasm for the god, runs the risk that his life may flow into too many channels, and as it flows be torn to shreds, hence coming to naught. Though when I say "flow" or "torn to shreds", no one must consider the bare meaning of the words and suppose that I mean a mere trickle of water or a thread of linen; rather, he must understand these words in another sense, that used by Plato, Plotinus, Porphyry, and the inspired Iamblichus. One who does not interpret them thus will laugh at them no doubt, but let me assure him that it will be a Sardonic laugh,[3] since he will be forever deprived of that knowledge of the gods which I hold to be more precious than to rule over the whole world, Roman and Barbarian put together. By Lord Helios I swear it. Once again, then, some god or another, by no choice of my own, has brought forth in me this Bacchic fervour.

Let us return to what led me to say all this. Whenever myths on sacred subjects are incongruous in thought, by that very fact they cry aloud, as it were, and summon us not to believe them literally

1. a lacuna of several words 2. cf. Plato, *Republic*, 382

3. A proverb for forced laughter, cf. *The Odyssey*, XX, 302; Plato, *Republic*, 337

but to study and track down their hidden meaning. In such myths, the incongruous element is even more valuable than the serious and straightforward, for when the latter is used there is risk of our regarding the gods as exceedingly great, noble, and good, certainly, but still as human beings. Whereas, when the meaning is expressed via the incongruous, there is some hope that, by surpassing the ostensible significance of the words, one may arrive at comprehension of the true nature of the gods and their pure intelligence, which transcends all existing things.

These, then, are the reasons why that branch of philosophy which is connected with initiation and the doctrines of the Mysteries ought by all means to be expressed in devout and serious language, while as regards the thought, the narrative may be expounded in a style that has stranger qualities. Yet one who is inventing tales for the purpose of reforming morals and inserts myths therein, does so not for men but for those who are children, whether in years or intelligence, and who on all accounts stand in need of such tales. If, however, you took us for children, myself, for instance, or Anatolius here, and you may reckon with us Memmorius, also, as well as Salutius and, if you will, all the others in due order, then you are in need of a voyage to Anticyra.[1]

For why should one pretend to be polite? Tell me, I ask, in the name of the gods, and of myth itself, or rather in the name of Helios the Lord of all the universe, what have you ever accomplished, great or small? When did you ever champion one who was threatened with death and had right on his side? When did you ever comfort the mourner and teach him by your arguments that death is not an evil either for him who has suffered it or for his friends? What youth will ever give you the credit for his temperance, and say that you have made him show himself sober instead of dissolute; beautiful not merely in body but far more in soul? What strenuous discipline have you ever embraced? What have you ever done to make you worthy of the staff of Diogenes, or, still more, by Zeus, of his freedom of speech? Do you really think it so great an achievement to carry a staff and let your hair grow, to haunt cities and camps uttering calumnies against the noblest men, and flattering the vilest? Tell me in the name of Zeus and of this audience now present, who are disgusted with philosophy because of men of your sort, why was it that you visited the late Emperor

1. Hellebore, a supposed cure for madness, grew at Anticyra, hence the proverb; cf. Horace, *Satires*, 2.3.166

Constantius in Italy but could not travel as far as Gaul? For, if you had come to me, you would at any rate have associated with one who was better able to comprehend your language. What do you gain by travelling about in all directions and wearing out the very mules you ride? Indeed, I hear that you wear out the mule drivers as well, and that they dread the sight of you Cynics even more than of soldiers. For I am told that some of you belabour them more cruelly with your staffs than do the soldiers with their swords, so that they are naturally more afraid of you.

Long ago I gave you a nickname and now I think I will write it down. It is "monks"[1] – a name applied to certain persons by the impious Galilæans. They are for the most part men who by making small sacrifices gain much, or rather, everything from all sources, and in addition secure honour, crowds of attendants, and flattery. Something akin to that is your method, except perhaps for uttering divine revelations, which is not your custom, though it is ours; for we are wiser than those insensate men. Perhaps, too, there is the difference that you have no excuse for levying tribute on specious pretexts as they do, which they call "alms", whatever that may mean. In all other respects, however, your habits and theirs are very much alike. Like them you have abandoned your country, you wander about all over the world, and you gave more trouble than they did at my headquarters, and were more insolent. For they were at any rate invited to come, but you we tried to drive away.

Furthermore, what good have you, or rather, what have the rest of us derived from all this? First arrived Asclepiades, then Serenianus, then Chytron, then a tall boy with blonde hair – I know not his name – then you, and with you all twice as many more. And now, my good sirs, what good has come from your journey? What city or individual has had any experience of your alleged freedom of speech? Was it not foolish of you to choose in the first place to make this journey to an Emperor who did not even wish to set eyes on you? Then, when you had arrived, did you not behave even more foolishly, ignorantly, and insanely in flattering and barking at me in the same breath, offering me your books, and, moreover, imploring that they should be taken to me? I do not believe that any one of you ever visited a philosopher's school as diligently as you did my secretary. In fact, the entrance to my residence stood for you in place of the Academy, the Lyceum, and the Portico.

1. Ἀποτακτιστάς = "recluse" or "solitaire"; Julian is of course referring to Christian monks who lived on charity

Have done with all this nonsense. At any rate, lay it aside now if not before, for you will gain no advantage at this point from your long hair and your staff. Shall I tell you how you have caused philosophy to become so despised? It is because the most ignorant of the rhetoricians, those whose tongues not even Lord Hermes himself could purify, and who Athena herself with the aid of Hermes could not make wise, acquire by their profession of wandering around in public places some semblance of knowledge, then – for they fail to perceive the enduring truth of the proverb "grapes ripen beside grapes"[1] – all hastily rush into Cynicism. They adopt the staff, the cloak, the long hair, the ignorance that now comes with these, the impudence, the insolence, and in a word everything of the sort. They say that they are travelling the short and ready road to virtue.[2] I would that you were going by the longer! For you would more easily arrive by that road than by this of yours. Are you not aware that shortcuts usually involve one in great difficulties? For just as is the case with the public roads, a traveller who is able to take a shortcut will more easily than other men go all the way round, whereas it does not at all follow that he who went around could always go via the shorter route; so too in philosophy, the end and the beginning are one, namely, to know oneself and to become like the gods. That is to say, the first principle is self-knowledge, and the end of conduct is the resemblance to the higher powers.

He who desires to be a Cynic, therefore, ought to despise all the usages and opinions of men and turn his mind first of all to himself and the gods. For him, gold is not gold, nor sand sand; and if one should enquire into their value with a view to exchanging them, leave it to him to rate them at their proper worth, for the Cynic knows that both of them are but earth. The fact that one is scarcer and the other easier to obtain he thinks to be merely the result of the vanity and ignorance of mankind. He will judge the baseness or nobility of an action, not by the applause or blame of men, but by its intrinsic nature. He avoids any excess in food, and renounces the pleasures of love. When he is forced to obey the needs of the body, he is not the slave of opinion; nor does he wait for the savoury smells and sauces of a cook; nor does he ever look about for Phryne,

1. A proverb to express emulation. Juvenal, *Satires*, 2.81, re the decay of morals in Rome: "this plague has come upon us by infection, and it will spread still further, just as in the fields the scab of one sheep, or the mange of one pig, destroys an entire herd; just as one bunch of grapes becomes tainted by the presence of its neighbour".

2. Plutarch, *Erotici*, pg. 759, says this of the Cynics; cf. Laërtius, 7.121

or Lais, or So-and-so's wife, or his young daughter, or his serving-maid. Rather, he satisfies his body's needs as far as possible with whatever comes to hand, and by thrusting aside all hindrances derived from the body, he contemplates from above, from the peaks of Olympus, those other men who are:

Ἄτης ἐν λειμῶνι κατὰ σκότον ἠλάσκοντας

"Wandering in darkness over the meadow of Ate."[1]

They, who, for the sake of a few wholly trifling pleasures, are undergoing torments greater than any by Cocytus or Acheron,[2] or those of which the most ingenious of the poets are forever telling us. Now, the true shortcut to philosophy is this: a man must step outside himself completely and recognise that he is of the divine; he must not only keep his mind untiringly and steadfastly fixed upon divine, virtuous, and pure thoughts, but he must also pay little heed to his body, and think it, in the words of Heraclitus, "more fitting to be cast out than dirt".[3] By the simplest means alone, he must satisfy his body's needs for so long as the god commands him to use it as an instrument.

So much for that, as the saying goes. Now, to return to the point at which I digressed. Since, as I was saying, myths ought to be addressed either to those who though grown men are like children in intellect, or to those who in actual years are mere children, we must take pains to utter before them no word that is offensive to gods or men, or anything impious, as was done recently. Moreover, we must in all cases apply careful tests to see whether the myth is plausible, pertinent to the matter discussed, and whether what is invented is really a myth. What you composed recently was not your own myth, though you boasted that it was. Rather, your myth was an old one and you did but adapt it to fresh circumstances, as I believe people are in the habit of doing who use tropes and figures of thought. The poet of Paros,[4] for instance, is much given to this style. It seems, then, that you did not even invent your myth, my clever friend, and that yours was an idle boast. For even nurses have their repartee. Yet I dare say that, if the mythical tales of Plutarch

1. Empedocles, fr. 21

2. Rivers within the Greek underworld, beyond which lies Hades

3. Heraclitus, fr. 96; Julian is likely exaggerating for effect, as Heracles was referring to a corpse and not a living body

4. Archilochus

had ever fallen into your hands, you would have doubtless failed to observe what a difference there is between inventing a myth from the beginning and adapting to one's own purpose a myth that already exists.

I must not detain you for even a moment, however, or hinder you on your way along that shortcut to wisdom by having you embark on books that are long and hard to read. You have not even heard of the myth used by Demosthenes, he of the Pæanian deme, to address the Athenians when the Macedonian demanded that the Athenian orators be given up. You ought to have invented something of that sort. In heaven's name, was it too hard for you to relate some little myth of the kind? Alas, you will force me, too, to become a myth-maker.

A certain wealthy man[1] had numerous flocks of sheep, herds of cattle, "ranging flocks of goats",[2] and many times ten thousand mares "grazed his marsh-meadows".[3] Many shepherds, too, he had, both slaves and hired freedmen, cowherds, goatherds, grooms for his horses, and many estates besides. Now much of all this his father had bequeathed to him, but he had himself acquired many times more, being eager to enrich himself – whether justly or unjustly – for little did he care for the gods. Several wives he had, and sons and daughters by them, among whom he divided his wealth before he died. He did not teach them how to manage it, however, or how to acquire more if it should be lost, or how to preserve what they had. For in his ignorance he thought that their mere numbers would suffice. He himself had no real knowledge of that type of craft, since he had not acquired his wealth by any rational principle but rather by use and wont, like second-rate doctors who try to cure their patients by relying on their experience only, so that many diseases escape them altogether.[4]

Accordingly, since he thought that a number of sons would suffice to preserve his wealth, he took no thought of how to make them virtuous. This very thing, of course, proved to be the beginning of their iniquitous behaviour towards one another. For every one of them desired to be as rich as his father and to possess the whole for himself alone, and so attacked the brother that was his neighbour. For a time they continued to behave thus. Their relatives also shared in the folly and ignorance of those sons, since they themselves had had no better education. Then ensued a

1. Constantine 2. *The Iliad*, II, 474 3. *The Iliad*, XX, 221
4. cf., Plato, *Charmides*, 156

general slaughter, and heaven brought the tragic curse[1] to fulfilment. For "by the edge of the sword they divided their patrimony" and everything was thrown into confusion. The sons demolished the ancestral temples which their father before them had despised and had stripped of the votive offerings that had been dedicated by many worshippers, but not least by his own ancestors. Further still, after demolishing the temples, they erected sepulchres[2] on both new sites and on the old sites of the temples, as though impelled by fate, or by an unconscious presentiment that before long they would need many such sepulchres, seeing as they so neglected the gods.

When all was in confusion, and many marriages that were not marriages were being concluded, and the laws of god and man alike had been profaned, Zeus was moved with compassion and, addressing himself to Helios, he said: "O my son, divine offspring more ancient than heaven and earth, are you still minded to resent the insolence of that arrogant and audacious mortal, who by forsaking you brought so many calamities upon himself and his race? Do you think that, though you do not show your anger and resentment against him, nor whet your arrows against his children, you are any less the author of his destruction in that you abandoned his house to desolation? Let us summon the Fates and enquire whether any help may be given the man".

Forthwith, the Fates obeyed the call of Zeus. Yet Helios, who was as if absorbed in thought and inward debate, gave constant heed, with eyes fixed upon Zeus. Then spoke the eldest of the Fates: "O father, both Piety and Justice restrain us. It is for you, therefore, to prevail upon them, since you ordered us to be subservient to them".

To which Zeus made answer: "truly they are my daughters, and it is only proper that I question them. What, then, have you to say, venerable goddesses?"

"It is, father" they replied "as you yourself ordain. Be careful, however, lest this wicked zeal for impious deeds should prevail universally among men."

"I shall look into both these matters myself" Zeus replied. Then the Fates approached and spun all as their father willed.

Next Zeus addressed Helios: "you see the child below"[3] – now,

1. The curse of Oedipus on his sons

2. Christian churches were so called since they were built over the tombs of martyrs

this was a certain kinsman of those brothers who had been cast aside and, though he was the nephew of that rich man and the cousin of his heirs, he was nonetheless despised – "this child" said Zeus "is your own offspring. Swear, then, by my sceptre and yours that you will care especially for him and cure him of this malady. For you see how he is, as it were, infected with smoke, filth, and darkness. There is danger that the spark of fire which you did implant in him will be quenched, unless you clothe him in fighting strength.[1] Take care of him, therefore, and rear him, for I and the Fates yield to you this task."

When King Helios heard this he was glad and delighted in the child, since he perceived that in him a small spark of himself was still preserved. Thereafter, he reared the child whom he had withdrawn "from the blood and noise of war and the slaughter of men".[2]

Father Zeus also bade Athena, the Motherless Maiden, share in the task of raising the child with Helios. When, thus reared, he had become a young man "with the first down on his chin and all the vigour of youth",[3] he learned of numerous disasters that had befallen his kinsmen and his cousins; he had all but hurled himself into Tartarus, so confounded was he by the extent of those calamities. Yet Helios of his grace, aided by Athena, Goddess of Forethought, threw him into a slumber or trance, and so diverted him from that end. Upon waking, he at once departed to the desert. There he found a stone and rested for a while, debating within himself how he might escape evils so numerous and so vast. For all things now appeared grievous to him and for the moment there was no hope anywhere.

Then Hermes, who had an affinity for the young man, appeared before him in the guise of a youth of his own age, and, greeting him kindly, said: "follow me, and I will guide you by an easier and smoother road as soon as you have surmounted this winding and rugged place, where you see all men stumbling and obliged to turn back". So the youth set out with great circumspection, carrying a sword, shield, and spear, though as yet his head was bare. Relying on Hermes, he went forward by a road that was smooth, untrodden, and very bright, overhung with fruits and many lovely flowers, such as are dear to the gods, with trees also – ivy, laurel, and myrtle. When Hermes had brought him to the foot of a great and lofty mountain, he said: "on the summit of this mountain dwells the

1. *The Iliad*, IX, 231 2. *The Iliad*, XI, 164 3. *The Iliad*, XXIV, 348

father of all the gods. Be careful then – for herein lies the greatest risk of all[1] – to worship him with the utmost piety and ask of him whatever you will. You will choose, my child, only what is best".

So saying, Hermes once more became invisible, though the young man was eager to learn from him what he ought to ask from the father of the gods. When he saw that the Wayfinder was no longer at his side, he said: "the advice, while incomplete, is good nonetheless. Therefore, let me by the grace of fortune ask for what is best, though I do not as yet see clearly the father of the gods. Father Zeus – or whichever name would best please that men should call you by[2] – show me the way that leads upwards to you. For fairer still, I suspect, is the region where you are, if I may judge the beauty of your abode by the splendour of the place whence I have come".

When he had uttered this prayer a sort of slumber or trance came over him. Zeus then revealed to the young man Helios himself. Awestruck by that vision, the youth exclaimed "for this and for all other favours I will dedicate myself to you, O Father of the Gods!" Then he cast his arms about the knees of Helios and would not let release his hold but kept entreating the god to save him. Helios called Athena and bade her first enquire of him what arms they young man had brought with him. When she saw his shield, sword, and spear, she said: "but where, my child, is your ægis[3] and your helmet?"

"Even these that I have" he replied "I procured with difficulty. For in the house of my kinsfolk there was none to aid one so despised."

"Know, then" said mighty Helios "that you must without fail return to that place". Thereupon the youth entreated him not to send him back again but to keep him there, since he would never be able to ascend a second time and would instead be overwhelmed by the ills of that world. As he wept and implored, Helios replied: "no, you are young and not yet initiated. Return, therefore, to your own people that you may be initiated and thereafter dwell among them in safety. For return you must. Cleanse away all impiety and invoke me, Athena, and the other gods to aid you".

When Helios had said this the young man remained silent. Then mighty Helios led him to a high peak whose uppermost region was filled with light, but the lower with the thickest mist

1. Plato, *Republic*, 618 2. cf. Æschylus, *Agamemnon*, 160

3. Literally "the Gorgon's head", which formed the centre of the ægis, or breastplate, of Athena

imaginable, through which, as through water, the light of the rays of Lord Helios penetrated but faintly.

"Do you see" said Helios "your cousin, the heir?"[1]

"I see him" the youth replied.

"Again, do you see there herdsmen and shepherds?"

The young man answered that he did.

"Then what do you think of the heir's disposition? And what of his shepherds and herdsmen?"

"He seems to me" replied the young man "to be for the most part asleep, sunk in forgetfulness and devoted to pleasure; and of his shepherds, a few are honest, but most are vicious and brutal. For they devour or sell his sheep, and doubly injure their master in that they not only ruin his flocks but moreover make great gain, returning him but little thereof, while they declare with loud complaint that they are defrauded of their wages. And yet it would be better if they should demand and obtain their full pay than destroy the flock."

"Now, what if I and Athena here" said Helios "obeying the command of Zeus, should appoint you to govern all these, in place of the heir?"

The youth merely clung to him again and earnestly entreated that he might remain there.

"Do not be obstinate in disobedience" said Helios "lest I should hate you as I have cherished you till now."[2]

The young man then spoke as follows: "O most mighty Helios, and you, Pallas Athena – and you, too, Father Zeus, do I call to witness – dispose of me as you will". Then Hermes suddenly appeared once more and inspired him with greater courage. For now, he thought that he had found a guide for the journey back, and the long path to rulership.

Then spoke Athena: "listen carefully, good youth, that are born of myself and of this god, your noble sire. The most virtuous of the shepherds do not please this heir, for flatterers and profligates have made him their slave and tool. So it is that he is not beloved by the good, and is most deeply wronged by those who are supposed to love him. Be careful, then, when you return, that he not make you his flatterer rather than his friend. This second warning you must also heed, my son. That man slumbers, and hence he is often deceived, so remain ever sober and vigilant,[3] lest the flatterer assume the frankness of a friend and thus deceive you. It is as

1. Constantius 2. *The Iliad*, III, 415 3. *Peter*, 1.5.8; *Thessalonians*, 1.5.6

though a smith covered with smoke and cinders should come draped in white garments, with his face painted white, and thus induce you to give him one of your daughters in marriage.[1] My third warning to you is this: with the utmost zeal keep watch over yourself; reverence us first, and among men only him who resembles us, and no one besides. You see how false shame and excessive timidity have injured this foolish man".

Then mighty Helios took up the tale and said: "once you have chosen your friends, treat them as friends and do not regard them as servants and attendants; let your conduct towards them be generous, candid, and honourable; say not one thing about them while you think another. You see that it was treachery to his friends that destroyed this heir. Love your subjects even as we love you. Prefer our worship to all other blessings. For we are your protectors, your friends, your preservers".

At these words the young man became calm and showed plainly that he was already obedient in all things to the gods.

"Come" said Helios "depart now with good hope. For everywhere we shall be with you, even I and Athena, and Hermes here, and with us all the gods that dwell upon Olympus, reside in the air, and upon the earth; indeed, the whole race of gods, so long as you remain pious towards us, loyal to your friends, and humane towards your subjects, ruling them and guiding them to what is best, never yielding to your own passions or becoming the slave of theirs.

"To accompany your departure and the armour that you brought here, receive from me first this torch, so that even below a great light may shine for you and ease your longing for the this place. From fair Athena here, take this ægis and helmet. For as you see, she has many, and she gives them to whom she will. Hermes, too, gifts to you a golden wand. Go, then, adorned thus in full armour over sea and land, steadfastly obeying our laws, and let no man or woman, kinsman or foreigner persuade you to neglect our commands. For while you abide by them, you will be loved and honoured by us, respected by our good servants, and formidable to the wicked and impious. Know that a mortal frame was given to you so that you might discharge these duties. For we desire, out of respect for your ancestors, to cleanse the house of your forefathers. Remember, therefore, that you possess an immortal soul that is our offspring, and that if you should follow us, you shall also be a god and with us shall behold our father."

1. An echo of Plato, *Republic*, 495

Now, whether this be a fable or a true narrative, I cannot say. In your composition, however, whom do you mean by Pan, and whom by Zeus, unless you and I are they, that is, you are Zeus and I am Pan? What an absurd counterfeit Pan! Yet you are still more absurd, by Asclepius, and very far indeed from being Zeus! Is not all this the utterance of a mouth that foams with morbid rather than inspired madness?[1] Do you not know that Salmoneus[2] in his day was punished by the gods for just this? For attempting, though a mortal man, to play the part of Zeus? Then, too, there is the account in Hesiod's poems of those who styled themselves by the names of the gods, even of Hera and of Zeus, but if you have not heard of it until this moment, I can excuse you for that. For you have not been well educated, nor did fate bestow on you such a guide to the poets as I had – by which I mean the philosopher[3] now present. Later, I arrived at the threshold of philosophy to be initiated therein by the teaching of one[4] whom I consider superior to all the men of my own time. He used to teach me to practise virtue before all else, and to regard the gods as my guides to all that is good. Of course, whether he accomplished anything of real benefit he himself must determine, or rather, the ruling gods must; but at least he purged me of such infatuate folly and insolence as yours, and tried to make me more temperate than I was by nature. Although I was, as you know, equipped[5] with great external advantages, I nevertheless submitted myself to my teacher, to his friends and peers, and to the philosophers of his school; I was eager to be instructed by all whose praises I heard uttered by him, and I read each and every book that he approved.

So it was that I found myself initiated by those guides, in the first place by a philosopher who trained me in the preparatory discipline, and next by that most perfect philosopher who revealed to me the entrance to philosophy. While I achieved a modest amount on account of the engrossing affairs that overwhelmed me from without, for all that I have still had the benefit of right training, and have not travelled by the short road as you say you have, but have gone all the way round. Though, in truth, as I call the gods to witness, I believe that the road I took was actually a shorter road to virtue than yours. For I, at any rate, if I may say so without bad taste, am standing at the entrance, whereas you are a

1. Plato, *Phædrus*, 244 2. *The Odyssey*, II, 235; Pindar, *Pythian*, 4.143; Salmoneus was destroyed by a thunder-bolt for imitating the thunder and lightning of Zeus
3. Maximus of Ephesus 4. Iamblichus 5. "Winged" in the original Greek

long way even from the entrance. "But as for virtue, you and your brethren..."[1] – omit the ill-sounding phrase and fill in the blank yourself. Or rather, if you will, bear with me when I "put it mildly"[2] by asking "what part or lot have you in it?"

You criticise everyone, though you yourself do nothing to deserve praise, while your praises are in worse taste than those of the most ignorant rhetoricians. They, because they have nothing to say and cannot invent anything from the matter in hand, are always dragging in Delos, and Leto with her children, then "swans singing their shrill song and the trees that echo them" and "dewy meadows full of soft, deep grass" and the "scent of flowers" and "the season of spring" and other figures of the same sort.[3] When did Isocrates ever do this in his panegyrics? Or when did anyone of those ancient writers who were genuine votaries of the Muses, unlike the writers of today? I omit what I might add, however, lest I should make them my enemies also, and offend at once the most worthless Cynics and the most worthless rhetoricians. Though, of course, I have nothing but friendly feelings for the truly virtuous Cynics, if indeed there be any nowadays. The same goes for all honest rhetoricians. Thus, while a vast number of illustrations of this sort flow into my mind – for anyone who desired to use them could certainly draw from an ample jar[4] – I shall refrain because of the present pressure of business. I do, nonetheless, still have somewhat to add to my discourse, like the balance of a debt; so before I turn to other matters, let me complete this treatise.

I ask you, then, what reverence for the names of the gods was shown by the Pythagoreans and by Plato? What was Aristotle's attitude in these matters? Is it not worthwhile to pay attention to this? Or surely no one will deny that he of Samos[5] was reverent? For he did not even allow the names of the gods to be used on a seal, nor oaths to be rashly uttered in the names of the gods. If I should go on to say that he also travelled to Egypt, visited Persia, and everywhere endeavoured to be admitted to the inner mysteries of the gods, to be initiated everywhere into every kind of rite, I shall be saying what is familiar and obvious to most people, though you may not have heard of it.

---

1. A direct quotation from Demosthenes, *De Corona*, 128; the word omitted by Julian is *κάθαρμα* = "offscourings" or "outcast" or "pariah"

2. An echo of Xenophon, *Anabasis*, 1.5.14

3. For this device of introducing cliched poetical and mythological allusions, cf. Themistius, 330, 336; Aristides, *Oration* 20, 428; Himerius, *Oration* 18; Epictetus, 3.282

4. A proverb for wealth, abundance; cf. Theocritus, 10.13

5. Pythagoras

Listen to what Plato says: "for my part, Protarchus, I feel a more-than-human awe, indeed, a fear beyond expression, of the names of the gods. Therefore, I will address Aphrodite by whatever name pleases her best; but as for pleasure, I know that it has many forms". This is what he says in the Philebus,[1] and he says the same sort of thing again in the Timæus.[2] For he states that we ought to believe directly and without proof what we are told, by which he means what the poets say about the gods. I have brought forward this passage for fear that Socrates may furnish you with an excuse – as I believe he does to many Platonists because of his natural tendency to irony – to slight the doctrine of Plato. For it is not Socrates who is speaking here, but Timæus, who had not the least tendency to irony. Though for that matter it is not a sound principle to enquire who says a thing and to whom, rather than the actual words.

Now, will you allow me to cite next that all-wise Siren, the living image of Hermes the god of eloquence, the man dear to Apollo and the Muses?[3] Well, he declares that all who raise the question or seek to enquire at all whether gods exist, ought not to be answered as though they were men but to be chastised as wild beasts. If, therefore, you had read that introductory sentence which was inscribed over the entrance to his school, like Plato's, you would most surely know that those who entered the Lyceum were warned to be reverent to the gods, to be initiated into all the mysteries, to take part in the most sacred ceremonies, and to be instructed in knowledge of every kind.

Furthermore, do not try to frighten me by bringing forward Diogenes as some sort of Mormo.[4] He was never initiated, they tell us, and replied to someone who once advised him to be initiated: "it is absurd of you, my young friend, to think that any tax-gatherer, if only he be initiated, can share in the rewards of the just in the next world, while Agesilaus and Epameinondas are doomed to lie in the mire".[5] These, my young friend, are profound words, and, I am persuaded, call for a more considered discussion. May the goddesses themselves grant us understanding thereof! Though, in truth, I think that has already been bestowed by them. For it is evident that Diogenes was not impious, as you aver, but resembled those philosophers whom I mentioned a moment ago. For having

1. *Philebus*, 12 2. *Timæus*, 40 3. Aristotle

4. *μορμολυκεῖον* = mormolyceum, also known as a mormo(n); a spirit in Greek folklore which was invoked to frighten children and keep them from misbehaving

5. Laërtius, 6.39

regard to the circumstances in which his lot was cast, and next paying heed to the commands of the Pythian god, knowing that the candidate for initiation must first be registered as an Athenian citizen, and, if he be not an Athenian by birth, must first become one by law, it was this he avoided, not initiation, because he considered that he was a citizen of the world; and, moreover, such was the greatness of his soul that he thought he ought to associate himself with the divine nature of all the gods who in common govern the whole universe, and not only with those whose functions are limited to certain portions of it.

Out of reverence for the gods, he did not transgress their laws, though he trampled on all other opinions and tried to give a new stamp to the common currency. Further still, he did not return to that servitude from which he had joyfully been released. What servitude do I mean? I mean that he would not enslave himself to the laws of a single city and submit himself to all that must befall one who had become an Athenian citizen. For is it likely that a man who in order to honour the gods journeyed to Olympia, and, like Socrates, embraced philosophy in obedience to the Pythian oracle – for he says himself that at home and in private he received the commands of that oracle, hence came his impulse to philosophy[1] – is it likely, I ask, that such a man would not very gladly have entered the temples of the gods but for the fact that he was trying to avoid submitting himself to any set of laws and making himself the slave of any one constitution?

Why, you will say, did he not assign this reason, but on the contrary a reason that detracted not a little from the dignity of the Mysteries? Perhaps one might bring this same reproach against Pythagoras as well, but the reasoning would be incorrect. For not everything ought to be told, indeed, even of those things that we are permitted to declare; some things, it seems to me, we ought to refrain from uttering to the common crowd. The explanation in this case, however, is obvious. For since he perceived that the man who exhorted him to be initiated neglected to regulate his own life aright, though he prided himself on having been initiated, Diogenes wished at the same time to reform his morals and to teach him that the gods reserve their rewards without stint for those whose lives have earned them the right to be initiated, even though they have not gone through the ceremony, whereas the wicked gain

1. Diogenes, like Socrates, claimed that he had a *δαιμόνιον* (daimon), a personal spirit to guide his conduct

nothing by penetrating within the sacred precincts. For this is what the hierophant proclaims, when he refuses the rite of initiation to him "whose hands are not pure or who for any reason ought not!"[1] Yet where would this discourse end if you are still unconvinced by what I have said?

1. This was the *πρόρρησις* or *præfatio sacrorum*; cf. Livy, 45.5

CONSOLATION ON THE DEPARTURE OF SALUTIUS

PREFACE

The *Consolation on the Departure of Salutius* was written in 359, shortly after Constantius had recalled Julian's quæstor from Gaul as a means of punishing and undermining his cousin. As the title suggests, Julian was devastated by the loss of a close friend, a trusted adviser, a brother-in-arms, and a fellow Hellene who would be best remembered for his Neo-Platonic treatise *On the Gods and the World*. The oration itself is a common type of sophistic composition – a "speech of consolation" – which Julian addressed to himself, but will surely have been read by Salutius.

It is notable that throughout the piece, Julian only ever refers to God in the singular (save for a passage framed as though it were spoken by Pericles and a few Homeric references). That the oration was presumably sent to Salutius, and thus could have been intercepted, lends credence to the idea that he did not wish to be too explicit lest his true religious beliefs be made public. Towards the end of the oration, when Julian offers a prayer on behalf of Salutius, God is referred to as "the God of Strangers" and "the Friendly One", two epithets for Zeus, which, though well-known, could plausibly have been denied. The two would be reunited after Julian became sole Augustus in 361, and when the Emperor received a mortal wound during his ill-fated Persia campaign two years later, Salutius remained by Julian's side in his final hours.

CONSOLATION ON THE DEPARTURE OF SALUTIUS

Ah, my beloved comrade, unless I tell you all that I said to myself when I learned that you were compelled to journey far from my side, I shall think I am deprived of some comfort; or rather, I shall consider that I have not even begun to procure some assuagement for my grief until I have first relayed it to you. For we two have shared in many hardships and also in many pleasant deeds and words, in affairs private and public, at home and in the field, and therefore for the present troubles, be they what they may, we must discover some cure, some remedy that both can share.

Yet who will imitate for us the lyre of Orpheus, who will echo for us the songs of the Sirens, or discover the drug nepenthe?[1] Though perhaps that was some tale full of Egyptian lore, or such a tale as the poet himself invented when, in what follows, he wove in the story of the sorrows of the Trojans, where Helen had learned it from the Egyptians. I do not mean a tale of all the woes that the Greeks and Trojans inflicted on one another, but rather tales such as they must be that will dispel the griefs of men's souls and have power to restore cheerfulness and calm. For pleasure and pain, it seems to me, are connected at their source[2] and succeed each other in turn. Indeed, philosophers assert that in all that befalls the wise man, the very greatest trials afford him as much felicity as vexation; and thus, as they say, does the bee extract sweet dew from the bitterest herb that grows on Hymettus and works it into honey. Even so, bodies that are naturally healthy and robust are nourished by any kind of food, and food that often seems unwholesome for others, far from injuring them, makes them strong. On the other hand, the slightest causes usually inflict very serious injuries on

1. *Odyssey*, IV, 227; a sophistic commonplace. The existence of Nepenthe, "that which chases away sorrow", is heavily disputed, as Julian alludes to here

2. Plato, *Phædo*, 60

persons who by nature or nurture, or owing to their habits, have an unsound constitution and are lifelong invalids. Just so with regard to the mind: those who have so trained it such that it is not altogether unhealthy but moderately sound, while it may not, in truth, exhibit the vigour of Antisthenes or Socrates, or the courage of Callisthenes, or the imperturbability of Polemon, it can, nevertheless, under the same conditions as theirs, adopt the golden mean, by which, I say, they will probably be able to remain cheerful in more trying conditions.

For my part, when I put myself to the test to find out how I am and shall be affected by your departure, I felt the same anguish as when at home I first left my preceptor.[1] For everything flashed across my mind at once: the labours that we shared and endured together; our unfeigned and candid conversation; our honest and upright exchanges; our co-operation in all that was good; our equally-matched and never-repented zeal and eagerness in opposing malefactors. How often we supported each other with one equal temper![2] How alike were our ways! How invaluable our friendship! Then, too, there came into my mind the words: "then was Odysseus left alone".[3] For now I am indeed like him, since the god has removed you, as with Hector,[4] beyond the range of the shafts which have so often been aimed at you by slanderers, or rather at me, since they desired to wound me through you; for they thought that only thus should I be vulnerable, if they should deprive me of the companionship of a faithful friend and devoted brother-in-arms, one who never on any pretext failed to share the dangers that threatened me. Moreover, the fact that you now have a smaller share than I in such labours and dangers does not, I think, make your grief less than mine; but you feel all the more anxiety for me and any harm that may befall my person.[5] For even as I never set your interests second to mine, so have I ever found you equally well disposed towards me. I am, therefore, naturally much chagrined that to you who with regard to all others can say "I heed them not, for my affairs are prosperous",[6] I alone occasion sorrow and anxiety. This sorrow, however, it seems we share equally, though you grieve only on my account, while I constantly feel the lack of your company and call to mind the friendship that we pledged to one another, that friendship which we ever cemented afresh, based as it was, first and foremost, on virtue, and secondly on the obligations

1. Mardonius 2. *The Iliad*, XVII, 720 3. *The Iliad*, XI, 401
4. *The Iliad*, XI, 163 5. *The Iliad*, XVII, 242 6. *Adespota fragmenta*, 430

which you continually conferred on me, and I on you. Not by oaths or by any such ties did we ratify it, like Theseus and Peirithous, but by being of the same mind and purpose, and that so far from forbearing to inflict injury on any citizen, we never even debated any such thing with one another. Though whether anything useful was done or planned by us in common, I will leave for others to say.

Now, that it is natural for me to be grieved by the present event, on being parted for even so short a time – and may God grant that it will be short – from one who is not only my friend but my loyal colleague, I think even Socrates, that great herald and teacher of virtue, will agree; so far at least as I may judge from the evidence on which we rely for our knowledge of him, that being the words of Plato. Regardless, what he says is: "ever more difficult did it seem to me to govern a state rightly. For neither is it possible to achieve anything without good friends and loyal colleagues, nor is it very easy to obtain enough of these".[1] And if Plato thought this more difficult than digging a canal through Mount Athos,[2] how must we expect to find it, we who in wisdom and knowledge are more inferior to him than he was to God? Yet it is not only when I think of the help in the administration that we gave one another in turn, and that which enabled us to bear more easily all that fate or our opponents brought to pass contrary to our purpose; but because I am destined soon to be bereft, also, of what has ever been my only solace and delight, it is natural that I am and have been cut to the very heart.[3] For in the future to what friend can I turn as loyal as yourself? With whose guileless and unaffected candour shall I now brace myself? Who now will give me prudent counsel, reprove me with affection, give me strength for good deeds without arrogance and conceit, and use frankness after extracting the bitterness from the words, like those who extract from medicines what is nauseating while leaving in what is beneficial?[4] These are the advantages that I reaped from your friendship! And now that I have been deprived of all these all at once, with what arguments shall I supply myself, so that when I am in danger of flinging away my life for loss of your counsel and kind heart,[5] they may persuade me to be calm and bear nobly whatever God has sent?[6] For in accordance

1. Julian paraphrases Plato, *Epistle* 7, 325
2. This feat of Xerxes became a rhetorical commonplace
3. Aristophanes, *Acharnians*, 1 4. A commonplace; Plato, *Laws*, 659
5. *The Odyssey*, XI, 20 6. Demosthenes, *De Corona*, 97

with the will of God, our mighty Emperor has surely planned this as all else. What, then, must my thoughts be, what spells must I find to persuade my soul to bear tranquilly the trouble with which it is now dismayed? Shall I imitate the discourses of Zamolxis, by which I mean those Thracian spells that Socrates brought to Athens and declared that he must utter them over the fair Charmides before he could cure him of his headache?[1] Or must we leave these alone as being, like large machinery in a small theatre, too lofty for our purpose and suited to greater troubles; and rather, from the deeds of old whose fame we have heard told, as the poet says,[2] shall we gather the fairest flowers as though from a variegated and many-coloured meadow, and thus console ourselves with such narratives, adding thereto some of the teachings of philosophy? For just as certain drugs are infused into things that have too saccharine a taste, and thus their cloying sweetness is tempered, so when tales like these are seasoned by the maxims of philosophy, we avoid seeming to drag in a tedious profusion of ancient history and a superfluous and uncalled-for flow of words.

"What first, what next, what last shall I relate?"[3] Shall I tell how the famous Scipio, who loved Lælius and was loved by him in return with equal yoke of friendship,[4] as the saying goes, not only took pleasure in his company, but undertook no task without first consulting with him and obtaining his advice as to how he should proceed? It was this, I understand, that furnished those who from envy slandered Scipio by saying that Lælius was the real author of his enterprises, and Africanus merely the actor. The same remark is made about ourselves, and, far from resenting this, I rather rejoice at it. For to accept another's good advice, Zeno held to be a sign of greater virtue than independently deciding oneself what one ought to do, and so he altered the saying of Hesiod. For Zeno says: "that man is best who follows good advice" instead of "decides all things for himself".[5] Not that the alteration is to my liking. For I am convinced that what Hesiod says is truer, and that Pythagoras was wiser than either of them when he originated the proverb and gave to mankind the maxim: "friends have all things in common".[6] By this he certainly did not mean property only, but also a partnership in intelligence and wisdom. So all that you suggested belongs just as much to me who adopted it, and whenever I was the actor who carried out your plans, you naturally have an equal share in the

1. Plato, *Charmides*, 156 2. *The Iliad*, IX, 524 3. *The Odyssey*, IX, 14
4. Theocritus, 12.15 5. Hesiod, *Works and Days*, 293 6. Laërtius, 8.10

accomplishment. In fact, to whichever of us the credit may seem to belong, it belongs equally to the other, and malicious persons will gain nothing from their idle talk.

Let me return now to Africanus and Lælius. When Carthage had been destroyed[1] and all Libya made subject to Rome, Africanus sent Lælius home, whereupon he embarked to carry the good news to their fatherland. Scipio was grieved at the separation from his friend, but he did not think his sorrow inconsolable. Lælius, too, was probably afflicted at having to embark alone, but he did not regard it as an intolerable calamity. Cato also made such a voyage and left his intimate friends at home, as did Pythagoras, Plato, and Democritus; indeed, they took with them no companion on their travels, though they left behind them at home many whom they dearly loved. Pericles also set out on his campaign against Samos without taking Anaxagoras, and he conquered Euboea by following the latter's advice; for while he had been trained by his instruction, the philosopher himself he did not drag along in his train as though he were part of the equipment needed for battle. And yet, in his case, too, we are told that much against his will the Athenians separated him from the company of his teacher. Wise man that he was, however, he bore the folly of his fellow citizens with fortitude and mildness. Indeed, he thought that he must of necessity bow to his country's will when, as a mother might, however unjustly, she still resented their close friendship. To which he probably reasoned as follows (you must take what I say next as if they were the very words of Pericles himself[2]):

"the whole world is my city and fatherland, and my friends are the gods, lesser divinities, and all good men, whoever and wherever they may be. Yet it is right to respect also the country where I was born, since this is the divine law, and to obey all her commands and not oppose them, or, as the proverb says, kick against the pricks. For inexorable, as the saying goes, is the yoke of necessity. Though we must not even complain or lament when her commands are harsher than usual, but rather consider the matter as it actually is. She now orders Anaxagoras to leave me and I shall see no more my close friend, on whose account the night was hateful to me because it did not allow me to see him,[3] whereas I was grateful to daylight

1. cf. Livy, 27.7

2. Cobet supposes this to be a gloss, but Julian may be echoing Plato, *Menexenus*, 246

3. A questionable application to Pericles of Critoboulos' speech in Xenophon, *Symposium*, 4.12

and the sun for they allowed me to see him whom I loved most. Yet, Pericles, if nature had given you eyes only as she has to wild beasts, it would be natural enough for you to feel tremendous grief. Since, however, she has breathed into you a soul, and implanted in you intelligence by means of which you now behold in memory many past events, even though they are no longer before you; and further, since your reasoning power discovers many future events and reveals them, as it were, to the eyes of your mind; and again, your imagination sketches for you not only those present events which are going on before your eyes and allows you to judge and survey them, but also reveals to you things at a distance and many thousands of stades[1] removed more clearly than what is going on at your feet, what need is there for such grief and resentment? To show that I have authority for what I say, the Sicilian[2] observed that 'the mind sees and the mind hears'; and mind is a thing so acute and endowed with such amazing speed that when Homer wishes to show us one of the gods employing incredible speed in travelling, he says:

Ὡς δ' ὅτ' ἂν ἀΐξῃ νόος ἀνέρος·

"Swift as a thought goes flashing through a man"[3]

Thus, if you employ your mind, you will easily see from Athens one who is in Ionia; and from the country of the Celts, one who is in Illyria or Thrace; likewise, from Thrace or Illyria, one who is in the country of the Celts. Moreover, though plants if removed from their native soil when the weather and season are unfavourable cannot be kept alive, it is not so with men, who can remove themselves from one place to another without completely deteriorating or changing their character, deviating thereby from the right principles that they had adopted prior. It is therefore unlikely that our goodwill shall become blunted, if indeed we do not love and cherish each other all the more for the separation. For "wantonness attends on satiety",[4] but fondness on want. So in this respect we shall be better off if our affection tends to increase, and we shall keep one another firmly set in our minds like sacred images. At one moment I shall see Anaxagoras, and the next he shall see me. Though nothing prevents our seeing one another at the same instant, of course, by which I do not mean our flesh and

1. The Attic stade was about 600 ft 2. Epicharmus, fr. 13 3. *The Iliad*, XV, 80
4. Theognis, 153

sinews, the "outline of forms and likeness in the chest"[1] of the original body, though perhaps there is no reason why these, too, should not become visible to our minds; rather, I mean our virtue, our deeds and words, our exchanges, and those conversations which we so often held with one another, when in perfect harmony we sang the praises of education, justice, and mind that governs all things mortal and human; when, too, we discussed the art of government, law, the different ways of being virtuous, and the noblest pursuits; in short, everything that occurred to us when, as occasion served, we mentioned these subjects. If we reflect on these things and nourish ourselves with these images, we shall probably pay no heed to the "visions of dreams in the night",[2] nor will the senses corrupted by the temperament of the body exhibit to our minds empty and vain phantoms. For we shall not employ the senses at all to assist and minister to us; instead, our minds will have escaped from them and so will be occupied by the themes I have mentioned, stimulated to comprehend and associate with things incorporeal. For by the mind we commune even with God, and by its aid we are enabled to see and to grasp things that escape the senses, being far apart in space, or rather, having no need of space; that is to say, all of us who have lived so as to deserve such a vision, conceiving it in the mind and laying hold thereof."

Ah, but Pericles, inasmuch as he was a man of lofty soul and was bred as became a free man in a free city, could take solace in such sublime arguments, whereas I, born of such men as now are,[3] must beguile and console myself with arguments more human. Thus I assuage the excessive bitterness of my sorrow, since I constantly endeavour to devise some comfort for the anxious and uneasy ideas which keep assailing me as they arise from this event, like a charm against some wild beast that is gnawing into my very vitals and my soul. First and foremost of the hardships that I shall have to face is that now I shall be bereft of our guileless exchanges and unreserved conversation. For I have no one now to whom I can talk with anything like the same confidence. What, you say, can I not easily converse with myself? Yet I wonder, will someone not rob me of even my thoughts, and compel me besides to think differently, and to admire what I prefer not to admire? Or does this robbery amount to a prodigy unimaginable, like writing on water or boiling a stone,[4] or tracing the course of the flight of birds on the wing?

1. Euripides, *Phoenissæ*, 165 2. *Adespota*, fr. 108 3. *The Iliad*, V, 304
4. Two common proverbs

Well then, since no one can deprive us of our thoughts, we shall surely commune with ourselves in some fashion, and perhaps God will suggest some alleviation. For it is not likely that he who entrusts himself to God will be utterly neglected and left wholly desolate. Rather, over him God stretches his hand,[1] endows him with strength, inspires him with courage, and puts into his mind what he must do. We know, too, how a divine voice accompanied Socrates and prevented him from doing what he ought not. While Homer also says of Achilles "she placed the thought in his mind",[2] implying that it is God who suggests our thoughts when the mind turns inwards and first communes with itself, then with God alone, by itself, hindered by nothing external. For the mind needs no ears to learn with, still less does God need a voice to teach us our duty; but apart from all sense-perception, communion with God is vouchsafed to the mind. How and in what manner I have not the leisure at this moment to inquire, yet that this does happen is evident, and there are sure witnesses thereof, men not obscure or only fit to be classed with the Megarians,[3] but such as have borne the palm for wisdom.

It follows, therefore, that since we may expect that God will be present with us in all our doings, and that we shall again renew our acquaintance, our grief must lose its sharpest sting. For indeed in the case of Odysseus,[4] too, who was imprisoned on the island for all those seven years and then bewailed his lot, I applaud him for his fortitude on other occasions, but I do not approve those lamentations. For of what avail was it for him to gaze on that fish-laden sea and shed tears?[5] To never abandon hope and despair of one's fate, but to play the hero in the extremes of toil and danger, does indeed seem to me more than can be expected of any human being. Yet it is wrong to praise and not imitate the Homeric heroes, or to think that whereas God was ever ready to assist them, he will disregard the men of our day if he sees that they are striving to attain that very virtue for which he favoured those others. For it was not physical beauty that he favoured, since in that case Nireus[6] would have been more approved; nor strength, for the Laëstrygons[7] and the Cyclops were infinitely stronger than Odysseus; nor riches,

1. *Iliad*, IX, 420 2. *The Iliad*, I, 55

3. The Megarians, upon inquiring as to their rank among Greeks from the Delphic oracle, were told that they were not in the reckoning at all; cf. Theocritus, 14.47

4. cf. Dio Chrysostom, 13.4 5. *The Odyssey*, V, 84 6. *The Iliad*, II, 673

7. *The Odyssey*, X, 119

for had that been so, Troy would never have been sacked. Why, however, should I myself labour to discover the reason why the poet says that Odysseus was beloved by the gods, when we can hear it from himself? It was "because you are prudent, keen of wit, and ever thoughtful".[1] It is evident, therefore, that if we have these qualities in addition, God on his side will not fail us, for in the words of the oracle once given of old to the Lacedæmonians:

καλούμενός τε καὶ ἄκλητος ὁ θεὸς παρέσται

"Invoked or not invoked, God will be with us"[2]

Now that I have consoled myself with these arguments, I will return to that other consideration which, though it may seem trivial, is nevertheless generally esteemed to not be ignoble. Even Alexander, we are told, felt a need for Homer; not, of course, to be his companion, but to be his herald, as he was for Achilles and Patroclus, the two Ajaxes, and Antilochus. Yet Alexander, ever despising what he had and longing for what he had not, could never be content with his contemporaries or be satisfied with the gifts that had been granted to him. Thus, even if Homer had fallen to his lot, he would probably have coveted the lyre of Apollo on which the god played at the nuptials of Peleus;[3] and he would not have regarded it as an invention of Homer's genius, but an actual fact that had been woven into the epic, as when, for instance, Homer says: "Dawn in her saffron robe came spreading light over all the world";[4] and "then uprose the Sun";[5] and "there is a land called Crete";[6] or other similar statements of poets about plain and palpable things partly existing to this very day, partly still happening.

In Alexander's case, however, whether a superabundance of virtue and an intelligence that matched the advantages with which he was endowed, we may ask, exalted his soul to such heights of ambition that he aimed at greater achievements than are within the scope of other men; or whether the cause was an excess of courage and valour that led him into ostentation bordering on arrogance, must be left as a general topic for consideration by those who desire to write either a panegyric of him, or a criticism; if, indeed, anyone thinks that criticism can properly be applied to him. I, on the contrary, can always be content with what I have

1. *The Odyssey*, XIII, 332 2. Thucydides, I.118 3. *The Iliad*, XXIV, 63
4. *The Iliad*, VIII, 1 5. *The Odyssey*, III, 1 6. *The Odyssey*, XIX, 172

and am the last to covet what I have not, and so am quite content when my praises are uttered by a herald who has been an eyewitness and comrade-in-arms in all that I have done; one who has never admitted any statements invented at random out of partiality or prejudice. Indeed, it is enough for me if he only speaks of his fondness for me, though on all else he were more silent than those initiated by Pythagoras.

Here, however, I am reminded of the current report that you are going not only to Illyria, but to Thrace also, and among the Greeks who dwell on the shores of that sea.[1] Among them I was born and brought up, hence I have a deep-rooted affection for them, for those lands, and for the cities there. It may be that in their hearts, also, there still remains no slight affection for me. I am therefore well assured that you will, as the saying goes, gladden their hearts by your arrival, and there will be a fair exchange, since they will gain in proportion as I lose by your leaving here. I say this not because I wish you to go, for it were far better if you should return to me by the same road without delay, but the thought in my mind is that even for this loss I shall not be without comfort or consolation, since I can rejoice with them on seeing you travel from us. I say "us" since on your account I now rank myself among the Celts,[2] seeing that you are worthy to be counted among the most distinguished Greeks for your upright administration and many other virtues; for your consummate skill in oration; in philosophy, too, you are thoroughly versed – a field wherein the Greeks alone have attained the highest rank, for they sought after truth, as its nature requires, by the aid of reason, and did not suffer us to pay heed to incredible fables or impossible miracles like most of the Barbarians.

Nevertheless, whatever the truth about it may be, I must also lay this subject aside for the present. As for you – for I must dismiss you with auspicious words – may God in his goodness be your guide wherever you may have to journey, and as the God of Strangers and the Friendly One,[3] may he receive you graciously and lead you safely by land; and if you must go by sea, may he smooth the waves![4] May you be loved and honoured by all you meet, welcomed when you arrive, regretted when you leave them! Though you retain your affection for me, may you never lack the company of a good comrade and faithful friend! And may God make the Emperor gracious to you, may he grant you all else

1. The Propontis 2. Salutius was a native of Gaul 3. Epithets for Zeus
4. Theocritus, 7.57

according to your desire, and make ready for you a safe and speedy journey home to us! In these prayers for you, I am echoed by all good and honourable men. Let me, then, add one last prayer: "health and great joy be with you, and may the gods give you all things good, even to come home again to your dear fatherland!"[1]

1. *The Odyssey*, XXIV, 402; X, 562

LETTER TO THE PHILOSOPHER THEMISTIUS

PREFACE

Themistius, under whom Julian studied as a young man, was a statesman, a philosopher, and a scholar who specialised in commentaries on the works of Aristotle. He was certainly not a Christian, though it is doubtful whether he was a practising Pagan either – at the very least not one who was especially outspoken or zealous, as evinced by his ability to maintain a friendship and correspondence with both Libanius and Gregory of Nazianzus. Under six consecutive Emperors, Themistius thrived, his long political and academic career indicative of a man who was widely respected and possessed no small amount of charisma.

Julian was clearly impressed by him and eager to meet his expectations. The letter itself may have been written either just after Julian became Emperor, or shortly after he arrived in Gaul to begin his Cæsarship. The persistent use of "God" in the singular and the absence of any mention of "gods" in the plural – a reference to one of Aristotle's treatises notwithstanding – does lend some weight to the latter, as does the topic of leisure versus toil, wherein Julian compares his life in Athens to that of his new surroundings.

LETTER TO THE PHILOSOPHER THEMISTIUS

I earnestly desire to fulfil your hopes of me, even as you express them in your letter, but I am afraid that I shall fall short of them, since the expectations you have raised both in the minds of others, and still more in your own, may be beyond my powers. There was a time when I believed that I ought to try and rival men who have been most distinguished for excellence – Alexander, for instance, or Marcus[1] – yet I shivered at the thought and was seized with terror lest I should fail entirely to reach the courage of the former, and should not make even the least approach to the latter's perfect virtue. With this in mind, I convinced myself that I preferred a life of leisure, thus I both gladly recalled the Attic manner of living, and thought myself to be in sweet accord with you who are my friends, just as those who carry heavy burdens lighten their labour by singing.[2] By your recent letter, however, you have increased my fears, and you point to an enterprise in every way more difficult. You say that God has placed me in the same position as Heracles and Dionysus of old who, being at once philosophers and kings, almost entirely purged both land and sea of the evils that infested them. You bid me shake off all thought of leisure and inactivity so that I may prove to be a good soldier worthy of so high a destiny. Besides those examples, moreover, you go on to remind me of lawgivers such as Solon, Pittacus, and Lycurgus, and you say that men have the right to expect greater things from me now than from any of these. When I read these words I was almost dumbfounded; for on the one hand I was sure that it was unlawful for you as a philosopher to flatter or deceive; while on the other hand, I am fully conscious that by nature there is nothing remarkable about me; there never was from the first, nor has there come to be now, but as regards philosophy I have only fallen in love with it (I say nothing of the fates that have intervened[3] to make that love so far ineffectual).

1. Marcus Aurelius 2. cf. Dio Chrysostom, *Oration* 1, 9 3. Euripides, *Orestes*, 16

I could not tell, therefore, how I ought to interpret such expressions, until God brought it into my mind that perhaps by your very praises you wished to exhort me, and to point out how great are those trials to which a statesman must inevitably be exposed each day of his life.

Alas, your method is more likely to discourage than to make one eager for such an existence. Suppose that a man were navigating your strait,[1] and were finding even that to be none too easy or safe; then suppose some professional soothsayer should tell him that he would have to traverse the Ægæan, then the Ionian Sea, before finally embarking on the outer sea. "Here", that prophet would say, "you see towns and harbours, but when you arrive there you will see not so much as a watch-tower or a rock, and you will be thankful to descry even a ship in the distance and to hail her crew. You will often pray to God that you might, however late, touch land and reach a harbour, even if that were to be the last day of your life. You will pray to be allowed to bring home your ship safe and sound, to restore your crew unscathed to their friends, and to then commit your body to the soil of your mother country. This may indeed happen, but you will not know for certain until that final day." Do you think that such a man, after being told all this, would choose to even live in a sea-port town? Would he not bid adieu to money-making and all the advantages of commerce, caring little for troops of friends and acquaintances abroad, and all that he might learn about nations and cities; would he not approve the wisdom of the son of Neocles[2] who bids us "live in obscurity"?

Indeed, you apparently perceived this, and by your abuse of Epicurus you tried to forestall me and eradicate beforehand any such purpose. For you go on to say that it was to be expected that so idle a man as he should commend leisure and conversations during walks. Now, for my part, I have long been firmly convinced that Epicurus was mistaken in that view of his, but whether it be proper to urge into public life any and every man, both him who lacks natural abilities and him who is not yet completely equipped, is a point that deserves the most careful consideration. We are told that Socrates dissuaded from the statesman's profession[3] many who had no great natural talent, including Glaucon, as Xenophon[4] tells us;

1. The Bosporus; Themistius was probably at Constantinople

2. Epicurus; his advice was λαθὲ βιώσας (literally "live unnoticed")

3. i.e. the stone on the Pnyx from which the Athenian orator addressed the people

4. *Memorabilia*, 3.6.1

and that he tried to restrain the son of Cleinias[1] also, but could not curb the youth's impetuous ambition. Shall we, then, try to force into that career men who are reluctant and conscious of their deficiencies, and urge them to be self-confident about such great tasks? For in such matters neither virtue alone nor a wise policy is paramount, but to a far greater degree Fortune holds sway throughout and compels events to incline as she wills. Chrysippus,[2] indeed, while in other respects he seems a wise man and to have been rightly so esteemed, by ignoring fortune and chance, along with all other such external causes that fall in to block the path of men of affairs, he uttered paradoxes wholly at variance with facts about which the past teaches us clearly by countless examples.

For instance, shall we call Cato a fortunate and happy man? Or shall we say that Dio of Sicily had a happy lot? It is true that for death they probably cared nothing, but they did care greatly about not leaving unfinished the undertakings which they had originally set afoot, and to secure that end there is nothing that they would have not endured. In that, they were disappointed, and I admit that they bore their lot with great dignity, as we learn, and derived no small consolation from their virtue; but happy one could not call them, seeing that they had failed in all those noble enterprises, except perhaps according to the Stoic conception of happiness. Further, with regard to that same Stoic conception, we must admit that to be applauded and to be counted happy are two very different things, and that if every living thing naturally desires happiness,[3] it is better to make it our aim to be congratulated on the score of happiness rather than to be applauded on the score of virtue. Yet happiness that depends on the chances of Fortune is very rarely secure. Thus men who are engaged in public life cannot, as the saying goes, so much as breathe unless she is on their side...[4] and they have created a merely verbal idea of a leader, one who is established somewhere above all the chances of Fortune in the sphere of things incorporeal and intelligible, just as men define the ideas, whether envisaging them truly, or falsely imagining them. Or again, they give us the ideal man, according to Diogenes: "the man without a city, without a home, bereft of a fatherland".[5] That is to say, a man who can gain nothing from Fortune, and on the other hand has nothing to lose. Though one whom we are in the habit of

1. Alcibiades 2. The Stoic 3. cf. Aristotle, *Nicomachean Ethics*, 1.10.6.
4. A lacuna of several words
5. Laërtius, 6.38, claims that this was a favourite quotation of Diogenes

calling, as Homer did first, "the man to whom the people have been entrusted and so many cares belong"[1] – how, I ask, shall we lead him beyond the reach of Fortune and keep his position secure? Then again, if he subject himself to Fortune, how great the provision he will think he must make, how great the prudence he must display so as to sustain with equanimity her variations in either direction, as a pilot must sustain the variations of the wind!

It is nothing exceptional, however, to withstand Fortune when she is merely hostile, but much more exceptional is it to show oneself worthy of the favours she bestows. By her favours, the greatest of kings, the conqueror[2] of Asia, was ensnared, showing himself more cruel and more insolent than Darius and Xerxes, after he had become the master of their empire. The shafts of her favours subdued and utterly destroyed the Persians, the Macedonians, the Athenian nation, Spartan magistrates, Roman generals, and countless absolute monarchs besides. It would be an endless business to enumerate all who have fallen victims to their wealth, to victories, and to luxury. As for those who, submerged by the tide of their misfortunes, from free men have become slaves, who have been humbled from their high estate after all their splendour, becoming poor and mean in the eyes of all men, what need now to go through the list of them as though I were copying it from a written record? Would that human life afforded no such instances! Yet it does not, nor will it ever lack such, so long as mankind endures.

To show that I am not the only one who thinks that Fortune has the upper hand in practical affairs, I will quote to you a passage from that admirable work, the Laws of Plato. You know it well and indeed taught it to me, but I have set down the speech which runs something like this, and offer it as a proof that I am not truly indolent: "God governs all things, and with God, Fortune and Opportunity govern all human affairs; but there is a milder view that Art must go with them and must be their associate".[3] He then indicates what must be the character of a man who is the craftsman and worker of noble deeds, and a divinely inspired king. Then he says: "Kronos, therefore, as I have already related, knew that human nature, when endowed with supreme authority, is never in any case capable of managing human affairs without being filled with insolence and injustice; therefore, having regard to this, he at that time set over our cities as kings and governors not men, but beings

1. *The Iliad*, II, 25 2. Alexander 3. Plato, *Laws*, 709

of a more divine and higher kind, that is, daimons; thus doing as we do now for our flocks and domestic herds. We never appoint certain oxen to rule over other oxen or goats to rule over goats, but we are their masters, a kind superior to theirs. In like manner, then, God, since he loves mankind, has set over us a class of beings superior to ourselves, that of daimons; and they, with great ease both to themselves and us, undertake the care of us, dispense peace and reverence, verily, and above all, justice without stint, thus they make the tribes of men harmonious and happy. That account is a true one which declares that in our day all cities that are governed not by a god but by a mortal man have no relief from ills and hardship. The lesson, then, is that we ought by every means in our power to imitate that life which is said to have existed in the days of Kronos; and in so far as the principle of immortality is in us, we ought to be guided by it in our management of public and private affairs, of our houses and cities, calling the distribution of mind 'law'.[1] Yet whether the government be in the hands of one man, an oligarchy, or a democracy, if it has a soul that seeks after pleasure and the lower appetites, and demands to indulge these, and if such a government rules over a city or individual having first trampled on the laws, there is no means of salvation".[2]

I have purposely set down the whole of this speech for you, lest you should think that I am cheating and defrauding by bringing forward ancient myths which may have some resemblance to the truth, but on the whole are not composed with regard to truth. What, however, is the true meaning of this narrative? You hear what it says, that even though a leader be by nature human, he must in his conduct be divine, a demi-god, and must completely banish from his soul all that is mortal and brutish, save that which must remain to safeguard the needs of the body. Now if, reflecting on this, one is afraid to be constrained to adopt a life from which so much is expected, do you therefore conclude that one admires the inaction recommended by Epicurus, the gardens and suburbs of Athens with its myrtles, or the humble home of Socrates? For never has anyone seen me prefer these to a life of toil. That toil of mine I would willingly recount to you, the hazards that threatened me from my friends and kinsfolk at the time when I began to study under you, if you did not yourself know them well enough. You are

1. A play on words: διανομή (issuance) and νόμος (law; ordinance) are both related to νέμω (to distribute)

2. Plato, *Laws*, 713; Julian condenses and slightly alters the original

well aware of what I did, in the first place, in Ionia, in opposition to one who was related to me by ties of blood, but even more closely by ties of friendship, and that on behalf of a foreigner with whom I was only very slightly acquainted, by which I mean the sophist. Did I not endure to leave the country for the sake of my friends? Indeed, you know how I took the part of Carterius when I went unsolicited to our friend Araxius to plead for him. While on behalf of the property of that admirable woman, Arete, and the wrongs she had suffered from her neighbours, did I not journey to Phrygia for the second time within two months, though I was physically very weak from the illness that had been brought on by former exertions?[1] Finally, before I went to Greece, while I was still with the army and running what most people would describe as the greatest possible risks, recall now what sort of letters I wrote to you, never filled with complaints or containing anything little, base, or servile. Then, when I returned to Greece, when everyone regarded me as an exile, did I not welcome my fate as though it were some high festival, and did I not say that the exchange to me was most delightful, that, as the saying goes, I had thereby gained "gold for bronze, the price of a hundred oxen for the price of nine"?[2] So great was my joy at obtaining the chance to live in Greece instead of my own home, though I possessed there no land or garden, or the humblest house.

Perhaps you think that, although I can bear adversity in the proper spirit, I show a poor and mean spirit towards the good gifts of Fortune, seeing that I prefer Athens to the pomp that now surrounds me; because, you will doubtless say, I approve the leisure of those days and disparage my present life due to the vast amount of work that the latter involves. Though perhaps you ought to judge me more accurately, and not consider the question of whether I am idle or industrious, but rather the precept "know thyself" and the saying "let every man practise the craft which he knows".[3]

To me, at any rate, it seems that the task of ruling is beyond man, and that a king requires a more divine character, as indeed Plato, too, used to say. Now, then, I will write out a passage from Aristotle to the same effect, not "bringing owls to the Athenians",[4] but in order to show you that I do not entirely neglect his writings. In his political treatises he says: "now even if one maintain the principle

1. We know nothing more of the events mentioned here

2. A proverb derived from *The Iliad*, 6.236, wherein Glaukos exchanges his golden armour for the bronze armour of Diomedes

3. Aristophanes, *Wasps*, 1431

4. A proverb; cf. "bringing coals to Newcastle"

that it is best for cities to be governed by a king, how will it be about his children? Ought his children to succeed him? And yet, if they prove to be no better than anybody else, that would be a bad thing for the city. But, you may ask, even though he has the power he will not leave the succession to his children? It is difficult indeed to believe that he will not; for that would be too hard for him, and demands a virtue greater than belongs to human nature".[1] While later on, when he is describing a so-called king who rules according to law, and says that he is both the servant and guardian of the laws, he does not call him a king at all, nor does he consider such a king as a distinct form of government; for he goes on to say: "now as for what is called absolute monarchy, that is to say, when a king governs all other men according to his own will, some people think that it is not in accordance with the nature of things for one man to have absolute authority over all the citizens, since those who are by nature equal must necessarily have the same rights".[2] Again, a little later he says: "It seems, therefore, that he who bids reason rule is really preferring the rule of God and the laws, whereas he who bids man rule adds an element of the beast. For desire is a wild beast, and passion warps even the best of men. It follows, then, that law is reason exempt from desire".

You see that the philosopher here seems clearly to distrust and condemn human nature. For he says it in so many words when he asserts that human nature is in no case worthy of such an excess of fortune. He thinks that it is too hard for one who is merely human to prefer the general wealth of the citizens to his own children; he says that it is not just that one man should rule over many who are his equals; and, finally, he puts the finishing stroke[3] to what he has just said when he asserts that "law is reason exempt from desire", and that political affairs ought to be entrusted to reason alone, not to any individual man whomsoever. For the reason that is in men, however good they may be, is entangled with passion and desire, those most savage beasts. These opinions, it seems to me, harmonise perfectly with Plato's: first, that he who governs ought to be superior to his subjects and surpass them not only in his acquired habits but also in natural endowment, a thing which is not easy to find among men...[4] thirdly, that he ought by every means in his power to observe the laws, not those that were framed to meet some sudden emergency, or established, as now

1. Aristotle, *Politics*, 3.15.1286 2. Ibid., 3.16.1287 3. cf. Plato, *Theætetus*, 153
4. Several words indicating the second point enumerated seem to have been lost

appears, by men whose lives were not wholly guided by reason. Instead, he must observe them only when the lawgiver in enacting those laws, having purified his mind and soul, keeps in view not merely the crimes of the moment or immediate contingencies, but rather recognises the nature of government and the essential nature of justice, and has carefully observed also the essential nature of guilt, then applies to his task all the knowledge thus derived, framing laws which have a general application to all the citizens without regard to friend or foe, neighbour or kinsman. Moreover, it is better that such a lawgiver should frame and promulgate his laws not for his contemporaries only but for posterity also, or for strangers with whom he neither has nor expects to have any private dealings. For instance, I hear that the wise Solon, having consulted his friends about the cancelling of debts, furnished them with an opportunity to make money, but brought on himself a disgraceful accusation.[1] So hard is it to avoid such blemishes, even when a man brings a passionless mind to the task of governing.

Since this sort of thing is what I dread, it is natural that I should often dwell on the advantages of my previous mode of life; and I am but obeying you when I reflect your own words, that I must not only emulate those famous men Solon, Lycurgus, and Pittacus, but also that I must now quit the shades of philosophy for the open air. This is as though, to a man who for his health's sake and by exerting himself to the utmost was able to take moderate exercise at home, you had announced: "now you have come to Olympia and have exchanged the gymnasium in your house for the stadium of Zeus, where for spectators you will have Greeks who have come from all parts, and foremost among them your own fellow citizens, on whose behalf you must contend for the prize; while certain Barbarians will be there, also, whom it is your duty to impress, showing them your fatherland in as formidable a light as lies in your power". You would have disconcerted him at once and made him nervous before the games began. Thus you may now suppose that I have been affected in the same manner by just such words from yourself. Accordingly, you will very soon inform me whether my present view is correct, or whether I am in part deceived as to my proper course, or, indeed, whether I am wholly mistaken.

Nevertheless, I should like to make clear to you the points in your letter by which I am puzzled, my dearest friend to whom I am

1. Before Solon's measure to cancel debts was widely known, some of his friends borrowed large sums in the knowledge that they would not have to repay them

especially bound to pay every honour, for I am eager to be more precisely informed about them. You said that you approve a life of action rather than the philosophic life, and you called to witness the wise Aristotle, who defines happiness as virtuous activity, and, discussing the difference between the statesman's life and the life of contemplation, showed a certain hesitation towards those lives. Therefore, though in others of his writings he preferred the contemplative life, in this place you say he approves the architects of noble actions. Yet it is you who assert that these are kings, whereas Aristotle does not speak in the sense of the words that you have introduced, and from what you have quoted one would rather infer the contrary. For when he says "we most correctly use the word 'act' of those who are the architects of public affairs by virtue of their intelligence",[1] we must suppose that what he says applies to lawgivers, political philosophers, and all whose activity consists in the use of intelligence and reason, but that it does not apply to those who do the work themselves or those who transact the business of politics. In their case, however, it is not enough that they should consider and devise, and instruct others as to what must be done, but it is their duty to undertake and execute whatever the laws ordain and circumstances may force on them, as often occurs. Unless, indeed, we call that man an architect who is "well versed in mighty deeds",[2] a phrase which Homer in his poems usually applies to Heracles, who was certainly of all men that ever lived most given to do the work himself.

If we conceive this to be true, or that only those who administer public affairs are happy, or who are in authority and rule over many, what then are we to say about Socrates? As for Pythagoras, Democritus, and Anaxagoras of Clazomenæ, you will perhaps say that they were happy in another sense of the word, because of their philosophic speculations. Yet as for Socrates who, having rejected the speculative life and embraced a life of action, had no authority over his own wife or son, can we say of him that he governed even two or three of his fellow citizens? Then will you assert that since he had no authority over any one, he accomplished nothing? On the contrary, I maintain that the son of Sophroniscus[3] performed greater tasks than Alexander, for to him I ascribe the wisdom of Plato, the generalship of Xenophon, the fortitude of Antisthenes, the Eretrian[4] and Megarian philosophies, Cebes, Simmias, Phædo

1. Aristotle, *Politics*, 7.3.1325 2. *The Odyssey*, XXI, 26 3. The father of Socrates
4. This school was founded by Phædo in Elis and later transferred to Eretria, Euboea

and a host of others; not to mention the offshoots derived from the same source, the Lyceum, the Stoa, and the Academies. Who, I ask, ever found salvation through the conquests of Alexander? What city was ever more wisely governed because of them, what individual improved? Many, in truth, you might find whom those conquests enriched, but not one whom they made wiser or more temperate than he was by nature, if indeed they have not made him more insolent and arrogant. Whereas all who now find their salvation in philosophy owe it to Socrates. Moreover, I am not the only person to perceive this fact and to express it, for Aristotle it seems did so before me, when he said that he had just as much right to be proud of his treatise on the gods as the conqueror[1] of the Persian Empire. And I think he was perfectly correct in that conclusion. For military success is due to courage and good fortune more than anything else, or, let us say, if you wish, to intelligence as well, though of the common everyday sort. To conceive true opinions about God, however, is an achievement that not only requires perfect virtue, but one might well hesitate as to whether it be proper to call one who attains to this a man or a god. For if the saying is true that it is the nature of everything to become known to those who have an affinity with it, then he who comes to know the essential nature of God would naturally be considered divine.

Now, because I seem to have hearkened back to the life of contemplation and to be comparing it with the life of action, though in the beginning of your letter you declined to make the comparison, I will remind you of those very philosophers whom you mentioned: Areius,[2] Nicolaus,[3] Thrasyllus,[4] and Musonius.[5] So far from any one of these governing his own city, Areius we are told refused the governorship of Egypt when it was offered to him, while Thrasyllus, by becoming intimate with the harsh and naturally cruel tyrant Tiberius, would have incurred indelible disgrace for all time, had he not cleared himself in the writings that he left behind him and so shown his true character, so little did his public career benefit him. Nicolaus did not personally do any great deeds, and he is known rather by his writings about such deeds; while Musonius became famous because he bore his sufferings with courage, and, by Zeus, sustained with firmness the cruelty of tyrants; and perhaps he was no less happy than those who administered great kingdoms. As for Areius, when he declined the governorship of Egypt he

1. Alexander 2. Themistius, 63 3. Historian under Octavian
4. Platonic philosopher and astrologer 5. Stoic philosopher exiled by Nero

deliberately deprived himself of the highest end, if he really thought that this was the most important thing. As for you yourself, may I ask, do you lead an inactive life because you are not a general or a public speaker and govern no nation or city? Of course not; no one with any sense would say so. For it is in your power by producing many philosophers, or even just three or four, to confer more benefit on the lives of men than many kings put together. To no trivial province is the philosopher appointed, and, as you said yourself, he does not only direct counsels or public affairs, nor is his activity confined to mere words; but if he confirms his words by deeds and shows himself to be such as he wishes others to be, he may be more convincing and more effective in making men act than those who urge them to noble actions by issuing commands.

Though I must return to what I said at the beginning and conclude this letter, which is perhaps already longer than it should be. The main point, then, is that it is not because I would avoid hard work or pursue pleasure, nor because I am in love with idleness and ease that I am averse to spending my life in administration. Rather, as I said when I began, it is because I am conscious that I have neither sufficient training nor natural talents above the ordinary; moreover, I am afraid of bringing reproach on philosophy, which, as much as I love it, I have never attained to, and which on other accounts hasn't the best of reputations among men of our day. For these reasons I wrote all this down some time ago, and now I have freed myself from your charges as far as I can.

May God grant me the happiest fortune possible, and wisdom to match my fortune! For now I think I need assistance from God above all, and also from philosophers such as yourself by all means in your power, since I have proved myself your leader and champion in danger. Should it be, however, that blessings greater than my means and the opinion that I now have of myself are granted to men by God through my agency, you must not resent my words. For being conscious of no good thing in me, save this only, that I do not even think that I possess the highest talent, and indeed have naturally none, I cry aloud and testify[1] that you must not expect great things of me, but must entrust everything to God. For thus shall I be free from censure for my shortcomings, and if everything should turn out favourably, I shall be discreet and moderate, not putting my name to the deeds of other men, but by giving God the glory for all, as is right; it is to him that I shall myself feel gratitude and I urge all of you to do the same.

1. Demosthenes, *De Corona*, 23

LETTER TO THE SENATE AND PEOPLE OF ATHENS

PREFACE

The following letter was written in Illyricum, in late 361, while Julian was attempting to seize the initiative in his struggle with Constantius. Of the manifestos sent to Athens, Rome, Corinth, and Sparta in an effort to preserve "by argument as well as by arms the superior merits of his cause"[1], only the first survived. Nevertheless, the letter provides an invaluable source for many of the events in Julian's life up to this point, as well as the first instance in which he ventured to speak forthrightly about Constantius. Julian doubtless hoped to win the support of the Athenians, whose history he so highly esteemed, and to preemptively clear his name of any accusation of disloyalty.

1. Gibbon, *Decline and Fall*, XXII

LETTER TO THE SENATE AND PEOPLE OF ATHENS

Many were the achievements of your forefathers of which you are still justly proud, even as they were of old; many were the trophies for victories raised by them, at one time for all Greece in common, at others separately for Athens herself, in those days when she contended single-handed against the rest of Greece as well as against the Barbarians; but there was no achievement and no display of courage on your part so prodigious that other cities cannot in their turn rival it. For they, too, wrought some such deeds in alliance with you, and some on their own account. Thus, that I may not by recalling these and then balancing them be thought either to pay more honour to one state than to another in the matters in which they are your rivals, or to praise less than they deserve those who proved inferior, in order to gain an advantage, after the manner of rhetoricians, I desire to bring forward on your behalf only this fact to which I can discover nothing that can be set against it on the part of the other Greek states, and which has been assigned to you by ancient tradition. When the Lacedæmonians were in power, you took that power away from them not by violence but by your reputation for justice; and it was your laws that nurtured Aristides the Just. Moreover, brilliant as were these proofs of your virtue, you confirmed them by yet more brilliant actions. For to be reputed just might perhaps happen to any individual, even if it were not true; and perhaps it would not be surprising that among many worthless citizens there should be found one virtuous man. For among the Medes, is not a certain Deioces[1] celebrated, and Abaris,[2] too, among the Hyperboreans, and Anacharsis[3] among the Scythians? In their case, of course, the surprising thing was that, born as they were among nations who knew nothing of

1. The first King of Media; reigned 709-656 B.C.

2. A legendary priest of Apollo from Hyperborea; cf. Herodotus, 4.36

3. A Scythian prince who visited Athens at the end of the sixth century B.C.; cf, Cicero, *Tusculan Disputations*, 5.32

justice, they nevertheless prized justice, two of them sincerely, though the third only pretended to do so out of self-interest. Yet it would be hard to find a whole people and city enamoured of just deeds and just words except your own. I wish, then, to remind you of one out of very many such deeds done in your city. After the Persian war, Themistocles[1] was planning to introduce a resolution to secretly set fire to the naval arsenals of the Greeks, only he did not dare propose it to the assembly. Instead, he agreed to confide the secret to any one man whom the people should elect by vote, and the people chose Aristides to represent them. Yet when he heard the scheme, he did not reveal what he had been told, but reported to the people that there could be nothing more abject or more unjust than that advice. Whereupon the city at once voted against it and rejected it, most nobly, by Zeus, as it behoved men to do who are nurtured under the eyes of the most wise goddess.[2]

If this was your conduct of old, then, and from that day to this there has been kept alive some small spark, as it were, of the virtue of your ancestors, it is natural that you should pay attention not to the magnitude merely of any performance, nor whether a man has travelled over the earth with incredible speed and unwearied energy as though he had flown through the air, but that you should rather consider whether one has accomplished this feat by just means, and then, if he seems to act with justice, you will perhaps all praise him both in public and private; whereas if he has slighted justice, he will naturally be scorned by you. For there is nothing so closely akin to wisdom as justice. Accordingly, those who slight her you will justly expel as showing impiety towards the goddess who dwells among you. For this reason I wish to report my conduct to you, though indeed you know it well, in order that if there is anything you do not know – and it is likely that some things you do not, those, in fact, which it is most important for all men to be aware of – it may become known to you and to the rest of the Greeks through you. Therefore, let no one think that I am trifling and wasting words if I try to give some account of things that have happened, as it were, before the eyes of all men, not only long ago but also just lately. For I wish none to be ignorant of anything that concerns me, and naturally not everyone can know every circumstance. First I will begin with my ancestors.

That on my father's side I am descended from the same stock as Constantius on his father's side is well known. Our fathers were

1. The story is told in Plutarch, *Themistocles* 2. Athena

brothers, sons of the same father. Yet close kinsmen as we were, how this most humane Emperor treated us! Six of my cousins and his, my father who was his own uncle, another uncle of both of us on my father's side, and my eldest brother, he put to death without a trial; and as for me and my other brother,[1] he intended to put us to death, but ultimately inflicted exile upon us. From that exile he released me, but my brother he stripped of the title of Cæsar just before he murdered him. Though why should I "recount" as though from some tragedy "all these unspeakable horrors?"[2] For he has repented, I am told, and is stung by remorse; he thinks that his unhappy state of childlessness is due to those deeds, and his ill success in the Persian war he also ascribes to that cause. This, at least, was the talk of the court at the time, and of those who were about the person of my brother Gallus of blessed memory, who is now for the first time so named. For after putting him to death in defiance of the laws, he neither suffered him to share the tombs of his ancestors nor granted him a pious remembrance.

As I said, they kept telling us and attempting to convince us that Constantius had acted thus, partly because he was deceived, and partly because he yielded to the violence and tumult of an undisciplined and mutinous army. Such was the line they took to soothe us when we had been imprisoned in a certain farm[3] in Cappadocia; when they allowed no one to come near us after they had summoned him from exile in Tralles and had dragged me from the schools, though I was still a mere boy. How shall I describe the six years we spent there? For we lived as though on the estate of a stranger, and were watched as if we were in some Persian garrison, since no stranger came to see us and not one of our old friends was allowed to visit us; thus we lived shut off from all genuine study and free exchange in a glittering servitude, sharing the exercises of our own slaves as though they were comrades. For no companion of our own age ever came near us or was allowed to do so.

From that place, barely and by the help of the gods, I was set free, and for a happier fate; but my brother was imprisoned at court and his fate was ill-starred above all men who have ever yet lived. Indeed, whatever cruelty or harshness was revealed in his disposition was increased by his having been brought up among those mountains. It is therefore, I think, only just that the Emperor should bear the blame for this, also, he who against our will allotted to us that sort of upbringing. As for me, the gods by means of

1. Gallus 2. Euripides, *Orestes*, 14 3. The estate at Macellum, Cappadocia

philosophy allowed me to remain untouched by it and unharmed; but on my brother no one bestowed this boon. For when he had come straight from the country to the court, the moment that Constantius had invested him with the purple robe, he at once began to be jealous of him, nor did he cease from that feeling until, not content with stripping him of the purple, he had destroyed him. Yet surely he deserved to live, even if he seemed unfit to govern. Though someone may say that it was necessary to deprive him of life as well. I admit it, only on condition that he had first been allowed to speak in his own defence as criminals are. For surely it is not the case that the law forbids one who has imprisoned bandits to put them to death, but says that it is right to destroy without a trial those who have been stripped of the honours that they possessed, having become mere individuals instead of rulers. What, I ask, if my brother had been able to expose those who were responsible for his errors? For there had been handed to him the letters of certain persons, and, by Heracles, what accusations against himself they contained! In his resentment at these, he gave way in a most unkingly fashion to uncontrolled anger, but he had done nothing to deserve being deprived of life itself. Is not this a universal law among all Greeks and Barbarians alike, that one should defend oneself against those who take the initiative in doing wrong to them? I admit that he did perhaps defend himself with too great a cruelty, but on the whole not more cruelly than might have been expected. For we have heard it said before[1] that an enemy may be expected to harm one in a fit of anger. Yet it was to gratify a eunuch,[2] his chamberlain who was also his chief cook, that Constantius gave over to his most inveterate enemies his own cousin, the Cæsar, his sister's husband, the father of his niece, the man whose own sister he had himself married in earlier days, and to whom he owed so many obligations connected with the gods of the family. As for me, he reluctantly let me go after dragging me here and there for seven whole months and keeping me under guard; such that, had not one of the gods desired that I should escape, and made the beautiful and virtuous Eusebia kindly disposed towards me, I could not have escaped from his hands by myself. And yet I call the gods to witness that my brother had pursued his course of action without my having a sight of him even in a dream. For I was not with him, nor did I visit him or travel to his country; while I used to write to him very seldom and on unimportant matters.

1. cf. Demosthenes, *Against Meidias*, 41

2. Eusebius; cf. Ammianus, 14.11; 22.3

Thinking, therefore, that I had escaped from that place, I set out for the house that had been my mother's. For of my father's estate nothing belonged to me, and I had acquired out of the great wealth that had naturally belonged to my father not the smallest clod of earth, not a slave, not a house. For the admirable Constantius had inherited in my place the whole of my father's property, and to me, as I was saying, he granted not the least trifle of it. Moreover, though he gave my brother a few things that had been his father's, he robbed him of the whole of his mother's estate.

Now, his whole behaviour towards me before he granted me that august title[1] – though in fact what he did was to impose on me the most galling and irksome slavery – you have heard, if not every detail, still the greater part. As I had begun to say, I was on my way home and was barely getting away safely, beyond my hopes, when a certain slanderer[2] turned up near Sirmium and fabricated the rumour against certain persons there that they were planning a revolt. You doubtless know by hearsay both Africanus[3] and Marinus; nor can you fail to have heard of Felix and what the fate of those men was. When Constantius was informed of the matter, then, and another false accuser, Dynamius, suddenly reported from Gaul that Silvanus was on the point of declaring himself his open enemy, in the utmost alarm and terror he forthwith sent for me; first he bade me retire for a short time to Greece, then he summoned me from there to the court once more. He had never seen me before except once in Cappadocia and once in Italy – a discussion which Eusebia had secured by her exertions so that I might feel confidence about my personal safety. And yet I lived for six months in the same city[4] as he did, and he had promised that he would see me again. However, that execrable eunuch,[5] his trusty chamberlain, unconsciously and involuntarily proved himself my benefactor. For he did not allow me to meet the Emperor often, nor perhaps did the latter desire it, though the eunuch was the chief reason. For what he dreaded was that if we had any interaction with one another I might be taken into favour, and when my loyalty became evident I might be given some place of trust.

From the first moment of my arrival from Greece, Eusebia of blessed memory continued to show me the utmost kindness through the eunuchs of her household. Shortly thereafter, when the Emperor returned – for the affair of Silvanus had been concluded – at last I was given access to the court, and, in the

1. Cæsar 2. Gaudentius 3. cf. Ammianus, 15.3 4. Mediolanum 5. Eusebius

words of the proverb, Thessalian persuasion[1] was applied to me. For when I firmly declined all interaction with the palace, some of them, as though they had come together in a barber's shop, cut off my beard, dressed me in a military cloak, and transformed me into a quite ridiculous soldier, as they thought at the time. For none of the adornments of those vermin suited me. I walked not like them, staring about me and strutting along, but gazing on the ground as I had been trained to do by the preceptor[2] who brought me up. At the time, then, I inspired their ridicule, but a little later their suspicion, and thereafter their jealousy was inflamed to the utmost.

This, however, I must not omit to tell here, how I submitted and how I consented to dwell under the same roof with those whom I knew to have ruined my whole family, and who, I suspected, would before long plot against myself also. Alas, what tears I shed and what laments I uttered when I was summoned, stretching out my hands to your Acropolis and imploring Athena to save her suppliant and to not abandon me. Many of you who were eye-witnesses can attest, and the goddess herself, above all others, is my witness that I even pleaded for death at her hands, there in Athens, rather than journey to the Emperor. That the goddess accordingly did not betray her suppliant or abandon him she proved by the event. For everywhere she was my guide, and on all sides she set a watch near me, bringing guardian angels from Helios and Selene.

What happened was as follows. When I came to Mediolanum I resided in one of the suburbs. While there, Eusebia sent me messages of good-will on several occasions, and urged me to write to her without hesitation about anything that I desired. Accordingly, I wrote her a letter, or rather, a petition containing vows like these: "may you have children to succeed you; may God grant you this and that, if only you send me home as quickly as possible!" Though I suspected that it was not safe to send to the palace letters addressed to the Emperor's wife. Therefore, I besought the gods to inform me at night whether I ought to send the letter to the Empress. They duly warned me that if I sent it I should meet the most ignominious death. I call all the gods to witness that what I write here is true. For this reason, then, I forbore to send the letter. Yet from that night there kept occurring to me an argument which it is perhaps worth your while, also, to hear. "Now", I said to myself, "I am planning to oppose the gods, and have imagined that I can devise wiser schemes for myself than those who know all things.

---

1. cf. Cicero, *Letter to Atticus*, 9.13. 2. Mardonius

And yet human wisdom, which looks only to the present moment, may be thankful if, with all its efforts, it succeeds in avoiding mistakes for even a short space of time. That is why no man takes thought for things that are to happen thirty years hence, or for things that are already past – for one is superfluous, while the other impossible – but only for what lies near at hand and has already some beginnings and seeds. Whereas the wisdom of the gods sees very far, or rather, sees the whole, and therefore directs aright and brings to pass what is best. For they are the causes of all that now is, and so likewise of all that is to be. Wherefore it is reasonable that they should have knowledge about the present."

So far, then, it seemed to me that on this reasoning my second determination was wiser than my first. Thus viewing the matter in the light of justice, I immediately reflected: "would you not be provoked if one of your own beasts were to deprive you of its services,[1] or were even to run away when you called it, a horse, or sheep, or calf, as the case might be? And will you, who pretended to be a man, and not even a man of the common herd or from the dregs of the people, but one belonging to the more noble and reasonable class, deprive the gods of your service, and not trust yourself to them to dispose of you as they please? Beware lest you not only fall into great folly, but also neglect your proper duties towards the gods. Where is your courage, and of what sort is it? A sorry thing it seems. At any rate, you are ready to flatter and wheedle from fear of death, and yet it is in your power to lay all that aside and leave it to the gods to work their will, dividing with them the care of yourself, as Socrates, for instance, chose to do. Furthermore, you might, while doing such things as best you can, commit everything to their charge, and seek to possess nothing, seize nothing, but accept simply what is vouchsafed to you by them". This course I thought not only safe but becoming to a reasonable man, since the response of the gods had suggested it. For to rush headlong into unseemly and foreseen danger while trying to avoid future plots seemed to me to court turbulence. Accordingly, I consented to yield. Immediately I was invested with the title and robe of Cæsar. The slavery that ensued and the fear for my very life that hung over me every day, Heracles, how great it was, and how terrible! My doors locked, warders to guard them, the hands of my servants searched lest one of them should convey to me the most trifling letter from my friends, strange servants to wait on me!

1. An echo of Plato, *Phædo*, 62   2. Oribasius

Only with difficulty was I able to bring with me to court four of my own domestics for my personal service, two of them mere boys and two older men, of whom only one knew of my attitude towards the gods, and, as far as he was able, secretly joined me in their worship. I had entrusted with the care of my books a certain physician,[2] since, having been allowed to leave home with me because it was not known that he was my friend, he was the only one with me of many loyal comrades and companions. This state of things caused me such alarm, so apprehensive was I about it, that though many of my friends really wished to visit me, I very reluctantly refused them admittance; for though I was most anxious to see them, I shrank from bringing disaster upon them and myself at the same time. Though this is somewhat foreign to my narrative. The following relates to the actual course of events.

Constantius gave me three hundred and sixty soldiers, and in the middle of winter[1] despatched me into Gaul, which was then in a state of great disorder. I was sent not as commander of the garrisons but rather as a subordinate of the generals stationed there. For letters had been sent to them and express orders given that they were to watch me as vigilantly as they did the enemy, for fear I should attempt to cause a revolt. Then, once all this had happened in the manner I have described, at about the summer solstice, he allowed me to join the army and to carry around with me his banner. Indeed, he had both said and written that he was not giving the Gauls a king but one who should convey to them his image.

Now when, as you have heard, the first campaign was concluded that year and great advantage gained, I returned to winter quarters,[2] and there was exposed to the utmost danger. For I was not even allowed to assemble the troops; rather, this power was entrusted to another, while I was quartered apart with only a few soldiers. Then, since the neighbouring towns begged for my assistance, I assigned to them the greater part of the force that I had, and so I myself was left isolated. Such was the condition of affairs at that time. When the commander-in-chief[3] of the forces subsequently fell under the suspicions of Constantius and was deprived by him of his command and superseded, I was thought to be by no means capable or talented as a general, merely because I had shown myself temperate and moderate. For I thought I should not fight against my yoke or interfere with the general in command, except when in some especially dangerous undertaking I saw that something was

1. 355 2. At Vienna, Gaul 3. Marcellus

being overlooked, or that something was being attempted that ought never to have been attempted at all. After certain persons had treated me with disrespect on multiple occasions, however, I decided that for the future I ought to show my own self-respect by keeping silence, and henceforth I contented myself with parading the imperial robe and the image. For I thought that to these at any rate I had been given a right.

Thereafter, Constantius, thinking that there would be some improvement, but not that so great a transformation would take place in the affairs of Gaul, handed over to me the command of all the forces in the beginning of spring.[1] Then, when the grain was ripe, I took the field; for a great number of Germans had settled themselves with impunity near the towns they had sacked in Gaul. Now, the number of the towns whose walls had been dismantled was about forty-five, without counting citadels and smaller forts. At that time, the Barbarians controlled on our side of the Rhine all the land that extends from its sources to the Ocean. Moreover, those who were settled nearest to us were as much as three hundred stades from the banks of the Rhine, and a district three times as wide as that had been left a desert by their raids, such that the Gauls could not even pasture their cattle there. There were also a number of cities deserted by their inhabitants, near which the Barbarians were not yet encamped. This, then, was the condition of Gaul when I took it over. I recovered the city of Agrippina[2] on the Rhine, which had been taken about ten months earlier, and also the neighbouring fort of Argentoratum,[3] near the foot-hills of the Vosges mountains, where I engaged the enemy not ingloriously. It may be that the fame of that battle has reached even your ears. There, though the gods gave into my hands as prisoner of war the king[4] of the enemy, I did not begrudge Constantius the glory of that success. And yet, though I was not allowed to triumph for it, I had it in my power to slay my enemy; moreover, I could have led him through the whole of Gaul and exhibited him to the cities, and have thus luxuriated, as it were, in the misfortunes of Chnodomar. I thought it my duty to do none of these things, but sent him at once to Constantius, who was returning from the country of the Quadi and the Sarmatians. So it came about that, though I had done all the fighting while he had only travelled in those parts and held friendly exchanges with the tribes who dwell on the borders of the Danube, it was not I but he who triumphed.

1. 357 2. Cologne 3. Strasbourg 4. Chnodomar

Then followed the second and third years of that campaign, by which time all the Barbarians had been driven out of Gaul, most of the towns had been recovered, and an entire fleet of ships had arrived from Britain. I had collected a fleet of six hundred ships, four hundred of which I had built in less than ten months, and I brought them all into the Rhine – no slight achievement, on account of the neighbouring Barbarians who kept attacking me. At least, it seemed so impossible to Florentius that he had promised to pay the Barbarians a fee of two thousand pounds in weight of silver in return for safe passage. When Constantius learned of this – for Florentius had informed him about the proposed payment – he wrote me to carry out the agreement, unless I thought it absolutely disgraceful. Yet how could it fail to be disgraceful when it seemed so even to Constantius, who was only too much in the habit of trying to conciliate the Barbarians? No payment was made to them. Instead, I marched against them, and since the gods protected me and were present to aid, I received the submission of part of the Salian tribe, drove out the Chamavi, and took many cattle, women, and children. I struck such fear into them all and made them tremble at my approach that I immediately received hostages from them and secured a safe passage for my food supplies.

It would take too long to enumerate everything and to write down every detail of the task that I accomplished within those four years. Though to sum it all up: three times, while I was still Cæsar, I crossed the Rhine; twenty thousand persons who were held as captives on the further side of the Rhine I demanded and received back; in two battles and one siege I took captive ten thousand prisoners, and those not of unserviceable age but men in the prime of life; I sent to Constantius four levies of excellent infantry, three more of infantry of only slightly less quality, and two very distinguished squadrons of cavalry. I have now with the help of the gods recovered all the towns, and by that time I had already recovered almost forty. I call Zeus and all the gods who protect our cities and our race to bear witness as to my behaviour towards Constantius and my loyalty to him, and that I behaved to him as I would have chosen that my own son should behave to me.[1] I have paid him more honour than any Cæsar has paid to any Emperor in the past. Indeed, to this very day he has no accusation to bring against me on that score, and though I have been entirely frank i n my dealings with him, he invents absurd pretexts for his

1. cf. Isocrates, *To Demonicus*, 14

resentment. He says "you have detained Lupicinus and three other men". Supposing I had even put them to death after they had openly plotted against me, he ought for the sake of keeping peace to have renounced his resentment at their fate. Yet I did those men not the least injury, and I detained them because they are by nature quarrelsome and belligerent. Further, though I am spending large sums of the public money on them, I have robbed them of none of their property. Observe how Constantius really lays down the law that I ought to proceed to extremities with such men! For by his anger on behalf of men who are not related to him at all, does he not rebuke and ridicule me for my folly in having served so faithfully the murderer of my father, my brothers, my cousins; the executioner, as it were, of his and my whole family and kindred? Consider, too, with what deference I have continued to treat him even since I became Augustus, as is shown in my letters.

How I behaved towards him before, that you shall now learn. Since I was well aware that whenever mistakes were made, I alone should incur the disgrace and danger, though most of the work was carried out by others, I first of all implored him, if he had made up his mind to that course and was altogether determined to proclaim me Cæsar, to provide me with good and able men to assist me. At first, however, he gave me the vilest wretches. Then, when one, the most worthless of them, had very gladly accepted and none of the others consented, he gave me with poor grace an officer who was indeed excellent, Salutius, who on account of his virtue fell at once under his suspicion. Yet since I was not satisfied with such an arrangement and saw how his manner to them varied, for I observed that he trusted one of them too much and paid no attention at all to the other, I clasped his right hand and his knees and said: "I have no acquaintance with any of these men nor have had so in the past. But I know them by report, and since you bid me, I regard them as my comrades and friends and pay them as much respect as I would to old acquaintances. Nevertheless, it is not just that my affair's should be entrusted to them or that their fortunes should be hazarded with mine. What then is my petition? Give me some sort of written rules as to what I must avoid and what you entrust to me to perform. For it is clear that you will approve of him who obeys you and punish him who is disobedient, though indeed I am very sure that no one will disobey you".

Now, I need not mention the innovations that Pentadius at once tried to introduce. I kept opposing him in everything and for that reason he became my enemy. Then Constantius chose another, and a second, and a third, and fashioned them for his purpose, by which I mean Paul and Gaudentius, those notorious maligners. He hired them to attack me and then took measures to remove Salutius, because he was my friend, and to appoint Lucilianus immediately as his successor. A little later, Florentius also became my enemy on account of his avarice which I would oppose. These men persuaded Constantius, who was perhaps already somewhat irritated by jealousy of my success, to remove me altogether from command of the troops. He wrote letters full of insults directed against me and threatening ruin to the Gauls. For he gave orders for the withdrawal from Gaul of, I might almost say, all of the most efficient troops without exception, and assigned this commission to Lupicinus, while to me he wrote that I must oppose them in nothing.

In what terms, then, shall I now describe to you the work of the gods? It was my intention, as they will bear me witness, to divest myself of all imperial splendour and state and remain in peace, taking no part whatsoever in public affairs. Yet I waited for Florentius and Lupicinus to arrive; for the former was at Vienne, the latter in Britain. Meanwhile, there was great excitement among the civilians and the troops, while someone wrote an anonymous letter to the town near where I was,[1] addressed to the Petulantes and the Celts – those were the names of the legions – full of invective against Constantius and of lamentations about his betrayal of the Gauls. Moreover, the author of the letter inveighed bitterly against the disgrace inflicted on myself. This letter when it arrived provoked all those who were most definitely on the side of Constantius to urge me in the strongest terms to send away the troops at once, before similar letters could be circulated amongst the rest of the legions. For there was no one there who might be expected to be well-disposed towards me, but only Nebridius, Pentadius, and Decentius, the latter of whom had been despatched for this very purpose by Constantius. Thus, when I replied that we ought to wait still longer for Lupicinus and Florentius, no one listened to me; rather, they all declared that we ought to do the very opposite, unless I wished to add this further proof and evidence for the suspicions that were already entertained about me. To which they added this argument: "if you send away the troops now it will be regarded as your measure, but when the others come, Constantius will give them the credit, not you, and you will be held

1. Lutetia

to blame". Therefore they persuaded, or rather, compelled me to write to him. For he alone may be said to be persuaded who has the power to refuse, but those who can use force have no need to persuade as well. Then again, where force is used there is no persuasion, but a man who is the victim of necessity. Thereupon we discussed by which road, since there were two, the troops had better march. I preferred that they should take one of these, but they immediately compelled them to take the other, for fear that the other route, if chosen, should give rise to mutiny among the troops and cause some disturbance, and that, once they had begun to mutiny, they might throw all into confusion. Indeed, such apprehension on their part seemed not altogether without grounds.

The legions arrived, and I, as was customary, went to meet them and exhorted them to continue their march. For one day they halted, and till that time I knew nothing at all of what they had determined. I call to witness Zeus, Helios, Ares, Athena, and all the other gods that no such suspicion even entered my mind until that very evening. It was already late when, at about sunset, the news was brought to me; suddenly the palace was surrounded and they all began to shout aloud, while I was still considering what I ought to do and feeling by no means confident. My wife was still alive and it happened that, in order to rest alone, I had gone to the upper room near hers. Then from there through an opening in the wall I prayed to Zeus. When the shouting grew still louder and all was in a tumult in the palace, I entreated the god to give me a sign, whereupon he showed me a sign[1] and bade me yield and not oppose myself to the will of the army. Nevertheless, even after these tokens had been vouchsafed to me, I did not yield without reluctance, but resisted as long as I could and would not accept either the salutation[2] or the diadem. Yet since I could not single-handedly control so many, and, moreover, the gods who willed that this should happen spurred on the soldiers, gradually softening my resolution, somewhere about the third hour some soldier or other gave me the torque, which I placed on my head before returning to the palace, as the gods know, groaning in my heart. Though it was surely my duty to feel confidence and to trust in the god after he had shown me that sign, I was terribly ashamed and ready to sink into the earth at the thought of not seeming to obey Constantius faithfully to the last.

Now, since there was the greatest consternation in the palace, to contrive a plot against me without delay, and so they distributed

1. *The Odyssey*, III, 173 2. i.e., the title of Augustus

the friends of Constantius thought they would seize the occasion money to the soldiers, expecting one of two things: either they would cause dissension between me and the troops, or the latter would no doubt attack me openly. However, when a certain officer belonging to those who commanded my wife's escort perceived that this was being secretly contrived, he first reported it to me and then, when he saw that I paid no attention to him, he became frantic, and like one possessed he began to cry aloud before the people in the market-place: "fellow soldiers, strangers, and citizens, do not abandon the Emperor!" Then the soldiers were inspired by a frenzy of rage and they all rushed to the palace under arms. When they found me alive, in their delight, like men who meet friends whom they had not hoped to see again, they pressed round me on this side and on that, and embraced me, and carried me on their shoulders. It was a sight worth seeing, for they were like men seized with a divine passion. Then after they had surrounded me on all sides, they demanded that I give up to them for punishment the friends of Constantius. What fierce opposition I had to fight down in my desire to save those persons is known to all the gods.

Further still, how did I behave to Constantius after this? Even to this day I have not yet used in my letters to him the title which was bestowed on me by the gods, but I have always signed myself Cæsar, and I have persuaded the soldiers to demand nothing more if only he would allow us to dwell peaceably in Gaul and would ratify what has already been done. All the legions with me sent letters to him praying that there might be harmony between us. Instead of this, however, he let loose against us the Barbarians, and among them proclaimed me his foe, paying them bribes so that the people of Gaul might be laid waste. Moreover, he wrote to the forces in Italy and bade them be on their guard against any who should come from Gaul; and on the frontiers of Gaul, in the cities nearby, he ordered three million bushels of wheat to be readied which had been ground at Brigantia,[1] plus the same amount near the Cottian Alps, with the intention of marching to oppose me. These are not mere words but deeds that speak plain. In fact, the letters that he wrote I obtained from the Barbarians who brought them to me; additionally, I seized the provisions that had been made ready, and the letters of Taurus. Besides, even now in his letters he addresses me as "Cæsar" and declares that he will never make terms with me, though he sent one Epictetus, a bishop of Gaul, to offer a guarantee of my personal

1. On Lake Constance, Bregenz, Austria

2. cf. "write in dust" or "write in water"

safety; and throughout his letters he keeps repeating that he will not take my life, but about my honour he says not a word. As for his oaths, I think they should, as the proverb says, be written in ashes,[2] so little do they inspire belief. Yet my honour I will not give up, partly out of regard for what is seemly and fitting, but also to secure the safety of my friends. All this, then, and I have not yet described the cruelty that he is practising throughout every country.

These, then, were the events that persuaded me; this was the conduct I thought just. First I imparted it to the gods who see and hear all things. Thereafter, when I had offered sacrifices for my departure, the omens were favourable on the very day on which I was to announce to the troops that they were to march; and since it was not only on behalf of my own safety, but far more for the welfare and freedom of all men, though in particular of the people of Gaul – for twice already he had betrayed them to the enemy and had not even spared the tombs of their ancestors, he who is so anxious to conciliate strangers – then, I say, I thought that I should add to my forces certain very powerful tribes and to obtain supplies of money, when I had a perfect right to coin, both gold and silver. Moreover, if even now he would welcome a reconciliation with me I would keep to what I at present possess; but if he should decide to go to war and will in no way relent from his earlier purpose, then I ought to do and to suffer whatever is the will of the gods, seeing that it would be more disgraceful to show myself his inferior through failure of courage or lack of intelligence than in mere numbers. For if he now defeats me by force of numbers that will not be his doing, but will be due to the larger army that he has at his command. If, on the other hand, he had surprised me waiting in Gaul, clinging to bare life, and, while I attempted to avoid danger, had attacked me on all sides, to the rear and on the flanks by means of the Barbarians, and in front by his own legions, I should, I believe, have had to face complete ruin; furthermore, the disgrace of such conduct is greater than any punishment – at least in the view of the wise.[1]

These are the views, men of Athens, which I have communicated to my fellow soldiers and which I am now writing to the whole body of the citizens throughout all Greece. May the gods who decide all things vouchsafe me the assistance which they have promised to the end, and may they grant to Athens all possible favours at my hands! May she always have such Emperors as will honour her and love her above and beyond all other cities!

---

1. Demosthenes, *Olynthiacs*, 1.27

FRAGMENT OF A LETTER TO A PRIEST

PREFACE

As *Pontifex Maximus*,[1] Julian believed that he had a duty to organise, instruct, and animate the Pagan priestly class, who in turn would be responsible for the care and edification of the broader population. His reformation was wide-sweeping, and sought to combine both traditional practices with more contemporary ideas, such as an institutional philanthropy which, though assuredly inspired by the Christians, was justified through an appeal to ancient Hellenic customs. As Evola observed:

> Julian yearned to implement his Pagan ideal within a stable and unitary imperial hierarchy, endowed with a dogmatic foundation, a system of disciplines and laws, and a priestly class. The priests were to have as their leader the Emperor himself who, having been renewed and elevated above the mere mortal condition by the Mysteries, embodied simultaneously spiritual authority and temporal power. According to this view, the Emperor was positioned as the *Pontifex Maximus*, an ancient term restored by Augustus.[2] The ideological presuppositions on which Julian's vision rested were thus: nature as a harmonious whole permeated by living but unseen forces; a state professed religion; and a body of philosophers – it would be better to call them wise men – capable of interpreting the traditional theology of ancient Rome and of actualising it through initiatory rites.[3]

This fragment, addressed to an unknown priest and likely written in 362 while he was resident in Antioch, shows the value Julian placed upon virtuous conduct and the importance of the priestly class to his designs.

1. Latin term meaning "head priest" or "supreme pontiff" 2. Octavian
3. Julius Evola, *The Emperor Julian*

FRAGMENT OF A LETTER TO A PRIEST

...only[1] that they chastise, then and there, any whom they see rebelling against their king. While the class of wicked daimons is appointed to punish those who do not worship the gods, and thus stung to madness by them, many of the godless are induced to court death in the belief that they will fly up to heaven when they have brought their lives to a violent end.[2] There are also some men who, though man is naturally a social and civilised being, seek out desert places instead of cities, since they have been given over to corrupting daimons and are led by them into this hatred of their own kind. Indeed, many of them have even devised fetters and stocks to wear; to such a degree does the wicked daimon to whom they have, of their own accord, given themselves over abet them in all ways, after they have rebelled against the everlasting and delivering gods. On this subject, however, what I have said is enough, and I shall return to the point at which I digressed.

Though just conduct in accordance with the laws of the state will evidently be the concern of the governors of cities, you in your turn must ensure by exhortation that men uphold the laws of the gods, since those are sacred. Moreover, inasmuch as the life of a priest ought to be more holy than the political life, you must guide and instruct men to adopt it. The better sort will naturally follow your guidance. Indeed, I pray that all men may; but, at the very least, I hope that those who are naturally good and upright will do so, for they will recognise that your teachings are particularly adapted to them.

You must above all exercise philanthropy, for from it result many other blessings, including that finest and greatest blessing of all, the good will of the gods. For just as those who are in agreement

1. The beginning is lost. Julian appears to have been describing the functions of different daimons, and here moves on to those whose task is to punish evil-doers

2. Julian seems to be referencing Christians in this passage, including those who purposefully sought out martyrdom in order to ascend to heaven

with their masters about their friendships, ambitions, and desires are more kindly treated than their fellow slaves, so we must suppose that God, who naturally loves human beings, has more kindness for those men who show goodwill to their fellows. Now, philanthropy has many divisions and is of many kinds. For instance, it is shown when men are punished in moderation with a view to the betterment of those punished, as schoolmasters punish children; and also in ministering to men's needs, even as the gods minister to our own. You see all the blessings of the earth that they have granted to us, food of all sorts, and in an abundance that they have not granted to all other creatures put together. Also, since we were born naked, they covered us with the hair of animals and with things that grow in the ground and on trees. Nor were they content to do this simply or spontaneously, as Moses bade men take coats of skins,[1] but you see how numerous are the gifts of Athena the Craftswoman. What other animals use wine, or olive oil? Except, indeed, in cases where we let them share in these things, even though we do not share them with our fellow men. What creature of the sea uses corn, what land animal uses things that grow in the sea? While I have not yet mentioned gold, bronze, or iron, though in all these the gods have made us very rich; though not to the end that we may bring reproach on them by disregarding the poor in our midst, especially when they happen to be of good character – men, for example, who have inherited no paternal estate, and are poor because in the greatness of their souls they do not covet wealth. Now, when the crowd see such men they blame the gods. Yet it is not the gods who are to blame for their poverty, but rather the insatiate greed of us men of property becomes the cause of this false conception of the gods among men, and of unjust blame of the gods besides. Of what use, I ask, is it for us to pray that God will rain gold on the poor as he did on the people of Rhodes?[2] For even if this should come to pass, we would at once set our slaves underneath to catch it, and put out vessels everywhere, and drive off all-comers so that we alone might seize upon the gifts of the gods meant for all in common. Anyone would naturally think it strange if we should ask for this, which is not in the nature of things, and is in every way unhelpful, while we do not do what is in our power. Who, I ask, ever became poor by giving to his neighbours? Indeed, I myself, who have often given generously to those in need, have recovered my gifts again many times over at the

1. *Genesis*, 3.21 2. Pindar, *Olympian Ode*, 7.49; this became a Sophistic commonplace

hands of the gods, though I am a poor man of business; nor have I ever repented of that ample giving. Of the present time I will say nothing, for it would be altogether irrational of me to compare the expenditure of private persons with that of an Emperor; but when I was myself still a private person, I know that this happened to me many times. My grandmother's estate, for instance, was kept for me untouched, though others had taken possession of it by violence, because I spent money on those in need and gave them a share of the little that I had.

We ought then to share our money with all men, but more generously with the good, and with those both helpless and poor so as to suffice for their need. Further, I will assert, even though it be paradoxical to say so, that it would be a pious act to share our clothes and food even with the wicked. For it is to the humanity in a man that we give, and not to his moral character. Hence, I think that even those who are shut up in prison have a right to the same sort of care, since this kind of philanthropy will not hinder justice. For when many have been shut up in prison to await trial, of whom some will be found guilty, while others will prove to be innocent, it would be harsh indeed if out of regard for the guiltless we should not bestow some pity on the guilty also; or again, if on account of the guilty we should also behave ruthlessly and inhumanly to those who have done no wrong. This too, when I consider it, seems to me altogether wrong; by which I mean that we call Zeus by the title "God of Strangers" while we show ourselves more inhospitable to strangers than are the very Scythians. How, I ask, can one who wishes to sacrifice to Zeus, the God of Strangers, even approach his temple? With what conscience can he do so, when he has forgotten the saying:

πρὸς γὰρ Διός εἰσιν ἅπαντες
Πτωχοί τε ξεῖνοί τε· δόσις δ' ὀλίγη τε φίλη τε·

"from Zeus come all beggars and strangers;
and a gift is precious though small"[1]

Again, the man who worships Zeus, the God of Comrades, and who, though he sees his neighbours in need of money, does not give them even so much as a *drachma*, how, I say, can he think that he is worshipping Zeus properly? When I observe this I am wholly amazed, since I see that these titles of the gods are from the

1. *The Odyssey*, VI, 207

beginning of the world their express images, yet in our practice we pay no attention to anything of the sort. The gods are called by us "gods of kindred" and Zeus the "God of Kindred" but we treat our kinsmen as though they were strangers. I say "kinsmen" because every man, willingly or otherwise, is akin to every other man, whether it be true, as some say, that we are all descended from one man and one woman, or whether it came about in some other way, and the gods created us all together at the beginning when the world began, not one man and one woman only, but many men and many women at once. For they who had the power to create one man and one woman, were able to create many men and women at once; since the manner of creating one man and one woman is the same as that of creating many men and many women. Thus one must have regard to the differences in our habits and laws, or still more to that which is higher, more precious, and more authoritative. By this I mean the sacred tradition of the gods which has been handed down to us by the theurgists of earlier days, namely that when Zeus was setting all things in order there fell from him drops of sacred blood, and from them, as they say, arose the race of men. It follows, therefore, that we are all kinsmen, whether, many men and women as we are, we come from two human beings, or whether, as the gods tell us, and as we ought to believe, since facts bear witness thereto, we are all descended from the gods. Moreover, that facts bear witness that many men came into the world at once, I shall maintain elsewhere, and precisely, but for the moment it will be enough to say this much: if we were descended from one man and one woman, it is not likely that our laws would show such great divergence; nor in any case is it likely that the whole earth was filled with people by one man; indeed, not even if the women used to bear many children at a time to their husbands, like swine. Yet when the gods all together had given birth to men, just as one man came forth, so in like manner came forth many men who had been allotted to the gods who rule over births; and they brought them forth, receiving their souls from the Demiurge out of eternity.[1]

It is proper, also, to bear in mind how many discourses have been devoted by men in the past to show that man is by nature a social animal. Shall we, then, after asserting this and enjoining it, bear ourselves unsociably to our neighbours? Then let everyone make the basis of his conduct moral virtues, and such actions as

1. Julian favours the Platonic account of creation in *Timæus* to the Biblical narrative

reverence towards the gods, benevolence towards men, and personal chastity; let him abound in pious acts, that is, by endeavouring always to have pious thoughts about the gods, by regarding the temples and images of the gods with due honour and veneration, and by worshipping the gods as though he beheld them truly present. For our fathers established images and altars, the maintenance of undying fire, and, generally speaking, everything of the sort, as symbols of the presence of the gods; not that we may regard such things as gods, but that we may worship the gods through them. For being in the body, it was in bodily form that we must perform our service to the gods, too, though they are themselves without bodies. Therefore, they revealed to us in the earliest images the class of gods next in rank to the first, those that revolve in a circle about the whole heavens. Yet since even to these due worship cannot be offered in bodily form – for by nature they want for nothing[1] – another class of images was invented on the earth, and by performing our worship to them, we shall make the gods propitious to ourselves. For just as those who make offerings to the statues of the Emperors, who also lack for nothing, nevertheless induce goodwill towards themselves thereby, so too those who make offerings to the images of the gods, though the gods need nothing, do nonetheless thereby persuade them to help and care for them. For zeal to do all that is in one's power is, in truth, a proof of piety, and it is evident that he who abounds in such zeal thereby displays a higher degree of piety; whereas he who neglects what is possible, and then pretends to aim at what is impossible, evidently does not strive after the impossible, since he overlooks the possible. For even though God stands in need of nothing, it does not follow on that account that nothing ought to be offered to him. He does not need the reverence that is paid in words. What then? Is it rational to deprive him of this also? By no means. It follows, then, that one ought not to deprive him of the honour that is paid to him through deeds either, an honour which not three years or three thousand years have ordained, but all past time among all the nations of the earth.

Therefore, when we look at the images of the gods, let us indeed not think they are mere stones or wood, but neither let us think they are the gods themselves; for we do not say that the statues of the Emperors are mere wood and stone and bronze, but still less do we say they are the Emperors themselves. He, therefore, who

1. cf. *Acts*, 17.25; "nor is he worshipped with men's hands, as if he needed anything"

loves the emperor delights to see the emperor's statue, and he who loves his son delights to see his son's statue, and he who loves his father delights to see his father's statue. It follows that he who loves the gods delights to gaze on the images of the gods and their likenesses, whereupon he feels reverence and shudders in awe of the gods who look at him from the unseen world. Thus, if any man thinks that because they have once been described as bearing a likeness to the gods, they are incapable of being destroyed, he is, it seems to me, altogether foolish, for surely in that case they were incapable of being made by men's hands. Yet what has been made by a wise and good man can be destroyed by a bad and ignorant man. Whereas those beings which were fashioned by the gods as the living images of their invisible nature, that is, the gods who revolve in a circle in the heavens, abide imperishable for all time. Therefore, let no man disbelieve in the gods because he sees and hears that certain persons have profaned their images and temples. Have they not in many cases put good men to death, like Socrates and Dio, and the great Empedotimus?[1] And yet I am quite sure that the gods cared more for these men than for the temples. Observe, however, that since they knew that the bodies of even these men were perishable, they allowed them to yield to nature and to submit, but later on they exacted punishment from their slayers; and this has happened in the sight of all, in our own day also, to those who have profaned the temples.

Then let no man deceive us with his sayings or trouble our faith in a divine providence. For as for those who make such profanation a reproach against us, by which I mean the prophets of the Jews, what have they to say about their own temple, which was overthrown three times and even now is not being raised up again? This I mention not as a reproach against them, for I myself, after so great a lapse of time, intended to restore it, in honour of the god whose name has been associated with it. Yet in the present case I have used this instance because I wish to prove that nothing made by man can be indestructible, and that the prophets who wrote such statements were uttering nonsense, as one who consorts with foolish old hags. In my opinion, there is no reason why their god should not be a mighty god, even though he does not happen to have wise prophets or interpreters. The real reason why they are not wise, however, is that they have not submitted their souls to be cleansed by the regular course of study, nor have they allowed those studies

1. Empedotimus of Syracuse

to open their tightly closed eyes, and to clear away the mist that hangs over them. Yet since these men see, as it were, a great light through a fog, not plainly or clearly, and since they think that what they see is not a pure light but a fire, failing thereby to discern all that surrounds it, they cry with a loud voice: "tremble, be afraid, fire, flame, death, a dagger, a broadsword!". Thus do they describe under many names the harmful might of fire. Though on this subject it will be better to demonstrate separately just how inferior these teachers of tales about the gods are to our own poets.

It is our duty to adore not only the images of the gods, but also their temples, sacred precincts, and altars. It is also reasonable to honour the priests as officials and servants of the gods; and because they minister to us what concerns the gods, lending strength to the gods' gift of good things to us. For they sacrifice and pray on behalf of all men. Therefore, it is right that we should pay them all not less, if not indeed more, than the honours that we pay to the magistrates of the state. If any one thinks that we ought to assign equal honours to them and to the magistrates of the state, since the latter are also in some way dedicated to the service of the gods, being guardians of the laws, we nevertheless ought to give the priests a far greater share of our good will. The Achæans, for instance, enjoined on their king[1] to reverence the priest, though he was one of the enemies, whereas we do not even reverence the priests who are our friends, and who pray and sacrifice on our behalf.

Though since my discourse has returned again to the beginning, as I have so long wished, I think it is worthwhile for me to describe next what sort of man a priest ought to be, in order that he may himself be justly honoured and may cause the gods to be honoured. For as concerns us, we ought not to investigate or enquire as to his conduct, and so long as a man is called a priest we ought to honour and cherish him, but if he proves to be wicked, we ought to permit his priestly office to be taken away from him, since he has shown himself unworthy of it. So long as he sacrifices for us, makes offerings, and stands in the presence of the gods, we must regard him with respect and reverence as the most highly honoured chattel[2] of the gods. For it would be absurd for us to pay respect to the very stones of which the altars are made, on account of their being dedicated to the gods, because they have a certain shape and form suited to the ritual for which they have been fashioned,

1. Agamemnon; *The Iliad*, I, 23   2. cf. Plato, *Phædo*, 62

and then not think that we ought to honour a man who has been dedicated to the gods.

Perhaps someone will object: "but suppose he does wrong and often fails to offer to the gods their sacred rites?" Then, indeed, I answer that we ought to convict a man of that sort, so that he may not by his wickedness offend the gods; but that we ought not to dishonour him until he has been convicted. Nor, in truth, is it reasonable that when we have set our hands to this business, we should take away their honour not only from these offenders but also from those who are worthy to be honoured. Therefore, let every priest, like every magistrate, be treated with respect, for there is also an oracle to that effect from the Didymæan god:[1] "as for men who with reckless minds work wickedness against the priests of the deathless gods and plot against their privileges with plans that fear not the gods, never shall such men travel life's path to the end, men who have shown contempt towards the blessed gods, whose honour and holy service those priests have in charge".[2] While again in another oracle the god says: "all my servants from harmful mischief I will protect"; and he says that on their behalf he will inflict punishment on the aggressors.

While there are many utterances of the god to the same effect, by means of which we may learn to honour and cherish priests as we ought, I shall speak on this subject elsewhere at greater length. For the present, then, it is enough to point out that I am not inventing anything extemporaneously, since I believe the declaration made by the god and the command expressed in his own words to be sufficient. Therefore, let any man who considers that as a teacher of such matters I am worthy to be believed show due respect to the god and obey him, and honour the priests of the gods above all other men.

Now I will try to describe what sort of man a priest himself ought to be, though not for your especial benefit. For if I did not already know from the evidence of both the high priest and of the most mighty gods that you administer this priestly office properly – at least in all matters that come under your management – I should not have ventured to confide in you a matter so important. I do so, however, in order that you may be able to instruct the other priests from what I say, not only in the cities but in the country districts, also, more convincingly and with complete freedom; since not of your own self do you alone devise these precepts and practise them,

1. Apollo 2. An oracle from an unknown source

but you have me as well to give you support. I, who by the grace of the gods am known as *Pontifex Maximus*, though I am in truth by no means worthy of so high an office, even as I desire and, moreover, constantly pray to the gods that I may be worthy. For the gods, you must know, hold out great hopes for us after death; and we must believe them absolutely. For they are always truthful, not only about the future life, but about the affairs of this life also. Further, since in the superabundance of their power they are both able to overcome the confusion that exists in this life and to regulate its disorders and irregularities, in that other life where conflicting things are reconciled, after the immortal soul has been separated from the body and the lifeless body has turned to earth, will they not be all the more able to bestow all those things for which they have held out hopes to mankind? Thus, since we know that the gods have granted to their priests a great recompense, let us make them responsible in all things for men's esteem of the gods, displaying their own lives as an example of what they ought to preach to the people.

The first thing we ought to preach is reverence towards the gods. For it is fitting that we should perform our service to the gods as though they were themselves present with us and beheld us, and though not seen by us could direct their gaze, which is more powerful than any light, even as far as our innermost thoughts. This saying is not my own[1] but the god's, and has been declared in many utterances; but for me it is certainly sufficient, by bringing forth one such utterance, to illustrate two things in one, namely how the gods see all things and how they rejoice in pious men: "on all sides extend the far-seeing rays of Phoebus. His swift gaze pierces through even solid rock, and travels through the dark blue sea, nor is he unaware of the starry multitude that passes in a endless circuit through the unwearied heavens by the statutes of necessity; nor of all the tribes of the dead in the underworld whom Tartarus has admitted within the misty dwelling of Hades, beneath the western darkness. For I delight in god-revering mortals as much as even Olympus itself".[2]

Now, in so far as all souls, but to a much higher degree the soul of man, is akin to and related to the gods, so much more likely is it that the gaze of the gods should penetrate through his soul easily and effectively. Observe the love of the god for mankind when he says that he delights in the disposition of god-revering men as

1. Euripides, fr. 488 2. An oracle from an unknown source

much as Olympus itself, most pure and bright. How, then, shall he not lead up our souls from the darkness and from Tartarus, if we approach him with pious awe? Indeed, he has knowledge of even those who have been imprisoned in Tartarus – for not even that region falls outside the power of the gods – and to the pious he promises Olympus instead of Tartarus. Wherefore we ought by all means to hold fast to deeds of piety, approaching the gods with reverence, and neither saying nor listening to anything base. Further, the priests ought to keep themselves pure not only from impure or shameful acts, but also from uttering words and hearing speeches of that character. Accordingly, we must banish all offensive jests and all licentious association. So that you may understand what I mean by this, let no one who has been consecrated a priest read either Archilochus or Hipponax,[1] or anyone else who writes such poems as theirs. While in old comedy, let him avoid everything of that type – for it is better thus – and indeed on all accounts philosophy alone will be appropriate for us priests; and of philosophers only those who chose the gods as guides of their mental discipline, like Pythagoras, Plato, Aristotle, and the school of Chrysippus and Zeno. For we ought not to give heed to them all, nor to the doctrines of all, but only to those philosophers and those of their doctrines that make men pious, and teach concerning the gods, first that they exist, secondly that they concern themselves with the things of this world, and further that they do no injury at all to either mankind or to one another, out of jealousy, envy, or enmity. By which I mean the sort of thing our poets in the first place have brought themselves into disrepute by writing, and in the second place such tales as the prophets of the Jews take pains to invent, and are admired for so doing by those miserable men who have attached themselves to the Galilæans.

For us, however, it will be appropriate to read such narratives as have been composed about deeds that have actually been done; while we must avoid all fictions in the form of narrative, such as were circulated among men in the past; for instance, tales concerned with the affairs of love, and generally everything of that sort. For just as not every road is suitable for consecrated priests, but the roads they travel ought to be duly assigned, so not every sort of reading is suitable for a priest. For words breed a certain sort of disposition in the soul; little by little it arouses desires, and then all of a sudden kindles a terrible blaze, against which one ought, in

1. Of Ephesus; a scurrilous poet who wrote in choliambics; cf. Horace, *Epochs*, 6.12

my opinion, to arm oneself well in advance.

Let us not admit discourses by Epicurus or Pyrrho; though, indeed, the gods have already in their wisdom destroyed their works, so that most of their books have ceased to be. Nevertheless, there is no reason why I should not, by way of example, mention these works too, to show what sort of discourse priests must especially avoid; and if such is spoken, then all the more must they avoid such thoughts. For an error of speech is, in my opinion, by no means the same as an error of the mind, though we ought to give heed to the mind first of all, since the tongue errs in company with it. We ought to learn by heart the hymns in honour of the gods – many and beautiful they are, composed by men of old and of our own time – though, in truth, we ought to also try to learn those which are being sung in the temples. For the greater number were bestowed on us by the gods themselves in answer to prayer, while a few were also written by men, having been composed in honour of the gods by the aid of divine inspiration and a soul unspoiled by things pernicious and low.

All this, at least, we ought to study to do, and we ought to pray often to the gods as well, both in private and in public, three times a day if possible, but if not so often, certainly at dawn and in the evening. For it is not fit that a consecrated priest should pass a day or a night without sacrifice; for dawn is the beginning of the day as twilight is of the night. Moreover, it is proper to begin both periods with sacrifice to the gods, even when we happen to not be assigned to perform the service. For it is our duty to maintain all the rituals of the temples that the law of our forefathers prescribes, and we ought to perform neither more nor less than that ritual; for eternal are the gods, thus we, too, ought to imitate their essential nature in order that thereby we may make them propitious.

Now, if we were pure of soul alone, and our bodies did not hinder us in any respect, it would be well to prescribe one sort of life for priests. Though since what he should practise when on duty concerns the individual priest alone, not priests generally, what should we concede to a man who has received the office of priest on occasions when he is not actually engaged in service at the temples? I think that a priest ought to keep himself pure from all contamination, for a night and a day, and then after purifying himself for another night following the first, with such rites of purification as the sacred laws prescribe, he should under these conditions enter the temple and remain there for as many days as the law commands (thirty is the number with us at Rome, but in other places the number varies). It is proper then, I think, that he should remain throughout all these days in the sacred precincts, devoting himself to philosophy; that he should not enter a house or a marketplace, or see even a magistrate, except in the precincts, but should concern himself with his service to the god, overseeing and arranging everything in person; and then, when he has completed the term of days, he should retire from his office in favour of another. When he turns again to the ordinary life of mankind, he may be allowed to visit a friend's house, and, when invited, to attend a feast, but only on the invitation of persons of the highest character. At this time, there would be nothing notable in his going occasionally to the marketplace and conversing with the governor or the chief magistrate of his tribe, and giving aid, as far as lies in his power, to those who have a good reason for needing it.

It is, in my opinion, fitting for priests to wear the most magnificent attire when they are performing services within the temple, but to wear ordinary dress without any extravagance when they are outside the sacred precincts. For it is not reasonable that we should misuse, in empty conceit and vain ostentation, what has been given to us for the honour of the gods. For this reason, then, we ought in the marketplace to abstain from costly attire and outward show, and, in short, from every sort of pretentiousness.

For consider how the gods rewarded Amphiaraus,[1] because they admired his perfect moderation, after they had decreed the destruction of that famous army. Despite knowing that it would be so, he went with the expedition and therefore did not escape his fated end, whereupon the gods, it is said, transformed him completely from what he had been and removed him to the sphere of the gods. For all the others who were in the expedition against Thebes engraved a device on their shields before they had conquered the enemy, and erected trophies to celebrate the downfall of the Cadmeans; whereas he, the associate of the gods, when he went to war had arms with no device; rather, he had compassion and temperance, as even the enemy bore witness. Hence, I think that we priests ought to show moderation in our dress in order that we may win the goodwill of the gods, since it is no slight offence that we commit against them when we wear in public the sacred dress and make it public property, thereby giving

1. cf. Aeschylus, *Seven Against Thebes*; Euripides, *Phoenissæ*, 1118

all men an opportunity to stare at it as though it were some sort of spectacle. For whenever this happens, many who are not purified come near us, and by this means the symbols of the gods are polluted. Moreover, what lawlessness it is, what arrogance towards the gods for us ourselves when we are not living the priestly life to wear the priestly dress! However, of this too I shall speak more particularly in another place; and what I am writing to you at the moment is only a mere outline of the subject.

No priest anywhere may be present at the licentious theatrical shows of the present day, nor introduce one into his own house, for that is altogether improper. Indeed, if it were possible to banish such shows absolutely from the theatres so as to restore to Dionysus those theatres pure as of old, I should certainly have endeavoured with all my heart to bring this about; but, as it is, since I believed this to be impossible, and that even if it should prove to be possible it would not on other accounts be expedient, I refrained entirely from this ambition. I do, nevertheless, demand that priests should withdraw themselves from the licentiousness of the theatres and leave them to the crowd. Therefore, let no priest enter a theatre, or have an actor or a charioteer for his friend; and let no dancer or mime[1] even approach his door. As for the sacred games, I permit anyone who wishes to attend only those in which women are forbidden not only to compete but even to be spectators. With regard to the hunting shows with dogs which are performed inside the city theatres, need I say that not only priests but even the sons of priests must keep away from them?

Now, it would perhaps have been better to say earlier from what class of men and by what method priests must be appointed; though it is quite appropriate that my remarks should end with this. I say that the most upright men in every city, by preference those who show most love for the gods, and next those who show most love for their fellow men, must be appointed, whether they be poor or rich. In this matter, let there be no distinction whatsoever whether they are unknown or well known. For the man who by reason of his gentleness has not won notice ought not to be barred by reason of his lack of fame. Even if he be poor and a man of the people, if he should possess within himself these two things, love for God and love for his fellow men, let him be appointed a priest. A proof of his love for God is his inducing his own people to show reverence to the gods; a proof of his love for his fellows is his

1. *μῖμος* referred to an actor who partook in farcical dramas full of mimicry

sharing cheerfully, even from a small store, with those in need, and his giving willingly thereof, seeking to do good to as many men as he is able.

We must pay especial attention to this point, and by this means effect a cure. For when it came about that the poor were neglected and overlooked by the priests, then I think the impious Galilæans observed this fact and devoted themselves to philanthropy. They have gained ascendancy in the worst of their deeds through the credit they win for such practices. For just as those who entice children with cake, and by throwing it to them two or three times induce them to follow them, and then, when they are far away from their friends, cast them on board a ship and sell them as slaves, whereby that which for the moment seemed sweet, proves to be bitter for all the rest of their lives. By the same method, I say, the Galilæans also begin with their so-called love-feast, or hospitality, or service of tables – for they have many ways of carrying it out and hence call it by many names – and the result is that they have led very many into godlessness...[1]

1. The conclusion is lost, and may have been suppressed by Christian copyists

LETTERS

1. TO PRISCUS[1]

(FROM GAUL, 359)

On receiving your letter, I at once despatched Archelaus and gave him letters to carry to you, along with the passport,[2] as you wished, for a longer time. If you are inclined to explore the ocean, everything, with the god's help, will be provided for you as you would wish, unless you dread the boorishness of the Gauls and the winter climate. This, however, will turn out as the god sees fit; though I swear to you by him who is the giver and preserver of all my good fortune that I desire to live only that I may in some degree be of use to you. When I say "you", I of course mean the true philosophers, convinced as I am that you are one of these. How much I have cherished and still cherish you, you well know, thus am I eager to see you. May Divine Providence preserve you in health for many a year, my dearest and best beloved brother! I salute the admirable Hippia and your children.[3]

2. TO PRISCUS

(FROM GAUL, 358-9)

As regards a visit to me from your good self, if you have it in mind, make your plans now, with the help of the gods, and exert yourself; for perhaps a little later I, too, shall have no time to spare. Hunt up for me all the writings of Iamblichus to his namesake. Only you can do this, for your sister's son-in-law owns a thoroughly revised version. Indeed, if I am not mistaken, while I was writing this sentence a marvellous sign was vouchsafed me. I entreat you to not let Theodorus[4] and his followers deafen you as well by their assertions that Iamblichus, that truly godlike man, who ranks next to Pythagoras and Plato, was worldly and self-seeking. Yet if it be rash to declare my own opinion to you, I may reasonably expect you

1. One of Ædesius' students whom Julian met in Pergamon. Priscus was one of those present with Julian in Persia when he died

2. Literally "token". This, like the Latin *tessera*, could be of various kinds, but here Julian is probably referring to a document comparable to the modern passport which he had ordered so that Priscus might proceed to Gaul

3. For the life of Priscus, cf. Eunapius, *Lives of the Sophists and Philosophers*

4. Theodorus of Asine was a disciple of the great Iamblichus; no such polemics as indicated here have survived

to excuse me, as one excuses those who are carried away by a divine enthusiasm. You are yourself an ardent admirer of Iamblichus for his philosophy and of his namesake for his theosophy. While I too think, like Apollodorus, that the rest are not worth mentioning compared with those two. As for your collection of the works of Aristotle, so much I will say, you have made me style myself your pupil, though I have no right to the title. For while Maximus of Tyre in six books was able to initiate me to some small extent into Plato's logic, you, with one book, have made me, perhaps I may even say, a complete initiate in the philosophy of Aristotle, but at any rate a thyrsus-bearer.[1] When you join me, I can prove the truth of my words by the great number of works that I wrote during this last winter.

3. TO EUMENIUS AND PHARIANUS[2]

(FROM GAUL, 359)

If anyone has persuaded you that there is anything more delightful or more beneficial for mankind than to pursue philosophy at one's leisure without interruptions, he is a deluded man trying to delude you. If, however, your old zeal still abides in you and has not been swiftly quenched like a brilliant flame, then I regard you as particularly blessed. Four years have already passed, and almost three months besides, since we parted from one another. It would give me pleasure to observe how far you have progressed in this period. As for my own progress, if I can still so much as speak Greek it is surprising, such a Barbarian have I become because of the places in which I have lived. Do not despise the study of mere words or be careless of rhetoric or fail to read poetry. Though you must devote still more attention to serious studies, and let your whole effort be to acquire understanding of the teachings of Aristotle and Plato. Let this be your task, the base, the foundation, the edifice, the roof. For all other studies are incidental, though they are completed by you with greater zeal than some bestow on truly important tasks. I call sacred Justice to witness that I give you this advice because I love you like brothers. For you were my fellow students and my very good friends. If, therefore, you do follow my advice, I shall love you all the

1. The *θύρσος* was a staff carried by the votaries of Dionysus. Plato, *Phædo*, 69, says that "many carry the thyrsus of Dionysus, but few are truly inspired".

2. Two students whom Julian probably met during his brief stay in Athens in 355

more, but if I see that you disregard it, I shall grieve. And grief, if it lasts, usually results in something that, for the sake of a happier augury, I forbear to mention.

4. TO ORIBASIUS[1]

(FROM LUTETIA, 359)

The divinely inspired Homer says[2] that there are two gates of dreams, and that with regard to future events we cannot trust them both equally. I think that this time, however, if ever before, you have seen clearly into the future; for I, too, this very day saw a vision of the same sort. I thought that in a certain very spacious room a tall tree had been planted, and that it was leaning down to the ground, while at its root had sprouted another, small and young, and very much flourishing. Now, I was very anxious on behalf of the small tree, lest someone in pulling up the large one should pull it up as well. In fact, when I came close I saw that the tall tree was lying at full length upon the ground, while the small one was still upright, but hung suspended away from the earth. When I saw this I said, in great anxiety: "alas for this tall tree! There is danger that not even its offspring will be preserved". Then one[3] who was altogether a stranger to me said: "look carefully and take courage. For since the root still remains in the earth, the smaller tree will be uninjured and will be established even more securely than before". So much then for my dreams. God knows what they portend.

As for that abominable eunuch,[4] I should be glad to learn when he said these things about me, whether it was before he met me, or since. So tell me whatever you can about this. with regard to my own behaviour towards him,[5] the gods know that often, when he wronged the provincials, I kept silence, at the expense of my own honour; to some charges I would not listen, others I would not

1. Julian's physician and friend who accompanied him to Gaul. Oribasius was considered one of the most important medical writers of the Græco-Roman period

2. *The Odyssey*, XIX, 562; Oribasius had evidently reported to Julian some dream of his which augured well for their hopes

3. Hermes, who was Julian's guide in his myth in *Against the Cynic Heraclius*

4. Possibly Eusebius, the chamberlain of Constantius. The epithet is unsuitable to Florentius, though some editors attribute it to him

5. In spite of the abruptness of the transition, Asmus and Wright believe, as is made quite clear from the text which follows, that Julian is now referring to Florentius

admit, others again I did not believe, while in some cases I imputed the blame to his associates. Yet when he thought fit to make me share in such infamy by sending those shameful and wholly abominable reports for me to sign, what was the right thing for me to do? Was I to remain silent, or to oppose him? The former course was foolish, servile, and odious to the gods; the latter was just, becoming of a man, and noble, but was not open to me on account of the affairs that engaged me. What then did I do? In the presence of many persons who I knew would report it to him I said: "such a one will certainly and by all means revise his reports, for they pass the bounds of decency". When he heard this, he was so far from behaving with discretion that he did things which, by heaven, no tyrant with any moderation would have done, and that, moreover, though I was so near to where he was. In such a case, what was the proper conduct for a man who is a zealous student of the teachings of Plato and Aristotle? Ought I to have looked on while the hapless people were being betrayed to thieves, or to have aided them as far as I could, for they were already singing their swan-song because of the criminal artifices of men of that sort? To me, at least, it seems a disgraceful thing that, while I punish my military tribunes when they desert their post – and indeed they ought to be put to death at once, and not even granted burial – I should myself desert my post, which is for the defence of such beleaguered people; for it is my duty to fight against thieves of his sort, especially when God is fighting on my side, since it was indeed he who posted me here. Further, if any harm to myself should result, it is no small consolation to have proceeded with a good conscience. Though I pray that the gods may let me keep the excellent Salutius![1] If, however, it transpires that because of this affair I should be removed from power, perhaps it will not grieve me. For it is better to do one's duty for a brief time honestly than for a long time dishonestly. The Peripatetic teachings are not, as some say, less noble than the Stoic. In my judgement, there is only this difference between them: the former are always more sanguine and not so much the result of deliberate thought, while the latter have a greater claim to practical wisdom, and are more rigidly consistent with the rules of conduct that they have laid down.

1. Salutius was recalled by Constantius in 359

5. TO PRISCUS

(FROM LUTETIA, 358-9)

I had only just recovered, by the providence of the All-Seeing One,[1] from a very severe and sharp attack of sickness, when your letters reached my hands, on the very day when I took my first bath. It was already evening when I read them, and it would be hard for you to tell how my strength began to return when I realised your pure and sincere affection. May I become worthy of it, that I may not shame your fondness for me! Your letters I read at once, though I was not very well able to do so, while those of Antonius to Alexander I saved for the following day. On the seventh day from their receipt, I began to write this to you, since my strength is improving reasonably well, thanks to Divine Providence. May the All-Seeing god preserve you, my dearest and most beloved brother. May I see you, my treasured friend!

(*Added with his own hand*) I swear by your well-being and my own, by the All-Seeing god, that I really feel as I have written. First among men, when can I see you and embrace you? For already, like devoted companions, I delight in your very name.

6. TO ALYPIUS, BROTHER OF CAESARIUS[2]

(FROM GAUL, PRE-JULY, 361)

Syloson, it is said,[3] went up to Darius, reminded him of his cloak, and asked him for Samos in return for it. Then Darius prided himself greatly on this, because he considered that he had given much for little; though after all it proved a grievous gift for Syloson.[4] Now consider my conduct compared with that of Darius. In the first place, I think that I have behaved better than he in one respect, that is, I did not wait to be reminded by another. Rather, after preserving the memory of your friendship so long undimmed, the first moment that the god granted me power I summoned you, not among the second

1. i.e. Helios-Mithras

2. According to Ammianus 23.1.2, Alypius was a native of Antioch. He is notable for having served as governor of Britannia, where he held the title of *Vicarius Uritanniarum*, an office subordinate to the prefect of the Gallic provinces

3. Herodotus, 3.139; the "cloak of Syloson" became a proverb for the overpayment of a benefit

4. The Persians devastated Samos before Syloson could benefit from the gift

but among the very first. So much for the past. Now, with reference to the future, will you allow me – for I am a prophet[1] – to foretell something? I think that it will be far more prosperous than in the case I spoke of, only let not Adrasteia[2] take offence when I say so! For you need no king to help you to conquer a city,[3] while I on the other hand need many to help me raise up again what has fallen on sorry days. Thus does my Gallic and Barbarian Muse jest for your benefit. But be of good cheer and come, and may the gods attend you.

(*Added with his own hand*) There is good spoil of deer and hunting of small sheep in the winter quarters.[4] Come to your friend who valued you even when he could not yet know your merit.

7. TO ALYPIUS, BROTHER OF CAESARIUS

It happened that when you sent me your map I had just recovered from my illness, though I was nonetheless glad on that account to receive the chart that you sent. For not only does it contain diagrams better than any hitherto made, but you have embellished it by adding those iambic verses, not such as "Sing the War of Bupalus",[5] as the poet of Cyrene[6] expresses it, but such as beautiful Sappho is wont to fashion for her songs. In fact, the gift is such as no doubt it well became you to give, while to me it is most agreeable to receive.[7] With regard to your administration of affairs, inasmuch as you study to act in all cases both energetically and humanely, I am very much pleased with it. For to blend mildness and moderation with courage and force, and to exercise the former towards the most virtuous, and the latter implacably in the case of the wicked for their reformation, is, as I am convinced, a task that calls for no slight natural endowment and virtue. I pray that you may ever hold fast to these ambitions and may adapt them both solely to what is fair and honourable. Not without reason did the most eloquent of the ancient writers believe that this is the end and aim set for all the virtues. May you continue in health and happiness as long as possible, my beloved and dear brother!

---

1. An echo of Plato, *Phædrus*, 343
2. Another name for Nemesis, goddess of divine retribution
3. Constantinople
4. This may be an allusion to Julian's plan to defeat the adherents of Constantius
5. For Bupalus, cf. Horace, *Epodes*, 6.14
6. Callimachus, fr. 90
7. An echo of Isocrates, *Nicocles*, 29

8. TO MAXIMUS THE PHILOSOPHER[1]

(FROM NAISSA, NOVEMBER, 361)

Everything crowds into my mind at once and chokes my utterance, as one thought refuses to let another precede it, whether you please to class such symptoms among psychological troubles, or to give them some other name. Let me arrange, then, what I have to tell in chronological order, though not till I have first offered thanks to the all-merciful gods, who at this moment have permitted me to write, and will also perhaps permit us to see one another. Directly after I had been made Emperor – against my will, as the gods know; and this I made evident then and there in every way possible – I led the army against the Barbarians.[2] That expedition lasted for three months, and when I returned to the shores of Gaul, I was ever on the watch and kept enquiring from all who came from that quarter whether any philosopher or any scholar wearing a philosopher's cloak or a soldier's tunic had arrived. Then I approached Besontio.[3] It is a little town that has lately been restored, but in ancient times it was a large city adorned with costly temples, and was fortified by a strong wall and further by the nature of the place, for it is encircled by the river Doubis.[4] It rises up like a rocky cliff in the sea, inaccessible, I might almost say, to the very birds, except in those places where the river, as it flows round it, throws out what one may call beaches that lie in front of it. Near this city there came to meet me a certain man who looked like a Cynic, with his long cloak and staff. When I first caught sight of him in the distance, I imagined that he was none other than yourself. Then, when I came nearer to him I thought that he had surely come from you. The man was in fact a friend of mine, though he fell short of what I had hoped and expected. This was one vain dream I had. Afterwards I thought that, because you were preoccupied with my affairs, I should certainly find you nowhere outside of Greece. Zeus be my witness, and great Helios, mighty Athena, and all the gods and goddesses, how on my way down to Illyricum from Gaul I shook, anxious of your safety! I also kept enquiring of the gods – not that I ventured to do this myself, for I could not endure to see or hear anything so terrible as one might have supposed would be happening to you at that time

1. Another of Ædesius' pupils. Julian sought Maximus out at Ephesus and quickly developed a strong friendship with the theurgist whom he regarded highly

2. Julian recrossed the Rhine in 360

3. cf. Julius Cæsar, *Bellum Gallicum*, 1.38

4. Doubs, eastern France

but I entrusted the task to others; and the gods did indeed show clearly that certain troubles would befall you; nothing terrible, however, nor to indicate that impious counsels would be carried out.[1]

Yet you see that I have passed over many important events. Above all, it is right that you should learn how I became at once conscious of the very presence of the gods, and in what manner I escaped the multitude of those who plotted against me, though I put no man to death, deprived no man of his property, and only imprisoned those whom I caught red-handed. All this, however, I ought perhaps to tell you rather than write it, but I think you will be very glad to be informed of it. I worship the gods openly, and the whole mass of the troops who are returning with me worship the gods;[2] I sacrifice oxen in public; I have offered to the gods many hecatombs as thank-offerings. The gods command me to restore their worship in its utmost purity, and I obey them, verily, and with a firm will. For they promise me great rewards for my labours, if only I am not remiss. Evagrius[3] has joined me...of the god whom we honour...

Many things occur to my mind, besides what I have written, but I must store up certain matters to tell you when you are with me. Come here, then, in the name of the gods, as quickly as you can, and use two or more public carriages. Moreover, I have sent two of my most trusted servants, one of whom will escort you as far as my headquarters; the other will inform me that you have set out and will forthwith arrive. Do yourself tell the youths which of them you wish to undertake which of these tasks.[4]

9. TO HIS UNCLE JULIAN[5]

(FROM NAISSA, LATE 361)

The third hour of the night has just begun, and as I have no scribe to dictate to because they are all occupied, I have with difficulty

1. Julian's friends in the East were in danger due to his quarrel with Constantius
2. cf. Libanius, *Oration* 18, 114 3. cf. Letter 25
4. Maximus did not join Julian at Naissa, but lingered instead at Ephesus in a vain attempt to secure favourable omens for the journey; he finally joined Julian at Constantinople in early 362; cf. Eunapius, *Life of Ædesius; Life of Chrysanthius*
5. The brother of Julian's mother, Basilina. After the death of Constantius, he was persuaded by his nephew to renounce Christianity and to devote himself to the restoration of the Hellenic religion. This he did with such zeal that he became particularly odious to the Christians. He died of a painful illness during Julian's visit to Antioch in 362-363

made the effort to write this to you myself. I am alive, by the grace of the gods, and have been freed from the necessity of either suffering or inflicting irreparable ill.[1] May Helios, whom of all the gods I besought most earnestly to assist me, and sovereign Zeus also, bear me witness that never for a moment did I wish to slay Constantius, but rather I wished the contrary. Why, then, did I come? Because the gods expressly ordered me, and promised me safety if I obeyed them, whereas if I stayed, what I pray no god may do to me! Furthermore, I came because, having been declared a public enemy, I meant to frighten him merely, and that our quarrel should result in an exchange on more friendly terms; but if we should have to decide the issue by battle, I intend to entrust the whole to Fortune and to the gods, and so await whatever their clemency might decide.

10. TO EUTHERIUS[2]

(FROM NAISSA, DECEMBER, 361)

I am alive, and have been saved by the gods. Therefore, offer sacrifices to them on my behalf, as thank-offerings. Your sacrifice will be not for one man only, but for the whole body of Hellenes.[3] If you have time to travel as far as Constantinople, I shall feel myself highly honoured by your presence.

11. TO LEONTIUS

(FROM NAISSA OR CONSTANTINOPLE, 361)

The Thurian historian[4] said that men's ears are to be trusted less than their eyes.[5] In your case, however, I hold the opposite opinion from this, since here my ears are more trustworthy than my eyes. For not if I had seen you ten times would I have trusted my eyes as I now trust my ears, instructed as I have been by a man who is in no way capable of speaking falsely;[6] that, while in all respects you show

1. A proverbial phrase; the sudden death of Constantius had averted further conflict

2. An Armenian Pagan who had been kidnapped, sold into slavery, and finally attained to the office of court official and confidential adviser to Constans and then Julian; he was employed by Julian as a trusted messenger to Constantius

3. i.e., Pagans 4. Herodotus 5. Herodotus, 1.8

6. An echo of Demosthenes, *Olynthiac*, 2.17

yourself a man, you surpass yourself in your achievements "with hand and foot" as Homer says.[1] I therefore entrust you with the employment of arms, and have despatched to you a complete suit of armour, such as is adapted for the infantry. Moreover, I have enrolled you in my household corps.[2]

12. TO THE PHILOSOPHER MAXIMUS

(FROM CONSTANTINOPLE, 361-2)

There is a tradition[3] that Alexander of Macedon used to sleep with Homer's poems under his pillow, in order that by night as well as by day he might busy himself with his martial writings. I, however, sleep with your letters as though they were healing drugs of some sort, and I do not cease to read them constantly as though they were newly written and had only just come into my hands. Therefore, if you are willing to furnish me with discourse by means of letters, as a semblance of your own companionship, write, and do not cease to do so continually. Or rather, come,[4] with heaven's help, and consider that while you are away I cannot be said to be truly alive, except in so far as I am able to read what you have written.

13. TO HERMOGENES, FORMERLY PREFECT OF EGYPT[5]

(FROM CONSTANTINOPLE, 361-2)

Suffer me to say, in the language of the poetical rhetoricians, O how little hope had I of safety! O how little hope had I of hearing that you had escaped the three-headed hydra! Zeus be my witness that I do not mean my cousin Constantius – indeed, he was what he was – but the wild beasts who surrounded him and cast their baleful eyes on all men; for they made him even harsher than he was by nature, even if on his own account he was by no means of a mild disposition, although he seemed so to many. Since he is now one of the blessed

---

1. *The Odyssey*, VIII, 148; in reference to the athletic sports of the Phæacians
2. i.e. the *protectores domestici*
3. Plutarch, *Alexander*, 12
4. cf. Ammianus, 22.7.3 for Julian's effusive greeting of Maximus
5. Hermogenes had been Prefect of Egypt before 328

dead, however, may the earth lie lightly on him, as the saying goes. Nor should I wish, Zeus be my witness, that these others should be punished unjustly; but since many accusers are rising up against them, I have appointed a court[1] to judge them. Come hither, my friend, and hasten, even if it task your strength. For, by the gods, I have long desired to see you, and now that I have learned to my great joy that you are safe and sound, I bid you come.

14. TO PROHAERESIUS[2]

(FROM CONSTANTINOPLE, 361-2)

Why should I not address the excellent Prohæresius, a man who has poured forth his eloquence on the young as rivers pour their floods over the plain; who rivals Pericles in his discourses, except that he does not agitate and embroil Greece[3] Though you must not be surprised that I have imitated Spartan brevity in writing to you. For though it becomes sages like you to compose very long and impressive discourses, from me to you even a few words are enough. Moreover, you must know that from all quarters at once I am inundated by affairs. As for the causes of my return,[4] if you are going to write a historical account, I will make a very precise report for you and hand over the letters[5] to you as written evidence. If, however, you have resolved to devote your energies to the last, till old age,[6] to your rhetorical studies and exercises, you will perhaps not reproach me for my silence.

1. The special commission appointed by Julian to try many of Constantius' ministers which was held at Chalcedon in the early winter of 361-2

2. The Armenian sophist, a Christian, who taught at Athens; cf. Eunapius, *Lives of the Sophists and Philosophers*

3. Aristophanes, *Acharnians*, 531

4. From Gaul to Constantinople

5. The correspondence between Julian and Constantius

6. Prohæresius was already in his late eighties by this stage

15. TO BISHOP AETIUS[1]

(FROM CONSTANTINOPLE, 362, JANUARY)

I have remitted their sentence of exile for all in common who were banished in whatever fashion by Constantius of blessed memory, on account of the folly of the Galilæans.[2] In your case, however, I not only remit your exile, but also, since I am mindful of our old acquaintance and association, I invite you to come to me. You will use a public conveyance[3] as far as my headquarters, and one extra horse.

16. TO THE HIGH-PRIEST THEODORUS

(FROM CONSTANTINOPLE, 361-2)

When I received your letter I was, of course, delighted. How could I feel otherwise on learning that my comrade and dearest friend is safe? Once I had removed the fastening from it and perused it many times, I cannot convey to you in words my feelings and state of mind. I was filled with serenity and felicity, and welcomed the letter as though I beheld in it an image, so to speak, of your noble disposition. To try to answer it point by point would take too long and perhaps I could not avoid excessive garrulity; but at any rate I shall not hesitate to say what it was that I especially approved. In the first place, that the insolent behaviour towards you from the Governor of Greece, if indeed a man of that sort can be called a Governor and not a tyrant, did not provoke your resentment, because you considered that none of these things concerned you. Then again, that you are willing and eager to aid that city[4] in which you had spent your time is a clear proof of the philosophic mind; such that in my opinion the former course is worthy of Socrates, the latter, I should say, of Musonius. For Socrates declared[5] that heaven would not permit a righteous man to be harmed by anyone inferior to him and worthless, while Musonius

1. A prominent member of the Anomoeans, a radical faction within the Arian sect which faced opposition and persecution from other Christians, including the more moderate Arians

2. Julian always scoffed at the disputes between the various sects of Christianity

3. i.e. he was given the privilege of using an official carriage, provided by the state

4. The city cannot be identified. Theodorus may have improved its water supply, which would explain the allusion to Musonius at Gyara thereafter

5. Plato, *Apology*, 30

concerned himself with the welfare of Gyara[1] when Nero decreed his exile. These two points in your letter I approve, but I am at a loss how to take the third. For you write to urge me to warn you whenever I think that you yourself do or say anything out of tune. For my part, I could give you many proofs that I believe myself to be more in need than you are of such advice at the present time, but I will put that off until later. Yet the request is perhaps not even suitable for you to make; for you have abundant leisure, excellent natural gifts, and you love philosophy as much as any man who ever lived. These three things combined sufficed to make Amphion known as the inventor of ancient music, namely, leisure, divine inspiration, and a love of poetry.[2] For not even the lack of instruments avails to offset these gifts, but one who had these three for his portion could also easily invent instruments. Indeed, have we not received the tradition by hearsay that this very Amphion invented not only harmonies, but besides these the lyre itself, by employing either an almost godlike intelligence or some gift[3] of the gods in a sort of extraordinary co-operation with them? For most of the great ones of old seem to have attained to genuine philosophy[4] by setting their hearts on these three things above all, and to have not needed anything else. Therefore, it is you who ought to stand by me, and in your letters show your willingness to advise me on what I ought to do and what not. For we observe in the case of soldiers that it is not those of them who are at peace who need allies, but, I should say, those who are hard pressed in war; while in the case of pilots, those who are not at sea do not call to their aid those who are at sea, but those who are navigating call on those who are at leisure. Thus it has from the very first seemed right that men who are at leisure should help and stand by those who are occupied with tasks, and should suggest the right course of action, that is, whenever they represent the same interests. It is well, then, that you should bear this in mind and act towards me as you think I should act towards you, and, if you like, let us make this compact: that I am to point out to you what are my views concerning all your affairs, and you in return are to do the same for me as regards my sayings and doings. Nothing, in my opinion, could be more valuable for us than this reciprocity. May divine Providence keep you in good health for long to come, my beloved brother! May I see you soon, as I pray to do!

1. Emperors banished offenders to this barren island, one of the Cyclades. For the discovery of water there by Musonius, cf. Philostratus, *Life of Apollonius*, 7.16

2. Possibly an echo of the lost play of Euripides, *Amphion*, fr. 192

3. Apollo is said to have given the lyre to Amphion

4. An echo of Plato, *Sophisti*, 216; *Laws*, 642

17. TO ZENO[1]

(FROM CONSTANTINOPLE, 362)

There is indeed abundant evidence of other kinds that you have attained to the first rank in the art of medicine and that your morals, uprightness, and temperate life are in harmony with your professional skill. Yet now has been added the crowning proof. Though absent, you are winning to your cause the whole city of Alexandria. So keen a sting, like a bee's, have you left in her.[2] This is natural, for I think that Homer was right when he said "one physician is worth many other men".[3] While you are not simply a physician, but also a teacher of that art for those who desire to learn, so that I might almost say that what physicians are as compared with the mass of men, you are, compared with other physicians. This is the reason for putting an end to your exile, and with very great distinction for yourself. For if it was owing to George that you were removed from Alexandria, you were removed unjustly, and it would be most just that you should return from exile. Do return, therefore, in all honour, and in possession of your former dignity; and let the favour that I bestow be acknowledged by both parties in common, since it restores Zeno to the Alexandrians and Alexandria to you.

18. TO AN OFFICIAL[4]

(FROM CONSTANTINOPLE, 362)

[5]...is it not right to pay to human beings the respect that we feel for things made of wood?[6] For let us suppose that a man who has obtained the office of priest is perhaps unworthy of it. Ought we not show forbearance until we have actually decided that he is wicked, and only then by excluding him from his official functions show that it was the ill-judged bestowal of the title of "priest" that was subject to punishment by censure, chastisement, and a fine? If you do not

1. A physician and professor of medicine at Alexandria. Zeno was driven from Alexandria by Bishop George in 360 for reasons unknown, and after George's murder by a mob of local citizens in December, 361, was recalled to his previous position at the request of the Alexandrians

2. A sophistic commonplace; cf. Eupolis 3. *The Iliad*, XI, 514

4. Julian had received an appeal from a high-priest, perhaps Theodorus, for protection for a priest who had been assaulted

5. The beginning of the letter is lost 6. i.e., images of the gods

know this you are not likely to have any proper sense at all of what is fitting. What experience can you have of the rights of men in general if you do not know the difference between a priest and a layman? And what sort of self-control can you have when you maltreated one at whose approach you ought to have risen from your seat? For this is the most disgraceful thing of all, and for it in the eyes of gods and men alike you are especially to blame. Perhaps the bishops and elders of the Galilæans sit with you, though not in public because of me, yet secretly and in the house; and perhaps the priest has actually been beaten by your order, for otherwise your high-priest would not, by Zeus, have come to make this appeal. Yet since what happened in Homer[1] seems to you merely mythical, listen to the oracular words of the Lord of Didymus,[2] so you may see clearly that, even as in bygone days he nobly exhorted the Hellenes in very deed, so too in later times he admonished the intemperate with these words: "whosoever with reckless mind works wickedness against the priests of the deathless gods and plots against their honours with plans that fear not the gods, never shall he travel life's path to the end, seeing that he has wronged the blessed gods whose honour and holy service those priests have in charge". Thus, then, the god declares that those who even deprive priests of their honours are detested by the gods, not to mention those who beat and insult them! For a man who strikes a priest has committed sacrilege. Wherefore, since by the laws of our fathers I am *Pontifex Maximus*, and, moreover, have but now received the function of prophecy from the god of Didymus,[3] I forbid you for three cycles of the moon to meddle in anything that concerns a priest. If during this period you appear to be worthy, and the high-priest of the city so writes to me, I will thereupon take counsel with the gods whether you may be received by us once more. This is the penalty that I award for your rash conduct. As for curses from the gods, men in days of old used to utter them and write them, but I do not think that this was well done, for there is no evidence at all that the gods themselves devised those curses. Besides, we ought to be the ministers of prayers, not curses. Therefore, I believe and join my prayers to yours that after earnest supplication to the gods you may obtain pardon for your errors.

1. Julian is probably referring to the wrong done to the priest Chryses which was avenged by Apollo in *The Iliad*, I

2. Apollo

3. The oracle of the Didymæan Apollo was at Didyma, Miletus, where an inscription on a column in honour of Julian has been discovered; cf. *Bulletin de correspondance hellenique*, 1877

19. TO A PRIEST[1]

(FROM CONSTANTINOPLE, 362)

I should never have favoured Pegasius unhesitatingly if I had not had clear proof that even in former days, when he had the title of Bishop of the Galilæans, he was wise enough to revere and honour the gods. This I do not report to you on hearsay from men whose words are always adapted to their personal dislikes and friendships, for much current talk of this sort about him has reached me, and the gods know that I once thought I should detest him above all other depraved persons.[2] When I was summoned[3] to his headquarters by Constantius of blessed memory, I was travelling by this route, and after rising at early dawn I came from Troas to Ilios about the middle of the morning. Pegasius came to meet me, as I wished to explore the city – this was my excuse for visiting the temples – and he was my guide, showing me all the sights. So now let me tell you what he did and said, and from it one may guess that he was not lacking in right sentiments towards the gods.

Hector has a hero's shrine there and his bronze statue stands in a tiny little temple. Opposite this they have set up a figure of the great Achilles in the unroofed court. If you have seen the spot, you will certainly recognise my description of it. You can learn from the guides the story that accounts for the fact that great Achilles was set up opposite to him and takes up the whole of the roofless court. Now, I found that the altars were still alight, I might almost say still blazing, and that the statue of Hector had been anointed till it shone. Thus I looked at Pegasius and asked: "what does this mean? Do the people of Ilios offer sacrifices?" This was to test him cautiously to find out his own views. He replied: "is it not natural that they should worship a brave man who was their own citizen, just as we worship the martyrs?" Now, the analogy was far from sound, but his point of view and intentions were those of a man of culture, if you consider the times in which we then lived. Observe what followed. "Let us go" said he "to the shrine of Athena of Ilios." Thereupon with the greatest eagerness he led me there and opened the temple, and as though he were producing evidence, he showed me all the statues in perfect preservation, nor did he behave at all as those impious men usually do, I mean when they make the sign on their profane

1. Asmus asserts that this is Theodorus, though there is no definitive proof

2. i.e. Christians, whom Julian often calls *πονηροί* ("knavish"; "depraved")

3. In the winter of 354, en route from Nicomedia to the court at Mediolanum

foreheads, nor did he hiss to himself as they do. For these two things are the quintessence of their theology, to hiss at daimons and make the sign of the cross on their foreheads.[1]

These are the two things that I promised to tell you. Though a third occurs to me which I feel I must not fail to mention. This same Pegasius went with me to the temple of Achilles, as well, and showed me the tomb in good repair, but I had been informed that this had also been pulled to pieces by him. Yet he approached it with great reverence; I saw this with my own eyes. Moreover, I have heard from those who are now his enemies that he also used to offer prayers to Helios and worship him in secret. Would you not have accepted me as a witness even if I had been merely a private citizen? Of each man's attitude towards the gods, who could be more trustworthy witnesses than the gods themselves? Should I have appointed Pegasius a priest if I had any evidence of impiety towards the gods on his part? Further, if in those past days, whether because he was ambitious for power, or, as he has often asserted to me, he clad himself in those rags in order to save the temples of the gods, and only pretended to be godless so far as the name of the thing went – indeed, it is clear that he never damaged any temple anywhere except for what amounted to a few stones, and that was as a blind, that he might be able to save the rest – well then, are we taking this into account, and are we not ashamed to behave towards him as Aphobius did, and as the Galilæans all pray to see him treated? If you care at all for my wishes, you will honour not him only but any others who are converted, in order that they may all the more readily heed me when I summon them to good works, and those others may have less cause to rejoice. If, however, we drive away those who come to us of their own free will, no one will be ready to heed when we summon.

20. TO THE HIGH-PRIEST THEODORUS[2]

(FROM CONSTANTINOPLE, 362-3)

I have written you a more familiar sort of letter than to the others, because you, I believe, have more friendly feelings than others towards me. For it means much that we had the same guide,[3] and I am

1. A clear allusion to Christians

2. Some regard this as belonging to the *Letter to a Priest*, the beginning of which is otherwise lost

3. Maximus, who initiated Julian and perhaps Theodorus into the Mithraic Mysteries

sure you remember him. A long time ago, when I was still living in the west,[1] I learned that he had the highest regard for you, and for that reason I counted you my friend; and yet because of their excessive caution, I have usually thought these words well said: "I never met the man or saw him".[2] Also: "before we love we must know and before we can know we must test by experience". Yet it seems that after all a certain other saying has most weight with me, namely: "the Master has spoken".[3] That is why I thought, even then, that I ought to count you among my friends, and now I entrust to you a task that is dear to my heart, while to all men everywhere it is of the greatest benefit. If, as I have the right to expect, you administer the office well, be assured that you will delight me greatly now and give me still greater hope for the future life. For I am certainly not one of those who believe that the soul perishes before the body or along with it, nor do I place my belief in any human being, but only the gods, for it is likely that they alone have the most perfect knowledge of these matters, if indeed we ought to use the word "likely" of what is inevitably true. After all, it is fitting for men to conjecture about such matters, but the gods alone have complete knowledge.

What, then, is this office which I say I now entrust to you? It is the governance of all the temples in Asia, with power to appoint the priests in every city and to assign to each what is fitting. Now, the qualities that befit one in this high office are, in the first place, fairness, and next, goodness and benevolence towards those who deserve to be treated thus. For any priest who behaves unjustly to his fellow men and impiously towards the gods, or is overbearing to all, must either be admonished with plain speaking or chastised with great severity. As for the regulations which I must make more complete for the guidance of priests in general, you as well as the others will soon learn them from me; in the meantime, however, I wish to make a few suggestions to you. You have good reason to obey me in such matters. Indeed, in such a case I very seldom act without forethought, as all the gods know, and no one could be more circumspect; and I avoid innovations in all things, so to speak, but more particularly in what concerns the gods. For I hold that we ought to observe the laws that we have inherited from our forefathers, since it is evident that the gods gave them to us. For they would not be as perfect as they are if they had been derived from mere men. Now, since it has come to pass that they have been

---

1. Gaul 2. *The Iliad*, IV, 374; *The Odyssey*, IV, 200

3. This Pythagorean phrase is the original of *ipse dixit* ("he, himself, said it") and denotes an assertion without proof

and corrupted, and wealth and luxury have become supreme, I believe I ought to consider them carefully as though from their cradle.[1] Therefore, when I saw that there is among us great indifference about the gods and that all reverence for the heavenly powers has been driven out by impure and vulgar luxury, I always secretly lamented this state of things. For I saw that those whose minds were turned to the doctrines of the Jewish religion are so ardent in their belief that they would choose to die for it, and to endure utter want and starvation rather than taste pork, or any animal that has been strangled or had the life squeezed out of it; whereas we are in such a state of apathy about religious matters that we have forgotten the customs of our forefathers, and as a consequence we actually do not know whether any such rule has ever been prescribed. These Jews, however, are in part god-revering, seeing that they worship a god who is truly most powerful and good, who governs this world of sense, and, as I well know, is worshipped by us also under other names.[2] They act as is right and seemly, in my opinion, if they do not transgress the laws; but in one thing they err, that is, while reserving their deepest devotion for their own god, they do not conciliate the other gods also. Instead, they believe the other gods have been allotted to us Gentiles only, to such a pitch of folly have they been brought by their barbaric conceit. Yet those who belong to the impious sect of the Galilæans, as if some disease...[3]

21. TO THE PEOPLE OF ALEXANDRIA[4]

(FROM CONSTANTINOPLE, JANUARY, 362)

If you do not revere the memory of Alexander, your founder, and yet more than him the great god, the most holy Serapis, how is it that you took no thought at least for the welfare of your community, for mankind, for decency? Furthermore, I will add that you took no thought for me either, though all the gods, and, above all, the great

1. A proverb; literally "from the hearth", i.e., from their origin

2. Julian never explicitly states which Pagan god he identifies with the Hebraic God

3. The conclusion of the sentence is lost, and may have been removed by a Christian because of a remark which was deemed to be profane

4. Julian admonishes the Alexandrians for having taken the law into their own hands and murdered the Arian Bishop, George of Cappadocia, who, admittedly, was loathed by Pagans and non-Arian Christians alike. Julian's censure is thus more concerned with the unlawful nature of the act than his death, per se

the great Serapis, judged it right that I should rule over the world. The proper course was for you to reserve for me the decision concerning the offenders. Though perhaps your anger and rage led you astray, since it often "turns reason out of doors and then does terrible things".[1] For after you had restrained your original impulse, you later introduced lawlessness to mar the wise resolutions which you had at first adopted, and were not ashamed, as a community, to commit the same rash acts as those for which you rightly detested your adversaries. For tell me, in the name of Serapis, what were the crimes for which you were incensed against George? You will doubtless answer: he agitated Constantius of blessed memory against you; then he brought an army into the holy city, whereby the general[2] in command of Egypt seized the most sacred shrine of the god, stripped it of its statues and offerings, and of all the ornaments in the temples. Then, when you were justly provoked and tried to succour the god, or rather the treasures of the god,[3] Artemius dared to send his soldiers against you, unjustly, illegally, and impiously, perhaps because he was more afraid of George than of Constantius; for the former was keeping a close watch on him to prevent his behaving too moderately and constitutionally towards you, but not to prevent his acting far more like a tyrant. Accordingly, you will say it was because you were angered for these reasons against George, the enemy of the gods, that you once more desecrated the holy city, when you might have subjected him to the votes of the judges. For in that case the affair would not have resulted in murder[4] and lawlessness, but in a lawsuit in due form, which would have kept you wholly free from guilt, while punishing that godless man for his inexpiable crimes; it would have checked all others who neglect the gods, and, moreover, those who lightly esteem cities like yours and flourishing communities, since they think that cruel behaviour towards these is a perquisite of their own power.

Now compare this letter of mine with the one[5] that I wrote to you a short time ago, and mark the difference well. What words of praise for you did I write then! Alas now, by the gods, though I wish to

1. Plutarch, *On the Restraint of Anger*, 453

2. Artemius, military prefect of Egypt; he was executed by Julian at the request of the Alexandrians in the summer of 362; Ammianus, 22.11

3. Serapis. The Serapeum was widely considered to be the most splendid temple in the ancient world; according to Ammianus, 22.16, "its splendour is such that mere words can only do it an injustice". The temple was reduced to rubble in 392 by a group of Christian fanatics

4. cf. Ammianus, 22.11.8

5. This letter has not survived

praise you, I cannot, because you have broken the law. Your citizens dare to tear a human being in pieces as dogs tear a wolf, and then are not ashamed to lift to the gods those hands still dripping with blood! But, you will say, George deserved to be treated in this fashion. Granted, and I might even admit that he deserved still worse and more cruel treatment. Yes, you will say, and on your account. To this I also agree; but if you say by your hands, I no longer agree. For you have laws which ought by all means to be honoured and valued by you all, to a man. Sometimes, no doubt, it happens that some persons break one or other of these laws; nevertheless, the state as a whole ought to be well governed and you ought to obey the laws and not transgress those that from the beginning were wisely established.

It is a fortunate thing for you, men of Alexandria, that this transgression of yours occurred in my reign, since by reason of my reverence for the god and out of regard for my uncle[1] and namesake, who governed the whole of Egypt and your city also, I preserve for you the affection of a brother. For power that ought to be respected, a truly strict and unswerving government would never overlook such an outrageous action of a people, but would rather purge it by bitter medicine, like a serious disease. However, for the reasons I have just mentioned, I administer to you the mildest of remedies, namely admonition and argument, by which I am quite sure that you will be all the more convinced if you really are, as I am told, originally Greeks, and even to this day there remains in your dispositions and habits a notable and honourable impression of that illustrious descent.

Let this be publicly proclaimed to my citizens of Alexandria.

22. TO ARSACIUS, HIGH-PRIEST OF GALATIA

(EN ROUTE TO ANTIOCH, 362)

The Hellenic religion does not yet prosper as I desire, and it is the fault of those who profess it, for the worship of the gods is on a splendid and magnificent scale, surpassing every prayer and every hope. May Adrasteia pardon my words, for indeed no one, just a little while ago, would have ventured to even pray for a change of such a kind or one so complete within so short a time. Why, then, do we think that this is enough, why do we not observe that it is their[2] benevolence to strangers, their care for the graves of the dead, and

1. Julian 2. Christians

the affected holiness of their lives that have done most to increase godlessness? I believe that we ought to genuinely and truly practise every one of these virtues. Further, it is not enough for you alone to practise them, but so must all the priests in Galatia, without exception. Either shame or persuade them into righteousness, or else remove them from their priestly office if they do not, together with their wives, children, and servants, attend to the worship of the gods, allowing instead for their servants or sons or wives to show impiety towards the gods and honour godlessness more than piety. In the second place, admonish them that no priest may enter a theatre, drink in a tavern, or control any craft or trade that is base and not respectable. Honour those who obey you, but those who disobey, expel from office. In every city, establish frequent hostels in order that strangers may profit by our benevolence; I do not mean for our own people only, but for others also who are in need of money. I have just now made a plan by which you may be well provided for this, for I have given directions that 30,000 modii of corn shall be assigned every year for the whole of Galatia, and 60,000 pints[1] of wine. I have ordered that one fifth of this be used for the poor who serve the priests, and the remainder be distributed by us to strangers and beggars. For it is disgraceful that, when no Jew ever has to beg, and the impious Galilæans support not only their own poor but ours as well, all men see that our people lack aid from us. Teach those of the Hellenic faith to contribute to public service of this sort, and the Hellenic villages to offer their first fruits to the gods; accustom those who love the Hellenic religion to these good works by teaching them that this was our practice of old. At any rate, Homer makes Eumæus say: "my friend, it is wrong, even if a baser man than you should come by, to dishonour a stranger. For from Zeus come all strangers and beggars, and a gift, though small, is precious".[2] So let us not, by allowing others to outdo us in good deeds, disgrace by such remissness, or rather, utter abandonment, the reverence due to the gods. If I hear that you are carrying out these orders I shall be filled with joy.

As for government officials, do not interview them often at their homes, but write to them frequently. When they enter the city, no priest must go to meet them, but only meet them within the vestibule when they visit the temples of the gods. Let no soldier march before them into the temple, but any who will may follow them, for the moment that one of them passes over the threshold of the sacred

1. Originally *modius* (approx. 9 litres) and *sextarius* (pint) 2. *The Odyssey*, XIV, 56

precinct, he becomes a private citizen. For you, as you are aware, have authority over what is within, since this is the bidding of the divine ordinance. Those who obey it are in truth god-revering, while those who oppose it with arrogance are vainglorious and empty-headed.

I am ready to assist Pessinus[1] if her people succeed in winning the favour of the Mother of the Gods. Though, if they neglect her, they are not only not free from blame, but, not to speak harshly, let them beware of reaping my enmity also. For "it is not lawful for me to cherish or pity men who are enemies of the deathless gods".[2] Therefore persuade them, if they claim my patronage, that the whole community must become suppliants of the Mother of the Gods.

23. TO ECDICIUS, PREFECT OF EGYPT[3]

(FROM CONSTANTINOPLE, JANUARY, 362)

Some men have a passion for horses, others for birds, others, again, for wild beasts; but I, from childhood, have been impelled by a passionate longing[1] to acquire books. It would thus be absurd if I should suffer these to be appropriated by men whose inordinate desire for wealth cannot be satiated by gold alone, and who unscrupulously design to steal these also. Therefore, grant me this personal favour, that all the books which belonged to George be sought out. For there were in his house many on philosophy, and many on rhetoric; many, also, on the teachings of the impious Galilæans. These latter I should wish to be utterly annihilated, though for fear that along with them more useful works may be destroyed by mistake, let all these also be sought for with the greatest care. Let George's secretary[5] take charge of this search for you, and if he hunts for them faithfully, let him know that he will obtain his freedom as a reward, but that if he prove in any way whatsoever dishonest in the business, he will be put to the test of torture. I know, moreover, what books George had – many of them, at any rate, if not all – for he lent me some of them to copy when I was in Cappadocia,[6] and those he received back.

1. This letter was likely written after Julian's visit to Pessinus en route to Antioch
2. *The Odyssey*, X, 73; Julian alters the original which is said by Æolus to Odysseus
3. Prefect of Egypt from 362-3; possibly also known as Olympus
4. A proverb; cf. Plato, *Menexenus*, 245 5. Possibly Porphyrius; cf. Letter 38
6. When Julian was interned at Macellum as a boy by Constantius

24. AN EDICT TO THE ALEXANDRIANS

(FROM CONSTANTINOPLE, 362)

One[1] who had been banished by so many imperial decrees, issued by many Emperors, ought to have waited for at least one imperial edict, then on the strength of that returned to his own country, and not displayed rashness and folly, insulting the laws as though they did not exist. For we have not, even now, granted to the Galilæans who were exiled by Constantius[2] of blessed memory to return to their churches, but only to their own countries. Yet I learn that the most audacious Athanasius, elated by his accustomed insolence, has again seized what is called among them the episcopal throne,[3] and that this is not a little displeasing to the god-revering citizens[4] of Alexandria. Wherefore we publicly warn him to depart from the city forthwith, on the very day that he shall receive this letter of our clemency. If, however, he should remain within the city, we publicly warn him that he will receive a much greater and more severe punishment.[5]

25. TO EVAGRIUS

(FROM CONSTANTINOPLE, 362)

A small estate of four fields in Bithynia was given to me by my grandmother, and this I give as a gift for your affection for me. It is too small to bring a man any great benefit on the score of wealth or to make him appear opulent, but even so it is a gift that cannot wholly fail to please you, as you will see if I describe its features to you one by one. There is, of course, no reason why I should not write in a light vein to you who are so full of the graces and amenities of culture. It is situated not more than twenty stades from the sea, so that no trader or sailor with his chatter and insolence disturbs the place. Yet it is not wholly deprived of the favours of Nereus either, for it has a constant supply of fish, fresh and still gasping; and if you walk up what may be called a hill away from the house, you will see the sea, the Propontis, the islands, and the city that bears the name of the noble Emperor;

---

1. Athanasius, an orthodox Christian who went into exile or hiding five times during his 47 years as bishop of Alexandria. As a staunch opponent of the Arians, he shared an especially bitter antagonism with George of Cappadocia

2. Constantius was an Arian and had appointed George to the see of Alexandria

3. Athanasius had installed himself in the church on 21st February, 362

4. i.e., Pagans

5. Athanasius withdrew from Alexandria, but not from Egypt

nor will you have to stand meanwhile on seaweed and brambles, or be annoyed by the filth that is always thrown out on to beaches and sands, which is so most unpleasant and even unmentionable; but you will stand on smilax, thyme, and fragrant herbage. Very peaceful it is to lie down there and glance at some book, and then, while resting one's eyes, it is equally agreeable to gaze at the ships and the sea. When I was still hardly more than a boy, I thought that this was the most delightful summer place, for it has, moreover, excellent springs, and a charming bath, garden, and trees. When I had grown to manhood, I used to long for my old manner of life there and visited it often, for our meetings there did not lack talks about literature. Moreover, there is, as a humble monument of my husbandry, a small vineyard there that produces a fragrant, sweet wine, which does not have to wait for time to improve its flavour. You will have a vision of Dionysus and the Graces. The grapes on the vine, and when they are being crushed in the press, smell of roses, and the newly made wine in the jars is a "rill of nectar", if one may trust Homer.[1] Then why is such a vine as this not abundant and growing over many acres?

Perhaps I was not a very industrious gardener. Though since my mixing bowl of Dionysus is inclined to soberness and calls for a large proportion of the nymphs,[2] I only provided enough for myself and my friends – and they are rather few. Well then, I now give this to you as a present, dear heart, and though it be small, as indeed it is, it is nonetheless precious as coming from a friend to a friend – "from home, homeward bound", in the words of the wise poet Pindar.[3] I have written this letter in haste, by lamplight, so if I have made any mistakes, do not criticise them too severely or as one rhetorician would another.

26. TO BASIL[4]

(FROM CONSTANTINOPLE, 362)

"Not of war is your report",[5] says the proverb; but I would add, from comedy: "O you whose words bring tidings of gold!"[6] Come

1. *The Odyssey*, IX, 359 2. i.e., of water 3. Pindar, *Olympian Ode*, 6.99; 7.5

4. Basil of Cæsarea, also known as Saint Basil the Great, was a Cappadocian Christian who later became bishop of Cæsarea. He and Julian were of about the same age and had been students together at Athens in 355. Despite the religious disagreement, the two appear to have been on good terms

5. Plato, *Phædrus*, 242; *Laws*, 102 6. Aristophanes, *Plutus*, 268

then, show it by your deeds and hasten to me, for you will come as friend to friend.[1] It is true that continuous attention to public business is thought to be a heavy burden on men who pursue it with all their energy; but those who share the task of administration with me are, I am convinced, honest and reasonable men, intelligent and entirely capable for all they have to do. So they give me leisure and the opportunity of resting without neglecting anything. For our association with one another is free from that hypocrisy of courts, of which alone you have, I think, had experience, that hypocrisy which leads men to praise one another even while they hate with a hatred more deadly than they feel for their worst enemies in war. Yet we, though we refute and criticise one another with appropriate frankness, whenever it is necessary, love one another as much as the most devoted friends. Hence I am able – if I may say so without odium – to work and yet enjoy relaxation, and when at work to be free from strain and sleep securely. For when I have kept vigil, it was less on my own behalf probably than on behalf of all my subjects.

Though perhaps I have been wearying you with my chatter and nonsense, displaying stupid conceit, for I have praised myself, like Astydamas.[2] I have, however, despatched this letter to you to convince you that your presence, wise man that you are, will be serviceable to me rather than any waste of my time. Make haste then, as I said, and use the state post. Then, when you have stayed with me as long as you desire, you shall go your way wheresoever you please, with an escort furnished by me, as is proper.

27. TO THE THRACIANS[3]

(FROM CONSTANTINOPLE, 362)

To an Emperor who had an eye solely to gain, your request would have appeared hard to grant, and he would not have thought that he should injure the public prosperity by granting a particular indulgence to any. Since, however, I have not made it my aim to collect the greatest possible sums from my subjects, but rather to be the source of the greatest possible blessings to them, this fact shall for you, too, cancel your debts. Nonetheless, it will not cancel the whole

1. Plato, *Menexenus*, 247 2. A proverb derived from *Philemon*, fr. 190

3. An answer to a petition. For Julian's popularity on account of his easing of the tax burden, cf. Ammianus, 25.4.15

sum absolutely, but there shall be a division of the amount, whereby part shall be remitted to you, and part shall be used for the needs of the army, since from it you yourselves assuredly gain no slight advantages, namely peace and security. Accordingly, I remit for you, down to the third assessment,[1] the whole sum that is in arrears for the preceding period. Thereafter, however, you will contribute as usual. The amount remitted is sufficient indulgence, while for my part I must not neglect the public interest. Concerning this, I have sent orders to the prefects also, in order that your indulgence may be carried into effect. May the gods keep you prosperous for all time!

28. ON BEHALF OF THE ARGIVES[2]

(FROM CONSTANTINOPLE, 362)

On behalf of the city of Argos, if one wished to recount her honours, many are the glorious deeds both old and new that one might relate. For instance, in the achievements of the Trojan War they may claim to have played the chief part, even as the Athenians and Lacedæmonians did later in the Persian War. For though both wars are held to have been waged by all Greece in common, it is nonetheless fitting that the leaders, just as they had the larger share of toils and anxiety, should have also a larger share of the praise. These events, however, may seem somewhat antiquated. Yet those that followed, by which I mean the return of the Heracleidæ, the taking of his birthright from the eldest,[3] the sending from Argos of the colony to Macedonia, and the fact that, though they were such near neighbours to the Lacedæmonians, they always preserved their city unenslaved and free, are proofs of no slight or common fortitude. Furthermore, all those great deeds accomplished by the Macedonians against the Persians might with justice be considered

---

1. i.e., the arrears are remitted to the year 359, but what is due thereafter must be paid

2. Probably addressed to the Proconsul of Achæa, Prætextatus. Under the Roman dominion, Greek cities had recourse to lawsuits in order to settle their disputes. Seven years before Julian's accession, Corinth had successfully claimed the right to tax Argos. The money was spent on wild beast shows and similar entertainment at Corinth. The Argives appealed to Julian for a revision of the case, and this was his response. While it seems unlikely, as some scholars have maintained, that the Argives appealed to him when he was a student at Athens in 355, the lack of a definitive proclamation on Julian's part leaves the possibility open

3. Temenus the Heraclid received Argos as his share; his descendants were expelled and colonised Macedonia; Herodotus, 8.137

to belong to this city; for this was the native land of the ancestors of Philip and Alexander,[1] those illustrious men. While in later days Argos obeyed the Romans, not so much because she was conquered as having the character of an ally, and, as I think, because she, like the other states, also shared in the independence and other rights which our rulers always bestow on the cities of Greece.

Now, however, the Corinthians, since Argos has been assigned to their territory by the sovereign city[2] – for this is the less invidious way of expressing it – have grown insolent in ill-doing and are compelling the Argives to pay them tribute. It has been seven years, as I am told, since they began this innovation, and they were not abashed by the immunity of Delphi or of the Eleans,[3] which was granted to them so that they might administer their sacred games. For there are, as we know, four very important and splendid games in Greece: the Eleans celebrate the Olympian games, the Delphians the Pythian, the Corinthians those at the Isthmus, and the Argives the Nemean festival. How, then, can it be reasonable that those others should retain the immunity that was granted to them in the past, whereas the Argives, who, in consideration of a similar outlay, had their tribute remitted in the past, or perhaps were not even subject to tribute originally, should now be deprived of the privilege of which they were deemed worthy? Moreover, Elis and Delphi are accustomed to contribute only once in the course of their far-famed four-year cycles, but in that period there are two celebrations of the Nemean games among the Argives, and likewise of the Isthmian among the Corinthians. Furthermore, in these days two other games of this sort have been established among the Argives, so that altogether there are four games in four years. How, then, is it reasonable that those others who bear the burden of this function only once should be left free from the tax, whereas the Argives are obliged to contribute to yet other games in addition to their fourfold expenditure at home, especially as the contribution is for a festival that is neither Hellenic nor of ancient date? For it is not to furnish gymnastic or musical contests that the Corinthians need so much money, but to buy bears and panthers for the hunting shows which they often exhibit in their theatres. Additionally, they themselves by reason of their wealth are naturally able to support these great

1. Alexander claimed to be an Argive. For the settling of Macedonia, Herodotus, 5.22

2. Rome. Corinth, which was made a colony by Octavian, claimed authority over certain cities that were not colonies; the Roman Proconsul often resided at Corinth

3. i.e. the Corinthians ought to have allowed similar immunity to Argos

expenses especially as many other cities, as is to be expected, help by contributing for this purpose – so that they purchase the pleasure of indulging their proud designs. Whereas the Argives are not so well off for money, and compelled as they are to slave for a foreign spectacle held in the country of others, will they not be suffering unjust and illegal treatment which is, moreover, unworthy of the ancient power and renown of their city? Being, as they are, near neighbours of Corinth, ought they not to be all the more kindly treated, if indeed the saying is true, "not so much as an ox would perish[1] except through the wrongdoing of one's neighbours"? Yet it appears that when the Argives bring these charges against the Corinthians, they are not raising a dispute about a single paltry ox, but about many heavy expenses to which they are not fairly liable.

And yet one might put this question to the Corinthians also, whether they think it right to abide by the laws and customs of ancient Greece, or rather by those which it seems they recently took over from the sovereign city? For if they respect the high authority of ancient laws and customs, it is no more fitting for the Argives to pay tribute to Corinth than for the Corinthians to pay it to Argos. If, on the other hand, by relying on the laws they now have, they claim that their city has gained advantages since they received the colony from Rome, then we will exhort them in moderate language to not be more arrogant than their fathers and to not break up the customs which their fathers with sound judgement maintained for the cities of Greece, or remodel them to the injury and detriment of their neighbours; especially since they are relying on a recent decision, and, in their avarice, regard as a piece of luck the ineptitude of the man who was appointed to represent the case of the city of Argos. For if he had appealed and taken the suit outside of the jurisdiction of Greece, the Corinthians would have had less influence; their rights would have been shown to be weak when investigated by these numerous and upright advocates,[2] and, swayed by these, it is likely that the judge would have been awed into giving the proper decision, especially as the renown of Argos would have also had weight.

As for the rights of the case with respect to the city, you[3] will learn them from the beginning from the orators if only you will consent to hear them and they are permitted to present their case, and then the situation will be correctly judged from their arguments. However, in order to show that we ought to place confidence in

1. cf. Hesiod, *Works and Days*, 348 2. The embassy led by Diogenes and Lamprias
3. Julian now addresses the Proconsul directly

those who have come on this embassy, I must add a few words concerning them. Diogenes and Lamprias are indeed philosophers equal to any in our time, and they have avoided the honours and lucrative offices of the state; but they are ever zealous to serve their country to the best of their ability, and whenever the city is in any great emergency, then they plead causes, assist in the government, go on embassies, and spend generously from their own resources. Thus by their actions they refute the reproaches brought against philosophy,[1] and disprove the common opinion that those who pursue philosophy are useless to the state. For their country employs them for these tasks and they are now endeavouring to aid her to obtain justice by my assistance, as I in turn by yours. Since this is indeed the only hope of safety left for the oppressed, that they may obtain a judge who has both the will and ability to give a fair decision. For if either of these qualities be lacking, so that he is either imposed on or faithless to his trust, then there is no help for it – the right must perish. Now, however, since we have judges who are all that we could wish for, and yet are not able to plead because they did not appeal at the time, they beg that this disability may first of all be removed for them, and that the lack of energy of him who at that time was the city's advocate and had the suit in charge may not be the cause of so great a detriment to her for all time to come.

We ought not to think it irregular that the case should again be brought to trial. For, though in the affairs of private persons it is expedient to somewhat forego one's advantage and the more profitable course, and to thereby purchase security for the future, since in their little life it is pleasant, even for a short while, to enjoy peace and quiet; moreover, it is a terrible thought that one may die while one's case is on trial before the courts and it may be handed down to one's heirs unsettled, such that it seems better to secure the half by any possible means than to die while struggling to gain the whole – cities on the other hand do not die, and unless there be found someone to give a just decision that will free them from their quarrels with one another, they must inevitably maintain undying ill-will, for their hatred is deep-rooted and gains strength with time.

I have had my say, as the orators express it. You must yourselves determine what is proper to do.

1. cf. Plato, *Republic*, 489

29. TO HIS UNCLE JULIAN
(FROM CONSTANTINOPLE, APRIL, 362)

If I set small store by your letters "then the gods themselves have destroyed my wits".[1] For all the virtues are displayed in them, goodwill, loyalty, truth, and what is more than all these, since without it the rest are nought, wisdom, displayed by you in all her various forms, shrewdness, intelligence, and good judgement. You reproached me for not answering them, but I have no time, heaven knows, and pray do not suppose that this is affectation or jest. The gods of eloquence bear me witness that, except for Homer and Plato, I have with me not so much as a pamphlet[2] on philosophy, rhetoric, or grammar, or any historical work of the sort that is in general use. While even these that I have are like personal ornaments or amulets, for they are always tied fast to me. For the rest I do not even offer up many prayers, though naturally I need now more than ever to pray very often and very long. Yet I am hemmed in and choked by public business, as you will perhaps see for yourself when I arrive in Syria.[3]

As for the business mentioned in your letter, I approve of everything and admire everything you propose; nothing of that must be rejected. Be assured, then, that with the aid of the gods I shall leave nothing undone.

First of all, set up the pillars of the temple of Daphne;[4] take those that are in any building anywhere and convey them thence; then set up in their places others taken from the recently occupied houses. If there are not enough even from that source, let us use cheaper ones for the meantime, of baked brick and plaster, casing them with marble,[6] for you are well aware that piety is to be preferred to splendour, and, when put in practice, secures much pleasure for the righteous in this life. Concerning the affair of Lauricius,[6] I do not think I need write you any instructions, but I give you just this word of advice: renounce all feeling of anger, trust all to justice, submitting

1. *The Iliad*, VII, 360 2. Literally "folding tablet"

3. Julian left for Antioch, where his uncle resided, in May

4. The famed temple of Apollo at Daphne, just outside Antioch, which was burned on 22nd October during Julian's visit, had fallen into disrepair under Constantius and Constantine, with its columns having been removed by Christians. Later, en route to Persia, Julian learned that Christians had robbed the temple of Asclepius at Ægæ of its columns and used them to build a church. He ordered the columns to be restored to the temple at the expense of the Christians (Zonaras, 13.12)

5. i.e. a coat of stucco made with marble dust

6. Possibly Bassidius Lauricius, a Christian and former governor of Isauria

your ears to his words with complete confidence in the right. Yet I do not deny that what he wrote to you was exasperating and full of every kind of insolence and arrogance; though put up with it you must. For it becomes a good and great-souled man to make no counter charge when he is maligned. For, just as missiles that are hurled against hard, well-built walls do not settle on them, or penetrate them, or stay where they strike, but rebound with increased force against the hand that throws them, just so every aspersion directed against an upright man – slander, calumny, or unmerited insolence – touches him not at all, but recoils on the head of him who made the aspersion. This is my advice to you, though the sequel will be for the law to decide. With regard, however, to the letters which he asserts you made public after receiving them from me, it seems to me ridiculous to bring them into court. For I call the gods to witness, I have never written to you or any other man a word that I am not willing to publish for all to see. Have I ever in my letters employed brutality or insolence, or abuse or slander, or said anything for which I need be ashamed? On the contrary, even when I have felt resentment against someone and my subject gave me a chance to use ribald language like a woman from a cart,[1] the sort of libels that Archilochus launched against Lycambes,[2] I have always expressed myself with more dignity and reserve than one observes even on a sacred subject. Further, if my letters did give emphatic proof of the kindly feeling that you and I have towards one another, did I wish this to be unknown or concealed? For what purpose? I call all the gods and goddesses to witness that I should not have resented it, even if someone had published abroad all that I ever wrote to my wife, so temperate was it in every respect. If this or that person has read what I wrote to my own uncle, it would be fairer to blame the man who ferreted it out with such malevolence, rather than me, the writer, or you, or any other who read it. Nevertheless, concede this to me, do not let it disturb your peace of mind, only look at the matter thus: if Lauricius is truly dishonest, get rid of him in a dignified way. If, however, he is a well-meaning person of average honesty, and has treated you badly, forgive him. For when men are honest in public life we must be on good terms with them, even if they do not behave properly to us in their private capacity. On the other hand, when men are dishonest in public affairs, even if they have won our favour,

1. A proverbial reference to the scurrilous language permitted to the women who rode in wagons in the Eleusinian processions; cf. Aristophanes, *Plutus*, 1014

2. cf. Horace, *Epodes*, 6.13

we must keep them under control. I do not mean that we must hate or avoid them, but rather keep careful watch on them, so that we may not fail to detect them when they misbehave; though if they are too hard to control in this way, we must not employ them at all. As for what you, as well as others, have written, that, though notorious for bad conduct, he masquerades as a physician, I did send for him thinking that he was trustworthy. Yet before he had an interview with me, his true character was detected, or rather he was denounced to me – when I meet you I will tell you by whom – and he was treated with contempt. For this, too, I have to thank you.

Instead of the estates that you asked for, since I have already given those away, as I call to witness the gods of our family and of friendship, I will give you some that pay far better, as you shall yourself discover.

30. TO PHILIP[1]

(FROM CONSTANTINOPLE, SPRING, 362)

I call the gods to witness that, when I was still Cæsar I wrote to you, and I think it was more than once. Indeed, I started to do so many times, but there were reasons that prevented me, of one kind at one moment, the next another; then followed that wolf's friendship that arose between myself and Constantius of blessed memory in consequence of the proclamation.[2] I was exceedingly careful not to write to anyone beyond the Alps for fear of getting him into serious trouble. So consider the fact that I did not write a proof of my goodwill. For it is often impracticable to make one's language harmonise with one's real sentiments. Then, too, letters from the Emperor to private persons might well lead to their display for bragging and making false pretences when they come into the hands of persons with no sense of propriety, who carry them about like seal-rings and show them to the inexperienced. Indeed, genuine friendship is produced first and foremost by similarity of disposition, but a second kind is when one feels true and not pretend admiration, for a humane, moderate, and virtuous man may be cherished by one who is his superior in fortune and intelligence. Moreover, letters of

1. Philip was perhaps the Cappadocian to whom Libanius wrote several extant letters, e.g., *Letter 1190*. For his zeal in aiding the restoration of Paganism he suffered persecution after the Julian's death

2. i.e. of himself as Augustus by the army in Gaul, in early 360

this sort are full of conceit and nonsense, and, for my part, I often blame myself for making mine too long, and for being too loquacious when I might discipline my tongue to Pythagorean silence.

I did indeed receive the tokens, namely a silver bowl weighing one *mina* and a gold coin.[1] I should be very glad to invite you to visit me as you suggest in your letter. Though the first signs of spring are here already, the trees are in bud, and the swallows, which are expected imminently, drive our band of campaigners outdoors as soon as they come, and remind us that we ought to be over the border. We shall travel through your part of the country,[2] so that you would have a better chance of seeing me, if the gods so will it, in your own home. This will, I think, be soon, unless some sign from heaven should forbid it. For this same meeting I am praying to the gods.

31. A DECREE CONCERNING PHYSICIANS[3]

(FROM CONSTANTINOPLE, MAY, 362)

That the science of medicine is salutary for mankind is plainly testified by experience. Hence the sons of the philosophers are right in proclaiming that this science is also descended from heaven. For by its means the infirmity of our nature and the disorders that attack us are corrected. Therefore, in accordance with reason and justice, we decree what is in harmony with the acts of former Emperors, and of our benevolence ordain that for the future you may live free from the burdens attached to senators.

32. TO THE PRIESTESS THEODORA

(FROM CONSTANTINOPLE OR ANTIOCH, 362)

I have received through Mygdonius the books that you sent me, alongside all the letters of recommendation[4] that you forwarded to me throughout the festival. Every one of these gives me pleasure, but you may be sure that more pleasant than anything else is the news

1. Such tokens were often sent to friends 2. En route to Antioch

3. This edict, preserved in the *Codex Theodosianus*, 13.3.4, was Julian's last known legislative act before he left Constantinople. It was probably meant to apply only to medical faculty heads, *archiatri*, as the Latin edict is addressed to them

4. Literally "tickets"; they were letters of recommendation for the use of travellers

about your excellent self, that by the grace of the gods you are in good physical health and are devoting yourself to the service of the gods more earnestly and energetically. As regards what you wrote to the philosopher Maximus, that my friend Seleucus[1] is ill-disposed towards you, believe me that he neither does nor says in my presence anything that he could possibly intend as slanderous. On the contrary, all that he tells me about you is favourable; and while I do not go so far as to say that he actually feels friendly to you – only he himself and the all-seeing gods can know the truth of that – I can still say with perfect sincerity that he does refrain from any such calumny in my presence. Therefore, it seems absurd to scrutinise what is thus concealed rather than what he actually does, and to search for proof of actions of which I have no shred of evidence. Since you have made so many accusations against him, however, and have plainly revealed to me a definite cause for your own hostility towards him, I do say this much to you frankly: if you are showing favour to any person, man or woman, slave or free, who neither worships the gods as yet, nor inspires in you any hope that you may persuade him to do so, you are wrong. For do but consider first how you would feel about your own household. Suppose that some servant for whom you feel affection should conspire with those who slandered and spoke ill of you, and showed deference to them, but abhorred and detested us who are your friends, would you not wish for his speedy destruction, or rather, would you not punish him yourself?[2] Well then, are the gods to be less honoured than our friends? You must use the same argument with reference to them; you must consider that they are our masters and we their servants. It follows, does it not, that if one of us who call ourselves servants of the gods has a favourite servant who abominates the gods and turns from their worship, we must in justice either convert him and keep him, or dismiss him from the house and sell him, in case someone does not find it easy to dispense with owning a slave? For my part, I would not consent to be loved by those who do not love the gods; wherefore I now say plainly that you and all who aspire to priestly offices must bear this in mind, and engage with greater energy in the temple worship of the gods. It is only reasonable to expect that a priest should begin with his own household in showing reverence, and first of all prove that it is wholly and throughout pure of such grave afflictions.

1. Seleucus of Cilicia. He was an old friend of the Emperor's and accompanied him on the Persian campaign. From the letters of Libanius, it seems that Julian had appointed Seleucus to some high priestly office in 362

2. An echo of Plato, *Euthyphro*, 13

33. TO THE MOST REVEREND THEODORA[1]

(FROM CONSTANTINOPLE, 362)

I was glad to receive all the books that you sent me, as well as your letters through the excellent Mygdonius.[2] Since I have hardly any leisure – as the gods know, I speak without affectation – I have written you these few lines. Now farewell, and may you always write me letters of the same sort!

34. TO THE PRIESTESS THEODORA[3]

(362)

I have received from you who are wisdom itself your letter telling me of the fair and blessed promises and gifts of the gods to us. First I acknowledged the great gratitude that I owed to the heavenly gods, and in the second place I rendered thanks to your generosity of soul, in that you are zealous, no one more so, in entreating the gods on my behalf; moreover, you lose no time but inform me without delay of the blessings that have been revealed where you are.

35. TO THE PHILOSOPHER ARISTOXENUS[4]

(EN ROUTE TO ANTIOCH, JUNE, 362)

Must you really wait for an invitation, then, and prefer to never come uninvited? Rather, see to it that you and I do not introduce this tiresome convention of expecting the same ceremony from our friends as from mere chance acquaintances. At this point, will somebody or other raise the question of how we came to be friends when we have never seen one another? My answer is how are we the friends of those who lived a thousand, or, by Zeus, even two thousand years ago? It is because they were all virtuous and of upright and noble character. While we, likewise, desire to be such as they, even though, to speak for myself, we completely fail in that aspiration. At any rate, however, this ambition does in some degree

1. The epithet as well as the preceding letter show that she was a priestess
2. Mygdonius protected Libanius in Constantinople in 343
3. Though unaddressed in the MSS, this letter was most likely written to Theodora
4. This Hellenic Cappadocian is otherwise unknown

rank us in the same category as those persons. Though why do I talk at length about these trifles? For if it is right that you should come without an invitation, you will certainly come; if, on the other hand, you really are waiting for an invitation, herewith you have from me an urgent summons. Therefore, meet me at Tyana, in the name of Zeus the god of friendship, and show me a genuine Hellene among the Cappadocians.[1] For I observe that, as yet, some refuse to sacrifice, and that, though some few are zealous, they lack knowledge.

36. RESCRIPT ON CHRISTIAN TEACHERS[2]

(FROM ANTIOCH, JUNE, 362)

I hold that a proper education results, not in laboriously acquired symmetry of phrases and language, but in a healthy condition of mind, that is, a mind which has understanding and true opinions about things good and ill, honourable and base. Therefore, when a man thinks one thing and teaches his pupils another, he fails in my opinion to educate exactly in proportion as he fails to be an honest man. If the divergence between a man's convictions and his utterances is merely in trivial matters, that can be tolerated somewhat, though it is wrong. If, however, in matters of the greatest importance a man has certain opinions yet teaches the contrary, what is that but the conduct of hucksters, of not honest but rather thoroughly dissolute men, in that they praise most highly the things which they believe to be most worthless, thus cheating and enticing by their praise those to whom they desire to transfer their worthless wares. Now, all who profess to teach anything whatsoever ought to be men of upright character, and ought not to harbour in their souls opinions irreconcilable with what they publicly profess; above all, I believe it is necessary that those who associate with the young and teach them rhetoric should be of that upright character, for they expound the writings of the ancients, whether they be rhetoricians or grammarians, and still more if they are sophists. For these people claim to teach, in addition to other things, not only the use of words, but morals also, and they assert that political philosophy is their particular field. Let us leave aside, for the moment, the question of whether this is true or not. For while I applaud them for aspiring to

1. By Julian's time, most of Cappadocia had become Christian

2. This version is almost certainly incomplete

such high pretensions, I should applaud them still more if they did not utter falsehoods and convict themselves of thinking one thing and teaching their pupils another. Indeed, was it not the gods who revealed all their learning to Homer, Hesiod, Demosthenes, Herodotus, Thucydides, Isocrates and Lysias? Did not these men think that they were consecrated, some to Hermes,[1] others to the Muses? I think it is absurd that men who expound the works of these writers should dishonour the gods whom they used to honour. Yet, though I think this absurd, I do not say that they ought to change their opinions and then instruct the young. Rather, I give them this choice: either do not teach what they do not think admirable, or, if they wish to teach, let them first truly persuade their pupils that neither Homer nor Hesiod, nor any of these writers whom they expound and have declared to be guilty of impiety, folly, and error in regard to the gods, is such as they declare. For since they earn money and even make a livelihood from the works of those writers, they thereby confess that they are most shamefully greedy of gain, and that, for the sake of a few *drachmæ*, they would put up with anything. It is true that, until now, there were many excuses for not attending the temples, and the terror that threatened on all sides absolved men for concealing the truest beliefs about the gods.[2] Since the gods have granted us liberty, however, it seems to me absurd that men should teach what they do not believe to be sound. For if they believe that those whose interpreters they are and for whom they sit, so to speak, in the seat of the prophets, were wise men, let them be the first to emulate their piety towards the gods. If, however, they think that those writers were in error with respect to the most honoured gods, then let them betake themselves to the churches of the Galilæans to expound Matthew and Luke, since you Galilæans are obeying them when you ordain that men should refrain from temple-worship. For my part, I wish that your ears and your tongues might be "born anew", as you would say, as regards these things;[3] and may I, and all who think and act as is pleasing to me, forever have a part in them.

For religious and secular teachers, let there be a general ordinance to this effect: any youth who wishes to attend the schools is not excluded; nor indeed would it be reasonable to shut out from the best way boys who are still too ignorant to know which way to

1. Hermes was, among other roles, the god of eloquence

2. Under the Christian Emperors Constantine and Constantius it was dangerous to worship the gods openly, specifically to perform certain rites

3. i.e. the beliefs held by the poets about the gods

turn, and to overawe them into being led against their will to the beliefs of their ancestors. Though indeed it might be proper to cure these, even against their will, as one cures the insane, except that we concede indulgence to all for this sort of disease.[1] For we ought, I think, to teach, but not punish, the demented.

37. TO ATARBIUS[2]

(362)

I affirm by the gods that I do not wish the Galilæans to be either put to death or unjustly beaten, or to suffer any other injury. Nevertheless, I do assert absolutely that the pious must be preferred to them. For through the folly of the Galilæans almost everything has been overturned, whereas through the grace of the gods we are all preserved. Wherefore we ought to honour the gods and the god-revering, both men and cities.

38. TO PORPHYRIUS[3]

(FROM ANTIOCH, 362)

The library of George was very large and complete, and contained philosophers of every school and many historians, especially, among these, numerous books of all kinds by the Galilæans. Therefore, make a thorough search for the whole library without exception and take care to send it to Antioch. You may be sure that you will yourself incur the severest penalty if you do not trace it with all diligence, and do not by every kind of enquiry, by every kind of sworn testimony and, further, by torture of the slaves, compel, if you cannot persuade, those who are in any way suspected of having stolen any of the books to bring them all forth. Farewell.[4]

1. Julian often referred to Christianity as a "sickness" which had infected the people of Rome by leading them away from their ancestral religion

2. A native of Ancyra and then administrator of the district of the Euphrates

3. Perhaps this is George's secretary mentioned in *Letter* 23. Geffcken thinks this letter was a Christian forgery as it seems to ignore the earlier order to Ecdicius

4. This uncharacteristic final phrase further undermines the authenticity of the letter; cf. Cumont. Admittedly, Julian's fondness for books was such that this level of impatience cannot be discounted entirely

39. TO THE CITIZENS OF BYZACIUM[1]

(362)

I have restored to you all your senators and councillors, whether they have abandoned themselves to the superstition of the Galilæans or have devised some other method of escaping from the senate, and have excepted only those who have filled public offices in the capital.

40. TO HECEBOLIUS[2]

(FROM ANTIOCH, LATE 362 OR EARLY 363)

I have behaved towards all the Galilæans with such kindness and benevolence that none of them has suffered violence anywhere, or been dragged into a temple, or threatened into anything else of the sort against his own will. Yet the followers of the Arian church, in the insolence bred by their wealth, have attacked the followers of Valentine[3] and have committed in Edessa such rash acts as could never occur in a well-ordered city. Since, therefore, by their most admirable law they are bidden to sell all they have and give to the poor so that they may attain more easily to the kingdom of the skies, I have, in order to aid those persons in that effort, ordered that all their funds, namely that which belongs to the church of the people of Edessa, are to be taken over so that they may be given to the soldiers, and that its property[4] be confiscated to the common purse.[5] This is in order that poverty may teach them to behave properly and that they may not be deprived of that heavenly kingdom for which they still hope. Moreover, I publicly command the citizens of Edessa to abstain from all feuds and rivalries, else you will provoke even my benevolence against yourselves, and being sentenced to the sword, to exile, and to fire as payment for the penalty of disturbing the good order of the commonwealth.

---

1. Byzacium was in the district of Tunis

2. This is unlikely to be the sophist to whom Julian addressed *Letter* 63. He was probably a leading official in Edessa, the capital of Osroene in Northern Mesopotamia. Constantius had favoured the Arians there and encouraged their fanatical sectarianism by handing over to them the great basilica of St. Thomas

3. Valentine founded one of the Gnostic sects in the 1st century

4. i.e., precious metal trinkets housed in the various churches in Edessa

41. TO THE CITIZENS OF BOSTRA[1]

(FROM ANTIOCH, AUGUST 1ST, 362)

I thought that the leaders of the Galilæans would be more grateful to me than to my predecessor in the administration of the Empire. For in his reign, it happened that the majority of them were sent into exile, prosecuted, and cast into prison, and, moreover, many whole communities of those who are called "heretics"[2] were actually butchered, as at Samosata and Cyzicus, in Paphlagonia, Bithynia, and Galatia, while among many other tribes, villages were also sacked and completely devastated; whereas, during my reign, the contrary has happened. For those who had been exiled have had their exile remitted, and those whose property was confiscated have, by a law of mine, received permission to recover all their possessions. Yet they have reached such a pitch of raving madness and folly that they are exasperated because they are not allowed to behave like tyrants or to persist in the conduct which they at one time indulged in against one another, carrying on thereafter towards us who revered the gods. They therefore leave no stone unturned, and have the audacity to incite the populace to disorder and revolt, whereby they both act with impiety towards the gods and disobey my edicts, humane though these are. At least I do not allow a single one of them to be dragged against his will to worship at the altars; indeed, I proclaim in so many words that, if any man of his own free will choose to take part in our lustral rites and libations, he ought first of all to offer sacrifices of purification and supplicate the gods that avert wickedness. So far am I from ever having wished or intended that anyone of those sacrilegious men should partake in the sacrifices that we most revere, until he has purified his soul by supplications to the gods, and his body by the purifications that are customary.

It is, at any rate, evident that the populace who have been led into error by those who are called "clerics" are in revolt because this license has been taken from them. For those who have till now behaved like tyrants are not content that they are not punished for their former crimes, but, longing for the power they had before, because they are no longer allowed to sit as judges, to draw up wills,[3] appropriating the inheritances of other men and assigning

1. Bostra, or Bosra. was one of the largest fortified cities in Arabia

2. Constantius persecuted Christians who did not belong to the Arian sect

3. Julian withdrew the right of Christian clerics to draw up wills for others, as well as a number of other privileges granted under Constantius and Constantine

everything to themselves, they pull every string[1] of disorder, and, as the proverb says, lead fire through a pipe to fire,[2] daring to add even greater crimes to their former wickedness by leading on the populace to disunion. Therefore, I have decided to proclaim to all communities of citizens, by means of this edict, and to make known to all, that they must not join in the feuds of the clerics or be induced by them to take stones in their hands or disobey those in authority; instead, they may hold meetings for as long as they please and may offer on their own behalf the prayers to which they are accustomed; while, on the other hand, if the clerics try to induce them to take sides on their behalf in quarrels, they must no longer consent to do so, if they wish to escape punishment.

I have been led to make this proclamation to the city of Bostra in particular, because their bishop Titus and the clerics, in the reports that they have issued, have made accusations against their own adherents, giving the impression that, when the populace were on the point of breaking the peace, they themselves admonished them not to cause sedition. Indeed, I have subjoined to this my decree the very words which he dared to write in his report: "although the Christians are a match for the Hellenes in numbers, they are restrained by our admonition that no one disturb the peace in any place". For these are the very words of the bishop about you. See how he says that your good behaviour was not of your own choice, since, as he at any rate alleged, you were restrained against your will by his admonitions! Thus, of your own free will, seize your accuser and expel him from the city,[3] but you, the populace, must live in agreement with one another, and let no man be quarrelsome or act unjustly. Neither let those of you who have strayed from the truth outrage those who worship the gods duly and justly, according to the beliefs that have been handed down to us from time immemorial; nor let those of you who worship the gods outrage or plunder the houses of those who have strayed rather from ignorance than of set purpose. It is by reason that we ought to persuade and instruct men, not by blows, or insults, or bodily violence. Wherefore, again and often, I admonish those who are zealous for the true religion not to injure the communities of the Galilæans or attack or insult them. Indeed, we ought to pity rather than hate men who in matters of the greatest importance are in such terrible plight. For in truth, the greatest of all blessings is reverence for the gods, as, on the other hand, irreverence

1. Literally "cable"; a proverb 2. i.e., "add fuel to fire"

3. Titus was still bishop of Bostra under Jovian in 363, cf. Socrates, *EH*, 3.25

is the greatest of all evils. It follows that those who have turned aside from the gods to corpses and relics[1] pay this as their penalty.[2] Wherefore, we suffer in sympathy with those who are afflicted by disease,[3] but rejoice with those who are being released and set free by the aid of the gods. *Given at Antioch on the First of August.*

42. TO CALLIXEINE

(FROM ANTIOCH, 362)

"Time alone proves the just man",[4] as we learn from men of old; though I would add the god-revering and pious man, also. However, you may say, the love of Penelope for her husband was also witnessed to by time. Now, who would rank a woman's piety second to her love for her husband without appearing to have drunk a very deep draught of mandragora?[5] And if one takes into account the conditions of the times and compares Penelope, who is almost universally praised for loving her husband, with pious women who not long ago hazarded their lives; and if one considers also that the period was twice as long, which was an aggravation of their sufferings; then, I ask, is it possible to make any fair comparison between yourself and Penelope? No, do not belittle my praises. All the gods will requite you for your hardships, while for my part I shall honour you with a double priesthood. For besides that which you held before of priestess to the most venerable goddess Demeter, I entrust to you the office of priestess to the most mighty Mother of the gods at Pessinus in Phrygia, beloved of the gods.

43. TO EUSTATHIUS THE PHILOSOPHER[6]

(FROM ANTIOCH, 362)

Perhaps the proverb "an honest man"[7] is too well-worn. I am sure you know the rest. More than this, you possess it, for, rhetorician

1. Julian's description of the Christian worship of martyrs and of Christ himself
2. i.e., in an ill state 3. Christianity, or more specifically, rejection of Hellenism
4. Sophocles, *Oedipus Rex*, 614
5. A proverb for sluggish wits; mandragora was also used as a stimulus for love
6. A Pagan, a distinguished orator, and a friend of Libanius
7. Euripides, fr. 902; "an honest man, though he dwell far away and I never see him with my eyes, him I count a friend"

and philosopher as you are, you know the words that come next, and you possess me for a friend, at least if we are both honest men. On your behalf, I would strenuously maintain that you are in that category, but about myself I say nothing. I only pray that others may find by experience that I am also honest! You ask why I go round in a circle as though I were going to say something extraordinary when I ought to speak out? Come, then, lose no time; fly here, as we say. A kindly god will speed you on your way with the aid of the Maiden of the Cross Roads, and the state post[1] will be at your disposal if you wish to use a carriage, plus two extra horses.

44. TO EUSTATHIUS

(FROM ANTIOCH, 362)

"Entreat kindly the guest in your house, but speed him when he would be gone".[2] Thus did wise Homer decree. Yet the friendship that exists between us two is stronger than that between guest and host, because it is inspired by the best education attainable and by our pious devotion to the gods. Therefore, no one could have fairly indicted me for transgressing the law of Homer if I had insisted that you should remain still longer with us. I see, however, that your weakened frame needs more care, and so I have given you permission to return to your own country,[3] and have provided for your comfort on the journey. That is to say, you are allowed to use a state carriage. May Asclepius and all the gods escort you on your way and grant that we may see you again.

45. TO ECDICIUS, PREFECT OF EGYPT

(FROM ANTIOCH, OCTOBER, 362)

As the proverb says: "you told me my own dream".[4] Thus I suspect that I am relating to you your own waking vision. The Nile, they tell me, has risen in full flood, cubits high, and has inundated the whole

1. The *cursus publicus* was the system of posting stations where horses were kept ready for the use of a select few. Eustathius evidently accepted the invitation

2. *The Odyssey*, XV, 74; this had become a proverb

3. Cappadocia. Eustathius was in poor health and died soon after

4. i.e., the imparting of news that is already well-known

of Egypt. If you want to hear the figures, it had risen fifteen cubits[1] on 20th September. Theophilus, the prefect, informs me of this. So, if you did not know it, hear it from me, and let it rejoice your heart.

46. TO ECDICIUS, PREFECT OF EGYPT

(FROM ANTIOCH, LATE 362)

Even though you do not write to me[2] on other matters, you ought at least to have written as regards that enemy of the gods, Athanasius,[3] especially since, for a long time now, you have known my just decrees. I swear by mighty Serapis that, if Athanasius, the enemy of the gods, does not depart from that city, or rather from all Egypt, before the December Kalends, I shall fine the cohort which you command a hundred pounds[4] of gold. You know well that, though I am slow to condemn, I am even slower to remit when I have once condemned.

Added with his own hand. It vexes me greatly that my orders are neglected. By all the gods there is nothing I should be so glad to see, or rather hear reported as achieved by you, as that Athanasius has been expelled beyond the frontiers of Egypt. Infamous man! He has had the audacity to baptise Greek women of noble standing during my reign! Let him be driven forth!

47. TO THE ALEXANDRIANS

(FROM ANTIOCH, LATE 362)

If your founder had been one of the Galilæans, men who have transgressed their own law[5] and have paid the penalties they deserved, since they elected to live in defiance of the law, having introduced a new doctrine and newfangled teaching, even then it

---

1. Pliny, *Natural History*, 5.9, says that a rise of 15 cubits gave Egypt security, while 16 was luxury; Ammianus, 22.15, says that cultivators feared a rise of more than 16 cubits. The Egyptian cubit was about 22 inches

2. Egypt was the property of Roman Emperors and reports were made by the prefect to them

3. Athanasius had disregarded the order to leave Alexandria, but on 24th October, he went into exile in Upper Egypt; Sozomen, 5.15

4. The Greek word used is the equivalent of the Latin *libra* (340 grams)

5. i.e., the Hebraic Law

would have been unreasonable for you to demand back Athanasius.[1] As it is, however, though Alexander founded your city and the lord Serapis is the city's patron god, together with his consort the Maiden, the Queen of all Egypt, Isis...[2] emulating not the healthy part of the city but the part that is diseased, has the audacity to arrogate to itself the name of the whole.

By the gods, I am overwhelmed with shame, O men of Alexandria, to think that even a single Alexandrian can admit that he is a Galilæan. The forefathers of the genuine Hebrews were the slaves of the Egyptians long ago, but in these days, men of Alexandria, you who conquered the Egyptians – for your founder was the conqueror of Egypt – you submit yourselves, despite your sacred traditions, in willing slavery to men who have set at nothing the teachings of their ancestors. You have, then, no recollection of those happy days of old when all Egypt held communion with the gods and we enjoyed many benefits therefrom. As for those who have but yesterday introduced among you this new doctrine, tell me of what benefit have they been to the city? Your founder was a god-revering man, Alexander of Macedon, who, by Zeus, was not like any of these persons, nor again did he resemble any Hebrews, though even the latter have shown themselves superior to the Galilæans. Indeed, Ptolemy,[3] son of Lagus, proved stronger than the Jews, while Alexander, if he had had to match himself with the Romans, would have made even them fight hard for supremacy. What, then, about the Ptolemies who succeeded your founder and nurtured your city from her earliest years as though she were their own daughter? It was certainly not by the preachings of Jesus that they increased her renown, nor by the teaching of the Galilæans, detested of the gods, did they perfect this administration which she enjoys and to which she owes her present good fortune. Thirdly, when we Romans became her masters and took her out of the hands of the Ptolemies, who were misgoverning her, Augustus visited your city and made the following speech to your citizens: "men of Alexandria, I absolve the city of all blame, because of my reverence for the mighty god Serapis, and further, for the sake of the people themselves and the great renown of the city. Though there is a third reason for my goodwill towards you, and that is my comrade Areius."[4] This Areius, by profession a philosopher, was a fellow citizen of yours and a familiar friend of Cæsar Augustus.

---

1. Athanasius had left Alexandria on 24th October, 362, shortly after which the Alexandrians petitioned Julian for his return. This is his answer to them.

2. A short lacuna 3. Ptolemy I took Jerusalem and led many Jews captive into Egypt

4. For the Alexandrian Stoic, Areius, cf. Philostratus, *Lives of the Sophists*

These, then, to sum them up briefly, are the blessings bestowed by the Olympian gods on your city in particular, though I pass over very many as they would take too long to describe. Yet the blessings that are vouchsafed by the visible gods to all in common, every day, not merely to a few persons or a single race, or to one city, but to the whole world at the same time, how can you fail to know what they are? Are you alone insensible to the beams that descend from Helios? Are you alone ignorant that summer and winter are from him? Or that all kinds of animal and plant life proceed from him? And do you not perceive what great blessings the city derives from her who is generated from and by him, even Selene who shaped the whole universe? Yet you have the audacity to not adore any one of these gods; and you think that one whom neither you nor your fathers have ever seen, even Jesus, ought to rank as 'God the Word'. While the god who from time immemorial the whole race of mankind has beheld and looked up to and worshipped, and from that worship prospered, by which I of course mean mighty Helios, his intelligible father's living image,[1] endowed with soul and intellect, cause of all good...[2] if you heed my admonition, lead yourselves even a little towards the truth. For you will not stray from the right road if you heed one who till his twentieth year walked that road of yours,[3] but for twelve years now has walked this road I speak of, by the grace of the gods.

Therefore, then, if it should please you to obey me, you will rejoice me all the more. If, however, you choose to persevere in the superstition and instruction of wicked men, at least agree among yourselves and do not crave for Athanasius. In any case, there are many of his pupils who can comfort well enough those itching ears of yours that yearn to hear impious words. I only wish that, along with Athanasius, the wickedness of his impious school had been suppressed. Yet as it is, you have a fine crowd of them and need have no trouble. For any man whom you elect from the crowd will be in no way inferior to him for whom you crave, at least for the teaching of the scriptures. Though if you have made these requests because you are so fond of the general subtlety of Athanasius – for I am informed that the man is a clever wretch – then you must know that for this very reason he has been banished from the city. For a meddlesome man is unfit by nature to be a leader of people. For if the leader is not even a man but only a contemptible puppet, like this great personage who thinks he

1. Julian is referring not to the visible sun, but to the "intellectual" (νοερὸς) Helios

2. Some words are lost, perhaps omitted by a Christian copyist as blasphemous

3. i.e., had been a Christian

is risking his head, this surely gives the signal for disorder. Wherefore, that nothing of the sort may occur in your case, as I long ago gave orders that he depart from the city, I now say, let him depart from the whole of Egypt.

Let this be publicly proclaimed to my citizens of Alexandria.

48. TO THE ALEXANDRIANS

(FROM ANTIOCH, EARLY 363)

I am informed that there is a granite obelisk[1] in your neighbourhood which, when it stood erect, reached a considerable height, but has been thrown down and now lies on the beach as though it were something entirely worthless. For this obelisk Constantius of blessed memory had a freight-boat built, because he intended to convey it to my native place, Constantinople. Though as, by the will of heaven, he has departed from this life to the next on that journey to which we are fated,[2] the city claims the monument from me because it is the place of my birth and more closely connected with me than with the late Emperor. For though he loved the place as a sister, I love it as a mother. I was, in fact, born there and brought up in the place, and I cannot ignore its claims. Well then, since I love you also, no less than my native city, I grant you permission to set up the bronze statue in your city.[3] A statue has lately been made of colossal size. If you set this up, you will have, instead of a stone monument, a bronze statue of a man whom you say you love and long for, and a human form instead of a quadrangular block of granite engraved with Egyptian characters. Moreover, the news has reached me that there are certain persons who worship there and sleep[4] at its very apex, and this convinces me beyond doubt that on account of these superstitious practices I ought to take it away. For men who see those persons sleeping there with so much filthy rubbish and careless and licentious behaviour in that place, not only do not believe that it[5] is sacred, but by the

1. This granite monolith, which stands in the hippodrome in Constantinople, was originally erected by Thothmes III (circa 1515 B.C.), probably at Heliopolis. The Alexandrians obeyed Julian's orders, but the boat carrying the obelisk was driven by a storm to Athens, where it remained until the reign of Theodosius (379-395)

2. Plato, *Phædo*, 117 3. Imperial permission was required for a city to erect a statue

4. Most likely Christian or Jewish ascetics, of which there were a considerable number in Alexandria, had settled near the obelisk; cf. Sozomen, 6.29; 1.12.

5. i.e. the obelisk, which was originally dedicated to the Sun

influence the superstition of those who dwell there, come to have less faith in the gods. For this very reason, therefore, it is all the more proper for you to assist in this business and to send it to my native city, which always receives you hospitably when you sail into the Pontus, and to contribute to its external adornment, even as you contribute to its sustenance. It cannot fail to give you pleasure to have something that has belonged to you standing in their city, and as you sail towards that city you will delight in gazing at it.

49. TO ECDICIUS, PREFECT OF EGYPT

(FROM ANTIOCH, LATE 362 OR EARLY 363)

If there is anything that deserves our fostering care, it is the sacred art of music.[1] Therefore, select from the citizens of Alexandria boys of good birth, and give orders that two artabæ[2] of corn are to be furnished every month to each of them, with olive oil also, and wine. The overseers of the Treasury will provide them with clothing. For the present, let these boys be chosen for their voices, but if any of them should prove capable of attaining to the higher study of the science of music, let them be informed that very considerable rewards for their work have been set aside at my court, also. For they must believe those who have expressed the right opinions on these matters that they themselves rather than we will be purified in soul by divinely inspired music, and benefit thereby. So much, then, for the boys. As for those who are now the pupils of Dioscorus the musician, urge them to apply themselves to the art with still more zeal, for I am ready to assist them in whatever they may wish.

50. TO NILUS, SURNAMED DIONYSIUS[3]

(FROM ANTIOCH, WINTER 362-363)

Your earlier silence was more creditable than your present defence; for then you did not utter abuse, though perhaps it was in your mind. Now, however, as though you were in travail, you have

1. For the study of music at Alexandria, cf. Ammianus, 22.16.17

2. The artaba, an Egyptian dry measure, was equivalent to about 0.16 cubic feet

3. Otherwise unknown. Perhaps to be identified with the Roman senator of whom Libanius says in *Oration* 18, 198, that Julian punished his impudence by a letter, when he might well have confiscated his property

poured out your abuse of me wholesale. For must I not regard it as abuse and slander that you supposed me to be like your own friends, to each of whom you offered yourself uninvited; or rather, by the first[1] you were not invited, and you obeyed the second[2] on his merely indicating that he wished to enlist you to help him. Nonetheless, whether I am like Constans and Magnentius, the event itself, as they say, will prove. As for you, however, from what you wrote it is very plain that, in the words of the comic poet, "you are praising yourself, lady, like Astydamas".[3]

For when you write about your "fearlessness" and "great courage" and say "would that you knew my real value and my true character" and, in short, all that sort of thing – for shame! What an empty noise and display of words this is. Pray tell, by the Graces and Aphrodite, if you are so brave and noble, why were you "so careful to avoid incurring displeasure" if need be "for the third time"?[4] For when men fall under the displeasure of princes, the lightest consequence – and, as one might say, the most agreeable to a man of sense – is that they are at once relieved from the cares of business; and if they have to pay a small fine as well, their stumbling block is merely money; while the culmination of the prince's wrath, and the "fate beyond all remedy" as the saying goes, is to lose their lives. Disregarding all these dangers, because, as you say, "you had come to know me in my private capacity for the man I am"[5] (and in my common and general capacity for the human being I am, though unknown to myself, late learner that I am) why, in heaven's name, did you say that you were careful to avoid incurring displeasure for the third time? For surely my anger will not change you from a good man into a bad. I should be enviable indeed, and with justice, if I had the power to do that; for then, as Plato says,[6] I could do the converse as well. Yet since virtue owns no master,[7] you ought not to have taken into account anything of the sort. Regardless, you think it is a fine thing to speak ill of all men, to abuse all without exception, and to convert the shrine of peace[8] into a workshop of war. Or do you think in this way to excuse yourself in the sight of all for your past sins, and that your courage now is a screen to hide your cowardice of old? You have heard the fable of Babrius: "once upon a time a weasel fell in love with a handsome youth".[9] The rest of the fable you may learn from

1. Constans 2. Magnentius 3. Philemon, fr. 190; this had become a proverb
4. i.e., after Constans and Magnentius 5. A quotation from Nilus' letter
6. Plato, *Crito*, 44 7. Plato, *Rep.*, 617 8. The Senate; cf. Xenophon, *Hell.*, 3.4.17
9. *Æsopica*, 32; the weasel, or cat, transformed into a woman, could not resist chasing a mouse

the book. However much you may say, you will never convince any man that you were not what you were, and such as many knew you to be in the past. As for your ignorance and audacity now, it was not, by heaven, philosophy that implanted them in you. On the contrary, it was what Plato calls a twofold lack of knowledge.[1] For though you really know nothing, just as I know nothing, you think forsooth that you are the wisest of all men, not only of those who are alive now, but also of those who have ever been, and perhaps of those who ever will be. To such a pitch of ignorance has your self-conceit grown.

As far as you are concerned, however, this that I have said is more than enough; though perhaps I ought to apologise on your account to the others since I too hastily summoned you to take part in public affairs. I am not the first or the only one, Dionysius, who has had this experience. Your namesake[2] deceived even great Plato; and Callippus the Athenian[3] also deceived Dio. For Plato says[4] that Dio knew he was a bad man but that he would never have expected in him such a degree of baseness. Why need I quote the experience of these men, when even Hippocrates,[5] the most distinguished of the sons of Asclepius, said: "the sutures of the head baffled my judgement". Now, if those famous men were deceived about persons whom they knew, and the physician was mistaken in a professional diagnosis, is it surprising that Julian was deceived when he heard that Nilus Dionysius had suddenly become brave? You have heard tell of the famous Phædo of Elis,[6] and you know his story. However, if you do not know it, study it more carefully; but at any rate, I will tell you this part. He thought that there is nothing that cannot be cured by philosophy, and that by her all men can be purified from all their modes of life, their habits, desires, in short from everything of the sort. If, indeed, she only availed those who are well born and well bred, there would be nothing marvellous about philosophy; but if she can lead up to the light men so greatly depraved, then I consider her marvellous beyond anything. For these reasons, my estimate of you, as all the gods know, inclined little by little to be more favourable; but even so, I did not count your sort in the first or the second class of the most virtuous. Perhaps you yourself know this; though if you

1. cf. Proclus, *Cratylus*, 65; Plato, *Apology*, 21; *Sophist*, 229
2. The tyrant of Syracuse
3. Callippus, who assassinated Dio in 353 B.C., was himself put to death by the Syracusans after he had usurped the government
4. Plato, *Epistle 7*, 351
5. Hippocrates, 5.3.561. This candid statement of Hippocrates, who had failed to find a wound in a patient's head, was often cited as proof of a great mind
6. He was a disciple of Socrates and wrote several dialogues; cf., Laërtius, 2.105

do not know it, enquire of the worthy Symmachus.[1] For I am convinced that he would never willingly tell a lie, since he is naturally disposed to be truthful in all things. If you are aggrieved that I did not honour you before all others, I for my part reproach myself for having ranked you even among the last in merit, and I thank all the gods and goddesses who hindered us from becoming associated in public affairs and from being familiar.[2] Indeed, though the poets have often said of Rumour that she is a goddess,[3] and let us grant, if you will, that she at least has daimonic power, not very much attention ought to be paid to her, because a daimon is not altogether pure or perfectly good, like the race of the gods, but has some share of the opposite quality. Further, even though it be not permissible to say this concerning the other daimons, I know that when I say of Rumour that she reports many things falsely as well as many truthfully, I shall never myself be convicted of bearing false witness.

As for your "freedom of speech", do you think that it is worth four *obols*, as the saying goes? Do you not know that Thersites also spoke his mind freely among the Greeks, whereupon the most wise Odysseus beat him with his staff,[4] while Agamemnon paid less heed to the drunken brawling of Thersites than a tortoise does to flies, as the proverb goes? For that matter it is no great achievement to criticise others, but rather to place oneself beyond the reach of criticism. Now, if you can claim to be in this category, prove it to me. Did you not, when you were young, furnish to your elders fine themes for talk about you? Like Electra in Euripides,[5] however, I keep silence about happenings of this sort. Yet when you came to the man's estate and betook yourself to the camp,[6] how, in the name of Zeus, did you behave? You say that you left it because you gave offence in the cause of truth. From what evidence can you prove this, as though many men and of the basest sort had not been exiled by the very persons by whom you yourself were driven away? O most wise Dionysius, it does not happen to a virtuous and temperate man to go away obnoxious to those in power! You would have done better if you had proved to us that men from their interactions with you were better behaved. Yet this was not in your power, no, by the gods, nor is it in the power of tens of thousands who emulate your way of life. For when rocks grind against rocks and stones against

1. Probably Aurelius Symmachus, the Roman senator and prefect of the city in 364-5

2. While there is no lacuna in the MSS, a section may be missing in which Julian, presumably, clarified that their association only existed as a rumour

3. Hesiod, *Work and Days*, 763 4. *The Iliad*, II, 265 5. *Orestes*, 16

6. i.e., to Constans

stones they do not benefit one another, and the stronger easily wears down the weaker.

I am not saying this in Laconic fashion[1] and concisely, am I? Indeed, I think that on your account I have shown myself even more talkative than Attic grasshoppers. Nevertheless, in return for your drunken abuse of myself, I will inflict on you the appropriate punishment, by the grace of the gods and our lady Adrasteia. What, then, is this punishment, and what has the greatest power to hurt your tongue and your mind? It is this: I will try, by erring as little as may be in word and deed, to not provide your slanderous tongue with so much foolish talk. And yet I am well aware that it is said that even the sandal of Aphrodite was satirised by Momus. Still, you will observe that, though Momus poured forth floods[2] of criticism, he could barely find anything to criticise in her sandal.[3] Even so, may you grow old fretting yourself over things of this sort, more decrepit than Tithonus, richer than Cinyras, more luxurious than Sardanapalus, so that in you may be fulfilled the proverb: "old men are twice children".

Why, however, does the divine Alexander seem to you so pre-eminent? Is it because you took to imitating him and aspired to that for which the youth Hermolaus[4] reproached him? Or rather, no one is so foolish as to suspect you of that. Yet the very opposite, that which Hermolaus lamented that he had endured, and which was the reason for his plotting, as they say, to kill Alexander – everyone believes this about you also, do they not? I call the gods to witness that I have heard many persons assert that they were very fond of you and who made many excuses for this offence of yours, but I have found just one person who did not believe it. Though he is that one swallow who does not make a spring. Perhaps the reason why Alexander seemed in your eyes a great man was that he cruelly murdered Callisthenes,[5] that Cleitus[6] fell victim to his drunken fury, and Philotas too, and Parmenio[7] and Parmenio's son; while the

1. The implication appears to be that Nilus had requested a brief answer

2. Or "burst with the effort"; cf. *rumpi invidia*

3. Philostratus, *Epistle* 37; Momus complained that Aphrodite's sandal squeaked

4. The page of Alexander, who was executed for plotting to assassinate the king. Some depict Hermolaus as uttering a diatribe against Alexander before his death

5. The historian who accompanied Alexander to the East

6. Cleitus was killed by Alexander at a banquet for quoting these verses from *Andromache*, 695, which continued: "it is not those who did the work that gain the credit, but rather the general wins all the glory"

7. Parmenio and his son Philotas were executed for treason; Arrian, *Anabasis*, 3.26

affairs of Hector,[1] who was smothered in the whirlpools of the Nile in Egypt or the Euphrates – the story is told of both rivers – I shall say nothing about, or of his other follies, lest I should seem to speak ill of a man who by no means maintained the ideal of rectitude, but nevertheless excelled as a general in the deeds of war. Whereas you are less endowed with both, namely good principles and courage, than a fish with hair. Now listen to my advice and do not resent it too much.

οὔ τοι τέκνον ἐμὸν δέδοται πολεμήϊα ἔργα·

"Not to you, my child have the deeds of war been given".[2]

The verse that follows I do not write out for you because, by the gods, to do so would be shameful. Nonetheless, I ask you to understand it as said. For it is only fair that words should follow on deeds, and that he who has never avoided deeds should not avoid the phrases that describe them.

Tell me, if you revere the pious memory of Magnentius and Constans, why do you wage war against the living and abuse those who excel in any way? Is it because the dead are better able than the living to avenge themselves on those who vex them? Regardless, it does not become you to say this. For you are, as your letter says: "very brave indeed". Yet if this is not the reason, perhaps there is a different one. Perhaps you do not wish to satirise them because they cannot feel it. Yet among the living, is there anyone so foolish or so cowardly as to demand that you should take any notice of him at all, and who will not prefer if possible to be altogether ignored by you; but if that should be impossible, to be abused by you, as indeed I am now abused rather than honoured? May I never be so ill-advised; may I never aspire to win praise rather than blame from you.

Perhaps you will say that the very fact that I am writing to you is proof that I am stung? No, I call the Redeeming Gods to witness that I am but trying to check your excessive audacity and boldness, the license of your tongue and the ferocity of your soul, the madness of your wits and your perverse fury on all occasions. In any case, it was in my power, if I had been stung, to chastise you with deeds and not merely with words,[3] and I would have been entirely within the law. For you are a citizen and of senatorial rank and you disobeyed a

1. According to Quintus Curtius, 5.8.7, Hector, a son of Parmenio, was accidentally drowned, though Julian ascribes his death to Alexander

2. *The Iliad*, V, 428, Zeus to Aphrodite

3. For Julian's leniency in such cases, cf. Ammianu, 25.4.9

command of your Emperor; while such behaviour was certainly not permissible to anyone who could not furnish the excuse of true necessity. Therefore, I was not satisfied with inflicting on you any sort of penalty for this conduct, but I thought I should write to you first, thinking that you might be cured by a short letter. Yet since I have discovered that you persist in the same errors, or rather, how great your frenzy is which I previously did not know...[1] lest you should be thought to be a man, when that you are not, or brimful of freedom of speech, when you are only full of insanity, or that you have had the advantage of education when you have not the smallest acquaintance with literature, as far, at any rate, as one may reasonably judge from your letters. For instance, no one of the ancients ever used φροῦδος[2] to mean "manifest" as you do here. As for the other blunders displayed in your letter, no one could describe them in even a long book, or that obscene and abominable character of yours that leads you to prostitute yourself. You tell me, indeed, that it is not those who arrive offhand or those who are hunting for public office whom we ought to choose, but those who use sound judgement and in accordance with this prefer to do their duty rather than those who are ready and eager to obey. Fair, truly, are the hopes you hold out for me, though I made no appeal to you, implying that you will yield if I again summon you to take part in public business. Yet I am so far from doing that, that, when the others were admitted, I never even addressed you at any time. Whereas I did address many who were known and unknown to me and dwell in Rome, beloved of the gods. Such was my desire for your friendship, so worthy of consideration did I think you! It is likely therefore that my future conduct towards you will be much the same. Indeed, I have written this letter now, not for your perusal alone, since I knew it was needed by many besides yourself, and I will give it to all, since all, I am convinced, will be glad to receive it. For when men see you more haughty and more insolent than befits your past life, they resent it.

You have here a complete answer from me, such that you can desire nothing more. Nor do I ask for any further communication from you. Once you have read my letters, then, use them for whatever purpose you please, for our friendship is at an end. Farewell, and divide your time between luxurious living and abuse of me.

---

1. Lacuna. Some reference to the letters written by Nilus is needed here

2. In Attic the word means "vanished" or "departed"

51. TO THE COMMUNITY OF THE JEWS[1]
(FROM ANTIOCH, LATE 362 OR EARLY 363)

In times past, by far the most burdensome thing in the yoke of your slavery has been the fact that you were subjected to unauthorised ordinances and had to contribute an untold amount of money to the accounts of the treasury. Of this I used to see many instances with my own eyes, and have learned of more, by finding the records which are preserved against you. Moreover, when a tax was about to be levied on you again I prevented it, and compelled the impiety of such obloquy to cease here; and I threw into the fire the records against you that were stored in my desks, so that it is no longer possible for anyone to aim at you such a reproach of impiety. My brother Constantius of honoured memory was not so much responsible for these wrongs of yours as were the men who used to frequent his table – Barbarians in mind, godless in soul. These I seized with my own hands and put them to death by thrusting them into the pit, such that not even any memory of their wickedness might linger amongst us. Further, since I wish that you should prosper yet more, I have admonished my brother Iulus, your most venerable patriarch, that the levy[2] which is said to exist among you should be prohibited, and that no one is any longer to have the power to oppress the masses of your people by such exactions; so that everywhere, during my reign, you may have security of mind, and in the enjoyment of peace may offer more fervid prayers for my reign to the most high God, the Maker, who has deigned to crown me with his own immaculate right hand. For it is natural that men who are distracted by any anxiety should be hampered in spirit, and should not have so much confidence in raising their hands to pray; but that those who are in all respects free from care should rejoice with their whole hearts and offer their suppliant prayers on behalf of my imperial office to mighty God, even to him who is able to direct my reign to the noblest ends, according to my purpose. This you ought to do, in order that, when I have successfully concluded the war with Persia, I may rebuild by my own efforts the sacred city of

1. Van Nuffelen believes this letter to be a fabrication. If it is authentic, Julian will have likely sought to exploit the mutual antagonism between Christians and Jews to undermine the former, his primary political and religious adversaries. To this end, he relieved the Jews of a targeted levy and promised to rebuild the temple at Jerusalem, a transparent move to discredit the prophecy of Christ that not one stone of the temple should remain on another. Despite his apparent overtures to the Jewish community, Julian's views on their religion were generally critical

2. Paid by Jews to maintain the Patriarchate, and later suppressed by Theodosius II

Jerusalem which for so many years you have longed to see inhabited, and may bring settlers there, and, together with you, may glorify the most high God therein.

52. TO LIBANIUS

(FROM ANTIOCH, WINTER 362)

Since you have forgotten your promise – at any rate, three days have gone by and the philosopher Priscus has not come himself but has sent a letter to say that he still delays – I remind you of your debt by demanding payment. The thing you owe is, as you know, easy for you to pay and very pleasant for me to receive. Therefore, send your discourse and your "divine counsel" and do so promptly, in the name of Hermes and the Muses, for I assure you, in these three days you have worn me out, if indeed the Sicilian poet[1] speaks the truth when he says: "those who long grow old in a day". If this be true, as in fact it is,[2] you have trebled my age, my good friend. I have dictated this to you in the midst of public business, for I was not able to write myself as my hand is lazier than my tongue.[3] Though, in truth, my tongue has also come to be somewhat lazy and inarticulate from lack of exercise. Farewell, brother, most dear and most cherished!

53. TO LIBANIUS

(FROM ANTIOCH, WINTER 362)

You have requited Aristophanes[4] for his piety towards the gods and his devotion to yourself by changing and transforming what was formerly a reproach against him so that it redounds to his honour, and not for today only but for the future also, since the malicious charges of Paul[5] and the verdict of So-and-so[6] have no force compared with words written by you. For their calumnies were detested even while they flourished, and perished along with their perpetrators; whereas your speeches are not only prized by genuine

1. Theocritus, 12.2 2. Plato, *Phædrus*, 242 3. Sophocles, *Philoctetes*, 97

4. Aristophanes of Corinth; cf. Libanius, *Letter* 758

5. Paul, a tool of Constantius nicknamed *Catena* "the chain", was burned alive on Julian's accession by order of the Chalcedon Commission; he was a Spaniard, malevolent, and inquisitorial; cf. Ammianus, 14.5.6; 22.3.11

6. The real name was suppressed, probably by a cautious editor

Hellenes today, but will still be prized in future times, unless I am mistaken in my verdict. For the rest, you shall judge whether you have convinced, or rather converted me on behalf of Aristophanes. I now agree not to believe that he is too weak to resist pleasure and money. What point would I not yield to the most philosophic and truth-loving of orators? Naturally you will proceed to ask me why, in that case, I do not alter his unhappy lot for the better and blot out the disgrace that attaches to him on account of his ill fortune. "Two walking together",[1] as the proverb says; namely, you and I, must take counsel. You have the right, moreover, not only to advise that we ought to assist a man who has honoured the gods so straightforwardly, but also as to how it ought to be done. Indeed, you did hint at this in an obscure way. Though it is perhaps better not to write about such matters, but to talk it over together. Farewell, brother, most dear and most cherished!

I read almost all of your speech yesterday before breakfast, then after breakfast, before resting, I gave myself up to reading the remainder. What a fortunate man to be able to speak so well, or rather to have such ideas! O what a discourse! What wit! What wisdom! What analysis! What logic! What method! What openings! What diction! What symmetry! What structure![2]

54. TO EUSTOCHIUS[3]

(FROM ANTIOCH, LATE 362)

The wise Hesiod[4] thinks that we ought to invite our neighbours to our feasts so that they may rejoice with us, since they sorrow and mourn with us when any unexpected misfortune befalls us. I say, however, that it is our friends that we ought to invite, rather than our neighbours; and for this reason, that it is possible to have a neighbour who is one's enemy, but that a friend should be an enemy is no more possible than for white to be black, or hot cold. If there were no other proof that you are my friend not now only, but for a long time past, and that you have steadily maintained your regard for me, the fact that my feeling for you has nevertheless been and is what it is, would be strong evidence of that friendship. Come, therefore, that you may

1. *The Iliad*, X, 224 2. Julian is likely referencing Marcus Aurelius, *To Fronto*

3. This is either Eustochius of Palestine, whose knowledge of law and eloquence is praised by Libanius, *Letter* 699, or a sophist from Cappadocia of the same name

4. *Works and Days*, 313

in person share my consulship.[1] The state post will bring you, and you may use one carriage and an extra horse. While in case we ought to pray for further aid, I have invoked for you the blessing of the goddess of the Crossroads[2] and the god of the Ways.[3]

55. TO PHOTINUS[4]

(FROM ANTIOCH, 362-363)

Moreover, the Emperor Julian, faithless to Christ, in his attack on Diodorus,[5] writes as follows to Photinus the heresiarch: O Photinus, you at any rate seem to maintain what is probably true, and come nearest to being saved, doing well to believe that he whom one holds to be a god can by no means be brought into the womb. Diodorus, meanwhile, a charlatan priest of the Nazarene, when he tries to give point to that nonsensical theory about the womb by artifices and juggler's tricks, is clearly a sharp-witted sophist of that cult of the country-folk. *A little further on he says:* but if only the gods and goddesses and all the Muses and Fortune will lend me their aid, I hope to show[6] that he is feeble and a corrupter of laws and customs, of Pagan[7] Mysteries and Mysteries of the gods of the underworld, and that this newfangled Galilæan god of his, whom he by a false myth styles eternal, has been stripped by his humiliating death and burial of the divinity falsely ascribed to him by Diodorus. *Then, just as people who are convicted of error always begin to invent, being the slaves of artifice rather than of truth, he goes on to say:* For the fellow sailed to Athens to the injury of the general welfare, then rashly took to philosophy and engaged in the study of literature; by the devices of rhetoric, he armed his hateful tongue against the heavenly gods, and being utterly ignorant of the Mysteries of the Pagans he, so to speak, imbibed most deplorably the whole mistaken folly of the base and ignorant cult-making fishermen. For this conduct he has long since been punished by the gods themselves. For many years past, he has

---

1. Julian, with Salutius as colleague, entered into the consulship on 1st January, 363

2. Hecate (Trivia in Latin)   3. Hermes

4. These fragments of a lost letter are preserved only in the Latin version of Facundus Hermianensis, a Christian who wrote at Constantinople sometime around 546. The italicised passages are the words of Facundus.

5. Bishop of Tarsus, a celebrated teacher; he was at Antioch in 362

6. This is a forecast of Julian's treatise *Against the Galilæans*

7. Twice in this letter, Facundus translates Julian's "Hellene" as "Pagan"

been in danger, having contracted a wasting disease of the chest, and he now suffers extreme torture. His whole body has wasted away. For his cheeks have fallen in and his body is deeply lined with wrinkles. Yet this is no sign of philosophic habits, as he wishes those who are deceived by him to believe, but most certainly a sign of justice done, of divine punishment which has stricken him down in suitable proportion to his crime, since he must live out to the very end his painful and bitter life, his appearance that of a man pale and wasted.[1]

56. EDICT ON FUNERALS[2]

(FROM ANTIOCH, FEBRUARY, 363)

It was my duty, after much reflection, to restore the ancient custom which I have now decided to confirm by a law. For when they considered the matter, the men of old, who made wise laws, believed that there is the greatest possible difference between life and death, perceiving that each of these two states has customs and practices uniquely appropriate to it. For they thought that death is an unbroken rest – and this is surely that "brazen sleep" of which the poets sing[3] – but that life, on the contrary, brings many pains and many pleasures, at one moment adversity, then greater prosperity the next. Considering thus, they enjoined that expiations connected with the departed should be conducted apart, and that apart from them the daily business of life should be carried on. Moreover, they held that the gods are the beginning and end of all things, and believed that while we live we are subject to the gods, and when we depart from this life we travel back to the gods. Though perhaps it is not right to speak openly about these matters, or to divulge whether both are in the hands of the same gods or one set of gods has charge of the living and another set the dead. Nevertheless, if, as the Sun is the cause of day and night, winter and summer by his departure and arrival, so also the most venerable one of the gods themselves, unto whom all things are and from whom all things proceed, has appointed rulers over the living and allotted lords over the dead,

1. The sometimes untranslatable writing of Facundus, an openly partisan agent, throws into some doubt the fidelity of the Latin text with respect to Julian's original

2. This is probably the earlier form of the Latin Edict in Codex Theodosianus, 9.17.5, dated 12th February, 363. It is not clear whether it was aimed at the Christians, but of course they had to observe it

3. *The Iliad*, XI, 241

then we ought to assign to both of these classes in turn what is fitting for them, and to imitate in our daily life the orderly arrangement of the gods in that which exists.

As I have said, death is rest; and night harmonises with rest. I think, therefore, it is fitting that business connected with the burials of the dead should be performed at night, since for many reasons we ought to forbid anything of the sort to go on by day. Throughout the city men are going to and fro, each on his own business, and all the streets are full of men going to the law-courts, to or from the market, sitting at work at their crafts, or visiting the temples to confirm the good hopes that the gods have vouchsafed. Then some persons or other, having laid a corpse on the bier, push their way into the midst of those who are busy about such matters. The thing is in every way intolerable. For those who meet the funeral are often filled with disgust, some because they regard it as an ill omen, while for others who are on the way to the temples, it is not permitted to approach for worship till they have cleansed themselves from the pollution. For after such a sight, it is not permitted to approach the gods who are the cause of life and of all things least akin to decay. I have still, moreover, to mention what is worse than this. What could that be? The sacred precincts and temples of the gods lie open; and it often happens that in one of them someone is sacrificing, pouring libations, or praying at the very moment when men carrying a corpse are passing close by the temple itself, whereupon the voice of lamentations and speech of ill omen is carried even to the altars.

Do you not understand that the functions belonging to the day and the night have been separated more than all other things? With good reason, therefore, has burial been taken out of the day and reserved for the night. For it is not right to deprecate the wearing of white for mourning and yet to bury the dead in the daytime and sunlight. The former was better, at least, if it was not offensive to any of the gods, but the latter cannot escape being an act of impiety towards all the gods. For thereby men wrongly assign burial to the Olympian gods and wrongly alienate it from the gods of the underworld, or whatever else the guardians and lords of souls prefer to be called. Furthermore, I know that those who are thoroughly versed and punctilious in sacred rites think it right to perform at night the ritual to the gods below, or in any case not until after the tenth hour of the day. If this is the better time for the worship of these gods, we will certainly not assign another time for the service of the dead.

What I have said suffices for those who are willing to obey. For now that they have learned what errors they used to commit, let them change to the better way. Yet if there be any man of such a character that he needs threat and penalty, let him know that he will incur the severest punishment if, before the tenth hour of the day, he should venture to perform the offices for the corpse of any dead person and to carry it through the city. Rather, let these things be done after sunset and before sunrise, and let the pure day be consecrated for pure deeds and the pure gods of Olympus.

57. TO ARSACES, SATRAP OF ARMENIA[1]

(FROM ANTIOCH, EARLY 363)

Make haste, Arsaces, to meet the enemy's battle line, and quicker than I tell you, arm your right hand against the madness of the Persians. For my military preparations and my set purpose are for one of two things: either to pay the debt of nature within the Parthian[2] frontier, after I have won the most glorious victories and inflicted on my foes the most terrible reverses, or to defeat them under the leadership of the gods and return to my native land as a conquering hero, after I have set up trophies of the enemy's defeat. Accordingly, you must discard all sloth and dishonesty, the Emperor Constantine of blessed memory, and the wealth of the nobles which was lavished in vain on you and on Barbarians of your character by the most luxurious and extravagant Constantius; and now I warn you, take heed of me, Julian, *Pontifex Maximus*, Cæsar, Augustus, servant of the gods and of Ares, destroyer of the Franks and Barbarians, liberator of the Gauls and of Italy. Should you form some other design – for I learn that you are a recreant[3] and a coward in war and a boaster, as the present condition of affairs proves; indeed, I have heard that you are secretly trying to conceal at your court a certain enemy of the public welfare – for the present I postpone this matter because of the fortune of war; since my alliance with the gods is enough to secure the destruction of the enemy. Though if Destiny

1. The King of Armenia during the reigns of Constantius and Julian. As Armenia was a buffer state between Rome and Persia, Arsaces was courted by both parties. His failure to arrive with auxiliaries to aid Julian at Ctesiphon contributed to the breakdown of the Persian campaign

2. "Persian" and "Parthian" were often either confused or used interchangeably

3. Arsaces was almost certainly a Christian; cf. Sozomen, 6.1

should also play some part in the decision – for the purpose of the gods is her opportunity – I will endure it fearlessly as a man ought to. Be assured that you will be an easy victim of the power of Persia when your hearth and home, your whole race and the kingdom of Armenia all blaze together. While the city of Nisibis[1] will also share in your misfortune, for this the heavenly gods long since foretold to me.

58. TO LIBANIUS, SOPHIST AND QUAESTOR

(FROM HIERAPOLIS, MARCH, 363)

I travelled as far as Litarbæ – it is a village of Chalcis – and came upon a road that still had the remains of a winter camp of Antioch. The road, I may say, was partly swamp, partly hill, but the whole of it was rough; there lay stones in the swamp which looked as though they had been thrown there purposely, for they lay together without any art, after the fashion followed by those who build public highways in cities and, instead of using cement, make a deep layer of soil, then place the stones close together as though they were making a boundary-wall. When I had passed over this with some difficulty and arrived at my first halting-place, it was about the ninth hour, after which I received at my headquarters the greater part of your senate.[2] You have perhaps learned already what we said to one another, and, if it be the will of heaven, you shall know it from my own lips.

From Litarbæ I proceeded to Beroea, and there Zeus, by showing a manifest sign from heaven, declared all things to be auspicious.[3] I stayed there for a day, wherein I saw the Acropolis and sacrificed to Zeus in imperial fashion a white bull.[4] Also, I conversed briefly with the senate about the worship of the gods. Yet though they all applauded my arguments, very few were converted by them, and these few were men who even before I spoke seemed to me to hold sound views. They were cautious, however, and would not disarm and lay aside their modest reserve, as though afraid of too frank a speech. For it is the prevailing habit of mankind, dear gods, to blush

1. After Julian's death, Jovian, his successor, ceded Nisibis to Persia. Shapur II, the Persian King, then captured and killed Arsaces

2. The Senators of Antioch followed Julian to plead for the city, which had exasperated him; cf. Libanius, *Oration 16*

3. Ammianus, 23.2, records certain fatal accidents at Hierapolis and Batnæ which were regarded as ill omens for the campaign

4. The Emperors would sacrifice white animals

for their noble qualities, manliness of soul and piety, and to plume themselves, as it were, on what is most depraved: sacrilege and weakness of mind and body.

Next, Batnæ entertained me, a place like nothing that I have ever seen in your country, except Daphne;[1] but that is now very like Batnæ, though not long ago, while the temple and statue were still unharmed, I should not have hesitated to compare Daphne with Ossa and Pelion, or the peaks of Olympus, or Thessalian Tempe, or even to have preferred it to all of them put together. Nevertheless, you have composed an oration[2] on Daphne such as no other man "of such sort as mortals now are"[3] could achieve, even though he used his utmost energies on the task, in truth, and I think not very many of the ancient writers either. Why, then, should I try to write about it now, when so brilliant a monody has been composed in its honour? Would that none had been needed! To return to Batnæ, however. Its name is barbarous but the place is Hellenic;[4] I say as much as throughout the whole country the fumes of frankincense arose on all sides, and everywhere I saw offerings ready for sacrifice. Yet while this gave me truly great pleasure, it rather looked to me like overstated zeal, and alien to proper reverence for the gods. For things that are sacred to the gods and holy ought to be off the beaten track and performed in peace and quiet, so that men may resort there to that end alone and not on the way to some other business. Though this matter will perhaps before long receive the attention that is appropriate.

Batnæ I saw to be a thickly wooded plain containing groves of young cypresses; and among these there was no old or decaying trunk, but all alike were in vigorous leafage. The imperial lodging was by no means sumptuous, for it was made only of clay and logs and had no decorations, but its garden, though inferior to that of Alcinous,[5] was comparable to the garden of Laërtes.[6] Inside it was a quite small grove full of cypresses, and along the wall many trees of this sort have been planted in a row one after the other. Then in the middle were beds, and in these, vegetables and trees bearing fruits of all sorts. What did I do there, you ask? I sacrificed in the evening and again at early dawn, as I am in the habit of doing practically every day. Then, since the omens were favourable, we kept on to Hierapolis where the inhabitants came to meet us. Here I am being entertained

1. A suburb of Antioch; its temple of Apollo was burned on 22nd October, 362
2. cf. Libanius, *On the Temple of Apollo at Daphne, Oration 60*
3. *The Iliad*, V, 304
4. i.e., it maintained its Pagan worship
5. *The Odyssey*, XII, 112
6. *The Odyssey*, XXIV, 245

by a friend who, though I have only lately met him for the first time, has long been dear to me. I know that you yourself are well aware of the reason, but for all that it gives me pleasure to tell you. For it is like nectar to me to hear and speak of these things continually. Sopater,[1] the pupil of the godlike Iamblichus, was a relative by marriage of this Sopater. To not love even as myself all that belonged to those men is in my opinion equivalent to the lowest baseness. Yet there is another more powerful reason than this. Though he often entertained my cousin and my half-brother,[2] and was often urged by them, naturally enough, to abandon his piety towards the gods, and though that is hard to withstand, he was not infected with this disease.[3]

So much, then, was I able to write to you from Hierapolis about my own affairs. As regards the military or political arrangements, you ought, I think, to have been present to observe and pay attention to them yourself. For, as you well know, the matter is too long for a letter, in fact, so vast that if one considered it in detail, it would not be easy to confine it to a letter even three times as long as this. Nonetheless, I will tell you of these matters also, summarily, and in very few words. I sent an embassy to the Saracens[4] and suggested that they could come if they wished. That is one affair of the sort I have mentioned. For another, I despatched men as wide-awake as I could obtain so that they might guard against anyone's leaving here secretly to go to the enemy and inform them that we are on the move. After that I held a court martial and, I am convinced, showed in my decision the utmost clemency and justice. I have procured excellent horses and mules and have mustered all my forces together. The boats to be used on the river are laden with corn, or rather, with baked bread and sour wine. You can understand at what length I should have to write in order to describe how every detail of this business was worked out and what discussions arose over every one of them. As for the number of letters I have signed, and papers – for these too follow me everywhere like my shadow – why should I take the trouble to enumerate them now?[5]

1. The elder Sopater was put to death by Constantine
2. Constantius and Gallus
3. i.e., Christianity, or more specifically the rejection of the gods
4. According to Ammianus, 23.3.8, the Saracens offered themselves to Julian as allies, but then apparently deserted later to the Persians
5. This is Julian's last extant letter. On leaving Hierapolis, he marched into Persia and began the campaign in earnest. On 26th June, he was fatally wounded in a battle beside the Tigris. His body was carried by his men back into Roman territory and buried at Tarsus in Cilicia

(UNDATED LETTERS)

59. TO THE PHILOSOPHER MAXIMUS

We are told in the myth that the eagle,[1] when he would test which of his brood are genuine, carries them still unfledged into the upper air and exposes them to the rays of the sun, to the end that he may become, by the testimony of the god, the sire of a true nursling and disown any spurious offspring. Just so, I submit my speeches to you as though to Hermes the god of eloquence; and, if they can bear the test of being heard by you, it rests with you to decide concerning them whether they are fit to take flight to other men also. If they are not, however, then fling them away as though disowned by the Muses, or plunge them into a river as bastards. Certainly the Rhine does not mislead the Celts,[2] for it sinks deep in its eddies their bastard infants, like a fitting avenger of an adulterous bed; but all those that it recognises to be of pure descent, it supports on the surface of the water and gives them back to the arms of the trembling mother, thus rewarding her with the safety of her child as incorruptible evidence that her marriage is pure and without reproach.

60. TO THE PHILOSOPHER EUGENIUS[3]

We are told that Dædalus dared to do violence to nature by his art, and moulded wings of wax for Icarus. Though for my part, while I applaud him for his art, I cannot admire his judgement. For he is the only man who ever had the courage to entrust the safety of his son to soluble wax. If it were granted me, in the words of the famous lyric poet of Teos,[4] to change my nature to a bird's, I should certainly not "fly to Olympus for Love" – no, not even to lodge a complaint against him – but I should fly to the very foothills of your mountains to embrace "you, my friend", as Sappho[5] says. Yet since nature has confined me in the prison of a human body[6] and refuses to lighten

---

1. A rhetorical commonplace; cf. Lucian, *The Fisherman*, 46

2. A commonplace of rhetoric; the ordeal was purportedly to strengthen their bodies as well as to test their legitimacy; cf. Claudian, *In Rufinum*, 2.112

3. A philosopher named Eugenius was the father of Themistius, a contemporary of Julian, but the familiar tone all but rules him out as a plausible recipient. Schwarz, Cumont, and Geffcken reject it on the ground of its sophistic mannerisms

4. Anacreon, fr. 22 5. Fr. 126 6. A Platonic commonplace

and raise me aloft, I approach you with such wings as I possess, the wings of words, and I write to you, and am with you in such fashion as I can. Surely for this reason and this only, Homer calls words "winged", such that they are able to go to and fro in every direction, darting where they will, like the swiftest of birds. Though so, for your part, write to me too, my friend! For you possess an equal if not larger share of the plumage of words, with which you are able to travel to your friends and from wherever you may be, just as though you were present, to cheer them.

61. TO SOPATER[1]

It is an occasion to rejoice all the more when one has the chance to address friends through an intimate associate. For then it is not only by what you write that you unite the image of your own soul with your readers. And this is what I myself am doing. For when I despatched the custodian of my children,[2] Antiochus, to you, I could not bear to leave you without a word of greeting. So that if you want to have news of me, you can have from him information of a more intimate sort. While if you care at all for your admirers, as I believe you do care, you will prove it by never missing an opportunity while you are able to write.

62. TO THE PHILOSOPHER EUCLEIDES[3]

In truth, when do you ever leave me, so that I need to write, or when do I not behold you with the eyes of the soul as though you were here with me? For not only do I seem to be with you continually and to converse with you, but I pay attention to my duties now just as zealously as when you were here to guide me. Yet if you do wish me to write to you, just as though you were not here, then take care that you do not yourself create the impression of not being with me all the more by your very wish that I should write. If, however, you do really find pleasure in it, I am willing to appease you in this also.

---

1. This letter is rejected by Schwarz, Cumont, and Geffcken

2. No forger would have referred to children of Julian's body, but the phrase may be in reference to his writings; cf. Libanius, *Epitaphius*

3. Libanius often mentions a native of Constantinople named Eucleides to whom this letter may be addressed. Schwarz and Cumont reject it on stylistic grounds

At any rate, by your request you will, as the proverb says, lead a galloping horse into the plain. Come then, see that you return like for like, and in answer to my counter-summons, do not grow weary of the unbroken series of letters exchanged between us. And yet I have no wish to hinder the zeal that you display on behalf of the public welfare. Nevertheless, in proportion as I keep you free for the pursuit of noble studies, I shall be thought, far from injuring it, to benefit the whole body of Hellenes at once; that is to say, if I leave you like a young and well-bred dog without interference, free to give all your time to tracking down, with a mind wholly free from all else, the art of writing discourses; but if you possess such swiftness that you need neither neglect your friends nor slacken in those other pursuits, come, take both courses and run at full speed!

63. TO HECEBOLIUS[1]

Pindar[2] thinks that the Muses are "silvery" and it is as though he likened the clearness and splendour of their art to the substance that shines most brilliantly. While the wise Homer calls silver "shining" and gives to water the epithet "silvery"[3] because it gleams with the very brightness of the reflected image of the sun, as though under its direct rays. Again, Sappho[4] the fair says that the moon is "silvery" and that because of this it dims the radiance of the other stars. Similarly, one might imagine silver to be more appropriate to the gods than gold; but that to man, at any rate, silver is more precious than gold and more familiar to them because it is not, like gold, hidden under the earth and does not avoid their eyes, but is both beautiful to the eye and more serviceable in daily life – this, I say, is not my own theory but was held by men of old. If, therefore, in return for the gold coin sent by you I give you a piece of silver of equal value, think not that the favour is less and do not imagine that, as with Glaucus,[5] the exchange is to your disadvantage; for perhaps not even Diomedes would have exchanged silver armour for golden, seeing that the former is far more serviceable than the latter, and like

1. Hecebolius was a sophist who taught Julian rhetoric when he was a boy at Constantinople in 342. Schwarz, Cumont, and Geffcken reject the letter because of its flowery style and lack of serious content

2. Fr. 212; cf. *Pythian*, 9.65, *Isthmian*, 2.13

3. These epithets are not in our version of Homer

4. Fr. 3

5. A sophistic commonplace; he exchanged bronze armour for gold; *The Iliad*, VI, 236

lead, well fitted to turn the points of spears.[1] All this I say in jest, and I take the cue for my freedom of speech from what you write yourself. Though if you really wish to send me gifts more precious than gold, write, and keep on writing regularly. For even a short letter from you I hold to be more precious than any other gift one could name.

64. TO LUCIAN THE SOPHIST[2]

Not only do I write to you, but I demand to receive payment in kind. Moreover, if I treat you ill by writing continually, then I beg you to ill-treat me in return and make me suffer in the same way.

65. TO ELPIDIUS THE PHILOSOPHER[3]

Even a short letter gives more pleasure when the writer's affection can be measured by the greatness of his soul, rather than by the meagre proportions of what he writes. So that if I now address you briefly, do not conclude that the accompanying affection is equally slight; rather, since you know the full extent of my fondness for you, forgive the brevity of my letter and do not hesitate to answer me in one equally short. For whatever you send me, however trifling, keeps alive in my mind a remembrance of all that is good.

66. TO GEORGE, A REVENUE OFFICIAL[4]

Well, let us grant that Echo is a goddess, as you say she is, and a chatterbox, and, if you like, the wife of Pan[5] also; for I shall not object. Thus, even though nature would fain inform me that Echo is only the sound of the voice answering back when the air is struck, bent back upon that which is opposite the ear that hears it, nevertheless, since I put my faith in the account given by men both ancient and modern, and in your own account no less, I am abashed

1. *The Iliad*, XI, 237 2. A conventional sophistic letter of compliment
3. In late 362, Elpidius was at Antioch and in Julian's confidence; cf. Libanius, *Letter* 758
4. Otherwise unknown. George was probably a sophist. This and the following letter are rejected by Schwarz, Cumont, and Geffcken, for their sophistic mannerisms
5. Moschus, *Idyll* 6

into admitting that Echo is a goddess.[1] What, in any case, would that matter to me, if only, in my expressions of friendship towards you, I excel Echo in a considerable degree? For she does not reply to all the sounds that she hears, but rather to the last syllables uttered by the voice, like a grudging sweetheart who returns her lover's kisses with the merest touch of her lips. I, on the other hand, in my correspondence with you, lead off gently, and then again, in reply to your challenge, I return you like for like as though I were throwing back a ball. Therefore, you cannot be too quick in recognising that your letters put you in default, and that it is yourself, since you receive more and give back very little, whom you consign to the similitude of the figure, and not me, since I am eager to outdo you in both ways.[2] Regardless, whether you give in just the same degree as you receive, or not, whatever I am permitted to receive from you is a boon, and is credited as sufficient to balance the whole.[3]

67. TO GEORGE, A REVENUE OFFICIAL[4]

"You have come, Telemachus!"[5] as the verse says; but in your letters I have already seen you and the image of your noble soul, and have received the impression thereof, as of an imposing device on a small seal. For it is possible for much to be revealed in little. Indeed, even Phidias the wise artist not only became famous for his statue at Olympia or at Athens, but he knew also how to confine a work of great art within the limits of a small piece of sculpture. For instance, they say that his grasshopper and bee, and, if you please, his fly also, were of this sort; for every one of these, though naturally composed of bronze, became through his artistic skill a living thing. In those works, however, the very smallness of the living models perhaps contributed the appearance of reality to his skilful art. Do, please, look at his Alexander[6] hunting on horseback, for its whole measurement is no larger than a fingernail. Yet the marvellous skill of the workmanship is so lavished on every detail that Alexander at one and the same time strikes his quarry and intimidates the

1. George had evidently used the figure of Echo, and accused Julian of imitating her
2. i.e. in both sending and receiving letters
3. The last two sentences may be a playful allusion to George's financial profession
4. Geffcken and Cumont reject this letter
5. *The Odyssey*, XVI, 23
6. The ascription to Pheidias the sculptor of works in the 'microtechnique' may be due to the confusion between the 5th century Pheidias with a gem-cutter of the same name from the 3rd century B.C. The anachronism here makes the letter suspect

spectator, scaring him by his whole bearing, while the horse, reared on the very tips of his hoofs, is about to take a step and leave the pedestal, and by creating the illusion of vigorous action is endowed with movement by the artist's skill. This is exactly the effect that you have on me, my excellent friend. For after having been crowned often, already, as victor over the whole course, so to speak, in the lists of Hermes, the God of Eloquence, you now display the highest pitch of excellence in a few written words. In truth, you imitate Homer's Odysseus, who, by merely saying who he was, was able to dazzle the Phæacians.[1] Though if even from me you require some of what you call "friendly smoke",[2] I shall not begrudge it. Surely the mouse who saved the lion in the fable[3] is proof enough that something useful may come even from one's inferiors.

68. TO DOSITHEUS

I am almost in tears; and yet the very utterance of your name ought to have been an auspicious sound, for I recall to mind our noble and wholly admirable father.[4] If you make it your aim to imitate him, not only will you yourself be happy, but you will also give to human life, as he did, an example of which it will be proud. Though if you are indolent, you will grieve me, and you will blame yourself when blaming will not avail.

69. TO HIMERIUS[5]

I could not read without tears the letter which you wrote after your wife's death, in which you told me of your overwhelming grief. For not only does the event in itself call for sorrow, when a young and

1. *The Odyssey*, IX, 19

2. George had perhaps referred to the longing of Odysseus to see even the smoke of his native land, and had compared his friend's letters to that smoke

3. Babrius, *Fable* 107; Æsop, *Fable* 256

4. Julian must be referring to someone who had taught them both. This was regular usage; the teacher of one's own teacher could be referred to as "grandfather"

5. This Himerius cannot be identified with certainty. It is probably not the famous Bithynian sophist whom Julian invited to join him at Antioch in 362 on account of the reference to a deceased wife. Cumont identifies him with the son, or son-in-law, of the philosopher Iamblichus

virtuous wife, the joy of her husband's heart,[1] and, moreover, the mother of precious children, is prematurely snatched away like a torch that has been kindled and shines brightly, but in a little while its flame dies down; yet over and above this, the fact that it is you to whom this sorrow has come seems to me to make it still more grievous. For least of all men did our good Himerius deserve to experience any affliction, excellent orator that he is, and of all my friends the best beloved. Further, if it were any other man to whom I had to write about this, I should certainly have had to use more words in dealing with it; for instance, I should have said that such an event is the common lot, that we must submit, that nothing is gained by excessive grief, and I should have uttered all the other commonplaces considered appropriate for the alleviation of suffering, that is, if I were exhorting one who did not know them. Since, however, I think it unbecoming to offer to a man who well knows how to instruct others the sort of argument by which one must school those who are too ignorant for self-control, see now, I will forbear all such phrases; but I will relate to you a fable, or it may be a true story, of a certain wise man, which perhaps is not new to you, though it is probably unfamiliar to most people; and if you will use this and this alone, as though it were a drug to relieve pain, you will find release from your sorrow, as surely as from that cup which the Spartan woman[2] is believed to have offered to Telemachus when his need was as great as your own. Now the story is that when Darius was in tremendous grief for the death of his beautiful wife, Democritus[3] of Abdera could not by any argument succeed in consoling him; and so he promised him that he would bring back the departed to life, if Darius were willing to undertake to supply him with everything necessary for the purpose. Darius bade him spare no expense but take whatever he needed and make good his promise. After waiting a little, Democritus said that he was provided with everything else for carrying out his task, but still needed one thing only, which he himself did not know how to obtain. Darius, however, as King of all Asia, would perhaps find it without difficulty. Then when the King asked him what it might be, this great thing which it was possible for only a king to know of, they say that Democritus in reply declared that if he would inscribe on his wife's tomb the names of three persons who had never mourned for anyone, she would immediately come to life again, since she could not disobey the authority of this

1. An echo of *The Iliad*, IX, 336 2. Helen, *The Odyssey*, IV, 220

3. The Atomistic philosopher

mystic rite. Then Darius was in a dilemma, and could not find any man who had not had to bear some great sorrow, whereupon Democritus burst out laughing,[1] as was his wont, and said: "why, then, O most absurd of men, do you mourn without ceasing, as though you were the only man who had ever been involved in so great a grief, you who cannot discover a single person of all who have ever lived who was without his share of personal sorrow?" But though it was necessary to say these things to Darius, a Barbarian and a man of no education, the slave both of pleasure and of grief, you, on the other hand, are a Greek, and honour true learning, thus you must find your remedy from within; for surely it would be a disgrace to the reasoning faculty if it had not the same potency as time.

70. TO DIOGENES[2]

Your son Diogenes, whom I saw after you went away, told me that you had been much irritated with him for some reason that would naturally make a father feel vexed with his child, and he implored me to act as mediator in a reconciliation between him and yourself. Now, if he has committed some error of a mild and not intolerable kind, do yield to nature, recognise that you are a father, and again turn your thoughts to your child. If, however, his offence is too serious to admit of immediate forgiveness, it is right for you yourself to decide, rather than me, whether you ought to bear even that with a generous spirit and overcome your son's purpose by wiser thoughts, or to entrust the offender's probation to a longer period of discipline.

71. TO COMMANDER GREGORIUS[3]

Even a short letter from you is enough to provide me with grounds for feeling greatly pleased. Accordingly, since I was exceedingly pleased with what you wrote to me, I in turn send you a letter of the same length, because in my judgement the friendly

1. Democritus was known as "the laughing philosopher"

2. Diogenes is otherwise unknown. Schwarz places this letter between January and June 362, when Julian was at Constantinople. The tone seems to imply that he was already Emperor, though the note is purely conventional

3. A Gregorius Dux was prætorian prefect in 336, according to *Codex Theodosianus*, 3.1.2, but this purely formal letter is probably addressed to a younger man

greetings of comrades ought to be rewarded not by length of letter so much as by magnitude of goodwill.

72. TO PLUTARCH[1]

In all respects my bodily health is fairly good, and indeed my state of mind is no less satisfactory. I wager there can be no better prelude than this to a letter sent from one friend to another. And to what is this the prelude? To a request, of course! And what is the request? It is for letters in return, and in their sentiments may they harmonise with my own letters and bring me similar news from you, and equally auspicious.

73. TO MAXIMINUS[2]

I have given orders that there shall be ships at Cenchreæ.[3] The number of these you will learn from the governor of the Greeks,[4] but as to how you are to discharge your commission you may now hear from me. It must be without bribery and without delay. I will myself, with the help of the gods, ensure that you do not regret having done your duty as I have indicated.

1. This may be the obscure Athenian philosopher; cf. Marinus, *Proclus*, 12

2. Nothing is known of Maximinus. If the letter is genuine, as is probable, it may refer to Julian's preparations for his march against Constantius in 361

3. A coastal town south-west of the Isthmus of Corinth

4. i.e., the proconsul of Achæa who resided at Corinth

EPIGRAMS AND FRAGMENTS

I. ON WINE MADE FROM BARLEY[1]

Who are you and whence, O Dionysus? By the true Bacchus I recognise you not; I know only the son of Zeus. He smells of nectar, but you smell of goat. Truly it was in their lack of grapes that the Celts brewed you from corn-ears. So we should call you Demetrius,[2] not Dionysus, wheat-born[3] not fire-born, barley god not boisterous god.[4]

Palatine Anthology 9.365, and in several manuscripts.

II. ON THE ORGAN

A strange growth of reeds do I behold. Surely they sprang all of a sudden from another brazen field, so wild are they. The winds that wave them are none of ours, but a blast leaps forth from a cavern of bull's hide and beneath the well-bored pipes travels to their roots. A dignified person, with swift moving fingers of the hand, stands there and handles the keys that pass the word to the pipes; then the keys leap lightly, and press forth the melody.[5]

The Greek Anthology vol. 3, 365, Paton; it is found in Parisinus, 690.

III. ON THE CONSTANTINIAN SOLDIERS

They only knew how to pray.[6]

Quoted by Zosimus, 3.3.2

1. Beer, which Julian encountered in Gaul and Germania
2. Son of Demeter, goddess of agriculture, and pertinently corn
3. *πῦρογενῆ*, not *πῠρογενῆ*, a play on words. cf. *The Greek Anthology*, Vol. 3
4. *βρόμος* means oats; Bromius "boisterous" was an epithet of Dionysus; it is impossible to reproduce the play on the words
5. A note in the MSS explains that Julian composed this poem during a procession as he was leaving the church of the Holy Apostles in Constantinople. He was then a mere boy, pursuing his education in the capital before his internment at Macellum
6. Said of the soldiers assigned to him by Constantius when he was sent to Gaul

III. RIDDLE ON A POLE PERFORMER

There is a tree between the lords, whose root has life and talks, and the fruits likewise. In a single hour it grows in a strange fashion, and ripens its fruit, and gets its harvest at the roots.[1]

Palatine Anthology vol. 2. p. 769.

IV. ON THE HOMERIC HEXAMETER

"The daughter of Icarius, prudent Penelope," appears with three fingers[2] and walks on six feet.

Anthology 2. 659.

V. ON FATE

Even as Fate the Sweeper wills to sweep you on, be you swept. For if you rebel, you will but harm yourself, and Fate still sweeps you on.

First ascribed to Julian, from Baroccianus, 133, by Cumont, Revue de Philologie, 1892. Also ascribed to St. Basil; cf. a similar epigram in Palatine Anthology 10. 73, ascribed to Palladas.

IX. TO THE CITIZENS WHO ACCLAIMED HIM IN THE TEMPLE OF FORTUNE[3]

When I enter the theatre unannounced, acclaim me if you will, but when I enter the temples, be silent and transfer your acclamations to the gods; or perhaps not even that, for indeed the gods do not require acclamations.

First published by Muratori in Anecdota Græca, Padua, 1709.

---

1. The performer balances on his forehead, between his temples, a pole at the end of which is a cage or bar, supporting a child or multiple children

2. There is a play of words on δάκτυλος: "finger" and "dactyl", a metrical foot. In the title, "foot" and "dactyl" are metrical terms; in the riddle they are used in the original, physical sense. The hexameter quoted has three dactyls

3. There were temples to Fortune in both Constantinople and Antioch; this admonition could have thus been directed at the citizens of either.

VII. ON THE HERCYNIAN FOREST[1]

We hastened to the Hercynian forest and it was a strange and immense sight that I beheld. At any rate, I do not hesitate to suggest that nothing of the sort has ever been seen in the Roman Empire, at least as far as is known. For if anyone considers Thessalian Tempe, or Thermopylæ, or the great and far-flung Taurus to be impassable, let me tell him that for difficulty of approach they are trivial indeed compared with the Hercynian forest.

Quoted by Suidas under Χρῆμα.

VIII. TO THE CORINTHIANS[2]

...My friendship with you dates from my father's time. For indeed my father lived in your city, and embarking thence, like Odysseus from the land of the Phæacians, had respite from his long-protracted wanderings[3]...there my father found repose.

Quoted by Libanius, Oration 14, 29, 30. For Aristophanes (of Corinth).

X. ON CHRISTIAN RHETORICIANS

...in the words of the proverb, we are stricken by our own arrows.[4] For from our own writings they take the weapons with which to engage in war against us.

Quoted by Theodoret, History of the Church, 3.4. with respect to Julian's ban on Christians teaching the classics.

1. An ancient and dense forest that stretched from Western Europe to the Carpathian Mountains. In the Germany of Julian's day, it extended from the Black Forest on the north-east to the Hartz Mountains.

2. This is all that remains of the manifesto sent to Corinth by Julian in 361.

3. Libanius says that Julian here spoke briefly about his father's "wicked stepmother", the Empress Helena, mother of Constantine. See Zosimus 2.8.

4. That is, the arrows are feathered from our plumage; cf. Aristophanes, Birds, 808. The figure is used by Byron, Waller, and Moore of a wounded eagle "which on the shaft that made him die, espied a feather of his own". The original is Æschylus, Myrmidons, frag. 139

AGAINST THE GALILAEANS

PREFACE

During the long winter nights of his residence in Antioch, Julian composed a treatise against the Christians, perhaps brought about in part by his experience in the Syrian capital, which was finally published in early 363. Unfortunately, only certain portions of the work have survived. Few such polemics, especially those directed at Christianity, managed to emerge from the Middle Ages intact. For the many examples of intellectual and cultural preservation that occurred – most notably in Byzantium – there are countless instances in which the works of heretics were resigned to the ashes. Julian's writings were no exception: "at this point in the book, there were thirteen leaves containing works by the apostate Julian; the abbot of the monastery of St. John the Baptist read them and realised that they were dangerous, so he threw them into the sea".[1]

In the case of *Against the Galilæans*, we are indebted to Cyril of Alexandria, who in the fifth century undertook a refutation of what he regarded to be an especially dangerous work, one which had "shaken many believers".[2] While only half of Cyril's text has survived, the quotations of Julian allowed Karl Johannes Neumann[3] to reconstruct a considerable portion of the original commentary. Naturally, the passages which Cyril chose to include will have been those he felt most capable of refuting. Nevertheless, it is the only version available to us and, save for the occasional lacuna in Julian's argument, a valuable resource.

The primary aims of Julian's treatise, then, was to expose what he perceived to be the inconsistencies in Christianity, to demonstrate that there is insufficient evidence in the Old Testament to validate the religion's existence, and to prove that the Hellenic faith offered a superior understanding of the divine. In this endeavour, Julian had been ably prepared by the Christians who tutored him during his confinement at Macellum. Indeed, only a person who was well versed in the Bible would understand the significance of Christians being called "Galilæans" – a pointed reference, no doubt, to the biblical verse "out of Galilee ariseth no prophet".[4]

1. N. G. Wilson, *Scholars of Byzantium*, pg. 12
2. Cyril of Alexandria, *Against Julian*
3. Karl Johannes Neumann was a German classical historian
4. John 7:52

Throughout, Julian contrasts Christians unfavourably with Hebrews and Pagans, repeatedly rebuking them for having abandoned both the Mosaic law and the Hellenic traditions of their ancestors. It should be noted, however, that in the extant version of this treatise, the Hebrews, and in particular their characterisation of God, receive extensive criticism, arguably more so than the Christians themselves. Otherwise, Julian's arguments share much in common with those employed by Celsus[1] and Porphyry in their respective refutations.

1. Celsus was one of the foremost critics of early Christianity. His second century work, *The True Word*, was much like Julian's in that it has survived only through the refutation, *Contra Celsum*, by Origen. Celsus was arguably even more scathing in his attack, commenting that those most receptive to the Christian message were "slaves, women, little children" and "the foolish, dishonourable, and stupid"

AGAINST THE GALILAEANS

It is, I think, expedient to set forth to all mankind the reasons by which I was convinced that the fabrication of the Galilæans is a fiction of men composed of deceit. Though it has nothing of the divine within it, by making full use of that part of the soul which loves fable and is both childish and foolish, it has induced men to believe that this absurd tale is drawn from truth. Now, since I intend to treat of all their first dogmas, as they call them, I wish to say in the first place that if my readers desire to try and refute me, they must proceed as if they were in a court of law and not drag in irrelevant matter, or, as the saying goes, bring counter-charges until they have defended their own views. For it will be better and clearer if, when they wish to censure any views of mine, they undertake that as a separate task, but when they are defending themselves against my censure, they bring no recriminations.

It is worthwhile, then, to recall in a few words whence and how we first arrived at a conception of god; next, to compare what is said about the divine among the Hellenes[1] and Hebrews; and finally, to enquire of those who are neither Hellenes nor Jews, but belong to the sect of the Galilæans, why they prefer the beliefs of the Jews to ours, and what, further, could be the reason why they do not even adhere faithfully to the Jewish beliefs, having abandoned them also to follow a way of their own. For they have not accepted a single admirable or important doctrine of those that are held either by us Hellenes, or by the Hebrews who derived them from Moses. Rather, from both religions they have gathered that which has been engrafted, as it were, like powers of corruption upon these nations: impiety from the Jewish levity, and a sordid and slovenly way of living from our heedlessness and vulgarity. This they desire should be called the noblest worship of the gods.

That man possesses his knowledge of god by nature and not from teaching is proved to us first of all by the universal yearning

1. Greco-Roman Pagans

for the divine that is in all men, whether private persons or communities, whether considered as individuals or as races. For all of us, without being taught, have attained to a belief in some sort of divinity, though it is not easy for all men to know the precise truth about it, nor is it possible for those who do know it to tell it to all men...[1] Surely, besides this conception which is common to all men, there is another also: that we are all by nature so closely dependent on the heavens and the gods that are revealed therein, that even if any man conceives of another god besides these, he in every case assigns to him the heavens as his dwelling-place. Not that he thereby separates him from the earth, but rather he establishes, so to speak, the Lord of All in the heavens, being the most honourable place of all, and conceives of him as overseeing from there the affairs of this world.

What need have I to summon Hellenes and Hebrews as witnesses of this? There exists no man who does not stretch out his hands towards the heavens when he prays; and whether he swears by one god or several, if he has any notion at all of the divine, he turns heavenward. It was only natural that men should feel thus. For they observed that in what concerns the heavenly bodies there is no increase, diminution, or mutability, and that they do not suffer any unregulated influence. Instead, their movement is harmonious and their arrangement in concert; the illuminations of the moon are regulated, and the risings and settings of the sun are regularly defined, always at regularly defined seasons. They naturally conceived, therefore, that the heaven is a god, or the throne of a god. For, since it is not subject to increase by addition, or to diminution by subtraction, and is stationed beyond all change due to alteration or mutability, a being of that sort is free from decay and generation, and inasmuch as it is immortal by nature and thus indestructible, it is pure from every sort of stain. Eternal and ever in movement, as we see, it travels in a circuit about the great Spirit,[2] whether it be impelled by a nobler and more divine soul that dwells therein, just as our own bodies are by the soul within us, or by having received its motion from the god himself, it wheels in its boundless circuit, in an unceasing and eternal act.

Now, it is true that the Hellenes invented myths about the gods – incredible and monstrous stories. For they said that Kronos

1. Some words are lost. This is the first of several lacunæ throughout the work

2. ψυχῆς; the spirit of the universe; the immaterial principle of movement and life; cf. Plato, Timæus, 34

swallowed his children and then disgorged them forth; and they even told of lawless unions, how Zeus had intercourse with his mother, and after having a child by her, married his own daughter,[1] or rather, did not even marry her, but simply had intercourse with her then handed her over to another.[2] Then, too, there is the legend that Dionysus was rent asunder and his limbs joined together again. This is the sort of thing described in the myths of the Hellenes. Compare with them the Jewish doctrine, how the garden planted by God and Adam was fashioned by Him, and next, for Adam, woman came to be. For God said:"it is not good that man should be alone. Let us make him a help-mate like him".[3] Yet so far was she from helping him at all that she deceived him, and was in part the cause of his and her own fall from their life of ease in the garden.

This is wholly preposterous. For is it probable that God did not know that the being he was creating as a helper would prove to be not so much a blessing as a misfortune to him who received her? Again, what sort of language are we to say that the serpent used when he talked with Eve? Was it the language of human beings? In what do such legends as these differ from the myths that were invented by the Hellenes? Moreover, is it not exceptionally strange that God should deny to the human beings whom he had fashioned the power to distinguish between good and evil? What could be more foolish than a being unable to distinguish good from bad? For it is evident that he would not avoid the latter, by which I mean evil, nor would he strive after the former, that is to say, good. In short, God refused to let man taste of wisdom, to which nothing is of more value for man. For that the power to distinguish between good and less good is the property of wisdom is surely evident even to the witless. Thus the serpent was a benefactor rather than a destroyer of man.

Furthermore, their God must be called envious. For when he saw that man had attained to a share of wisdom, he cast him out of the garden so that he might not, God declared, taste of the tree of life, saying in so many words:"behold, Adam has become as one of us, because he knows good from bad; let him not put forth his hand and take also of the tree of life and thus live forever".[4] Accordingly, unless every one of these legends is a myth that involves some hidden interpretation, as I indeed believe, they are filled with many blasphemous sayings about God. For in the first place to be ignorant that she who was created as a help-mate would be the

1. Persephone 2. Hades 3. *Genesis*, 2.18 4. *Genesis*, 3.22

cause of the fall; secondly, to refuse the knowledge of good and bad, when knowledge alone seems to give coherence to the mind of man; and lastly, to be jealous lest man should eat from the tree of life and from mortal become immortal – this is unduly grudging and envious.

Next, to consider the views that are correctly held by the Jews, as well as those that our fathers handed down to us from the beginning. Our account has in it the immediate maker[1] of this universe, as the following shows...[2] Moses has said nothing whatsoever about the gods who are superior to this maker; indeed, he has not even ventured to say anything about the nature of the angels. That they serve God he has asserted in many ways and often, but whether they were generated or ungenerated, whether they were generated by one god and appointed to serve another, or in some other way, he has nowhere said definitely. He does, however, describe fully in what manner the heavens, the earth, and all therein were set in order. In part, he says, God ordered them to be, such as light and the firmament; and in part, he says, God made them, such as the heavens and the earth, the sun and the moon, and that all things which already existed but were hidden away for the time being, he separated, such as water and dry land. Apart from these, alas, he did not venture to say a word about the generation or the making of the Spirit, but only this: "and the Spirit of God moved upon the face of the waters". Whether that spirit was ungenerated or had been generated, though, he does not make at all clear.

Let us now compare the utterances of Plato. Observe, then, what he says about the maker, and what words he has him speak at the time of the generation of the universe, in order that we may compare Plato's account of that generation with that of Moses. For in this way it will be apparent who was the nobler and more worthy of communion with god, Plato who paid homage to images, or he of whom the scripture says that God spoke with him mouth to mouth.[3]

---

1. δημιουργόν; the Platonic Demiurge ("craftsman"), a divinity responsible for fashioning and maintaining the physical, perceptible universe after the model of the Ideas. While the Demiurge is juxtaposed with the Abrahamic God throughout this treatise, its role is that of creator and not of a personal divinity, nor does it represent the Unmoved Mover, as with the Judeo-Christian God; cf. Plato, *Timæus*

2. According to Asmus, the Pagan theory is missing as is part of the Jewish one

3. *Numbers*, 12.8: "with him will I speak mouth to mouth"

> "In the beginning, God created heaven and earth. And the earth was invisible and without form, and darkness was upon the face of the deep. And the spirit of God moved upon the face of the waters. And God said, let there be light; and there was light. And God saw the light that it was good; and God divided the light from the darkness. And God called the light Day, and the darkness he called Night. And the evening and the morning were the first day. And God said, Let there be a firmament in the midst of the waters. And God called the firmament Heaven. And God said, Let the waters under the heaven be gathered together unto one place, and let the dry land appear; and it was so. And God said, Let the earth bring forth grass for fodder, and the fruit-tree yielding fruit. And God said, let there be lights in the firmament of the heaven that they may be for a light upon the earth. And God set them in the firmament of the heaven to rule over the day and over the night."[1]

In all this, you observe, Moses does not say that the deep was created by God, or the darkness, or the waters. After saying in relation to light that God ordered it to be, and thus it was, surely he ought to have gone on to speak of night also, and the deep, and the waters. Of them, however, he says not a word to imply that they were not already in existence, though he often mentions them. Furthermore, he does not mention the birth or creation of the angels, or in what manner they were brought into being, but deals only with the heavenly and earthly bodies. It follows that, according to Moses, God is the creator of nothing that is incorporeal, but is only the disposer of matter that already existed. For the words "and the earth was invisible and without form" can only mean that he regards the wet and dry substance as the original matter, and that he introduces God as the disposer of this matter.

On the other hand, let us hear what Plato says about the universe:

> "the whole heaven, or cosmos – or whichever other name would be most acceptable to it, so let it be named by us – has it existed eternally, having no beginning of generation, or has it come into being, starting from some beginning? It has come into being. For it is visible, tangible, and possessed of a body; and all such things are the objects of sensation, and such objects of sensation, being apprehensible by opinion with the

1. *Genesis*, 1-17, with certain omissions

> aid of sensation, come into existence, as we saw, and are generated...[1] It follows, therefore, according to this reasonable theory, that we ought to affirm that the universe came into being as a living creature possessing soul and intelligence in truth, both by the providence of god."[2]

Let us but compare them, point by point. What sort of speech does the god make in the account of Moses, and what of the god in the account of Plato?

> "And God said, let us make man in our image, and our likeness; and let them have dominion over the fish of the sea, and over the fowl of the air, and over the cattle, and over all the earth, and over every creeping thing that creepeth upon the earth. So God created man, in the image of God he created him; male and female he created them, and said, be fruitful and multiply and replenish the earth, and subdue it; and have dominion over the fish of the sea, and over the fowl of the air, and over all the cattle and over all the earth."[3]

Now, I say, let us hear the speech which Plato puts in the mouth of the Maker of All:

> "Gods of gods! Those works whose creator and father I am will abide indissoluble, so long as it is my will. All that has been fastened may be loosed, yet to will to loose that which is harmonious and in good state were the deed of an evil being. Wherefore, since you have come into being, you are not immortal or indissoluble altogether, nevertheless you shall by no means be disjoined or meet with the doom of death, since you have found in my will a bond more mighty and more potent than those wherewith you were bound when you came into being. Now, then, hearken to the words which I declare to you: three kinds of mortal beings still remain ungenerated, and unless these have birth the heaven will be incomplete. For it will not have within itself all the kinds of living things. Yet if these should come into being and receive a share of life at my hands, they would become equal to gods. Therefore, in order that they may be mortal, and that this All may be All in truth, turn yourself according to your nature to the forming of living things, imitating my power even as I showed it in generating you. Now such part of them as is fitted to receive the same name

1. *Timæus*, 28 2. *Timæus*, 30 3. *Genesis*, 26-28

> as the immortals, which is called divine, and the power in them that governs all who are willing ever to follow justice, this part I will deliver to you, having sowed it and given it origin. For the rest, do you, weaving the mortal with the immortal, form and generate living beings; then by giving them sustenance increase them, and when they perish receive them back again".[1]

Before you begin to consider whether this is just a dream, learn first the meaning thereof. Plato gives the name gods to those that are visible – the sun and moon, the stars and the heavens – but these are only the likenesses of the unseen[2] gods. The sun which is visible to our eyes is the likeness of the intelligible and unseen sun,[3] and again, the moon which is visible to our eyes and every one of the stars are likenesses of the intelligible. Accordingly, Plato knows of those intelligible and unseen gods which are immanent in and coexist with the maker himself and were begotten and proceeded from him. Naturally, therefore, the maker in Plato's account says "gods" when he is addressing the unseen beings, and "of gods," meaning by this, evidently, the visible gods. The common creator of both these is he who fashioned the heavens, the earth, the sea, and the stars, and begat in the intelligible world the archetypes of these.

Observe, then, that what follows is well said also. "For", he says, "there remain three kinds of mortal things" meaning, clearly, human beings, animals, and plants; for each one of these has been set in accordance with its own distinct purpose and measure. "Now," he goes on to say, "if each one of these also should come to exist by me, it would of necessity become immortal." Indeed, in the case of the intelligible gods and the visible universe, no other cause for their immortality exists than that they came into existence by the act of the maker. When, therefore, he says "such part of them as is immortal must be given to these by the creator" he means the reasoning soul. "For the rest," he says, "weave mortal with immortal." It is therefore clear that the creative gods received from their father their creative power, and so begat on earth all living things that are mortal. For if there were to be no difference between the heavens and mankind – and animals too, by Zeus, and all the way down to the very order of reptiles and the little fish that swim

1. *Timæus*, 41. There are slight variations from our *Timæus*
2. Ἀφᾰνής ("not manifest")
3. cf. *Hymn to Helios* for exposition of this theory held by the late Neo-Platonists

in the sea – then there would have had to be one and the same creator for them all. If, however, there is a great gulf fixed between immortals and mortals, and this cannot become greater by addition or less by subtraction, nor can it be mixed with what is mortal and subject to fate, it follows that one set of gods were the creative cause of mortals, and another of immortals.

Accordingly, since Moses has also failed, as it seems, to give a complete account of the immediate architect of this universe, let us proceed to set one against another the opinion of the Hebrews and that of our fathers about these nations.

Moses says that the creator of the universe chose the Hebrew nation, that to that nation alone did he pay heed and care for it, and he gives him charge of it alone. Yet how and by what sort of gods the other nations are governed he has said not a word, unless, indeed, one should concede that he did assign to them the sun and moon.[1] Of this, however, I shall speak a little later. For now I will only point out that Moses himself, the prophets who came after him, and Jesus the Nazarene – and, yes, Paul also, who surpassed all the magicians and charlatans of every place and every time – assert that he is the God of Israel alone and of Judæa, and that the Jews are his chosen people. Listen to their own words, and first to the words of Moses: "and thou shalt say unto Pharaoh, Israel is my son, my firstborn. And I have said to thee, Let my people go that they may serve me. But thou didst refuse to let them go".[2] And a little later: "and they say unto him, The God of the Hebrews hath summoned us; we will go therefore three days' journey into the desert, that we may sacrifice unto the Lord our God".[3] Soon he speaks again in the same way: "the Lord the God of the Hebrews hath sent me unto thee, saying, Let my people go that they may serve me in the wilderness."[4]

That from the beginning God cared only for the Jews and that he chose them as his portion, has been clearly asserted not only by Moses and Jesus, but by Paul as well; though in Paul's case this is strange. For according to circumstances he keeps changing his views about God, as the polypus changes its colours to match the rocks.[5] At one moment he insists that the Jews alone are God's portion, and then, when he is trying to persuade the Hellenes to take sides with him, he says: "do not think that he is the God of Jews only, but also of Gentiles; yea of Gentiles also".[6] Therefore, it is

---

1. *Deuteronomy*, 4.19 2. *Exodus*, 4.22 3. *Exodus*, 4.23 4. *Exodus*, 5.3
5. A proverb 6. *Romans*, 3.29; *Galatians*, 3.28

quite fair to ask of Paul why God, if he was not the God of the Jews only but also of the Gentiles, sent the blessed gift of prophecy to the Jews in abundance and gave them Moses, the oil of anointing, the prophets, the law, and the incredible and monstrous elements in their myths? For you hear them crying aloud: "man did eat angels' food".[1] Finally, God sent to them Jesus, also, but to us no prophet, no oil of anointing, no teacher, no herald to announce his love for man which should one day, though late, reach even to us as well. Indeed, he even looked on for myriads, or, if you prefer, for thousands of years, while men in extreme ignorance served 'idols', as you call them, from where the sun rises to where he sets, from North to South, save only that little tribe which less than two thousand years before had settled in one part of Palestine. For if he is the God of all of us alike, and the creator of all, why did he neglect us?

Wherefore it is natural to think that the God of the Hebrews was not the begetter of the whole universe with lordship over all, but rather, as I said before, that he is confined within limits, and that since his empire has bounds, we must conceive of him as merely one among a crowd of other gods. Are we then to pay further heed to you because you or one of your stock imagined the God of the universe, though in any case you attained only to a basic conception of him? Is not all this partiality? God, you say, is a jealous God. But why is he so jealous, even avenging the sins of the fathers on the children?[2]

Consider now our teaching in comparison with this of yours. Our writers say that the creator is the common father and lord of all things, but that the other functions have been assigned by him to national gods of the peoples and gods that protect the cities; each one of whom administers his own domain in accordance with his own nature. For in the father all things are complete and all things are one, while in the separate deities one quality or another predominates; thus Ares rules over the warlike nations, Athena over those that are wise as well as warlike, Hermes over those that are more shrewd than adventurous, and in short the nations over which the gods preside follow each the essential character of their proper god. Now, if experience does not bear witness to the truth of our teachings, we should grant that our traditions are a figment and a misplaced attempt to convince, and then we ought to approve the doctrines held by you. If, however, quite the contrary is true, and

1. *Psalms*, 78.25 2. *Exodus*, 20.5

from the remotest past, experience bears witness to our account and in no case does anything appear to harmonise with your teachings, why do you persist in maintaining a pretension so enormous?

Come, tell me why it is that the Celts and the Germans are fierce, while the Greeks and Romans are, generally speaking, inclined to political life and humane, though at the same time unyielding and warlike? Why the Egyptians are more intelligent and more given to crafts, and the Syrians unwarlike and effeminate, but at the same time intelligent, hot-tempered, vain, and quick to learn? For if there is anyone who does not discern a reason for these differences among the nations, but rather declaims that all this so befell spontaneously, how, I ask, can he still believe that the universe is administered by a providence? If, however, there is any man who maintains that there are reasons for these differences, let him tell me them, in the name of the maker himself, and instruct me.

As for the laws of men, it is evident that men have established them to correspond with their own natural dispositions; that is to say, constitutional and humane laws were established by those in whom a humane disposition had been fostered above all else, savage and inhumane laws by those in whom there lurked and was inherent the contrary disposition. For lawgivers have succeeded in adding but little by their discipline to the natural characters and aptitudes of men. Accordingly, the Scythians would not receive Anacharsis[1] among them when he was inspired by religious fervour, and with very few exceptions you will not find that any men of the Western nations have any great inclination for philosophy, or geometry, or any studies of that sort, although the Roman Empire has so long now been paramount. Yet those who are unusually talented delight only in debate and the art of rhetoric, and do not adopt any other study; so strong, it seems, is the force of nature. Whence, then, come these differences of character and laws among the nations?

Of the dissimilarity of language, Moses has given a wholly implausible explanation. For he said that the sons of men came together intending to build a city, with a great tower therein, only for God to respond that he must go down and confound their

1. A Scythian prince who travelled in search of knowledge and was counted by some among the seven sages. On his return to Thrace he is said to have been killed while celebrating the rites of Cybele, which were new to the Scythians; cf. Herodotus, 4.76; Lucian, *Anacharsis*

languages. So that no one may think I am falsely accusing him of this, I shall read directly from the book of Moses: "and they said, go to, let us build us a city and a tower, whose top may reach unto heaven; and let us make us a name, before we be scattered abroad upon the face of the whole earth. And the Lord came down to see the city and the tower, which the children of men had built. And the Lord said, behold, the people is one, and they have all one language; and this they have begun to do; and now nothing will be withheld from them which they purpose to do. Go to, let us go down, and there confound their language, that no man may understand the speech of his neighbour. So the Lord God scattered them abroad upon the face of all the earth: and they left off to build the city and the tower".[1] Then you demand that we should believe this account, while you yourselves disbelieve Homer's narrative of the Aloadæ, namely that they planned to set three mountains atop one another "so that the heavens might be scaled".[2]

For my part, I say that this tale is almost as fantastic as the other. If, however, you accept the former, why in the name of the gods do you discredit Homer's fable? For I suppose that to men so ignorant as you, I must say nothing about the fact that, even if all men throughout the inhabited world ever employ one speech and one language, they will not be able to build a tower that will reach to the heavens, even if they should turn the entire earth into bricks. For such a tower would need countless bricks of a mass equal to the entire earth if they were to succeed in reaching to the orbit of the moon. For let us assume that all mankind came together, employing but one language and speech, and that they made the entire earth into bricks, hewing out stones – when would it reach as high as the heavens, even if they spun it out and stretched it until it was finer than a thread? Then do you, who believe that this obvious fable is true, and, moreover, think that God was threatened by the actions of men, for which reason he came down to earth to confound their languages, do you, I say, still venture to boast of your knowledge of God?

Regardless, I will return again to the question of how God confounded their languages. The reason why he did so, Moses has declared, namely, that God was afraid that if they should have one language and were of one mind, they would first construct for themselves a path to the heavens and then engage in some misdeed against him. How he carried this out, Moses does not say at all;

1. *Genesis*, 11.4-8 2. *The Odyssey*, XI, 316

only that he first came down from heaven – because he could not, as it seems, do it from on high, without coming down to earth. With respect to the existing differences in characters and customs, neither Moses nor anyone else has enlightened us. Yet among mankind the difference between the customs and the political constitutions of the nations is in every way greater than the difference in their languages. What Greek, for instance, ever tells us that a man ought to marry his sister, or his daughter, or his mother? While in Persia this is accounted virtuous. Yet why need I go over their various characteristics, or describe the love of liberty and lack of discipline of the Germans, the docility and tameness of the Syrians, the Persians, the Parthians, and in short of all the Barbarians in the East and the South, and of all nations who possess and are contented with a somewhat despotic form of government?

Now, if these differences that are greater and more important came about without the aid of a higher and more divine providence, why do we vainly trouble ourselves about and worship one who takes no thought for us? For is it fitting that he who cared nothing for our lives, our characters, our manners, our good government, our political constitution, should still claim to receive honour at our hands? Certainly not. You see to what an absurdity your doctrine comes. For of all the blessings that we behold in the life of man, those that relate to the soul come first, and those that relate to the body are secondary. If, therefore, he paid no heed to our spiritual blessings, took no thought for our physical conditions, and, moreover, sent to us neither teachers nor lawgivers as he did for the Hebrews, such as Moses and the prophets who followed him, for what shall we properly feel gratitude to him?

Consider, however, whether God has not given to us gods and noble guardians of whom you have no knowledge; gods in no way inferior to him who from the beginning has been held in honour among the Hebrews of Judæa, the only land that he chose to take thought for, as Moses and those who came after him declared, down to our own time. Though even if he who is honoured among the Hebrews really was the immediate creator of the universe, our beliefs about him are higher than theirs, and he has bestowed on us greater blessings than on them, with respect both to the soul and to externals. Of these, however, I shall speak a little later. Furthermore, he sent to us lawgivers not inferior to Moses, if indeed many of them were not far superior.

Therefore, as I said, unless for every nation separately some presiding national god (and under him an angel, a daimon, a hero, and a particular order of spirits which obey and work for the higher powers)[1] established the differences in our laws and characters, you must demonstrate to me how these differences arose by some other agency. Moreover, it is not sufficient to say "God spake and it was so". For the natures of things that are created ought to harmonise with the commands of God. I will say more clearly what I mean: did God ordain that fire should mount upwards by chance and earth sink down? Was it not necessary, in order that the ordinance of God should be fulfilled, for the former to be light and the latter to weigh heavy? While in the case of other things, also, this is equally true... Likewise with respect to things divine.

The reason, then, is that mankind is perishable and doomed to death. Accordingly, the works of men are also naturally perishable, mutable, and subject to every kind of alteration. Since God is eternal, though, it follows that of such sort are his ordinances also. As they are such, they are either the nature of things or are accordant with the nature of things. For how could nature be at variance with the ordinance of God? How could it fall out of harmony therewith? If, therefore, he did ordain that even as our languages are confounded and do not harmonise with one another, so too should it be with the political constitutions of the nations, then it was not by a special, isolated decree that he gave these constitutions their essential characteristics, or framed us also to match this lack of agreement. For different natures must first have existed in all those things that among the nations were to be differentiated. This, at any rate, is seen if one observes how very different in their bodies are the Germans and Scythians from the Libyans and Ethiopians. Can this also be due to a mere decree, and does not the climate or the country have a joint influence with the gods in determining what sort of complexion they have?

Furthermore, Moses also consciously drew a veil over this sort of enquiry, and did not assign the confusion of dialects to God only. For he says[2] that God did not descend alone, but that there descended with him not one but several, and he did not say who

---

1. Plato, *Laws*, 713, defines daimons as beings superior to man but inferior to gods who watch over human affairs and act as intermediaries between man and the divine. The distinction with angels is unclear; Proclus placed them cosmologically and metaphysically higher. Julian's triad of "angels, daimons, heroes" was a fixture of later Platonic theory

2. *Genesis*, 11.7

these were. It is evident, nonetheless, that he assumed that the beings who descended with God resembled him. If, therefore, it was not the Lord alone but his associates with him who descended for the purpose of confounding the dialects, it is very evident that for the confusion of men's characters, also, it was not the Lord alone but those who together with him confounded the dialects that would reasonably be considered responsible for this division.

So, why have I discussed this matter at such length, though it was my intention to speak briefly? For this reason: if the immediate creator of the universe be he who is proclaimed by Moses, then we hold nobler beliefs concerning him, inasmuch as we consider him to be the master of all things in general, but that there are besides national gods who are to him as viceroys are to a king, each administering separately his own province; and, moreover, we do not make him the regional rival of the gods whose station is subordinate to his. If, however, Moses first pays honour to a regional god, and then makes the lordship of the whole universe contrast with his power, then it is better to believe as we do, and to recognise the God of All, though not without apprehending also the God of Moses. This is better, I say, than to honour one who has been assigned the lordship over a very small portion instead of the architect of all things.

Now, as to the admirable law of Moses, by which I mean the famous decalogue. "Thou shalt not steal"; "thou shalt not kill"; "thou shalt not bear false witness". Let me write out, word for word, every one of the commandments which he says were written by God himself: "I am the Lord thy God, which have brought thee out of the land of Egypt".[1] Then follows the second: "thou shalt have no other gods but me"; "thou shalt not make unto thee any graven image".[2] Then he adds the reason: "for I the Lord thy God am a jealous God, visiting the iniquity of the fathers upon the children unto the third generation". Then: "thou shalt not take the name of the Lord thy God in vain"; "remember the sabbath day"; "honour thy father and thy mother"; "thou shalt not commit adultery"; "thou shalt not kill"; "thou shalt not steal"; "thou shalt not bear false witness"; "thou shalt not covet anything that is thy neighbour's".[3]

Except for the command "thou shalt not worship other gods" and "remember the sabbath day", what nation is there, I ask in the name of the gods, which does not think that it ought to keep the

1. *Exodus*, 20.2-3 2. *Exodus*, 20.4 3. *Exodus*, 20.13-17

other commandments? So much so that penalties have been ordained against those who transgress them, sometimes more severe, and sometimes similar to those enacted by Moses, though they are at times more humane.

As for the commandment "thou shalt not worship other gods", to this he surely adds a terrible libel upon God. "For I am a jealous God" he says, and in another place again: "our God is a consuming fire".[1] Hence, if a man is jealous and envious you think him blameworthy, whereas if God is called jealous you think it a divine quality? How can it be reasonable to speak falsely of God in a matter that is so evident? For if he is indeed jealous, then against his will are all other gods worshipped, and against his will do all the remaining nations worship their gods. How is it, then, that he did not himself restrain them, if he is so jealous and does not wish that the others should be worshipped, but only himself? Can it be that he was not able to do so, or did he not wish, even from the beginning, to prevent the other gods from also being worshipped? The first explanation, however, is impious, that is, to suggest that he was unable; while the second is in accordance with what we ourselves do. Lay aside this nonsense and do not draw down on yourselves such terrible blasphemy. For if it is God's will that none other should be worshipped, why do you worship this spurious son of his whom he has never yet recognised or considered as his own? This I shall easily prove. You, I know not why, foist on him a counterfeit son...[2]

Nowhere[3] is God shown as angry, resentful, or wrathful, or as taking an oath, inclining first to this side, then suddenly to that, or as turned from his purpose, as Moses tells us happened in the case of Phinehas. If any of you have read the Book of Numbers, you will know what I mean. For when Phinehas had seized with his own hand and slain the man who had dedicated himself to Baal-peor, along with him the woman who had persuaded him, striking her with a shameful and most painful wound through the belly, as Moses tells us, then God is made to say: "Phinehas, son of Eleazar, son of Aaron the priest, hath turned my wrath away from the children of Israel, for he was jealous with my jealousy among them; and I consumed not the children of Israel in my jealousy".[4] What

1. *Deuteronomy*, 4.24; *Hebrews*, 12.29

2. According to Cyril's summary, Julian next reproaches the Christians for having forsaken the Greek doctrines about God

3. i.e., in the Greek accounts of the gods

4. *Numbers*, 25.11

could be more trivial than the reason for which God was falsely represented as angry by the writer of this passage? What could be more irrational, even if ten or fifteen persons, or even, let us suppose, a hundred – for they certainly will not say that there were a thousand, though let us assume that even as many persons as that ventured to transgress one of the laws laid down by God – was it right that on account of this one thousand, six hundred thousand should be utterly destroyed? For my part I think it would be better in every way to preserve one bad man along with a thousand virtuous men than to destroy the thousand together with that one...[1]

For if the anger of just one hero or unimportant daimon is hard to bear for entire countries and cities, who could have endured the wrath of so mighty a God, whether it were directed against daimons, or angels, or mankind? It is worthwhile to compare his behaviour with the mildness of Lycurgus and the forbearance of Solon, or the kindness and benevolence of the Romans towards transgressors. Observe also from what follows how far superior are our teachings to theirs. The philosophers bid us imitate the gods so far as we can, and they teach us that this imitation consists in the contemplation of realities. That this sort of study is remote from passion and is indeed based on freedom from passion, is, I suppose, evident, even without my saying it. It follows then, having been assigned to the contemplation of realities, that as we attain to freedom from passion, in so far do we become like God. Yet what sort of imitation of God is praised among the Hebrews? Anger, wrath, and fierce jealousy. For God says: "Phinehas hath turned away my wrath from the children of Israel, in that he was jealous with my jealousy among them". For God, on finding one who shared his resentment and his grief, thereupon, it would appear, laid aside his resentment. These words and others like them about God, Moses is frequently made to utter in the scripture.

Additionally, observe from what follows that God did not take thought for the Hebrews alone, but though he cared for all nations, he bestowed on the Hebrews nothing considerable or of great value, whereas on us he bestowed gifts far higher and surpassing theirs. The Egyptians, for example, as they tally the names of not a few wise men among themselves, can boast that they possess many successors of Hermes, by which I mean Hermes who

1. According to Cyril, Julian then argued that the Creator ought not to have given way so often to violent anger against and even wished to destroy his people

in his third manifestation visited Egypt.[1] The Chaldæans and Assyrians, meanwhile, can boast of the successors of Oannes[2] and Belos;[3] the Greeks can boast of countless successors of Cheiron[4] For thereafter all Hellenes were born with an aptitude for the mysteries and theology, in the very way, you observe, which the Hebrews claim as their own unique boast...[5]

Yet has God granted to you the origination of any science or philosophical study? Why, what is it? For the theory of the heavenly bodies was perfected among the Greeks, after the first observations had been made among the Barbarians in Babylon.[6] The study of geometry arose in the measurement of the land in Egypt, and from this grew to its present importance. Arithmetic began with the Phoenician merchants, and among the Greeks over the course of time acquired the aspect of a regular science. These three the Greeks combined with music into one science, for they connected astronomy with geometry and adapted arithmetic to both, perceiving the principle of harmony within it. Hence they laid down the rules for their music, since they had discovered for the laws of harmony, with reference to the sense of hearing, an agreement that was infallible, or something very near to it.[7]

Need I list their names man by man, or under their professions? By which I mean, either the individual men, such as Plato, Socrates, Aristeides, Cimon, Thales, Lycurgus, Agesilaus, Archidamus, or should I speak instead of the class of philosophers, of generals, of artists, of lawgivers? For it will be found that even the most wicked and most brutal of the generals behaved more mildly to the greatest offenders than Moses did to those who had done no wrong. And of what monarchy shall I report to you? Shall it be that of Perseus, or Æacus, or Minos of Crete, who purified the sea of pirates, and expelled and drove out the Barbarians as far as Syria and Sicily, advancing in both directions the frontiers of his realm,

1. A reference to Hermes Trismegistus, "thrice greatest Hermes", whom the Greeks identified with the Egyptian god Thoth. The Neo-Platonists ascribed certain mystic writings to this legendary being and regarded him as a sage

2. A Babylonian fish-god described by Berosus in his *History of Babylonia*. He was supposed to have taught the Chaldæans the arts of civilisation

3. This is the Greek version of the Assyrian *bil* ("lord"), the Baal of the Bible

4. The Centaur who taught Achilles

5. According to Cyril's summary, Julian then ridicules David and Samson and says that they were not really brave warriors, but far inferior to the Hellenes and Egyptians, and their dominion was very limited

6. The Hellenes perfected the astronomy of the Chaldæans and Egyptians

7. They had discovered the laws of musical intervals

ruling not only over the islands but also over the dwellers along the coasts? He, dividing with his brother Rhadamanthus, not indeed the earth, but the care of mankind, laid down the laws as he received them from Zeus, but left to Rhadamanthus to fill the part of judge...[1]

After her[2] founding, when many wars encompassed her, she won and prevailed in them all; and thereafter she increased in size relative to her very dangers and need for greater security. Then Zeus[3] set over her the great philosopher Numa.[4] This, of course, was the excellent and upright Numa, who dwelt in deserted groves and ever communed with the gods in the pure thoughts of his own heart...it was he who established most of the laws concerning temple worship. These blessings, derived from a divine possession and inspiration which proceeded both from the Sibyl and others who at that time uttered oracles in their native tongue, were manifestly bestowed on the city by Zeus. As to the shield which fell from the clouds,[5] and the head which appeared on the hill,[6] from which, I believe, the seat of mighty Zeus received its name, are we to reckon these among the very highest or among secondary gifts? And yet, you misguided men, though there is preserved among us that weapon which flew down from heaven, which mighty Zeus or father Ares sent down to give us a pledge, not in word but in deed, that he will forever hold his shield before our city, you have ceased to adore and reverence it, but you adore instead the wood of the cross, drawing its likeness on your foreheads and engraving it on your house-fronts.

Would not any man be justified in detesting the more intelligent among you, or pitying the more foolish, who, by following you, have sunk to such depths of ruin that they have abandoned the everlasting gods and have gone over to the corpse of the Judæan...for I say nothing about the Mysteries of the Mother of the Gods, and I admire Marius...for the spirit that comes to men from

1. According to Cyril, Julian then related stories about Minos, the myth of Dardanus, the account of Æneas' journey to Italy, and the founding of Rome

2. i.e., Rome 3. i.e., Jupiter

4. Numa Pompilius, a legendary king who succeeded Romulus; various portents manifested the favour of the gods towards Numa

5. A small shield, *ancile*, on whose preservation the power of Rome was claimed to depend, was said to have fallen from the sky in Numa's reign

6. When the foundations were dug for the temple of Jupiter, a human head, *caput*, was found; this was regarded as an omen, and hence the Capitoline Hill received its name; cf. Livy, 1.55

the gods is present, but seldom and in few; it is not easy for every man to share in it, nor at every time. So it is that the prophetic spirit has ceased among the Hebrews, nor is it maintained among the Egyptians, either, down to the present. We even see that the indigenous oracles[1] of Greece have similarly fallen silent and yielded to the course of time. At this, our gracious lord and father, Zeus, took thought, and, that we might not be wholly deprived of communion with the gods, has granted us through the sacred arts[2] a means of enquiry by which we may obtain the aid that suffices for our needs.

I had almost forgotten the greatest of the gifts of Helios and Zeus. Though naturally I kept it for the last. In truth, it is not exclusive to us Romans only, but we share it, I believe, with the Greeks, our kinsmen. I refer to how Zeus engendered Asclepius from himself among the intelligible gods, and through the life of generative Helios he revealed him to the world. Asclepius, having made his visitation to earth from the sky, appeared singly at Epidaurus in the form of a man; thereafter he multiplied himself, and by his visitations stretched out over the whole land his saving right hand. He came to Pergamon, to Ionia, to Tarentum afterwards, and later he came to Rome. He travelled to Cos and thence to Ægæ. Next, he became present everywhere on land and sea. He visits not one of us separately, and yet he sets right souls that are lost and bodies that are sick.

Yet what great gift of this sort do the Hebrews boast of as bestowed on them by God, the people who have persuaded you to desert to them? If you had at any rate paid heed to their teachings, you would not have fared altogether ill, and though worse than you did before, when you were with us, still your condition would have been bearable and supportable. For you would be worshipping one god instead of many, not a man, or rather many wretched men;[3] and though you would be following a law that is harsh, containing much that is savage and barbarous, instead of our mild and humane laws, not to mention the other respects in which you would be inferior to us, you would at least be more holy and pure than in your current forms of worship. Now, however, it has come to pass that like leeches you have sucked the worst blood from that source and left the purer. For Jesus, who won over the least worthy of you, has been known by name for little more than three hundred years.

1. Julian is likely referring to the oracle of Delphi which he had sought to restore
2. i.e. practices such as augury and *haruspicina* 3. i.e., the martyrs

During his lifetime, he accomplished nothing worth hearing of, unless anyone thinks that to heal crooked and blind men, or to exorcise those who were under the influence of daimons in villages such as Bethsaida and Bethany can be classed as a mighty achievement.

As for purity of life, you do not know whether he so much as mentioned it, yet you emulate the rages and the bitterness of the Jews, overturning temples and altars, slaughtering not only those of us who remained true to the teachings of their fathers, but also men who were as much astray as yourselves, heretics, because they did not wail over the corpse[1] in the same fashion as yourselves. These are rather your own doings, for nowhere did either Jesus or Paul hand down to you such commands. The reason for this is that they never even imagined that you would one day attain to such power as you have. They were content if they could delude maidservants and slaves, and through them the women, and men like Cornelius[2] and Sergius.[3] If you can show me that even one of these men is mentioned by the well-known writers of that time – these events happened during the reign of Tiberius or Claudius – then you may consider that I speak falsely about all matters.

I know not whence I was, as it were, inspired to utter these remarks. Nevertheless, let us return to the point at which I digressed, when I asked: "why were you so ungrateful to our gods as to abandon them for the Jews?" Was it because the gods granted the sovereign power to Rome, permitting the Jews to be free for a short time only, and then to forever be enslaved and outsiders? Look at Abraham: was he not an alien in a strange land? And Jacob: was he not a slave, first in Syria, then after that in Palestine, and in his old age in Egypt? Does not Moses say that he led them forth from the house of bondage out of Egypt "with a stretched out arm"?[4] After their sojourn in Palestine, did they not change their fortunes more frequently than observers say the chameleon changes its colour, at one moment subject to the judges,[5] then enslaved to foreign races the next? As for when they began to be governed by kings, well, let me for the present postpone asking how they were governed. For, as the Scripture tells us,[6] God did not willingly allow them to have kings, but only when constrained by them, and after protesting to them beforehand that they would thus be governed ill. Still, they did at any rate inhabit their own

1. Christ, or a martyr 2. *Acts*, 10 3. *Acts*, 13
4. *Exodus*, 6.6 5. *Judges*, 12.16 6. 1 *Samuel*, 8

country and tilled it for a little over three hundred years. After that they were enslaved first to the Assyrians, then to the Medes, later to the Persians, and now at last to ourselves. Even Jesus, who was proclaimed among you, was one of Cæsar's subjects. If you do not believe me, I will prove it a little later, or rather, let me simply assert it now. You admit, after all, that with his father and mother he registered his name in the governorship of Cyrenius.[1]

When he became a man what benefits did he confer on his own kinsfolk? Ah, the Galilæans answer, the Jews refused to hearken unto Jesus. What? How was it that this hardhearted[2] and stiff-necked people hearkened unto Moses, but Jesus, who commanded the spirits[3] and walked upon the sea, drove out malevolent daimons and, as you yourselves assert, made the heavens and the earth – for not one of his disciples ventured to say this concerning him, save only John, and he did not say it clearly or distinctly; still, let us at any rate admit that he said it – could not this Jesus change the dispositions of his own friends and kinsfolk to the end that he might save them?

Regardless, I will consider this again shortly when I begin to examine specifically the miracle-working and fabrication of the gospels. For now, answer me this: is it better to be continuously free and rule over the greater part of the earth and the sea for two thousand whole years, or to be enslaved and to live in obedience to the will of others? No man is so lacking in self-respect as to choose the latter by preference. Again, will anyone think that victory in war is less desirable than defeat? Who is so stupid? If this that I assert is the truth, then, point out to me among the Hebrews a single general like Alexander or Cæsar! You have no such man. Indeed, by the gods, I am well aware that I am insulting these heroes by the question, but I mentioned them because they are well known. For the generals who are inferior to them are unknown to the multitude, and yet every one of them deserves more admiration than all the generals put together whom the Jews have had.

Further, as regards the constitution of the state and the fashion of the law-courts, the administration of cities and the excellence of the laws, progress in learning and the cultivation of the arts, were not all these things in a miserable and barbarous state among the Hebrews? And yet the wretched Eusebius[4] will have it that poems in hexameters are to be found even among them, and constructs a

1. *Luke*, 2.2 2. *Ezekiel*, 3.7 3. *Mark*, 1.27

4. Eusebius, *Præparatio Evangelica*, 11.5.5

claim that the study of logic exists among the Hebrews on the basis that he has heard among the Greeks the word they use for logic. What kind of healing art has ever appeared among the Hebrews, like that of Hippocrates among the Greeks, and of certain other schools that came after him?

Is their "wisest" man Solomon at all comparable with Phocylides, Theognis, or Isocrates among the Greeks? Certainly not. At least, if one were to compare the exhortations of Isocrates with Solomon's proverbs, you would, I am very sure, find that the son of Theodoras is superior to their "wisest" king. "But" they answer "Solomon was also proficient in the secret cult of God." What then? Did not this Solomon serve our gods also, deluded by his wife, as they assert?[1] What great virtue! What wealth of wisdom! He could not rise above pleasure and so the arguments of a woman led him astray! If, then, he was deluded by a woman, do not call this man wise. If, however, you are convinced that he was wise, do not believe that he was deluded by a woman, but that, trusting to his own judgement and intelligence, and the teaching that he received from the God who had been revealed to him, he served the other gods also. For envy and jealousy do not come near even the most virtuous men, and much more are they remote from angels and gods. Yet you concern yourselves with incomplete and partial powers,[2] which if anyone should call daimonic he does not err. For in them are pride and vanity, but in the gods there is nothing of the sort.

If the reading of your own scriptures is sufficient for you, why do you nibble at the learning of the Greeks? Though it was better to keep men away from such learning than from the eating of sacrificial meat. For by that, as even Paul says,[3] he who eats thereof is not harmed, but the conscience of the brother who sees him might be offended, according to you, O most wise and arrogant men. This learning of ours, however, has caused every noble being that nature has produced among you to abandon impiety. Accordingly, everyone who possessed even a small fraction of innate virtue has speedily abandoned your godlessness. It would, therefore, have been better for you to keep men from learning, rather than from sacrificial meats. Yet you yourselves know, it seems to me, the very different effect on the intelligence of your writings as compared with ours; that from studying yours, no man could

1. *1 Kings*, 11.4; 3.1

2. Julian seems to be referring to the saints

3. *1 Corinthians*, 8.7-13

attain to excellence or even to ordinary goodness, whereas from studying ours, every man would become better than before, even if he were altogether without natural fitness. Though when a man is naturally well endowed, and in addition receives the education of our literature, he becomes in fact a gift of the gods to mankind, either by kindling the light of knowledge, or by founding some form of political constitution; by routing numbers of his country's foes, or even by travelling far over the earth and far by sea, and thereby proving himself a man of heroic mould...[1]

Now this would be clear proof: select children from among you then train and educate them in your scriptures, and if, when they come to manhood, they prove to have nobler qualities than slaves, then you may believe that I am talking nonsense and am suffering from spite. Yet you are so misguided and foolish that you regard those chronicles of yours as divinely inspired, though by their help no man could ever become wiser, braver, or better than he was before; while, on the other hand, writings by whose aid men can acquire courage, wisdom, and justice, these you ascribe to Satan and to those who serve Satan!

Asclepius heals our bodies; the Muses with the aid of Asclepius, Apollo, and Hermes, the god of eloquence, train our souls; Ares fights for us in war, with Enyo also; Hephæstus apportions and administers the crafts; and Athena, the Motherless Maiden, with the aid of Zeus, presides over them all. Consider, then, whether we are not superior to you in every single one of these things, by which I mean in the arts, in wisdom, and intelligence. This is true, whether you consider the useful arts, or the imitative arts whose end is beauty, such as the sculptor's art, painting, or household management, and the art of healing derived from Asclepius, whose oracles are found everywhere on earth, the god granting to us a share in them perpetually. At any rate, when I have been unwell, Asclepius has often cured me by prescribing remedies – of this Zeus is witness. Therefore, if we who have not given ourselves over to the spirit of apostasy fare better than you in soul, body, and external affairs, why do you abandon these teachings of ours and go over to those others?

Moreover, why is it that you do not abide even by the traditions of the Hebrews, or accept the law which God has given to them? Indeed, you have forsaken their teaching even more than ours,

1. Some words are missing. The summary of Cyril suggests that Julian next attacked the Old Testament and ridiculed it because of its language

abandoning the religion of your forefathers and giving yourselves over to the predictions of the prophets. For if any man should wish to examine the truth concerning you, he will find that your impiety is compounded of the rashness of the Jews, and the indifference and vulgarity of the Gentiles. From both sides you have drawn what is by no means their best, but rather their inferior teaching, and so have made for yourselves a border[1] of wickedness.

For the Hebrews have precise laws concerning religious worship, as well as countless sacred things and observances which demand the priestly life and profession. Though their lawgiver forbade them to serve all the gods save only that one, whose "portion is Jacob, and Israel an allotment of his inheritance",[2] he did not, perhaps, say this only, but I suspect also added: "thou shalt not revile the gods".[3] Yet the shamelessness and audacity of later generations, desiring to root out all reverence from the mass of the people, has held the view that blasphemy ought to accompany the neglect of worship. This, in fact, is the only thing that you have drawn from this source, for in all other respects you and the Jews have nothing in common. Indeed, it is from the novel teaching of the Hebrews that you have seized upon this blasphemy of the gods who are honoured among us. While the reverence for every higher nature, characteristic of our religious worship, combined with the love of the traditions of our forefathers, you have cast off, and have acquired only the habit of eating all things "even as the green herb". To tell the truth, however, you have taken pride in outdoing our vulgarity (this, I believe, is something which comes to pass among all nations eventually), thinking that you must adapt your ways to the lives of the baser sort, such as pedlars, tax-collectors, dancers, and libertines.

That not only the Galilæans of our day, but also those of the earliest time who were the first to receive the teaching from Paul, were men of this sort is evident from the testimony of Paul himself in a letter addressed to them. For unless he actually knew that they had committed all these disgraceful acts, he was not, I think, so impudent as to write to those men concerning their conduct in language for which, even though in the same letter he included as many eulogies of them, he ought to have blushed. This would be true even if those eulogies were deserved, while if they were false and fabricated, then he ought to have sunk into the ground

1. παρυφή, Latin *clavus*, is the woven border of a garment

2. cf. *Deuteronomy*, 32.9 3. *Exodus*, 22.28

to escape seeming to behave with wanton flattery and slavish adulation. Regardless, the following are the very words that Paul wrote concerning those who had heard his teaching, and were addressed to the men themselves: "be not deceived: neither idolaters, nor adulterers, nor effeminates, nor abusers of themselves with men, nor thieves, nor covetous, nor drunkards, nor revilers, nor extortioners, shall inherit the kingdom of God. And of this ye are not ignorant, brethren, that such were you also; but ye washed yourselves, but ye were sanctified in the name of Jesus Christ".[1]

Do you see that he says that these men, too, had been of such sort, but that they "had been sanctified" and "had been washed" as if water, finding its way to the soul, were able to cleanse, thoroughly purge, and instil knowledge. Further, as baptism does not take away his leprosy from the leper, or scabs, pimples, warts, gout, dysentery, dropsy, whitlow, or in fact any disorder of the body, great or small, then shall it do away with adultery and theft, and in short all the transgressions of the soul?...[2]

Now, since the Galilæans say that, though they are different from the Jews, they are still, precisely speaking, Israelites in accordance with their prophets, and that they obey Moses above all, alongside the prophets who in Judæa succeeded him, let us see in what respect they chiefly agree with those prophets. Let us begin with the teaching of Moses, who himself also, as they claim, foretold the birth of Jesus that was to be. Moses, then, not once, or twice, or thrice, but very many times says that men ought to honour one God only, and in fact names him the Highest; though that they ought to honour any other god he nowhere says. He speaks of angels and lords, and moreover of several gods, but from these he chooses the first and does not assume any god as second, either like or unlike him, such as you have invented. If among you, perchance, you possess a single utterance of Moses with respect to this, you ought to produce it. For the words "a prophet shall the Lord your God raise up unto you of your brethren, like unto me; to him shall ye hearken"[3] were certainly not said of the son of Mary. And even though, to please you, one should concede that they were said of him, Moses states that the prophet will be like him and not like God; a prophet like himself and born of men, not of a god. Further, the words "the sceptre shall not depart from Judah, nor a leader from his loins"[1] were most certainly not said of the son of Mary, but

1. 1 *Corinthians*, 6.9-11 2. A short lacuna 3. *Acts*, 3.22; *Deuteronomy*, 18.18

of the royal house of David, which, you observe, came to an end with King Zedekiah.

While certainly the Scripture can be interpreted in two ways when it says "until there comes what is reserved for him", you have wrongly interpreted it as "until he comes for whom it is reserved".[2] Nevertheless, it is very clear that not one of these sayings relates to Jesus, for he is not even from Judah. How could he be when according to you he was not born of Joseph but of the Holy Spirit? For though in your genealogies you trace Joseph back to Judah, you could not invent even this plausibly. For Matthew and Luke are refuted by the fact that they disagree concerning his genealogy.[3] As I intend to examine closely the truth of this matter in my second book, however, I shall leave it until then.[4] All the same, if one grants that he really is "a sceptre from Judah" then he is not "God born of God", as you are in the habit of saying, nor is it true that "all things were made by him; and without him was not any thing made".[5] But, say you, we are told in the Book of Numbers also: "there shall arise a star out of Jacob, and a man out of Israel".[6] It is certainly clear that this relates to David and to his descendants, for David was a son of Jesse.

If you should try to prove anything from these writings, show me a single saying that you have drawn from that source whence I have drawn very many. That Moses believed in one God, the God of Israel, he says in Deuteronomy: "so that thou mightest know that the Lord thy God he is one God; and there is none else beside him".[7] Moreover, he says besides: "and lay it to thine heart that this the Lord thy God is God in the heaven above and upon the earth beneath, and there is none else".[8] And again: "hear, O Israel: the Lord our God is one Lord".[9] Once more: "see that I am and there is no God save me."[10] These, then, are the words of Moses when he insists that there is only one God. Perhaps the Galilæans will reply: "but we do not assert that there are two gods or three". Yet I will show that they do assert this also, and I call John to witness, who says: "in the beginning was the Word, and the Word was with God, and the Word was God".[10] You see that the Word is said to be with God? Now whether this is he who was born of Mary or someone

1. *Genesis*, 49.10 2. Or "whose it is"; Julian follows the Septuagint

3. cf. *Matthew*, 1.1-17; *Luke*, 3.23-38

4. Cyril's reply to this part of Julian's Second Book is lost, so that the Emperor's more detailed discussion cannot be reconstructed

5. *John*, 1.3 6. *Numbers*, 24.17 7. *Deuteronomy*, 4.35 8. ibid. 4.39

9. ibid. 6.4 10. ibid. 32.39 11. *John*, 1.1

else – that I may answer Photinus[1] at the same time – this now makes no difference. Indeed, I leave the dispute to you; but it is enough to bring forward the evidence that he says "with God" and "in the beginning". How, then, does this agree with the teachings of Moses?

"But" say the Galilæans "it agrees with the teachings of Isaiah. For Isaiah says, 'behold the virgin shall conceive and bear a son'."[2] Granted this is said about a god, though it is by no means so stated; for a married woman who before her conception had lain with her husband was no virgin – but let us concede that it is said about her – does Isaiah anywhere say that a god will be born of the virgin? So why do you not cease to call Mary the mother of God, if Isaiah nowhere says that he who is born of the virgin is the "only begotten Son of God"[3] and "the firstborn of all creation"?[4] As for the saying of John: "all things were made by him; and without him was not any thing made that was made"[5] – can anyone point this out among the utterances of the prophets? Listen, however, to the sayings that I point out to you from those same prophets, one after another: "O Lord our God, make us thine; we know none other beside thee".[6] While Hezekiah the king has been represented by them as praying as follows: "O Lord God of Israel, that sittest upon the Cherubim, thou art God, even thou alone".[7] Does he leave any place for the second god? Yet if, as you believe, the Word is God born of God and proceeded from the substance of the Father, why do you say that the virgin is the mother of God? For how could she bear a god since she is, according to you, a human being? Moreover, when God declares plainly "I am he, and there is none that can deliver beside me",[8] do you dare to call her son saviour?

That Moses refers to the angels as gods you may hear from his own words: "the sons of God saw the daughters of men that they were fair; and they took them wives of all which they chose".[9] While a little further on: "after that, when the sons of God came in unto the daughters of men, and they bare children to them, the same became the giants which were of old, the men of renown".[10] That he means the angels is evident, and this has not been foisted on him from without, but it is clear also from his saying that not men but giants were born from them. For it is clear that if he had

1. The heretical bishop Photinus of Sirmium was tried under Constantius before the synod at Mediolanum in 351 for denying the divinity of Christ

2. *Isaiah*, 7.14 3. *John*, 1.18 4. *Colossians*, 1.15 5. *John*, 1.3 6. *Isaiah*, 26.13 7. *Isaiah*, 37.16 8. *Deuteronomy*, 32.39 9. *Genesis*, 6.2 10. *Genesis*, 6.4

thought that men and not beings of some higher and more powerful nature were their fathers, he would not have said that the giants were their offspring. For it seems to me that he declared that the race of giants arose from the mixture of mortal and immortal. Again, when Moses speaks of many sons of God and calls them not men but angels, would he not then have revealed to mankind, if he had known thereof, God the "only begotten Word", or a son of God, or however you title him?

Is it, then, because he did not think this of great importance that he says concerning Israel: "Israel is my firstborn son"?[1] Why did not Moses say this about Jesus also? He taught that there was only one God, but that he had many sons who divided the nations among themselves. Yet the Word as firstborn son of God, or as a God, or any of those fictions which have been invented by you since, he neither knew at all, nor taught openly thereof. You have now heard Moses himself and the other prophets. Moses, therefore, utters many sayings to the following effect and in many places: "thou shalt fear the Lord thy God and him only shalt thou serve".[2] How, then, has it been handed down in the Gospels that Jesus commanded "go ye therefore and teach all nations, baptising them in the name of the Father, and of the Son, and of the Holy Ghost"[3] if they were not intended to serve him also? Your beliefs are also in harmony with these commands, when along with the Father you pay divine honours to the son...[4]

Observe again how much Moses says about the deities that avert evil: "and he shall take two he-goats of the goats for a sin-offering, and one ram for a burnt offering. And Aaron shall bring also his bullock of the sin-offering, which is for himself, and make an atonement for himself and for his house. And he shall take the two goats and present them before the Lord at the door of the tabernacle of the covenant. And Aaron shall cast lots upon the two goats; one lot for the Lord and the other lot for the scape-goat"[5] so as to send him forth, says Moses, as a scape-goat, and let him loose into the wilderness. Thus is sent forth the goat that is sent as a scape-goat. Of the second goat, then, Moses says: "then shall he kill the goat of the sin-offering that is for the people before the Lord, and bring his blood within the veil, and shall sprinkle the blood upon the altar-step,[6] and shall make an atonement for the holy place, because of the uncleanness of the children of Israel and

1. *Exodus*, 4.22 2. *Deuteronomy*, 6.13 3. *Matthew*, 28.19 4. A short lacuna
5. cf. *Leviticus*, 16.5-8 6. "Mercy-seat"

because of their transgressions in all their sins".[1] Accordingly, it is evident from what has been said that Moses knew the various methods of sacrifice. Further, to show that he did not think them impure as you do, listen again to his own words: "but the soul that eateth of the flesh of the sacrifice of peace-offerings that pertain unto the Lord, having his uncleanness upon him, even that soul shall be cut off from his people".[2] So cautious is Moses himself with regard to the eating of the flesh of sacrifice.

Now, however, I had better remind you of what I said earlier, on account of my having said all this. Why is it, I repeat, that after deserting us you do not accept the law of the Jews or abide by the sayings of Moses? No doubt some sharp-sighted person will answer: "the Jews do not sacrifice either". Yet I will convict him of being terribly dull-sighted, for in the first place I reply that neither do you observe any of the other customs observed by the Jews; secondly, that the Jews do sacrifice in their own houses, and even to this day everything that they eat is consecrated. Moreover, they pray before sacrificing, and give the right shoulder to the priests as the first fruits. Since they have been deprived of their temple, however, or, as they are accustomed to call it, their holy place, they are prevented from offering the first fruits of the sacrifice to God. Why, then, do you not sacrifice, given that you have invented your new kind of sacrifice and do not need Jerusalem at all? Though it was superfluous to ask you this question, since I said the same thing at the beginning when I wished to show that the Jews agree with the Gentiles, except that they believe in only one God. That is indeed unique to them and strange to us; for all the rest we have, in a manner, in common with them – temples, sanctuaries, altars, purifications, and certain precepts. With respect to these, we differ from one another either slightly or not at all...[3]

Why in your diet are you not as pure as the Jews, and why do you say that we ought to eat everything "even as the green herb", putting your faith in Peter, because, as the Galilæans say, he declared: "what God hath cleansed, that make not thou common"?[4] What proof is there of this, that of old God held certain things abominable, but now has made them clean? For Moses, when he is laying down the law concerning four-footed things, says that "whatsoever parteth the hoof and is cloven-footed

1. *Leviticus*, 16.15 2. *Leviticus*, 7.20

3. According to Cyril, Julian then says that the Christians in worshipping not one or many gods, but three, have strayed from both Jewish and Hellenic teaching

4. *Acts*, 10.15

and cheweth the cud"[1] is pure, but that which is not of this sort is impure. If, therefore, as per the vision of Peter, the pig has now taken to chewing the cud, then let us obey Peter, for it is verily a miracle if it has taken to that habit. If, on the other hand, he spoke falsely when he claimed to have seen this revelation – to use your own way of speaking – in the house of the tanner, why are we so ready to believe him in such important matters? Was it so hard a thing that Moses enjoined on you when, besides the flesh of swine, he forbade you to eat winged things and things that dwell in the sea, declaring to you that besides the flesh of swine these also had been cast out by God and shown to be impure?

Why do I discuss at length these teachings of theirs,[2] when we may easily see whether they have any validity? They assert that God, after the earlier law, appointed the second. For, say they, the former arose with a view to a certain occasion and was circumscribed by definite periods of time, but this later law was revealed because the law of Moses was circumscribed by time and place. That they say this falsely I will clearly show by quoting from the books of Moses – not merely ten but ten thousand passages as evidence – where he says that the law is for all time. Listen, then, to a passage from Exodus: "and this day shall be unto you for a memorial; and ye shall keep it a feast to the Lord throughout your generations; ye shall keep it a feast by an ordinance forever; the first day shall ye put away leaven out of your houses..."[3]

Many passages to the same effect are still left, but, on account of their number, I shall refrain from citing them to prove that the law of Moses was to last for all time. Will you, by contrast, point out to me where there is any statement by Moses of what was later rashly uttered by Paul, by which I mean that "Christ is the end of the law".[4] Where does God announce to the Hebrews a second law besides that which was established? Nowhere does it occur, not even a revision of the established law. For listen again to the words of Moses: "Ye shall not add unto the word which I command you, neither shall ye diminish aught from it. Keep the commandments of the Lord your God which I command you this day".[5] Further: "cursed be every man who does not abide by them all".[6] Yet you have thought it a slight thing to diminish and add to that which was written in the law; and to transgress it completely you have

1. *Leviticus*, 11.13 2. i.e., of the Christians

3. *Exodus*, 12.14; Julian went on to quote several more passages, but these are lost

4. *Romans*, 10.14 5. *Deuteronomy*, 4.2 6. *Deuteronomy*, 27.26

thought yourselves to be in every way more courageous and high-souled, because you do not look to the truth but to that which will persuade all men.[1]

So misguided are you, however, that you have not even remained faithful to the teachings that were handed down to you by the apostles. These, too, have been altered by those who came after so as to be worse and more ungodly. At any rate, neither Paul, nor Matthew, nor Luke, nor Mark ventured to call Jesus God. Yet the worthy John, having perceived that a great number of people in many of the towns of Greece and Italy had already been infected by this disease,[2] and because he heard, I believe, that even the tombs of Peter and Paul were being worshipped – secretly, it is true, but still he did hear this – he, I say, was the first to venture to call Jesus God. After he had spoken briefly about John the Baptist, he referred again to the Word which he was proclaiming, and said: "and the Word was made flesh, and dwelt among us".[3] Quite how, he does not say, because he was doubtless ashamed. Though nowhere does he refer to him as either Jesus or Christ, so long as he calls him God and the Word. Nevertheless, he does, as it were, insensibly and secretly steal away our ears, saying that John the Baptist bore this witness on behalf of Jesus Christ, that in very truth it is he whom we must believe to be God the Word.

That John says this concerning Jesus Christ, I for my part do not deny. Yet certain of the impious think that Jesus Christ is quite distinct from the Word that was proclaimed by John. That, however, is not the case. For he whom John himself calls God the Word, this is he who was recognised by John the Baptist to be Jesus Christ. Observe accordingly how cautiously, how quietly and insensibly he introduces into the drama the crowning word of his impiety; and he is so rascally and deceitful that he rears his head once more to add: "no man hath seen God at any time; the only begotten Son which is in the bosom of the Father, he hath declared him".[4] Then is this only begotten Son which is in the bosom of the Father the same God who is the Word and became flesh? If, moreover, as I think, it is indeed he, then you have certainly beheld God. For "he dwelt among you, and ye beheld his glory".[5] Why, then, do you add to this that "no man hath seen God at any time"?

---

1. According to Cyril, Julian next ridicules Peter and calls him a hypocrite, convicted by Paul of living at once according to Greek, then to Hebrew, customs

2. i.e., Christianity and the abandoning of Hellenism 3. *John*, 1.14

4. *John*, 1.18 5. *John*, 1.19

For you have certainly seen, if not God the Father, still God who is the Word. Then again, if the only begotten Son is one person and the God who is the Word another, as I have heard from some among you, then it appears that not even John made that rash statement.[1]

Nonetheless, this baneful doctrine did originate with John. Though who could detest, as they deserve, all those doctrines that you have invented as a sequel, when you keep adding many corpses newly dead to the corpse of long ago?[2] You have filled the whole world with tombs and sepulchres, yet in your scriptures it is nowhere said that you must grovel among tombs[3] and pay them honour. Indeed, you have gone so far in iniquity that you think you need not listen even to the words of Jesus of Nazareth on this matter. Listen, then, to what he says about sepulchres: "woe unto you, scribes and Pharisees, hypocrites! for ye are like unto whited sepulchres; outward the tomb appears beautiful, but within it is full of dead men's bones, and of all uncleanness".[4] If Jesus said that sepulchres are full of uncleanness, how can you invoke God at them?...[5]

Why, then, since this is so, do you grovel among tombs? Do you wish to hear the reason? It is not I who will tell you, but the prophet Isaiah: "they lodge among tombs and in caves for the sake of dream visions".[6] You will observe, then, how ancient this work of witchcraft – namely sleeping among tombs for the sake of dream visions – was among the Jews. In truth, it is likely that your apostles, after their teacher's death, practised this and handed it down to you from the beginning. I refer here to those who first adopted your faith, and how they themselves performed their spells more skilfully than you do, displaying openly to those who came after them the places in which they performed this witchcraft and abomination.

You, however, though you practise that which God from the first abhorred, as he showed through Moses and the prophets, have

---

1. i.e., that Jesus was God

2. For the collection of the "bones and skulls of criminals" and the apotheosis of the martyrs as it struck a contemporary Pagan, cf. Eunapius, *Lives*, pg. 424

3. cf. Plato, *Phædo*, 81; Eunapius, *Lives*, says of this practice: "they collected the bones and skulls of criminals who had been put to death for numerous crimes, men whom the law courts of the city had condemned to punishment, made them out to be gods, haunted their sepulchres, and thought that they became better by defiling themselves at their graves"

4. *Matthew*, 23.27

5. According to Cyril, Julian quoted *Matthew*, 8.21: "let the dead bury their dead"

6. *Isaiah*, 65.4

refused nevertheless to sacrifice at the altar or make offerings. "Yes" say the Galilæans "because fire will not descend to consume the sacrifices as in the case of Moses". Only once, I answer, did this happen in the case of Moses;[1] and again after many years in the case of Elijah the Tishbite.[2] For I will prove in a few words that Moses himself thought that it was necessary to bring fire from outside for the sacrifice, and, even before him, Abraham the patriarch as well...[3]

This, moreover, is not the only instance, for when the sons of Adam also offered first fruits to God, the scripture says: "and the Lord had respect unto Abel and to his offerings; but unto Cain and to his offerings he had not respect. And Cain was very wrath, and his countenance fell. And the Lord God said unto Cain, Why art thou wrath? And why is thy countenance fallen? Is it not so, if thou offerest rightly, but dost not cut in pieces rightly, thou hast sinned?"[4] Do you then desire to hear also what their offerings were? "And at the end of days it came to pass that Cain brought of the fruits of the ground an offering unto the Lord. And Abel, he also brought of the firstlings of his flock and of the fat thereof."[5]

You see, say the Galilæans, it was not the sacrifice but the division thereof that God disapproved when he said to Cain: "if thou offerest rightly, but dost not cut in pieces rightly, hast thou not sinned?" This is what one of your most learned bishops[6] told me. Yet in the first place he was deceiving himself, as well as other men besides. For when I asked him in what way the division was blameworthy, he did not know how to get out of it, or how to offer me even a formal explanation. Therefore, when I saw that he was having great difficulty, I said: "God rightly disapproved the thing you speak of. For the zeal of the two men was equal, in that they both thought that they ought to offer up gifts and sacrifices to God. But in the matter of their division one of them hit the mark and the other fell short of it. How, and in what manner? Why, since of things on the earth some have life and others are lifeless, and those that have life are more precious than those that are lifeless to the living God, who is also the cause of life, inasmuch as they also have a share of life and have a soul more akin to his – for this reason God was more graciously inclined to him who offered a perfect sacrifice".

1. *Leviticus*, 9.24 2. *1 Kings*, 18.38

3. Cyril says that Julian recounted the sacrifice of Isaac by Abraham in *Genesis*, 22

4. *Genesis*, 4.4-7 5. *Genesis*, 4.3-4 6. This was perhaps Ætius

Now, I must take up this other point and ask them: why, pray tell, do you not practise circumcision? "Paul" they answer "said that circumcision of the heart but not of the flesh was granted unto Abraham because he believed.[1] For it was not now of the flesh that he spoke, and we ought to believe the pious words that were proclaimed by him and by Peter." On the other hand, hear again that God is said to have given circumcision of the flesh to Abraham for a covenant and a sign: "this is my covenant which ye shall keep, between me and thee, and thy seed after thee in their generations. Ye shall circumcise the flesh of your foreskin, and it shall be in token of a covenant betwixt me and thee, and betwixt me and thy seed..."[2] Therefore, when he[3] has undoubtedly taught that it is proper to observe the law, and threatened with punishment those who transgress one commandment, what manner of defending yourselves will you devise, you who have transgressed them all without exception? For either Jesus will be found to speak falsely, or rather you will be found in all respects and in every way to have failed to preserve the law. "The circumcision shall be of thy flesh" says Moses.[4] Yet the Galilæans do not heed him, and they say: "we circumcise our hearts". By all means. For there is among you no ill-doer, no reprobate; so thoroughly do you circumcise your hearts. They say: "we cannot observe the rule of unleavened bread or keep the Passover, for on our behalf Christ was sacrificed once and for all". Very well! Then did he forbid you to eat unleavened bread?

I myself, as I call the gods to witness, am one of those who avoid keeping their festivals with the Jews. Nevertheless, I always pay respect to the God of Abraham, Isaac, and Jacob,[5] who being themselves Chaldæans, of a sacred race, skilled in theurgy, had learned the practice of circumcision while they travelled as strangers among the Egyptians. They revered a God who was ever favourable to me and those who worshipped him as Abraham did, for he is a very great and powerful God, but he has nothing to do with you. For you do not imitate Abraham by erecting altars to him, or by building altars of sacrifice and worshipping him as Abraham did with offerings. For Abraham used to sacrifice even as we Hellenes do, always and continually, using as he did the method

1. cf. *Romans*, 4.11; 2.29

2. cf. *Genesis*, 17.10; according to Cyril, Julian then quoted *Matthew*, 5.17, 19 to prove that Christ did not come to destroy the law but uphold it

3. Christ 4. cf. *Genesis*, 17.13

5. cf. *Letter 20*, where Julian says that the Hebrew god "is worshipped by us under other names". It is unclear to which Pagan god(s) Julian is referring

of divination from shooting stars. This is probably also a Hellenic custom. For higher things, however, he augured from the flight of birds. While he also possessed a steward of his house who set signs for himself.[1] If one of you doubts this, the very words which were uttered by Moses concerning it will show him clearly:

> "after these sayings the word of the Lord came unto Abraham in a vision of the night, sayings Fear not, Abraham: I am thy shield. Thy reward shall be exceeding great. And Abraham said. Lord God what wilt thou give me? For I go childless, and the son of Masek the slave woman will be my heir. And straightaway the word of the Lord came unto him saying, this man shall not be thine heir, but he that shall come forth from thee shall be thine heir. And he brought him forth and said unto him, look now towards heaven, and tell the stars, if thou be able to number them; and he said unto him, so shall thy seed be. And Abraham believed in the Lord, and he counted to him for righteousness".[2]

Tell me now why he who dealt with him, whether angel or God, brought him forth and showed him the stars? For while still within the house, did he not know how great the multitude of stars is, being at night ever visible and shining? I think, perhaps, it was because he wished to show him the shooting stars, so that as a visible pledge of his words he might offer to Abraham the decision of the heavens that fulfils and sanctions all things. Additionally, lest any man should think that such an interpretation is forced, I will convince him by adding what comes next to the above passage. For it is written: "and he said unto him, I am the Lord that brought thee out of the land of the Chaldees, to give thee this land to inherit it. And he said, Lord God, whereby shall I know that I shall inherit it? And he said unto him, Take me an heifer of three years old, and a she-goat of three years old, and a ram of three years old, and a turtle-dove and a pigeon. And he took unto him all these, and divided them in the midst, and laid each piece one against another; but the birds divided he not. And the fowls came down upon the divided carcasses, and Abraham sat down among them".

You see how the announcement of the angel or god who had appeared was strengthened by means of the augury from birds, and how the prophecy was completed, not haphazardly as happens with you, but with the accompaniment of sacrifices? Furthermore, he

1. *Genesis*, 24.2, 10, 43 2. *Genesis*, 15

says that by the flocking together of the birds he showed that his message was true. Thus Abraham accepted the pledge, and, moreover, declared that a pledge that lacked truth seemed to be mere folly and imbecility. For it is not possible to behold the truth from speech alone, but some clear sign must follow on what has been said, a sign that by its appearance shall guarantee the prophecy that has been made concerning the future...[1]

For your indolence in this matter, then, there remains for you one single excuse, namely that you are not permitted to sacrifice if you are outside Jerusalem, though for that matter Elijah sacrificed[2] on Mount Carmel, and not in the holy city...[3]

1. According to Cyril, Julian then claimed to have been informed by an augury that he was to become Augustus

2. *1 Kings*, 18.19 3. The extant material ends here

FRAGMENTS

I.

Such things[1] have often happened and still happen; how, therefore, can these be signs of the end of the world?[2]

Neumann fragment 3; from Julian, Book 2, derived from Cyril, Book 12. Quoted by Theodorus, bishop of Mopsuestia, in his Commentary on the New Testament. Neumann thinks that Theodorus probably wrote a refutation of Julian at Antioch in around 378.

II.

Moses, after fasting for forty days, received the law;[3] and Elijah, after fasting for the same period, was granted to see God face to face.[4] Yet what did Jesus receive after a fast of the same length?[5]

Neumann fragment 4; from the same source as I.

III.

And how could he lead Jesus to the pinnacle of the Temple when Jesus was in the wilderness?[6]

Neumann fragment 6. From the same source as I and II.

IV.

Furthermore, Jesus prays in such a language as would be used by a pitiful wretch who cannot bear misfortune with serenity; and though he is a god, he is reassured by an angel. Who told you, Luke, the story of the angel, if indeed this ever happened? For those who were there when he prayed could not see the angel, for they were asleep. Therefore, when Jesus came from his prayer he found them fallen asleep from their grief, whereupon he said: "why

1. i.e. wars, famines, etc 2. cf. *Matthew*, 24.3-14 3. *Exodus*, 31.18
4. 1 *Kings*, 19.9 5. *Matthew*, 4.2 6. *Matthew*, 4.5

do ye sleep? Arise and pray" and so forth. Then: "and while he was yet speaking, behold a multitude and Judas".[1] That is why John did not write about the angel, for neither did he see it.

Neumann frag. 7. From the same source as 3.

V.

Listen to a fine statesman-like piece of advice: "sell all that ye have and give to the poor; provide yourselves with bags which wax not old".[2] Can anyone quote a more fanciful ordinance than this? For if all men were to obey you, who would there be to buy? Can anyone praise this teaching when, if it were carried out, no city, no nation, not a single family would hold together? For, if everything has been sold, how can any house or family be of any value? Moreover, the fact that if everything in the city were being sold at once there would be no one to trade is obvious, without being mentioned.

Neumann, frag. 12. From Cyril, Book 18, quoted by Photius.

VI.

How did the Word of God take away sin[3] when it caused many to commit the atrocity of killing their fathers, and many their children?[4] Mankind is thus compelled to either uphold their ancestral customs and cling to the pious tradition that they have inherited from the ages, or to accept this innovation. Is this not true of Moses also, who came to take away sin, but has been found to have increased the number of sins?[5]

Not in Neumann. Reconstructed by him from the polemical writings of Archbishop Arethas of Caesarea, who wrote in refutation of Julian in the 10th century. First published by Cuinont, Recherches sur la tradition manuscrite de l'empereur Julien, Brussels, 1898. Neumann's reconstruction is in Theologische Litteraturzeitung, 10. 1899.

---

1. *Luke*, 22.42-47 2. *Luke*, 12.33 3. Julian is criticising the Gospel of St. John

4. *Matthew*, 10.21. "And the brother shall deliver up the brother to death, and the father the child; and the children rise up against their parents, and cause them to be put to death"

5. cf. *Leviticus*, 16

VII.

The words that were written concerning Israel,[1] Matthew the Evangelist transferred to Christ[2] so that he might mock the simplicity of those among the Gentiles who believed.

Neumann fragment 15. Preserved by the 5th century writer, Hieronymus, in his Latin Commentary on Hosea 3. 11.

1. *Hosea*, 11.1 2. *Matthew*, 2.15

HYMN TO LORD HELIOS

PREFACE

In 362, on the occasion of the *Natale Solis Invicti*,[1] Julian composed a theological treatise on the subject of the sun god, Helios, who had risen to a position of supreme importance within the Roman pantheon during the reign of Aurelian. According to the classification of the rhetorician Menander, Julian's oration is a φυσικὸς ὕμνος, that is, a hymn or ode which describes the qualities of a god as they manifest in the material or natural world. The god in question, Helios, was not the only deity to have been associated with the sun in Greco-Roman Paganism, however, with Apollo and Mithras being two other prominent examples. As an initiate of the Mithraic Mysteries, it is the latter which Julian identifies primarily with Helios.

The worship of Mithras, a deity widely assumed to have been inspired by, but otherwise quite removed from the Indo-Iranian divinity Mithra, first appeared among the Romans in the first century B.C. The bull-slaying god was to become especially popular within the Imperial army, where devotees of Mithras were highly regarded as temperate and disciplined soldiers who had formed an unbreakable bond with their fellow worshippers.[2] For the Romans, the Mithraic cult provided the ideals of purity, devotion, and self-control which the other cults had lacked. Those who practised Mithraism were taught to contend against the powers of evil, and to submit themselves to severe moral discipline, the reward for which was to become as pure as the gods to whom they would ascend after death.[3] Julian himself had a Mithræum constructed within the imperial palace shortly after becoming Emperor.

The hymn itself is divided into three parts: first, the origin and substance of Helios; second, the activities and powers of the god; and finally, his property and his patronage of Rome.[4] Julian's grounding in Neo-Platonic theory is fundamental to the oration. As with Plotinus and Iamblichus, he regards the "One" (ἓν) or the "Good" (τὸ ἀγαθὸν) as the supreme principle which presides over

1. A festival in honour of the sun god, *Sol Invictus*, which was celebrated on 25th December

2. *Mithras in the Roman Legions, The Gale Encyclopedia*

3. W. C. F. Wright

4. Francesco Massa, re *Discorso su Helios* by Attilio Mastrocinque

the intelligible world, itself ruled by the intelligible gods. Over the intermediary world, first introduced by Iamblichus, preside the intellectual gods, upon whom the supreme god and metaphysical centre, Helios-Mithras, bestows the intellectual, creative, and unifying forces which originate with his transcendental counterpart among the intelligible gods. The final member of the triad is the world of sense-perception, which is governed by the Sun, the visible manifestation of Helios.[1]

While Julian was unquestionably a devotee of Mithras, his conception of the supreme solar deity is informed by a broader set of ideas and traditions. As Attilio Mastrocinque noted[2], for as influential as Mithraism was on Julian's thinking, his hymn to Helios ought to be viewed not as a Mithraic treatise, but rather as the theo-philosophical foundation of his religious and political project. In a similar vein, Julius Evola summarised the oration thus:

> Helios was the power to which Julian dedicated his hymn, whose name he invoked even in his dying words. Helios is the sun, conceived not as a deified physical star, but rather as a symbol of metaphysical light and transcendent power. This power manifests itself in man and in those who have been regenerated as a sovereign *nous* and supra-natural force from above. In ancient days, and in Rome itself via an Iranian influence, this force was considered to be strictly associated with the authority of the sovereign. The true meaning of the imperial Roman cult which Julian attempted to restore and to institutionalise over and against Christianity can only be appreciated in this context. The central idea is that the true and legitimate leader is the only one who is endowed with an almost supra-natural, ontological superiority and who is an image of the King of the Heavens, namely Helios himself. When this occurs – and only then – authority and hierarchy are justified; the *regnum* is sanctified; and a luminous centre of gravity is established, which draws to itself a system of human and natural forces.[3]

Some have perceived Julian's vision to be approaching a form of monotheism, with the various gods of the Romano-Hellenic pantheon reduced, it might be argued, to mere aspects of the supreme deity, Helios. It may be more accurate, however, to

---

1. Wright 2. Attilio Mastrocinque, *Giuliano l'Apostata, Discorso su Helios*
3. Julius Evola, *The Emperor Julian*

characterise the system as a hierarchy in which the myriad forces and beings present in the world are unified in the figure of the first and highest. Furthermore, while Julian's conception certainly places greater emphasis on one particular god, the idea is not entirely at odds with earlier tradition:

> In many cases, Homer, and of course later Hellenism, attributes the instigation of important events to "gods" in general (θεῷ) or to "god" (θεός). The latter expression does not at all imply a definite personality, in the monotheistic sense, but rather bears the same meaning as the first – the unity of the divine world as it communicates itself, despite its diverse manifestations, to living sensibilities. When Diomedes sharply rebukes Agamemnon for his counsel to desist from war, and Sthenelus offers the solemn assurance that they would in any case fight to the end, "for as much as it was with god that we made our way here", he speaks with trust in the higher world which stands above man.[1]

By having Helios, a definite being, represent the centre and the pinnacle of that transcendent order, Julian's beliefs are undeniably closer to the monotheistic conception. Nevertheless, the other deities are not held to be less important or deserving of worship as a consequence, and Julian will have assuredly viewed their relationship to Helios, the unifier, as a refinement of earlier understanding, one that was consistent with previous traditions. Indeed, his insistence on the divine inspiration of Homer, Hesiod, and Plato[2] necessitated the inclusion and preservation of all the gods. How such a theological system may have developed over the fullness of time is open to speculation, of course, yet it should be recognised that Julian's professed intentions were to reform and revitalise an explicitly polytheistic order.

---

1. Walter F. Otto, *The Homeric Gods*, pg.171 2. W. C. F. Wright

HYMN TO LORD HELIOS

What I am about to say I consider to be of the greatest importance for all things "that breathe and move upon the earth",[1] and that have a share in existence, a reasoning soul,[2] and intelligence, though above all others it is of importance to myself. For I am a follower of Lord Helios. Of this fact I possess within me, known to myself alone, proofs more certain than I can give.[3] Yet this at least I am permitted to say without sacrilege, that from my childhood an extraordinary longing for the rays of the god penetrated deep into my soul; and from my earliest years my mind was so completely swayed by the light that illumines the heavens that not only did I desire to gaze intently at the sun, but whenever I walked abroad in the night season, when the firmament was clear and cloudless, I abandoned all else without exception and gave myself up to the beauty of the heavens; nor did I understand what anyone might say to me, nor heed what I was doing myself. I was considered to be overly curious about these matters and to pay too much attention to them, such that people went as far as to regard me as an astrologer when my beard had only just begun to grow. And yet, I call heaven to witness, never had a book on this subject come into my hands, nor at that time did I even know what that branch of science was. Why, then, do I mention this, when I have more important things to tell, if I should relate how, in those days, I thought about the gods? Let that darkness be buried in oblivion;[4] but let what I have said bear witness to this fact, that the heavenly light shone all about me, and that it roused and urged me on to its contemplation, so that even then I recognised of myself that the movement of the moon was in the opposite direction to the universe, though as yet I had met no one of those who are wise in these matters. Now, for my part, I envy the good fortune of any man

1. *The Iliad*, XVII, 447

2. As opposed to the unreasoning soul, *ἄλογος ψυχή*, that is in animals other than man. Plato, Aristotle, Plotinus, and Porphyry allowed some form of soul to plants, but this was questioned by Iamblichus, and in turn Julian and Salutius

3. He is alluding to his initiation into the Mithraic Mysteries

4. When he still presented publicly as a Christian

to whom the god has granted to inherit a body built of the seed of holy and inspired ancestors, so that he may unlock the treasures of wisdom; nor do I despise that lot with which I was myself endowed by the god Helios, that I should be born of a house that rules and governs the world in my time; but further, I regard this god, if we may believe the wise, as the common father of all mankind. For it is said with truth that man and the sun together beget man,[1] and that the god sows this earth with souls which proceed not from himself alone but from the other gods also;[2] and for what purpose, the souls reveal by the kind of lives that they choose. Now, the best thing by far is when someone is fortunate enough to have inherited the service of the god, even before the third generation, from a long and unbroken line of ancestors; yet it is not a thing to be disparaged when someone, recognising that he is by nature intended to be the servant of Helios, either alone of all men, or in company with but few, devotes himself to the service of his master.

Come then, let me celebrate, as best I may, his festival which the Imperial city[3] adorns with annual sacrifices.[4] It is difficult, as I well know, to merely comprehend how great the Unseen is, if one judges by his visible self, and to tell it is perhaps impossible, even though one should consent to fall short of what is his due. For well I know that no one in the world could attain to a description that would be worthy of him, and to not fall short of a certain measure of success in his praises is the greatest height to which human beings can attain in the power of utterance. As for myself, however, may Hermes, the god of eloquence, stand by my side to aid me, and the Muses, also, and Apollo, leader of the Muses, since he too has oratory for his province; thus may they grant that I utter only what the gods approve that men should say and believe about them. What, then, shall be the manner of my praise? Or is it not evident that if I describe his substance and his origin, his powers and actions, both visible and invisible, and the gift of blessings which he bestows throughout all the worlds,[5] I shall compose an encomium not wholly displeasing to the god? With these, then, let me begin.

This divine and wholly beautiful universe, from the highest vault of heaven to the lowest limit of the earth, is held together by the continuous providence of the god, it has existed from eternity

1. Aristotle, *Physics*, 2.2 2. Plato, *Timæus*, 42 3. Rome 4. 25th December

5. i.e. the intelligible world, *νοητός*, comprehended only by pure reason; the intellectual, *νοερός*, endowed with intelligence; and thirdly the world of sense-perception *αἰσθητός*. The first of these worlds was derived from Plato, *Republic*, 508; the second was introduced by Iamblichus

ungenerated, is imperishable for all time to come, and is guarded immediately by nothing else than the Fifth Substance,[1] whose culmination is the beams of the sun;[2] and in the second and higher degree, so to speak, by the intelligible world. Though in a still loftier sense it is guarded by the Lord of the whole universe, who is the centre of all things that exist. He, whether it is right to call him the Supra-Intelligible, or the Idea of Being, and by Being I mean the whole intelligible domain, or the One, since the One seems somehow to be prior to all the rest, or, to use Plato's name for him, the Good. Regardless, this uncompounded cause of the whole reveals to all existence beauty, perfection, oneness, and irresistible power; and in virtue of the primal creative substance that abides within it, produced, as middle among the middle and intellectual, creative causes, Helios, the most mighty god, proceeding from itself and in all things like unto itself. Just as the divine Plato believed, when he writes: "therefore, said I, when I spoke of this, understand that I meant the offspring of the Good, which the Good begat in his own likeness, and that what the Good is in relation to pure reason and its objects in the intelligible world, such is the sun in the visible world in relation to sight and its objects".[3]

Accordingly, his light has the same relation to the visible world as truth has to the intelligible world. While he himself, as a whole, since he is the son of what is first and greatest, namely, the Idea of the Good, and subsists from eternity in the region of its abiding substance, has also received dominion among the intellectual gods, and himself dispenses to the intellectual gods those things of which the Good is the cause for the intelligible gods. Now, the Good is, I believe, the cause for the intelligible gods of beauty, existence, perfection, and oneness, connecting these and illuminating them with a power that works towards the good. These, accordingly, Helios bestows on the intellectual gods also, since he has been appointed by the Good to rule and govern them, even though they came forth and came into being together with him, and this was, I suppose, in order that the cause which resembles the Good may guide the intellectual gods to blessings for them all, and may regulate all things according to pure reason.

Yet this visible disc also, third[1] in rank, is clearly, for the objects of sense-perception, the cause of preservation, and this visible

1. Aristotle proposed a fifth element superior to the other four which he referred to as "æther" or "first element", *De Coelo*, 1.3.270; Iamblichus then developed this theory further, cf. *Theologumenæ Arithmetic*, 35,22

2. Pindar, fr. 107; Sophocles, *Antigone*, 100

3. *Republic*, 508

Helios is the cause for the visible gods[1] of just as many blessings as we said mighty Helios bestows on the intellectual gods. Of this there are clear proofs for one who studies the unseen world in the light of things seen. For in the first place, is not light itself a sort of incorporeal and divine form of the transparent in a state of activity? As for the transparent itself, whatever it may be, since it is the underlying basis, so to speak, of all the elements, and is a form belonging uniquely to them, it is not like the corporeal or compounded, nor does it admit qualities particular to corporeal substance.[2] One would not, therefore, say that heat is a property of the transparent,[3] or its opposite cold, nor would one assign to it hardness or softness, or any other of the various attributes connected with touch, taste, or smell.[4] A nature of this sort is obvious to sight alone, since it is brought into activity by light. For light is a form of this substance, so to speak, which is the substratum of and coextensive with the heavenly bodies. While of light, itself incorporeal, the culmination and flower, so to speak, is the sun's rays.

Now, the doctrine of the Phoenicians, who were wise and learned in sacred lore, declared that the rays of light everywhere diffused are the undefiled incarnation of pure mind. In harmony with this is our theory, seeing that light itself is incorporeal, where one should regard its fountainhead, not as corporeal, but as the undefiled activity of mind[5] pouring light into its own abode. This is assigned to the middle of the whole firmament, whence it sheds its rays and fills the heavenly spheres with vigour of every kind, illuminating all things with light divine and undefiled. The activities proceeding from it and exercised among the gods have been, in some measure at least, described already and will shortly be spoken of further. Yet all that we see merely with the sight at first is a name only, deprived of activity, unless we add thereto the guidance and aid of light. For what, speaking generally, could be seen, were it not first brought into touch with light in order that, I suppose, it may receive a form, as matter is brought under the

1. Julian conceives of the sun in three ways: first as transcendental, in which his form he is indistinguishable from the Good in the intelligible world; secondly as Helios-Mithras, ruler of the intellectual gods; and thirdly as the visible sun

2. i.e., celestial bodies

3. An echo of *De Anima*, 419, where Aristotle says that light is the actualisation or positive determination of the transparent medium

4. *De Anima*, 418

5. Mind, νοῦς, is identified here with Helios; cf. Macrobius, *Saturnalia*, 1.19.9: *Sol mundi mens est* (the sun is the mind of the universe); Iamblichus, *Protrepticus*, 21,11

hand of a craftsman? Indeed, molten gold in its crude form is simply gold, and not yet a statue or an image, until the craftsman has given it its proper shape. So, too, all the objects of sight, unless they are brought under the eyes of the beholder together with light, are altogether deprived of visibility. Accordingly, by giving the power of sight to those who see, and the power of being seen to the objects of sight, it brings to perfection, by means of a single activity, two faculties, namely vision and visibility.[1] Thus in forms and substance are expressed its perfecting powers.

This, however, is perhaps somewhat subtle; whereas for that guide whom we all follow, ignorant and unlearned, philosophers and rhetoricians, what power in the universe has this god when he rises and sets? Night and day he creates, and before our eyes changes and sways the universe. To which of the other heavenly bodies does this power belong? How then can we now fail to believe, in view of this, in respect also to things more divine, that the unseen and divine tribes of intellectual gods above the heavens are filled with power that works for good by him, even by him to whom the whole band of the heavenly bodies yields place, and whom all generated things follow, piloted by his providence? For that the planets dance about him as their king, in certain intervals, fixed in relation to him, and revolve in a circle with perfect accord, making certain halts, and pursuing to and fro their orbit,[2] as those who are learned in the study of the spheres call their visible motions; and that the light of the moon waxes and wanes varying in proportion to its distance from the sun, is, I think, clear to all. Is it not natural, then, that we should suppose that the more venerable ordering of bodies among the intellectual gods corresponds to this arrangement?

Let us comprehend, therefore, out of all his functions, first his power to perfect, from the fact that he makes visible the objects of sight in the universe, for through his light he perfects them; secondly, his creative and generative power from the changes wrought by him in the universe; thirdly, his power to link together all things into one whole, from the harmony of his motions towards one and the same goal; fourthly, his middle station we can comprehend from himself, who is midmost; and fifthly, the fact that he is established as king among the intellectual gods, from his middle station among the planets. Now, if we see that these powers,

---

1. Julian echoes Plato, *Republic*, 507, 508

2. the stationary positions and the direct and retrograde movements of the planets

or powers of similar importance, belong to any one of the other visible deities, let us not assign to Helios leadership among the gods. If, however, he has nothing in common with those other gods except his beneficent energy, and of this too he gives them all a share, then let us call to witness the priests of Cyprus who set up common altars to Helios and Zeus; yet even before them, let us summon as witness Apollo, who sits in council with our god. For this god declares: "Zeus, Hades, Helios Serapis, three gods in one godhead!"[1] Let us then assume that, among the intellectual gods, Helios and Zeus have a joint, or rather, a single sovereignty. Hence, I think that with reason Plato called Hades a wise god.[2] We call this same god Hades Serapis, also, namely the Unseen and Intellectual, to whom Plato[3] says the souls of those who have lived most righteously and justly mount upwards. For let no one conceive of him as the god at whom legends teach us to shudder, but rather as one who is mild and kind, since he completely frees our souls from generation; and the souls that he has thus freed he does not nail to other bodies,[4] punishing them and exacting penalties, but he carries aloft and lifts up our souls to the intelligible world.

This doctrine, moreover, is not wholly new, for both Homer and Hesiod, those most venerable of poets, held it before us, whether this was their own view or, like seers, they were lead by divine inspiration towards the truth, as is evident from the following. Hesiod, in tracing his genealogy, said[5] that Helios is the son of Hyperion and Thea, intimating thereby that he is the true son of him who is above all things. For who else could Hyperion[6] be? And is not Thea herself, in another fashion, said to be most divine of beings? Yet as for a union or marriage, let us not conceive of such a thing, since that is the incredible and paradoxical trifling of the poetic Muse. Instead, let us believe that his father and sire was the most divine and supreme being; and who else could have this nature save him who transcends all things, the central point and goal of all things that exist? Equally, Homer calls him Hyperion after his father[7] and shows his unconditioned nature, superior to all constraint. For Zeus, as Homer says, since he is lord of all, constrains the other gods. When, therefore, in the course of the

1. This oracular verse is quoted as Orphic by Macrobius, *Saturnalia*, 1.18.18; but Julian, no doubt following Iamblichus, substitutes Serapis for Dionysus

2. *Phædo*, 80; in *Cratylus*, 403, Plato discusses the etymology of "Hades"

3. *Cratylus*, 403 4. *Phædo*, 83 5. *Theogony*, 371; cf. Pindar, *Isthmian*, 4.1

6. Ὑπερίων means "he that walks above" 7. *The Iliad*, VIII, 480; *The Odyssey*, I, 8

myth,[1] Helios says that on account of the impiety of the comrades of Odysseus[2] he will forsake Olympus, Zeus no longer says "with the very earth and the sea withal would I draw you up",[3] nor does he threaten him with fetters or violence, but he says that he will inflict punishment on the guilty and bids Helios go on shining among the gods. Does he not thereby declare that besides being unconditioned, Helios has also the power to perfect? For why do the gods need him unless by sending his light, himself unseen, on their substance and existence, he fulfils for them the blessings of which I spoke? For when Homer says that "ox-eyed Hera, queen of the heavens, sent unwearied Helios, all unwilling, to sink into the depths of Oceanus",[4] he means that, by reason of a heavy mist, it was thought to be night before the proper time. This mist, then, is surely the goddess herself, for in another place in the poem he also says: "Hera spread before them a thick mist".[5] Though let us leave the stories of the poets alone. For along with what is inspired, they contain much also that is merely human. Instead, let me now relate what the god himself seems to teach us, both about himself and the other gods.

The region of the earth bears being in a state of becoming. Yet who endows it with imperishability? Is it not he[6] who keeps all things together by means of definite limits? For that the nature of being should be unlimited was not possible, since it is neither uncreated nor self-subsistent. Moreover, if out of being something were generated absolutely without ceasing and nothing were resolved back into it, the substance of things generated would fail. Accordingly, this god, moving in due measure, raises up and stimulates this substance when he approaches it, and when he departs to a distance he diminishes and destroys it; or rather, he himself continually revivifies it by giving it movement and flooding it with life. His departure and turning in the other direction, therefore, is the cause of decay for things that perish. Yet ever does his gift of blessings descend evenly upon the earth. For now one country then another receives them, to the end that becoming may not cease, nor does the god ever benefit less or more than is his custom this changeful world. For immutability, as of being so also

1. *The Odyssey*, XII, 387   2. They had devoured the oxen of the sun; ibid, XII, 352

3. *The Iliad*, VII, 24; Zeus utters this threat against the gods if they should aid either the Trojans or the Achæans

4. *The Iliad*, XVII, 239   5. *The Iliad*, XXI, 6

6. Julian now describes the substance or essential nature, *οὐσία*, of Helios

of activity, exists among the gods, and above all the others in the case of the Lord of All, Helios, who makes the simplest movement of all the heavenly bodies that travel in a direction opposite to the whole. In fact, this is the very thing that the celebrated Aristotle makes a proof of his superiority compared with the others. Nevertheless, from the other intellectual gods also, forces clearly discernible descend to this world. What does this mean? Are we not excluding the others when we assert that the leadership has been assigned to Helios? No, far rather do I think it right from the visible to have faith about the invisible. For even as this god is seen to complete and to adapt to himself and to the universe the powers that are bestowed on the earth from the other gods, after the same fashion we must believe that among the invisible gods also there is interaction with one another; his mode of interaction being that of a leader, while the modes of interaction of the others are at the same time in harmony with his. For since we said that the god is established midmost among the midmost intellectual gods, may Lord Helios himself grant us to tell what is the nature of that middleness among things of which we must regard him as the middle.

Now "middleness"[1] we define not as that mean which in opposites is seen to be equally remote from the extremes, as, for instance, in colours, tawny or beige, and warm in the case of hot and cold, and the like, but that which unifies and links together what is separate. For example, the type of thing that Empedocles[2] means by Harmony when from it he altogether eliminates Strife. Thus, what does Helios link together, and of what is he the middle? I assert that he is midway between the visible gods who surround the universe and the immaterial and intelligible gods who surround the Good – for the intelligible and divine substance is, as it were, multiplied without external influence and without addition. For that the intellectual and wholly beautiful substance of Lord Helios is middle in the sense of being unmixed with extremes, complete in itself, and distinct from the whole number of the gods, manifested and unmanifested, both those perceptible by sense and those which are intelligible only. This, then, is the sense in which we must conceive of his middleness. If, however, I must also describe

1. The μεσότης, or middleness, which Helios possesses makes him the mediator and connecting link, while also being midway between the two worlds and the centre of the intellectual gods

2. cf. Empedocles, fr. 18

these things one by one, in order that we may discern with our intelligence how his intermediary nature, in its various forms, is related both to the highest and the lowest, even though it is not easy to recount it all, let me try to say what can be said.

Wholly one is the intelligible world, pre-existent from all time, and it combines all things together in the One. Again, is not our whole world also one complete living organism, entirely full of soul and intelligence throughout, "perfect, with all its parts perfect"?[1] Midway, then, between this uniform two-fold perfection – by which I mean that one kind of unity holds together in one all that exists in the intelligible world, while the other kind of unity unites in the visible world all things into one and the same perfect nature – between these, I say, is the uniform perfection of Lord Helios, established among the intellectual gods. There is, however, next in order, a sort of binding force in the intelligible world of the gods, which orders all things into one. Again, is there not visible in the heavens also, travelling in its orbit, the nature of the Fifth Substance, which links and compresses[2] together all the parts, holding together things that by nature are prone to scatter and to fall away from one another? These existences, therefore, which are two causes of connection, one in the intelligible world, while the other appears in the world of sense-perception, Lord Helios combines into one, imitating the essential power of the former among the intellectual gods, seeing that he proceeds from it, and subsisting prior to the latter which is seen in the visible world. Then must not the unconditioned also, which exists primarily in the intelligible world, and finally among the visible bodies in the heavens, possess midway between these two the unconditioned substance of Lord Helios? And from that primary creative substance, do not the rays of his light, illuminating all things, descend to the visible world? Again, to take another point of view, the creator of the whole is one, but many are the creative gods[3] who revolve in the heavens. Thus midmost of these, also, we must place

1. Plato, *Timæus*, 33

2. In *Timæus*, 58 it is the revolution of the whole which compresses all matter together, but Julian had that passage in mind. In Empedocles, fr. 38, it is the Titan, Æther, i.e. the Fifth Substance, that "binds the globe"

3. In *Timæus*, 41, Plato distinguishes "the gods who revolve before our eyes" from "those who reveal themselves so far as they will". Julian regularly describes, as here, a triad: every one of his three worlds has its own unconditioned being (*αὐθυπόστατον*); its own creative power (*δημιουργία*); its own power to generate life (*γόνιμον τῆς ζωῆς*); and in every case, the middle is Helios as a connecting link in his capacity as an intellectual god (*νοερός*)

the creative activity which descends into the world from Helios. Additionally, the power of generating life is abundant and overflowing in the intelligible world; and our world also appears to be full of generative life. It is evident, therefore, that the life-generating power of Lord Helios is also midway between both worlds, and the phenomena of our world bear witness to this. For some forms he perfects, others he makes, or adorns, or wakes to life, thus there is no single thing which, independent of the creative power derived from Helios, can come to light and to birth. Further, besides this, if we should comprehend the pure, undefiled, and immaterial substance[1] among the intelligible gods – to which nothing external is added, nor has any foreign thing a place therein, but it is filled with its own unstained purity – and if we should comprehend also the pure, unpolluted nature of unsullied and divine substance, whose elements are wholly unmixed, and which, in the visible universe, surrounds the substance that revolves,[2] here, we should discover the radiant and immaculate substance of Lord Helios, midway between the two; that is to say, midway between the immaterial purity that exists among the intelligible gods, and that perfect purity, unstained and free from birth and death, that exists in the world which we can perceive. The greatest proof of this is that not even the light which comes down nearest to the earth from the sun is mixed with anything, nor does it admit dirt and defilement, but remains wholly pure and without stain, free from external influences among all existing things.

We must, now, go on to consider the immaterial and intelligible forms,[3] as well as those visible forms which are united with matter or the substratum. Here again, the intellectual will be found to be midmost among the forms that surround mighty Helios, by which forms in their turn the material forms are aided; for they could never have existed or been preserved had they not been brought, by his aid, into connection with being. Consider: is not he the cause of the separation of the forms, and of the combination of matter, in that he not only permits us to comprehend his very self, but also to behold him with our eyes? For the distribution of his rays over the whole universe, and the unifying power of his light, prove him to be the master craftsman who gives an individual existence to

1. Julian now describes the three kinds of substance (*οὐσία*) and its three forms (*εἴδη*) in the three worlds

2. i.e. the visible heavenly bodies

3. Helios connects the forms (Plato's Ideas) which exist in the intelligible world with those which in our world ally themselves with matter

everything that is created. Now, while there are many more blessings connected with the substance of the god, each apparent to us, which show that he is midway between the intelligible and the mundane gods,[1] let us proceed to his last visible province. His first province in the last of the worlds is, as though by way of a pattern, to give form and personality to the sun's angels.[2] Next is his province of generating the world of sense-perception, of which the more honourable part contains the cause of the heavens and the heavenly bodies, while the inferior part guides this, our world of becoming, and from eternity contains in itself the uncreated cause of that world. Now, to describe all the properties of the substance of this god, even if the god himself were to grant one to comprehend them, is impossible, seeing that to even grasp them all with the mind is, in my opinion, beyond our power.

Since I have already described many of them, however, I must set a seal, as it were, on this discourse, now that I am about to pass to other subjects that demand no less investigation. What, then, that seal is, and what is the knowledge of the god's substance that embraces all these questions, and, as it were, sums them up under one head, may he himself suggest to my mind, since I desire to describe in a brief summary both the cause from which he proceeded, his own nature, and those blessings with which he fills the visible world. Thus we must declare that Lord Helios is One and proceeds from one god, even from the intelligible world which is itself One; that he is midmost of the intellectual gods, stationed in their midst by every kind of mediacy that is harmonious and friendly, and that joins what is sundered; and that he brings together into one the last and the first, having in his own person the means of completeness, of connection, of generative life, and of uniform being. Further, that for the world which we can perceive he initiates blessings of all sorts, not only by means of the light with which he illumines it, adorning it and giving it its splendour, but also because he calls into existence, along with himself, the substance of the Sun's angels; and that finally in himself he comprehends the ungenerated cause of things generated, and moreover, prior to this, the ageless and abiding cause of the life of the imperishable bodies.

As for what was right to say about the substance of this god, though the greater part has been omitted, much has nonetheless been said. Yet since the multitude of his powers and the beauty of

1. i.e., the visible 2. These angels combine the idea and its hypostazisation

his activities is so great, such that we shall now exceed the limit of what we observed about his substance – for it is natural that when divine things come forth into the region of the visible they should be multiplied, in virtue of the superabundance of life and life-generating power in them – consider what I have to do. For now I must strip for a plunge into this fathomless sea, though I have barely, and as best I might, taken breath after the first part of this discourse. Nevertheless, venture I must, and, putting my trust in the god, endeavour to handle this theme.

We must assume that what has just been said about his substance applies equally to his powers. For it cannot be that a god's substance is one thing, and his power another, and his activity, by Zeus, a third thing besides these. Since all that he wills he is, and can do, and puts into action. For he does not will what is not, nor does he lack the power to do what he wills, nor does he desire to put into action what he cannot. In the case of a human being, however, this is otherwise. For his is a two-fold contending nature of soul and body compounded into one, the former divine, the latter dark and clouded. Naturally, therefore, there is a battle and a feud between them. Indeed, Aristotle himself states[1] that this is why neither the pleasures nor the pains in us harmonise with one another. For he says that what is pleasant to one of the natures within us is painful to the nature which is its opposite. Yet among the gods there is nothing of this sort. From their very nature what is good belongs to them, and perpetually, not intermittently. In the first place, then, all that I said when I tried to show forth his substance, I must be considered to have said about his powers and activities also. Additionally, since in such cases the argument is naturally convertible, all that I observe next concerning his powers and activities must be considered to apply not only to his activities, but to his substance also. For verily there are gods related to Helios and of like substance who sum up the immaculate nature of this god, and though in the visible world they are plural, in him they are one. Now, listen first to what is asserted by those who look at the heavens, not like horses and cattle, or some other unreasoning and unknowing animal,[2] but from it draw their conclusions about the unseen world. Even before this, however, consider, if you will, his supra-mundane powers and activities, and out of a countless number, observe but a few.

First, then, of his powers through which he reveals the whole

1. *Nicomachean Ethics*, 7.14.1154 2. cf. *Timæus*, 47, *Republic*, 529

intellectual substance throughout as one, since he brings together its extremes. For even as in the world of sense-perception, we can clearly discern air and water set between fire and earth[1] as the link that binds together the extremes. Would one not reasonably suppose, then, that in the case of the cause which is separate from elements and prior to them – and though it is the principle of generation, is not itself generation – it is so ordered that, in that world also, the extreme causes which are wholly separate from elements are bound together into one through certain modes of mediation, by Lord Helios, and are united about him as their centre? While the creative power of Zeus also coincides with him, by reason of which in Cyprus, as I mentioned earlier, shrines are founded and assigned to them in common. Apollo himself we also called to witness our statements, since it is certainly likely that he knows better than we about his own nature. For he too abides with Helios and Zeus by reason of the singleness of his thoughts, the stability of his substance, and the consistency of his activity.

Yet Apollo, too, appears to separate in no respect the dividing creative function of Dionysus[2] from Helios. Since, moreover, he always subordinates it to Helios and so indicates that Dionysus is his partner on the throne, Apollo is the interpreter for us of the fairest purposes that are to be found with our god. Further, since he comprehends in himself all the principles of the fairest intellectual synthesis, Helios is himself Apollo, leader of the Muses. Finally, as he fills the whole of our life with fair order, he begat Asclepius in the world, though even before the beginning of the world he had him by his side.

While one should survey many other powers that belong to this god, never could one investigate them all. It is enough to have observed the following: that there is an equal and identical dominion of Helios and Zeus over the separate creation which is prior to substances, that is to say, of the absolute causes which, separated from visible creation, existed prior to it; secondly, we observed the singleness of his thoughts which is bound up with the abiding immutability and imperishableness that he shares with Apollo; thirdly, the dividing part of his creative function which he shares with Dionysus who controls divided substance; then we

1. *Timæus*, 32; Plato says that to make the universe solid, "god set air and water between fire and earth"

2. Proclus, *On Timæus*, 203, says that because Dionysus was torn asunder by the Titans, his function is to divide wholes into their parts and to separate the forms

observed the power of the leader of the Muses, revealed in fairest symmetry and blending of the intellectual; and finally, we comprehended that Helios, with Asclepius, fulfils the fair order of the whole of life.

So it is, truly, with respect to those powers of his that existed before the beginning of the world; and co-ordinate with these are his works over the entire visible world, in that he fills it with all that is good. For since he is the genuine son of the Good and from it has received his blessed lot in fullness of perfection, he himself distributes that blessedness to the intellectual gods, bestowing on them a beneficent and perfect nature. This, then, is one of his works.

A second work of the god is his most perfect distribution of intelligible beauty among the intellectual and immaterial forms. For when the generative substance[1] which is visible in our world desires to beget in the Beautiful,[2] and to bring forth offspring, it is further necessary that it should be guided by the substance that, in the region of intelligible beauty, does this very thing eternally and always, not intermittently, at one moment fruitful, at another barren. For all that is beautiful in our world only at times, is beautiful always in the intelligible world. We must therefore assert that the ungenerated offspring, intelligible and eternal in beauty, guides the generative cause in the visible world; the offspring[3] of which this god[4] called into existence and keeps at his side, and to it he assigns perfect reason also. For just as through his light he gives sight to our eyes, so also among the intelligible gods through his intellectual counterpart – which he causes to shine far more brightly than his rays in our upper air – he bestows, as I believe, on all the intellectual gods the faculty of thought and of being comprehended by thought. Besides these, another marvellous activity of Helios the Lord of All is that by which he endows with superior lot the nobler races – that is, angels, daimons,[5] heroes, and those divided souls[6] which remain in the category of model and archetype, never giving themselves over to bodies. I have now described the substance of our god that is prior to the world and his powers and activities, celebrating Helios the Lord of All in so far as it was possible for me to compass his praise. Yet since eyes, as the

1. The sun 2. Plato, *Symposium*, 206 3. Intellectual Helios 4. Intelligible Helios
5. Plato, *Laws*, 713, defines daimons as beings superior to man but inferior to gods who watch over human affairs, acting as intermediaries between man and the divine
6. i.e. the individual souls; by using this term, derived from the Neo-Platonists and Iamblichus, Julian implies that there is an indivisible world soul; cf. Plotinus 4.8.8

saying goes, are more trustworthy than hearing – although they are, of course, less trustworthy and weaker than intelligence – come, let me endeavour to tell also of his visible creative function, though first I must entreat him to grant that I speak with some measure of success.

From eternity there subsisted, surrounding Helios, the visible world, and from eternity the light that encompasses the world has its fixed station, not shining intermittently, nor in different ways at different times, but always in the same manner. Thus if one desired to comprehend, as far as the mind may, this eternal nature from the point of view of time, one would understand most easily of how many blessings for the world throughout eternity he, Helios the Lord of All, who shines without cessation, is the cause. Now, I am aware that the great philosopher Plato,[1] and after him a man who, though he is later in time, is by no means inferior to him in genius – I mean Iamblichus of Chalcis, who through his writings initiated me not only into other philosophic doctrines but these also – I am aware that they employed as a hypothesis the conception of a generated world, and assumed for it, so to speak, a creation in time in order that the magnitude of the works that arise from Helios might be recognised.

However, apart from the fact that I fall short altogether of their ability, I must by no means be so rash; especially since the glorious hero Iamblichus thought it was not without risk to assume, even as a bare hypothesis, a temporal limit for the creation of the world. For indeed the god came forth from an eternal cause, or rather, brought forth all things from the everlasting, engendering by his divine will and with untold speed and unsurpassed power, from the invisible all things now visible in present time. Then he assigned as his own station the mid-heavens, in order that from all sides he may bestow equal blessings on the gods who came forth by his agency and in company with him; and that he may guide the seven spheres[2] in the heavens alongside the eighth sphere[3] also, and, as I believe, the ninth creation too, namely our world which revolves for ever in a continuous cycle of birth and death. For it is evident that the planets, as they dance in a circle about him, preserve as the measure of their motion a harmony between this

1. *Timæus*, 37; the Creator invented Time as an attribute of "divided substance"

2. Kronos (Saturn), Zeus (Jupiter), Ares (Mars), Helios (the Sun), Aphrodite (Venus), Hermes (Mercury), Selene (the Moon) are the seven celestial spheres; though Helios guides the others he is counted with them

3. i.e. the fixed stars; cf. Iamblichus, *Theologumena Arithmeticæ*, 56.4

god and their own movements such as I shall now describe; and that the whole heaven also, which adapts itself to him in all its parts, is full of gods who proceed from Helios. For this god is lord of five zones in the heavens, and when he traverses three of these he begets in them the three Graces.[1] The remaining zones, meanwhile, are the scales of mighty Necessity.[2]

To the Greeks what I say is perhaps incomprehensible – as though one were obliged to say to them only what is known and familiar. Yet even this is not altogether strange to them as one might suppose. For who, in your opinion, are the Dioscuri, O you most wise, you who accept without question so many of your traditions? Do you not call them "alternate of days"[3] because they may not both be seen on the same day? It is obvious that by this you mean "yesterday" and "today". Yet what, in the name of those same Dioscuri, does this mean? Let me apply it to some natural object, so that I may not say anything empty and senseless; though no such object would one ever find, however carefully one might search for it. For the theory that some have supposed to be held by the theogonists, that the two hemispheres of the universe are its significance, has no meaning. For how one could call each one of the hemispheres "alternate of days" is not easy to imagine, since the increase of their light in each separate day is imperceptible. Let us consider, then, a question on which some may think that I am innovating. We say correctly that those persons for whom the time of the sun's course above the earth is the same in one and the same month share the same day. Consider, therefore, whether the expression "alternate of days" cannot be applied both to the tropics and the other, the polar, circles. Yet someone will object that it does not apply equally to both. For though the former are always visible, and both of them are visible at once to those who inhabit that part of the earth where shadows are cast in an opposite direction,[4] in the case of the latter, those who see the one do not see the other.

Let us not to dwell too long on the same subject; since he causes the winter and summer solstice, Helios is, as we know, the father of the seasons; and since he never forsakes the poles, he is Oceanus,

---

1. The Graces are often associated with spring; Julian seems to be describing obscurely the annual course of the sun

2. Necessity played an important part in the cult of Mithras and was sometimes identified with the constellation Virgo, who holds the scales of Justice

3. The Odyssey, 11, 303

4. i.e. the Torrid Zone. On the equator, shadows fall due north at noon in the winter, and due south in the summer

the lord of two-fold substance. My meaning here is not obscure, is it, seeing that before my time Homer said the same thing? "Oceanus who is the father of all things".[1] Indeed, for mortals and for the blessed gods too, as he himself would say; and what he says is true. For there is no single thing in the whole of existence that is not the offspring of the substance of Oceanus. But what has that to do with the poles? Shall I tell you? It were better indeed to keep silence, but for all that I will speak.[2]

Some say, then, even though all men are not ready to believe it, that the sun travels in the starless heavens far above the region of the fixed stars. According to this theory, he will not be stationed midmost among the planets but midway between the three worlds; that is, according to the hypothesis of the mysteries, if indeed one ought to use the word "hypothesis" instead of "established truths", reserving the word "hypothesis" for the study of the heavenly bodies. For the priests of the mysteries tell us what they have been taught by the gods or mighty daimons, whereas the astronomers make plausible hypotheses from the harmony that they observe in the visible spheres. It is proper, no doubt, to approve the astronomers as well, but where any man thinks it better to believe the priests of the mysteries, him I admire and revere, both in jest and earnest. So much for that, as the saying goes.[3]

Now, besides those whom I have mentioned, there is in the heavens a great multitude of gods who have been recognised as such by those who survey the heavens, not casually, nor like cattle. For as he divides the three spheres by four through the zodiac,[4] which is associated with every one of the three, so he divides the zodiac also into twelve divine powers; once more, he divides every one of these twelve by three, so as to make thirty-six gods in all. Hence, as I believe, there descends from above, from the heavens to us, a three-fold gift of the Graces; that is, from the spheres, for this god, by thus dividing them by four, sends to us the fourfold glory of the seasons, which express the changes of time. Indeed, on our earth the Graces imitate a circle[5] in their statues. It is Dionysus who is the giver of the Graces, and in this very connection he is said to reign with Helios. Why, then, should I go on to speak to you of Horus[6] and of the other names of gods, all of which belong to

1. *The Iliad*, XIV, 246 2. An allusion to the esoteric knowledge of mystery cults
3. Plutarch, *Demosthenes*, 4, quotes this phrase as notably Platonic; cf. *Laws*, 676
4. *ζῳοφόρος* ("life-bearer"), Aristotle's phrase for the zodiac
5. There is a play on the word *κύκλος*, which means both "sphere" and "circle"
6. The Egyptian sun-god whose worship was introduced into Greece and later Rome

Helios? For from his works men have learned to know this god, who makes the whole heavens perfect through the gift of intellectual blessings, and gives it a share of intelligible beauty; furthermore, taking the heavens as their starting-point, they have learned to know him both as a whole and by his parts also, from his abundant bestowal of good gifts. For he exercises control over all movement, even to the lowest plane of the universe. While everywhere he makes all things perfect – nature, soul, and everything that exists. Thus, marshalling together this great army of the gods into a single commanding unity, he handed it over to Athena Pronaia,[1] who, as the legend says, sprang from the head of Zeus, though I would say that she was sent forth wholly from Helios, from his whole being, having been contained within him. I disagree with the legend, however, only insofar as I assert that she came forth not from his highest part, but whole from the whole of him. For in other respects, since I believe that Zeus is in no way different from Helios, I agree with that ancient tradition. Moreover, in using this very phrase Athena Pronaia, I am not innovating, if I rightly understand the words: "he came to Pytho and to grey-eyed Pronaia".[2] This proves that the ancients also thought that Athena Pronaia shared the throne of Apollo, who, as we believe, differs in no way from Helios. Indeed, did not Homer reveal this truth by divine inspiration – for he was, we may suppose, influenced by a god – when he says often in his poems: "may I be honoured even as Athena and Apollo were honoured".[3] By Zeus, that is to say, who is identical with Helios? For just as Lord Apollo, through the singleness of his thoughts, is associated with Helios, so also we must believe that Athena has received her nature from Helios, and that she is his intelligence in perfect form; thus she binds together the gods who are assembled about Helios and brings them without confusion into unity with him, the Lord of All; finally, she distributes and is the channel for immaculate and pure life throughout the seven spheres, from the highest vault of the heavens as far as Selene the Moon.[4] For Selene is the last of the heavenly spheres which Athena fills with wisdom, and by her aid Selene beholds the intelligible which is higher than the heavens, and adorns with its forms the realm of matter that lies below her, thus does she do away with its savagery, confusion, and disorder.

1. Athena as goddess of Forethought was worshipped at Delphi, but her earlier epithet was *Pronaia*, "the one before (the temple)"; cf. Æschylus, *Eumenides*, 21

2. This verse was quoted from an unknown source by Eustathius, *On The Iliad*

3. *The Iliad*, VIII, 538; XIII, 827 4. cf. Proclus, *On Timæus*, 258

To mankind, moreover, Athena gives the blessings of intelligence, wisdom, and the creative arts. Surely, therefore, she dwells in the capitols of cities because, through her wisdom, she has established the community of the state. I have still to say a few words about Aphrodite, who, as the wise men among the Phoenicians affirm, and, as I believe, assists Helios in his creative function. She is, in truth, a synthesis of the heavenly gods, and in their harmony she is the spirit of love and unity.[1] For she is very near to Helios,[2] and when she pursues the same course as he and approaches him, she fills the skies with fair weather, giving generative power to the earth. For she herself takes thought for the continuous birth of living things; and while Lord Helios is the primary creative cause of that continuous birth, Aphrodite is the joint cause with him, she who enchants our souls with her charm and sends down to earth from the upper air rays of light most sweet and pure, indeed, more lustrous than gold itself. I desire to mete out to you still more of the theology of the Phoenicians, and whether it be to some purpose, my argument as it proceeds will show. The inhabitants of Emesa,[3] a place from time immemorial sacred to Helios, associate with Helios in their temples Monimos and Azizos.[4] Iamblichus, from whom I have taken this and all besides, a little from a great store, says that the secret meaning to be interpreted is that Monimos is Hermes, and Azizos is Ares, the aides of Helios, who are the channel for many blessings to our region of the world.

Such, then, are the works of Helios in the heavens, and, when completed by means of the gods whom I have named, they reach even unto the furthest bounds of the earth. Yet to tell the number of all his works in the region below the moon would take too long. Nevertheless, I must describe them also in a brief summary. I am aware that I mentioned them earlier when I claimed that from things visible we could observe the invisible properties of the god's substance, but the argument demands that I should expound them now, also, in their proper order.

I explained, then, that Helios holds sway among the intellectual gods in that he unites into one, about his own undivided substance, a great multitude of the gods; further, I demonstrated that among the gods whom we can perceive, who revolve eternally in their most

1. cf. Proclus, On *Timæus*, 155; 259, where Aphrodite is referred to as "the binding goddess" *συνδετικήν*, and "harmoniser" *συναρμοστικήν*

2. i.e., as the planet Venus

3. Emesa was famous for its temple to Baal, the sun god

4. The god of the morning star

blessed path, he is leader and lord, since he bestows on their nature its generative power, and fills the whole heavens not only with visible rays of light but with countless other blessings that are invisible; and, moreover, that the blessings which are abundantly supplied by the other visible gods are made perfect by him, and that even prior to this the visible gods themselves are made perfect by his unspeakable and divine activity. In the same manner, we must believe that on this, our world of generation certain gods have alighted who are linked together with Helios. These gods guide the four-fold nature of the elements, and inhabit, together with the three higher races, those souls which are upborne by the elements. Yet for the divided souls also, of myriad blessings is he the cause. For he extends to them the faculty of judging, and guides them with justice, purifying them by his brilliant light. Again, does he not set in motion the whole of nature and kindle life therein by bestowing on it generative power from on high? While for the divided natures also, is not he the cause that they journey to their appointed end?[1] For Aristotle says that man is begotten by man and the sun together.[2] Accordingly, the same theory about Lord Helios must surely apply to all the other activities of the divided souls. Again, does he not produce for us rain and wind, and the clouds in the skies, by employing, as though it were matter, the two kinds of vapour? For when he heats the earth he draws up steam and smoke, and from these there arise not only the clouds but also all the physical changes on our earth, both great and small.

Why, however, do I deal with the same questions at such length, when I am free at last to come to my goal, though not till I have first celebrated all the blessings that Helios has given to mankind? For from him are we born, and by him are we nourished. As for his more divine gifts, all that he bestows on our souls when he frees them from the body and lifts them up on high to the region of those substances that are akin to the god; the fineness and vigour of his divine rays, which are assigned as a sort of vehicle for the safe descent of our souls into this world of generation; all this, I say, let others celebrate in fitting strains, but let me believe it rather than demonstrate its truth. Though I needn't hesitate to discuss so much as is known to all. Plato says[3] that the sky is our instructor in wisdom. For from its contemplation we have learned the nature of numbers, whose distinguishing characteristics we know only from the course of the sun. Plato himself says that day and night were

1. i.e. their ascent after death to the gods 2. *Physics*, 2.2.194 3. *Republic*, 529;

created first.[1] Next, from observing the moon's light, which was bestowed on the goddess by Helios, we progressed still further in the understanding of these matters, in every case conjecturing the harmony of all things with this god. For Plato himself says somewhere[2] that our race was by nature doomed to toil, and so the gods pitied us and gave us Dionysus and the Muses as companions. Thus we recognised that Helios is their common lord, since he is celebrated as the father of Dionysus and the leader of the Muses. For has not Apollo, who is his colleague in empire, set up oracles in every part of the earth, and given to men inspired wisdom, and regulated their cities by means of religious and political ordinances? Furthermore, he has civilised the greater part of the world by means of Greek colonies, and so made it easier for the world to be governed by the Romans. For not only do the Romans themselves belong to the Greek race, but the sacred ordinances and the pious belief in the gods which they have established and maintained are, from beginning to end, also Greek. Beside this, they have established a constitution not inferior to that of any one of the best governed states, if indeed it be not superior to all others that have ever been put into practice. For which reason I myself recognise that our city is Greek, both in descent and as to its constitution.

Shall I now go on to tell you how Helios took thought for the health and safety of all men by begetting Asclepius to be the saviour of the whole world? How he bestowed on us every kind of excellence by sending down to us Aphrodite together with Athena, and thus laid down for our protection what is almost a law, that we should only unite to beget our kind? Surely it is for this reason that, in agreement with the course of the sun, all plants and all tribes of living things are stirred to bring forth their kind. What need is there for me to glorify his beams and his light? For surely everyone knows how terrible is night without the moon or stars, and so from this he can appraise how great a boon for us is the light of the sun. It this very light he supplies at night, without ceasing, and directly, from the moon in those upper spaces where it is needed, while he grants us through the night a truce from toil. Yet there would be no limit to the account if one should endeavour to describe all his gifts of this sort. For there is no single blessing in our lives which we do not receive as a gift from this god, either perfect from him alone, or, through the other gods, perfected by him.

He, moreover, is the founder of our city.[3] For not only does

1. i.e. as a unit of measurement; *Timæus*, 39, 47 2. *Laws*, 653, 665 3. Rome

Zeus, who is glorified as the father of all things, inhabit its citadel[1] together with Athena and Aphrodite, but Apollo also dwells on the Palatine Hill, and, of course, Helios himself under this name of his which is commonly known to all and familiar to all. I could say much to prove that we, the sons of Romulus and Æneas, are in every way and in all respects connected with him, but I will mention briefly only what is most familiar. According to the legend, Æneas is the son of Aphrodite, who is herself subordinate to Helios and his kinswoman. The tradition has been handed down that the founder of our city was the son of Ares, and the paradoxical element in the tale has been believed because of the portents which later appeared to support it. For a she-wolf, they say, suckled him. Now, I am aware that Ares, who is called Azizos by the Syrians that inhabit Emesa, precedes Helios in the sacred procession, though I mentioned it before, so I think I may let that pass. Why, however, is the wolf sacred only to Ares and not to Helios? Yet men call the period of a year "lycabas"[2] which is derived from "wolf". For not only Homer[3] and the famous men of Greece call it by this name, but also the god himself, when he says: "with dancing does he bring to a close his journey of twelve months, even the lycabas". Now, do you wish me to bring forward a still greater proof that the founder of our city was sent down to earth, not by Ares alone, though perhaps some noble daimon with the character of Ares did take part in the fashioning of his mortal body, even he who is said to have visited Silvia[4] when she was carrying water for the bath of the goddess,[5] but the whole truth is that the soul of the god Quirinus[6] came down to earth from Helios. For we must, I think, believe the sacred tradition. The close conjunction of Helios and Selene, who share the empire over the visible world, even as it had caused his soul to descend to earth, in like manner caused to mount upwards him whom it received back from the earth, after blotting out with fire from a thunderbolt[7] the mortal part of his body. So clearly did

1. The famous temple of Jupiter on the Capitoline. The three shrines in this temple were dedicated to Jupiter, Minerva, and Juno, but Julian introduces Aphrodite in Juno's place for her connection with Æneas

2. The accepted etymology of "lycabas" is "path of light"

3. *The Odyssey*, XIV, 161. The word was also used on Roman coins to mean "year"

4. Silvia the Vestal virgin gave birth to twins, Romulus and Remus, whose father was claimed to be Mars (Ares)

5. Vesta, the Greek Hestia, the goddess of the hearth

6. The name given to Romulus after his apotheosis

7. For the legend of his ascension, cf. Livy 1.16; Plutarch, *Romulus*, 21;

she who creates earthly matter, she whose place is at the furthest point below the sun, receive Quirinus when he was sent down to earth by Athena, goddess of Forethought; and when he took flight again from earth, she led him back at once to Helios, the Lord of All.

Do you wish me to mention yet another proof of this, by which I mean the work of King Numa?[1] In Rome, maiden priestesses[2] guard the undying flame of the sun at different hours in turn; they guard the fire that is produced on earth by the agency of the god. Furthermore, I can tell you a still greater proof of the power of this god, which is the work of that most divine king himself. The months are reckoned from the moon by, one may say, all other peoples; but we and the Egyptians alone reckon the days of every year according to the movements of the sun. If, after this, I should say that we also worship Mithras, and celebrate games in honour of Helios every four years, I shall be speaking of customs that are somewhat recent.[3] Perhaps, then, it is better to cite a proof from the remote past. The beginning of the cycle of the year is placed at different times by different peoples. Some place it at the vernal equinox, others at the height of summer, and many in the late autumn; but they each and all sing the praises of the most visible gifts of Helios. One nation celebrates the season best adapted for work in the fields, when the earth bursts into bloom and exults, when all the crops are just beginning to sprout and the sea begins to be safe for sailing, while the disagreeable, gloomy winter puts on a more cheerful aspect; others, again, award the crown to the summer season,[4] since at that time they can safely feel confidence about the yield of the fruits, when the grains have already been harvested, midsummer is now at its height, and the fruits on the trees are ripening. Others, indeed, with still more subtlety, regard as the close of the year the time when all the fruits are in their perfect prime and decay has already set in. For this reason they celebrate the annual festival of the New Year in late autumn. Our forefathers, however, from the time of the most divine king Numa, paid still greater reverence to the god Helios. They ignored the question of mere utility, I think, because they were naturally religious and

1. Numa Pompilius, the legendary king who reigned after Romulus, and to whom the Romans ascribed the foundation of many of their religious ceremonies

2. The Vestal Virgins

3. The Heliaia, *Agon Solis*, was founded by the Emperor Aurelian at Rome in 274, though the "unconquered sun", *Sol Invictus*, had been worshipped there for fully a century before Aurelian's foundation

4. The Attic year began with the summer solstice

endowed with remarkable intelligence. Nevertheless, they saw that he is the cause of all that is useful, and so ordered the observance of the New Year to correspond with the present season; that is to say, when Lord Helios returns to us again, leaving the region furthest south and, rounding Capricorn as though it were a goal-post, advances to the north to give us our share of the year's blessings. That our forefathers, because they comprehended this correctly, thus established the beginning of the year, one may perceive from the following. For it was not, I think, the time when the god turns, but rather the time when he becomes visible to all men, as he travels from south to north, that they appointed for the festival. For still unknown to them was the nicety of those laws which the Chaldæans and Egyptians discovered, and which Hipparchus[1] and Ptolemy[2] perfected; they simply judged by sense-perception, and were limited to what they could actually see.

The truth of these facts was recognised, as I said, by a later generation. Before the beginning of the year, at the end of the month which is called after Kronos,[3] we celebrate in honour of Helios the most splendid games, and we dedicate the festival to *Sol Invictus*. After this, it is not lawful to perform any of the shows that belong to the last month, melancholy as they are, though necessary. Next in the cycle, then, immediately after the end of the Kronia,[4] follows the Heliaia. That festival may the ruling gods grant me to praise and to celebrate with sacrifice! And above all the others may Helios himself, the Lord of All, grant me this, he who from eternity has proceeded from the generative substance of the Good; who is midmost of the midmost intellectual gods; who fills them with continuity, endless beauty, a superabundance of generative power, and perfect reason, verily with all blessings at once, independent of time! For now he illumines his own visible abode, which from eternity moves as the centre of the vast heavens, and bestows a share of intelligible beauty on the entire visible world, filling the whole of the heavens with the same number of gods as he contains within himself in intellectual form. Thus without division they reveal themselves in manifold form surrounding him, though they are attached to him and form a unity.

1. A Greek astronomer who flourished in the middle of the second century B.C.

2. Claudius Ptolemy, an astronomer at Alexandria circa 127-151

3. i.e., December

4. The festival of Saturn, Saturnalia, was celebrated from 17th to 23rd December; Saturn was identified with the Greek god Kronos, hence Julian's use of Kronia

Indeed, through his perpetual generation and the blessings that he bestows from the heavenly bodies, he holds together the region beneath the moon. For he cares for the whole of mankind in common, but especially for my own city,[1] even as he also brought into being my soul from eternity, and made it his follower. All this, therefore, that I prayed for a moment ago, may he grant, and further may he, of his grace, endow my city as a whole with eternal existence, so far as is possible, and protect her; while for myself personally, may he grant that, so long as I am permitted to live, I may prosper in my affairs both human and divine; finally, may he grant me to live and serve the state with my life, so long as it is pleasing to himself, proper for me, and of benefit to Rome.

This discourse, friend Salutius,[2] I composed in three nights at most, in harmony with the three-fold creative power of the god,[3] as far as possible just as it occurred to my memory. I have ventured to write it down and to dedicate it to you because you thought my earlier work on the Kronia[4] was not wholly worthless. If, however, you wish to meet with a more complete and mystical treatment of the same theme, then read the writings of the inspired Iamblichus on this subject,[5] and you will find there the most consummate wisdom which man can achieve. May mighty Helios grant that I, too, may attain to no less perfect knowledge of himself, and that I may instruct all men, speaking generally, but especially those who are worthy to learn. And so long as Helios grants, let us all in common revere Iamblichus, beloved of the gods. For he is the source for what I have here set down, a few thoughts from many, as they occurred to my mind. Yet I know well that no one can utter anything more perfect than he, indeed, not though he should labour long at the task and say very much that is new. For he will naturally diverge thereby from the truest knowledge of the god. Thus it would probably have been a vain undertaking to compose anything after Iamblichus on the same subject, if I had written this discourse for the sake of giving instruction. Since, however, I wished to compose a hymn to express my gratitude to the god, I thought that this was the best place in which to tell, to the best of my power, of his essential nature. I think, therefore, that not in vain

1. Rome

2. Julian's friend and fellow Neo-Platonist to whom this work was addressed

3. For the threefold creative force, cf. Proclus, *On Timæus*, 94. Here Julian means that there are three modes of creation exercised by Helios across the three worlds

4. This work is lost

5. i.e. his treatise *On the Gods*, which is not extant

has this discourse been composed. For the saying "to the extent of your powers offer sacrifice to the immortal gods"[1] I apply not to sacrifice only, but also to the praises that we offer to the gods. For the third time, then, I pray that Helios, the Lord of All, may be gracious to me in recompense for this my zeal; and may he grant me a virtuous life, more perfect wisdom, and inspired intelligence, and, when fate wills, the gentlest exit that may be from life, at a fitting hour; and that I may ascend to him thereafter and abide with him, for ever if possible, though if that be more than the actions of my life deserve, for many periods of many years!

1. Hesiod, *Works and Days*, 336

HYMN TO THE MOTHER OF THE GODS

PREFACE

Julian's second hymn, composed in 362 at Pessinus, in Phrygia, is dedicated to Cybele, the appellated Mother of the Gods. The cult of the Phrygian goddess was the first Oriental religion to be adopted by the Romans, who bestowed upon her the name of *Magna Mater Deorum*. Her arrival in Rome during the Second Punic War, at the very end of third century, is recounted by Julian with due reverence and a rather uncharacteristic adherence to the traditional story, including its more supra-natural elements. Nevertheless, as a Neo-Platonist first and foremost, the aim of his hymn was to integrate the popular cult into his worldview and to provide its Mysteries with a philosophic interpretation[1].

The various historical accounts of Cybele's arrival in Rome from Asia Minor focus upon the power of the goddess and how the piety of the Romans was rewarded – the victory over Carthage was attributed in part to the fulfilment of a Sibylline prophecy. She is described as having neither a consort, nor a priesthood, and appears wholly Romanised from the very beginning. Since the Romans believed Cybele to be the mother-goddess of ancient Troy, the ancestral home, according to mythology, of the Roman people, "the cult was eventually installed in a temple on the Palatine Hill, in the very centre of the city of Rome. The goddess had come to join the Trojan descendants in Italy; she had come back home".[2] It is understandable, then, why Julian would be eager to incorporate Cybele into his theology and give her pride of place next to Helios atop the pantheon. The obstacles to doing so, however, were by no means inconsiderable.

While the *Magna Mater* herself was very much welcome within the Eternal City, her consort and priesthood were not. According to the legend which will have originated in the Near East,[3] Cybele appeared before a young mortal man by the name of Attis, who at once fell into a frenzy, her resplendence such that, in his madness, he was driven to castrate himself. After his death, caused by the extraordinary act of self-emasculation, Attis was brought back to eternal life through the intervention of Cybele, whereupon he became the consort of the goddess. Attis was thus a central figure in the cult of the *Magna Mater*.

---

1. W.C.F. Wright 2. Mary Beard, *The Roman and the Foreign* 3. ibid.

The priesthood of Cybele, known individually as *gallus* and collectively as *galli*, took inspiration from the myth, and sought to emulate Attis as part of their devotion to the goddess. These priests were a "flamboyantly foreign, and often unsettling presence in the city of Rome"[1], their behaviour wholly at odds with the temper and mores of Roman society. Their religious rituals entailed not merely ecstatic dancing, but frenetic self-flagellation and, in the most extreme instances, self-castration in imitation of Attis: "on March 24th, the *dies sanguinis* was celebrated, a mournful observance in which the *galli* would shed their blood and sometimes mutilate themselves in commemoration of the wound that had caused Attis' death".[2] One can only imagine the distaste this would have provoked among the local populous. The emasculated, decidedly un-Roman devotees of Cybele "stalk the pages of Latin literature as mad, frenzied, foreign eunuchs"[3], the practitioners of a cult which could never be truly integrated into Rome's religious tradition. Under the Emperor Hadrian, for example, castration of any man, free or slave, was explicitly forbidden. To the Roman mind, "the eunuch *gallus* was both a non-man and a man who broke the rules of proper male behaviour".[4] It would not be unreasonable to suggest that, at the time of her introduction, they had been unaware of the true nature of the cult they were importing: "the Romans had brought their ancestral – that is, Trojan – goddess to the new country and provided her with proper accommodation, only to then discover how widely and profoundly their own attitude differed from that of the Near East".[5]

The task before Julian, then, was by no means straightforward. The frenzied rituals, intemperance, and ostentation were entirely at odds with his own values of propriety, self-restraint, and considered reflection; while the emasculating, matriarchal aspects of the cult of the pre-Indo-European goddess was fundamentally in opposition to the "virile, Apollonian"[6] element of Rome. Julian needed, by means of a philosophic interpretation, to render both the myth and the *Magna Mater* priesthood compatible with his religious vision, and to make the aforementioned not merely tolerable but compelling to the Romano-Hellenic faithful.

---

1. Mary Beard, *The Roman and the Foreign*
2. Franz Cumont, *Oriental Religions in Roman Paganism*
3. Mary Beard, *The Roman and the Foreign* 4. ibid.
5. Vermaseren, 1977 6. Evola, *Rome and the Sibylline Books*

His hymn in honour of Cybele consequently devotes far more attention to Attis and, by extension, the practice of the *galli*. For all Julian's attempts to recontextualise, sanitise, and rationalise the story of Attis, however, the myth, and the barbaric practices associated with it, remain inherently objectionable, not only to most modern observers, but assuredly to a contemporary Roman audience. As the oration progresses, Julian loses himself in an "excessive use of allegory" and "extravagant symbolism"[1] indicative of the impossible purpose with which he had burdened himself. This is arguably one instance in which Julian would have benefited from allowing a cult to be resigned to the pages of history.

1. Franz Cumont, *Oriental Religions in Roman Paganism*

HYMN TO THE MOTHER OF THE GODS

Ought I to say something on this subject, also? Shall I write, then, about things not to be spoken of and divulge what ought not to be divulged? Shall I utter the unutterable? Who is Attis[1] or Gallus,[2] who is the Mother of the Gods,[3] and what is the manner of their ritual of purification? Furthermore, why was it introduced in the beginning among us Romans? It was handed down by the Phrygians in very ancient times, and was first taken over by the Greeks; not by any ordinary Greeks, but by Athenians who had learned by experience that they were wrong to jeer at one who was celebrating the Mysteries of the Mother. For it is said that they wantonly insulted and drove out Gallus on the ground that he was introducing a new cult, because they did not understand what sort of goddess they were dealing with, nor that she was that very Deo whom they worship, with Rhea and Demeter, too. Then followed the wrath of the goddess and the propitiation of her wrath. For the priestess of the Pythian god who guided the Greeks in all noble conduct, bade them propitiate the wrath of the Mother of the Gods. Thus, we are told, the Metroum was built where the Athenians used to keep all their state records.[4] After the Greeks, the Romans took over the cult, since the Pythian god had advised them in turn to bring the goddess from Phrygia as an ally in their war against Carthage.[5] Perhaps there is no reason why I should not include here a brief account of what happened. When they learned the response of the oracle, the inhabitants of Rome, that city beloved of the gods, sent an embassy to ask from the kings of Pergamon,[6] who then

1. The Phrygian god of vegetation who corresponds to the Syrian Adonis. His name is said to mean "father", and he is at once the lover and son of the Mother of the Gods. His death and resurrection were celebrated in spring

2. The name of the eunuch priests of Cybele and Attis

3. The Phrygian Cybele, the Near Eastern goddess of fertility; the chief seat of her worship was Pessinus in Phrygia

4. After the mid 5th century B.C.; before that records were kept in the Acropolis

5. In 204 B.C.; cf. Livy, 29.10; Ovid, Fasti, 4.255

6. The Attalids

ruled over Phrygia, and from the Phrygians themselves the most holy statue[1] of the goddess. Once they had received it, they brought back their most sacred freight, putting it on a broad cargo-boat which could sail smoothly over those wide seas. Thus she crossed the Ægean and Ionian Seas, sailed round Sicily and over the Etruscan Sea, and so entered the mouth of the Tiber. The people and the Senate with them poured out of the city, and in front of all the others there came to meet her every priest and priestess in suitable attire, according to their ancestral custom. In excited suspense they gazed at the ship as she ran before a fair wind, and about her keel they could discern the foaming wake as she cleft the waves. They greeted the ship as she sailed in and adored her from afar, each from where they happened to be standing. Yet the goddess, as though she desired to show the Roman people that they were not bringing a lifeless image from Phrygia, but that what they had received from the Phrygians and were now bringing home possessed greater and more divine powers than an image, stayed the ship when she touched the Tiber, and suddenly it was as though she were rooted mid-stream. So they tried to tow her against the current, but she did not follow. Then they tried to push her off, thinking they had grounded on a shoal, but for all their efforts she did not move. Next, every possible device was brought to bear, but in spite of it all she remained immovable. Thereupon a terrible and unjust suspicion fell on the maiden who had been consecrated to the most sacred office of priestess, and they began to accuse Claudia[2] – for that was the name of that noble maiden[3] – of having not kept herself pure and unblemished for the goddess; wherefore they said that the goddess was angry and was plainly declaring her wrath. For by this time it seemed to all to be the intervention of a divine power.

Now, at first she was filled with shame at the mere name of the thing and the suspicion; so very far was she from such shameless and lawless behaviour. Yet when she saw that the charge against her was gaining strength, she took off her girdle and fastened it about the prow of the ship, and, like one divinely inspired, bade all stand aside; then she besought the goddess not to suffer her to be thus implicated in unjust slanders. Next, as the story goes, she cried

1. A black meteoric stone embodied the goddess of Pessinus

2. *Claudia, turritæ rara ministra deæ.* "Claudia, you peerless priestess of the goddess with the embattled crown", *Propertius*, 4.11.52

3. A matron in other versions

aloud as though it were some nautical word of command "O Goddess Mother, if I am pure, follow me!" And lo, she not only made the ship move, but even towed her for some distance up stream. Two things, I think, the goddess showed the Romans on that day: first that the freight they were bringing from Phrygia had no small value, but was priceless; that this was no work of men's hands but truly divine, not lifeless clay but a thing possessed of life and divine powers. This, I say, was one thing that the goddess showed them. The other was that none of the citizens could be with or without virtue and she not know thereof. Moreover, the war of the Romans against the Carthaginians forthwith took a favourable turn, so that the third war was waged only for the walls of Carthage itself.[1]

As for this narrative, though some will think it incredible and wholly unworthy of a philosopher or a theologian, nevertheless let it here be related. For besides the fact that it is commonly recorded by most historians, it has been preserved, too, on bronze statues in mighty Rome, beloved of the gods.[2] Though I am well aware that some overly wise persons will call it an old wives' tale, not to be credited. For my part, however, I would rather trust the traditions of cities than those self-certain people, whose tiny souls are keen-sighted enough, but never do they see anything that is sound.[3]

I am told that on this same subject of which I am impelled to speak at the very season of these sacred rites, Porphyry too has written a philosophic treatise. Since, however, I have never met with it, I do not know whether at any point it may chance to agree with my discourse. Yet him whom I call Gallus, or Attis, I discern of my own knowledge to be the substance of generative and creative Mind which engenders all things down to the lowest plane of matter,[4] and comprehends in itself all the concepts and causes of the forms that are embodied in matter. For truly the forms of all things are not in all things, and in the highest and first causes we do not find the forms of the lowest and last, after which there is nothing save privation[5] coupled with a dim idea. Now, there are many substances and very many creative gods, but the nature of the third creator,[6] who contains in himself the separate concepts of the forms that are embodied in matter as well as the connected chain

1. In the Third Punic War (149-6 B.C.), Carthage was sacked by the Romans
2. A relief in the Capitoline Museum shows Claudia in the act of pulling the ship
3. Plato, *Republic*, 519 4. i.e. the world of sense-perception
5. cf. Plotinus 1.8.4 6. Helios; Attis here is identified with the light of the sun

of causes, by which I mean that nature which is last in order, and through its superabundance of generative power descends even unto earth through the upper region from the stars – this is he whom we seek, Attis himself. Though perhaps I ought to distinguish more clearly what I mean. We assert that matter exists and also form embodied in matter. Yet if no cause be assigned prior to these two, we should be introducing, unconsciously, the Epicurean doctrine. For if there be nothing of higher order than these two principles, then a spontaneous motion and chance brought them together. "But", says some acute Peripatetic like Xenarchus, "we see that the cause of these is the fifth or cyclic substance. Aristotle is absurd when he investigates and discusses these matters, and Theophrastus likewise. At any rate, he overlooked the implications of a well-known utterance of his. For when he came to incorporeal and intelligible substance, he stopped short and did not inquire into its cause, and merely asserted that this is what it is by nature; surely in the case of the fifth substance, also, he ought to have assumed that its nature is to be thus, and he ought not to have gone on to search for causes, but should have stopped at these, not falling back on the intelligible, which has no independent existence by itself, and in any case represents a bare supposition". This is the sort of thing that Xenarchus says, as I remember having heard. Now, whether what he says is correct or not, let us leave to the extreme Peripatetics to refine. That his view is not agreeable to me, however, is, I think, clear to everyone. For I hold that the theories of Aristotle himself are incomplete unless they are brought into harmony with those of Plato;[1] or rather, we must make these also agree with the oracles that have been vouchsafed to us by the gods.

It is perhaps worthwhile to inquire into this, how the cyclic substance[2] can contain the incorporeal causes of the forms that are embodied in matter. For that, apart from these causes, it is not possible for generation to take place is, I think, clear and manifest. For why are there so many kinds of generated things? Whence arise masculine and feminine? Whence the distinguishing characteristics of things according to their species in well-defined types, if there are not pre-existing and pre-established concepts, and causes which

1. Julian here sums up the tendency of the philosophy of his age. The Peripatetics had been merged in the Platonists and Neo-Platonists, and Themistius the Aristotelian commentator often speaks of the reconciliation, in contemporary philosophy, of Plato and Aristotle; cf. 235, 236, 366

2. i.e. æther, the fifth substance

existed beforehand to serve as a pattern?[1] Thus if we discern these causes but dimly, let us still further purify the eyes of the soul. The right kind of purification, then, is to turn our gaze inwards and to observe how the soul and embodied Mind are a sort of mould[2] and likeness of the forms that are embodied in matter. For in the case of the corporeal, or of things that though incorporeal come into being and are to be studied in relation to the corporeal, there is no single thing whose mental image the mind cannot grasp independently of the corporeal. Yet this it could not have done if it did not possess something naturally akin to the incorporeal forms. Indeed, it is for this reason that Aristotle himself called the soul the "place of the forms",[3] only he said that the forms are there not actually but potentially. Now, a soul of this sort, one that is allied with matter, must possess these forms potentially only, but a soul that should be independent and unmixed in this way we must believe would contain all the concepts, not potentially but actually. Let us make this clearer by means of the example which Plato himself employed in the Sophist, with reference certainly to another theory, though still he did employ it. I bring forward the illustration, therefore, not to prove my argument, for one must not try to grasp it by demonstration, but only by apprehension. For it deals with the first causes, or at least those that rank with the first, if indeed, as it is right to believe, we must regard Attis also as a god. What then, and of what sort is this illustration? Plato says[4] that if any man whose profession is imitation desires to imitate in such a way that the original be exactly reproduced, this method of imitation is troublesome and difficult, and, by Zeus, borders on the impossible; but pleasant, easy, and quite possible is the method which only seems to imitate real things. For instance, when we take up a mirror and turn it round we easily get an impression of all objects, and are shown the general outline of every single thing. From this example, let us go back to the analogy I spoke of and let the mirror stand for what Aristotle calls the "place of the forms" potentially.

Now, the forms themselves must certainly subsist actually before they subsist potentially. If, therefore, the soul in us, as Aristotle himself believed, contains potentially the forms of

1. i.e. the causes of the forms embodied in matter have a prior existence as Ideas

2. An echo of Plato, *Theætetus*, 191, 196; *Timæus*, 50

3. *De Anima*, 3.4.429; Aristotle quotes the phrase with approval and evidently attributes it to Plato; the precise expression is not to be found in Plato, though in *Parmenides*, 132, he says that the Ideas are "in our souls"

4. *Sophist*, 235 a; cf. *Republic*, 596

existing things, where shall we place the forms in that previous state of actuality? Shall it be in material things? No, for the forms that are in them are evidently the last and lowest. Therefore, it only remains to search for immaterial causes which exist in actuality prior to and of a higher order than the causes that are embodied in matter. For our souls must subsist in dependence on these and come forth together with them, and so receive from them the concepts of the forms, as mirrors show the reflections of things; then, with the aid of nature, it bestows them on matter and on these material bodies of our world. For we know that nature is the maker of bodies, with each being part of the All; while that the individual nature of each is the maker of particulars is plainly evident. Yet nature exists in us in actuality without a mental image, whereas the soul, which is superior to this nature, possesses a mental image besides. If, therefore, we admit that nature contains in herself the cause of things of which she has no mental image, why, in heaven's name, are we not to assign to the soul these same forms, only in a still higher degree, and with priority over nature, seeing that it is in the soul that we recognise the forms by means of mental images, and comprehend them by means of the concept? Who, then, is so contentious as to admit on the one hand that the concepts embodied in matter exist in nature – even though not all and equally in actuality, yet all potentially – while on the other hand he refuses to recognise that the same is true of the soul? If, therefore, the forms exist in nature potentially, but not actually, and if they also exist potentially in the soul,[1] albeit in a still purer sense and more completely separated, such that they can be comprehended and recognised, yet exist in actuality nowhere at all, to what, I ask, shall we hang the chain of perpetual generation, and on what shall we base our theories of the imperishability of the universe?

Now, the cyclic substance itself is composed of matter and form. It must therefore follow that, even though in actuality these two, matter and form, are never separate from one another, for our intelligence the forms must have prior existence and be regarded as of a higher order. Accordingly, since for the forms embodied in matter a wholly immaterial cause has been assigned, which leads these forms under the hand of the third creator – who for us is the lord and father not only of these forms but also of the visible fifth substance – from that creator we distinguish Attis, the cause which

1. For the superiority of the soul to nature, cf. *De Mysteriis*, 8.7.270; and for the theory that the soul gives form to matter, cf. Plotinus, 4.3.20

descends even unto matter, and we believe that Attis, or Gallus, is a god of generative powers. Of him the myth relates that, after being exposed at birth near the eddying stream of the river Gallus, he grew up like a flower, and when he had grown to be fair and tall, he was beloved by the Mother of the Gods. She entrusted all things to him, and moreover set on his head the starry cap.[1] Thus, if our visible sky covers the crown of Attis, must one not interpret the river Gallus as the Milky Way?[2] For it is there, they say, that the substance which is subject to change mingles with the passionless revolving sphere of the fifth substance. Only as far as this did the Mother of the Gods permit this fair, intellectual god Attis, who resembles the sun's rays, to leap and dance. Yet when he passed beyond this limit and came even to the lowest region, the myth says that he had descended into the cave, and had wedded the nymph. This nymph, then, is to be interpreted as the dampness of matter; though the myth does not here mean matter itself, but the lowest immaterial cause which subsists prior to matter. Indeed, Heraclitus also says: "it is death to souls to become wet". We mean, therefore, that this Gallus, the intellectual god, the connecting link between forms embodied in matter beneath the region of the moon, is united with the cause that is set over matter, though not in the sense that one sex is united with another, but like an element that is gathered to itself.

Who, then, is the Mother of the Gods? She is the source of the intellectual and creative gods, who in their turn guide the visible gods; she is both the mother and the partner of mighty Zeus; she came into being next to and together with the great creator; she has power over of every form of life, and is the cause of all generation; she easily brings to perfection all things that are made; without pain she brings to birth, and with the father's aid creates all things that are; she is the motherless maiden,[3] enthroned at the side of Zeus, and in very truth is the Mother of all the Gods. For having received into herself the causes of all the gods, both intelligible and supramundane, she became the source of the intellectual gods. Now, this goddess, who is also Forethought, was inspired with a passionless love for Attis. For not only the forms embodied in matter, but to a still greater degree the causes of those forms, voluntarily serve her and obey her will. Accordingly, the myth relates the following: that

1. cf. Salutius, *On the Gods and the World*, 4.16.1 2. ibid. 4.14.25

3. Hence she is the counterpart of Athena. Athena is Forethought among the intellectual gods; Cybele is Forethought among the intelligible gods

she who is the Providence, who preserves all that is subject to generation and decay, loved their creative and generative cause, and commanded that cause to beget offspring rather in the intelligible region; and she desired that it should turn towards herself and dwell with her, yet condemned it to dwell with no other thing. For only thus would that creative cause strive towards the uniformity that preserves it, and at the same time avoid that which inclines towards matter. She bade that cause look towards her, the source of the creative gods, and not be dragged down or allured into generation. For in this way was mighty Attis destined to be an even mightier creation, seeing that in all things the conversion to what is higher produces more power to effect than the inclination to what is lower. Moreover, the fifth substance itself is more creative and more divine than the elements of our earth, for the reason that it is more nearly connected with the gods. Not that anyone, surely, would venture to assert that any substance, even if it be composed of the purest æther, is superior to soul undefiled and pure, like that of Heracles, for instance, as it was when the creator sent it to earth. For that soul of his both seemed to be and was more vigorous than after it had bestowed itself on a body. Since even Heracles, now that he has returned, one and indivisible, to his father, more easily controls his own province than formerly when he wore the garment of flesh and walked among men. This shows that in all things the conversion to the higher is more powerful than the propensity to the lower. This, then, is what the myth aims to teach us when it says that the Mother of the Gods exhorted Attis not to leave her or to love another. Yet he went further, and descended even to the lowest limits of matter. Since, however, it was necessary that his limitless course should cease and halt at last, mighty Helios, the true Corybant,[1] who is enthroned alongside the Mother and with her creates all things, has providence for all things, and does no thing apart from her, persuaded the Lion[2] to reveal the matter. And who is this Lion? Verily we are told that he is flame-coloured.[3] He is, therefore, the cause that subsists prior to the hot and fiery, whose task it was to contend against the nymph and to be jealous of her union with Attis (and who the nymph is, I have said). Further, the myth says that the Lion serves the creative Providence of the world,

1. Corybantes were the Phrygian priests of Cybele, who at Rome were called *Galli*

2. The Near Eastern deities, especially Cybele, are often represented holding lions, or in cars drawn by them; cf. Catullus, 63.76

3. *The Iliad*, X, 23

which evidently means the Mother of the Gods. Then it says that by detecting and revealing the truths he caused the youth's castration. What is the meaning of this act? It is the checking of the unlimited. For now was generation confined within definite forms checked by creative Providence. This, moreover, would not have happened without the so-called madness of Attis, which overstepped and transgressed due measure, and thereby made him become weak so that he had no control over himself. It is not surprising that this should come to pass when we have to do with the cause that ranks lowest among the gods. For consider the fifth substance, which is subject to no change of any sort, in the region of the light of the moon, that is, where our world of continuous generation and decay borders on the fifth substance. We perceive that in the region of her light it seems to undergo certain alterations and to be affected by external influences. Therefore, it is not contradictory to suppose that our Attis is also a sort of demigod – for that is actually the meaning of the myth – or rather, for the universe he is wholly god, for he proceeds from the third creator, and after his alteration is led upwards again to the Mother of the Gods. Yet though he seems to lean and incline towards matter, one would not be mistaken in supposing that, though he is the lowest in order of the gods, he is nevertheless the leader of all the tribes of divine beings. The myth, however, calls him a demigod to indicate the difference between him and the unchanging gods. He is attended by the Corybants who are assigned to him by Cybele; they are the three leading personalities of the higher races that are next in order to the gods. Attis also rules over the lions, who together with the Lion, who is their leader, have chosen for themselves the hot and fiery substance, and so are, first and foremost, the cause of fire. Through the heat derived from fire, they are the causes of motive force and of preservation for all other things that exist. While Attis encircles the heavens like a crown, and thence sets out as though to descend to earth.

This, then, is our mighty god Attis. This explains his once lamented flight and concealment, his disappearance and descent into the cave. In proof of this, let me cite the time of year at which it happens. For we are told that the sacred tree[1] is felled on the day when the sun reaches the height of the equinox. Thereupon the trumpets are sounded;[2] and on the third day the sacred and

1. A sacred pine was felled on 22nd March; cf. Frazer, *Attis, Adonis, and Osiris*, p. 222
2. 23rd March

unspeakable sacrifice of the god Gallus is severed.[1] Next comes, they say, the Hilaria[2] and the festival. That this castration, so much discussed by the crowd, is really the halting of his unlimited course, is evident from what happens directly as mighty Helios touches the cycle of the equinox, where the bounds are most clearly defined (for the even is bounded, but the uneven is without bounds, and there is no way through or out of it). At that time, precisely, according to the account we have, the sacred tree is felled. Thereupon, in their proper order, all the other ceremonies take place. Some of them are celebrated with the secret ritual of the Mysteries, but others by a ritual that can be told to all. For instance, the cutting of the tree belongs to the story of Gallus and not to the Mysteries at all, but it has been taken over by them. This, I think, is because the gods wished to teach us, in symbolic fashion, that we must pluck the fairest fruits from the earth, namely, virtue and piety, and offer them to the goddess to be the symbol of our well-ordered constitution here on earth. For the tree grows from the soil, but it strives upwards as though to reach the upper air; it is fair to behold and gives us shade in the heat; and casts before us and bestows on us its fruits as a boon. Such is its superabundance of generative life. Accordingly, the ritual enjoins on us, who by nature belong to the heavens but have fallen to earth, to reap the harvest of our constitution here on earth, namely, virtue and piety, and then strive upwards to the goddess of our forefathers, to her who is the principle of all life.

Immediately after the sacrifice, then, the trumpet sounds the recall for Attis and for all of us who once flew down from heaven and fell to earth. After this signal, when Lord Attis stays his limitless course by his castration, the god bids us also root out the unlimited in ourselves and imitate the gods our leaders, hastening back to the defined and uniform, and, if it be possible, to the One itself. After this, the Hilaria must by all means follow. For what could be more blessed, what more joyful than a soul which has escaped from limitlessness, generation, and inward storm, and has been translated up to the very gods? For Attis himself was such a one, and the Mother of the Gods by no means allowed him to advance unregarded further than was permitted. Indeed, she made him turn towards herself, and commanded him to set a limit to his limitless course.

---

1. 24th March, the *dies sanguinis,* during which the Galli shed their blood and in extreme instances engaged in riualistic self-mutilation

2. 25th March was the resurrection of Attis and the freeing of souls from generation (*γένεσις*), which was celebrated with the feast of the Hilaria

Let no one suppose my meaning to be that this was ever done or happened in a way that implies that the gods themselves are ignorant of what they intend to do, or that they have to correct their own errors. Yet our ancestors in every case tried to trace the original meaning of things, whether with the guidance of the gods or independently – though perhaps it would be better to say that they sought them under the leadership of the gods – then when they had discovered those meanings they clothed them in paradoxical myths. This was in order that, by means of the paradox and the incongruity, the fiction might be detected and we might be induced to search out the truth. Now, I think ordinary men derive benefit enough from the myth, which instructs them through symbols alone; while those who are more highly endowed with wisdom will find the truth about the gods helpful, though only on condition that such a man examine, discover, and comprehend it under the leadership of the gods. If by such riddles as these he is reminded that he must search out their meaning, and so attains to the goal and summit of his quest through his own research, he must not be modest and put faith in the opinions of others rather than in his own mental powers.

What shall I say now by way of summary? Because men observed that, as far as the fifth substance, not only the intelligible world but also the visible bodies of our world must be classed as unaffected by the external and divine, they believed that, as far as the fifth substance, the gods are uncompounded. Additionally, then, by means of that generative substance, the visible gods came into being, and, from everlasting, matter was produced along with those gods, from them and through their agency, by reason of the superabundance in them of the generative and creative principle. Then the Providence of the world, she who from everlasting is of the same essential nature as the gods, she who is enthroned by the side of Lord Zeus, and moreover is the source of the intellectual gods, set in order, corrected, and changed for the better all that seemed lifeless and barren, the refuse and offscourings, so to speak, of things, their dregs and sediment; and this she did by means of the last cause derived from the gods, in which the substances of all the gods come to an end.

For it is evident that Attis of whom I speak, who wears the crown set with stars, took for the foundation of his own dominion the functions of every god as we see them applied to the visible world. Thus in his case, all is undefiled and pure as far as the Milky

Way. Yet, at this very point, that which is troubled by passion begins to mingle with the passionless, and from that union matter begins to subsist. Therefore the association of Attis with matter is the descent into the cave, nor did this take place against the will of the gods and the Mother of the Gods, though the myth says that it was against their will. For by their nature the gods dwell in a higher world, and the higher powers do not desire to drag them hence down to our world; rather, through the condescension of the higher, they desire to lead the things of our earth upwards to a higher plane more favoured by the gods. In fact, the myth does not say that the Mother of the Gods was hostile to Attis after his limitation; rather it says that, though she is no longer angry, she was angry at the time on account of his condescension, in that he who was a higher being and a god had given himself to that which was inferior. Yet when, after staying his limitless progress, he has set in order the chaos of our world through his sympathy with the cycle of the equinox, where mighty Helios controls the most perfect symmetry of his motion within due limits, then the goddess gladly leads him upwards to herself, or rather, keeps him by her side. Never did this happen save in the manner that it happens now; but forever is Attis the servant and charioteer of the Mother; forever he yearns passionately towards generation; and forever he cuts short his unlimited course through the cause whose limits are fixed, even the cause of the forms. In like manner, the myth says that he is led upwards as though from our earth, and again resumes his ancient sceptre and dominion; not that he ever lost it, or ever loses it now, for the myth says that he lost it on account of his union with that which is subject to passion and change.

Perhaps, then, it is worthwhile to raise the following question also. There are two equinoxes, but men pay more honour to the equinox in the sign of Capricorn than to that in the sign of Cancer.[1] Surely the reason for this is evident. Since the sun begins to approach us immediately after the spring equinox – I need not mention that the days then begin to lengthen – this seemed the more agreeable season. For apart from the explanation which says that light accompanies the gods, we must believe that the uplifting rays of the sun are nearly akin to those who yearn to be set free from generation. Consider it clearly: the sun, by his vivifying and marvellous heat, draws up all things from the earth, calls them

1. Porphyry, *On the Cave of the Nymph*, 22, says that Cancer and Capricorn are the two gates of the sun; that souls descend through Cancer and rise through Capricorn

forth, and makes them grow; he separates, I think, all corporeal things to the utmost degree of tenuity, and makes things weigh light that naturally have a tendency to sink. We ought, then, to make these visible things proofs of his unseen powers. For if among corporeal things he can bring this about through his material heat, how should he not draw and lead upwards the souls of the blessed by the agency of the invisible, wholly immaterial, divine, and pure substance which resides in his rays? We have seen that this light is nearly akin to the god, and to those who yearn to mount upwards; moreover, that this light increases in our world, so that when Helios begins to enter the sign of Capricorn, the day becomes longer than the night. It has also been demonstrated that the god's rays are by nature uplifting; and this is due to his energy, both seen and unseen, by which very many souls have been lifted up out of the region of the senses, since they were guided by that sense which is clearest of all and most nearly like the sun. For when with our eyes we perceive the sun's light, not only is it welcome and useful for our lives, but also, as the divine Plato said[1] when he sang its praises, it is our guide to wisdom. Additionally, if I should also touch on the secret teaching of the Mysteries in which the Chaldæan,[2] divinely enthused, celebrated the God of the Seven Rays, that god through whom he lifts up the souls of men, I should be saying what is unintelligible, indeed, wholly unintelligible to the common herd, but familiar to the happy theurgists.[3] Thus I will for the present be silent on that subject.

Now, I was saying before that we ought not to suppose that the ancients appointed the season of the rites irrationally, but rather as far as possible with plausible and true grounds of reason; and, indeed, a proof of this is that the goddess herself chose as her province the cycle of the equinox. For the most holy and secret Mysteries of Deo and the Maiden[4] are celebrated when the sun is in the sign of Libra, and this is quite natural. For when the gods depart we must consecrate ourselves afresh, so that we may suffer no harm from the godless power of darkness that now begins to gain the upper hand. At any rate, the Athenians celebrate the Mysteries of Deo twice in the year, the Lesser Mysteries as they call them in the sign of Capricorn, and the Great Mysteries when the sun is in the

1. *Phædrus*, 250, *Timæus*, 47, *Republic*, 507

2. Chaldæan astrology and oracles are often cited with respect by Neo-Platonists

3. e.g. Iamblichus and especially Maximus of Ephesus

4. The Eleusinian Mysteries of Demeter and Persephone; the Lesser were celebrated in February, and the greater in September

sign of Cancer, the latter for the reason that I have just mentioned. I believe that these Mysteries are called Great and Lesser for several reasons, but especially, as is natural, they are called great when the god departs rather than when he approaches, and so the Lesser are celebrated only by way of reminder.[5] By which I mean that when the saving and uplifting god approaches, the preliminary rites of the Mysteries take place. A little later, the rites of purification follow, one after another, and the consecration of the priests. Then, when the god departs to the antipodes, the most important ceremonies of the Mysteries are performed, for our protection and salvation. Observe the following: as in the festival of the Mother where the instrument of generation is severed, so too with the Athenians, those who take part in the secret rites are wholly chaste and their leader, the hierophant, forswears generation. For he must not have anything to do with the progress to the unlimited, but only with the substance whose bounds are fixed, so that it abides forever and is contained within the One, immaculate and pure. On this subject I have said enough.

It only remains now to speak, as is fitting, about the sacred rite itself, and the purification, so that from these, also, I may borrow whatever contributes to my argument. For example, everyone believes that the following is ridiculous: the sacred ordinance allows men to eat meat, but it forbids them to eat grains and fruits. What, say they, are not the latter lifeless, whereas the former was once possessed of life? Are not fruits pure, whereas meat is full of blood and of much else that offends eye and ear? Yet most important of all, is it not the case that, when one eats fruit nothing is hurt, while the eating of meat involves the sacrifice and slaughter of animals who naturally suffer pain and torment? So would say many even of the wisest. Yet the following ordinance is ridiculed by the most impious of mankind also. They observe that whereas vegetables that grow upwards can be eaten, roots are forbidden – turnips, for instance; and they point out that figs are allowed, but not pomegranates or apples, either. I have often heard many men saying this in whispers, and I, too, in former days have said the same, but now it seems that I alone of all men am bound to be deeply grateful to the ruling gods, to all of them, surely, but above all the rest to the Mother of the Gods. For all things am I grateful to her, and for this among the rest, that she did not disregard me when I wandered, as it were, in darkness. For first she bade me sever no part of my body, but rather,

1. Plato, *Gorgias*, 497; Plutarch, *Demetrius*, 900

by the aid of the intelligible cause that subsists prior to our souls, all that was superfluous and vain in the impulses and motions of my own soul. That cause gave me, to aid my understanding, certain beliefs which are perhaps not wholly out of harmony with the true and sacred knowledge of the gods. It looks, however, as though, not knowing what to say next, I were turning round in a circle. I can, nevertheless, give clear and manifest reasons in every single case why we are not allowed to eat this food which is forbidden by the sacred ordinance, and presently I will do this. For the moment, however, it is better to bring forward certain forms and regulations, so to speak, which we must observe in order to be able to decide about these matters; though perhaps, owing to my haste, my argument may pass by some evidence.

First, I had better remind you in a few words who Attis is; what his castration means; what is symbolised by the ceremonies that occur between the sacrifice and the Hilaria; and what is meant by the rite of purification. Attis, then, was declared to be an original cause and a god, the direct creator of the material world, who descends to the lowest limits and is checked by the creative motion of the sun as soon as that god reaches the precisely limited circuit of the universe, which is called the equinox because of its effect in equalising night and day. I explained that the castration meant the checking of limitlessness, which could only be brought about through the summons and resurrection of Attis to the more venerable and commanding causes. I also said that the end and aim of the rite of purification is the ascent of our souls.

For this reason, then, the ordinance forbids us first to eat those fruits that grow downwards below the earth. For the earth is the last and lowest of things. Plato himself says[1] that evil, exiled from the gods, now moves on earth; and in the oracles, the gods often call the earth refuse, and exhort us to escape thence. Thus, in the first place, the life-generating god who is our providence does not allow us to nourish our bodies using fruits that grow under the earth; and thereby enjoins that we turn our eyes towards the heavens, or rather, beyond the heavens.[2] One kind of fruit of the earth, however, some people do eat, that is, fruit in pods, because they regard this as a vegetable rather than a fruit, since it grows with a sort of upward tendency and is upright, and not rooted below the soil, by which I mean that it is rooted like the fruit of the ivy that hangs on a tree or of the vine that hangs on a stem. For this reason,

1. *Theætetus*, 176 2. i.e. to the intelligible world and the One

then, we are forbidden to eat seeds and certain plants, but we are allowed to eat fruit and vegetables, specifically not those that grow upon the ground, but those that are raised up from the earth and hang high in the air. It is surely for this reason that the ordinance bids us also avoid that part of the turnip which inclines to the earth, for it belongs to the under world, yet allows us to eat that part which grows upwards and attains to some height, since by that very fact it is pure. In fact, it allows us to eat any vegetables that grow upwards, but forbids us roots, and especially those which are nourished in and influenced by the earth. Moreover, in the case of trees, it does not allow us to destroy and consume apples, for these are sacred and golden, being the symbols of secret and mystical rewards. Rather, they are worthy to be reverenced and cherished as models of creation. Pomegranates, too, are forbidden because they belong to the under-world; and the fruit of the date-palm, perhaps one might say because the date-palm does not grow in Phrygia where the ordinance was first established. My own theory, however, is that it is because this tree is sacred to the sun, and is perennial, that we are forbidden to use it to nourish our bodies during the sacred rites. Besides these, the use of all kinds of fish is forbidden. This is a question of interest to the Egyptians as well as to ourselves. Now, my opinion is that for two reasons we ought to abstain from fish, at all times if possible, but above all during the sacred rites. One reason is that it is not fitting that we should eat what we do not use in sacrifices to the gods. Perhaps I need not be afraid that hereupon some greedy person who is the slave of his belly will take me up, though as I remember that very thing happened to me once before; at which I heard someone object: "what do you mean? Do we not often sacrifice fish to the gods?" Yet I had an answer ready for this question also: "my good sir," I said, "it is true that we make offerings of fish in certain mystic sacrifices, just as the Romans sacrifice the horse and many other animals, too, both wild and domesticated, while both the Greeks and the Romans also sacrifice dogs to Hecate. Among other nations, also, many other animals are offered in the mystic cults; and sacrifices of that sort take place publicly in their cities once or twice a year. But that is not the custom in the sacrifices which we honour most highly, in which alone the gods deign to join us and to share our table. In those most honoured sacrifices, we do not offer fish for the reason that we do not tend fish, nor look after the breeding of them, since we do not keep flocks of fish as we do of sheep and cattle. For since we foster these animals and they multiply accordingly, it is only right that they should serve for all our uses and above all for the sacrifices that we honour most". This, then, is one reason why I think we ought not to use fish for food at the time of the rite of purification. The second reason, which, I think, is even more in keeping with what I have just said, is that, since fish also, in a manner of speaking, go down into the lowest depths, they, even more than seeds, belong to the under-world. Thus he who longs to take flight upwards and to mount aloft above this atmosphere of ours, even to the highest peaks of the heavens, would do well to abstain from all such food. He will rather pursue and follow after things that tend upwards towards the air, that strive to the utmost height, and, if I may use a poetic phrase, look upward to the heavens. Birds, for example, we may eat, save only those few which are commonly held sacred,[1] and ordinary four-footed animals, except the pig. This animal is banned as food during the sacred rites because by its shape and way of life, and the very nature of its substance – for its flesh is impure and coarse – it belongs wholly to the earth. Consequently, men came to believe that it was an acceptable offering to the gods of the under-world. For this animal does not look up at the sky, not only because it has no such desire, but because it is so made that it can never look upwards. These, therefore, are the reasons that have been given by the divine ordinance for abstinence from such food as we ought to renounce. So we who have come to this understanding share our knowledge with those who know the nature of the gods.

As to the question of what food is permitted, then, I will only say this. The divine law does not allow all kinds of food to all men, but takes into account what is possible to human nature and allows us to eat most animals, as I have said. It is not as though we must all of necessity eat all kinds – for perhaps that would not be convenient – but we are to use first what our physical powers allow; secondly, what is at hand in abundance; thirdly, we are each to exercise our own will. At the season of the sacred ceremonies, however, we ought to exert our will to the utmost, so that we may attain to what is beyond our ordinary physical powers and thus may be eager and willing to obey the divine ordinances. For it is by all means more effective for the salvation of the soul itself that one should pay greater heed to its safety than to the safety of the body.

1. Porphyry, *On Abstinence*, 3.5, gives a list of these sacred birds; e.g., the owl was sacred to Athena, the eagle to Zeus, and the crane to Demeter

Moreover, the body, too, seems thereby to share insensibly in that great and marvellous benefit. For when the soul abandons itself wholly to the gods, and entrusts its own concerns absolutely to the higher powers, then follows the sacred rites – these too being preceded by the divine ordinances – then, I say, since there is nothing to hinder or prevent, in that moment the divine light illumines our souls; for all things reside in the gods, all things subsist in relation to them, and all things are filled with the gods. Thus endowed with divinity, they impart a certain vigour and energy to the breath[1] implanted in them by nature; and so that breath is hardened, as it were, and strengthened by the soul, hence it gives health to the whole body. For I think not one of the sons of Asclepius would deny that all diseases, or at any rate very many and those the most serious, are caused by disturbances to and irregularity of one's breathing. Some doctors assert that all diseases, others that the greater number, including the most serious and hardest to cure, are due to this. Moreover, the oracles of the gods bear witness thereto, which is to say that by the rite of purification, not the soul alone, but the body as well is greatly benefited and preserved. Indeed, the gods, when they exhort those theurgists who are especially pious, announce to them that their "mortal husk of raw matter"[2] shall be preserved from perishing.

Now, what is left for me to say? Especially since it was granted me to compose this hymn at a breath,[3] in the short space of one night, without having read anything on the subject beforehand, or having thought it over. Indeed, I had not even planned to speak thereof until the moment that I asked for these writing-tablets. May the goddess bear witness to the truth of my words! Nevertheless, as I said before, does there not still remain for me to celebrate the goddess in her union with Athena and Dionysus? For the sacred law established their festivals at the very time of her sacred rites. Thus I recognise the kinship of Athena and the Mother of the Gods through the similarity of the forethought that inheres in the substance of both goddesses. Further, I discern also the divided creative function of Dionysus, which great Dionysus received from the single and abiding principle of life that is in mighty Zeus. For from Zeus he proceeded, and he bestows that life on all things

1. cf. Aristotle, *On the Generation of Animals*, 736, for the breath (πνεῦμα) that envelops the disembodied soul and resembles æther

2. This phrase probably occurred in an oracular verse

3. Demosthenes, *De Corona*, 308

visible, controlling and governing the creation of the whole divisible world. Together with these gods we ought to celebrate Hermes Epaphroditus.[1] For so this god is entitled by the initiated, who say that he kindles the torches for wise Attis. I ask, then, who has a soul so dense as to not understand that through Hermes and Aphrodite are invoked all generated things everywhere, since in all places and throughout they have a purpose which is uniquely appropriate to the Logos?[2] Yet is not this Logos Attis, who not long ago was out of his senses, but now through his limitation is called wise? Indeed, he was out of his senses because he preferred matter and presided over generation, yet he is wise because he adorned and transformed this refuse, our earth, with such beauty as no human art or craft could imitate. How, then, shall I conclude my discourse? Surely with this hymn to the Great Goddess.

O Mother of gods and men, you who are the assessor of Zeus and share his throne; O source of the intellectual gods, who pursue your course with the pure substance of the intelligible gods; who receives from each of them the common cause of things, thereby bestowing it on the intellectual gods; O life-giving goddess who are the counsel, the providence, and the creator of our souls; who loved great Dionysus, and saved Attis when exposed at birth, leading him back when he had descended into the cave of the nymph; O you who gives all good things to the intellectual gods and fills with all things this sensible world, giving us with the others all things good! May you grant to all men happiness, and that highest happiness of all, the knowledge of the gods; grant to the Roman people in general that they may cleanse themselves of the stain of impiety; grant them a blessed lot, and help them to guide their Empire for many thousands of years! While for myself, grant me as fruit of my worship of you that I may have true knowledge in the doctrines of the gods. Make me perfect in theurgy. Lastly, in all that I undertake, in the affairs of the state and the army, grant me virtue and good fortune, and that the close of my life may be painless and glorious, in the good hope that it is to you, the gods, that I journey!

1. The epithet means "favoured by Aphrodite"

2. λόγος here may mean "Reason"

MISOPOGON

PREFACE

Julian arrived in the Syrian city of Antioch in July, 362, where he would remain resident until March the following year when he finally departed on the ill-fated Persia campaign. His stay in the provincial capital was certainly eventful, and provided the Emperor with all manner of frustrations. While the "splendid jewel of the Orient"[1] was undeniably an important commercial centre, with the considerable wealth that such attends, her glory was, in Julian's eyes, dependant on two things: the famous shrine of Apollo in nearby Daphne, and its esteemed school of rhetoric.[2] Regrettably, both of these had been neglected by the "frivolous"[3] Antiochians. The culture of the city was, with few exceptions, wholly confounding and objectionable to the disappointed Julian. At the same time, "his austere personality and mode of life repelled the populace and the corrupt officials of Antioch".[4]

During the New Year's celebrations of 363, many of the citizens engaged, as was customary, in mirthful, if somewhat anarchic and libertine, public festivities that were not looked upon with terribly great appreciation by certain of its residents. The Antiochians "ridiculed decency, violated judicial authority, laughed at public opinion, made sport with the whole world watching, and in so doing claimed that all was in jest".[5] On this particular occasion, it was Julian who bore the worst of their abuse, with the mocking and jeering of the crowds crossing at times into outright invective. Needless to say, the Emperor was not overly impressed by the conduct of the offenders with whom he had already lost all patience. Following the advice of his long-time companion and doctor, Oribasius, who had supposedly counselled him "that even if he felt anger, he should never show it in his eyes or his voice",[6] Julian decided to respond in kind. Since the Antiochians had satirised him in anapæstic verse, Julian accordingly composed a festive satire on the city of Antioch, albeit one framed as self-mockery, hence the title *Misopogon* (Beard-Hater).

---

1. Ammianus, 22.9.14 2. W. C. F. Wright

3. The Emperor Hadrian had been particularly offended by the levity of Antioch's citizens, while John Chrysostom expressed much the same view as Julian.

4. W. C. F. Wright 5. Gleason, *Festive Satire*

6. Brown, *Power and Persuasion in Late Antiquity*, pg. 59

Julian could not resist rebuking the city and its citizens in a more direct fashion[1], however, and the satire of his own character and habits is consequently not maintained throughout, devolving at points into outright censure. Nevertheless, the work is, if something of an oddity to modern readers, reflective of a restrained approach to rulership. When viewing the satire in isolation and from a modern perspective, some have struggled with how best to interpret *Misopogon*, even seeing in the parodical invective directed by Julian against himself a troubled mind, or at the very least a troubled Emperor. In actuality, "far from revealing the tortured psyche of Julian, it should be read as testimony to the skill with which late Roman rulers displayed, on occasion, the civilised good humour that contemporaries liked to associate with a moderate, because secure, style of rule".[2]

The Emperor's satire – what might be referred to as an "edict of chastisement"[3] – was posted publicly in the city for all to read. One could almost view it as a farewell letter, for indeed Julian was to leave Antioch just a few months later, to the great relief of both Augustus and citizen alike.

---

1. It should be noted that Roman satire was not merely intended to provoke laughter, but also contempt, hence the poet Decimus Juvenalis describing satires as "*facit indignatio versum*", that is, exciting indignation

2. Brown, *Power and Persuasion in Late Antiquity*, pg. 59

3. Gleason, *Festive Satire*

MISOPOGON

Anacreon the poet composed many delightful songs, for a luxurious life was allotted to him by the Fates; whereas the god did not permit Alcæus and Archilochus of Paros[1] to devote their muse to mirth and pleasure. For constrained as they were to endure toil, at once of one sort, then of another, and by abusing those who wronged them they lightened the burdens imposed on them by heaven. As for me, however, the law forbids me to accuse by name those who, though I have done them no wrong, try to show their hostility towards me; while on the other hand, the fashion of education that now prevails among the well-born deprives me of the use of the music that consists in song. For in these days men think it more degrading to study music than at one point in the past they thought it to be rich by dishonest means. Nevertheless, I will not on that account renounce the aid that it is in my power to win from the Muses. Indeed, I have observed that even the Barbarians across the Rhine sing savage songs composed in a language not unlike the croaking of harsh-voiced birds, and that they delight in such songs. For I think it is always the case that inferior musicians, though they annoy their audiences, give very great pleasure to themselves. With this in mind, I often say to myself, like Ismenias – for though my talents are not equal to his, I have as I persuade myself a similar independence of soul – "I sing for the Muses and myself".[2]

The song that I now sing, however, has been composed in prose, and it contains much violent abuse, directed not, by Zeus, against others – how could it be so, since the law forbids it? – but against the poet and author himself. For there is no law to prevent one's writing either praise or criticism of oneself. Now, as for praising myself, though I should be very glad to do so, I have no reason for that; but for criticising myself I have countless reasons, and first I will begin with my face. For though nature did not make this all too handsome or well-favoured, or give it the bloom of youth,

1. In the seventh century B.C. Alcæus and Archilochus suffered exile, and the latter fell in battle against Naxos. For the misfortunes of Alcæus, cf. Horace, *Odes*, 2.13

2. For Ismenias of Thebes, cf. Plutarch, *Pericles*; the saying became a proverb

I myself out of sheer petulance and ill-temper have added to it this long beard of mine, to punish it, as it would seem, for this very crime of not being handsome by nature. For the same reason, I put up with the lice that scamper about in it as though it were a thicket for wild beasts. As for eating greedily or drinking with my mouth wide open, it is not in my power; for I must take care, I suppose, or else before I know it I shall eat up some of my own hairs along with my crumbs of bread. In the matter of being kissed and kissing I suffer no inconvenience whatsoever. And yet for this as for other purposes a beard is evidently troublesome, since it does not allow me to press shaven "lips to other lips more sweetly" – because they are smooth, I suppose – as has been said already by one of those who, with the aid of Pan and Calliope, composed poems in honour of Daphnis.[1] Though you say that I ought to twist ropes from it. Well, I am willing to provide you with ropes if only you have the strength to pull them and their roughness does not do dreadful damage to your "unworn and tender hands".[2] For let no one suppose that I am offended by your gibes. Indeed, I myself furnish you with an excuse for it by wearing my chin as goats do, when I might, I suppose, make it smooth and bare as handsome youths wear theirs, and all women, who are endowed by nature with loveliness. Whereas you, since even in your old age you emulate your own sons and daughters by your soft and delicate way of living, or perhaps by your effeminate dispositions, carefully make your chins smooth, and your manhood you barely reveal, indicating it slightly by your foreheads, not by your jaws as I do.

Yet as if the mere length of my beard were not enough, my head is dishevelled besides, and I seldom have my hair cut or my nails, while my fingers are nearly always black from using a pen. Further, if you would like to learn something that is usually a secret, my chest is shaggy, and covered with hair, like the breasts of lions who among wild beasts are monarchs like me; never in my life have I made it smooth, so ill-conditioned and shabby am I, nor have I made any other part of my body smooth or soft. If I had a wart like Cicero,[3] I should tell you so; but as it happens I have none. Though by your leave I will tell you something else. I am not content with having my body in this rough condition, but in addition, the mode of life that I practise is very strict indeed. I banish myself from

1. Daphnis is the hero of bucolic poetry; Julian echoes Theocritus, 12.32

2. *The Odyssey*, XXII, 151

3. cf. Plutarch, *Cicero*, who says that Cicero had a wart on his nose

the theatres, such a dolt am I, and I do not admit the thymele[1] within my court, except on the first day of the year, because I am too stupid to appreciate it, like some country fellow who from his small means has to pay a tax or render tribute to a harsh master. What's more, even when I do enter the theatre, I look like a man who is expiating a crime. Then again, although I am called a mighty emperor, I employ no one to govern the actors and charioteers as my lieutenant or general throughout the inhabited world. Thus observing this recently, "you now recall that youth of his, his wit and wisdom".[2]

Perhaps you had another grievance and clear proof of the worthlessness of my disposition – for I am ever adding more novel characteristics – such as that I hate horse-races as men who owe money hate the marketplace. I therefore seldom attend them, only during the festivals of the gods; and I do not stay the whole day as my cousin[3] used to do, and my uncle,[4] my brother, and my father's son.[5] Six races are all that I stay to see, and not even those with the air of one who loves the sport, or even, by Zeus, with the air of one who does not hate and loathe it, and I am glad to get away.

Yet all these things are externals; and indeed what a small fraction of my offences against you have I described! Though to turn to my private life within the court. Sleepless nights on a pallet and a diet that is anything rather than overindulging make my temper harsh and unfriendly to a luxurious city like yours. It is not, however, in order to set an example to you that I adopt these habits. Rather, in my childhood a strange and senseless delusion came over me and persuaded me to war against my belly, so that I do not allow it to fill itself with a great quantity of food. Thus it has happened to me most rarely of all men to vomit my food; and though I remember having this experience once, after I became Cæsar, it was by accident and was not due to over-eating. It may be worthwhile to tell the story which is not in itself very graceful, but for that very reason is especially suited to me.

I happened to be in winter quarters at my beloved Lutetia – for that is how the Celts refer to the capital of the Parisians. It is a small island lying in the river; a wall entirely surrounds it, and wooden bridges lead to it on both sides. The river seldom rises and falls, but

1. i.e. the altar of Dionysus which was set up in the orchestra

2. Cratinus, *Eunidæ*, fr. 1; Julian refers to Constantius, with whom the people of Antioch now compare him

3. Constantius 4. Julian 5. Gallus

is usually the same depth in the winter as in the summer season, while it provides water which is very clear to the eye and most pleasant for one who wishes to drink. For since the inhabitants live on an island, they have to draw their water chiefly from the river. The winter, too, is rather mild there, perhaps from the warmth of the ocean, which is not more than nine hundred stades distant, and it may be that a slight breeze from the water is wafted so far; for sea water seems to be warmer than fresh. Whether from this or from some other cause obscure to me, the fact is, as I say, that those who live in that place enjoy a warmer winter. Additionally, an excellent type of vine grows thereabouts, and some persons have even managed to make fig-trees grow by covering them in winter with a sort of garment of wheat straw and other things of that sort, such as are used to protect trees from the harm that is done them by the cold wind. As I was saying then, the winter was more severe than usual, and the river kept bringing down blocks of ice like marble. You are familiar, I presume, with the white stone that comes from Phrygia; the blocks of ice were very much like it, of great size, and drifted down one after another; in fact, it seemed likely that they would make an unbroken path and bridge the stream. The winter, then, was more inclement than usual, but the room where I slept was not warmed in the way that most houses are heated, that is, by furnaces underground, even though it was conveniently arranged for letting in heat from such a fire. Yet it so happened that, because I was, I suppose, awkward then as now, I displayed disregard first of all, as was natural, towards myself. For I wished to accustom myself to bear the cold air without needing this aid. And though the winter weather prevailed and continually increased in severity, even so I did not allow my servants to heat the house, because I was afraid of drawing out the dampness in the walls; instead, I ordered them to carry in fire that had burned down and to place in the room a very moderate number of hot coals. Yet these coals, though there were not very many of them, brought out from the walls quantities of steam and this made me fall asleep. Since my head was filled with the fumes, I was almost choked. Then I was carried outside, and as the doctors advised me to throw up the food I had just swallowed – and it was little enough, by Zeus – I vomited it and at once began to recover, so that I had a more comfortable night, and the next day could do whatever I pleased.

After this fashion, then, even when I was among the Celts, like the ill-tempered man in Menander, "I myself kept heaping troubles on my own head". Yet whereas the boorish Celts used to easily put up with these ways of mine, they are naturally resented by a gay, prosperous, crowded city in which there are numerous dancers and flute players, more actors than ordinary citizens, and no respect at all for those who govern. For the blush of modesty befits the unmanly, but manly fellows like you it befits to begin your revels at dawn, to spend your nights in pleasure, and to show not only by your words but by your deeds also that you despise the laws. For indeed it is only by means of those in authority that the laws inspire fear in men, so that he who insults one who is in authority, over and above this, tramples on the laws. That you take pleasure in this sort of behaviour you show clearly on many occasions, but especially in the marketplaces and theatres; the mass of the people by their clapping and shouting, while those in office show it by the fact that, on account of the sums they have spent on such entertainments, they are more widely known and more talked about by all men than Solon the Athenian ever was on account of his interview with Croesus, King of the Lydians.[1] Moreover, all of you are handsome and tall, smooth-skinned and beardless; for young and old alike, you are emulous of the happiness of the Phæacians, and rather than righteousness you prefer "changes of raiment, warm baths, and soft beds".[2]

"What then?" you answer, "did you really suppose that your boorish manners and savage ways and clumsiness would harmonise with these things? O most ignorant and quarrelsome of men, is it so senseless then and so stupid, that puny soul of yours which men of poor spirit call temperate, and which you forsooth think it your duty to adorn and deck out with temperance? You are wrong; for in the first place we know not what temperance is and we hear only its name, while the real thing we cannot perceive. If it is the sort of thing that one must practise, however, if it consists in knowing that men must be enslaved to the gods and the laws; in behaving with fairness to those of equal rank and bearing with mildness any superiority among them; in studying and taking thought that the poor may suffer no injustice whatsoever at the hands of the rich; in putting up with all the annoyances that you will naturally often meet with – hatred, anger, and abuse – to attain this; then, in bearing these also with firmness, and not resenting them or giving way to your anger, but in training yourself as far as possible to

1. For Solon's visit to Croesus at Sardis, cf. Herodotus, 1.29

2. The Odyssey, VIII, 249

practise temperance; if, again, one also defines as the effect of temperance that one must abstain from every pleasure, even if it be not excessively unbecoming or considered blameworthy when openly pursued, because you are convinced that it is impossible for a man to be temperate in his private life and in secret, if in public and openly he is willing to be licentious and delights in the theatres; if, in short, temperance is really of this sort, then you have ruined yourself and, moreover, you are ruining us, who cannot bear in the first place to even hear the name of obedience, whether it be obedience to the gods or the laws. For sweet is liberty in all things!

"But what an affectation of humility is yours! You say that you are not our master and you will not let yourself be so called, and what's more, you resent the very idea, such that you have actually persuaded the majority of men who have long grown accustomed to it, to rid themselves of this word 'government' as though it were something invidious; and yet you compel us to be enslaved to magistrates and laws. Yet how much better it would be for you to accept the name of master, while in actual fact allowing us to be free, you who are so very mild about the names we use and very strict about the things we do! Then again, you harass us by forcing the rich to behave with moderation in the law-courts, while you keep the poor from making money by informing.[1] Further, by ignoring the stage, actors, and dancers, you have ruined our city, thus we receive nothing from you except your harshness; and this we have had to put up with these seven months, such that we have left it to the old crones who grovel among the tombs to pray that we may be entirely rid of so great a curse, though we ourselves have accomplished it by our own ingenious insolence, by shooting our gibes at you like arrows. How, noble sir, will you face the darts of Persians, when you take flight at our ridicule?"

Come, I am ready to make a fresh start in abusing myself. "You, sir, go regularly to the temples, ill-tempered, petulant, and wholly worthless as you are! It is your doing that the masses stream into the sacred precincts, yes, and most of the magistrates as well, and they give you a splendid welcome, greeting you with shouts and clapping in the precincts as though they were in the theatres. Then why do you not treat them kindly and praise them? Instead of that, you try to be wiser in such matters than the Pythian god,[2] making

1. i.e. bringing false accusations, which was the trade of the defamer or blackmailer
2. Apollo who was worshipped at Daphne near Antioch

harangues to the crowd and with harsh words rebuking those who shout. These are the very words you use towards them: 'you hardly ever assemble at the shrines to do honour to the gods, but to do me honour you rush here in crowds and fill the temples with much disorder. Yet it becomes prudent men to pray in orderly fashion, and to ask blessings from the gods in silence. Have you never heard Homer's maxim: "in silence, to yourselves"?[1] Or how Odysseus checked Eurycleia when she was stricken with amazement by the greatness of his success: "restrain yourself, old woman, and rejoice in your heart. Utter no cry aloud"?[2] Again, Homer did not show us the Trojan women praying to Priam or to any one of his daughters or sons, indeed, not even to Hector himself (though he does, in truth, say that the men of Troy were wont to pray to Hector as a god); but in his poems he did not show us either women or men in the act of prayer to him, rather he says that to Athena all the women lifted up their hands with a loud cry.[3] This was in itself a barbaric thing to do and suitable only for women, though at any rate it displayed no impiety towards the gods, as does your conduct. For you applaud men instead of the gods, or rather, instead of the gods you flatter me who am a mere man. Yet it would be best, I think, not to flatter even the gods but to worship them with temperate hearts.'"

See, there I am again, busy with my usual phrase-making! I do not even allow myself to speak out in the moment fearlessly and freely, but with my usual awkwardness I am laying out information against myself. It is thus and in words like these that one ought to address men who want to be free, not only with respect to those who govern them, but to the gods also, in order that one may be considered well-disposed towards them, "like an indulgent father",[4] even if one is by nature an ill-conditioned person like myself. "Bear with them, then, when they hate and abuse you in secret or even openly, since you thought that those who applauded you with one accord in the temples were only flattering you. For surely you did not suppose that you would be in harmony with the pursuits, or the lives, or the temperaments of these men. I grant that. Yet who will bear with this other habit of yours? You always sleep alone at night, and there is no way of softening your savage and uncivilised temper – since all avenues are closed to anything that might sweeten your disposition – and the worst of all these

1. *The Iliad*, VII, 195 2. *The Odyssey*, XXII, 411 3. *The Iliad*, VI, 301
4. *The Odyssey*, V, 12

evils is that you delight in living that sort of life and have laid pleasure under a general ban. Then can you feel aggrieved if you hear yourself spoken of in such terms? No, you ought to feel grateful to those who out of kindness of heart admonish you wittily in anapæstic verse to shave your cheeks smooth, and then, beginning with yourself, to show first to this laughter-loving people all sorts of fine spectacles – impressionists, dancers, shameless women, boys who in their beauty emulate women, and men who have not only their jaws shaved smooth but their whole bodies too, so that those who meet them may think them smoother than women; yes and feasts, too, and general festivals, not, by Zeus, the sacred ones at which one is bound to behave with sobriety. No, we have had enough of those, like the oak tree in the proverb;[1] we are completely surfeited with them. The Emperor sacrificed once in the temple of Zeus, then in the temple of Fortune, while he visited the temple of Demeter three times in succession." (I have, in fact, forgotten how many times I entered the shrine of Daphne, which had been first abandoned owing to the carelessness of its guardians, and then destroyed by the audacious acts of godless men.[2]) "The Syrian New Year arrived, and again the Emperor went to the temple of Zeus the Friendly One. Then came the general festival, and the Emperor went to the shrine of Fortune. Then, after refraining on the forbidden day,[3] again he goes to the temple of Zeus the Friendly One, and offers up prayers according to the custom of our ancestors. Now, who could put up with an Emperor who goes to the temples so often when it is in his power to disturb the gods only once or twice, and to celebrate the general festivals which are for all the people in common, those in which not only men whose profession it is to have knowledge of the gods can take part, but also the people who have crowded into the city? For pleasure is here in abundance, and delights whose fruits one could only enjoy continuously; for instance, the sight of men and pretty boys dancing, and any number of charming women."

When I take all this into account, I do indeed congratulate you on your good fortune, though I do not reproach myself. For perhaps

---

1. The phrase δρῦς καὶ πέτρα, literally, "the oak tree and the rock" became a proverb for something hackneyed; cf. Hesiod, *Theogony*, 35

2. Christians vandalised the temple at Daphne and constructed a church beside it. When Julian removed the church in an attempt to restore the sanctuary, both the temple and the statue of Apollo were burned down, possibly by Christians

3. Literally the "day not to be mentioned"; i.e., the "unholy day" (*nefandus dies*), on which business was suspended

it is some god who has made me prefer my own ways. Be assured, then, that I have no grievance against those who quarrel with my way of life and my choice. Though I myself add, as far as I can, to the sarcasms against myself and with a more free hand I pour down on my own head these abusive charges. For it was due to my own folly that I did not understand what has been the temper of this city from the beginning; and this in spite of the fact that I am convinced I have turned over quite as many books as any man of my own age. You know of course the tale that is told about the king who gave his name to this city, or rather, whose name the city received when it was colonised, for it was founded by Seleucus, though it takes its name from the son[1] of Seleucus. They say,[2] then, that out of excessive softness and luxury, the latter was constantly falling in love and being loved, and finally he conceived a dishonourable passion for his own step-mother. Though he wished to conceal his condition, he could not, and little by little his body began to waste away and disappear, his powers began to wane, and his breathing was feebler than usual. Yet what could be the matter with him was, I think, a sort of riddle, since his malady had no visible cause, or rather, its nature was not at all apparent, though the youth's weakness was manifest. Then the physician of Samos[3] was set a difficult problem, namely to discover what was the nature of the malady. Suspecting what the nature of "cares that devour the limbs" is from the words of Homer,[4] how in many cases it is not a bodily weakness but an infirmity of soul that causes a wasting of the body, and seeing, moreover, that the youth was very susceptible to love because of his time of life and his habits, he took the following way of tracking down the disease. He sat near the youth's couch and watched his face, having ordered handsome young men and women to walk past him, beginning with the queen[5] herself. Now, when she entered, apparently to see how he was, the young man at once began to show the symptoms of his malady. He breathed like one who is being choked, for though he was very anxious to control his agitated breathing, he could not, thus it became disordered and a deep blush spread over his face. Upon seeing this, the physician laid his hand to his chest and found that his heart was beating terribly fast, almost as if it were trying to burst forth from his breast. Such were his symptoms while she was present;

1. i.e. Antiochus 2. cf. Plutarch, *Demetrius* 3. i.e. Erasistratus

4. The phrase appears in Hesiod, *Works and Days*, 66, but not in our version of Homer

5. Stratonica

but when she had gone away and others came in, he remained calm and was like a man in a normal state of health. Then Erasistratus saw what ailed him and told the king, who out of love for his son said that he would give up his wife to him. At first, the young man refused, but when his father died not long after, he sought with the greatest vehemence the favour which he had so honourably declined when it was first offered to him.[1]

Since this was the conduct of Antiochus, then, I have no right to be angry with his descendants when they emulate their founder or him who gave his name to the city. For just as in the case of plants, it is natural that their qualities should be transmitted for a long time, or rather that, in general, the succeeding generation should resemble its ancestors; so too, in the case of human beings, it is natural that the morals of descendants should resemble those of their ancestors. I myself, for example, have found that the Athenians are the most ambitious for honour and the most humane of all the Greeks. Indeed, I have observed that these qualities exist in an admirable degree among all the Greeks, and I can say for them that they more than all other nations love the gods, and are hospitable to strangers. By this I mean all the Greeks generally, but among them the Athenians most especially, as I myself can bear witness. Therefore, if they still preserve in their characters the image of their ancient virtue, surely it is natural that the same thing should be true of the Syrians also, and the Arabs, the Celts, the Thracians, the Pæonians, and those who dwell between the Thracians and the Pæonians, that is, the Mysians on the very banks of the Danube, from whom my own family is derived, a stock wholly boorish, austere, awkward, without charm, and abiding immovably by its decisions; all such qualities which are proofs of terrible boorishness.

I therefore ask for forgiveness, in the first place for myself, and in my turn I grant it to you, also, since you emulate the manners of your forefathers, nor do I bring it against you as a reproach when I say that you are "liars and dancers, well skilled to dance in a chorus";[2] on the contrary, it is in the place of a panegyric that I ascribe to you emulation of the practice of your forefathers. For Homer, too, is praising Autolycus when he says that he surpassed all men "in stealing and perjury".[3] As for my own awkwardness, ignorance, and ill-temper, and my inability to be influenced, or to

---

1. In Plutarch's version, Antiochus married Stratonica during his father's lifetime

2. *The Iliad*, XXIV, 261

3. *The Odyssey*, XIX, 396

mind my own business when people beg me to do so, or try to deceive me and that I cannot yield to their clamour – even such reproaches I gladly accept. Whether your ways or mine are more supportable, however, is perhaps clear to the gods, for among men there is no one capable of arbitrating in our disagreement. For such is our self-love that we shall never believe him, since every one of us naturally admires his own ways and despises those of other men. In fact, he who grants indulgence to one whose aims are the opposite of his own is, in my opinion, the most considerate of men.

Though now that I come to ponder the matter, I find that I have committed yet other terrible sins. For although I was coming to a free city which cannot tolerate unkempt hair, I entered it unshaven and with a long beard, like men who are at a loss for a barber. One would have thought it was some Smicrines[1] he saw, or some Thrasyleon, some ill-tempered old man or crazy soldier, when by beautifying myself I might have appeared as a blooming boy and transformed myself into a youth, if not in years, at any rate in manners and effeminacy of features. "You do not know", you answer, "how to mix with people, and you cannot approve of the maxim of Theognis,[2] for you do not imitate the polypus which takes on the colours of the rocks. Rather, you behave to all men with the proverbial Myconian[3] boorishness, ignorance, and stupidity. Are you not aware that we here are far from being Celts or Thracians or Illyrians? Do you not see what a number of shops there are in this city? Though you are hated by the shopkeepers because you do not allow them to sell provisions to the common people and those who are visiting the city at a price as high as they please. The shopkeepers blame the landowners for the high prices, but you make these men your enemies also by compelling them to do what is just. Again, those who hold office in the city are subject to both penalties; I mean that just as, before you came, they obviously used to enjoy profits from both sources, both as land-owners and as shopkeepers, so naturally they are now aggrieved on both accounts, since they have been robbed of their profits from both sources. Then the whole body of Syrian citizens are discontented because they cannot get drunk and dance the cordax.[4] You, however,

1. Smicrines is a typical name in New Comedy for an avaricious old man; Thrasyleon is said to have been used by Menander as the name of a boasting soldier, *Miles Gloriosus*

2. *Theognis*, 215, advises men to imitate the adaptability of the polypus

3. The inhabitants of the island Mykonos were proverbial for poverty and greed

4. The cordax was a lascivious dance

think that you are feeding them well enough if you provide them with plenty of corn. Another charming thing about you is that you do not even take care that the city should have shellfish. What's more, when someone complained the other day that neither shellfish nor much poultry could be found in the market, you laughed very maliciously and said that a well-conducted city needs bread, wine, and olive oil, but meat only when it is growing luxurious.[1] For you said that even to speak of fish and poultry is the extreme of luxury and of profligacy such as was beyond the reach of even the suitors in Ithaca; and that anyone who did not enjoy eating pork and mutton[2] would fare very well if he took to vegetables.[3] You must have thought that you were laying down these rules for Thracians, your own fellow citizens, or for the uncultured people of Gaul who – so much the worse for us – trained you to be 'a heart of maple, a heart of oak'; though not indeed 'one who fought at Marathon'[4] also, but rather to be half Acharnian and altogether an unpleasant and ungracious fellow. Would it not be better that the marketplace should be fragrant with myrrh when you walk there, and that you should be followed by a troop of handsome boys at whom the citizens could stare, and by choruses of women like those that exhibit themselves every day in our city?"

No, my temperament does not allow me to look wanton, casting my eyes in all directions in order that in your sight I may appear beautiful, not indeed in soul but in visage. For, in your judgement, true beauty of soul consists in a wanton life. I, however, was taught by my tutor to look at the ground when I was on my way to school; and as for a theatre, I did not see one until I had more hair on my chin than on my head.[5] Then, even at that age, it was never on my own account and by my own wish, but on three or four occasions, if you must know, the governor, who was my kinsman and near relative, "doing a favour for Patroclus", ordered me to attend; this while I was still a private individual.[6] Therefore forgive me. For I hand over to you, instead of myself, one whom you will more justly detest, that being the curmudgeon, my tutor, who even used to harass me by teaching me to walk in one straight path and now he is responsible for my quarrel with you. It was he who

1. Plato, *Republic*, 372 2. The suitors of Penelope lived on pork and mutton

3. Literally "pulses"

4. Aristophanes, *Acharnians*, 180, uses these words to describe the older, more robust generation of Athenians

5. Xenophon, *Symposium*, 4.28 6. i.e., before he had been appointed Cæsar

wrought in my soul and as it were carved therein what I did not then desire, though he was very zealous in implanting it, as if he were producing some charming characteristic; while boorishness he called dignity, lack of taste he called sobriety, and not yielding to one's desires or achieving happiness by that means he called manliness. I assure you, by Zeus and the Muses, that while I was still a mere boy, my tutor would often say to me: "never let the crowd of your playmates who flock to the theatres lead you into the mistake of craving for such spectacles as these. Have you a passion for horse races? There is one in Homer,[1] very cleverly described. Take the book and study it. Do you hear them talking about dancers in pantomime? Leave them alone! Among the Phæacians the youths dance in more manly fashion. For a citharode[2] you have Phemius; for a singer Demodocus. Moreover, there are in Homer many plants more delightful to hear of than those that we can see: 'one time did I see, so fair, the shoot of a young palm tree near the altar of Apollo at Delos'.[3] Consider the wooded island of Calypso, the caves of Circe, and the garden of Alcinous; be assured that you will never see anything more delightful than these".

Now do you want me to tell you my tutor's name, also, and the nationality of the man who used to say these things? He was a Barbarian, by the gods and goddesses; by birth he was a Scythian, and he had the same name[4] as the man who persuaded Xerxes to invade Greece. Moreover, he was a eunuch, a word which, twenty months ago,[5] was constantly heard and revered, though it is now applied as an insult and a term of abuse. He had been brought up under the patronage of my grandfather, in order that he might instruct my mother[6] in the poems of Homer and Hesiod. And since she, after giving birth to me her first and only child, died a few months later, snatched away while she was still a young girl by the motherless maiden[7] from so many misfortunes that were to come, I was handed over to him after my seventh year. From that time he won me over to these views of his, and led me to school by one straight path; and since neither he himself desired to know any other nor allowed me to travel by any other path, it is he who

1. The chariot race in *The Iliad*, XXIII

2. The citharode played and sang to the lyre: Phemius was at the court of Odysseus in Ithaca; Demodocus in Phæacia

3. Odysseus refers to Nausicaa thus in *The Odyssey*, 6.162

4. i.e. Mardonius

5. Constantius was under the influence of the powerful eunuchs of his court; they had been expelled by Julian, but Mardonius was an exception to his class

6. Basilinia

7. Athena

has caused me to be hated by all of you. If you agree, however, let us make a truce with him, you and I, and make an end of our quarrel. For he neither knew that I should visit you nor did he anticipate that, even supposing I was likely to come here, it would be as a ruler, and that over so great an empire as the gods bestowed on me; though they did not do so, believe me, without using great compulsion both towards him who offered and him who accepted it. For neither of us had the air of being willing; since he who offered that honour or favour or whatever you may please to call it, was unwilling to bestow it, while he who received it was sincere in steadfastly refusing it. This matter, however, is and shall be as the gods will. Though perhaps if my tutor had foreseen this he would have exercised much forethought to the end that I might, as far as possible, seem agreeable in your eyes.

What then, you will ask, is it not possible even now for me to lay aside my character, and to repent of the boorish temper that was bred in me in earlier days? Habit, as the saying goes, is second nature. Yet to fight with nature is rather hard; and to shake off the training of thirty years is very difficult, especially when it was carried on with such painful effort, and I am already more than thirty years old. "Well and good," you answer, "but what is the matter with you that you try to hear and decide cases about contracts? For surely your tutor did not teach you this also, as he did not even know whether you would govern." Yes, it was that terrible old man who convinced me that I ought to do so; thus you would do well to help me abuse him, since he is of all men most responsible for my way of life; though he too, you must know, had in his turn been misled by others. Theirs are names that you have often met when they are ridiculed in comedy – that is, Plato and Socrates, Aristotle and Theophrastus. This old man in his folly was first convinced by them, and then he got hold of me, since I was young and loved literature, and convinced me that if I would emulate those famous men in all things I should become better, not perhaps than other men – for it was not with them that I had to compete – but certainly better than my former self. Accordingly, since I had no choice in the matter, I obeyed him, and now I am no longer able to change my character, though indeed I often wish I could, and I blame myself for not granting to all men impunity for all wrong-doing. But then the words of the Athenian stranger in Plato come to mind: "though he who does no wrong himself is worthy of honour, he who does not allow the wicked to do wrong is worthy of more than twice as much honour. For whereas the former is responsible for one man only, the latter is responsible for many others besides himself, when he reports to the magistrates the wrong-doing of the rest. Thus he who as far as he can helps the magistrates to punish wrong-doers, himself being the great and powerful man in the city, let him I say be proclaimed as winner of the prize for virtue. Just so, we ought to utter the same eulogy with regard to temperance also, and wisdom, and all the other good qualities that such a man possesses, and which are such that he is able not only to have them himself but also to impart them to other men".[1]

These things he taught me when he thought that I would be a private citizen. For he certainly did not foresee that there would be assigned to me by Zeus this lot in life, to which the god has now brought me and has set me therein. Nevertheless, because I was ashamed to be less virtuous as a ruler than I had been as a private citizen, I have unconsciously given you the benefit of my own boorishness, though there was no necessity. While another of Plato's laws has made me take thought for myself and so become hateful in your eyes, by which I mean the law stating that those who govern, and also the older men, ought to train themselves in respect for others and in self-control, in order that the masses may look to them and thereby order their own lives properly. Now since I alone, or rather in company with a few others, am now pursuing this course, it has had a very different result and has naturally become a reproach against me. For we here are only seven persons, strangers and newcomers in your city – though indeed one of our number is a fellow citizen of yours, a man dear to Hermes and to me, an excellent craftsman of discourses.[2] Furthermore, we have business dealings with no man, nor do we go by any road that does not lead to the temples of the gods; and seldom, and even then not all of us, do we go to the theatres, since we have adopted the most inglorious line of conduct and the most unpopular aim and end of life. The wise men of Greece will surely allow me to repeat some of the sayings current among you, for I have no better way of illustrating what I mean. We have stationed ourselves in the middle of the road, so highly do we prize the opportunity to collide with you and to be disliked, when we ought instead to try to please and

1. Plato, *Laws*, 730

2. Julian is referring to Libanius. the famous rhetorician; also with him were Maximus of Ephesus, Priscus, Himerius, and Oribasius the physician

flatter you. "So-and-so has oppressed So-and-so. Fool! What business is it of yours? When it was in your power to win his goodwill by becoming the partner in his wrong-doing, you let the profit go and incurred hatred besides; and when you do this, you think that you are doing right and are wise about your own affairs. You ought to have taken into account that, when men are wronged, not one of them ever blames the magistrates but only the man who has wronged him; whereas the man who seeks to do wrong and is prevented from it, far from blaming his proposed victim, turns his grievance against the magistrates.

"All this when it was in your power by the aid of such careful reasoning to refrain from compelling us to do what is just; when you might have allowed every man to do whatever he pleases and has the power to do – for the temper of the city is surely like that, excessively independent – do you then, I say, fail to understand this and assert that the citizens ought to be wisely governed? Have you not even observed what great independence exists among the citizens, even down to the very asses and camels? The men who hire them out lead even these animals through the porticoes as though they were brides. For the unroofed alleys and the broad highways were certainly not made for the use of pack-animals, rather they are provided merely for show and as an extravagance; but in their independence, the asses prefer to use the porticoes, and no one keeps them out of any one of these for fear he should be robbing them of their independence, so independent is our city! And yet you think that even the charming youths in the city ought to keep quiet and, if possible, think whatever you like, but at any rate utter only what is agreeable for you to hear. Whereas it is their independence that makes them hold revels; and this they always do handsomely, albeit during festivals they revel more than usual."

Once upon a time, the citizens of Tarentum paid to the Romans the penalty for this sort of jesting, seeing that, when drunk at the festival of Dionysus, they insulted the Roman ambassadors.[1] Yet you are in all respects more fortunate than the citizens of Tarentum, for you give yourselves up to pleasure throughout the whole year, instead of for a few days; and instead of foreign ambassadors, you insult your own sovereign, indeed, even the very hairs on his chin and the devices engraved on his coins.[2] Well done, O wise citizens,

---

1. Rome took Tarentum in 272 B.C.

2. The people of Antioch ridiculed Pagan symbols, such as the figure of Helios, the sun god, which Julian had engraved on his coinage

both you who make such jests and you who welcome and find profit in the jesters! For it is evident that uttering them gives pleasure to the former, while the latter rejoice to hear jests of this sort. I share your pleasure in this unanimity, and you do well to be a city of one mind in such matters, since it is not at all dignified or an enviable task to restrain and chastise the licentiousness of the young. For if one were to rob human beings of the power to do and say what they please, that would be to take away and to curtail the first principle of independence. Therefore, since you knew that men ought to be independent in all respects, you acted quite rightly, in the first place when you permitted the women to govern themselves, so that you might profit by their being independent and licentious to excess; secondly, when you entrusted to them the bringing up of children, for fear that if they had to experience any harsher authority they might later turn out to be slaves; and as they grew up to be boys might be taught first of all to respect their elders, then under the influence of this bad habit might show too much reverence for the magistrates, and finally might have to be classed not as men but as slaves; thus, becoming temperate, well-behaved, and orderly, they might, before they knew it, be altogether corrupted. Then what effect have the women on the children? They induce them to revere the same things as they do by means of pleasure, which is, it seems, the most blessed thing and the most highly honoured, not only by men but by beasts also. It is for this reason, I think, that you are so very happy, because you refuse every form of slavery: first you begin by refusing slavery to the gods, secondly to the laws, and thirdly to me who am the guardian of the laws. For I should indeed be eccentric if, when the gods suffer the city to be so independent and do not chastise her, I should be resentful and angry. For be assured that the gods have shared with me in the disrespect that has been shown to me in your city.

"The Chi", say the citizens, "never harmed the city in any way, nor did the Kappa." Now the meaning of this riddle which your wisdom has invented is hard to understand, but I obtained interpreters from your city and was informed that these are the first letters of names, and that the former is intended to represent Christ, the latter Constantius. Bear with me, then, if I speak frankly. In one thing Constantius did harm you, in that when he had appointed me as Cæsar he did not put me to death. As for the rest, may the gods grant to you alone of all the many citizens of Rome to have experience of the avarice of many a Constantius, or I should say rather, of the avarice of his friends. For the man was my cousin and dear to me; but after he had chosen enmity with me instead of friendship, and then the gods with the utmost benevolence arbitrated our contention with one another, I proved myself a more loyal friend to him than he had expected to find me before I became his enemy. Why, then, do you think that you are annoying me by your praises of him, when I am truly angry with those who slander him? As for Christ, you love him, you say, and adopt him as the guardian of your city instead of Zeus, and the god of Daphne, and Calliope,[1] who revealed your clever intention. Did those citizens of Emesa who set fire to the tombs of the Galilæans long for Christ?[2] And what citizens of Emesa have I ever annoyed? I have, however, annoyed many of you – I might almost say all – the Senate, the wealthy citizens, and the common people. The latter, indeed, since they have chosen godlessness, hate me for the most part, or rather, all of them hate me because they see that I adhere to the ordinances of the sacred rites which our forefathers observed; the powerful citizens hate me because they are prevented from selling everything at a high price; but all of you hate me on account of the dancers and the theatres. Not because I deprive others of these pleasures, but because I care less for things of that sort than for frogs croaking in a pond.[3] Therefore, is it not natural for me to accuse myself, when I have furnished so many handles for your hatred?

Cato the Roman,[4] however – how he wore his beard I do not know, but he deserves to be praised in comparison with anyone who prides themselves on their temperance, their nobility of soul, and above all on their courage – he, I understand, once visited this populous, luxurious, and wealthy city. When he saw the youths in the suburb drawn up in full array, and with them the magistrates, as though for some military display, he thought your ancestors had made all those preparations in his honour. So he quickly dismounted from his horse and came forward, though at the same time he was vexed with those of his friends who had preceded him, for they informed the citizens that Cato was approaching and so induced them to hasten forth. While he was in this position, then, feeling slightly embarrassed and flushed, the master of the

1. There was a statue of Calliope in the market place at Antioch

2. The people of Emesa burned the Christian churches and spared only one, which they converted into a temple of Dionysus

3. A proverb to express complete indifference

4. The anecdote which follows is told by Plutarch in *Cato the Younger* and *Pompeius*

gymnasium ran to meet him and called out: "stranger, where is Demetrius?" Now, this Demetrius was a freedman of Pompey, who had acquired a very large fortune; and if you want to know the amount of it – for I suppose that, of all that I am now telling you, you are most anxious to hear this – I will tell you who has related the story. Damophilus of Bithynia has written compositions of this sort, and in them, by culling anecdotes from many books, he has produced tales that give the greatest delight to anyone who loves to listen to stories, whether he be young or old. For old age usually revives in the elderly that love of tales which is natural to the young; and this, I think, is the reason why both the old and the young are equally fond of stories.

Well, then, to return to Cato. Do you want me to tell you how he greeted the master of the gymnasium? Do not imagine that I am slandering your city; for the story is not my own. If any rumour has come round, even to your ears, of the man of Chæronea,[1] who belongs to that worthless class of men who are called by impostors philosophers – I myself never attained to that class, though in my ignorance I claimed to be a member of it and to have a part in it – well he, as I was saying, related that Cato answered not with a word, but only cried aloud "alas for this ill-fated city!" like a man stricken with madness and out of his senses, whereupon he took himself off.

Do not be surprised, therefore, if I now feel towards you as I do, for I am more uncivilised than he, and more fierce and headstrong in proportion as the Celts are more so than the Romans. He was born in Rome and was nurtured among the Roman citizens until he was on the threshold of old age. As for me, however, I had to do with Celts and Germans and the Hercynian forest[2] from the moment that I was reckoned a grown man, and I have by now spent a long time there, like some huntsman who associates with and is entangled among wild beasts. There I met with temperaments that know not how to wheedle or flatter, but only how to behave simply and frankly to all men alike. After my nurture in childhood, my path as a boy took me through the discourses of Plato and Aristotle, which are not at all suited for the reading of communities who think that on account of their luxury they are the happiest of men. I then had to work hard myself among the most warlike and high-spirited of all nations, where men have knowledge of Aphrodite, goddess of Wedlock, only for the purpose of marrying and having

1. Plutarch 2. cf. Cæsar, *Bellum Gallicum*, 6.24.479

children, and know Dionysus the Drink-Giver, only for the sake of just so much wine as each can drink at a draught. While in their theatres no licentiousness or insolence exists, nor does any man dance the cordax on their stage.

A story is told of them that not long ago a certain Cappadocian was exiled from here to that place, a man who had been brought up in your city in the house of the goldsmith – you know of course whom I mean – and had learned, as he naturally did learn there, that one ought not to have intercourse with women but to pay attention to youths. Thus, after doing and suffering here I know not what, when he went to the court of the king in that country, he took with him to remind him of your habits a number of dancers and other such delights from this city; then finally, since he still needed a cotylist[1] – you know the word and that to which it refers – he invited him also from here, because of his longing and love for the austere mode of life that prevails among you. Now, the Celts never made the acquaintance of the cotylist, since he was at once admitted into the palace; but when the dancers began to display their art in the theatre, the Celts gave them a wide berth because they thought that they were like men stricken with nympholepsy. For the theatre seemed to the men in that country highly ridiculous, just as it does to me; but whereas the Celts were a few ridiculing many, here, I along with a few others seem absurd in every way to all of you.

This is a fact which I do not resent. Indeed, it would be unjust of me not to make the best of the present state of things, after having so greatly enjoyed life among the Celts. For they were so fond of me, on account of the similarity of our dispositions, that not only did they venture to take up arms on my behalf, but they gave me many valuable things besides; and when I would have declined it, they almost forced me to take it, and in all things readily obeyed me. Though most wonderful of all, a great report of me travelled thence to your city, and all men proclaimed loudly that I was brave, wise, and just, not only terrible to encounter in war, but also skilful in turning peace to my account, approachable and mild-tempered. Yet now you have sent them tidings from here in return, to the effect that firstly the affairs of the whole world have been turned upside down by me – though indeed I am not conscious of turning anything upside down, either voluntarily or involuntarily; secondly, that I ought to twist ropes from my beard; lastly, that I war against the Chi and that you begin to regret the Kappa. Now, may the

1. κοτύλη (cup; joint-socket). It is not known what a cotylist performance entailed

guardian gods of this city grant you a double allowance of the Kappa![1] For besides this you falsely accused the neighbouring cities, which are holy and the servants of the gods, like myself, of having produced the satires which were composed against me; though I know well that those cities love me as their own sons, for they at once restored the shrines of the gods and overturned all the tombs of the godless,[2] on the signal that was given by me the other day. So excited were they in mind and so exalted in spirit that they even attacked those who were offending against the gods with more violence than I would have wished.

Though consider now your own behaviour. Many of you overturned the altars of the gods which had only just been erected, and with difficulty did my indulgent treatment teach you to keep quiet. When I sent away the body from Daphne,[3] some of you, in expiation of your conduct towards the gods, handed over the shrine of the god of Daphne to those who were aggrieved about the relics of the body, and the rest of you, whether by accident or on purpose, hurled against the shrine that fire which made the strangers who were visiting your city shudder, but gave pleasure to the mass of your citizens, and was ignored – and is still ignored – by your Senate. Now, in my opinion, even before that fire, the god had forsaken the temple, for when I first entered it his holy image gave me a sign thereof. I call mighty Helios to bear me witness of this before all doubters. Next I wish to remind you of yet another reason for your hatred of me, then to abuse myself – a thing which I usually do fairly well – and to both accuse and blame myself with regard to that hatred.

In the tenth month, according to your reckoning – Loos, I think you call it – there is a festival founded by your forefathers in honour of this god, and it was your duty to be zealous in visiting Daphne. Accordingly, I hastened there from the temple of Zeus Kasios,[4] thinking that at Daphne, if anywhere, I should enjoy the sight of your wealth and public spirit. Thus I imagined in my own mind the sort of procession it would be, like a man seeing visions

1. i.e. may they have two such rulers as Constantius

2. The sepulchres over which the Christian churches were built

3. Babylas, Bishop of Antioch, had been reburied in the grove of Daphne, beside the sanctuary of Apollo. When the church over his tomb was removed by Julian, he transported the body of St. Babylas to its original resting place in Antioch, and that night (22nd October, 362) the temple of Apollo which Julian had restored was set on fire. Julian suspected the Christians, but no culprit was ever found

4. Kasios was the name of a mountain near Antioch where a temple of Zeus stood

in a dream – beasts for sacrifice, libations, choruses in honour of the god, incense, and the youths of your city there surrounding the shrine, their souls adorned with all holiness and themselves attired in white and splendid raiment. Yet when I entered the shrine I found there no incense, not so much as a cake, not a single beast for sacrifice. For that moment I was amazed; I thought that I was still outside the shrine and that you were waiting for the signal from me, doing me that honour because I am *Pontifex Maximus*. When I began to inquire, however, as to what sacrifice the city intended to offer to celebrate the annual festival in honour of the god, the priest answered: "I have brought with me from my own house a goose as an offering to the god, but the city this time has made no preparations".

Thereupon, being fond of making enemies, I made in the Senate a very unseemly speech, which it may perhaps be pertinent to quote to you now. "It is a terrible thing", I said, "that so important a city should be more neglectful of the gods than any village on the borders of the Pontus. Your city possesses ten thousand lots of privately owned land, and yet when the annual festival in honour of the god of her forefathers is to be celebrated for the first time since the gods dispelled the cloud of impiety, she does not produce on her own behalf a single bird, though she ought if possible to have sacrificed an ox for every tribe, or if that were too difficult, the whole city in common ought at any rate to have offered to the god one bull on her own behalf. Yet every one of you delights to spend money privately on dinners and feasts; and I know very well that many of you squandered very large sums of money on dinners during the May festival. Nevertheless, on your own behalf and on behalf of the city's welfare, not one of the citizens offers a private sacrifice, nor does the city offer a public sacrifice, but only this priest! Though I think that it would have been more just for him to go home carrying portions from the multitude of beasts offered by you to the god. For the duty assigned by the gods to priests is to do them honour by their nobility of character and by the practice of virtue, and also to perform to them the service that is due; but it befits the city, I think, to offer both private and public sacrifice. As it is, however, every one of you allows his wife to carry everything out of his house to the Galilæans, and when your wives feed the poor at your expense, they inspire a great admiration for godlessness in those who are in need of such aid – and of such sort are, I think, the great majority of mankind – while as for yourselves, you think that you are doing nothing unusual when in the first place you are careless of the honours due to the gods, and not one of those in need goes near the temples – for there is nothing there, I think, with which to feed them – and yet when any one of you gives a birthday feast, he provides dinner and breakfast without stint and welcomes his friends to a costly table. Conversely, when the annual festival arrived, no one furnished olive oil for a lamp for the god, or a libation, or a beast for sacrifice, or incense. Now, I do not know how any good man could endure to see such things in your city, and for my part I am sure that it is displeasing to the gods also."

This is what I remember having said at the time, and the god bore witness to the truth of my words – would that he had not! – when he forsook your suburb which for so long he had protected, and again during that time of storm and stress[1] when he turned in the wrong direction the minds of those who were then in power and forced their hands. Though I acted foolishly in making myself odious to you. For I ought to have remained silent as, I think, many of those who came here with me did, and I ought not to have been meddlesome or found fault. Yet I poured down all these reproaches on your heads for no purpose, owing to my rashness and a ridiculous desire to flatter – for it is surely not to be believed that out of goodwill towards you I spoke those words to you then; rather I was, I think, hunting after a reputation for piety towards the gods and for sincere good-will towards you, which is, I believe, the most absurd form of flattery. Therefore, you treat me justly when you defend yourselves against those criticisms of mine and choose a different place for making your defence. For I abused you under the god's statue near his altar and the footprints of the holy image, in the presence of few witnesses; whereas you abused me in the marketplace, in the presence of the whole populace, and with the help of citizens who were capable of composing such pleasant witticisms as yours. For you must be well aware that all of you, those who uttered the sayings about me and those who listened to them, are equally responsible; and he who listened with pleasure to those slanders, since he had an equal share of the pleasure, though he took less trouble than the speaker, must share the blame.

Throughout the whole city, then, you both uttered and listened to all the jests that were made about this miserable beard of mine,

1. Julian is probably alluding to the riot which took place at Antioch in 354 on account of the famine, when the populace killed Theophilus the Governor and were punished for the murder by Constantius

and about one who has never displayed to you, nor ever will display among you, the sort of life that you always live and also desire to see among those who govern you. Next, with respect to the slanders which both privately and publicly you have poured down on my head, when you ridiculed me in anapæstic verse, since I too have accused myself, I permit you to employ that method with even greater frankness; for I shall never on that account do you any harm, by slaying or beating, fettering or imprisoning you, or punishing you in any way. Why indeed should I? For now that in showing you myself, in company with my friends, behaving with sobriety – a most sorry and unpleasing sight to you – I have failed to show you any beautiful spectacle, I have decided to leave this city and to retire from it. Not, in truth, because I am convinced that I shall be in all respects pleasing to those to whom I am going, but because I judge it more desirable, in case I should fail at least to seem to them an honourable and good man, to give all men in turn a share of my unpleasantness,[1] and not to annoy this happy city with the evil odour, as it were, of my moderation and the sobriety of my friends.

For not one of us has bought a field or garden in your city, or built a house, or married or given in marriage among you, or fallen in love with any of your handsome youths, or coveted the wealth of Assyria, or awarded court patronage;[2] nor have we allowed any of those in office to exercise influence over us, or induced the populace to organise banquets or theatrical shows; rather, we have procured for them such luxurious ease that, since they have respite from want, they have had leisure to compose their anapæsts against the very author of their well-being. Again, I have not levied gold or demanded silver or increased the tribute; but in addition to the arrears, one-fifth of the regular taxes has been in all cases remitted. Moreover, I do not think it enough that I myself practise self-restraint, but I have an usher also who, by Zeus and the other gods, is especially moderate, as I believe; though he has been finely scolded by you, because, being an old man and slightly bald in front, in his perversity he is too modest to wear his hair long at the back, as Homer made the Abantes wear theirs.[3] While I have with me at my court two or three other men, also, who are not at all inferior to him, indeed, four or even five now, if you please.

1. Demosthenes, *Against Meidias*, 153

2. *προστασία* may be in reference to the Imperial protection of a municipal guild

3. *The Iliad*, II, 542

As for my uncle and namesake, did he not govern you most justly, for so long as the gods allowed him to remain with me and to assist me in my work? Did he not with utmost foresight administer all the business of the city? For my part, I thought these were admirable things, that is, mildness and moderation in those who govern, and I supposed that by practising these I should appear admirable in your eyes. Since the length of my beard is displeasing to you, however, as is my unkempt locks, and the fact that I do not put in an appearance at the theatres, and that I require men to be reverent in the temples; and since more than all these things my constant attendance at trials displeases you, as well as the fact that I try to banish greed from the marketplace, I willingly go away and leave your city to you. For when a man changes his habits in his old age it is not easy, I think, for him to escape the fate that is described in the legend about the kite. The story goes that the kite once had a note like that of other birds, but it aimed at neighing like a high-spirited horse; then, because it had forgotten its former note and could not quite attain to the other sound, it was deprived of both, and hence the note it now utters is less musical than that of any other bird. This, then, is the fate that I am trying to avoid, that is, failing to be either truly boorish or truly accomplished. For already, as you can see for yourselves, I am, since Heaven so wills, near the age "when on my head, white hairs mingle with black", as the poet of Teos said.[1]

Enough of that. Now then, in the name of Zeus, God of the Agora[2] and Guardian of the City, render me an account of your ingratitude. Were you ever wronged by me in any way, either all in common or as individuals, and is it because you were unable to avenge yourselves openly that you now assail me with abuse in your marketplaces in anapæstic verse, just as comedians drag Heracles and Dionysus on the stage and make a public show of them? Or can you say that, though I refrained from any harsh conduct towards you, I did not refrain from speaking ill of you, so that you, in your turn, are defending yourselves by the same methods? What, I ask, is the reason for your antagonism and your hatred of me? For I am very sure that I have done no terrible or incurable injury to any one of you, either separately, as individuals, or to your city as a whole; nor have I uttered any disparaging word, but I have even praised

1. Anacreon, fr. 77

2. The agora ("gathering-place") was the centre of athletic, artistic, commercial, social, religious, and political life in the ancient Greek city states

you, as I thought I ought to, and have bestowed on you certain advantages, as was natural for one who desires, as far as he can, to benefit many men. Yet it is impossible, as you know well, to both remit all taxes to the taxpayers and to give everything to those who are accustomed to receive gifts. Therefore, when it is seen that I have diminished none of the public subscriptions which the imperial purse is accustomed to contribute, but have remitted not a few of your taxes, does this business not seem like a riddle?

It becomes me, however, to be silent about all that I have done for my subjects in common, lest it should seem that I am purposely singing my praises with my own lips, as it were, and that no less after announcing that I should pour down on my own head many most opprobrious insults. As for my actions with respect to you as individuals, which, though the manner of them was rash and foolish, nevertheless did not by any means deserve to be repaid by you with ingratitude, it would, I think, be becoming for me to bring them forward as reproaches against myself; and these reproaches ought to be more severe than those I uttered before, those that related to my unkempt appearance and my lack of charm, inasmuch as they are more genuine since they have especial reference to the soul. That is, before I came here I used to praise you in the strongest possible terms, without waiting to have actual experience of you, nor did I consider how we should feel towards one another; indeed, since I believed you to be sons of Greeks, and I myself, though my family is Thracian, am a Greek in my habits, I assumed that we would regard one another with the greatest possible affection. This example of my rashness must therefore be counted as a reproach against me. Next, after you had sent an embassy to me – and it arrived not only later than all the other embassies, but even later than that of the Alexandrians who dwell in Egypt – I remitted large sums of gold and of silver also, and all the tribute money for you separately apart from the other cities; moreover, I increased the register of your Senate by two hundred members and spared no man;[1] for I was planning to make your city greater and more powerful.

I therefore gave you the opportunity to elect and to have in your Senate the richest men among those who administer my own revenues and have charge of coining the currency. Yet rather than elect the capable men among these, you instead seized the opportunity to act like a city by no means well-ordered, albeit quite

1. The Senatorship was an expensive burden

in keeping with your character. Would you like me to remind you of a single example? You nominated a Senator, and then before his name had been placed on the register, and the scrutiny of his character was still pending, you thrust this person into the public service. Then you dragged in another from the marketplace, a man who was poor and who belonged to a class which in every other city is counted as the very dregs, but who among you, since in your excessive wisdom you exchange rubbish for gold, enjoys a moderate fortune; and this man you elected as your colleague. Many such offences did you commit with regard to the nominations, and then when I did not consent to everything, not only was I deprived of the thanks due for all the good that I had done, but I also incurred your dislike on account of everything from which, in justice, I refrained.

Of course, these were very trivial matters and could not so far make the city hostile to me. My greatest offence of all, however, and what aroused that violent hatred of yours, was the following. When I arrived among you the populace in the theatre, who were being oppressed by the rich, first of all cried aloud: "everything plentiful; everything dear!" On the following day, I had an interview with your most powerful citizens and tried to persuade them that it is better to despise unjust profits and to benefit the citizens and strangers in your city. They duly promised to take charge of the matter, but though for three successive months I took no notice and waited, they neglected the matter in a way that no one would have thought possible. Then, when I saw that there was truth in the outcry of the populace, and that the pressure in the market was due not to any scarcity but to the insatiate greed of the rich, I appointed a fair price for everything, and made it known to all men. Further, since the citizens had everything else in great abundance – wine, for instance, and olive oil, and all the rest – but were short of corn, because there had been a terrible failure of the crops owing to the previous droughts, I decided to send to Chalcis, Hierapolis, and the cities nearby, and from them I imported for you four hundred thousand measures of corn. When this, too, had been used up, I first expended five thousand, then later seven thousand, and once more ten thousand bushels – *modii*[1] as they are called in my country – all of which was my very own property. Moreover, I gave to the city corn which had been brought for me from Egypt, and the price which I set on it was a silver piece, not

1. The *modius* was a bushel measure

for ten measures but for fifteen, that is to say, the same amount that had formerly been paid for ten measures. For if in the summer, in your city, that same number of measures is sold for that sum, what could you reasonably have expected at the season when, as the Boeotian poet says, "it is a cruel thing for famine to be in the house"?[1] Would you not have been thankful to get five measures for that sum, especially when the winter had set in so severe?

Yet what did your rich men do? They secretly sold the corn in the country for an exaggerated price, and they oppressed the community by the expenses that private persons had to incur. The result is that not only the city but most of the country people too are flocking in to buy bread, which is the only thing to be found cheap and in abundance. For indeed, who remembers fifteen measures of corn having been sold among you for a gold piece, even when the city was in a prosperous condition? It was for this conduct that I incurred your hatred; because I did not allow people to sell you wine, vegetables, and fruit for gold, or the corn which had been locked away by the rich in their granaries to be sold for their benefit. For they managed the business finely outside the city, and so procured for men "famine that grinds down mortals",[2] as the god said when he was accusing those who behave in this fashion. So the city now enjoys plenty only as regards bread, and nothing else.

I knew well even then that when I acted thus I should not please everybody, only I cared nothing about that. For I thought it was my duty to assist the mass of the people who were being wronged, and the strangers who kept arriving in the city both on my account and on account of the high officials who were with me. Yet since it is now the case, I think, that the latter have departed, and the city is of one mind with respect to me – for some of you hate me and the others whom I fed are ungrateful – I leave the whole matter in the hands of Adrasteia[3] and I will betake myself to some other nation, to citizens of another sort. Nor will I even remind you how you treated one another when you asserted your rights nine years ago; how the populace with loud clamour set fire to the houses of those in power and murdered the Governor; and how later they were punished for these things because, though their anger was justified, what they did exceeded all limits.[4]

1. This does not occur in our versions of Hesiod or Pindar
2. A phrase from an unknown oracular source
3. The avenging goddess who is better known as Nemesis
4. i.e., the murder of Theophilus, the Governor of Syria, in 354

Why, I repeat, in heaven's name, am I treated with ingratitude? Is it because I feed you from my own purse, a thing which before this day has never happened to any city, and, moreover, feed you so generously? Is it because I increased the register of Senators? Or because, when I caught you in the act of stealing, I did not proceed against you? Let me, if you will, remind you of one or two instances, so that no one may think that what I say is a pretext or mere rhetoric or a false claim. You said, I believe, that three thousand lots of land were uncultivated, and you asked to have them; and when you had received them, you all divided them amongst yourselves, though you did not need them. This matter was investigated and brought to light beyond any doubt. Then I took the lots away from those who held them unjustly and made no inquiries about the lands which they had acquired beforehand – land for which they paid no taxes, though they most certainly ought to have been taxed – and I appointed these men to the most expensive public services in the city. Even now, they who breed horses for you every year hold nearly three thousand lots of land exempt from taxation. This is due in the first place to the judgement and management of my uncle and namesake, but also to my own kindness; and since this is the way in which I punish swindlers and thieves, I naturally seem to you to be turning the world upside down. For you know very well that clemency towards men of this sort increases and fosters wickedness among mankind.

Well then, my discourse seems to have come back around again to the point at which I wished to arrive. Which is to say that I am myself responsible for all the wrong that has been done to me, because I transformed your graciousness to ungracious ways. This, therefore, is the fault of my own folly and not of your licence. For in my future dealings with you, then, I shall indeed endeavour to be more sensible; but to you, in return for your good will towards me and the honour wherewith you have publicly honoured me, may the gods duly pay the recompense!

THE CAESARS

PREFACE

The Cæsars, also referred to as *Symposium* or *Saturnalia*, is the only other surviving satire written by Julian. It was composed in 361 at Constantinople, shortly after he had become Emperor, and was probably addressed to Salutius, to whom Julian had sent his lost work *The Kronia*. The interlocutor at the beginning of *The Cæsars* is almost certainly intended to be Salutius.[1]

Of Julian's extant writings, *The Cæsars* may reasonably be described as his wittiest, most light-hearted and playful work. The keen student of history is evidently in his element with the large cast of former Emperors at his disposal. Admittedly, the licence with which he portrays the gods, while doubtless appropriate to the festival, does seem to conflict somewhat with the admonitions addressed to priests and Cynics in his other writings.[2] Julian's defence would presumably be that his use of the gods as characters was entirely reverential, consistent with traditional portrayals, and befitting the context of the narrative.

In his 1683 work *Les Cesars de l'empereur Julien*, Spanheim explores the distinction between the Greek *satyr*, a dramatic piece which was acted after the tragedy, and the Roman *satura*, a miscellaneous composition in either prose or verse that sought to inspire amusement, indignation, or both at once. While *The Cæsars* of Julian seems slightly out place in either class, it of course owes far more to the later Roman tradition.

1. W.C.F. Wright 2. Julian, *Letter to a Priest* and *To the Cynic Heraclius*

THE CAESARS

"It is the season of the Kronia,[1] during which the god allows us to make merry. Yet, my dear friend, as I have no talent for amusing or entertaining, I feel I must take pains not to talk mere nonsense."

"But Cæsar, can there be anyone so dull and stupid as to take pains over jesting? I had always thought that such recreation was a relaxation for the mind and a relief from pains and cares."

"Yes, and no doubt your view is correct, but that is not how the matter strikes me. For by nature I have no turn for raillery, or parody, or raising a laugh. Yet since I must obey the ordinance of the god of the festival, should you like me to relate to you by way of entertainment a myth in which there is perhaps much worth hearing?"

"I shall listen with great pleasure, for I too am not one to despise myths, and I am far from rejecting those that have the right tendency; indeed, I am of the same opinion as you and your admired, or rather, the universally admired, Plato. He also often conveyed a serious lesson in his myths."

"By Zeus, that is indeed true!"

"What, then, is your myth and of what type?"

"It is not one of those old-fashioned ones, such as Æsop[2] wrote. Though whether you should call mine an invention of Hermes – for it was from him that I learned what I am about to tell you – or whether it is really true, or a mixture of truth and fiction, the upshot, as the saying goes, will decide."

"This is indeed a fine preface that you have composed, just the thing for a myth, not to say an oration! Now, however, pray tell me the tale itself, whatever its type may be."

"Give heed, then, if you will."

At the festival of the Kronia, Romulus held a banquet, and invited not only all the gods, but the Emperors as well. For the gods, couches had been prepared on high, at the very apex, so to speak,

---

1. Better known by its Latin name Saturnalia. Saturn is the Greek Kronos

2. i.e. not a fable with a moral nor an animal fable

of the sky,[1] upon "Olympus, where the seat of the gods is said to be, abiding and eternal".[2] For we are told that after Heracles, Quirinus also ascended there, since we must give Romulus the name of Quirinus in obedience to the divine will. For the gods, then, the banquet had been made ready there. Yet just below the moon, in the upper air, he had decided to entertain the Emperors. The lightness of the bodies with which they had been invested, along with the revolution of the moon sustained them. Four couches were there made ready for the superior gods. That of Kronos was made of gleaming ebony, which concealed in its blackness a lustre so intense and divine that no one could endure to gaze thereon. For in looking at that ebony, the eyes suffered as much, I suspect, from its excess of radiance as from the sun when one gazes too intently at his disc. The couch of Zeus was more brilliant than silver, but paler than gold; whether one ought to call this "electron",[3] however, or give it some other name, Hermes could not inform me precisely. On either side of these sat the mother and daughter upon golden thrones, Hera beside Zeus, and Rhea beside Kronos. As for the beauty of the gods, not even Hermes tried to describe it in his tale; he merely said that it transcended description, and must be comprehended by the eye of the mind, for in words it was hard to portray and impossible to convey to mortal ears. Never, indeed, will there be or appear an orator so gifted that he could describe such surpassing beauty as shines forth on the countenance of the gods.

For the other gods had been prepared a throne or couch, for each according to his seniority. Nor did any dispute arise as to this, but as Homer correctly said,[4] no doubt instructed by the Muses themselves, every god has his seat on which it is irrevocably ordained that he shall sit, firmly and immovably fixed; and though they rise on the entrance of their father, they never confounded or changed the order of their seats, or infringe on one another's, since every one knows his appointed place.

When the gods were seated in a circle, Silenus, amorous, I think, of Dionysus, ever fair and ever young, who sat close to Zeus his father, took his seat next to him on the pretext that he had raised him and was his tutor. Thus, since Dionysus loves jesting and laughter and is the giver of the Graces, Silenus cheered the god with an endless stream of witticisms and jests, and in other ways besides.

1. cf. Plato, *Phædrus*, 247 2. *The Odyssey*, VI, 42

3. cf. Martial, VIII, 51.5; it is uncertain whether electron means amber, or a combination of gold and silver

4. This is not in our version of Homer; Julian may have in mind *The Iliad*, XI, 76

Once the banquet had been arranged for the Emperors also, Julius Cæsar entered first, and such was his passion for glory that he seemed ready to contend with Zeus himself for dominion. Whereupon Silenus, observing him, said: "take care, Zeus, lest this man in his lust for power be minded to rob you of your empire. He is, as you see, tall and handsome, and if he resembles me in nothing else, round about his head he is very much like me".[1] While Silenus, to whom the gods paid very little attention, was jesting thus, Octavian entered, changing colour continually, like a chameleon, turning at first pale then red; one moment his expression was gloomy, sombre, and overcast, the next he unbent and showed all the charms of Aphrodite and the Graces. Moreover, in the glances of his eyes he was fain to resemble mighty Helios, for he preferred that none who approached should be able to meet his gaze.[2] "Good Heavens!" exclaimed Silenus, "what a changeable monster is this! What mischief will he do us?"

"Cease trifling", said Apollo, "after I have handed him over to Zeno[3] here, I shall promptly transform him for you into gold without alloy. Come, Zeno," he ordered, "take charge of my nursling". Zeno obeyed, and thereupon, by reciting over Octavian a few of his doctrines,[4] in the fashion of those who mutter the incantations of Zamolxis,[5] he made him wise and temperate.

The third to hasten in was Tiberius, with countenance solemn and grim, and an expression at once sober and martial. As he turned to sit down, however, his back was seen to be covered with countless scars, burns, and sores, painful welts and bruises, while ulcers and abscesses were as though branded thereon, the result of his self-indulgent and cruel life.[6] Silenus at once cried out, "far different, friend, you appear now than before",[7] and seemed more serious than he had wont.

"Pray tell, why so solemn, dear little father?" said Dionysus.

"It was this old satyr", he replied, "he shocked me and made me forget myself then introduce Homer's Muse."

"Take care", said Dionysus, "he will pull your ear, as he is said to have done to a certain grammarian."[8]

---

1. Silenus is usually represented as bald 2. Suetonius, *Augustus*, 16 3. The Stoic
4. Julian is likely alluding to the influence of Athenodorus the Stoic on Octavian
5. A deity among the Thracians who, according to one tradition, had been a slave of Pythagoras; cf. Herodotus, 4.94; Plato, *Charmides*, 156
6. cf. Plato, *Gorgias*, 525; *Republic*, 611 c, Tacitus, *Annales*, 6.6; Lucian, *Cataplus*, 27
7. *The Odyssey*, 16. 181 8. i.e., Seleucus; cf. Suetonius, *Tiberius*, 56, 70

"Plague take him", said Silenus, "in his little island" – he was alluding to Capri – "let him scratch the face of that wretched fisherman".[1] While they were still joking together, there came a fierce monster.[2] Thereupon all the gods averted their eyes from the sight, and the next moment Justice handed him over to the Avengers who hurled him into Tartarus. So Silenus had no chance to say anything about him. Yet when Claudius came in, Silenus began to sing certain verses from the Knights of Aristophanes,[3] toadying Claudius, as it seemed, instead of Demos. The he looked at Quirinus and said, "Quirinus, it is not kind of you to invite your descendant to a banquet without his freedmen Narcissus and Pallas.[4] Come", he went on, "send and fetch them, and please send, too, for his spouse Messalina, for without them this fellow is like a lay-figure in a tragedy; I might almost say lifeless."[5] While Silenus was speaking, Nero entered, lyre in hand and wearing a wreath of laurel. Whereupon Silenus turned to Apollo and said: "you see he models himself on you".

"I shall soon remove that wreath", replied Apollo, "for he does not imitate me in all things, and even when he does, he does so poorly." Then his wreath was taken off and Cocytus instantly swept him away.

After Nero, many Emperors of many sorts came crowding in together – Vindex, Galba, Otho, Vitellius – so that Silenus exclaimed: "where, dear gods, have you found such a swarm of monarchs? We are being suffocated with their smoke, for brutes of this sort spare not even the temple of the gods".[6] Then Zeus turned to his brother Serapis, and pointing to Vespasian said, "send this miser from Egypt forthwith to extinguish the flames. As for his sons, bid the eldest[7] sport with Aphrodite Pandemos, and chain the younger[8] in the stocks like the Sicilian monster."[9] Next entered an old man,[10] beautiful to behold; for even old age can be radiantly beautiful. Very mild were his manners, most just his dealings. In Silenus he inspired such awe that he fell silent.

"What!" said Hermes, "have you nothing to say to us about this man?"

"Yes, by Zeus," he replied, "I blame you gods for the injustice of

1. Suetonius, *Tiberius*, 60 2. Caligula 3. Aristophanes, *Knights*, 1111
4. Their riches were proverbial; cf. Juvenal, 1.100; 14.32 5. Tacitus, *Annales*, 11.12
6. An allusion partly to the smoke of civil war, partly to the burning of the temple of Jupiter Capitoline under Vitellius, restored by Vespasian; Tacitus, *Annales*, 4.81
7. Titus 8. Domitian 9. Phalaris of Agrigentum 10. Nerva

allowing that blood-thirsty monster to rule for fifteen years, while you granted this man scarcely one whole year."

"Careful where you lay blame," said Zeus, "for I shall bring in many virtuous rulers after him." Accordingly, Trajan entered forthwith, carrying on his shoulders the trophies of his wars with the Getæ and the Parthians. Silenus, when he saw him, said in a whisper which he meant to be heard, "now is the time for Zeus our master to look out, if he wishes to keep Ganymede for himself".

Next entered an austere-looking man[1] with a long beard, one adept in all the arts, but especially music, one who was always gazing at the heavens and prying into hidden things. Silenus when he saw him said: "what think you of this sophist? Can he be looking here for Antinous? One of you should tell him that the young man is not here, and make him cease from his madness and folly". Thereupon a man[2] entered of temperate character, I do not say in affairs of love but in affairs of state. When Silenus caught sight of him he exclaimed: "bah! Such fussing over trifles! This old man seems to me the sort of person who would split cumin seed".[3] Next entered the pair of brothers, Verus[4] and Lucius.[5] Silenus scowled horribly because he could not jeer or scoff at them, especially not at Verus; but he would not ignore his errors of judgement in the case of his son[6] and his wife,[7] in that he mourned the latter beyond what was becoming, particularly considering that she was not even a virtuous woman, while he failed to see that his son was ruining the Empire as well as himself; this, moreover, despite Verus having an excellent son-in-law who would have administered the state better, and would also have managed the youth better than he could manage himself. Yet although he refused to ignore these errors, he reverenced the exalted virtue of Verus. His son, conversely, he considered not worth even ridicule and so let him pass. Indeed, he fell to earth of his own accord because he could not keep on his feet or accompany the heroes.

Then Pertinax came in to the banquet still bewailing his violent end. Thus Justice took pity on him and said: "come, the authors of this deed shall not long exult. Though Pertinax, you too were guilty, since, at least so far as conjecture went, you were privy to the plot that was aimed at the son of Marcus". Next came Severus, a man of excessively harsh temper and delighting to punish. "Of

1. Hadrian 2. Antonius Pius 3. A proverb for miserliness; cf. Theocritus 10.50
4. Verus was the family name of Marcus Aurelius 5. Lucius Verus
6. Commodus 7. Faustina

him", said Silenus, "I have nothing to say, for I am terrified by his forbidding and implacable countenance". When his sons would have entered with him, Minos kept them at a distance. Once he had clearly discerned their characters, however, he let the younger[1] pass, but sent away the elder[2] to atone for his crimes. Next Macrinus, assassin and fugitive, and after him the little boy from Emesa[3] were driven far away from the sacred enclosure. Though Alexander the Syrian sat down somewhere in the lowest ranks and loudly lamented his fate.[4] Silenus made fun of him and exclaimed: "O fool and madman! Exalted as you were, you could not govern your own family, but gave your revenues to your mother;[5] nor could you be persuaded how much better it was to bestow them on your friends than to hoard them".

"I, however," said Justice, "will consign to torment all who were accessory to his death." Then the youth was left in peace. Next entered Gallienus and his father,[6] the latter still dragging the chains of his captivity, the other with the dress and languishing gait of a woman. Seeing Valerian, Silenus cried, "who is this with the white plume that leads the army's van?"[7] Then he greeted Gallienus with, "he who is all decked with gold and dainty as a maiden".[8] Though Zeus ordered the pair to depart the feast.

Next came Claudius, at whom all the gods gazed; in admiration of his greatness of soul, they had granted the Empire to his descendants, since they thought it just that the posterity of such a lover of his country should rule as long as possible. Then Aurelian came rushing in as though trying to escape from those who would detain him before the judgement seat of Minos. For many charges of unjust murders were brought against him, and he was in flight because he could ill defend himself against the indictments. Yet Lord Helios, who had assisted him on other occasions, now came to his aid once more and declared before the gods: "he has paid the penalty, or have you forgotten the oracle uttered at Delphi, 'if his punishment should match his crime, justice has been done'?"[9]

With Aurelian entered Probus, who in less than seven years restored seventy cities and was in many ways a wise administrator. Since he had been unjustly treated by impious men, the gods paid

1. Geta 2. Caracalla 3. Heliogabalas

4. Alexander Severus was assassinated in 235 5. Mammæa

6. Valerian died in captivity among the Persians 7. Euripides, *Phoenissæ*, 120

8. Slightly altered from our version of *The Iliad*, II, 872

9. An oracular verse ascribed to Rhadamanthus by Aristotle, *Nicomachean Ethics*, 5.5.3; it became a proverb

him honours, and, moreover, exacted the penalty from his assassins. For all that, Silenus tried to jest at his expense, though many of the gods urged him to be silent. In spite of them he called out: "now let those that follow him learn wisdom from his example. Probus, do you not know that when physicians give bitter medicines they mix them with honey?[1] Yet you were always too austere and harsh and never displayed tolerance. Therefore your fate, though unjust, was natural enough. For no one can govern horses, cattle, or mules, still less men, unless he sometimes yields to them and gratifies their wishes; just as physicians humour their patients in trifles so that they may make them obey in things more essential".

"What now, dear little father," exclaimed Dionysus, "have you turned up as our philosopher?"

"Why, my son," he replied, "did I not make a philosopher of you? Do you not know that Socrates, also, who was so much like me,[2] carried off the prize for philosophy from his contemporaries, at least if you believe that your brother[3] tells the truth? Thus you must allow me to be serious on occasion and not always jocular."

While they were talking, Carus and his sons tried to slip into the banquet, but Justice drove them away. Next, Diocletian advanced in pomp, bringing with him the two Maximians and my grandfather Constantine. These latter held one another by the hand and did not walk alongside Diocletian, but formed a sort of chorus around him. Then, when they wished to run before him as bodyguards, he prevented them, since he did not think himself entitled to more privileges than they. When he realised that he was growing weary, however, he gave over to them all the burdens that he carried on his shoulders, and, admiring their unanimity, permitted them to sit far in front of many of their predecessors. Maximian was so grossly intemperate that Silenus wasted no jests on him, and he was not allowed to join the Emperors at their feast. For not only did he indulge in vicious passions of all sorts, but he proved meddlesome and disloyal, and often introduced discord. So he went I know not where, for I forgot to interrogate Hermes on this point. Nevertheless, into that harmonious symphony of four there crept a terribly harsh and dissonant strain. For this reason, Justice would not suffer the two[4] so much as to approach the door of

1. Plato, *Laws*, 659; a rhetorical commonplace 2. cf. Plato, *Symposium*, 215
3. The oracle of Apollo declared that Socrates was the wisest man of his time
4. i.e. the two Maximians, the colleagues of Diocletian

that assembly of heroes. As for Licinius, he came as far as the door, but as his misdeeds were many and monstrous, Minos forthwith drove him away.

Constantine, however, did enter and sat for some time, then came his sons.[1] Magnentius was refused admission because he had never done anything truly laudable, though much that he achieved had the appearance of merit. So the gods, who perceived that these achievements were not based on any virtuous principle, sent him packing, to his deep chagrin. When the feast had been prepared as I have described, the gods lacked nothing, since all things are theirs. Then Hermes proposed to examine the heroes personally and Zeus was of the same mind. Quirinus thereupon requested that he might summon one of their number to his side. "Quirinus," said Heracles, "I will not have it. For why did you not invite to the feast my beloved Alexander also? Zeus, if you are minded to introduce into our presence any of these Emperors, send, I beg of you, for Alexander. For if we are to examine the merits of men generally, why do we not throw open the competition to the better man?" Zeus considered that what the son of Alcmena said was only just. So Alexander joined the company of heroes, but neither Cæsar nor anyone else yielded his place to him. Nevertheless, he found and took a vacant seat which the son[2] of Severus had taken for himself – he had been expelled for fratricide. Then Silenus began to rally Quirinus and said: "let us now see whether all these Romans can match this one Greek".[3]

"By Zeus," retorted Quirinus, "I consider that many of them are as good as he! It is true that my descendants have admired him so much that they hold that he alone of all foreign generals is worthy to be styled 'the Great'. That, however, we shall very soon find out by examining these men." Even as he spoke, Quirinus was becoming flushed, and was evidently extremely anxious on behalf of his descendants, fearing that they might come away with second prize.

Then Zeus asked the gods whether it would be better to summon all the Emperors to enter the lists, or whether they should follow the custom of athletic contests, that he who defeats the winner of many victories, though he should overcome only that one competitor, is held thereby to have proved himself superior to all who have been previously defeated; and, moreover, that they have not wrestled with the winner, but only shown themselves

1. Constantine II, Constans, and Constantius 2. Caracalla 3. cf. Plato, *Laws*, 730

inferior to an antagonist who has been defeated. All the gods agreed that this was a very suitable sort of test. Hermes then summoned Cæsar to appear before them, then Octavian, and thirdly Trajan, these being the greatest warriors. In the silence that followed, Kronos turned to Zeus and said that he was astonished to see that only martial Emperors were summoned to the competition, and not a single philosopher. "For my part," he added, "I like philosophers just as much. So tell Marcus[1] to come in too." Accordingly, Marcus was summoned and came in looking exceptionally dignified and showing the effect of his studies in the expression of his eyes and his lined brows. His aspect was unutterably noble from the very fact that he was careless of his appearance and unadorned by art; for he wore a very long beard, his dress was plain and sober, and from lack of indulgence, his body was very much shining, almost translucent, like light most pure and immaculate. When he, too, had entered the sacred enclosure, Dionysus said: "Lord Kronos and Father Zeus, can any incompleteness exist among the gods?" And when they replied that it could not: "then", said he, "let us bring in here some votary of pleasure as well".

"Out of the question", answered Zeus. "It is not permitted that any man should enter here who does not model himself on us".

"In that case," said Dionysus, "let them be tried at the entrance. Let us summon by your leave a man not unwarlike but a slave to pleasure and enjoyment. Let Constantine come as far as the door." When this had been agreed upon, opinions were offered as to the manner in which they were to compete. Hermes thought that everyone ought to speak for himself in turn, after which the gods should vote. Though Apollo did not approve of this plan, because he said the gods ought to test and examine the truth, not plausible rhetoric and the devices of the orator. Zeus wished to please them both and at the same time to prolong the assembly, so he said: "there is no harm in letting them speak if we measure each a small allowance of water,[2] then later on we can cross-examine them and test the disposition of each one". Whereupon Silenus added sardonically: "take care, or Trajan and Alexander will think it is nectar and so drink up all the water and leave none for the others".

"It was not my water", retorted Poseidon, "but your vines of which these two were fond. Thus you had better tremble for your vines rather than for my springs." Silenus was greatly piqued and had no answer ready, but thereafter turned his attention to the

1. Aurelius 2. A reference to the water-clock, *clepsydra*

disputants. Then Hermes made the following proclamation:

"The trial that begins
Awards to him who wins
The fairest prize today.
And lo, the hour is here
And summons you, appear!
You may no more delay;
Come hear the herald's call
You rulers one and all.
Many the tribes of men
To you submissive then!
How keen in war your swords!
But now 'tis wisdom's turn;
So let your rivals learn
How keen can be your words.
Wisdom, thought some, is bliss
Most sure in life's short span;
Others did hold no less
That power to ban or bless
Is happiness for man.
Yet some set Pleasure high,
Idleness, feasting, love,
All that delights the eye;
Their raiment soft and fine,
Their hands bejewelled did shine,
Such bliss did they approve.
But whose the victory won
Shall Zeus decide alone"[1]

While Hermes had been making this proclamation, the lots were drawn, and it so happened that the first lot favoured Cæsar's passion for being first. This made him triumphant and prouder than before. Whereas the effect on Alexander was that he almost withdrew from the competition, had not mighty Heracles encouraged him and prevented him from leaving. Alexander drew the lot to speak second, but the lots of those who came next coincided with the order in which they had lived. Cæsar then began as follows: "it was my fortune, O Zeus and you other gods, to be born, following a number of great men, in a city so illustrious

1. In this comic rhyme made up of tags of anapaestic verse, Julian reproduces in the first five and last two verses of the proclamation made at the Olympic games. The first three verses occur in Lucian, *Demonax*, 65

that she rules more subjects than any other city has ever ruled; and, indeed, other cities are quite pleased to rank as second to her. What other city, I ask, began with three thousand citizens and in less than six centuries carried her victorious arms to the ends of the earth? What other nation ever produced so many brave and warlike men or such lawgivers? What nation ever honoured the gods as they did? Observe then that, though I was born in a city so powerful and so illustrious, my achievements not only surpassed the men of my own day, but all the heroes who ever lived. As for my fellow citizens, I am confident that there is none who will challenge my superiority. Though if Alexander here is is presumptuous, which of his deeds does he pretend to compare with mine? His Persian conquests, perhaps, as though he had never seen all those trophies I gathered when I defeated Pompey! And pray tell, who was the more skilful general, Darius or Pompey? Which of them led the bravest troops? Pompey had in his army the most martial of the nations formerly subject to Darius,[1] but he reckoned them no better than Carians, for he also led those European forces which had many times repulsed all of Asia when she invaded Europe, and, indeed, he had the bravest of them all – Italians, Illyrians, and Celts. Since I have mentioned the Celts, then, shall we compare the exploits of Alexander against the Getæ with my conquest of Gaul? He crossed the Danube once, I crossed the Rhine twice. The German conquest, again, is all my doing. No one opposed Alexander, but I had to contend against Ariovistus. I was the first Roman who ventured to sail the outer sea.[2] Perhaps this achievement was not so impressive, yet it was a daring deed that may well command your admiration; further, a more glorious action of mine was when I leapt ashore from my ship before all the others.[3] Of the Helvetians and Iberians I say nothing. Moreover, I have still said not a word about my campaigns in Gaul, when I conquered more than three hundred cities and no less than two million men! Though great as these achievements of mine were, that which followed was still greater and more daring. For I had to contend against my fellow citizens themselves, and to subdue the invincible, the unconquerable Romans. Again, if we are judged by the number of our battles, I fought three times as many as Alexander, even reckoning by the boasts of those who embellish his exploits. If one counts the cities captured, I reduced the greatest number, not only in Asia but

1. Darius III 2. The "inner" sea was the Mediterranean

3. Cæsar, *Bellum Gallicum*, 4.25, ascribes this to the standard bearer of the 10th legion

in Europe as well. Alexander only visited Egypt as a sight-seer, whereas I conquered her at the same time I was arranging drinking-parties. Are you pleased to inquire which of us showed more clemency after victory? I forgave even my enemies, and for what I suffered at their hands in consequence, Justice has taken vengeance. Yet Alexander did not even spare his friends, much less his enemies. I ask, are you still capable of disputing the first prize with me? Then since you will not, like the others, yield place to me, you compel me to say that whereas I was humane towards the Helvetians, you treated the Thebans cruelly. You burned their cities to the ground, but I restored the cities that had been burned by their own inhabitants. What's more, it was not at all the same thing to subdue ten thousand Greeks, and to withstand the onset of a hundred and fifty thousand men. Much more could I add both about myself and Alexander, but I have not had leisure to practise public speaking. Wherefore you ought to pardon me, though from what I have said, you ought, forming that decision which equity and justice demand, to award me the first prize".

When Cæsar had spoken to this effect, he still wished to go on talking, but Alexander, who had with difficulty hitherto restrained himself, now lost patience, and with some agitation and combativeness began speaking: "how long," said he, "O Zeus and you other gods, must I endure in silence the insolence of this man? There is, as you see, no limit to his praise of himself or his abuse of me. It would have better become him perhaps to refrain from both, since both are alike insupportable, but especially from disparaging my conduct, all the more since he imitated it. Yet he has arrived at such a pitch of impudence that he dares to ridicule the model of his own exploits. Come, Cæsar, you ought to have remembered those tears you shed upon hearing of the monuments that had been consecrated to my glorious deeds.[1] Since then, however, Pompey has inflated you with pride, the very same Pompey who thought he was the idol of his countrymen, but was in fact wholly insignificant. Take his African triumph: that was no great exploit, but the feebleness of the consuls in office made it seem glorious. Then the famous Servile War[2] was waged not against men but the vilest of slaves, and its successful conclusion was due to others, by which I mean Crassus and Lucius,[3] though Pompey

1. At Gades, upon seeing a statue of Alexander; cf. Suetonius, *Julius Cæsar*, 7
2. Led by Spartacus, 73-71 B.C.; Appian, *Civil Wars*, I, 116-120
3. Lucius Gellius; Plutarch, *Crassus*

gained the reputation and the credit for it. Again, Armenia and the neighbouring provinces were conquered by Lucullus,[1] yet for these, also, Pompey triumphed. Then he became the idol of the citizens and they called him 'the Great'. Greater, I ask, than whom of his predecessors? What achievement of his can be compared with those of Marius,[2] or of the two Scipios, or of Furius,[3] who sits over there by Quirinus because he rebuilt his city when it was almost in ruins? Those men did not make their reputation at the expense of others, as happens with public buildings built at the public expense; that is, one man lays the foundation, another finishes the work, while the last man who is in office, though he has only whitewashed the walls, has his name inscribed on the building. Not thus, I repeat, did those men gain credit for the deeds of others. They were themselves the architects and artificers of their schemes and deserved their illustrious titles. Well then, it is no wonder that you vanquished Pompey, who used to scratch his head with his finger-tip[4] and was in all respects more of a fox than a lion. When he was deserted by Fortune, who had so long favoured him, you easily overcame him, thus unaided. It is evident that it was not to any superior ability of yours that you owed your victory, since after running short of provisions[5] – no small blunder for a general to make, as I need not tell you – you fought a battle and were beaten. Further, if from imprudence or lack of judgement or inability to control his countrymen, Pompey neither postponed a battle when it was in his interest to protract the war, nor followed up a victory when he had won,[6] it was due to his own errors that he failed, and not your strategy.

The Persians, on the contrary, though on all occasions they were well and wisely equipped, had to submit to my valour. Moreover, since it becomes a virtuous man and a king to pride himself not merely on his exploits, but also on the justice of those exploits, it was on behalf of the Greeks that I took vengeance on the Persians; and when I made war on the Greeks, it was not because I wished to injure Greece, but only to chastise those who tried to prevent me from marching through and from calling the Persians to account. You, however, while you subdued the Germans and Gauls, were preparing to fight against your own

1. Lucinius Lucullus, conqueror of Mithridates

2. Caius Marius, the rival of Sulla

3. Furius Camillus repulsed the Gauls, 390 B.C.

4. A proverb for effeminacy; cf. Plutarch, *Pompeius*, 48; Juvenal, 9.133

fatherland. What could be worse or more infamous? And since you have alluded as though insultingly to 'ten thousand Greeks', I am aware that you Romans are yourselves descended from the Greeks, and that the greater part of Italy was colonised by Greeks; though on that fact I do not insist. At any rate, did not you Romans think it most important to have as friends and allies one insignificant tribe of those very Greeks, namely the Ætolians, my neighbours? Then, later, when you had gone to war with them for whatever reason, did you not have great trouble in making them obey you? Well then, if in the old age, as one may say, of Greece, you were barely able to reduce not the whole nation but an insignificant state which was hardly heard of when Greece was in her prime, what would have happened to you if you had had to contend against the Greeks when they were in full vigour and united? You know how cowed you were when Pyrrhus crossed to invade you. And if you think the conquest of Persia such a trifle and disparage an achievement so glorious, tell me why, after a war of more than three hundred years, you Romans have never conquered a small province beyond the Tigris which is still governed by the Parthians? Shall I tell you why? It was the arrows of the Persians that checked you. Ask Antony to give you an account of them, since he was trained for war by you. I, on the other hand, in less than ten years conquered not only Persia, but India too. After that, do you dare to dispute the prize with me, who from childhood have commanded armies, whose exploits have been so glorious that the memory of them – though they have not been worthily recounted by historians – will nevertheless live forever, like those of the Invincible Hero,[1] my king, whose follower I was, on whom I modelled myself? Achilles, my ancestor, I strove to rival, but Heracles I ever admired and followed, so far as a mere man may follow in the footsteps of a god.

"This much, dear gods, I was bound to say in my own defence against this man; though indeed it would have been better to ignore him. And if some things I did seemed cruel, it was never towards the innocent, but only to those who had often and in many ways thwarted me and had made no proper or fitting use of their opportunities. While even my offences against these, which were due to the emergency of the time, were followed by Remorse, that very wise and divine preserver of men who have erred. As for those whose ambition it was to show their enmity continually and to thwart me, I considered that I was justified in chastising them".

1. Heracles

When Alexander, in his turn, had made his speech in martial fashion, Poseidon's attendant carried the water-clock to Octavian, but gave him a smaller allowance of water, partly because time was precious, yet still more because he bore him a grudge for the disrespect he had once shown to the god.[1] Octavian with his usual sagacity understood this, so without stopping to say anything that did not concern himself, he began: "For my part, Zeus and you other gods, I shall not stay to disparage and belittle the actions of others, but shall speak only of what concerns myself. Like the noble Alexander here, I was but a youth when I was called to govern my country. Like Cæsar over there, my father,[2] I conducted successful campaigns against the Germans. When I became involved in civil dissensions, I conquered Egypt in a sea-fight off Actium; I defeated Brutus and Cassius at Philippi; while the defeat of Sextus, Pompey's son, was a mere incident in my campaign. I showed myself so gentle to the guidance of philosophy that I even put up with the plain speaking of Athenodorus,[3] and instead of resenting it, I was delighted with it and revered the man as my preceptor, or rather, as though he were my own father. Areius I counted my friend and close companion, and in short I was never guilty of any offence against philosophy. Yet because I saw that more than once before Rome had been brought to the verge of ruin by internal quarrels, I so administered her affairs as to make her strong as adamant for all time, unless indeed, O dear gods, you will otherwise. For I did not give way to boundless ambition and aim at enlarging her empire at all costs, but assigned for it two boundaries defined, as it were, by nature herself, the Danube and the Euphrates. Then after conquering the Scythians and Thracians, I did not employ the long reign that you gods vouchsafed me in making projects for war after war, but devoted my leisure to legislation and to reforming the ills that war had caused. For in this I thought that I was no less well advised than my predecessors, or rather, if I may make bold to say so, I was better advised than any who have ever administered so great an empire. For some of these, when they might have remained quiet and not taken the field, kept making one war an excuse for the next, like quarrelsome people and their lawsuits; and so they perished in their campaigns. Others when they had a war on their

1. Suetonius, *Augustus*, 16; during the campaign against Pompey, when his fleet was lost in a storm, Octavian swore he would win in spite of Neptune

2. Augustus was Julius Caesar's nephew, and his son only by adoption

3. A Stoic philosopher; cf. Pseudo-Lucian, *Long Lives*, 21.23; Suetonius, *Augustus*;

hands gave themselves up to indulgence, and preferred such base indulgence not only to future glory, but even to their personal safety. When I reflect on all this, I do not think myself entitled to the lowest place. Though whatever shall seem right to you, O dear gods, it surely becomes me to accept with good grace".

Trajan was allowed to speak next. Though he had some talent for oration, he was so indifferent to it that he had been in the habit of letting Sura write most of his speeches for him; thus he shouted rather than spoke, and meanwhile displayed to the gods his Getic and Parthian trophies, while he accused his old age of not having allowed him to extend his Parthian conquests.

"You cannot take us in", said Silenus; "you reigned for twenty years and Alexander here only twelve. Why, then, do you not put it down to your own love of ease, instead of complaining of your short allowance of time?"

Stung by the taunt, since he was not deficient in eloquence, though intemperance often made him seem more stupid than he was, Trajan began again: "O Zeus and you other gods, when I took over the Empire, it was in a sort of lethargy and much disordered by the tyranny that had long prevailed at home, and by the insolent conduct of the Getæ. I alone ventured to attack the tribes beyond the Danube, whereby I subdued the Getæ, the most warlike race that ever existed, which is due partly to their physical courage, partly to the doctrines that they have adopted from their admired Zamolxis. For they believe that they do not die but only change their place of abode, thus they meet death more readily than other men undertake a journey. Yet I accomplished that task in a matter of five years or so. That of all the Emperors who came before me I was regarded as the mildest in the treatment of my subjects is, I imagine, obvious, and neither Cæsar here nor any other will dispute it with me. Against the Parthians, I thought I should not employ force until they had put themselves in the wrong, but when they did so I marched against them, undeterred by my age, though the laws would have allowed me to quit the service. Since, then, the facts are as I have said, do I not deserve to be honoured before all the rest, first because I was so mild to my subjects, secondly because more than others I inspired terror in my country's foes, thirdly because I revered your daughter, divine Philosophy?"

When Trajan had finished this speech, the gods decided that he excelled all the rest in clemency; and evidently this was a virtue particularly pleasing to them.

When Marcus Aurelius began to speak, Silenus whispered to Dionysus: "let us hear which one of his paradoxes and wonderful doctrines this Stoic will produce".

Marcus, however, simply turned to Zeus and the other gods and said: "It seems to me, O Zeus and you other gods, that I have no need to make a speech or compete. If you did not know all that concerns me, it would indeed be fitting for me to inform you. But since you know it and nothing at all is hidden from you, do of your own accord assign me such honour as I deserve". Thus Marcus showed that, admirable as he was in other respects, he was wise also beyond the rest, for he knew "when it is time to speak and when to be silent".[1]

Constantine was allowed to speak next. On first entering the lists, he was confident enough. Yet when he reflected on the exploits of the others, he saw that his own were wholly trivial. He had defeated two tyrants, but, to tell the truth, one of them[2] was untrained in war and effeminate, the other[3] a poor creature and enfeebled by old age, while both alike were odious to gods and men. Moreover, his campaigns against the Barbarians covered him with ridicule. For he paid them tribute, so to speak, while he gave all his attention to Pleasure, who stood at a distance from the gods, near the entrance to the moon. Of her, indeed, he was so enamoured that he had no eyes for anything else, and cared not at all for victory. As it was his turn, however, and he had to say something, he began: "in the following respects I am superior to these others. To the Macedonian in having fought against Romans, Germans, and Scythians, instead of Asiatic Barbarians; to Cæsar and Octavian in that I did not, like them, lead a revolution against brave and good citizens, but attacked only the most cruel and wicked tyrants. As for Trajan, I should naturally rank higher on account of those same glorious exploits against the tyrants, while it would only be fair to regard me as his equal on the score of that territory which he added to the Empire, and I recovered; if indeed it be not more glorious to regain than to gain. As for Marcus here, by saying nothing for himself, he yields precedence to all of us".

"But Constantine," said Silenus, "are you not offering us mere gardens of Adonis[4] as exploits?"

"What do you mean", he asked, "by gardens of Adonis?"

"I mean", said Silenus, "those that women plant in pots, in

1. Euripides, fr. 417 2. Maxentius 3. Licinius
4. A proverb for whatever perished quickly; cf. Theocritus, 15

honour of the lover of Aphrodite, by scraping together a little earth for a garden bed. They bloom for a little space and fade forthwith." At this Constantine blushed, for he realised that this was exactly his own performance.

Silence was then proclaimed, and the Emperors thought they had only to wait until the gods decided to whom they would vote the first prize. Yet the latter agreed that they must bring to light the motives that had governed each, and not judge them by their actions alone, since Fortune had the greatest share in these. That goddess was herself standing near and kept reproaching all of them, with the single exception of Octavian; he, she said, had always been grateful to her. Accordingly, the gods decided to entrust this enquiry to Hermes also; he was told to begin with Alexander and to ask him what he considered the finest of all things, and what had been his object in doing and suffering all that he had done and suffered.

"To conquer the world", he replied.

"Well," asked Hermes, "do you think you accomplished this?"

"I do indeed", said Alexander.

Whereupon Silenus with a malicious laugh exclaimed: "Yet you were often conquered yourself by my daughters!", by which he meant his vines, alluding to Alexander's love of wine and intemperate habits. Alexander was well stocked with Peripatetic subterfuges, however, and retorted: "inanimate things cannot conquer; nor do we contend with such, but only with the whole race of men and beasts".

"Ah," said Silenus, "behold the chicanery of logic! But tell me in which class you place yourself, the inanimate or the animate and living?"

At this he seemed mortified and said: "hush! Such was my greatness of soul that I was convinced that I should become, or rather that I already was, a god".

"At any rate," said Silenus, "you were often defeated by yourself."

"Except," retorted Alexander, "to conquer oneself or be defeated by oneself amounts to the same thing. I was talking of my victories over other men."

"No more of your logic!" cried Silenus. "How adroitly you detect my sophisms! Yet when you were wounded in India,[1] and,

1. At the storming of the capital of the Mallians (probably modern Multan), in 326 B.C.; cf. Plutarch, *Alexander*

with Peucestes[1] laying near you, they carried you out of the town at your last gasp, were you defeated by him who wounded you, or did you conquer him?"

"I conquered him, and what is more I sacked the town as well."

"Not you, exactly, you immortal," said Silenus, "for you were lying like Homer's Hector, powerless and at your last gasp. It was your soldiers who fought and conquered."

"Indeed, but I led them", said Alexander.

"How so? When you were being carried away almost dead?" Then Silenus recited the passage in Euripides,[2] beginning: "alas, how unjust is the custom of the Greeks, when an army triumphs over the enemy–" but Dionysus interrupted him, saying: "stop, dear little father, say no more, or he will treat you as he treated Cleitus". At that Alexander turned red, his eyes became suffused with tears and he said no more. Thus their conversation ended.

Next Hermes began to question Cæsar, asking: "And you, Cæsar, what was the end and aim of your life?"

"To hold the first place in my own country," he replied, "and to neither be nor thought to be second to any man."

"This", said Hermes, "is not quite clear. Tell me, was it in wisdom that you wished to be first, or in oratorical skill, or in military science, or the science of government?"

"I should have liked well", said Cæsar, "to be first of all men in all of these; but as I could not attain to that, I sought to become the most powerful of my fellow citizens."

"And did you become so very powerful?" asked Silenus.

"Certainly," he replied, "since I made myself their master."

"Yes, that you were able to do; but you could not make yourself beloved by them, even though you played the philanthropic role as if you were acting in a stage-play, and flattered them all shamefully."

"What!" cried Cæsar. "Not beloved by the people? When they punished Brutus and Cassius!"

"That was not for murdering you," replied Silenus, "since for that they elected them consuls![3] No, it was because of the money you left them. When they had heard your will read, they perceived what a fine reward was offered them in it for such resentment of your murder."

---

1. Peucestes was wounded but saved Alexander's life; Pliny, 34.8

2. *Andromache*, 695, which continued: "it is not those who did the work that gain the credit, but rather the general wins all the glory"; Cleitus was killed by Alexander for quoting these verses

3. The senate gave Brutus and Cassius proconsul power in their provinces

When this dialogue ended, Hermes next accosted Octavian. "Now for you", he said. "Will you please tell us what you thought to be the finest thing in the world?"

"To govern well", he replied.

"You must say what you mean by 'well', Augustus. Govern well! The most wicked of tyrants claim to do that. Even Dionysius,[1] I suppose, thought that he governed well, and so did Agathocles,[2] who was a still greater criminal."

"You know, O dear gods," said Octavian, "that when I parted with my grandson,[3] I prayed for you to give him the courage of Cæsar, the cleverness of Pompey, and my own good fortune."

"Truly," cried Silenus, "how many things needed from the saving gods have been jumbled together by this figurine-maker!"

"Why, pray tell, do you give me that ridiculous name?" asked Octavian.

"Because" he replied, "just as they model nymphs, did you not model gods,[4] Augustus, and first and foremost Cæsar here?" At this Octavian seemed abashed and said no more.

Then Hermes, addressing Trajan, said: "now you, tell us what the principle was that guided all your actions?"

"My aims", he replied, "were the same as Alexander's, though I acted with more prudence."

"Hardly", said Silenus. "You were the slave of more ignoble passions. Anger was nearly always his weak point, but yours was pleasure of the vilest and most infamous sort."

"Plague take you!" exclaimed Dionysus. "You keep railing at them all and you do not let them say a word for themselves. In their case, however, there was some ground for your sarcasms, but now consider well what you can find to criticise in Marcus. For in my opinion he is a man, to quote Simonides, 'four-square and made without a flaw'."[5]

Then Hermes addressed Marcus and said: "and you, Verus, what did you consider to be the noblest ambition in life?" In a low voice he answered modestly: "to imitate the gods". This answer they at once agreed was highly noble and in fact the best possible. Even Hermes did not wish to cross-examine him further, since he was convinced that Marcus would answer every question equally well. The other gods were of the same mind; only Silenus cried "by

1. Tyrant of Syracuse, 405–367 B.C. 2. Tyrant of Syracuse, 317–289 B.C.

3. Caius Cæsar 4. Julian is referring to the custom of deifying Emperors

5. Simonides, fr. 5

Dionysus I shall not let this sophist off so easily. Why, then, did you eat bread and drink wine, and not ambrosia and nectar like us?"

"Because", he replied "it was not in the fashion of my meat and drink that I thought to imitate the gods. Rather, I nourished my body because I believed, perhaps falsely, that even your bodies require to be nourished by the fumes of sacrifice. Not that I believed I ought to imitate you in that respect, but rather with respect to your minds." For the moment Silenus was at a loss as though he had been hit by a skilled boxer;[1] then he said: "there is perhaps something in what you say; but now tell me what you thought was really meant by 'imitating the gods'".

"Having the fewest possible needs, and doing good to the greatest possible number."

"Do you mean to say", he asked, "that you had no needs at all?"

"I", said Marcus, "had none, but my poor body had a few perhaps." Since in this, also, Marcus seemed to have answered wisely, Silenus was at a loss, but finally fastened on what he thought was foolish and unreasonable in the Emperor's behaviour to his son and wife, that is, in enrolling the latter among the deified and entrusting the Empire to the former.

"Yet in that also", said Marcus, "I did but imitate the gods. I adopted the maxim of Homer when he says 'the good and prudent man loves and cherishes his own wife',[2] while as to my son, I can quote the excuse of Zeus himself when he is rebuking Ares: 'Long ago,' he says, 'I should have struck you with a thunderbolt, had I not loved you because you are my son'.[3] Besides, I never thought my son would prove so wicked. Youth ever vacillates between the extremes of vice and virtue, and if in the end he inclined to vice, he was not vicious when I entrusted the Empire to him; it was only after receiving it that he became corrupted. Therefore, my behaviour to my wife was modelled on that of the divine Achilles, and that to my son was in imitation of highest Zeus. Moreover, in neither case did I introduce any novelty. It is the custom to hand down the succession to a man's sons, and all men desire to do so; as for my wife, I was not the first to decree divine honours to a wife, for I followed the example of many others. It is perhaps absurd to have introduced any such custom, but it would be almost an injustice to deprive one's nearest and dearest of what is now long established. Though I forget myself when I make such a lengthy explanation to you, O Zeus and you other gods, for

1. Plato, *Protagoras*, 339 2. *The Iliad*, IX, 343 3. A paraphrase of *The Iliad*, V, 897

you know all things. Forgive me this forwardness."

When Marcus had finished his speech, Hermes next asked Constantine: "and what was the height of your ambition?"

"To amass great wealth", he answered, "and then to spend it liberally so as to gratify my own desires and the desires of my friends." At this, Silenus burst into a loud laugh, and said: "if it was a banker that you wanted to be, how did you so far forget yourself as to lead the life of a pastry-cook and hairdresser? Your locks and your fair favour[1] betokened this all along, but what you say about your motives convicts you". Thus did Silenus sharply reprove Constantine.

Then silence was proclaimed and the gods cast a secret ballot. It transpired that Marcus had most of the votes. After conferring apart with his father,[2] Zeus bade Hermes make a proclamation as follows: "know all you mortals who have entered this contest, that according to our laws and decrees, the victor is allowed to exult but the vanquished must not complain. Depart, then, wherever you please, and in future live every one of you under the guidance of the gods. Let every man choose his own guardian and guide".

After this announcement, Alexander hastened to Heracles, and Octavian to Apollo, but Marcus attached himself closely to Zeus and Kronos. Cæsar wandered about for a long time, pacing this way and that, till mighty Ares and Aphrodite took pity on him and summoned him to them. Trajan hastened to Alexander and sat down near him. As for Constantine, he could not discover among the gods the model of his own career, but when he caught sight of Pleasure, who was not far off, he ran to her. She received him tenderly and embraced him, then after dressing him in raiment of many colours and otherwise making him beautiful, she led him away to Incontinence. There, too, he found Jesus, who had taken up his abode with her and cried aloud to all-comers: "he that is a seducer, he that is a murderer, he that is sacrilegious and infamous, let him approach without fear! For with this water will I wash him and will straightaway make him clean. And though he should be guilty of those same sins a second time, let him but smite his breast and beat his head and I will make him clean again". To him Constantine came gladly, once he had conducted his sons forth from the assembly of the gods. Yet the avenging deities nevertheless punished both him and them for their impiety, and extracted the penalty for the shedding of the blood of their

1. *The Iliad*, III, 55 2. Kronos

kindred, until Zeus granted them a respite for the sake of Claudius and Constantius.[1]

"As for you," Hermes said to me, "I have granted you the knowledge of your father, Mithras. Keep his commands, and thus secure for yourself confidence and sure anchorage throughout your life; and when you must depart from this world, you can with good hope, and the god's grace, adopt him as your guardian."

1. Constantius Chlorus

"So the gods weep, weep the goddesses all
That the beautiful perishes, that the perfect dies;
Yet glorious still is a lament from beloved lips,
For the ignoble goes soundless down to Orcus"

– Schiller, *Nänie*

OTHER TITLES FROM INVICTUS PUBLISHING

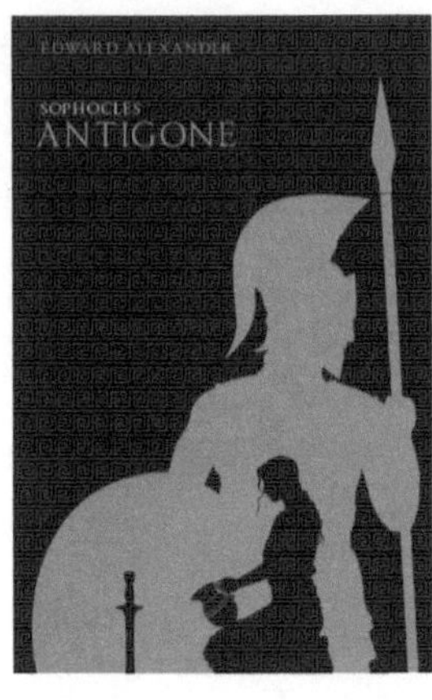

Antigone (Sophocles)
Edward Alexander

In the aftermath of a brutal war, the city of Thebes is in chaos. When the new king, Creon, declares that the body of Antigone's traitorous brother must be left unburied to rot in the sun, she boldly defies his order – an act of rebellion which sets in motion the tragic showdown between the daughter of Oedipus and the king. Sophocles' timeless tragedy explores the conflict between individual will and the power of the state, between the gods of the hearth and the polis, between loyalty to family and to fatherland. With themes of morality, justice, and duty at its core, Antigone stands among the crowning achievements of European literature, as compelling today as in the age of Periclean Athens.

Edward Alexander's masterful verse translation is accompanied by an extensive essay detailing the themes of Antigone and its relationship to Athenian history, the Homeric epics, and Ancient Greek religion. Also included in this edition is the full play in the original Greek.

OTHER TITLES FROM INVICTUS PUBLISHING

The Samurai: History, Bushidō, and the Way of the Sword
William Ashcroft

William Ashcroft's "The Samurai" traces the long and storied history of Japan's famous warrior class, detailing the great battles, legendary figures, and key developments that shaped the samurai over the centuries, together with an exploration of bushidō – the Way of the Warrior – and the art of swordsmanship, drawing on works by Yamamoto Jōchō and Miyamoto Musashi.

Ashcroft's concise history expertly charts the emergence of the samurai during the early imperial age, their rise to national dominance, and their eventual dissolution upon the founding of the modern Japanese state. Traversing over a thousand years of history, The Samurai covers such subjects as seppuku, the daring feats of Minamoto no Yoshitsune, the last stand of Kusunoki Masashige, the tumultuous Sengoku Jidai ("Age of the Country at War"), the famed vendetta of the forty-seven rōnin, and the Satsuma Rebellion – the last samurai uprising and the last civil war in Japanese history.

OTHER TITLES FROM INVICTUS PUBLISHING

Polybius and the Roman Conquest of Greece: How Hellenic Disunity Gave Rise to Roman Rule

Fustel de Coulanges

Less than two centuries after the death of Alexander the Great, Greece had been reduced to a province of the nascent Roman empire. In Polybius and the Roman Conquest of Greece, Fustel de Coulanges explores the key social and political conditions which led to Greece's subjugation, from the fierce divisions that had long plagued Ancient Greek society, to the unassailable disunity between the Hellenic city-states. Uncompromising in his analysis, Coulanges details the fractured resistance to Roman conquest through the lens of Polybius' writings, exploring how "the last historian of a free Greece" would ultimately come to view Rome as the solution to the deep disorders of his homeland.

www.ingramcontent.com/pod-product-compliance
Lightning Source LLC
Chambersburg PA
CBHW030916120726
47906CB00002B/359

* 9 7 8 1 0 6 8 4 1 6 3 2 3 *